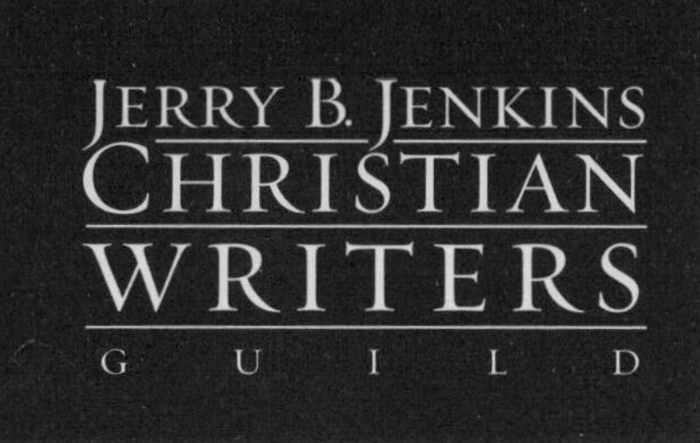

THE CHRISTIAN WRITER'S MARKET GUIDE 2014

YOUR COMPREHENSIVE RESOURCE FOR GETTING PUBLISHED

JERRY B. JENKINS

TYNDALE HOUSE PUBLISHERS, INC.
CAROL STREAM, ILLINOIS

Visit Tyndale online at www.tyndale.com.

Visit Jerry B. Jenkins Christian Writers Guild at www.christianwritersguild.com.

E-mail: marketguide@christianwritersguild.com

The 2014 Christian Writer's Market Guide: Your Comprehensive Resource for Getting Published

Designed by Jennifer Phelps

Edited by Erin Gwynne

ISSN 1080-3995

ISBN 978-1-4143-8735-2

Printed in the United States of America

19 18 17 16 15 14 13
7 6 5 4 3 2 1

Contents

PART 2: PERIODICAL PUBLISHERS

PART 3: SPECIALTY MARKETS

PART 4: SUPPORT FOR WRITERS

Introduction

Hardly any industry has ever changed as much in so short a time as publishing has in the last few years. Traditional methods of seeing your writing get to the printed page have broadened so dramatically that many veterans hardly recognize the publishing landscape anymore. Besides royalty-paying book publishers and fee-paying periodical markets, opportunities abound for anyone who wants to be published electronically, on demand, in blogs, or through self-, vanity-, or subsidy-publishing means.

Regardless, good writing rises like cream and must be crafted, edited, proofread, honed, and polished.

Some publishers say writers who submit to them don't read their guidelines first—some even drop their listings from this guide for that reason. Most publishers carry their guidelines on their websites, so most of our listings include the addresses to find those. Carefully read the guidelines before submitting—a critical step if you want to sell in today's tighter market.

More and more publishers are dropping their fax numbers or even their addresses and depend almost entirely on e-mail or website contacts.

A number of periodical publishers are accepting assignments only, so it is important that you establish a reputation in your areas of interest and expertise. Once you have acquired credits in a given field, write to some of those assignment-only editors, asking for an assignment.

Carefully check out agents before signing with them. See the introduction to the agent section for tips on that. Because agents have become more important in a writer's quest for publication, we list which conferences have agents in attendance.

Attending conferences is one of the best ways to contact agents as well as publishers.

If you are new to this guide or only want to find specific markets for your work, check out the supplementary lists throughout the book. Read through the glossary and learn terms.

Also be sure to study the "How to Use This Book" section. It will save you time, and it's full of helpful hints.

One of the most common complaints from publishers is that the material they receive is not appropriate for their needs. Editors tell me they are looking for writers who understand their periodical or publishing house and its unique approach to the marketplace. With a little time and effort, you can meet an editor's expectations, distinguish yourself as a professional, and sell what you write.

Godspeed to you as you travel the exciting road to publication. You have been given a mission for which you might often feel inadequate. Just remember that the writing assignments God has given you could not be written the same by anyone else.

Finally, special thanks to my executive assistant Debbie Kaupp for developing and overseeing the database we use to produce the guide. Through her efforts the listings are as up to date as they can be, and the guide has been streamlined to be easier to use than ever. Thanks also to Janice Mitchell, Tanya Shtatman, and Andy Scheer for their help.

Jerry B. Jenkins
PO Box 88288, Black Forest, CO 80908
719.495.5835
Fax: 719.494.1299
Christian Writers Guild: 719.495.5177 or 866.495.5177
E-mail: marketguide@jerryjenkins.com
Website: www.christianwritersguild.com
Blog: www.jerry-jenkins.com
Facebook: facebook.com/jerry.b.jenkins
Twitter: twitter.com/JerryBJenkins

For additional books to help with your specific writing needs, visit the bookstore at www.christianwritersguild.com.

How to Use This Book

The 2014 Christian Writer's Market Guide is designed to make it easier for you to sell your writing. It will serve you well if you use it as a springboard for becoming thoroughly familiar with those markets best suited to your style and areas of interest and expertise.

Start by getting acquainted with the setup of the guide. The beginnings of chapters 1 and 5 carry comprehensive listings of periodical and book topics. Cross-referencing may be helpful. For example, if you have a novel that deals with doctor-assisted suicide, you might look at the list for adult fiction and the list for controversial issues and look for publishers on both lists.

Read listings carefully to see whether your target market pays, requires an agent, etc. Each book publisher listing carries the following information (as available):

- Name of publisher
- Address, phone and fax numbers, e-mail address, website
- Denomination or affiliation
- Name of editor—This may include the main editor, followed by another editor to whom submissions should be sent. In some cases, several editors are listed with the types of books each is responsible for. (It's always best to submit to a specific person, never just "Sir" or "Madam" or "To Whom It May Concern.")
- Statement of purpose
- List of imprint names
- Number of inspirational/religious titles published per year, followed by formats of books published (hardcover, trade paperbacks, mass-market paperbacks, coffee table books). Note that coffee table books are also represented in the topical listings.
- Number of submissions received annually
- Percentage of books published from first-time authors
- (Usually) whether the publisher accepts, prefers, requires, or doesn't accept manuscripts through agents
- Percentage of books from freelance authors they subsidy publish (if any). This does not refer to percentage paid by author. If percentage of subsidy is over 50 percent, the publisher will be listed in a separate section under "Subsidy Publishers."
- Whether they reprint out-of-print books from other publishers
- Preferred manuscript length in words or pages; "pages" refers to double-spaced manuscript pages; figure approximately 250 words per page.
- Average amount of royalty, if provided, and whether it is based on the retail (cover price) of the book or on the net receipts (wholesale price to bookstores or distributors)
- Average amount paid for advances and whether the publisher pays an advance against royalties. Not all publishers answer this, so if nothing is mentioned, that doesn't necessarily mean none is offered.
- Whether they pay flat fees rather than royalties
- Average number of copies in first printing
- Average length of time between acceptance of a manuscript and publication
- Whether they consider simultaneous submissions. This means you can send a query or proposal or even a complete manuscript simultaneously, as long as you indicate to each that you are doing so.
- Length of time it should take them to respond to a query/proposal or to a complete manuscript (when two lengths of time are given, the first refers to a query and the latter to a complete

manuscript). Give them a one-month grace period beyond that, and then send a polite follow-up letter.
- Whether a publisher "accepts," "prefers," or "requires" manuscripts sent electronically. (Sending hard copies is almost unheard of now.)
- Which Bible version the publisher prefers
- Whether they do print-on-demand publishing
- Availability and cost of writer's guidelines and book catalogs. Most of these will be available online or via e-mail, but if the publisher offers hard copies, ask directly whether there's a charge, postage costs, etc.
- Nonfiction and Fiction sections indicate preference for query letter, book proposal, or complete manuscript, and whether they accept phone, fax, or e-queries. (Most do not.) If they want a query letter, send a letter describing your project. If they want a query letter/proposal, add a chapter-by-chapter synopsis and 2-3 sample chapters.
- Special Needs
- Ethnic Books—Specifies which groups they target
- Also Does—Indicates which publishers also publish booklets, pamphlets, tracts, or e-books
- Photos/Artwork—Indicates whether they accept freelance photos for book covers.
- Tips

At the end of some listings you will find an indication that the publisher receives book proposals from www.ChristianManuscriptSubmissions.com (see website or index) or The Writer's Edge.

In each periodical listing you will find the following information (as available) in this format:

- Name of periodical
- Address, phone and fax numbers, e-mail address, website
- Denomination or affiliation
- Name of editor to submit to
- Theme of publication
- Format, frequency of publication, number of pages, and circulation size
- Subscription rate for a one-year subscription. (You might want to subscribe to at least one of your primary markets every year to become acquainted with its focus.)
- Date established, if 2007 or later
- Openness to freelance submissions; percentage of unsolicited freelance submissions accepted versus assigned articles
- Preference for query or complete manuscript also tells whether they want a cover letter with complete manuscripts and whether they accept phone or e-mail queries. If there is no mention of cover letters or phone or e-mail queries, assume they do not accept them.
- Payment schedule, payment on acceptance or publication, and rights purchased. (See glossary for definitions.)
- If a publication does not pay or pays in copies or subscription, that is indicated in bold capital letters.
- If a publication is not copyrighted, you should ask that your copyright notice appear with your published piece so your rights will be protected.
- Preferred word lengths and average number of manuscripts purchased per year (in parentheses)
- Response time—The time they usually take to respond to your query or manuscript submission
- Seasonal and holiday material—should reach them by at least the specified length of time in advance.

- Acceptance of simultaneous submissions and reprints—whether they accept submissions sent simultaneously to several publishers. It's best to send to non-overlapping markets (such as denominational), and be sure to indicate that it is a simultaneous submission. Reprints are pieces you have sold previously but to which you hold the rights (which means you sold only first or one-time rights to the original publisher and the rights reverted to you).
- Whether they accept, prefer, or require submissions electronically. Most prefer them now. Some indicate whether they want submissions as attached files or copied into the message.
- Average kill-fee amount (see glossary)
- Whether they use sidebars (see glossary)
- Their preferred Bible version, if any. See glossary for "Bible versions."
- Whether they accept submissions from children or teens. "Young-Writer Markets" are also found in the topical listings.
- Availability and cost for writer's guidelines, theme lists, and sample copies—most now have guidelines available by e-mail or website.
- Poetry—Name of poetry editor. Average number of poems bought each year. Types of poetry. Number of lines. Payment rate. Maximum number of poems you may submit at one time.
- Fillers—Name of fillers editor. Types of fillers accepted; word length. Payment rate.
- Columns/Departments—Name of column editor. Names of columns in the periodical (information in parentheses gives focus of column); word-length requirements. Payment rate. Be sure to see sample before sending ms or query. Most columns require a query letter first.
- Special Issues or Needs
- Ethnic
- Contest Information. See "Contests" chapter for full list of contests.
- Tips

Adhering closely to the guidelines set out in these listings will mark you as a professional.

If your manuscript is completed, be sure the slant fits the publisher you have in mind.

If you have an idea for an article, short story, or book but you have not written it yet, the topical listing will help you decide on a possible slant or approach. If your idea is for an article, do not overlook writing on the same topic for different periodicals listed under that topic. For example, you could write on money management for a general adult magazine, a teen magazine, a women's publication, or a magazine for pastors. Each would require a different slant, but you would get a lot more mileage from that idea.

If you run into words you're not familiar with, check the glossary at the back of the book.

If you need someone to evaluate your material or to give it a thorough editing, look up "Editorial Services." That often will make the difference between success or failure in publishing.

If you are a published author, you may be interested in finding an agent. Some agents consider unpublished authors (their listing will indicate that), but even they require you to have a completed manuscript before being considered (see agent list). The list also includes secular agents who handle religious/inspirational material.

Check the "Clubs/Groups" list to find a chapter to join in your area.

Go to the "Conferences" list to find one you might attend this year. Attending a conference every year or two is almost essential to your success.

Do not rely solely on the information provided in this guide. Use it to familiarize yourself with target markets, but then interact personally with an editor to be sure you're providing what they want. It is important to your success that you learn to use writer's guidelines and study book catalogs or sample copies before submitting to any publisher.

PART 1

Book Publishers

1

Topical Listings of Book Publishers

One of the most difficult aspects of marketing your writing is determining which publishers might be interested in your book. This list will help you do that.

If you don't find your area of interest listed, check the table of contents for related topics. Next, secure writer's guidelines and book catalogs from those publishers. Just because a particular publisher is listed under your topic, don't assume it would automatically be interested in your book. You must determine whether your approach will fit the scope of that publisher's mission. It is also helpful to visit a Christian bookstore or a website to peruse the books produced by each publisher you are considering submitting to.

(a) before a listing indicates the publisher accepts submissions only through agents.

AFRICAN AMERICAN MARKETS

(a) Abingdon Press
(a) Doubleday Relig.

American Binding
Booklocker.com
Bridge Logos
CLC Publications
Franciscan Media
InterVarsity Press
Judson Press
Lift Every Voice
Moody Publishers
New Hope
Praeger Publishers
Tate Publishing
Whitaker House

APOLOGETICS

(a) Bethany House
(a) FaithWords
(a) Kregel
(a) Nelson, Thomas

Aaron Book
Abingdon Press
ACW Press
Ambassador Intl.
American Binding
AMG Publishers
Blue Dolphin
BMH Books
Booklocker.com
Bridge Logos
Brown Books
Canticle Books
Charisma House
Christian Heritage
Creation House
Crossway
CSS Publishing
Discovery House
Earthen Vessel
Eerdmans Pub., Wm. B.
Essence
Fairway Press
Faith Books & More
Grace Acres Press
Guardian Angel
Hensley Publishing
Hope Publishing
Howard Books
InterVarsity Press
Lighthouse Publishing
Lighthouse Trails
Lutheran Univ. Press
Magnus Press
NavPress
New Leaf
Our Sunday Visitor
P&R Publications
Parson Place
Randall House
Salt Works
Tate Publishing
Trail Media
VBC Publishing
Whitaker House
WinePress
Word Alive
Zoë Life Publishing

ARCHAEOLOGY

(a) Baker Academic
(a) Baker Books
(a) Doubleday Relig.
(a) HarperOne
(a) Kregel

Aaron Book
Abingdon Press
ACW Press
American Binding
Blue Dolphin
BMH Books
Booklocker.com
Brown Books
Christian Writer's Ebook
Comfort Publishing
Conciliar Press
Eerdmans Pub., Wm. B.
Essence
Fairway Press

Faith Books & More
Lighthouse Publishing
NavPress
New Leaf
Pacific Press
Tate Publishing
VBC Publishing
White Fire Publishing
WinePress
Word Alive
Yale Univ. Press

ART, FREELANCE

Aaron Book
Abingdon Press
Ambassador Books
Ambassador Intl.
AMG Publishers
Blue Dolphin
Booklocker.com
CrossLink Publishing
Dawn Publications
Dove Inspirational
Earthen Vessel
Eerdmans/Yg Readers
Essence
Faith Books & More
Focus on the Family
Grace Acres Press
Group Publishing
Guardian Angel
Halo Publishing Intl.
JourneyForth/BJU
Judson Press
Legacy Press
Lighthouse Publishing
New Leaf
Parson Place
Parsons Publishing
Pauline Kids
Pelican Publishing
Players Press
Rainbow Publishers
Randall House
Ravenhawk Books
Salt Works
Sunpenny Publishing
VBC Publishing
Warner Press
WinePress

AUTOBIOGRAPHY

(a) Baker Books
(a) Doubleday Relig.
(a) FaithWords
(a) HarperOne
(a) Nelson, Thomas
(a) WaterBrook Press

Aaron Book
ACW Press
Ambassador Intl.
American Binding
Blue Dolphin
Bold Vision Books
Bondfire Books
Booklocker.com
Bridge Logos
Brown Books
Chalfont House Publishing
Charisma House
Christian Heritage
Christian Writer's Ebook
CLC Publications
Comfort Publishing
Creation House
CrossLink Publishing
Deep River Books
Earthen Vessel
Essence
Evergreen Press
Fairway Press
Faith Books & More
Grace Acres Press
Kirk House
Lighthouse Publishing
Lighthouse Trails
Morgan James Publishing
Pacific Press
Parson Place
Parsons Publishing
Tate Publishing
Trail Media
White Fire Publishing
WinePress
Word Alive
Zoë Life Publishing

BIBLE/BIBLICAL STUDIES

(a) Baker Academic
(a) Baker Books
(a) Bethany House
(a) Cook, David C.
(a) Doubleday Relig.
(a) Kregel
(a) WaterBrook Press

Aaron Book
Abingdon Press
ACW Press
Ambassador Books
Ambassador Intl.
American Binding
AMG Publishers
Blue Dolphin
BMH Books
Bold Vision Books
Bondfire Books
Booklocker.com
Bridge Logos
Brown Books
Canticle Books
Chalfont House Publishing
Christian Writer's Ebook
Conciliar Press
Contemporary Drama
CrossLink Publishing
CSS Publishing
DCTS Publishers
Deep River Books
Discovery House
Earthen Vessel
Eerdmans Pub., Wm. B.
Essence
Evergreen Press
Fairway Press
Faith Books & More
Grace Publishing
Group Publishing
Hannibal Books
Harrison House
Hensley Publishing
Inkling Books
InterVarsity Press
JourneyForth/BJU
Lift Every Voice
Lighthouse Publishing
Lutheran Univ. Press
Magnus Press
NavPress
New Hope
On My Own Now
Our Sunday Visitor

Pacific Press
P&R Publications
Parson Place
Parsons Publishing
Pauline Kids
Randall House Digital
Salt Works
Tate Publishing
Trail Media
VBC Publishing
Wesleyan Publishing
Whitaker House
WinePress
Word Alive
Write Integrity Press
Yale Univ. Press
Zoë Life Publishing
Zondervan

BIBLE COMMENTARY

(a) Baker Books
(a) B&H Publishing
(a) Cook, David C.
(a) Doubleday Relig.
(a) Kregel
(a) Tyndale House

Aaron Book
Abingdon Press
ACW Press
Ambassador Books
Ambassador Intl.
American Binding
AMG Publishers
Blue Dolphin
BMH Books
Bondfire Books
Booklocker.com
Bridge Logos
Brown Books
Christian Writer's Ebook
Conciliar Press
CrossLink Publishing
CSS Publishing
Discovery House
Eerdmans Pub., Wm. B.
Essence
Fairway Press
Faith Books & More
Harrison House
Inkling Books
InterVarsity Press
Lighthouse Publishing
Lutheran Univ. Press
NavPress
Our Sunday Visitor
P&R Publications
Tate Publishing
VBC Publishing
WinePress
Word Alive
Yale Univ. Press
Zoë Life Publishing
Zondervan

BIOGRAPHY

(a) Baker Books
(a) Ballantine
(a) Doubleday Relig.
(a) HarperOne
(a) Nelson, Thomas
(a) WaterBrook Press

Aaron Book
ACW Press
Ambassador Intl.
American Binding
Blue Dolphin
Bondfire Books
Booklocker.com
Bridge Logos
Brown Books
Chalfont House Publishing
Charisma House
Christian Heritage
Christian Writer's Ebook
CLC Publications
Comfort Publishing
Conciliar Press
Creation House
CrossLink Publishing
Deep River Books
Discovery House
Eerdmans Pub., Wm. B.
Essence
Fairway Press
Faith Books & More
Franciscan Media
Grace Acres Press
Guideposts Books
Hannibal Books
Hope Publishing
Inkling Books
Kirk House
Lighthouse Publishing
Lighthouse Trails
New Leaf
On My Own Now
Pacific Press
Parson Place
Parsons Publishing
Pauline Books
Pauline Kids
Ravenhawk Books
Tate Publishing
Trail Media
Whitaker House
White Fire Publishing
WinePress
Word Alive
Yale Univ. Press
Zoë Life Publishing

BOOKLETS

Aaron Book
American Binding
Bold Vision Books
Bondfire Books
Chalfont House Publishing
Charisma House
Christian Writer's Ebook
Creation House
Essence
Evergreen Press
Fruitbearer Pub.
Grace Publishing
InterVarsity Press
Life Cycle Books
Lighthouse Trails
Our Sunday Visitor
Pacific Press
P&R Publications
Randall House
Salt Works
Tate Publishing
Trinity Foundation
WinePress
Word Alive

CANADIAN/FOREIGN

Essence
Sunpenny Publishing
Word Alive

CELEBRITY PROFILES

(a) Baker Books
(a) FaithWords
(a) Hay House
(a) Nelson, Thomas

Aaron Book
ACW Press
American Binding
Blue Dolphin
Bold Vision Books
Bondfire Books
Booklocker.com
Brown Books
Charisma House
Christian Writer's Ebook
Comfort Publishing
Deep River Books
Essence
Fairway Press
Faith Books & More
Grace Acres Press
Howard Books
Lighthouse Publishing
On My Own Now
Ravenhawk Books
Tate Publishing
Whitaker House
WinePress
Word Alive

CHARISMATIC

(a) Nelson, Thomas

Aaron Book
ACW Press
American Binding
Blue Dolphin
Booklocker.com
Bridge Logos
Canticle Books
Charisma House
Chosen Books
Comfort Publishing
Creation House
CSS Publishing
Destiny Image (books)
Eerdmans Pub., Wm. B.
Essence
Fairway Press
Faith Books & More
Fruitbearer Pub.
Harrison House
Lighthouse Publishing
Lutheran Univ. Press
Magnus Press
Parsons Publishing
Salvation Publisher
Tate Publishing
Whitaker House
WinePress
Word Alive
Zoë Life Publishing

CHILDREN'S BOARD BOOKS

Ambassador Books
Eerdmans/Yg Readers
Faith Books & More
Halo Publishing Intl.
Morgan James Publishing
Pauline Kids
Tate Publishing
WinePress
Word Alive

CHILDREN'S DEVOTIONALS

Bondfire Books
Essence
Grace Publishing
New Leaf
Pauline Books
Trail Media
Warner Press
Zoë Life Publishing

CHILDREN'S EASY READERS

(a) Baker Books
(a) Cook, David C.
(a) Tyndale House

Aaron Book
Ambassador Books
Booklocker.com
Brown Books
Charisma House
Conciliar Press
Creation House
Dawn Publications
Deep River Books
Essence
Evergreen Press
Fairway Press
Faith Books & More
Grace Publishing
Guardian Angel
Inkling Books
JourneyForth/BJU
Legacy Press
Lift Every Voice
Lighthouse Publishing
Our Sunday Visitor
Pacific Press
Pauline Books
Pauline Kids
Pelican Publishing
Standard Publishing
Tate Publishing
Trail Media
VBC Publishing
Warner Press
Word Alive
Zoë Life Publishing

CHILDREN'S PICTURE BOOKS (nonfiction)

(a) Baker Books
(a) Bethany House
(a) Cook, David C.
(a) Tyndale House
(a) WaterBrook Press

Aaron Book
Abingdon Press
Ambassador Books
Bridge Logos
Brown Books
Conciliar Press
Creation House
Dove Inspirational
Eerdmans Pub., Wm. B.
Eerdmans/Yg Readers
Essence
Evergreen Press
Faith Books & More
Fruitbearer Pub.
Guardian Angel
Halo Publishing Intl.
Lighthouse Publishing
Lighthouse Trails
Morgan James Publishing
New Leaf

Pauline Books
Pauline Kids
Pelican Publishing
Standard Publishing
Tate Publishing
Trail Media
Warner Press
WinePress
Zoë Life Publishing

CHRIST

(a) Bethany House
(a) Cook, David C.
(a) Doubleday Relig.
(a) Nelson, Thomas

Aaron Book
ACW Press
Ambassador Intl.
American Binding
Barbour
Blue Dolphin
BMH Books
Bondfire Books
Booklocker.com
Brown Books
Canticle Books
Chalfont House Publishing
Charisma House
Christian Heritage
Christian Writer's Ebook
CLC Publications
Creation House
CrossLink Publishing
CSS Publishing
Deep River Books
Discovery House
Earthen Vessel
Eerdmans Pub., Wm. B.
Essence
Fairway Press
Faith Books & More
Grace Acres Press
Guardian Angel
Guideposts Books
JourneyForth/BJU
Lift Every Voice
Lighthouse Publishing
Lutheran Univ. Press
Magnus Press
NavPress
New Leaf
Our Sunday Visitor
P&R Publications
Parson Place
Pauline Kids
Salt Works
Tate Publishing
VBC Publishing
WinePress
Word Alive
Yale Univ. Press
Zoë Life Publishing

CHRISTIAN BUSINESS

(a) Cook, David C.
(a) Doubleday Relig.
(a) Nelson, Thomas
(a) WaterBrook Press

Aaron Book
ACW Press
Ambassador Intl.
American Binding
Blue Dolphin
BMH Books
Bold Vision Books
Bondfire Books
Booklocker.com
Brown Books
Charisma House
Christian Writer's Ebook
Comfort Publishing
Creation House
CSS Publishing
Cupola Press
Deep River Books
Eerdmans Pub., Wm. B.
Essence
Evergreen Press
Fairway Press
Faith Books & More
Grace Acres Press
Hannibal Books
Howard Books
InterVarsity Press
JourneyForth/BJU
Kirk House
Lift Every Voice
Lighthouse Publishing
Lutheran Univ. Press
Morgan James Publishing
NavPress
New Leaf
Ravenhawk Books
Salvation Publisher
Tate Publishing
Trail Media
Trinity Foundation
VBC Publishing
Whitaker House
White Fire Publishing
WinePress
Word Alive
Zoë Life Publishing

CHRISTIAN EDUCATION

(a) Baker Academic
(a) Baker Books
(a) Cook, David C.
(a) Doubleday Relig.
(a) Kregel

Aaron Book
ACW Press
Ambassador Intl.
American Binding
Blue Dolphin
Bold Vision Books
Bondfire Books
Booklocker.com
Brown Books
Christian Heritage
Christian Writer's Ebook
Church Growth Inst.
Contemporary Drama
CSS Publishing
DCTS Publishers
Eerdmans Pub., Wm. B.
Essence
Fairway Press
Faith Books & More
Grace Acres Press
Grace Publishing
Group Publishing
Halo Publishing Intl.
Hensley Publishing
InterVarsity Press
Judson Press
Kirk House
Lift Every Voice
Lighthouse Publishing
Lutheran Univ. Press

Meriwether
New Leaf
Our Sunday Visitor
Pacific Press
Rainbow Publishers
Reference Service
Salvation Publisher
Standard Publishing
Tate Publishing
Trail Media
Trinity Foundation
VBC Publishing
White Fire Publishing
WinePress
Word Alive
Zoë Life Publishing

CHRISTIAN HOMESCHOOLING

(a) Baker Books

Aaron Book
ACW Press
American Binding
Blue Dolphin
BMH Books
Bondfire Books
Booklocker.com
Brown Books
Christian Writer's Ebook
CrossHouse
CSS Publishing
Eerdmans Pub., Wm. B.
Essence
Fairway Press
Faith Books & More
Fruitbearer Pub.
Grace Acres Press
Grace Publishing
Hannibal Books
Inkling Books
Lift Every Voice
Lighthouse Publishing
Morgan James Publishing
New Leaf
Pacific Press
Parsons Publishing
Standard Publishing
Tate Publishing
Trail Media
White Fire Publishing
WinePress
Word Alive
Zoë Life Publishing

CHRISTIAN LIVING

(a) Baker Books
(a) B&H Publishing
(a) Bethany House
(a) Cook, David C.
(a) Doubleday Relig.
(a) FaithWords
(a) HarperOne
(a) Multnomah
(a) Nelson, Thomas
(a) Revell
(a) Tyndale House
(a) WaterBrook Press

Aaron Book
Abingdon Press
ACW Press
Ambassador Books
Ambassador Intl.
American Binding
Barbour
Blue Dolphin
Bold Vision Books
Bondfire Books
Booklocker.com
Brown Books
Canticle Books
Chalfont House Publishing
Charisma House
Christian Writer's Ebook
CLC Publications
Comfort Publishing
Creation House
CrossLink Publishing
Crossway
CSS Publishing
Cupola Press
DCTS Publishers
Deep River Books
Destiny Image (books)
Discovery House
Eerdmans Pub., Wm. B.
Essence
Evergreen Press
Fairway Press
Faith Books & More
Franciscan Media
Grace Acres Press
Grace Publishing
Guideposts Books
Hope Publishing
Howard Books
Inheritance Press
InterVarsity Press
JourneyForth/BJU
Judson Press
Life Cycle Books
Lift Every Voice
Lighthouse Publishing
Lighthouse Trails
Lutheran Univ. Press
Magnus Press
Moody Publishers
Morgan James Publishing
NavPress
New Hope
New Leaf
On My Own Now
Our Sunday Visitor
Parsons Publishing
Pauline Kids
Port Hole Public.
Randall House
Salvation Publisher
Standard Publishing
Sunpenny Publishing
Tate Publishing
Trail Media
VBC Publishing
Wesleyan Publishing
White Fire Publishing
WinePress
WingSpread
Word Alive
Write Integrity Press
Zoë Life Publishing

CHRISTIAN SCHOOL BOOKS

(a) Baker Books

Aaron Book
ACW Press
American Binding
Blue Dolphin
Bondfire Books
Booklocker.com
Christian Writer's Ebook

CrossLink Publishing
CSS Publishing
Eerdmans Pub., Wm. B.
Essence
Fairway Press
Faith Books & More
Grace Acres Press
Grace Publishing
Inkling Books
JourneyForth/BJU
Lighthouse Publishing
Our Sunday Visitor
Pacific Press
Pauline Kids
Tate Publishing
Trinity Foundation
White Fire Publishing
WinePress
Word Alive
Zoë Life Publishing

CHRISTMAS BOOKS

Bondfire Books
Cupola Press
Essence
Grace Publishing
Trail Media
Warner Press
White Fire Publishing
Write Integrity Press
Zoë Life Publishing

CHURCH GROWTH

(a) Kregel

Aaron Book
Ambassador Intl.
Booklocker.com
Brown Books
CrossHouse
Dove Inspirational
Eerdmans/Yg Readers
Essence
Faith Books & More
Grace Acres Press
Grace Publishing
Guardian Angel
Legacy Press
NavPress
New Leaf
P&R Publications
Pauline Kids
Pelican Publishing
Randall House
Salt Works
White Fire Publishing
WinePress
WingSpread
Zoë Life Publishing

CHURCH HISTORY

(a) Baker Books
(a) B&H Publishing
(a) Doubleday Relig.
(a) HarperOne
(a) Kregel

Aaron Book
Abingdon Press
ACW Press
Ambassador Intl.
American Binding
Blue Dolphin
Bondfire Books
Booklocker.com
Christian Heritage
Christian Writer's Ebook
Creation House
CrossHouse
CrossLink Publishing
Crossway
CSS Publishing
Earthen Vessel
Eerdmans Pub., Wm. B.
Essence
Fairway Press
Faith Books & More
Franciscan Media
Hannibal Books
InterVarsity Press
Kirk House
Lighthouse Publishing
Loyola Press
Lutheran Univ. Press
NavPress
Our Sunday Visitor
Pacific Press
Pauline Books
Randall House
Tate Publishing
Trinity Foundation
White Fire Publishing
WinePress
Word Alive
Yale Univ. Press
Zoë Life Publishing
Zondervan

CHURCH LIFE

(a) Baker Books
(a) Bethany House
(a) Doubleday Relig.
(a) HarperOne
(a) Kregel
(a) Nelson, Thomas

Aaron Book
Abingdon Press
ACW Press
Ambassador Intl.
American Binding
Blue Dolphin
Bondfire Books
Booklocker.com
Charisma House
Christian Writer's Ebook
CLC Publications
Creation House
Crossway
CSS Publishing
DCTS Publishers
Deep River Books
Discovery House
Earthen Vessel
Eerdmans Pub., Wm. B.
Essence
Fairway Press
Faith Books & More
Grace Acres Press
Hannibal Books
Harrison House
Hope Publishing
Howard Books
InterVarsity Press
Judson Press
Kirk House
Lift Every Voice
Lighthouse Publishing
Lutheran Univ. Press
NavPress
New Hope
Pacific Press
P&R Publications

Pauline Kids
Randall House
Tate Publishing
Wesleyan Publishing
White Fire Publishing
WinePress
WingSpread
Word Alive
Zoë Life Publishing

CHURCH MANAGEMENT

(a) B&H Publishing
(a) Doubleday Relig.
(a) Kregel

Aaron Book
Abingdon Press
ACW Press
Ambassador Intl.
American Binding
Blue Dolphin
BMH Books
Booklocker.com
Charisma House
Christian Heritage
CLC Publications
Creation House
CSS Publishing
Eerdmans Pub., Wm. B.
Essence
Fairway Press
Faith Books & More
Grace Acres Press
Group Publishing
Hannibal Books
Harrison House
Hope Publishing
JourneyForth/BJU
Judson Press
Kirk House
Lighthouse Publishing
Lutheran Univ. Press
Our Sunday Visitor
Randall House
Tate Publishing
Wesleyan Publishing
White Fire Publishing
WinePress
Word Alive
Zoë Life Publishing

CHURCH RENEWAL

(a) Baker Books
(a) Doubleday Relig.
(a) HarperOne
(a) Kregel

Aaron Book
Abingdon Press
ACW Press
Ambassador Intl.
American Binding
Blue Dolphin
BMH Books
Bondfire Books
Booklocker.com
Bridge Logos
Canticle Books
Christian Writer's Ebook
Church Growth Inst.
CLC Publications
Creation House
CSS Publishing
Deep River Books
Destiny Image (books)
Earthen Vessel
Eerdmans Pub., Wm. B.
Essence
Fairway Press
Faith Books & More
Grace Acres Press
Hannibal Books
Hope Publishing
Howard Books
InterVarsity Press
Judson Press
Lighthouse Publishing
Lutheran Univ. Press
Magnus Press
NavPress
Pacific Press
Parson Place
Randall House
Salvation Publisher
Tate Publishing
Wesleyan Publishing
White Fire Publishing
WinePress
WingSpread
Word Alive
Zoë Life Publishing

CHURCH TRADITIONS

(a) Baker Books
(a) Doubleday Relig.
(a) Kregel
(a) Nelson, Thomas

Aaron Book
Abingdon Press
ACW Press
Ambassador Intl.
American Binding
Blue Dolphin
Booklocker.com
Christian Heritage
Christian Writer's Ebook
Conciliar Press
Creation House
CSS Publishing
Deep River Books
Earthen Vessel
Eerdmans Pub., Wm. B.
Essence
Fairway Press
Faith Books & More
Franciscan Media
Howard Books
Inkling Books
InterVarsity Press
Lighthouse Publishing
Lutheran Univ. Press
NavPress
Our Sunday Visitor
Pacific Press
Pauline Kids
Praeger Publishers
Tate Publishing
White Fire Publishing
WinePress
Word Alive
Zoë Life Publishing

COFFEE TABLE BOOKS

Aaron Book
ACW Press
Ambassador Intl.
Brown Books
Creation House
Deep River Books
Essence
Halo Publishing Intl.
Kirk House

Lutheran Univ. Press
Players Press
Salt Works
WinePress
Zoë Life Publishing

COMPILATIONS

(a) Doubleday Relig.
(a) WaterBrook Press

Aaron Book
ACW Press
Ambassador Intl.
American Binding
Barbour
Bondfire Books
Booklocker.com
Charisma House
Christian Heritage
Christian Writer's Ebook
CLC Publications
Creation House
Cupola Press
Deep River Books
Earthen Vessel
Eerdmans Pub., Wm. B.
Essence
Fairway Press
Faith Books & More
Group Publishing
InterVarsity Press
Lighthouse Publishing
NavPress
Salt Works
Tate Publishing
White Fire Publishing
WinePress
Word Alive
Zoë Life Publishing

CONTROVERSIAL ISSUES

(a) Baker Books
(a) Doubleday Relig.
(a) FaithWords
(a) HarperOne
(a) Hay House
(a) Kregel

Aaron Book
ACW Press
American Binding
AMG Publishers
Blue Dolphin
Bondfire Books
Booklocker.com
Bridge Logos
Canticle Books
Chalfont House Publishing
Charisma House
Christian Writer's Ebook
Comfort Publishing
Conciliar Press
Creation House
Deep River Books
Destiny Image (books)
Earthen Vessel
Eerdmans Pub., Wm. B.
Essence
Fairway Press
Faith Books & More
Hannibal Books
Hope Publishing
Howard Books
Inkling Books
InterVarsity Press
Judson Press
Life Cycle Books
Lighthouse Publishing
Lighthouse Trails
Magnus Press
MountainView
NavPress
Ravenhawk Books
Salt Works
Tate Publishing
Trail Media
White Fire Publishing
WinePress
Word Alive
Write Integrity Press
Zoë Life Publishing

COOKBOOKS

(a) Ballantine
(a) Nelson, Thomas

Aaron Book
Adams Media
American Binding
Barbour
Booklocker.com
Bridge Logos
Brown Books
Charisma House
Christian Writer's Ebook
CrossHouse
Dove Inspirational
Essence
Evergreen Press
Fairway Press
Faith Books & More
Grace Publishing
Guardian Angel
Halo Publishing Intl.
Hannibal Books
Pacific Press
Pelican Publishing
Sunpenny Publishing
Tate Publishing
WinePress
Word Alive
Zoë Life Publishing

COUNSELING AIDS

(a) Baker Books
(a) Kregel
(a) Nelson, Thomas

Aaron Book
ACW Press
Ambassador Intl.
American Binding
Blue Dolphin
Bold Vision Books
Bondfire Books
Booklocker.com
Bridge Logos
Brown Books
Chalfont House Publishing
Charisma House
Christian Writer's Ebook
CSS Publishing
Deep River Books
Eerdmans Pub., Wm. B.
Essence
Evergreen Press
Fairway Press
Faith Books & More
Grace Publishing
InterVarsity Press
JourneyForth/BJU
Langmarc
Life Cycle Books

Lighthouse Publishing
Morgan James Publishing
On My Own Now
P&R Publications
Randall House
Reference Service
Tate Publishing
WinePress
WingSpread
Word Alive
Zoë Life Publishing

CREATION SCIENCE

Aaron Book
ACW Press
Ambassador Intl.
American Binding
Blue Dolphin
BMH Books
Bold Vision Books
Bondfire Books
Booklocker.com
Bridge Logos
Chalfont House Publishing
Charisma House
Christian Writer's Ebook
Eerdmans Pub., Wm. B.
Essence
Fairway Press
Faith Books & More
Hope Publishing
Inkling Books
Lighthouse Publishing
New Leaf
Pacific Press
Parson Place
Salt Works
Tate Publishing
Trail Media
Whitaker House
WinePress
Word Alive
Zoë Life Publishing

CULTS/OCCULT

(a) Baker Books
(a) HarperOne
(a) Kregel

Aaron Book
ACW Press
American Binding
Booklocker.com
Christian Writer's Ebook
CLC Publications
Comfort Publishing
Conciliar Press
Eerdmans Pub., Wm. B.
Essence
Fairway Press
Faith Books & More
Lighthouse Publishing
Ravenhawk Books
Tate Publishing
Whitaker House
WinePress
Word Alive

CURRENT/SOCIAL ISSUES

(a) Baker Academic
(a) Baker Books
(a) B&H Publishing
(a) Bethany House
(a) Doubleday Relig.
(a) FaithWords
(a) HarperOne
(a) Kregel
(a) Nelson, Thomas
(a) Tyndale House

Aaron Book
ACW Press
American Binding
AMG Publishers
Ampelos Press
Blue Dolphin
Bondfire Books
Booklocker.com
Bridge Logos
Brown Books
Chalfont House Publishing
Charisma House
Christian Writer's Ebook
Comfort Publishing
Conari Press
Creation House
CrossLink Publishing
DCTS Publishers
Deep River Books
Eerdmans Pub., Wm. B.
Essence
Fairway Press
Faith Books & More
Hannibal Books
Howard Books
Inkling Books
InterVarsity Press
JourneyForth/BJU
Judson Press
Life Cycle Books
Lighthouse Publishing
Loyola Press
Lutheran Univ. Press
NavPress
New Hope
New Leaf
On My Own Now
Ravenhawk Books
Salt Works
Tate Publishing
Trail Media
VBC Publishing
Whitaker House
White Fire Publishing
WinePress
Word Alive
Write Integrity Press
Yale Univ. Press
Zoë Life Publishing

CURRICULUM

(a) Cook, David C.

Aaron Book
Bondfire Books
CrossLink Publishing
Eerdmans Pub., Wm. B.
Fairway Press
Gospel Light
Grace Acres Press
Group Publishing
Hannibal Books
Inheritance Press
Lighthouse Publishing
Lighthouse Trails
New Leaf
Randall House Digital
Standard Publishing
Tate Publishing
WinePress

Word Alive
Zoë Life Publishing

DATING/SEX

(a) Ballantine
(a) Bethany House
(a) Cook, David C.
(a) Doubleday Relig.
(a) FaithWords
(a) HarperOne
(a) Kregel
(a) Nelson, Thomas
(a) WaterBrook Press

Aaron Book
ACW Press
American Binding
Barbour
Blue Dolphin
Bondfire Books
Booklocker.com
Bridge Logos
Chalfont House Publishing
Charisma House
Christian Writer's Ebook
Comfort Publishing
Deep River Books
Destiny Image (books)
Eerdmans Pub., Wm. B.
Essence
Evergreen Press
Fairway Press
Faith Books & More
Lift Every Voice
Lighthouse Publishing
NavPress
On My Own Now
P&R Publications
Pauline Books
Tate Publishing
Trail Media
Whitaker House
White Fire Publishing
WinePress
Word Alive
Zoë Life Publishing

DEATH/DYING

(a) Baker Books
(a) Cook, David C.
(a) Doubleday Relig.
(a) HarperOne
(a) Kregel
(a) Nelson, Thomas
(a) WaterBrook Press

Aaron Book
Abingdon Press
ACW Press
American Binding
Blue Dolphin
Bondfire Books
Booklocker.com
Bridge Logos
Brown Books
Chalfont House Publishing
Charisma House
Christian Writer's Ebook
Comfort Publishing
Creation House
CSS Publishing
Cupola Press
Deep River Books
Discovery House
Eerdmans Pub., Wm. B.
Essence
Evergreen Press
Fairway Press
Faith Books & More
Guardian Angel
Halo Publishing Intl.
Hope Publishing
Life Cycle Books
Lift Every Voice
Lighthouse Publishing
Loyola Press
Lutheran Univ. Press
NavPress
Pacific Press
P&R Publications
Pauline Books
Tate Publishing
Trail Media
Whitaker House
White Fire Publishing
WinePress
Word Alive
Zoë Life Publishing

DEVOTIONAL BOOKS

(a) Baker Books
(a) Bethany House
(a) Cook, David C.
(a) Doubleday Relig.
(a) FaithWords
(a) HarperOne
(a) Kregel
(a) Nelson, Thomas
(a) Tyndale House
(a) WaterBrook Press

Aaron Book
Abingdon Press
ACW Press
Ambassador Books
Ambassador Intl.
American Binding
Ampelos Press
Barbour
Blue Dolphin
Bold Vision Books
Bondfire Books
Booklocker.com
Brown Books
Chalfont House Publishing
Charisma House
Christian Heritage
Christian Writer's Ebook
CLC Publications
Contemporary Drama
Creation House
CrossLink Publishing
CSS Publishing
Cupola Press
Deep River Books
Discovery House
Eerdmans Pub., Wm. B.
Essence
Evergreen Press
Fairway Press
Faith Books & More
Franciscan Media
Fruitbearer Pub.
Grace Publishing
Group Publishing
Guideposts Books
Hannibal Books
Harrison House
Howard Books
Inheritance Press
Inkling Books
Judson Press
Legacy Press

Lift Every Voice
Lighthouse Publishing
MOPS Intl.
Morgan James Publishing
NavPress
New Hope
New Leaf
On My Own Now
P&R Publications
Parson Place
Parsons Publishing
Pauline Books
Salt Works
Salvation Publisher
Standard Publishing
Tate Publishing
Trail Media
VBC Publishing
Warner Press
Wesleyan Publishing
White Fire Publishing
WinePress
WingSpread
Word Alive
Zoë Life Publishing

DISCIPLESHIP

(a) Baker Books
(a) B&H Publishing
(a) Bethany House
(a) Cook, David C.
(a) Doubleday Relig.
(a) HarperOne
(a) Kregel
(a) Nelson, Thomas
(a) WaterBrook Press

Aaron Book
Abingdon Press
ACW Press
Ambassador Intl.
American Binding
Barbour
Blue Dolphin
BMH Books
Bold Vision Books
Bondfire Books
Booklocker.com
Bridge Logos
Brown Books
Chalfont House Publishing
Charisma House
Christian Heritage
Christian Writer's Ebook
CLC Publications
Comfort Publishing
Creation House
Crossway
CSS Publishing
Cupola Press
DCTS Publishers
Deep River Books
Destiny Image (books)
Discovery House
Eerdmans Pub., Wm. B.
Essence
Evergreen Press
Fairway Press
Faith Books & More
Grace Acres Press
Grace Publishing
Group Publishing
Harrison House
Hensley Publishing
Howard Books
Inheritance Press
Inkling Books
InterVarsity Press
JourneyForth/BJU
Judson Press
Lift Every Voice
Lighthouse Publishing
Lutheran Univ. Press
Moody Publishers
Morgan James Publishing
NavPress
New Hope
New Leaf
On My Own Now
Pacific Press
P&R Publications
Parson Place
Pauline Books
Randall House
Salt Works
Salvation Publisher
Standard Publishing
Tate Publishing
Trail Media
Whitaker House
White Fire Publishing
WinePress
WingSpread
Word Alive
Zoë Life Publishing

DIVORCE

(a) Baker Books
(a) Bethany House
(a) Cook, David C.
(a) Kregel
(a) Nelson, Thomas
(a) WaterBrook Press

Aaron Book
ACW Press
Ambassador Books
Ambassador Intl.
American Binding
Blue Dolphin
Bold Vision Books
Bondfire Books
Booklocker.com
Bridge Logos
Brown Books
Chalfont House Publishing
Charisma House
Christian Writer's Ebook
Comfort Publishing
Creation House
CSS Publishing
Deep River Books
Earthen Vessel
Eerdmans Pub., Wm. B.
Essence
Fairway Press
Faith Books & More
Grace Publishing
Guideposts Books
Halo Publishing Intl.
InterVarsity Press
Lighthouse Publishing
Pacific Press
P&R Publications
Pauline Books
Tate Publishing
Trail Media
WinePress
WingSpread
Word Alive
Zoë Life Publishing

DOCTRINAL

(a) Baker Books
(a) Bethany House
(a) Doubleday Relig.
(a) Kregel
(a) Tyndale House

Aaron Book
ACW Press
Ambassador Intl.
American Binding
Blue Dolphin
Booklocker.com
Brown Books
Canticle Books
Christian Heritage
Christian Writer's Ebook
CLC Publications
Creation House
Crossway
DCTS Publishers
Earthen Vessel
Eerdmans Pub., Wm. B.
Essence
Fairway Press
Faith Books & More
InterVarsity Press
Lighthouse Publishing
Lutheran Univ. Press
Pacific Press
Randall House
Tate Publishing
Trinity Foundation
VBC Publishing
White Fire Publishing
WinePress
Word Alive
Zoë Life Publishing

DRAMA

(a) Kregel

Aaron Book
American Binding
Contemporary Drama
Fairway Press
Faith Books & More
Guardian Angel
Halo Publishing Intl.
Lighthouse Publishing
Meriwether
Ravenhawk Books
Salt Works
Tate Publishing
WinePress
Word Alive

E-BOOKS

(a) Tyndale House

Ambassador Intl.
Blue Dolphin
Bold Vision Books
Bondfire Books
Booklocker.com
Chalfont House Publishing
Christian Writer's Ebook
Comfort Publishing
CSS Publishing
Cupola Press
Faith Books & More
Grace Acres Press
Grace Publishing
Guardian Angel
InterVarsity Press
Lighthouse Publishing
NavPress
New Leaf
Randall House Digital
Salt Works
Sunpenny Publishing
Trail Media
Westbow Press
White Fire Publishing
White Rose
Word Alive
Zoë Life Publishing

ECONOMICS

(a) Baker Books

Aaron Book
ACW Press
American Binding
Blue Dolphin
Booklocker.com
Brown Books
Christian Writer's Ebook
Creation House
Deep River Books
Eerdmans Pub., Wm. B.
Essence
Evergreen Press
Fairway Press
Faith Books & More
Lighthouse Publishing
New Hope
New Leaf
Praeger Publishers
Salvation Publisher
Tate Publishing
Trinity Foundation
WinePress
Word Alive
Zoë Life Publishing

ENCOURAGEMENT

(a) Doubleday Relig.
(a) WaterBrook Press

Aaron Book
ACW Press
American Binding
Barbour
Blue Dolphin
Bold Vision Books
Bondfire Books
Booklocker.com
Brown Books
Chalfont House Publishing
Charisma House
CLC Publications
Comfort Publishing
Creation House
CSS Publishing
Cupola Press
Discovery House
Earthen Vessel
Eerdmans Pub., Wm. B.
Essence
Fairway Press
Faith Books & More
Grace Acres Press
Guardian Angel
Howard Books
JourneyForth/BJU
Lift Every Voice
Lighthouse Publishing
NavPress
New Hope
On My Own Now
Parson Place
Players Press

Port Hole Public.
Randall House
Salvation Publisher
Tate Publishing
Trail Media
VBC Publishing
White Fire Publishing
WinePress
WingSpread
Word Alive
Zoë Life Publishing

ENVIRONMENTAL ISSUES

(a) Baker Books
(a) Doubleday Relig.

Aaron Book
ACW Press
American Binding
Blue Dolphin
Bold Vision Books
Booklocker.com
Christian Writer's Ebook
Cladach Publishing
Dawn Publications
Deep River Books
Eerdmans Pub., Wm. B.
Essence
Fairway Press
Faith Books & More
InterVarsity Press
Judson Press
Lighthouse Publishing
New Leaf
Praeger Publishers
Ravenhawk Books
Sunpenny Publishing
Tate Publishing
WinePress
Word Alive

ESCHATOLOGY

(a) Baker Books
(a) Kregel
(a) Nelson, Thomas

Aaron Book
ACW Press
American Binding
Blue Dolphin
BMH Books
Booklocker.com
Bold Vision Books
Bridge Logos
Chalfont House Publishing
Charisma House
Christian Heritage
Christian Writer's Ebook
Creation House
CSS Publishing
DCTS Publishers
Eerdmans Pub., Wm. B.
Essence
Fairway Press
Faith Books & More
Grace Acres Press
Kirk House
Lighthouse Publishing
Lighthouse Trails
Lutheran Univ. Press
Nelson, Thomas
Pacific Press
Parson Place
Strong Tower
Tate Publishing
VBC Publishing
WinePress
Word Alive
Zoë Life Publishing

ETHICS

(a) Baker Books
(a) Kregel

Aaron Book
ACW Press
American Binding
Blue Dolphin
Bold Vision Books
Bondfire Books
Booklocker.com
Chalfont House Publishing
Christian Heritage
Christian Writer's Ebook
CLC Publications
Conciliar Press
Creation House
Crossway
Deep River Books
Earthen Vessel
Eerdmans Pub., Wm. B.
Essence
Fairway Press
Faith Books & More
Franciscan Media
Grace Acres Press
Guardian Angel
Hannibal Books
Howard Books
Inkling Books
InterVarsity Press
Kirk House
Life Cycle Books
Lift Every Voice
Lighthouse Publishing
Lutheran Univ. Press
Our Sunday Visitor
Pacific Press
Paragon House
Randall House
Ravenhawk Books
Salt Works
Tate Publishing
Trinity Foundation
Whitaker House
White Fire Publishing
WinePress
Word Alive
Yale Univ. Press
Zoë Life Publishing

ETHNIC/CULTURAL

(a) Baker Books
(a) Doubleday Relig.
(a) HarperOne
(a) Kregel

Aaron Book
ACW Press
American Binding
Blue Dolphin
Bold Vision Books
Booklocker.com
Bridge Logos
Christian Writer's Ebook
CLC Publications
Creation House
Deep River Books
Eerdmans Pub., Wm. B.
Essence
Fairway Press
Faith Books & More
Franciscan Media
Guardian Angel

Howard Books
InterVarsity Press
Judson Press
Kirk House
Lift Every Voice
Lighthouse Publishing
Lutheran Univ. Press
Moody Publishers
NavPress
New Hope
Pacific Press
Praeger Publishers
Standard Publishing
Sunpenny Publishing
Tate Publishing
Whitaker House
WinePress
Word Alive
Yale Univ. Press
Zoë Life Publishing
Zondervan

EVANGELISM/WITNESSING

(a) Baker Books
(a) Cook, David C.
(a) Kregel
(a) Nelson, Thomas
(a) Tyndale House

Aaron Book
ACW Press
Ambassador Intl.
American Binding
Blue Dolphin
BMH Books
Bold Vision Books
Bondfire Books
Booklocker.com
Bridge Logos
Chalfont House Publishing
Charisma House
Christian Heritage
Christian Writer's Ebook
Church Growth Inst.
CLC Publications
Creation House
CrossHouse
CrossLink Publishing
CSS Publishing
DCTS Publishers
Deep River Books
Discovery House
Earthen Vessel
Eerdmans Pub., Wm. B.
Essence
Evergreen Press
Fairway Press
Faith Books & More
Grace Acres Press
Group Publishing
InterVarsity Press
Judson Press
Lift Every Voice
Lighthouse Publishing
Lutheran Univ. Press
Moody Publishers
Morgan James Publishing
NavPress
New Hope
Pacific Press
P&R Publications
Parson Place
Randall House
Salt Works
Tate Publishing
VBC Publishing
Wesleyan Publishing
White Fire Publishing
WinePress
WingSpread
Word Alive
Write Integrity Press
Yale Univ. Press
Zoë Life Publishing

EXEGESIS

(a) Baker Books
(a) Doubleday Relig.
(a) Kregel

Aaron Book
Abingdon Press
ACW Press
American Binding
Blue Dolphin
BMH Books
Bondfire Books
Booklocker.com
Canticle Books
Christian Writer's Ebook
CLC Publications
CSS Publishing
Deep River Books
Earthen Vessel
Eerdmans Pub., Wm. B.
Essence
Fairway Press
Faith Books & More
Grace Acres Press
InterVarsity Press
Lighthouse Publishing
Lutheran Univ. Press
Salt Works
Tate Publishing
VBC Publishing
WinePress
Word Alive
Yale Univ. Press
Zoë Life Publishing

EXPOSÉS

(a) Baker Books

Aaron Book
ACW Press
American Binding
Blue Dolphin
Booklocker.com
Christian Writer's Ebook
Eerdmans Pub., Wm. B.
Fairway Press
Faith Books & More
Lighthouse Publishing
Lighthouse Trails
Ravenhawk Books
Salt Works
WinePress
Word Alive
Zoë Life Publishing

FAITH

(a) Baker Books
(a) B&H Publishing
(a) Bethany House
(a) Doubleday Relig.
(a) FaithWords
(a) HarperOne
(a) Kregel
(a) Nelson, Thomas
(a) Tyndale House
(a) WaterBrook Press

Aaron Book
Abingdon Press

ACW Press
Ambassador Books
Ambassador Intl.
American Binding
Barbour
Blue Dolphin
Bold Vision Books
Bondfire Books
Booklocker.com
Bridge Logos
Brown Books
Chalfont House Publishing
Charisma House
Christian Heritage
Christian Writer's Ebook
CLC Publications
Comfort Publishing
Creation House
CrossLink Publishing
Cupola Press
DCTS Publishers
Deep River Books
Destiny Image (books)
Discovery House
Earthen Vessel
Eerdmans Pub., Wm. B.
Essence
Evergreen Press
Fairway Press
Faith Books & More
Fruitbearer Pub.
Grace Acres Press
Grace Publishing
Group Publishing
Guardian Angel
Guideposts Books
Halo Publishing Intl.
Harrison House
Hensley Publishing
Howard Books
Inheritance Press
InterVarsity Press
JourneyForth/BJU
Judson Press
Lift Every Voice
Lighthouse Publishing
Loyola Press
Lutheran Univ. Press
Magnus Press
Morgan James Publishing
NavPress
New Hope
On My Own Now
Pacific Press
Parson Place
Parsons Publishing
Pauline Books
Randall House
Salt Works
Salvation Publisher
Tate Publishing
Trail Media
VBC Publishing
Wesleyan Publishing
Whitaker House
White Fire Publishing
WinePress
WingSpread
Word Alive
Write Integrity Press
Zoë Life Publishing

FAMILY LIFE

(a) Baker Books
(a) B&H Publishing
(a) Bethany House
(a) Cook, David C.
(a) FaithWords
(a) HarperOne
(a) Kregel
(a) Nelson, Thomas
(a) Tyndale House
(a) WaterBrook Press

Aaron Book
Abingdon Press
ACW Press
Ambassador Books
Ambassador Intl.
American Binding
Barbour
Blue Dolphin
Bold Vision Books
Bondfire Books
Booklocker.com
Bridge Logos
Brown Books
Chalfont House Publishing
Charisma House
Christian Writer's Ebook
Cladach Publishing
Comfort Publishing
Conari Press
Creation House
CrossLink Publishing
Crossway
Cupola Press
DCTS Publishers
Deep River Books
Destiny Image (books)
Discovery House
Dove Inspirational
Eerdmans Pub., Wm. B.
Essence
Evergreen Press
Fairway Press
Faith Books & More
Focus on the Family
Franciscan Media
Grace Acres Press
Grace Publishing
Guardian Angel
Guideposts Books
Halo Publishing Intl.
Hannibal Books
Hensley Publishing
Hope Publishing
Howard Books
InterVarsity Press
JourneyForth/BJU
Judson Press
Langmarc
Legacy Press
Life Cycle Books
Lift Every Voice
Lighthouse Publishing
Loyola Press
MOPS Intl.
Morgan James Publishing
MountainView
NavPress
New Hope
New Leaf
Our Sunday Visitor
Pacific Press
P&R Publications
Pauline Books
Pelican Publishing
Port Hole Public.
Randall House

Salvation Publisher
Tate Publishing
Trail Media
VBC Publishing
Vision Forum
Whitaker House
White Fire Publishing
WinePress
WingSpread
Word Alive
Write Integrity Press
Zoë Life Publishing

FICTION: ADULT/GENERAL

(a) Ballantine
(a) FaithWords
(a) HarperOne
(a) Kregel
(a) Multnomah
(a) Nelson, Fiction, Thomas

Aaron Book
Ambassador Intl.
American Binding
Blue Dolphin
Bold Vision Books
Bondfire Books
Brown Books
BRP Publishing
Chalfont House Publishing
Charisma House
Cladach Publishing
Comfort Publishing
Creation House
Essence
Evergreen Press
Halo Publishing Intl.
Howard Books
Lighthouse Publishing
Lighthouse Trails
Love Inspired
Morgan James Publishing
MountainView
New Leaf
Parson Place
Ravenhawk Books
Whitaker House
White Fire Publishing
Write Integrity Press

FICTION: ADULT/RELIGIOUS

(a) Baker Books
(a) Ballantine
(a) B&H Publishing
(a) Bethany House
(a) Doubleday Relig.
(a) FaithWords
(a) HarperOne
(a) Kregel
(a) Multnomah
(a) Nelson, Fiction, Thomas
(a) Revell
(a) WaterBrook Press

Aaron Book
ACW Press
Adams Media
Ambassador Books
Ambassador Intl.
American Binding
Barbour
Bold Vision Books
Bondfire Books
Booklocker.com
Bridge Logos
Brown Books
BRP Publishing
Chalfont House Publishing
Charisma House
Christian Writer's Ebook
Cladach Publishing
Comfort Publishing
Creation House
CrossHouse
Deep River Books
Destiny Image (books)
Earthen Vessel
Eerdmans Pub., Wm. B.
Essence
Evergreen Press
Fairway Press
Faith Books & More
Focus on the Family
Fruitbearer Pub.
Grace Publishing
Guideposts Books
Halo Publishing Intl.
Hannibal Books
Howard Books
Lift Every Voice
Lighthouse Publishing
Lighthouse Trails
Love Inspired
Moody Publishers
Morgan James Publishing
MountainView
NavPress
New Leaf
OakTara
Pacific Press
Parson Place
Parsons Publishing
Port Hole Public.
Salt Works
Sunpenny Publishing
Tate Publishing
Trail Media
Vision Forum
Whitaker House
White Fire Publishing
White Rose
WinePress
Word Alive
Write Integrity Press
Zoë Life Publishing

FICTION: ADVENTURE

(a) Baker Books
(a) Multnomah
(a) WaterBrook Press

Aaron Book
ACW Press
Ambassador Books
Ambassador Intl.
American Binding
Barbour
Bold Vision Books
Bondfire Books
Booklocker.com
Bridge Logos
Brown Books
BRP Publishing
Chalfont House Publishing
Charisma House
Christian Writer's Ebook
Comfort Publishing
Creation House
Deep River Books
Eerdmans/Yg Readers
Essence

Evergreen Press
Fairway Press
Faith Books & More
Grace Publishing
Halo Publishing Intl.
Howard Books
JourneyForth/BJU
Lift Every Voice
Lighthouse Publishing
Morgan James Publishing
MountainView
New Leaf
P&R Publications
Parson Place
Parsons Publishing
Pauline Kids
Port Hole Public.
Ravenhawk Books
Salt Works
Sunpenny Publishing
Tate Publishing
White Fire Publishing
WinePress
Write Integrity Press
Zoë Life Publishing

FICTION: ALLEGORY

(a) Baker Books
(a) Multnomah

Aaron Book
ACW Press
American Binding
Barbour
Bondfire Books
Booklocker.com
Bridge Logos
Brown Books
Chalfont House Publishing
Charisma House
Christian Writer's Ebook
Creation House
Deep River Books
Destiny Image (books)
Essence
Evergreen Press
Fairway Press
Faith Books & More
Howard Books
Lighthouse Publishing
OakTara
Port Hole Public.
Salt Works
Tate Publishing
WinePress
Zoë Life Publishing

FICTION: BIBLICAL

(a) Baker Books
(a) Multnomah
(a) Nelson, Fiction, Thomas
(a) WaterBrook Press

Aaron Book
Abingdon Press
ACW Press
Ambassador Intl.
American Binding
Bold Vision Books
Bondfire Books
Booklocker.com
Bridge Logos
Brown Books
BRP Publishing
Chalfont House Publishing
Charisma House
Christian Writer's Ebook
Cladach Publishing
Creation House
Deep River Books
Destiny Image (books)
Earthen Vessel
Eerdmans Pub., Wm. B.
Eerdmans/Yg Readers
Essence
Evergreen Press
Fairway Press
Faith Books & More
Guideposts Books
Hannibal Books
Howard Books
Lift Every Voice
Lighthouse Publishing
Lighthouse Trails
Moody Publishers
Morgan James Publishing
NavPress
OakTara
Pacific Press
P&R Publications
Parsons Publishing
Port Hole Public.
Salt Works
Tate Publishing
Trail Media
WinePress
Write Integrity Press
Zoë Life Publishing

FICTION: CHICK LIT

(a) Multnomah
(a) Nelson, Fiction, Thomas
(a) WaterBrook Press

Aaron Book
ACW Press
Ambassador Books
Ambassador Intl.
American Binding
Bondfire Books
Booklocker.com
Brown Books
BRP Publishing
Chalfont House Publishing
Charisma House
Christian Writer's Ebook
Creation House
Deep River Books
Essence
Faith Books & More
Lighthouse Publishing
Love Inspired Suspense
Morgan James Publishing
Port Hole Public.
Ravenhawk Books
Whitaker House
WinePress
Write Integrity Press
Zoë Life Publishing

FICTION: CONTEMPORARY

(a) Avon Inspire
(a) Baker Books
(a) Ballantine
(a) B&H Publishing
(a) Bethany House
(a) FaithWords
(a) Kregel
(a) Multnomah
(a) Nelson, Fiction, Thomas
(a) Revell
(a) Tyndale House
(a) WaterBrook Press

Aaron Book
ACW Press
Ambassador Books
American Binding
AMG Publishers
Barbour
Bold Vision Books
Bondfire Books
Booklocker.com
Brown Books
BRP Publishing
Chalfont House Publishing
Charisma House
Christian Writer's Ebook
Creation House
Deep River Books
Desert Breeze Pub.
Destiny Image (books)
Eerdmans/Yg Readers
Essence
Fairway Press
Faith Books & More
Focus on the Family
Grace Publishing
Howard Books
JourneyForth/BJU
Lift Every Voice
Lighthouse Publishing
Love Inspired
Moody Publishers
Morgan James Publishing
MountainView
NavPress
New Leaf
OakTara
Parson Place
Pauline Books
Pauline Kids
Port Hole Public.
Ravenhawk Books
Salt Works
Sunpenny Publishing
Tate Publishing
Whitaker House
White Fire Publishing
WinePress
Write Integrity Press
Zoë Life Publishing

FICTION: COZY MYSTERIES

Ambassador Intl.
Bold Vision Books
Bondfire Books
BRP Publishing
Chalfont House Publishing
Comfort Publishing
Essence
Grace Publishing
Write Integrity Press
Zoë Life Publishing

FICTION: ETHNIC

(a) Baker Books
(a) Ballantine
(a) Multnomah

Aaron Book
ACW Press
American Binding
Booklocker.com
Chalfont House Publishing
Charisma House
Christian Writer's Ebook
Deep River Books
Essence
Evergreen Press
Fairway Press
Faith Books & More
Focus on the Family
Lift Every Voice
Lighthouse Publishing
Sunpenny Publishing
Tate Publishing
White Fire Publishing
WinePress
Zoë Life Publishing

FICTION: FABLES/PARABLES

(a) HarperOne

Aaron Book
ACW Press
American Binding
Blue Dolphin
Booklocker.com
Brown Books
BRP Publishing
Chalfont House Publishing
Deep River Books
Essence
Faith Books & More
Lighthouse Publishing
Parson Place
Pauline Books
Salt Works
Tate Publishing
White Fire Publishing
WinePress
Zoë Life Publishing

FICTION: FANTASY

(a) Ballantine
(a) Multnomah
(a) WaterBrook Press

Aaron Book
ACW Press
American Binding
AMG Publishers
Barbour
Bondfire Books
Booklocker.com
BRP Publishing
Chalfont House Publishing
Charisma House
Christian Writer's Ebook
Comfort Publishing
Creation House
Deep River Books
Desert Breeze Pub.
Destiny Image (books)
Eerdmans Pub., Wm. B.
Essence
Fairway Press
Faith Books & More
Lighthouse Publishing
MountainView
OakTara
P&R Publications
Parsons Publishing
Port Hole Public.
Ravenhawk Books
Tate Publishing
Whitaker House
WinePress
Zoë Life Publishing

FICTION: FRONTIER

(a) Baker Books
(a) Bethany House

(a) Multnomah
(a) Nelson, Fiction, Thomas

Aaron Book
ACW Press
Ambassador Intl.
American Binding
AMG Publishers
Bold Vision Books
Booklocker.com
Brown Books
BRP Publishing
Chalfont House Publishing
Charisma House
Christian Writer's Ebook
Cladach Publishing
Deep River Books
Essence
Fairway Press
Faith Books & More
Guardian Angel
JourneyForth/BJU
Lighthouse Publishing
MountainView
Parson Place
Port Hole Public.
Ravenhawk Books
Tate Publishing
Trail Media
Whitaker House
WinePress
Zoë Life Publishing

FICTION: FRONTIER/ROMANCE

(a) Baker Books
(a) Bethany House
(a) Multnomah
(a) Nelson, Fiction, Thomas

Aaron Book
ACW Press
Ambassador Intl.
American Binding
AMG Publishers
Barbour
Bold Vision Books
Bondfire Books
Booklocker.com
Brown Books
BRP Publishing
Chalfont House Publishing
Charisma House
Christian Writer's Ebook
Deep River Books
Desert Breeze Pub.
Essence
Fairway Press
Faith Books & More
Lighthouse Publishing
MountainView
Parson Place
Port Hole Public.
Ravenhawk Books
Tate Publishing
Whitaker House
White Fire Publishing
White Rose
WinePress
Zoë Life Publishing

FICTION: HISTORICAL

(a) Avon Inspire
(a) Baker Books
(a) Ballantine
(a) B&H Publishing
(a) Bethany House
(a) FaithWords
(a) Kregel
(a) Multnomah
(a) Nelson, Fiction, Thomas
(a) Revell
(a) WaterBrook Press

Aaron Book
Abingdon Press
ACW Press
Ambassador Books
Ambassador Intl.
American Binding
AMG Publishers
Blue Dolphin
Bold Vision Books
Bondfire Books
Booklocker.com
Bridge Logos
Brown Books
BRP Publishing
Chalfont House Publishing
Charisma House
Christian Writer's Ebook
Cladach Publishing
Comfort Publishing
Deep River Books
Earthen Vessel
Eerdmans Pub., Wm. B.
Eerdmans/Yg Readers
Essence
Fairway Press
Faith Books & More
Focus on the Family
Grace Publishing
Hannibal Books
Howard Books
JourneyForth/BJU
Lift Every Voice
Lighthouse Publishing
Moody Publishers
Morgan James Publishing
MountainView
NavPress
OakTara
Parson Place
Parsons Publishing
Pauline Books
Pauline Kids
Port Hole Public.
Ravenhawk Books
Salt Works
Sunpenny Publishing
Tate Publishing
Trail Media
Vision Forum
Whitaker House
White Fire Publishing
WinePress
Zoë Life Publishing

FICTION: HISTORICAL/ROMANCE

(a) Baker Books
(a) B&H Publishing
(a) Bethany House
(a) Multnomah
(a) Nelson, Fiction, Thomas
(a) Tyndale House
(a) WaterBrook Press

Aaron Book
Abingdon Press
ACW Press
Ambassador Intl.
American Binding

AMG Publishers
Barbour
Bold Vision Books
Bondfire Books
Booklocker.com
Brown Books
BRP Publishing
Chalfont House Publishing
Charisma House
Christian Writer's Ebook
Comfort Publishing
Deep River Books
Desert Breeze Pub.
Essence
Fairway Press
Faith Books & More
Grace Publishing
Hannibal Books
Lift Every Voice
Lighthouse Publishing
Morgan James Publishing
MountainView
Parson Place
Port Hole Public.
Ravenhawk Books
Tate Publishing
Whitaker House
White Fire Publishing
White Rose
WinePress
Zoë Life Publishing

FICTION: HUMOR

(a) Baker Books
(a) Ballantine
(a) FaithWords
(a) Multnomah

Aaron Book
ACW Press
Ambassador Books
American Binding
Bold Vision Books
Bondfire Books
Booklocker.com
BRP Publishing
Chalfont House Publishing
Charisma House
Christian Writer's Ebook
Creation House
Deep River Books
Eerdmans/Yg Readers
Essence
Evergreen Press
Fairway Press
Faith Books & More
Halo Publishing Intl.
JourneyForth/BJU
Lighthouse Publishing
MountainView
Parson Place
Parsons Publishing
Port Hole Public.
Ravenhawk Books
Salt Works
Sunpenny Publishing
Tate Publishing
White Fire Publishing
WinePress
Write Integrity Press
Zoë Life Publishing

FICTION: JUVENILE (Ages 8-12)

(a) Baker Books
(a) Kregel
(a) Tyndale House

Aaron Book
ACW Press
Ambassador Books
American Binding
AMG Publishers
Barbour
Blue Dolphin
Booklocker.com
Brown Books
Chalfont House Publishing
Charisma House
Comfort Publishing
Creation House
CrossHouse
Deep River Books
Eerdmans Pub., Wm. B.
Eerdmans/Yg Readers
Essence
Evergreen Press
Fairway Press
Faith Books & More
Fruitbearer Pub.
Grace Publishing
Guardian Angel
Halo Publishing Intl.
JourneyForth/BJU
Lift Every Voice
Lighthouse Publishing
Moody Publishers
Morgan James Publishing
Pacific Press
P&R Publications
Parson Place
Pauline Books
Pauline Kids
Port Hole Public.
Salt Works
Standard Publishing
Tate Publishing
Warner Press
WinePress
Word Alive
Zoë Life Publishing

FICTION: LITERARY

(a) Baker Books
(a) Ballantine
(a) Bethany House
(a) FaithWords
(a) HarperOne
(a) Multnomah
(a) Nelson, Fiction, Thomas
(a) WaterBrook Press

Aaron Book
ACW Press
Ambassador Books
American Binding
Bold Vision Books
Bondfire Books
Booklocker.com
Brown Books
BRP Publishing
Chalfont House Publishing
Charisma House
Christian Writer's Ebook
Deep River Books
Eerdmans Pub., Wm. B.
Eerdmans/Yg Readers
Essence
Fairway Press
Faith Books & More
Focus on the Family
JourneyForth/BJU
Lighthouse Publishing

Moody Publishers
NavPress
Port Hole Public.
Ravenhawk Books
Salt Works
Sunpenny Publishing
Tate Publishing
WinePress
Zoë Life Publishing

FICTION: MYSTERY/ROMANCE

(a) Baker Books
(a) Ballantine
(a) B&H Publishing
(a) Bethany House
(a) Kregel
(a) Multnomah
(a) Nelson, Fiction, Thomas
(a) Summerside Press

Aaron Book
ACW Press
American Binding
Barbour
Bold Vision Books
Bondfire Books
Booklocker.com
Brown Books
BRP Publishing
Chalfont House Publishing
Charisma House
Christian Writer's Ebook
Comfort Publishing
Deep River Books
Desert Breeze Pub.
Essence
Fairway Press
Faith Books & More
Grace Publishing
Guideposts Books
Howard Books
Lift Every Voice
Lighthouse Publishing
Love Inspired Suspense
Morgan James Publishing
MountainView
Parson Place
Port Hole Public.
Tate Publishing
White Fire Publishing
White Rose
WinePress
Write Integrity Press
Zoë Life Publishing

FICTION: MYSTERY/SUSPENSE

(a) Baker Books
(a) Ballantine
(a) B&H Publishing
(a) Bethany House
(a) Kregel
(a) Multnomah
(a) Revell
(a) Tyndale House

Aaron Book
ACW Press
Ambassador Books
American Binding
Blue Dolphin
Bold Vision Books
Booklocker.com
Brown Books
BRP Publishing
Chalfont House Publishing
Charisma House
Christian Writer's Ebook
Comfort Publishing
Creation House
Deep River Books
Desert Breeze Pub.
Eerdmans/Yg Readers
Essence
Fairway Press
Faith Books & More
Focus on the Family
Grace Publishing
Guideposts Books
Howard Books
JourneyForth/BJU
Lift Every Voice
Lighthouse Publishing
Love Inspired Suspense
Moody Publishers
Morgan James Publishing
MountainView
New Leaf
OakTara
Parson Place
Parsons Publishing
Pauline Books
Pauline Kids
Port Hole Public.
Ravenhawk Books
Salt Works
Sunpenny Publishing
Tate Publishing
White Fire Publishing
WinePress
Write Integrity Press
Zoë Life Publishing

FICTION: NOVELLAS

(a) Baker Books

Aaron Book
ACW Press
American Binding
Barbour
Bondfire Books
Booklocker.com
BRP Publishing
Chalfont House Publishing
Christian Writer's Ebook
Essence
Fairway Press
Faith Books & More
Halo Publishing Intl.
Lighthouse Publishing
MountainView
Salt Works
WinePress
Zoë Life Publishing

FICTION: PLAYS

American Binding
CSS Publishing
Essence
Fairway Press
Guardian Angel
Meriwether
Players Press
Salt Works

FICTION: ROMANCE

(a) Baker Books
(a) Ballantine
(a) Bethany House
(a) Multnomah
(a) Nelson, Fiction, Thomas
(a) Summerside Press

(a) Tyndale House
(a) WaterBrook Press

Aaron Book
ACW Press
American Binding
Barbour
Bold Vision Books
Bondfire Books
Booklocker.com
Brown Books
BRP Publishing
Chalfont House Publishing
Charisma House
Christian Writer's Ebook
Comfort Publishing
Creation House
Deep River Books
Essence
Fairway Press
Faith Books & More
Hannibal Books
Lift Every Voice
Lighthouse Publishing
Love Inspired
Love Inspired Suspense
Morgan James Publishing
MountainView
OakTara
Parson Place
Port Hole Public.
Sunpenny Publishing
Tate Publishing
Whitaker House
White Fire Publishing
White Rose
WinePress
Write Integrity Press
Zoë Life Publishing

FICTION: SCIENCE FICTION

(a) WaterBrook Press

Aaron Book
ACW Press
American Binding
Bondfire Books
Booklocker.com
BRP Publishing
Chalfont House Publishing
Charisma House
Christian Writer's Ebook
Comfort Publishing
Creation House
Deep River Books
Desert Breeze Pub.
Essence
Evergreen Press
Fairway Press
Faith Books & More
Lighthouse Publishing
MountainView
OakTara
Port Hole Public.
Sunpenny Publishing
Tate Publishing
White Fire Publishing
WinePress
Zoë Life Publishing

FICTION: SHORT STORY COLLECTIONS

(a) Baker Books
(a) Ballantine

Aaron Book
ACW Press
American Binding
Bondfire Books
Booklocker.com
BRP Publishing
Chalfont House Publishing
Christian Writer's Ebook
Comfort Publishing
Deep River Books
Earthen Vessel
Eerdmans Pub., Wm. B.
Essence
Fairway Press
Faith Books & More
MountainView
Parson Place
Pauline Books
Pauline Kids
Port Hole Public.
Salt Works
Tate Publishing
Trail Media
White Fire Publishing
White Rose
WinePress
Zoë Life Publishing

FICTION: SPECULATIVE

(a) Baker Books
(a) Multnomah

Aaron Book
ACW Press
American Binding
Booklocker.com
Chalfont House Publishing
Charisma House
Christian Writer's Ebook
Deep River Books
Essence
Faith Books & More
Lighthouse Publishing
MountainView
OakTara
Port Hole Public.
Salt Works
Tate Publishing
White Fire Publishing
WinePress
Zoë Life Publishing

FICTION: TEEN/YOUNG ADULT

(a) Baker Books
(a) FaithWords
(a) Kregel
(a) Multnomah
(a) Nelson, Fiction, Thomas
(a) WaterBrook Press

Aaron Book
ACW Press
Ambassador Books
American Binding
AMG Publishers
Barbour
Blue Dolphin
Bondfire Books
Booklocker.com
BRP Publishing
Chalfont House Publishing
Charisma House
Christian Writer's Ebook
Comfort Publishing
Creation House

Deep River Books
Eerdmans Pub., Wm. B.
Eerdmans/Yg Readers
Essence
Fairway Press
Faith Books & More
Fruitbearer Pub.
Grace Publishing
JourneyForth/BJU
Kirk House
Legacy Press
Lift Every Voice
Lighthouse Publishing
Lighthouse Trails
Moody Publishers
Morgan James Publishing
MountainView
NavPress
P&R Publications
Parson Place
Parsons Publishing
Ravenhawk Books
Tate Publishing
Trail Media
Warner Press
Watershed Books
White Fire Publishing
WinePress
Word Alive
Zoë Life Publishing

FICTION: WESTERNS

(a) Baker Books
(a) Multnomah

Aaron Book
ACW Press
American Binding
Bold Vision Books
Booklocker.com
Brown Books
BRP Publishing
Chalfont House Publishing
Charisma House
Christian Writer's Ebook
Deep River Books
Desert Breeze Pub.
Essence
Fairway Press
Faith Books & More
JourneyForth/BJU
Lighthouse Publishing
MountainView
Parson Place
Ravenhawk Books
Salt Works
Tate Publishing
Trail Media
Whitaker House
WinePress
Zoë Life Publishing

FORGIVENESS

(a) B&H Publishing
(a) Doubleday Relig.
(a) FaithWords
(a) HarperOne
(a) Kregel
(a) Nelson, Thomas

Aaron Book
Abingdon Press
ACW Press
Ambassador Intl.
American Binding
Barbour
Blue Dolphin
Bold Vision Books
Bondfire Books
Booklocker.com
Bridge Logos
Brown Books
Chalfont House Publishing
Charisma House
Christian Writer's Ebook
CLC Publications
Comfort Publishing
Creation House
CrossLink Publishing
CSS Publishing
Cupola Press
DCTS Publishers
Deep River Books
Destiny Image (books)
Discovery House
Eerdmans Pub., Wm. B.
Essence
Fairway Press
Faith Books & More
Grace Acres Press
Grace Publishing
Guardian Angel
Halo Publishing Intl.
Hensley Publishing
Howard Books
InterVarsity Press
JourneyForth/BJU
Judson Press
Lift Every Voice
Lighthouse Publishing
Lutheran Univ. Press
Morgan James Publishing
NavPress
New Hope
On My Own Now
Pacific Press
Parson Place
Parsons Publishing
Pauline Books
Salt Works
Salvation Publisher
Tate Publishing
VBC Publishing
White Fire Publishing
WinePress
WingSpread
Word Alive
Write Integrity Press
Zoë Life Publishing

GAMES/CRAFTS

(a) Baker Books

Booklocker.com
Contemporary Drama
Essence
Fairway Press
Faith Books & More
Group Publishing
Guardian Angel
Legacy Press
Lighthouse Publishing
Players Press
Rainbow Publishers
Standard Publishing
Tate Publishing
Warner Press
Zoë Life Publishing

GIFT BOOKS

Aaron Book
Blue Dolphin
Bold Vision Books

Bridge Logos
Brown Books
Charisma House
Creation House
Cupola Press
Eerdmans Pub., Wm. B.
Essence
Faith Books & More
Fruitbearer Pub.
Howard Books
Lighthouse Publishing
Ravenhawk Books
Salt Works
WinePress
WingSpread
Write Integrity Press
Zoë Life Publishing

GRANDPARENTING

(a) Bethany House
(a) Nelson, Thomas

Aaron Book
Abingdon Press
ACW Press
American Binding
Blue Dolphin
Bold Vision Books
Bondfire Books
Booklocker.com
Bridge Logos
Brown Books
Chalfont House Publishing
CLC Publications
Comfort Publishing
Creation House
CrossLink Publishing
Cupola Press
Discovery House
Eerdmans Pub., Wm. B.
Essence
Faith Books & More
Howard Books
Lighthouse Publishing
New Hope
Parson Place
Salvation Publisher
VBC Publishing
Whitaker House
White Fire Publishing
WinePress
WingSpread
Write Integrity Press
Zoë Life Publishing

GRIEF

(a) Bethany House

Aaron Book
ACW Press
American Binding
Blue Dolphin
BMH Books
Bold Vision Books
Bondfire Books
Booklocker.com
Chalfont House Publishing
Charisma House
Comfort Publishing
Creation House
CrossLink Publishing
Cupola Press
Discovery House
Eerdmans Pub., Wm. B.
Essence
Faith Books & More
Franciscan Media
Grace Publishing
Howard Books
Lift Every Voice
Lighthouse Publishing
Morgan James Publishing
NavPress
Pauline Books
Port Hole Public.
Ravenhawk Books
Salvation Publisher
White Fire Publishing
WinePress
WingSpread
Zoë Life Publishing

GROUP STUDY BOOKS

(a) Baker Books

Aaron Book
Abingdon Press
ACW Press
American Binding
AMG Publishers
BMH Books
Bold Vision Books
Bondfire Books
Booklocker.com
Bridge Logos
Chalfont House Publishing
Christian Writer's Ebook
CrossHouse
CrossLink Publishing
CSS Publishing
Deep River Books
Eerdmans Pub., Wm. B.
Essence
Evergreen Press
Fairway Press
Grace Acres Press
Grace Publishing
Group Publishing
Hannibal Books
Hensley Publishing
InterVarsity Press
Judson Press
Lighthouse Publishing
Morgan James Publishing
New Hope
Pacific Press
Parson Place
Randall House
Salt Works
Tate Publishing
Trail Media
White Fire Publishing
WinePress
Word Alive
Zoë Life Publishing

HEALING

(a) Baker Books
(a) Cook, David C.
(a) FaithWords
(a) Hay House
(a) Nelson, Thomas

Aaron Book
ACW Press
American Binding
Blue Dolphin
Booklocker.com
Bridge Logos
Brown Books
Canticle Books
Chalfont House Publishing
Charisma House

Christian Heritage
Christian Writer's Ebook
CLC Publications
Comfort Publishing
Creation House
CSS Publishing
Cupola Press
Deep River Books
Destiny Image (books)
Eerdmans Pub., Wm. B.
Essence
Fairway Press
Faith Books & More
Harrison House
Hope Publishing
Lighthouse Publishing
Loyola Press
Lutheran Univ. Press
Magnus Press
NavPress
Pacific Press
Parson Place
Parsons Publishing
Pauline Books
Salvation Publisher
Tate Publishing
Whitaker House
White Fire Publishing
WinePress
WingSpread
Word Alive
Zoë Life Publishing

HEALTH

(a) Baker Books
(a) Ballantine
(a) FaithWords
(a) Hay House
(a) Nelson, Thomas

Aaron Book
ACW Press
Ambassador Books
American Binding
Blue Dolphin
Bold Vision Books
Booklocker.com
Brown Books
Canticle Books
Charisma House
Christian Writer's Ebook
Cladach Publishing
Comfort Publishing
Creation House
Deep River Books
Destiny Image (books)
Eerdmans Pub., Wm. B.
Essence
Evergreen Press
Fairway Press
Faith Books & More
Franciscan Media
Grace Publishing
Guardian Angel
Hope Publishing
Langmarc
Life Cycle Books
Lighthouse Publishing
Loyola Press
Magnus Press
Morgan James Publishing
MountainView
New Hope
Pacific Press
Parsons Publishing
Salvation Publisher
Sunpenny Publishing
Tate Publishing
VBC Publishing
WinePress
Word Alive
Zoë Life Publishing

HISPANIC MARKETS

(a) Doubleday Relig.

Abingdon Press
American Binding
B&H Publishing
Booklocker.com
Bridge Logos
Charisma House
InterVarsity Press
Judson Press
Pacific Press
Parsons Publishing
Praeger Publishers
Tate Publishing
Tyndale Español
Whitaker House

HISTORICAL

(a) Baker Academic
(a) Baker Books
(a) Doubleday Relig.
(a) HarperOne
(a) Kregel
(a) Nelson, Thomas

Aaron Book
ACW Press
Ambassador Books
American Binding
AMG Publishers
Blue Dolphin
Bold Vision Books
Booklocker.com
Bridge Logos
Brown Books
Chalfont House Publishing
Christian Heritage
Christian Writer's Ebook
Comfort Publishing
Conciliar Press
Creation House
CrossLink Publishing
Earthen Vessel
Eerdmans Pub., Wm. B.
Essence
Fairway Press
Faith Books & More
Inkling Books
InterVarsity Press
Kirk House
Lift Every Voice
Lighthouse Publishing
Loyola Press
Lutheran Univ. Press
Salt Works
Sunpenny Publishing
Tate Publishing
Trinity Foundation
Vision Forum
WinePress
Word Alive
Yale Univ. Press
Zoë Life Publishing

HOLIDAY/SEASONAL

(a) Cook, David C.
(a) FaithWords
(a) HarperOne

Aaron Book
Abingdon Press
ACW Press
Ambassador Books
American Binding
Barbour
Blue Dolphin
Bondfire Books
Booklocker.com
Charisma House
Christian Writer's Ebook
CSS Publishing
Deep River Books
Discovery House
Essence
Evergreen Press
Fairway Press
Faith Books & More
Grace Publishing
Guardian Angel
Guideposts Books
Howard Books
Judson Press
Lighthouse Publishing
Meriwether
New Hope
Pauline Books
Ravenhawk Books
Salt Works
Standard Publishing
Tate Publishing
Trail Media
Warner Press
WinePress
Word Alive
Write Integrity Press

HOLINESS

(a) Bethany House

Aaron Book
ACW Press
Ambassador Intl.
American Binding
Blue Dolphin
Bondfire Books
Booklocker.com
Bridge Logos
Brown Books
Chalfont House Publishing
Charisma House
Christian Heritage
CLC Publications
Creation House
Eerdmans Pub., Wm. B.
Essence
Faith Books & More
Grace Acres Press
Howard Books
InterVarsity Press
Lighthouse Publishing
NavPress
Parson Place
Parsons Publishing
Pauline Books
Salt Works
Salvation Publisher
Tate Publishing
Wesleyan Publishing
White Fire Publishing
WinePress
WingSpread
Write Integrity Press

HOLY SPIRIT

(a) Kregel
(a) Nelson, Thomas

Aaron Book
ACW Press
American Binding
Blue Dolphin
Bold Vision Books
Bondfire Books
Booklocker.com
Bridge Logos
Canticle Books
Chalfont House Publishing
Charisma House
Christian Heritage
Christian Writer's Ebook
CLC Publications
Comfort Publishing
Creation House
CSS Publishing
Deep River Books
Destiny Image (books)
Eerdmans Pub., Wm. B.
Essence
Fairway Press
Faith Books & More
Harrison House
InterVarsity Press
Lift Every Voice
Lighthouse Publishing
Lutheran Univ. Press
Magnus Press
Morgan James Publishing
NavPress
Pacific Press
Parson Place
Parsons Publishing
Salvation Publisher
Tate Publishing
VBC Publishing
Whitaker House
White Fire Publishing
WinePress
WingSpread
Word Alive
Zoë Life Publishing

HOMESCHOOLING RESOURCES

(a) Baker Books

Aaron Book
ACW Press
American Binding
Bondfire Books
Booklocker.com
Christian Writer's Ebook
CrossHouse
CrossLink Publishing
Eerdmans Pub., Wm. B.
Essence
Fairway Press
Faith Books & More
Grace Acres Press
Grace Publishing
Guardian Angel
Hannibal Books
JourneyForth/BJU
Lighthouse Publishing
Lighthouse Trails
New Leaf
Salt Works
Tate Publishing
Trail Media
WinePress
Word Alive
Zoë Life Publishing

HOMILETICS

(a) Baker Books
(a) Kregel

Aaron Book
Abingdon Press
ACW Press
American Binding
Bondfire Books
Booklocker.com
Christian Writer's Ebook
CSS Publishing
DCTS Publishers
Deep River Books
Earthen Vessel
Eerdmans Pub., Wm. B.
Essence
Fairway Press
Faith Books & More
Judson Press
Lighthouse Publishing
Lutheran Univ. Press
NavPress
Salt Works
Tate Publishing
VBC Publishing
WinePress
Word Alive
Zoë Life Publishing

HOW-TO

(a) Baker Books
(a) Ballantine
(a) Nelson, Thomas
(a) Revell

Aaron Book
ACW Press
Adams Media
American Binding
Blue Dolphin
Bold Vision Books
Bondfire Books
Booklocker.com
Bridge Logos
Christian Writer's Ebook
Church Growth Inst.
Deep River Books
Essence
Evergreen Press
Fairway Press
Faith Books & More
Gospel Light
Guardian Angel
Halo Publishing Intl.
Howard Books
Inkling Books
Kirk House
Lighthouse Publishing
Meriwether
Morgan James Publishing
MountainView
Our Sunday Visitor
Pacific Press
Parson Place
Players Press
Salt Works
Salvation Publisher
Standard Publishing
Tate Publishing
VBC Publishing
WinePress
Word Alive
Write Integrity Press
Zoë Life Publishing

HUMOR

(a) Baker Books
(a) Ballantine
(a) Cook, David C.
(a) FaithWords
(a) Nelson, Thomas

Aaron Book
ACW Press
Ambassador Books
American Binding
Barbour
Blue Dolphin
Bold Vision Books
Bondfire Books
Booklocker.com
Bridge Logos
Christian Writer's Ebook
Comfort Publishing
Creation House
Cupola Press
Deep River Books
Essence
Evergreen Press
Fairway Press
Faith Books & More
Guideposts Books
Kirk House
Lighthouse Publishing
Loyola Press
Meriwether
MOPS Intl.
Morgan James Publishing
NavPress
On My Own Now
Pacific Press
Parson Place
Salt Works
Salvation Publisher
Tate Publishing
Trail Media
White Fire Publishing
WinePress
Word Alive
Write Integrity Press
Zoë Life Publishing

INSPIRATIONAL

(a) Baker Books
(a) Bethany House
(a) Doubleday Relig.
(a) FaithWords
(a) Hay House
(a) Nelson, Thomas
(a) Tyndale House
(a) WaterBrook Press

Aaron Book
Abingdon Press
ACW Press
Adams Media
Ambassador Books
American Binding
Barbour
Blue Dolphin
Bold Vision Books
Bondfire Books
Booklocker.com
Bridge Logos
Brown Books
Canticle Books
Chalfont House Publishing
Charisma House
Christian Writer's Ebook
CLC Publications
Comfort Publishing
Creation House

CrossHouse
CrossLink Publishing
CSS Publishing
Cupola Press
DCTS Publishers
Deep River Books
Destiny Image (books)
Discovery House
Dove Inspirational
Earthen Vessel
Essence
Evergreen Press
Fairway Press
Faith Books & More
Franciscan Media
Fruitbearer Pub.
Grace Publishing
Guardian Angel
Harrison House
Hope Publishing
Howard Books
JourneyForth/BJU
Judson Press
Kirk House
Langmarc
Lighthouse Publishing
Loyola Press
Lutheran Univ. Press
Magnus Press
Morgan James Publishing
MountainView
NavPress
New Leaf
On My Own Now
Pacific Press
Parson Place
Parsons Publishing
Pauline Books
Pelican Publishing
Port Hole Public.
Ravenhawk Books
Salt Works
Salvation Publisher
Sunpenny Publishing
Tate Publishing
VBC Publishing
Wesleyan Publishing
Whitaker House
White Fire Publishing
WinePress
WingSpread
Word Alive
Write Integrity Press
Zoë Life Publishing

LAY COUNSELING

Bold Vision Books
Bondfire Books
Chalfont House Publishing
Randall House
WingSpread
Zoë Life Publishing

LEADERSHIP

(a) Baker Books
(a) B&H Publishing
(a) Bethany House
(a) Cook, David C.
(a) Kregel
(a) Nelson, Thomas
(a) WaterBrook Press

Aaron Book
Abingdon Press
ACW Press
Ambassador Intl.
American Binding
Blue Dolphin
BMH Books
Bold Vision Books
Bondfire Books
Booklocker.com
Bridge Logos
Chalfont House Publishing
Charisma House
Christian Writer's Ebook
Church Growth Inst.
CLC Publications
Creation House
CrossLink Publishing
Crossway
CSS Publishing
DCTS Publishers
Deep River Books
Eerdmans Pub., Wm. B.
Essence
Evergreen Press
Fairway Press
Faith Books & More
Grace Acres Press
Grace Publishing
Group Publishing
Guardian Angel
Harrison House
InterVarsity Press
Judson Press
Kirk House
Lift Every Voice
Lighthouse Publishing
Lutheran Univ. Press
Morgan James Publishing
NavPress
New Hope
New Leaf
Parson Place
Parsons Publishing
Randall House
Ravenhawk Books
Salt Works
Salvation Publisher
Standard Publishing
Tate Publishing
Trail Media
VBC Publishing
Wesleyan Publishing
Whitaker House
White Fire Publishing
WinePress
WingSpread
Word Alive
Zoë Life Publishing

LIFESTYLE

Bondfire Books
Chalfont House Publishing
Cladach Publishing
Comfort Publishing
Grace Publishing
Halo Publishing Intl.
Morgan James Publishing
NavPress
New Leaf
Zoë Life Publishing

LITURGICAL STUDIES

(a) Baker Books
(a) Doubleday Relig.

Aaron Book
ACW Press
American Binding
American Cath. Press

Bondfire Books
Booklocker.com
Chalfont House Publishing
Christian Heritage
Christian Writer's Ebook
Conciliar Press
CSS Publishing
Eerdmans Pub., Wm. B.
Fairway Press
Faith Books & More
Group Publishing
InterVarsity Press
Lighthouse Publishing
Lutheran Univ. Press
Parson Place
Ravenhawk Books
Salt Works
Tate Publishing
Trail Media
White Fire Publishing
WinePress
Word Alive
Zoë Life Publishing

MARRIAGE

(a) Baker Books
(a) B&H Publishing
(a) Bethany House
(a) Cook, David C.
(a) Doubleday Relig.
(a) FaithWords
(a) HarperOne
(a) Kregel
(a) Nelson, Thomas
(a) Revell
(a) Tyndale House
(a) WaterBrook Press

Aaron Book
ACW Press
Ambassador Books
Ambassador Intl.
American Binding
Barbour
Blue Dolphin
Bold Vision Books
Bondfire Books
Booklocker.com
Brown Books
Chalfont House Publishing
Charisma House
Christian Writer's Ebook
Comfort Publishing
Creation House
CrossHouse
CrossLink Publishing
Crossway
CSS Publishing
Cupola Press
Deep River Books
Destiny Image (books)
Discovery House
Earthen Vessel
Eerdmans Pub., Wm. B.
Essence
Evergreen Press
Fairway Press
Faith Books & More
Focus on the Family
Franciscan Media
Grace Acres Press
Grace Publishing
Guideposts Books
Halo Publishing Intl.
Hannibal Books
Hensley Publishing
Hope Publishing
Howard Books
InterVarsity Press
JourneyForth/BJU
Judson Press
Lift Every Voice
Lighthouse Publishing
Loyola Press
MOPS Intl.
Morgan James Publishing
NavPress
New Hope
New Leaf
Pacific Press
Parson Place
Parsons Publishing
Randall House
Standard Publishing
Tate Publishing
Trail Media
VBC Publishing
Whitaker House
White Fire Publishing
WinePress
WingSpread
Word Alive
Zoë Life Publishing

MEMOIRS

(a) Baker Books
(a) Ballantine
(a) Doubleday Relig.
(a) FaithWords
(a) HarperOne
(a) Nelson, Thomas

Aaron Book
ACW Press
Ambassador Intl.
American Binding
Bondfire Books
Booklocker.com
Brown Books
Chalfont House Publishing
Christian Heritage
Christian Writer's Ebook
Cladach Publishing
Creation House
Deep River Books
Essence
Fairway Press
Faith Books & More
Franciscan Media
Fruitbearer Pub.
Grace Acres Press
Guideposts Books
Halo Publishing Intl.
Inheritance Press
Lighthouse Publishing
Lighthouse Trails
Morgan James Publishing
On My Own Now
Pacific Press
Salvation Publisher
Sunpenny Publishing
Tate Publishing
Trail Media
White Fire Publishing
WinePress
Word Alive
Zoë Life Publishing

MEN'S BOOKS

(a) Baker Books
(a) B&H Publishing
(a) Bethany House

(a) Doubleday Relig.
(a) Kregel
(a) Nelson, Thomas
(a) WaterBrook Press

Aaron Book
ACW Press
Ambassador Books
American Binding
AMG Publishers
Barbour
Blue Dolphin
BMH Books
Bold Vision Books
Bondfire Books
Booklocker.com
Bridge Logos
Chalfont House Publishing
Charisma House
Christian Writer's Ebook
Comfort Publishing
Creation House
CrossLink Publishing
Crossway
Deep River Books
Eerdmans Pub., Wm. B.
Essence
Evergreen Press
Fairway Press
Faith Books & More
Franciscan Media
Grace Publishing
Halo Publishing Intl.
Hensley Publishing
Howard Books
Inkling Books
InterVarsity Press
Lift Every Voice
Lighthouse Publishing
Loyola Press
NavPress
New Leaf
Pacific Press
Parson Place
Randall House
Ravenhawk Books
Tate Publishing
Trail Media
VBC Publishing
Whitaker House
White Fire Publishing
WinePress
WingSpread
Word Alive
Zoë Life Publishing

MINIBOOKS

American Binding
Bold Vision Books
Charisma House
Grace Publishing
Harrison House
Legacy Press
Lighthouse Publishing
Salt Works
Tate Publishing
Trail Media

MIRACLES

(a) Baker Books
(a) HarperOne

Aaron Book
ACW Press
American Binding
Blue Dolphin
Bondfire Books
Booklocker.com
Chalfont House Publishing
Charisma House
Christian Heritage
Christian Writer's Ebook
Comfort Publishing
Creation House
CrossLink Publishing
CSS Publishing
Deep River Books
Destiny Image (books)
Essence
Evergreen Press
Fairway Press
Faith Books & More
Guideposts Books
Harrison House
Lighthouse Publishing
Loyola Press
On My Own Now
Pacific Press
Parson Place
Parsons Publishing
Salvation Publisher
Tate Publishing
Whitaker House
White Fire Publishing
WinePress
Word Alive
Zoë Life Publishing

MISSIONS/MISSIONARY

(a) Baker Books

Aaron Book
ACW Press
Ambassador Intl.
American Binding
Ampelos Press
Bold Vision Books
Bondfire Books
Booklocker.com
Brown Books
Chalfont House Publishing
Charisma House
Christian Heritage
Christian Writer's Ebook
CLC Publications
Comfort Publishing
Creation House
CrossHouse
CSS Publishing
Deep River Books
Discovery House
Earthen Vessel
Eerdmans Pub., Wm. B.
Essence
Evergreen Press
Fairway Press
Faith Books & More
Grace Acres Press
Hannibal Books
Hope Publishing
InterVarsity Press
Lift Every Voice
Lighthouse Publishing
Lighthouse Trails
Lutheran Univ. Press
NavPress
Pacific Press
P&R Publications
Parson Place
Parsons Publishing
Randall House
Salt Works
Tate Publishing

Trail Media
VBC Publishing
White Fire Publishing
WinePress
Word Alive
Yale Univ. Press
Zoë Life Publishing

MONEY MANAGEMENT

(a) Baker Books
(a) Cook, David C.
(a) FaithWords
(a) Nelson, Thomas
(a) WaterBrook Press

Aaron Book
ACW Press
Ambassador Intl.
American Binding
Barbour
Blue Dolphin
BMH Books
Bold Vision Books
Bondfire Books
Booklocker.com
Charisma House
Christian Writer's Ebook
Creation House
Deep River Books
Eerdmans Pub., Wm. B.
Essence
Evergreen Press
Fairway Press
Faith Books & More
Grace Publishing
Hannibal Books
Hensley Publishing
JourneyForth/BJU
Judson Press
Lift Every Voice
Lighthouse Publishing
Moody Publishers
Morgan James Publishing
MountainView
NavPress
New Hope
New Leaf
Pacific Press
Parson Place
Ravenhawk Books
Reference Service
Salvation Publisher
Tate Publishing
VBC Publishing
WinePress
Word Alive
Zoë Life Publishing

MUSIC-RELATED BOOKS

(a) Baker Books

Aaron Book
American Cath. Press
Blue Dolphin
BMH Books
Booklocker.com
Christian Writer's Ebook
Contemporary Drama
Deep River Books
Destiny Image (books)
Eerdmans Pub., Wm. B.
Essence
Fairway Press
Faith Books & More
Guardian Angel
Lighthouse Publishing
Lutheran Univ. Press
Players Press
Standard Publishing
Tate Publishing
WinePress
Word Alive
Zoë Life Publishing

NOVELTY BOOKS FOR KIDS

(a) Baker Books

Brown Books
Fairway Press
Guardian Angel
Legacy Press
Lift Every Voice
Salt Works
Standard Publishing
Tate Publishing
Word Alive
Zoë Life Publishing

PAMPHLETS

Chalfont House Publishing
Christian Writer's Ebook
Essence
Fruitbearer Pub.
Lift Every Voice
Our Sunday Visitor
Salt Works
Trinity Foundation

PARENTING

(a) Baker Books
(a) Ballantine
(a) B&H Publishing
(a) Bethany House
(a) Cook, David C.
(a) FaithWords
(a) Kregel
(a) Nelson, Thomas
(a) Revell
(a) Tyndale House
(a) WaterBrook Press

Aaron Book
ACW Press
Adams Media
Ambassador Books
Ambassador Intl.
American Binding
AMG Publishers
Barbour
Blue Dolphin
Bold Vision Books
Bondfire Books
Booklocker.com
Brown Books
Chalfont House Publishing
Christian Writer's Ebook
Comfort Publishing
Conari Press
Conciliar Press
Creation House
CrossLink Publishing
Cupola Press
Deep River Books
Destiny Image (books)
Discovery House
Eerdmans Pub., Wm. B.
Essence
Evergreen Press
Fairway Press
Faith Books & More
Focus on the Family
Franciscan Media

Grace Acres Press
Grace Publishing
Halo Publishing Intl.
Harrison House
Hensley Publishing
Howard Books
InterVarsity Press
JourneyForth/BJU
Langmarc
Lift Every Voice
Lighthouse Publishing
MOPS Intl.
NavPress
New Hope
New Leaf
Our Sunday Visitor
Pacific Press
P&R Publications
Parsons Publishing
Pauline Books
Port Hole Public.
Randall House
Salt Works
Standard Publishing
Sunpenny Publishing
Tate Publishing
Trail Media
VBC Publishing
Whitaker House
White Fire Publishing
WinePress
WingSpread
Word Alive
Write Integrity Press
Zoë Life Publishing

PASTORS' HELPS

(a) Baker Academic
(a) Baker Books
(a) B&H Publishing
(a) Kregel

Aaron Book
ACW Press
Ambassador Intl.
American Binding
Blue Dolphin
Bold Vision Books
Booklocker.com
Bridge Logos
Christian Writer's Ebook
Church Growth Inst.
Creation House
CrossLink Publishing
CSS Publishing
DCTS Publishers
Deep River Books
Earthen Vessel
Eerdmans Pub., Wm. B.
Essence
Fairway Press
Faith Books & More
Grace Publishing
Group Publishing
Lighthouse Publishing
Lutheran Univ. Press
NavPress
Randall House
Standard Publishing
Tate Publishing
VBC Publishing
Wesleyan Publishing
White Fire Publishing
WinePress
WingSpread
Word Alive
Zoë Life Publishing
Zondervan

PERSONAL EXPERIENCE

(a) Baker Books
(a) HarperOne
(a) Kregel
(a) Nelson, Thomas

Aaron Book
ACW Press
Ambassador Intl.
American Binding
Ampelos Press
Blue Dolphin
Bondfire Books
Booklocker.com
Bridge Logos
Canticle Books
Chalfont House Publishing
Charisma House
Christian Writer's Ebook
Comfort Publishing
Creation House
CrossLink Publishing
Cupola Press
DCTS Publishers
Deep River Books
Essence
Fairway Press
Faith Books & More
Fruitbearer Pub.
Guideposts Books
Halo Publishing Intl.
Hannibal Books
Lighthouse Publishing
Lighthouse Trails
On My Own Now
Pacific Press
Ravenhawk Books
Salvation Publisher
Tate Publishing
Trail Media
White Fire Publishing
WinePress
Word Alive

PERSONAL GROWTH

(a) Baker Books
(a) B&H Publishing
(a) Bethany House
(a) FaithWords
(a) HarperOne
(a) Hay House
(a) Kregel
(a) Nelson, Thomas
(a) Tyndale House
(a) WaterBrook Press

Aaron Book
ACW Press
Ambassador Books
Ambassador Intl.
American Binding
AMG Publishers
Barbour
Blue Dolphin
BMH Books
Bold Vision Books
Bondfire Books
Booklocker.com
Bridge Logos
Canticle Books
Chalfont House Publishing
Charisma House
Christian Writer's Ebook
CLC Publications

Comfort Publishing
Conari Press
Creation House
CrossLink Publishing
Cupola Press
DCTS Publishers
Deep River Books
Destiny Image (books)
Discovery House
Essence
Evergreen Press
Fairway Press
Faith Books & More
Franciscan Media
Grace Publishing
Guideposts Books
Halo Publishing Intl.
Hannibal Books
Hensley Publishing
Howard Books
InterVarsity Press
JourneyForth/BJU
Lift Every Voice
Lighthouse Publishing
Morgan James Publishing
NavPress
New Hope
On My Own Now
Pacific Press
Parson Place
Parsons Publishing
Pauline Books
Ravenhawk Books
Tate Publishing
Trail Media
White Fire Publishing
WinePress
WingSpread
Word Alive
Write Integrity Press

PERSONAL RENEWAL

(a) Baker Books
(a) HarperOne
(a) Kregel
(a) Tyndale House

Aaron Book
ACW Press
American Binding
Barbour
Blue Dolphin
BMH Books
Bold Vision Books
Bondfire Books
Booklocker.com
Bridge Logos
Canticle Books
Chalfont House Publishing
Charisma House
Christian Writer's Ebook
Cladach Publishing
CLC Publications
Comfort Publishing
Conari Press
Creation House
DCTS Publishers
Deep River Books
Destiny Image (books)
Essence
Evergreen Press
Fairway Press
Faith Books & More
Grace Publishing
Halo Publishing Intl.
Hannibal Books
Hensley Publishing
Howard Books
Kirk House
Lift Every Voice
Lighthouse Publishing
NavPress
New Hope
On My Own Now
Pacific Press
Ravenhawk Books
Tate Publishing
Trail Media
White Fire Publishing
WinePress
WingSpread
Word Alive
Write Integrity Press
Zoë Life Publishing

PHILOSOPHY

(a) Baker Books
(a) Doubleday Relig.
(a) HarperOne
(a) Kregel

Aaron Book
ACW Press
American Binding
Blue Dolphin
Bondfire Books
Booklocker.com
Christian Writer's Ebook
Creation House
Deep River Books
Eerdmans Pub., Wm. B.
Essence
Fairway Press
Faith Books & More
Inkling Books
InterVarsity Press
Lighthouse Publishing
Lutheran Univ. Press
Paragon House
Port Hole Public.
Salt Works
Tate Publishing
Trinity Foundation
White Fire Publishing
WinePress
Word Alive
Zoë Life Publishing

PHOTOGRAPHS (FOR COVERS)

Abingdon Press
Ambassador Books
Ambassador Intl.
American Binding
Blue Dolphin
Booklocker.com
Bridge Logos
Chalfont House Publishing
Charisma House
Church Growth Inst.
Comfort Publishing
Conciliar Press
Creation House
CrossHouse
CrossLink Publishing
Earthen Vessel
Essence
Faith Books & More
Fruitbearer Pub.
Guardian Angel
Lift Every Voice

Lighthouse Publishing
Lutheran Univ. Press
Morgan James Publishing
MountainView
New Hope
Our Sunday Visitor
Parson Place
Pauline Kids
Players Press
Ravenhawk Books
Sunpenny Publishing
Tate Publishing
Trinity Foundation
WinePress
Zoë Life Publishing

POETRY

Aaron Book
ACW Press
American Binding
Blue Dolphin
Bondfire Books
Booklocker.com
Christian Writer's Ebook
Creation House
Earthen Vessel
Eerdmans Pub., Wm. B.
Essence
Fairway Press
Faith Books & More
Halo Publishing Intl.
Lighthouse Publishing
Port Hole Public.
Tate Publishing
WinePress
Word Alive
Zoë Life Publishing

POLITICS

(a) Baker Books
(a) Doubleday Relig.
(a) HarperOne
(a) Nelson, Thomas

Aaron Book
ACW Press
American Binding
AMG Publishers
Blue Dolphin
Bondfire Books
Booklocker.com
Christian Writer's Ebook
Creation House
Deep River Books
Eerdmans Pub., Wm. B.
Essence
Fairway Press
Faith Books & More
Howard Books
Inkling Books
Lighthouse Publishing
Praeger Publishers
Ravenhawk Books
Salt Works
Tate Publishing
Trinity Foundation
White Fire Publishing
WinePress
Word Alive
Yale Univ. Press
Zoë Life Publishing

POPULAR CULTURE

Bondfire Books
Chalfont House Publishing
Comfort Publishing
Essence
Pauline Books
White Fire Publishing
Zoë Life Publishing

POSTMODERNISM

Chalfont House Publishing
Essence
White Fire Publishing
Zoë Life Publishing

PRAYER

(a) Baker Books
(a) Bethany House
(a) Cook, David C.
(a) Doubleday Relig.
(a) FaithWords
(a) HarperOne
(a) Kregel
(a) Nelson, Thomas
(a) Tyndale House
(a) WaterBrook Press

Aaron Book
Abingdon Press
ACW Press
Ambassador Books
Ambassador Intl.
American Binding
Ampelos Press
Barbour
Blue Dolphin
BMH Books
Bold Vision Books
Bondfire Books
Booklocker.com
Bridge Logos
Chalfont House Publishing
Charisma House
Christian Heritage
Christian Writer's Ebook
CLC Publications
Creation House
CrossHouse
CrossLink Publishing
CSS Publishing
Cupola Press
DCTS Publishers
Deep River Books
Destiny Image (books)
Discovery House
Earthen Vessel
Eerdmans Pub., Wm. B.
Essence
Evergreen Press
Fairway Press
Faith Books & More
Franciscan Media
Fruitbearer Pub.
Grace Publishing
Guideposts Books
Halo Publishing Intl.
Harrison House
Hensley Publishing
Hope Publishing
Howard Books
InterVarsity Press
JourneyForth/BJU
Legacy Press
Lift Every Voice
Lighthouse Publishing
Loyola Press
Lutheran Univ. Press
Moody Publishers
NavPress
On My Own Now

Our Sunday Visitor
Pacific Press
Pauline Books
Pauline Kids
Port Hole Public.
Salvation Publisher
Standard Publishing
Tate Publishing
VBC Publishing
Wesleyan Publishing
Whitaker House
White Fire Publishing
WinePress
WingSpread
Word Alive
Write Integrity Press
Zoë Life Publishing

PRINT-ON-DEMAND

Aaron Book
ACW Press
American Binding
Blue Dolphin
Booklocker.com
Bridge Logos
Christian Writer's Ebook
CrossLink Publishing
CSS Publishing
Evergreen Press
Faith Books & More
Grace Publishing
Hannibal Books
Inkling Books
Lighthouse Publishing
OakTara
Players Press
Randall House Digital
Ravenhawk Books
Salvation Publisher
Strong Tower
VBC Publishing
WingSpread
Word Alive
Write Integrity Press

PROPHECY

(a) Baker Books
(a) Kregel

Aaron Book
ACW Press
American Binding
Blue Dolphin
BMH Books
Bold Vision Books
Bondfire Books
Booklocker.com
Bridge Logos
Chalfont House Publishing
Charisma House
Christian Writer's Ebook
Comfort Publishing
Creation House
CSS Publishing
Deep River Books
Destiny Image (books)
Eerdmans Pub., Wm. B.
Essence
Fairway Press
Faith Books & More
Harrison House
Lighthouse Publishing
Lutheran Univ. Press
Pacific Press
Parson Place
Parsons Publishing
Ravenhawk Books
Salvation Publisher
Tate Publishing
White Fire Publishing
WinePress
Word Alive
Write Integrity Press
Zoë Life Publishing

PSYCHOLOGY

(a) Baker Academic
(a) Kregel
(a) Tyndale House

Aaron Book
ACW Press
Adams Media
American Binding
Blue Dolphin
Bold Vision Books
Bondfire Books
Booklocker.com
Chalfont House Publishing
Christian Writer's Ebook
Comfort Publishing
Creation House
Deep River Books
Eerdmans Pub., Wm. B.
Essence
Evergreen Press
Fairway Press
Faith Books & More
Hope Publishing
InterVarsity Press
Lighthouse Publishing
MountainView
On My Own Now
Paragon House
Tate Publishing
White Fire Publishing
WinePress
Word Alive
Zoë Life Publishing

RACISM

(a) Baker Books

Aaron Book
ACW Press
American Binding
Blue Dolphin
Booklocker.com
Chalfont House Publishing
Charisma House
Christian Writer's Ebook
DCTS Publishers
Deep River Books
Eerdmans Pub., Wm. B.
Essence
Fairway Press
Faith Books & More
Hope Publishing
Howard Books
InterVarsity Press
Judson Press
Kirk House
Lift Every Voice
Lighthouse Publishing
New Hope
Salt Works
Tate Publishing
White Fire Publishing
WinePress
Word Alive
Zoë Life Publishing

RECOVERY

(a) Baker Books
(a) HarperOne
(a) Tyndale House
(a) WaterBrook Press

Aaron Book
ACW Press
Ambassador Books
American Binding
Blue Dolphin
Bold Vision Books
Bondfire Books
Booklocker.com
Brown Books
Chalfont House Publishing
Charisma House
Christian Writer's Ebook
Comfort Publishing
Creation House
CSS Publishing
Deep River Books
Earthen Vessel
Eerdmans Pub., Wm. B.
Essence
Evergreen Press
Fairway Press
Faith Books & More
Grace Publishing
Halo Publishing Intl.
Hannibal Books
Hope Publishing
Howard Books
Langmarc
Lighthouse Publishing
NavPress
Parsons Publishing
Pauline Books
Randall House
Tate Publishing
VBC Publishing
WinePress
WingSpread
Word Alive
Zoë Life Publishing

REFERENCE

(a) Baker Academic
(a) Baker Books
(a) Bethany House
(a) Cook, David C.
(a) Doubleday Relig.
(a) HarperOne
(a) Kregel
(a) Tyndale House

Aaron Book
Abingdon Press
ACW Press
Ambassador Intl.
American Binding
AMG Publishers
Barbour
BMH Books
Bondfire Books
Booklocker.com
Bridge Logos
Christian Heritage
Christian Writer's Ebook
Creation House
CrossLink Publishing
Eerdmans Pub., Wm. B.
Essence
Fairway Press
Faith Books & More
Guardian Angel
Hope Publishing
InterVarsity Press
Life Cycle Books
Lighthouse Publishing
Our Sunday Visitor
Paragon House
Reference Service
Tate Publishing
VBC Publishing
White Fire Publishing
WinePress
Word Alive
Zoë Life Publishing
Zondervan

RELATIONSHIPS

(a) Bethany House
(a) FaithWords
(a) Kregel
(a) Nelson, Thomas

Aaron Book
ACW Press
Adams Media
Ambassador Books
Ambassador Intl.
American Binding
Barbour
Blue Dolphin
Bold Vision Books
Bondfire Books
Booklocker.com
Bridge Logos
Brown Books
Chalfont House Publishing
Charisma House
Church Growth Inst.
Cladach Publishing
CLC Publications
Comfort Publishing
Creation House
CrossHouse
CrossLink Publishing
Cupola Press
Discovery House
Eerdmans Pub., Wm. B.
Essence
Evergreen Press
Faith Books & More
Grace Publishing
Halo Publishing Intl.
Hannibal Books
Hensley Publishing
Howard Books
InterVarsity Press
Judson Press
Lift Every Voice
Lighthouse Publishing
MOPS Intl.
NavPress
New Hope
New Leaf
On My Own Now
P&R Publications
Pauline Books
Port Hole Public.
Randall House
Ravenhawk Books
Salt Works
Tate Publishing
Trail Media
Whitaker House
White Fire Publishing
WinePress
WingSpread
Zoë Life Publishing

RELIGION

(a) Baker Academic
(a) Baker Books
(a) Ballantine
(a) B&H Publishing
(a) Doubleday Relig.
(a) FaithWords
(a) HarperOne
(a) Nelson, Thomas
(a) Revell
(a) Tyndale House
(a) WaterBrook Press

Aaron Book
Abingdon Press
ACW Press
Ambassador Books
Ambassador Intl.
American Binding
American Cath. Press
Blue Dolphin
Bondfire Books
Booklocker.com
Brown Books
Chalfont House Publishing
Charisma House
Christian Heritage
Christian Writer's Ebook
Church Growth Inst.
CLC Publications
Comfort Publishing
Creation House
CrossLink Publishing
CSS Publishing
Deep River Books
Eerdmans Pub., Wm. B.
Essence
Fairway Press
Faith Books & More
Grace Acres Press
Halo Publishing Intl.
Harrison House
InterVarsity Press
Kirk House
Life Cycle Books
Lighthouse Publishing
Loyola Press
Lutheran Univ. Press
NavPress
New Leaf
Our Sunday Visitor
Pacific Press
Parsons Publishing
Pauline Books
Praeger Publishers
Salt Works
Tate Publishing
Trinity Foundation
Whitaker House
White Fire Publishing
WinePress
Word Alive
Yale Univ. Press
Zoë Life Publishing

RELIGIOUS TOLERANCE

(a) Baker Books
(a) FaithWords

Aaron Book
ACW Press
American Binding
Blue Dolphin
Bondfire Books
Booklocker.com
Chalfont House Publishing
Charisma House
Christian Writer's Ebook
Creation House
Deep River Books
Eerdmans Pub., Wm. B.
Essence
Fairway Press
Faith Books & More
Howard Books
Judson Press
Lighthouse Publishing
On My Own Now
Paragon House
Tate Publishing
White Fire Publishing
WinePress
Word Alive
Yale Univ. Press
Zoë Life Publishing

RETIREMENT

(a) Baker Books

Aaron Book
ACW Press
American Binding
Blue Dolphin
Bold Vision Books
Bondfire Books
Booklocker.com
Charisma House
Christian Writer's Ebook
Cladach Publishing
Cupola Press
Eerdmans Pub., Wm. B.
Essence
Fairway Press
Faith Books & More
Kirk House
Lighthouse Publishing
Tate Publishing
WinePress
Word Alive
Zoë Life Publishing

SCHOLARLY

(a) Baker Academic
(a) Baker Books
(a) Cook, David C.
(a) Doubleday Relig.
(a) Kregel

Aaron Book
Abingdon Press
ACW Press
American Binding
Blue Dolphin
Bondfire Books
Booklocker.com
Christian Heritage
Christian Writer's Ebook
Deep River Books
Eerdmans Pub., Wm. B.
Essence
Fairway Press
Faith Books & More
Grace Acres Press
Guardian Angel
Inkling Books
InterVarsity Press
Life Cycle Books
Lighthouse Publishing
Lutheran Univ. Press
Paragon House
Tate Publishing
Trinity Foundation
VBC Publishing
White Fire Publishing

WinePress
Word Alive
Yale Univ. Press
Zoë Life Publishing
Zondervan

SCIENCE

(a) Baker Books
(a) Doubleday Relig.

Aaron Book
ACW Press
American Binding
Blue Dolphin
Booklocker.com
Chalfont House Publishing
Christian Writer's Ebook
Eerdmans Pub., Wm. B.
Essence
Fairway Press
Faith Books & More
Guardian Angel
Inkling Books
InterVarsity Press
Lighthouse Publishing
New Leaf
Parsons Publishing
Salt Works
Tate Publishing
Trinity Foundation
WinePress
Word Alive
Zoë Life Publishing

SELF-HELP

(a) Baker Books
(a) Ballantine
(a) HarperOne
(a) Hay House
(a) Nelson, Thomas
(a) Revell
(a) Tyndale House
(a) WaterBrook Press

Aaron Book
ACW Press
Adams Media
Ambassador Books
American Binding
Blue Dolphin
Bold Vision Books
Bondfire Books
Booklocker.com
Bridge Logos
Brown Books
Chalfont House Publishing
Charisma House
Christian Writer's Ebook
CLC Publications
Comfort Publishing
Creation House
CrossLink Publishing
Cupola Press
DCTS Publishers
Deep River Books
Essence
Evergreen Press
Fairway Press
Faith Books & More
Franciscan Media
Grace Publishing
Guideposts Books
Halo Publishing Intl.
Howard Books
Langmarc
Lighthouse Publishing
Morgan James Publishing
MountainView
On My Own Now
Salvation Publisher
Tate Publishing
Trail Media
VBC Publishing
WinePress
WingSpread
Word Alive
Zoë Life Publishing

SENIOR ADULT CONCERNS

(a) Baker Books
(a) Cook, David C.

Aaron Book
ACW Press
American Binding
Blue Dolphin
Bold Vision Books
Bondfire Books
Booklocker.com
Chalfont House Publishing
Charisma House
Christian Writer's Ebook
Cupola Press
Deep River Books
Discovery House
Eerdmans Pub., Wm. B.
Essence
Evergreen Press
Fairway Press
Faith Books & More
Focus on the Family
Grace Publishing
Langmarc
Lighthouse Publishing
New Hope
Tate Publishing
WinePress
WingSpread
Word Alive
Zoë Life Publishing

SERMONS

(a) Baker Books
(a) Kregel

Aaron Book
Abingdon Press
ACW Press
American Binding
Bondfire Books
Booklocker.com
Chalfont House Publishing
Christian Writer's Ebook
Church Growth Inst.
CrossLink Publishing
CSS Publishing
DCTS Publishers
Deep River Books
Earthen Vessel
Eerdmans Pub., Wm. B.
Essence
Fairway Press
Faith Books & More
Group Publishing
Judson Press
Lighthouse Publishing
MountainView
NavPress
Pacific Press
Salt Works
Salvation Publisher
Tate Publishing
WinePress

Word Alive
Zoë Life Publishing

SINGLES' ISSUES

(a) Baker Books
(a) Bethany House
(a) Cook, David C.
(a) FaithWords
(a) Kregel

Aaron Book
ACW Press
Ambassador Books
American Binding
Barbour
Blue Dolphin
Bold Vision Books
Bondfire Books
Booklocker.com
Chalfont House Publishing
Charisma House
Christian Writer's Ebook
Creation House
Deep River Books
Eerdmans Pub., Wm. B.
Essence
Evergreen Press
Fairway Press
Faith Books & More
Fruitbearer Pub.
Grace Publishing
Hensley Publishing
InterVarsity Press
Judson Press
Lift Every Voice
Lighthouse Publishing
NavPress
New Hope
On My Own Now
Pacific Press
P&R Publications
Parsons Publishing
Pauline Books
Salt Works
Tate Publishing
Trail Media
VBC Publishing
Whitaker House
White Fire Publishing
WinePress
WingSpread
Word Alive
Write Integrity Press
Zoë Life Publishing

SMALL-GROUP RESOURCES

Bold Vision Books
Bondfire Books
Chalfont House Publishing
Essence
Franciscan Media
Grace Acres Press
Grace Publishing
Morgan James Publishing
NavPress
Randall House
WingSpread
Zoë Life Publishing

SOCIAL JUSTICE ISSUES

(a) Baker Books
(a) FaithWords
(a) HarperOne
(a) Nelson, Thomas

Aaron Book
ACW Press
American Binding
Ampelos Press
Blue Dolphin
Bondfire Books
Booklocker.com
Chalfont House Publishing
Charisma House
Christian Writer's Ebook
Comfort Publishing
DCTS Publishers
Deep River Books
Destiny Image (books)
Eerdmans Pub., Wm. B.
Essence
Fairway Press
Faith Books & More
Hope Publishing
Howard Books
Inkling Books
InterVarsity Press
Judson Press
Life Cycle Books
Lift Every Voice
Lighthouse Publishing
NavPress
New Hope
On My Own Now
Our Sunday Visitor
Ravenhawk Books
Tate Publishing
Trail Media
WinePress
Word Alive
Yale Univ. Press
Zoë Life Publishing

SOCIOLOGY

(a) Baker Books

Aaron Book
ACW Press
American Binding
Blue Dolphin
Bondfire Books
Booklocker.com
Charisma House
Christian Writer's Ebook
Deep River Books
Eerdmans Pub., Wm. B.
Essence
Fairway Press
Faith Books & More
InterVarsity Press
Life Cycle Books
Lighthouse Publishing
On My Own Now
Tate Publishing
Trail Media
White Fire Publishing
WinePress
Word Alive
Zoë Life Publishing

SPIRITUAL GIFTS

(a) Baker Books
(a) B&H Publishing
(a) Kregel
(a) Nelson, Thomas

Aaron Book
ACW Press
Ambassador Books
American Binding
Blue Dolphin
Booklocker.com
Bridge Logos

Brown Books
Canticle Books
Chalfont House Publishing
Charisma House
Christian Writer's Ebook
Church Growth Inst.
CLC Publications
Comfort Publishing
Creation House
CrossHouse
CrossLink Publishing
CSS Publishing
Deep River Books
Destiny Image (books)
Eerdmans Pub., Wm. B.
Essence
Fairway Press
Faith Books & More
Grace Acres Press
Group Publishing
Guardian Angel
Halo Publishing Intl.
Harrison House
Hensley Publishing
Howard Books
InterVarsity Press
Lift Every Voice
Lighthouse Publishing
Lutheran Univ. Press
Magnus Press
NavPress
New Hope
Pacific Press
Parson Place
Parsons Publishing
Salvation Publisher
Tate Publishing
Whitaker House
WinePress
WingSpread
Word Alive
Write Integrity Press
Zoë Life Publishing

SPIRITUALITY

(a) Baker Books
(a) Ballantine
(a) Bethany House
(a) Doubleday Relig.
(a) FaithWords
(a) HarperOne
(a) Hay House
(a) Kregel
(a) Nelson, Thomas
(a) Tyndale House
(a) WaterBrook Press

Aaron Book
Abingdon Press
ACW Press
Ambassador Books
American Binding
Blue Dolphin
Bondfire Books
Booklocker.com
Bridge Logos
Brown Books
Canticle Books
Chalfont House Publishing
Charisma House
Christian Heritage
Christian Writer's Ebook
CLC Publications
Comfort Publishing
Conari Press
Creation House
CrossLink Publishing
CSS Publishing
Deep River Books
Destiny Image (books)
Discovery House
Eerdmans Pub., Wm. B.
Essence
Evergreen Press
Fairway Press
Faith Books & More
Franciscan Media
Grace Acres Press
Grace Publishing
Guardian Angel
Halo Publishing Intl.
Howard Books
InterVarsity Press
Kirk House
Lighthouse Publishing
Loyola Press
Lutheran Univ. Press
Magnus Press
NavPress
New Hope
On My Own Now
Pacific Press
Paragon House
Parsons Publishing
Pauline Books
Ravenhawk Books
Salt Works
Sunpenny Publishing
Tate Publishing
WinePress
WingSpread
Word Alive
Write Integrity Press
Zoë Life Publishing

SPIRITUAL LIFE

(a) B&H Publishing
(a) Bethany House
(a) FaithWords
(a) HarperOne
(a) Kregel
(a) Nelson, Thomas
(a) WaterBrook Press

Aaron Book
Abingdon Press
ACW Press
Ambassador Books
American Binding
Barbour
Blue Dolphin
BMH Books
Bold Vision Books
Bondfire Books
Booklocker.com
Bridge Logos
Brown Books
Canticle Books
Chalfont House Publishing
Charisma House
Christian Writer's Ebook
Church Growth Inst.
CLC Publications
Comfort Publishing
Creation House
CrossHouse
CrossLink Publishing
CSS Publishing
Deep River Books
Destiny Image (books)
Eerdmans Pub., Wm. B.
Essence

Evergreen Press
Fairway Press
Faith Books & More
Grace Acres Press
Grace Publishing
Guardian Angel
Halo Publishing Intl.
Harrison House
Howard Books
Inheritance Press
InterVarsity Press
JourneyForth/BJU
Judson Press
Lift Every Voice
Lighthouse Publishing
Morgan James Publishing
NavPress
New Hope
New Leaf
On My Own Now
Parsons Publishing
Pauline Books
Port Hole Public.
Randall House
Salvation Publisher
Tate Publishing
Trail Media
Wesleyan Publishing
Whitaker House
White Fire Publishing
WinePress
WingSpread
Word Alive
Write Integrity Press
Zoë Life Publishing

SPIRITUAL WARFARE

(a) Baker Books
(a) B&H Publishing
(a) Nelson, Thomas

Aaron Book
ACW Press
American Binding
Blue Dolphin
Booklocker.com
Bridge Logos
Brown Books
Chalfont House Publishing
Charisma House
Christian Writer's Ebook
CLC Publications
Comfort Publishing
Creation House
CrossLink Publishing
Destiny Image (books)
Earthen Vessel
Eerdmans Pub., Wm. B.
Essence
Evergreen Press
Fairway Press
Faith Books & More
Grace Acres Press
Grace Publishing
Harrison House
Hensley Publishing
Lighthouse Publishing
Morgan James Publishing
NavPress
New Hope
On My Own Now
Parson Place
Parsons Publishing
Salvation Publisher
Tate Publishing
VBC Publishing
Whitaker House
White Fire Publishing
WinePress
WingSpread
Word Alive
Write Integrity Press
Zoë Life Publishing

SPORTS/RECREATION

(a) Baker Books
(a) Ballantine

Aaron Book
ACW Press
Ambassador Books
American Binding
Blue Dolphin
Booklocker.com
Brown Books
Charisma House
Christian Writer's Ebook
Cladach Publishing
Comfort Publishing
Deep River Books
Earthen Vessel
Essence
Evergreen Press
Fairway Press
Faith Books & More
Guardian Angel
Halo Publishing Intl.
Judson Press
Lighthouse Publishing
Ravenhawk Books
Reference Service
Sunpenny Publishing
Tate Publishing
WinePress
Word Alive
Zoë Life Publishing

STEWARDSHIP

(a) Baker Books
(a) Bethany House
(a) Kregel

Aaron Book
ACW Press
Ambassador Intl.
American Binding
Blue Dolphin
BMH Books
Bold Vision Books
Booklocker.com
Brown Books
Chalfont House Publishing
Christian Writer's Ebook
Church Growth Inst.
CLC Publications
Creation House
CrossLink Publishing
CSS Publishing
Deep River Books
Eerdmans Pub., Wm. B.
Essence
Evergreen Press
Fairway Press
Faith Books & More
Grace Acres Press
Grace Publishing
Group Publishing
Hensley Publishing
Hope Publishing
InterVarsity Press
Judson Press
Kirk House
Lift Every Voice

Lighthouse Publishing
Lutheran Univ. Press
Morgan James Publishing
NavPress
New Hope
On My Own Now
Our Sunday Visitor
Pacific Press
Parson Place
Parsons Publishing
Randall House
Salvation Publisher
Tate Publishing
VBC Publishing
White Fire Publishing
WinePress
WingSpread
Word Alive
Zoë Life Publishing

THEOLOGY

(a) Baker Books
(a) Bethany House
(a) Cook, David C.
(a) Doubleday Relig.
(a) HarperOne
(a) Kregel
(a) Multnomah
(a) Nelson, Thomas
(a) Tyndale House

Aaron Book
Abingdon Press
ACW Press
Ambassador Intl.
American Binding
American Cath. Press
Blue Dolphin
BMH Books
Bondfire Books
Booklocker.com
Brown Books
Canticle Books
Chalfont House Publishing
Christian Heritage
Christian Writer's Ebook
CLC Publications
Conciliar Press
Creation House
CrossLink Publishing
Crossway
CSS Publishing
Deep River Books
Earthen Vessel
Eerdmans Pub., Wm. B.
Essence
Fairway Press
Faith Books & More
Grace Acres Press
Inkling Books
InterVarsity Press
Kirk House
Lift Every Voice
Lighthouse Publishing
Lighthouse Trails
Lutheran Univ. Press
Magnus Press
Meriwether
NavPress
Pacific Press
Randall House
Ravenhawk Books
Tate Publishing
Trinity Foundation
VBC Publishing
Wesleyan Publishing
White Fire Publishing
WinePress
WingSpread
Word Alive
Yale Univ. Press
Zoë Life Publishing
Zondervan

TIME MANAGEMENT

(a) Baker Books
(a) Cook, David C.
(a) Nelson, Thomas

Aaron Book
ACW Press
American Binding
Barbour
Blue Dolphin
Bold Vision Books
Booklocker.com
Brown Books
Charisma House
Christian Writer's Ebook
CrossHouse
Cupola Press
DCTS Publishers
Deep River Books
Essence
Evergreen Press
Fairway Press
Faith Books & More
Grace Acres Press
Grace Publishing
Hensley Publishing
Judson Press
Kirk House
Lighthouse Publishing
Morgan James Publishing
NavPress
New Hope
On My Own Now
Salvation Publisher
Tate Publishing
VBC Publishing
WinePress
Word Alive
Zoë Life Publishing

TRACTS

Chalfont House Publishing
Christian Writer's Ebook
Essence
Fruitbearer Pub.
Life Cycle Books
Trinity Foundation
Word Alive

TRAVEL

(a) Baker Books
(a) Ballantine

Aaron Book
ACW Press
American Binding
Booklocker.com
Brown Books
Christian Heritage
Christian Writer's Ebook
Cladach Publishing
Essence
Fairway Press
Faith Books & More
Grace Publishing
Hope Publishing
Lighthouse Publishing
New Leaf
Sunpenny Publishing

Tate Publishing
Trail Media
White Fire Publishers
WinePress
Word Alive
Zoë Life Publishing

TWEEN BOOKS

Aaron Book
ACW Press
Ambassador Books
Ambassador Intl.
American Binding
Barbour
Bondfire Books
Booklocker.com
Chalfont House Publishing
Comfort Publishing
Eerdmans Pub., Wm. B.
Essence
Faith Books & More
Fruitbearer Pub.
Legacy Press
Lighthouse Publishing
Parsons Publishing
Pauline Books
Tate Publishing
Trail Media
WinePress
Zoë Life Publishing

WOMEN'S ISSUES

(a) Baker Academic
(a) Baker Books
(a) Ballantine
(a) B&H Publishing
(a) Bethany House
(a) Cook, David C.
(a) Doubleday Relig.
(a) FaithWords
(a) HarperOne
(a) Kregel
(a) Nelson, Thomas

Aaron Book
ACW Press
Adams Media
Ambassador Books
American Binding
AMG Publishers
Barbour
Blue Dolphin
BMH Books
Bold Vision Books
Bondfire Books
Booklocker.com
Bridge Logos
Brown Books
Chalfont House Publishing
Charisma House
Christian Writer's Ebook
Comfort Publishing
Creation House
CrossHouse
CrossLink Publishing
Crossway
Cupola Press
Deep River Books
Discovery House
Eerdmans Pub., Wm. B.
Essence
Evergreen Press
Fairway Press
Faith Books & More
Focus on the Family
Franciscan Media
Fruitbearer Pub.
Grace Publishing
Halo Publishing Intl.
Hensley Publishing
Hope Publishing
Howard Books
Inkling Books
InterVarsity Press
JourneyForth/BJU
Judson Press
Kirk House
Langmarc
Life Cycle Books
Lift Every Voice
Lighthouse Publishing
Loyola Press
Moody Publishers
Morgan James Publishing
NavPress
Nelson, Thomas
New Hope
On My Own Now
Parson Place
Pauline Books
Port Hole Public.
Praeger Publishers
Ravenhawk Books
Reference Service
Sunpenny Publishing
Tate Publishing
Trail Media
VBC Publishing
Whitaker House
White Fire Publishing
WinePress
WingSpread
Word Alive
Write Integrity Press
Zoë Life Publishing

WORLD ISSUES

(a) Baker Books
(a) Doubleday Relig.
(a) HarperOne
(a) Kregel
(a) Tyndale House

Aaron Book
ACW Press
American Binding
AMG Publishers
Ampelos Press
Blue Dolphin
Booklocker.com
Bridge Logos
Chalfont House Publishing
Charisma House
Christian Writer's Ebook
Comfort Publishing
Creation House
CrossLink Publishing
Deep River Books
Eerdmans Pub., Wm. B.
Essence
Fairway Press
Faith Books & More
Halo Publishing Intl.
InterVarsity Press
Kirk House
Lift Every Voice
Lighthouse Publishing
NavPress
New Hope
Ravenhawk Books
Salt Works
Tate Publishing

Trail Media
VBC Publishing
White Fire Publishing
WinePress
Word Alive
Write Integrity Press
Yale Univ. Press
Zoë Life Publishing

WORSHIP

(a) B&H Publishing
(a) Bethany House
(a) Cook, David C.
(a) Kregel
(a) Nelson, Thomas

Aaron Book
Abingdon Press
ACW Press
American Binding
Barbour
BMH Books
Bold Vision Books
Bondfire Books
Booklocker.com
Bridge Logos
Chalfont House Publishing
Charisma House
Christian Heritage
Christian Writer's Ebook
CLC Publications
Creation House
CrossLink Publishing
CSS Publishing
Deep River Books
Eerdmans Pub., Wm. B.
Essence
Fairway Press
Faith Books & More
Grace Acres Press
Group Publishing
Halo Publishing Intl.
Harrison House
InterVarsity Press
JourneyForth/BJU
Judson Press
Lift Every Voice
Lighthouse Publishing
Lutheran Univ. Press
NavPress
New Hope
Pacific Press
Parsons Publishing
Salt Works
Tate Publishing
VBC Publishing
WinePress
WingSpread
Word Alive

WORSHIP RESOURCES

(a) Baker Books
(a) B&H Publishing
(a) Kregel

Aaron Book
Abingdon Press
ACW Press
American Binding
American Cath. Press
Bondfire Books
Booklocker.com
Christian Writer's Ebook
CSS Publishing
DCTS Publishers
Deep River Books
Eerdmans Pub., Wm. B.
Essence
Fairway Press
Faith Books & More
Group Publishing
InterVarsity Press
Judson Press
Lighthouse Publishing
Lutheran Univ. Press
Meriwether
NavPress
Our Sunday Visitor
Parsons Publishing
Salt Works
Standard Publishing
Tate Publishing
WinePress
Word Alive
Zoë Life Publishing

WRITING HOW-TO

Aaron Book
American Binding
Bold Vision Books
Bondfire Books
Booklocker.com
Christian Writer's Ebook
Deep River Books
Essence
Evergreen Press
Fairway Press
Faith Books & More
Grace Publishing
Lighthouse Publishing
Morgan James Publishing
Parson Place
Tate Publishing
WinePress
Word Alive
Zoë Life Publishing

YOUTH BOOKS (Nonfiction)

Note: Listing denotes books for 8- to 12-year-olds, junior highs, or senior highs. If all three, it will say "all." If no age group is listed, none was specified.

(a) Baker Books
(a) WaterBrook Press (All)

Aaron Book (8-12/Jr. High)
ACW Press (All)
Ambassador Books (All)
American Binding (Jr./Sr. High)
Barbour (8-12/Jr. High)
Bondfire Books
Booklocker.com (All)
Brown Books (All)
Chalfont House Publishing (All)
Christian Writer's Ebook (All)
Comfort Publishing (All)
Conciliar Press (8-12)
Contemporary Drama
Creation House (All)
CrossHouse (All)
Dawn Publications (Jr. High)
Deep River Books (All)
Eerdmans Pub., Wm. B. (All)
Essence (All)
Evergreen Press
Faith Books & More (All)
Focus on the Family (Sr. High)
Guardian Angel (8-12)

Halo Publishing Intl. (All)
Legacy Press (8-12)
Life Cycle Books (8-12)
Lift Every Voice (All)
Lighthouse Publishing (All)
Lighthouse Trails (All)
Meriwether (Jr./Sr. High)
Moody Publishers
NavPress (Sr. High)
New Leaf (All)
On My Own Now (Sr. High)
Pacific Press
P&R Publications (All)
Pauline Kids (8-12)
Ravenhawk Books (Jr./Sr. High)
Tate Publishing (All)
Trail Media (All)
Warner Press (All)
WinePress (All)
Word Alive (All)
Zoë Life Publishing

YOUTH PROGRAMS

(a) Baker Books
(a) Kregel
ACW Press
American Binding
Christian Writer's Ebook
Church Growth Inst.
Contemporary Drama
CrossLink Publishing
Fairway Press
Group Publishing
Randall House Digital
Standard Publishing
Tate Publishing
Zoë Life Publishing

BONUS SECTION

Writer's Helps

Your Calling

A Middle-Aged Mom Goes to Hollywood

by Kathryn Mackel

I TOOK MY FIRST plane ride when I was forty-five. I rode first class, paid for by Twentieth Century Fox. I was provided a nice car and luxury lodging at the Beverly Wilshire Hotel. I made the rounds of eight studios, heard Steven Spielberg read the riot act to some hapless assistant, and learned that meeting-wear in the film business was jeans and T-shirts instead of my business suit.

I was the flavor of the week, despite the fact that I was forty-five and had never been west of New York City. How did a middle-aged mom get to Hollywood?

Clearly, God has a sense of humor.

I had no concept of becoming a screenwriter—though I had literally grown up in a movie theater. My father was a projectionist who babysat me while my mother worked. I rode my bike up and down the aisles while he swept floors, cleaned bathrooms, and got the films ready to show. When the lights darkened, I watched the movies from the back row. (To this day, I still prefer the back row.) When certain cues flickered on the screen, I ran up to the booth to wait for the switch to the next reel. I loved running the rewind machine. Learning the mechanics of projecting dreams onto a screen never robbed me of wonder.

I loved movies for their power to stir imagination, inspire emotion, make me dream. As a child, I directed countless productions with the neighborhood kids. When I reached my twenties, I was still making up stories in my head. If were a writer, I would write—correct? But I didn't write, therefore I concluded I was not a writer. I was just weird.

Dreams Revisited

I married, had children, found Jesus. And stayed *silently* weird. I became a technical writer, the complete opposite of a fiction writer. But those stories kept coming to me. "Grow up," I told myself, and enrolled in a master's program for professional writing. When the program didn't offer anything in my field, I decided to take my first fiction workshop.

I was forty-one years old and scared silly.

My classmates included a journalist, a novelist, a published short-story writer, and other confident, experienced writers. Completely intimidated, I would have dropped the class if my secretary hadn't browbeaten me into staying.

I had fun indulging the *weird*. When the next semester rolled around, I joined my intimidating classmates in screenwriting.

"Start with an image," our professor said. "What do you see?"

I saw a little girl I coached in Little League softball, picking daisies while a fly ball fell a foot from her head. She never looked up. And then I saw a story unfold about an elite pitcher who moves to a town without softball. She has to teach eleven random girls how to play so she can have a team.

As they would say in a Hollywood pitch session, it was the *Bad News Bears meets Jenny Finch* (US Olympic gold medal–winning softball pitcher).

Beating the Odds

Professor Larry Maness gave me the tools to channel my *weird*. After writing four screenplays just for fun, I decided I should try to sell one. "It'll be easier if you sell a novel first," Larry said. So I wrote a middle-reader novel about a young softball pitcher who is so good and powerful that none of her teammates can catch her.

The month I turned forty-five, I sold my first novel, *A Season of Comebacks,* which a publishing company found in their slush pile. The editor told me it was a million-to-one shot that they bought something that hadn't been submitted through a literary agent.

Three weeks later I sold my first screenplay, *Mother Ship*, out of Hollywood's equivalent of the slush pile. A studio exec told me it was a million-to-one shot that they bought something that didn't come in through an agent.

Do the math.

Only God could send a middle-aged mom to Hollywood. And if he sent me, why couldn't he send you?

Does God Still Want Me to Write?

by Sandra P. Aldrich

Do you long to add "writer" to your list of accomplishments but wonder if God is calling you to that? Have you prayed but remain undecided? That you are reading *The Christian Writer's Market Guide* may reveal not only your longing, but also your calling.

Psalm 37:4 says, "Delight yourself in the Lord; and He will give you the desires of your heart" (NASB). I'm convinced God places those desires within the hearts of his children. So, yes, he wants you to write. Yes, he wants you to share his reality and his truth.

Start by recognizing the treasure of your experience. Alex Haley, the late author of *Roots*, said, "When an old person dies, it's like a library burning." You embody volumes of experience the next generation needs.

Whose Voice?

If it is God who is calling you to write, his voice will be encouraging and persistent. Each day will present another reminder of his beckoning.

The enemy's voice will be negative. "What makes you think you have anything to write about?" "Who's gonna read your stuff?" "You're too old."

Ignore the voice that predicts defeat. What could be sadder than "if only" and "I wish"? Don't let regrets—or the enemy—win.

Words of Encouragement

Think you're too old? Consider Helen Hooven Santmyer. In 1982, when she was eighty-seven, she wrote the novel . . . *And Ladies of the Club*, which appeared on the *New York Times* Best Sellers List for thirty-seven weeks. She realized her dream because she refused to let advancing years stop her.

We can find even greater encouragement in Matthew 7:7: "Ask and it will be given to you; seek and you will find; knock and the door will be opened to you" (NIV). Notice the verbs of action: ***ask, seek,*** and ***knock***. Start taking action and watch for good results to follow.

Actions to Take

In addition to asking for God's direction and reading this *Guide*,

- join a local critique group,
- attend a writers conference,
- take an online course,
- study the markets in which you'd like to be published, and
- start submitting your work.

What Shall I Write About?

Pray about possible topics. If God has placed this longing within you, he will provide numerous ideas, if you ask.

Ponder your interests. I'm an Appalachian, so the hills of southeastern Kentucky dominate my stories. What area calls to you?

What story tugs at your heart? Everyone has a story. Write yours. Don't worry about what others are writing.

What are your favorite memories? What personal stories do you enjoy telling?

What have you learned through experience? Often wisdom comes at an emotional or physical cost. What you've learned can provide examples for others.

What fascinates you about people? As you watch others, imagine their lives. Ask "Why?" and "What if?" Why is that couple sad? What if that father stopped talking on his phone and smiled at the little girl by his side? What if . . . ?

What truth do you want to pass to the next generation? My cousins and I now have silver hair, but we still quote our grandmother.

What skills do you possess? Cabinetmaking? Creative parenting? Gardening? Teaching? Accounting? Readers need your expertise.

Extend your horizons. Even beyond your experiences, wisdom, and skills, don't be afraid to explore subjects about which you've always wondered.

If you're hesitant, ponder the ten lepers in Luke 17. When they called to Jesus, asking for his pity, he told them to go and show themselves to the priests. The end of verse 14 says, "And as they went, they were cleansed" (NIV).

So write. Will the journey be easy? No. But you can show God's reality to this hurting world and make a difference for eternity—regardless your age.

Writing Gift, Spiritual Gift?

by Joyce K. Ellis

WHEN I STARTED WRITING FOR PUBLICATION, I applied pen to tablet with my best Palmer Method handwriting script. Today I make words dance across a computer screen in twelve-point Times New Roman. But one thing hasn't changed: why I write.

God planted in me the desire to write for him—then steered me to magazines and manuals and mentors to help me polish that rough talent.

But is writing a spiritual gift? The question often surfaces among Christian writers.

If writing is a spiritual gift, what if you've been writing for some time, but are beginning to doubt it's *your* gift?

If writing is not a spiritual gift, what is it?

Definitions

Scripture teaches that the Holy Spirit has given each believer at least one spiritual gift—a special ability entrusted to believers (1 Corinthians 12:11) that he knows we can use. He expects us to use these to enhance his Kingdom—within the church and in the world.

The lists in Romans 12, 1 Corinthians 12, Ephesians 4, and 1 Peter 4 may not be exhaustive, but they reveal the types of gifts that come from the Holy Spirit. We find general categories: teaching, encouraging, and leading—not specifics, such as spring break beach witnessing, singing with a worship team, or even writing.

We can use each spiritual gift in many ways. Paul wrote, "There are different kinds of gifts . . . different kinds of service . . . different kinds of working, but the same God works all of them in all [of us]" (1 Corinthians 12:4-6, NIV).

Devoting Our Gifts

I don't believe that writing is one of the spiritual gifts, but it is one avenue through which we can express them.

Just as some pastor-teachers use their gifts of preaching, teaching, exhorting, etc., orally before large congregations, others in jails, others at racetracks, and others in children's work, some use them in print. Other writers apply the gifts of encouragement, evangelism, prophecy, healing, or hospitality.

A believer may exercise one gift in multiple venues. Paul applied his teaching gift in preaching, in small-group settings, in follow-up after his evangelism, and in his writing. With his spiritual gift of encouragement, he restored John Mark to service. He wrote the Epistle to the Philippians from a prison cell, showing Christians how to find joy in difficult circumstances.

Direction

If we learn about the spiritual gifts God has given us, we may find direction for our writing. If one writer identifies his spiritual gifts as leadership, giving, and mercy, he will find himself writing about those topics. But the Lord may also lead him to write direct-appeal letters for relief organizations. Perhaps he'll be drawn to write personality features about people in need, including sidebars about practical ways to help.

If another writer's spiritual gifts are teaching and encouragement, she may find her best opportunities in expository articles, devotionals, or how-tos on Christian living.

Detours

Writing frustrations may come from working outside our gifts. A recently retired pastor showed me his writing projects. Although his five-hundred-word devotionals were okay, they fell short in various ways, and he became discouraged with quick rejections. A brilliant theologian with an obvious gift of teaching, he could have been writing expository articles and books—clarifying deep truths with which he had wrestled.

I have read articles by writers who surely have the gift of hospitality or mercy because as I read, they immediately put me at ease. I felt they were walking beside me, not preaching at me or even teaching. All Christian writers should communicate that way, but writers with those gifts excel.

Defeating the Enemy

Our gifts also equip us for the spiritual warfare we encounter in writing. David wrote, "Praise be to the LORD my Rock, who trains my hands for war, my fingers for battle" (Psalm 144:1, NIV). Can't you see him—if he were writing psalms today—slaving over a keyboard and praying that God would defeat the enemy, who wants so desperately to keep us from glorifying Christ?

As Christian writers, we can be confident that our eternal Commander in Chief has outfitted each of us with unique equipment to bring about his ultimate victory. Some of us will capture souls for Christ. Some will build up the troops. Some will tend the wounded. We can do these through our writing—depending on the equipment God gave us. Peter says, "Each one should use whatever gift he has received to serve others, faithfully administering God's grace in its various forms" (1 Peter 4:10, NIV).

So unwrap your spiritual gift and look for ways to use it in your writing.

This previously appeared in the November/December 2004 issue of *Advanced Christian Writer*.

Is God Calling You to Write?

by Judy Bodmer

A WOMAN IN HER LATE SIXTIES approached me at a writers conference and told me her son had made her attend. "He thinks I need to follow my dream of becoming a writer. But how do I know this is what God wants me to do?"

I've been asked this by people of all ages, but older writers know they don't have ten years to spend learning a new craft—only to be rejected. If they're going to invest time and effort, they want some assurances of success—or at least to know they're following God's voice.

Ask Yourself

How can any of us know we're doing the right thing when we begin following our dream to be a writer? These questions might help.

- *Have you prayed about this?* God's Word says if we ask, he will give us wisdom (see James 1:5).
- *Have you felt this passion for a long time?* If your longing to write persists, it's worth pursuing. God plants dreams in our hearts. Why not discover if this desire is from him?
- *Are you a voracious reader?* The best writers were readers first, enjoying a wide variety of authors and styles.
- *Have others urged you to write?* Maybe you get comments on your letters or e-mails.
- *Have you been writing all along?* Maybe you've contributed to the church newsletter or written skits for the children's ministry or Bible studies for the women's group. Maybe you're like Emily Dickinson, stuffing poems away in a drawer, feeling they aren't worthy for anyone else's eyes.
- *Do you have a message God has given you?* Writing of your youth for your family may be all you'll ever do, but what a legacy for your children! Imagine a grandchild yet unborn reading your testimony and giving her life to God. Isn't that worth the sacrifice to learn to communicate clearly?

Take Steps

Still unsure? Step out in obedience. Take a class. Join a local writers group. The camaraderie of other writers might inspire you to great things. Frank McCourt wrote about his experiences growing up (*Angela's Ashes*) and won the Pulitzer Prize for literature when he was sixty-seven.

Laura Ingalls Wilder's daughter started her mother writing. At age sixty-five she penned her first book, *Little House in the Big Woods*. Maybe you should listen to the urging of your son or daughter.

What to Write?

I took my first writing class because I wanted to write a book about marriage. I hadn't a clue how to get published—or that there were other ways to communicate my story. Like me, many people start out with the aim of writing books. That's fine. Books are a way to communicate our big message.

But publishing a book can take years. Meanwhile, why not hone your skills by writing articles? Start small. Lydia began by writing fillers, book reviews, recipes for children's magazines, and devotions. She now has a regular column and has published a Bible study.

Kathy started by writing inspirational pieces. She likes this type of article because they require little research. She writes what God has done in her life—and touches the lives of readers, even bringing people to Christ.

Kate's passion is fiction. Her first endeavor was a novel. She rewrote it until she thought it was perfect. She faced many rejections but finally found a publisher. She's now about to publish her third novel.

I wrote articles, how-tos, and personal experience pieces for years before I finally wrote that marriage book.

Don't limit yourself to one type of writing. Search the listings in the *Market Guide* and learn what publishers are seeking. You might discover article topics that fit your style, and they won't take as long as a book-length project. Then build on that success.

Three Tests to Determine Whether You're Called to Write

by Dennis E. Hensley, PhD

I DIRECT A UNIVERSITY PROFESSIONAL WRITING PROGRAM, so hundreds of times each year, prospective students visit and ask, "Is it right for me to feel God can use me as a Christian author?" It's a fair question, and I've come up with three tests to discover the answer.

Feeling God's Pleasure

First, apply what I call the Eric Liddell analysis. Liddell won the four hundred meters Olympic gold medal in Paris in 1924. His sister urged him to give up competitive running and accompany her to China as a missionary. But Eric told her, "God made me fast. And when I run, I feel his pleasure." So he continued to run, and he used his fame to attract crowds who would listen to him preach. Eventually he did go to China as a missionary, but he continued to run even there.

If you feel God's pleasure and power within you when you are engrossed in your writing, take that as a sign that you are in your zone for what God wants you to do.

Within Your Gifts

Second, be honest about whether God has gifted you in this area. I'd like to be a major-league pitcher or the world's greatest classical guitarist. But I'm not gifted in those areas. The same holds true for some people and writing. Many would love to see their name on the cover of a book, but they lack the ability to create phenomenal plots and to write with proper grammar, syntax, spelling, and punctuation.

Training is necessary even if you have natural talent. But if after several attempts you cannot put a story on paper with logic, organization, and unique creativity, admit that your gifts lie elsewhere.

More Than a Chore

Third, I ask people how much they write "anyway." If a person says, "I keep a journal and I maintain a blog and I write book reviews for my local newspaper and I write the newsletter for our church," I know this person has a passion for writing. It isn't a chore—it's a delight. This sort of person would rather write than watch TV, bake a pie, knit a sweater, or repair a car engine. Writing is a natural love enabled by God, so this person should channel it into even more productive outlets. He or she can take it from a hobby to a career.

Are you considering a career in writing? If it's in your blood, then it was probably put there by the one who created that blood. Pursue it.

If it's not a genuine passion, there's no shame in admitting that. Explore until you find what *is* in your blood. It may be editing, and then you can be a taskmaster for the rest of us.

What to Write When . . . and Why

I teach at a lot of writing conferences and workshops. Whether a person is entering this field at twenty-eight or seventy-eight, there is always a concern about making the best use of what time is available. I get asked where a person should focus his or her writing energies. I say it isn't a matter of preferences; it's a matter of practicality.

Let's say a person is fifty and wants to become established as a working writer—but also has dreams of one day writing some major work. The two seem contradictory, since it might take two years to write a five hundred–page nonfiction book, revise and edit it, then start to market it. And then what if it doesn't sell? What a waste of time!

There's nothing wrong with wanting to write a book, but why stop all else in the process? Instead, write it progressively:

- First, create a table of contents that lists the topics you want to cover.
- Second, begin writing each chapter as a separate feature article (or two articles, or an article with sidebars).
- Third, start selling the articles to magazines.

You'll accomplish three things at once:

1. You will begin to build a platform as a published expert on your book's topic.
2. You will get byline exposure and also earn cash.
3. You will be writing your book.

This system has worked for me in writing more than twenty of my fifty-four published books. Try it! Use your time wisely.

Never Too Late to Start

by Kathryn Mackel

YOU KNOW THE SIGNS. Gray hair. Smile lines. Joint replacements. The first time we're called Ma'am or Sir.

Does looking down the barrel of maturity mean it is too late to start a writing career? Absolutely not! Your first gray hair or your inability to Tweet may be just the signal you need to *start* writing.

One survey of mainstream novelists shows the first sale happened at an average age of thirty-six.* My experience at Christian writers conferences suggests many pursuing the craft are over forty.

Forty and Older

Vickie McDonough started writing at forty-seven and made her first sale at fifty. Donita K. Paul began writing when she was forty-six. Other names of novelists you might know who were published at age forty or older include Nancy Moser, James A. Michener, Sunni Jeffers, Louise Gouge, Raymond Chandler, Belva Plain, Jillian Kent, Alex Haley, Tamera Alexander, Annie Proulx, Richard Adams, DiAnn Mills, Henry Miller, Sharon Hinck, Jill Elizabeth Nelson.

If forty is far in your rearview mirror, consider Martha Rogers who sold her first novel at seventy-three. Of the fourteen years between first submission and sale, she says, "Age became a challenge as I approached seventy with no contract in sight. Who would want to take a chance on someone that old? Galatians 6:9 became my life verse: 'Let us not grow weary while doing good, for in due season we shall reap if we do not lose heart' (NKJV)."

What keeps someone who has majored in life from considering a writing career?

The clock and the calendar. Learning the craft takes time. You may write a perfectly wonderful first novel that has no market. If you put a year or more into this effort, you now see fewer years available for starting again. But now you have more experience spiritually, emotionally, psychologically. So don't count backwards; you have hard-earned wisdom to share.

Perceived irrelevance. Perhaps you think, *I'm so old, no one will care what I have to say*. Think again. Deborah Raney says, "I'm not sure I could have written a salable novel in my genre without forty years of life under my belt."

If you feel out of touch, pay closer attention. If you can't write teen dialogue, go to the mall or your church's youth group meeting. Listen. Travel. Look in corners, watch life happen. Clothing and speech and technology change rapidly, but the human heart remains the same.

Momentum. Pursuing a brand-new or long-simmering vocation is daunting at an age when you might rather take a breather. Looking at a tortuous road of revision and marketing can take the *oomph* out of any writer. Commit to a single page. Do the same tomorrow. Watch one page become another, and those pages become a book.

Physical limitations. Because of arthritis, I have made many accommodations—including eight finger-joint replacements—to keep writing. Use common sense. Get a good chair, use good light. Explore different keyboards. Use speech recognition software. Take breaks. Write outside.

Know when you're at your best—morning, evening, or midday—and write then.

If you worry about running out of steam, consider Veronica Heley. She turned in her seventy-second book two months before her eightieth birthday. She says her publishers "tell me I can keep on telling stories as long as I want to."

You're just too old. Really? Tamera Alexander says, "When I first started, a twentysomething publicist skipped up to me and said, 'You're a little old to be starting now, aren't you?'

"I said, 'I'm forty-two, honey. I'm not dead.'"

If you want to start writing, *do* it. And don't count gray hairs or wrinkles or birthdays. Count only words.

*"First Novel Survey Results, *Jim C. Hines: Fantasy Author*, www.jimchines.com/2010/03/survey-results.

It's Time for Your Dream

by DiAnn Mills

"Stop telling me someday you're going to write a book," my husband said. "Do it now. Quit your job. I'll give you one year to get anything published. I believe in you."

I was forty-six, and my youngest son was a senior in high school. I'd felt the urge to write for at least five years, but I was afraid to get started, afraid of failure, afraid I was too old.

But I wanted to write. I could taste the words.

Fully Employed

I devised a plan. I viewed my writing goals like a full-time job. If I were to reach my goal of publication, I'd have to soar to the top of the slush pile—that collection of unsolicited manuscripts publishers assign to first readers to evaluate.

I organized my day around writing, studying how-to books, reading in my genre, and exploring what conferences would teach me the most and provide the best exposure to agents, editors, and other writers. I even started a critique group.

During the first year, I wrote devotions, articles, a short story, and a historical novel. Sure, I received rejections, but I never went back to my old job. Two years later, in 1998, my first novel was published. The excitement of tearing into the box of author copies! A dream come true. That was fifty-eight books ago.

Don't think it's been easy. Each novel is a little tougher to write. The characterization must be deeper. The plot twists more unexpected. The setting more intense. The dialogue and emotion like a sword fight. My two nonfiction books felt like clawing my way up a cliff.

Making Sacrifices

I believe God purposed me to write. Obedience is a big thing to him. The tools of the craft weren't drop-shipped into my brain. I suffered through lots of rewrites. I still do.

Your commitment to writing means getting started now. Let others know you're entering a new career, a special interest that's not just a hobby. Join a writers group, and send your work out to be critiqued.

Don't allow age to hold you back. Be courageous and toss off those shackles. Now is the time to pursue your dream.

How to Grasp the Dream

The older we get, the more valuable our life experiences, our spiritual legacy. But our increase of wisdom comes with a downside. We must be more focused on what we write.

How do we choose the path best suited? Some writers prefer poetry, greeting cards, children's works, magazine articles, screenplays, fiction, nonfiction, or something in between. You may be drawn to entertaining, while others desire to instruct.

A schoolteacher may dream of writing for children. A grandmother may be interested in developing a blog for grandparents or providing instructions for crafts. A pastor may have a novel simmering. A banker may also be an expert fly fisherman. A couple may have spent a lifetime developing recipes, and a cookbook is buried in their hearts.

These questions will help you explore your deepest passion for writing and help you decide where to concentrate your efforts:

- What have I done that I'd like to share?
- What have I discovered that's especially valuable?
- Am I passionate about being transparent and allowing others to learn from my strengths, weaknesses, victories, challenges, and failures?
- How would my values, beliefs, and insights shape my writing?
- What do I like to read?
- What excites me about writing?

The Birth of a Writing Idea

by Roger Palms

I'M SITTING IN A COFFEE SHOP enjoying the moment. I left the nine-to-five world when I retired, so my time is my own. But I'm still—and always will be—a writer.

At a nearby table, I overhear two women. One says, "I'm over fifty now. If anything is going to happen in my life, I have to make it happen."

I grab a napkin and start scribbling notes. There is an article here—or more. The culture tells us, "You have to make it happen." God says to us, "You are mine. Trust in me with all your heart. Don't simply lean on your own understanding, and I will direct your path."

The difference in thinking is sharp and clear. But do people understand that difference? Do Christians practice it?

Many Options

I don't yet know how I'll develop this idea. It might become an article about trusting God to lead us—or a nonfiction book about a life lived under God's direction—or a novel contrasting one character who follows God with another who goes through life saying, "I'm going to make it happen."

Now my writing juices are flowing. I trust that as I start to outline this idea about who will direct our lives, I will know what genre will best convey this polarity.

When I get home, I transcribe my napkin notes and find myself adding much more. Online I find quotes and essays that offer additional insights on what is rapidly developing in my mind and on my computer.

Driven by Passion

The writing passion drives me. It drives every writer. It sometimes takes only a thought or a comment before the next project is in the works.

Maybe illness will strike tomorrow and I'll never finish this work. Maybe someone else will work with my notes. Or maybe my best writing is about to happen and I will finish one of the most influential projects I've ever undertaken.

I have committed to God all that he has poured into me through the years—all that makes me the person I am with the writing voice I have.

God put me in the right place to overhear a conversation that is now shaping my thinking in fresh ways. I thank God for the idea, and I promise to discipline myself to work with that idea—and praise him for the gifts that enable me to develop and write about it.

I'm a writer. I have to write. And God knows that I am willing to write what he gives me.

What and How?

What shall I write? How shall I write it?

- Does the idea stay with me?
- Is there another side to the issue?
- Have I detected something in the culture that's shaping people's thinking?
- Am I hearing a lot about that new idea or changes in peoples' behavior?
- If I don't write this, who will?
- Is this idea better explored through fiction or nonfiction?
- Is this best suited to a blog, a magazine article, or a book?
- Am I willing to invest the time to write this well?

Ideas come at us from everywhere. We hear snatches of conversation, see a television program, or watch people respond to an action by Congress or a Little League umpire.

What shall I do with that idea? Is there more behind what I experienced that will help readers if I explore that subject well?

Writers are always self-motivated and usually self-employed. Do I know myself, my discipline, and my time commitments well enough to identify what projects I can and should take on?

Every day writers should take inventory of

- their time;
- what is driving them to write; and
- their willingness to invest in the current writing project.

As long as God knows we are ready, he may be about to give us our next big idea.

Writing as Stewardship

by Terry White

"AMATEURS SIT AND WAIT FOR INSPIRATION," Stephen King says in his book *On Writing,* "the rest of us just get up and go to work."

Some people—a very few—seem compelled to write. For them, writing is the oxygen that sustains them.

I've never understood that. My view of writing is much more utilitarian. I see it as good stewardship.

It's Only Practical

If you have a good idea, or if you see one in action, or if you come across a remarkable person or story that can help others, it only makes sense to write about it and get it published—on paper or on the web—to reach an audience vastly greater than you ever could in person.

"How do you know God is calling you to write?" is not a question I struggle with. Because I have a modest ability with words and with a camera—and because I learned to type early in life—opportunities have always been there.

Abundant Opportunities

Often they don't pay—or don't pay much. A newsletter for my homeowner's association. Reporting my children's sports for the local paper. Creating a press release for an aspiring singer. But seeking to be mission-driven in my writing has led to wonderful opportunities.

Because I grew up studying the Bible, my first trip to Israel put me in awe of what I was seeing. So I shared it with others in a handbook of Bible lands and customs that enlarged my own knowledge and helped eager Bible students.

When I worked in prison ministry, I often encountered people who wanted to write to prisoners but were wary about how much information to share, how to keep inmates from taking advantage of them, and how to minister without being misunderstood. So I helped develop a manual for pen pals—how to visit prison in an envelope, complete with guidelines, sample first letters, sample ways of sharing the gospel, and a glossary of prison language.

I belonged to a church that seemed to burst with creative programming and effective new methods of ministry. I didn't think them up, but I wrote about them. And I shared them widely in denominational publications, regional Christian periodicals, and channels that reached ministry professionals seeking fresh ideas.

Early on, God also gave me a burden for planting a love of effective communication in younger people. So a life of

One Event, Multiple Articles

A creative group in my church developed a Bible-character-based curriculum for vacation Bible school. Elders, pastors, and church leaders in costume delivered first-person messages of biblical characters. Everyone enjoyed creating a first-century village and sharing Bible stories in creative ways.

Here's how I leveraged their creativity:

1. I wrote the story and submitted it, with several photographs, to the local newspaper. They printed it on the front page.
2. I submitted it as a photo-essay to our denominational publication, which ran it as a two-page spread.
3. Our regional Christian newspaper printed a version of the local story and photo.
4. Recast as a transferrable idea for VBS leaders, it appeared in a Christian education magazine for youth and children's ministry leaders.
5. All the children had their photos taken with one of the costumed biblical characters, and at the end of the week, each was given a framed print. Some stayed on family refrigerators for years.
6. Our church used the photos the following year on postcards promoting the next VBS.

This was before social media, so now the reach could be extended even further with e-zines, e-mails, Facebook, Twitter, church websites, and other digital venues. Still, our little effort resulted in the feeding of five thousand (or more)!

teaching, mentoring, and encouraging has resulted in a wonderfully satisfying roster of former students who are making an impact for Christ through their writing and editing.

Equipped to Write

One advantage of growing older is having a lifetime of experiences from which to draw. Our house burned down—an opportunity to reflect on recovery and the transient nature of possessions. Our daughter died—an opportunity to reflect on parenting in a way that results in few regrets. I lost my job—another opportunity to share hope and optimism, highlighting God's sovereignty. There is always someone who needs that message today who didn't need it yesterday.

Keeping a journal builds writing muscle and discipline. In thirty years of journaling I've also seen it provide a well of reflections that can be mined for articles.

Like the sower in the Matthew 13 parable, if we continually write effective words that fall on good soil, God will produce a harvest. That's good stewardship.

2

Alphabetical Listings of Book Publishers

If you do not find the publishers you are looking for, check the General Index. Check out any publisher thoroughly before signing a contract.

(*) before a listing indicates unconfirmed or no information update.

AARON BOOK PUBLISHING, 1104 Bristol Caverns Hwy., Bristol TN 37620. (423) 212-1208. E-mail: info@aaronbookpublishing.com. Website: www.AaronBookPublishing.com. Lidany Rouse, acq. ed. Professional self-publishing, print-on-demand. Book covers, formatting, editing, printing, and marketing products. **100% royalty from net sales.** Considers simultaneous submissions. Hardcover, paperback, coffee table books. Prefers mss by e-mail. Guidelines on website.

Nonfiction/Fiction: Query first; proposal/2-3 chapters; e-query.

Special Needs: Books of good content. Strong characters, great story line.

Artwork: Open to queries from freelance artists.

Tips: Open to almost any topic.

ABINGDON PRESS, 201 Eighth Ave. S., PO Box 801, Nashville TN 37202. (615) 749-6000. E-mail: [first initial and last name]@umpublishing.org. Website: www.abingdonpress.com. United Methodist Publishing House/Cokesbury. Mary C. Dean, ed-in-chief. Editors: Ramona Richards, fiction; Ron Kidd, study resources; Michael Stephens, Bible reference; Kathryn Armistead, theology; Constance Stella, leadership; Lil Copan, Christian living. Books and church supplies directed primarily to a mainline religious market. Publishes 120 titles/yr.; hardcover, trade paperbacks. Receives 2,000 submissions annually. Less than 5% of books from first-time authors. Accepts mss through agents only for fiction and Christian living. No reprints. **Royalty 7.5% on net.** Average first printing 2,500-4,000. Publication within 18 mos. Requires requested ms electronically. Prefers Common English Bible or a variety of which CEB is one. Guidelines on website; free catalog.

Nonfiction: Proposal/3 chapters; no phone/fax/e-query.

Fiction: Solicited or agented material only.

Ethnic Books: African American, Hispanic, Native American, Korean.

Music: See guidelines on website.

Tips: "We develop and produce materials to help more people in more places come to know and love God through Jesus Christ and to choose to serve God and neighbor."

This publisher serviced by ChristianManuscriptSubmissions.com.

***ADAMS MEDIA CORP.,** 57 Littlefield St., Avon MA 02322. (508) 427-7100. Toll-free fax (800) 872-5628. Website: www.adamsmedia.com. Division of F + W Publications. Jill Alexander, sr. ed.; submit to Paula Munier. Publishes 250 titles/yr. Receives 6,500 submissions annually. 40% of books from first-time authors. Accepts mss through agents or authors. **Royalty; variable advance; or outright purchase.** Publication within 12-18 mos. Considers simultaneous submissions. Responds in 3 mos. to queries. No mss accepted by e-mail. Guidelines on website ("Submissions"); catalog for 9 x 12 SAE/5 stamps.

Nonfiction: Query first by mail; no phone/fax/e-query.

Tips: General publisher that does some inspirational books.

***AMBASSADOR BOOKS, INC.**, 997 Macarthur Blvd., Mahwah NJ 07430. Toll-free (800) 218-1903. (201) 825-7300. Toll-free fax (800) 836-3161. Fax (201) 825-8345. E-mail: info@paulistpress.com. Website: www.paulistpress.com. Catholic/Paulist Press. Gerry Goggins, adult ed. (ggoggins@paulist press.com); Jennifer Conlan, children's ed. (jconlan@paulistpress.com). Books of intellectual and spiritual excellence. Publishes 12 titles/yr.; hardcover, trade paperbacks. Receives 1,000 submissions annually. 50% of books from first-time authors. Accepts mss through agents or authors. No reprints. **Royalty 8-10% of net; advance $500-1,000.** Publication within 1 yr. Considers simultaneous submissions. Responds in 3-4 mos. Prefers NRSV. Guidelines by mail/e-mail/website ("Manuscript Submission"); free catalog (or on website).

Nonfiction: Query; no phone/fax/e-query.

Fiction: Query. Juvenile, young adult, adult; picture books & board books.

Photos/Artwork: Accepts freelance photos for book covers; open to queries from freelance artists.

Tips: "Our mission for adult books is to celebrate the spiritual dimension of this world by witnessing to the reality of the Way, the Truth, and the Life. For children, it is to foster the knowledge that they are precious to the Lord while encouraging a friendship with Him that will last a lifetime."

***AMBASSADOR INTERNATIONAL** (formerly Ambassador-Emerald Intl.), 427 Wade Hampton Blvd., Greenville SC 29609. (864) 235-2434. Fax (864) 235-2491. E-mail: publisher@emerald house.com. Website: www.ambassador-international.com. Sam Lowry, ed. Dedicated to spreading the gospel of Christ and empowering Christians through the written word. Publishes 30+ titles/yr.; hardcover, trade paperbacks, mass-market paperbacks, coffee table books, digital. Receives 350-400 submissions annually. 65% of books from first-time authors. Accepts mss through agents or authors. Subsidy publishes 40-50%; no print-on-demand. No reprints. Prefers 30,000+ wds. or 100-250 pgs. **Royalty 10-18% of net; no advance.** Average first printing 2,000-3,000. Publication within 3 mos. Considers simultaneous submissions. Prefers requested ms by e-mail. Responds in up to 30 days. Prefers KJV, NIV, ESV, NKJV, NASB. Guidelines by mail/e-mail/website ("Get Published"/"submission guidelines" in text); free catalog.

Nonfiction: E-mail proposal/3 chapters; phone/fax/e-query OK.

Fiction: E-mail proposal/3 chapters; phone/fax/e-query OK. For adults.

Special Needs: Business, finance, biographies, novels, inspirational, devotional, topical, Bible studies.

Also Does: DVDs.

Photos/Artwork: Accepts freelance photos for book covers; open to queries from freelance artists.

Tips: "We're most open to a book which has a clearly defined market and the author's total commitment to the project. We do well with first-time authors. We have full international coverage. Many of our titles sell globally."

***AMERICAN CATHOLIC PRESS**, 16565 State St., South Holland IL 60473-2025. (708) 331-5485. Fax (708) 331-5484. E-mail: acp@acpress.org. Website: www.acpress.org or www.leafletmissal.com. Catholic worship resources. Father Michael Gilligan, ed. dir. Publishes 4 titles/yr.; hardcover. Receives 10 submissions annually. Reprints books. **Pays $25-100 for outright purchases only.** Average first printing 3,000. Publication within 1 yr. No simultaneous submissions. Responds in 2 mos. Prefers NAS. No guidelines; catalog for SASE.

Nonfiction: Query first; no phone/fax/e-query.

Tips: "We publish only materials on the Roman Catholic liturgy. Especially interested in new music for church services. No poetry or fiction."

***AMG PUBLISHERS/LIVING INK BOOKS**, 6815 Shallowford Rd., Chattanooga TN 37421. Toll-free (800) 266-4977. (423) 894-6060. Toll-free fax (800) 265-6690. (423) 648-2244. E-mail:

ricks@amgpublishers.com, info@amgpublishers.com, or through website: www.amgpublishers.com. AMG International. Rick Steele, product development & acquisitions; Dr. Warren Baker, sr. ed. To provide biblically oriented books for reference, learning, and personal growth. Imprints: Living Ink Books; God and Country Press. Publishes 30-35 titles/yr.; hardcover, trade paperbacks, and oversized Bible studies. Receives 2,500 submissions annually. 30% of books from first-time authors. Accepts mss through agents or authors. Reprints books. Prefers 40,000-60,000 wds. or 176-224 pgs. **Royalty 10-16% of net; average advance $2,000.** Average first printing 3,500. Publication within 18 mos. Accepts simultaneous submissions. Prefers accepted ms by e-mail. Responds in 1-4 mos. Prefers KJV, NASB, NIV, NKJV, NLT. Guidelines by e-mail/website; catalog for 9 x 12 SAE/5 stamps.

Nonfiction: Query letter first; e-query preferred. "Looking for historical fiction and nonfiction for our God and Country Press imprint. Need more reference-type works; Bible studies 4-8 weeks in length; and YA fiction."

Fiction: Query letter first; e-query preferred. "Always looking for YA fantasy and historical fiction for adults."

Special Needs: Bible studies and reference—especially reference.

Also Does: Bible software, Bible audio cassettes, CD-ROMs.

Artwork: Open to queries from freelance artists.

Tips: "Most open to a book that is well thought out, clearly written, and finely edited. A professional proposal, following our specific guidelines, has the best chance of acceptance. Spend extra time in developing a good proposal. AMG is always looking for something new and different—with a niche. Write, and rewrite, and rewrite, and rewrite again."

This publisher serviced by ChristianManuscriptSubmissions.com and The Writer's Edge.

***AVON INSPIRE,** HarperCollins, 10 E. 53rd St., New York NY 10022. (212) 207-7000. Website: www.harpercollins.com. Cynthia DiTiberio, ed. Inspirational women's fiction. Publishes 8-10 titles/yr. Agented submissions only.

Fiction: Historical & contemporary; Amish.

BAKER ACADEMIC, 6030 E. Fulton Rd., Ada MI 49301. (616) 676-9185. Fax (616) 676-9573. E-mail: submissions@bakeracademic.com. Website: www.bakeracademic.com. Imprint of Baker Publishing Group. Jim Kinney, ed. dir. Publishes religious academic books and professional books for students and church leaders. Publishes 50 titles/yr.; hardcover, trade paperbacks. 10% of books from first-time authors. Accepts mss through agents, submission services, or editor's personal contacts at writers' conferences. **Royalty; advance.** Publication within 1 yr. Guidelines on website ("Contact"/"Submitting a Proposal"); catalog on website.

Nonfiction: No unsolicited queries.

This publisher serviced by ChristianManuscriptSubmissions.com.

BAKER BOOKS, 6030 E. Fulton Rd., Ada MI 49301. (616) 676-9185. Fax (616) 676-2315. Website: www.bakerbooks.com. Imprint of Baker Publishing Group. Publishes ministry and Christian living for the church. Publishes hardcover, trade paperbacks. No unsolicited proposals. Catalog on website. Submit only through an agent, Authonomy.com, The Writer's Edge, or ChristianManuscript Submissions.com.

***BALLANTINE PUBLISHING GROUP,** 1745 Broadway, 18th Fl., New York NY 10019. (212) 782-9000. Website: www.randomhouse.com/BB. A Division of Random House. Submit to Religion Editor. General publisher that does a few religious books. Mss from agents only. No e-query. **Royalty 8-15%; variable advances.** Nonfiction & fiction. Guidelines on website; no catalog.

***B&H PUBLISHING GROUP,** 127—9th Ave. N., Nashville TN 37234-0115. E-mail: Manuscript Submission@lifeway.com. Website: www.bhpublishinggroup.com. Twitter: @BHpub. Facebook: www.facebook.com/bhpublishing. B&H Publishing Group, a division of LifeWay Christian Resources, is a team of mission-minded people with a passion for taking God's Word to the world. Because we believe Every Word Matters, we seek to provide innovative, intentional content that is grounded in biblical truth. Imprints: B&H Books, B&H Academic, Holman Bible Publishers, Holman Reference, Broadman ChurchSupplies, B&H Español. Publishes 90-100 titles/yr.; hardcover, trade paperback. Receives 3,000 submissions annually. 10% of books from first-time authors. **Royalty on net; advance.** Publication within 18 mos. Considers simultaneous submissions. Responds in 2-3 mos. Prefers HCSB. Guidelines by mail/e-mail.

Nonfiction: Query first; no phone/fax query.

Fiction: Query first; no phone/fax query.

Also Does: Licensing, Kindle Reader, some audio.

Blog: blog.bhpublishinggroup.com/

Tips: "Follow guidelines when submitting. Be informed that the market in general is very crowded with the book you might want to write. Do the research before submitting."

This publisher serviced by ChristianManuscriptSubmissions.com and The Writer's Edge.

***BANTAM BOOKS**. See Doubleday Religious on p. 77.

***BARBOUR PUBLISHING INC.,** 1810 Barbour Dr., PO Box 719, Uhrichsville OH 44683. (740) 922-6045. Fax (740) 922-8065. Mission statement: To publish and distribute inspirational products offering exceptional value and biblical encouragement to the masses. E-mail: submissions@barbourbooks.com. Guidelines by website, www.barbourbooks.com (click on "Contact Us"/"How do I submit my manuscript for publishing?"). Accepts fiction proposals only through agents. Publishes 300+ titles/yr.; fiction, nonfiction, Bible reference, devotions, gift books, Christian classics, children's titles; hardcover, flexibound, trade paperbacks, mass market paperbacks. Considers simultaneous submissions & reprints.

This publisher serviced by The Writer's Edge.

BETHANY HOUSE PUBLISHERS, a division of Baker Publishing Group, 6030 E. Fulton Rd., Ada MI 49301. Website: www.bethanyhouse.com. Offering inspiration and encouragement to readers through story and spiritual insight, Bethany House titles help Christians apply biblical truth in all areas of life. Publishes approx. 90 titles/yr.; hardcover, trade paperbacks. 10% of books from first-time authors. Accepts mss through agents. **Negotiable royalty on net; negotiable advance.** Publication within 18 mos. Considers simultaneous submissions. Catalog available on website.

Nonfiction: "Seeking well-planned and developed books in the following categories: personal growth, deeper-life spirituality, contemporary issues, women's issues, reference, applied theology, and inspirational."

Fiction: See website for fiction guidelines.

Tips: "We do not accept unsolicited queries or proposals."

This publisher serviced by WritersEdgeService.com, ChristianManuscriptSubmissions.com, and The Writer's Edge.

***BLUE DOLPHIN PUBLISHING, INC.,** PO Box 8, Nevada City CA 95959. (530) 477-1503. Fax (530) 477-8342. E-mail: Bdolphin@bluedolphinpublishing.com. Website: www.bluedolphinpublishing.com. Paul M. Clemens, pub. Imprints: Pelican Pond (fiction & poetry), Papillon Publishing (juvenile), and Symposium Publishing (nonfiction). Books that help people grow in their social and spiritual awareness. Publishes 20-24 titles/yr. (includes 10-12 print-on-demand). Receives 4,800 submissions annually. 90% of books from first-time authors. Prefers about 60,000 wds. or 200-300 pgs. **Royalty 10-15% of net; no advance.** Average first printing 300, then on demand. Publication within 10 mos. Considers simultaneous submissions. Requires requested ms on disk. Responds in 3-6 mos. Guidelines by e-mail/website (scroll down right side to "About Blue Dolphin"/"Guidance for Authors"); catalog for 8.5 x 11 SAE/2 stamps.

Nonfiction: Query or proposal/1 chapter; no phone/e-query. "Looking for books that will increase people's spiritual and social awareness. We will consider all topics."

Fiction: Query/2-pg. synopsis. Pelican Pond Imprint. For teens and adults; no children's board books or picture books.

Also Does: E-books.

Photos/Artwork: Accepts freelance photos for book covers; open to queries from freelance artists.

Tips: "Looking for mature writers whose focus is to help people lead better lives. Our authors are generally professionals who write for others—not just for themselves. We look for topics that would appeal to the general market, are interesting, different, and will aid in the growth and development of humanity. See website before submitting."

Note: This publisher also publishes books on a range of topics, including cross-cultural spirituality. They also may offer a copublishing arrangement, not necessarily a royalty deal.

BMH BOOKS, PO Box 544, Winona Lake IN 46590. (574) 268-1122. Fax (574) 268-5384. E-mail: lcgates@bmhbooks.com. Website: www.BMHbooks.com. Fellowship of Grace Brethren Churches. Liz Cutler Gates, ed./pub. Trinitarian theology; dispensational eschatology; emphasis on exegesis. Publishes 3-5 titles/yr.; hardcover, trade paperbacks. Receives 30 submissions annually. 50% of books from first-time authors. Accepts mss through agents or authors. Seldom reprints books. Prefers 50,000-75,000 wds. or 128-256 pgs. **Royalty 8-10% on retail; rarely pays an advance.** Average first printing 2,000. Publication within 1 yr. Prefers not to consider simultaneous submissions. Responds in 3 mos. Prefers KJV or NIV. Requires accepted mss by e-mail. Guidelines by mail/e-mail; free catalog.

Nonfiction: Proposal/2 chapters; no phone/fax query; e-query OK. "Most open to a small-group study book or text for Bible college/Bible institute."

Tips: "Most open to biblically based, timeless discipleship material."

BOLD VISION BOOKS, PO Box 2011, Friendswood TX 77549-2011. (281) 797-5832. E-mail: boldvisionbooks@gmail.com. Website: www.boldvisionbooks.com. Karen Porter, sr. ed. Imprint: Bold Vision Books. Publishes 10 titles/yr. Receives 100 submissions/yr. 50% of books from first-time authors. Accepts books submitted by agents. Hardcover, trade paperbacks, mass-market paperbacks, coffee table books, digital. Reprints books. Preferred book length 35,000 wds. **Royalty 5-25% on net.** No advance. Publication within 6 mo. Considers simultaneous submissions. Responds 1-3 mos. $2 for catalog. Writers guidelines on website.

Nonfiction: Compelling stories of life change and spiritual growth. Query letter first. Accept e-mail queries. Require mss by e-mail.

Fiction: Adult. Looking for strong story skills with compelling characters who experience life change.

Tips: "Bold Vision Books is interested in fresh voices from authors who write with the reader in mind. Your best opportunity with BVB is strong writing and a powerful takeaway message. Bold Vision Books exists to bring personal publishing solutions to authors with strong, fresh expressions of faith and purpose. To be noticed by our editors, write in crisp, tight, and authoritative language and offer answers that lead to transformation."

BONDFIRE BOOKS, Parent co. Alive Communications, 7680 Goddard St., Ste. 220, Colorado Springs CO 80920. (719) 260-7080. Fax: (719) 260-8223. E-mail: submissions@bondfirebooks.com. Website: www.bondfirebooks.com. Chief Kindler, ed. Bondfire Books is an e-publisher focused on kindling thought and action through Christian and inspirational content while maximizing digital prospects for authors. Publish 50+/yr. Receives 5,000 proposals/yr. 10% first-time authors. Accepts books submitted by agents. Digital. Will reprint. Preferred book length 150,000 wds. **Royalty 50% based on net.** E-books 50%. No advance. Avg. time to publication 2 mos. Considers simultaneous submissions. Responds 2-4 wks. Catalog on website. Guidelines on website. Open to queries from freelance artists.

Nonfiction: proposal with 2 chap. E-mail queries. Requires mss by e-mail.

Fiction: teens/adults. Query letter ONLY. Proposal with 2 chap.

Special Needs: Memoir, fiction, nonfiction, tie-ins to news events. News makers. Out of print with rts. reverted, in print works with available elec. rights.

Tips: "Publishers and agents are being much more selective with what they say yes to. And yet amidst increased competition, the cream always rises to the top. The great books get noticed and picked up." Contemporary fiction or big nonfiction book tied to a news maker. Primarily interested in working with authors with established platforms and audiences.

BRAZOS PRESS, 6030 E. Fulton Rd., Ada MI 49301. (616) 676-9185. Fax (616) 676-9573. Website: www.brazospress.com. Imprint of Baker Publishing Group. Publishes thoughtful, theologically grounded books on subjects of importance to the church and the world. Publishes hardcover, trade paperbacks. Guidelines on website ("Contact"/"Submitting a Proposal"). Catalog on website.

***BRIDGE LOGOS,** 17750 N.W. 115th Ave., Bldg. 200, Ste. 220, Alachua FL 32615. (386) 462-2525. Fax (586) 462-2535. E-mail: editorial@bridgelogos.com or phildebrand@bridgelogos.com. Website: www.bridgelogos.com. Peggy Hildebrand, acq. ed. Publishes classics, books by Spirit-filled authors, and inspirational books that appeal to the general evangelical market. Imprint: Synergy. Publishes 40 titles/yr.; hardcover, trade paperbacks, mass-market paperbacks. Receives 200+ submissions annually. 30% of books from first-time authors. Accepts mss through agents or authors. Subsidy publishes to 5%; does very little print-on-demand. Reprints books. Prefers 250 pgs. **Royalty 10% on net; rarely pays $500 advance.** Average first printing 4,000-5,000. Publication within 6-12 mos. Considers simultaneous submissions. Responds in 6 wks. Prefers accepted mss by e-mail. Guidelines on website ("Information"/"Manuscript Submission"); free catalog.

Nonfiction: Proposal/3-5 chapters; no phone/fax query; e-query OK. "Most open to evangelism, spiritual growth, self-help, and education." Charges a $50 manuscript submission/evaluation fee.

Fiction: Proposal/3-5 chapters; no phone/fax query; e-query OK.

Special Needs: Reference, biography, current issues, controversial issues, church renewal, women's issues, and Bible commentary. Also teen, preteen, and kids' books.

Ethnic Books: African American & Hispanic.

Photos: Accepts freelance photos for book covers.

Tips: "Looking for well-written, timely books that are aimed at the needs of people and that glorify God. Have a great message, a well-written manuscript, and a specific plan and willingness to market your book. Looking for previously published authors with an active ministry who are experts on their subject."

BRP PUBLISHING GROUP, PO Box 822674, Vancouver WA 98682. (208) 352-0396. Fax (208) 246-3962. E-mail: publisher@barkingrainpress.org. Website: www.barkingrainpress.org. Ti Locke, ed. dir. Imprints: Barking Rain Press, Virtual Tales, Nitis Books. Publishes 12-15 bks./yr. Receives 100+ ms/yr. 60% first-time authors. Accepts bks. submitted by agents and unsolicited mss from authors. Hardcover, trade paperbacks, digital, reprints. Prefers 20,000-100,000 wds. **Royalty 50-60%.** Advance for est. authors. Exclusively POD services & e-books. Publication within 12 mos. No simultaneous submissions. Responds 30-60 days. Catalog on website. Guidelines on website.

Fiction: Only book proposal w/4 chapters. Open submissions: January, May, September. Elec. submissions only. Sign up for reminder list on website.

Special Needs: Non-erotic romance, YA, speculative fiction.

Tips: Well written, good plot and story arc, no POV issues (head-hopping). Barking Rain Press is a nonprofit publisher. Our mission is to help new authors and midlist authors further their writing careers. Freelance openings posted on website.

CANTICLE BOOKS, 1647 Shire Ave., Oceanside CA 92057. (760) 806-3743. Fax (760) 806-3689. E-mail: magnuspress@aol.com. Website: www.magnuspress.com. Imprint of Magnus Press. Warren Angel, ed. dir. To publish biblical studies by Catholic authors that are written for the average person and that minister life to Christ's Church. Publishes 2 titles/yr.; trade paperbacks. Receives 60 submissions annually. 50% of books from first-time authors. Accepts mss through agents or authors. Reprints books. Prefers 105-300 pgs. **Graduated royalty on retail; no advance.** Average first printing 2,500. Publication within 1 yr. Considers simultaneous submissions. Accepts requested ms on disk. Responds in 1 mo. Guidelines by mail/e-mail/website ("Canticle Book Submissions"); free catalog.

Nonfiction: Query or proposal/3 chapters; fax query OK. "Looking for spirituality, thematic biblical studies, unique inspirational books."

Tips: "Our writers need solid knowledge of the Bible and a mature spirituality that reflects a profound relationship with Jesus Christ. Most open to well-researched, popularly written biblical studies geared to Catholics, or personal experience books that share/emphasize a person's relationship with Christ."

CHALFONT HOUSE PUBLISHING, PO Box 84, Dumfries VA 22026. (800) 728-9893. Fax: (800) 728-9893. E-mail: info@chalfonthouse.com. Website: www.chalfonthouse.com. Lynellen Perry, pres. Imprint: HopeSprings Books. We are focused on publishing quality books that don't shy away from tough topics. Publishes 6-12 titles/yr. Receives 50 submissions/yr. 100% from first-time authors. Accepts books submitted by agents. Trade, mass-market, digital. Reprints books. Prefers up to 100,000 wds. **Royalty based on net. E-books based on net.** Guidelines on website.

Photos: Accepts freelance photos for book covers.

Nonfiction: Proposal with 3 sample chapters. E-mail query. Accepts mss by e-mail.

Fiction: Proposal with 3 sample chapters or complete mss. E-mail query.

Tips: "In fiction, a good story is key. We look for characters who draw you in and keep you reading. We're open to discussion of topics that are often considered 'off limits,' and we enjoy transformational and reality-based fiction, because we understand that Christians aren't perfect and we don't expect fictional Christians to be either. In nonfiction, you need to have a fairly established platform, or at least a good idea of how to develop one already in place. There needs to be something unique about your proposal that sets your work apart from the other similar books out there already."

CHARISMA HOUSE (formerly Strang Book), 600 Rinehart Rd., Lake Mary FL 32746. (407) 333-0600. Fax (407) 333-7100. E-mail: creationhouse@charismamedia.com or charismahouse@charismamedia.com. Website: www.charismamedia.com. Communications. Submit to Acquisitions Assistant. To inspire and equip people to live a Spirit-led life and walk in the divine purpose for which they were called. This house has 8 imprints, which are listed with descriptions/details. Publishes 150 titles/yr.; hardcover, trade paperbacks, mass-market paperbacks. Receives 1,500 submissions annually. 65% of books from first-time authors. Prefers mss through agents. Reprints books. Prefers 55,000 wds. **Royalty on net or outright purchase; advance.** Average first printing 7,500. Publication within 9 mos. Considers simultaneous submissions. Accepts requested ms on disk or on website. Responds in 6-10 wks. Guidelines by mail/e-mail/website (under "Submit Book Proposal"); free catalog.

Nonfiction: Proposal or complete ms; by mail or e-query OK; no phone query. Book proposal application on website. "Open to any books that are well written and glorify Jesus Christ."

Fiction: Proposal or complete ms; by mail or e-query OK; no phone query. Book proposal application on website. "For all ages. Fiction must have a biblical worldview and point the reader to Christ."

Photos: Accepts freelance photos for book covers.

Charisma House: Books on Christian living, mainly from a Charismatic/Pentecostal perspective. Topics: Christian living, work of the Holy Spirit, prophecy, prayer, Scripture, adventures in evangelism and missions, popular theology.

Siloam: Books about living in good health—body, mind, and spirit. Topics: alternative medicine; diet and nutrition; and physical, emotional, and psychological wellness. We prefer manuscripts from certified doctors, nutritionists, trainers, and other medical professionals. Proof of credentials may be required.

Frontline: Books on contemporary political and social issues from a Christian perspective.

Creation House: Copublishing imprint for a wide variety of Christian books. Author is required to buy a quantity of books from the first press run. This is not self-publishing or print-on-demand.

Realms: Christian fiction in the supernatural, speculative genre. Full-length adult novels, 80,000-120,000 wds. Will also consider historical or biblical fiction if supernatural element is substantial.

Excel: Publishes books that are targeted toward success in the workplace and businesses.

Casa Creación: Publishes and translates books into Spanish. (800) 987-8432. E-mail: casacreacion@charismamedia.com. Website: www.casacreacion.com.

Publicaciones Casa: Publishes the same as Creation House and is for people who like to copublish in Spanish. Contact info same as Casa Creación.

This publisher serviced by ChristianManuscriptSubmissions.com and The Writer's Edge.

***THE CHARLES PRESS, PUBLISHERS,** 230 N. 21st St., Ste. 202, Philadelphia PA 19103-1095. (215) 561-2786. E-mail: submissions@charlespresspub.com. Website: www.charlespresspub.com. Lauren Metzler, pub. (lauren@charlespresspub.com). Responds in 4-16 wks. Guidelines on website ("Book Proposal Submission Guidelines"); catalog.

Nonfiction: Submit a letter of inquiry first; no fax submissions.

CHICKEN SOUP FOR THE SOUL BOOKS. See listing in Periodicals section.

CHOSEN BOOKS, Division of Baker Publishing Group, 3985 Bradwater St., Fairfax VA 22031-3702. (952) 829-2550. E-mail: jcampbell@chosenbooks.com. Website: http://bakerpublishinggroup.com/chosen. Jane Campbell, editorial dir. Charismatic; Spirit-filled–life titles and a few thematic narratives. No autobiographies. No unsolicited mss, but will respond to e-mail queries. Credentials and platform vital.

This publisher is serviced by The Writer's Edge.

***CHRISTIAN HERITAGE SOCIETY,** PO Box 519, Baldwin Place NY 10505. Phone/fax (914) 962-3287. E-mail: gtkurian@aol.com. Website: www.encyclopediasociety.com. George Kurian, ed. Publishes 6 titles/yr.; hardcover, trade paperbacks. Receives 100 submissions annually. 50% of books from first-time authors. Prefers mss through agents. No subsidy. Reprints books. Prefers 120,000 wds. **Royalty 10-15% on net; no advance.** Average first printing 10,000. Publication within 1 yr. Considers simultaneous submissions. Responds in 3 mos. Guidelines by mail; free catalog.

Nonfiction: Query; e-query OK. "Looking for Christian history, reference books, memoirs, devotionals, and evangelism."

***CHRISTIAN WRITER'S EBOOK NET,** PO Box 446, Ft. Duchesne UT 84026. (435) 772-3429. E-mail: editor@writersebook.com or through website: www.writersebook.com. Nondenominational/evangelical Christian. Linda Kay Stewart Whitsitt, ed-in-chief (linda@webtechdg.com); M. P. Whitsitt, asst. ed. (MP@webtechdg.com); Terry Gordon Whitsitt, asst. to ed. (terry@webtechdg.com). Gives first-time authors the opportunity to bring their God-given writing talent to the Christian market. Publishes 25 titles/yr. Receives 150 submissions annually. 95% of books from first-time authors. Accepts mss through agents or authors. Subsidy publishes 25%. Reprints books. Prefers 60+ pgs. **Royalty 35-50%; no advance.** E-books only for Kindle and other e-reader formats. Publication within 6 mos. Considers simultaneous submissions. Electronic queries and submissions only; mss need to be in electronic form (MS Word, WordPerfect, ASCII, etc.) to be published; send by e-mail (preferred). No mail submissions accepted without contact by e-mail first. Responds in 1-2 mos. Guidelines on website ("Publishing" on right side).

Nonfiction/Fiction: E-query only. Any topic or genre.

Also Does: Booklets, pamphlets, tracts. E-books.

Tips: "Make sure your work is polished and ready for print. The books we publish are sold in our online store at Amazon and Ebay. If you are not sure what an e-book is, check out our website's FAQ page."

***CHURCH GROWTH INSTITUTE,** PO Box 7, Elkton MD 21922-0007. (434) 525-0022. Fax (434) 525-0608. E-mail: info@churchgrowth.org. Website: www.ChurchGrowth.org. Ephesians Four Ministries. Cindy G. Spear, product development dir. Providing practical tools for leadership, evangelism, and church growth. Publishes 3 titles/yr.; trade paperbacks/other. Receives 20 submissions annually. 7% of books from first-time authors. No mss through agents. Prefers 64-160 pgs. **Royalties vary; 6% on retail or outright purchase; no advance.** Average first printing 100. Publication within 1 yr. Considers simultaneous submissions. Responds in 3 mos. Requires requested ms on disk or by e-mail. Guidelines sent after query/outline is received by e-mail. No printed catalog; full product listing on website.

Nonfiction: Query; no phone/fax query; e-query OK. "We prefer our writers to be experienced in what they write about."

Special Needs: New or unique ministries (how-to). Self-discovery and evaluation tools, such as our Spiritual Gifts Inventory and Spiritual Growth Survey, Friendship Skills Assessment.

Photos: Rarely use freelance photos.

Tips: "Currently concentrating on own Team Ministry/Spiritual Gifts resources. Accept very few unsolicited submissions. Most open to ministry how-to manuals or audio albums (CDs/audiotapes and workbooks) for ministry leaders—something unique with a special niche. Must be practical and different from anything else on the same subject—or must be a topic/slant few others have published. May consider evaluation tools as mentioned above. No devotionals, life testimonies, commentaries, or studies on books of the Bible."

CLADACH PUBLISHING, PO Box 336144, Greeley CO 80633. (970) 371-9530. E-mail: staff@cladach.com. Website: www.cladach.com. Independent, small Christian press. Catherine Lawton, pub. (cathyl@cladach.com). Seeks to influence those inside and outside the body of Christ by giving a voice to talented writers with a clear, articulate, and Christ-honoring vision. Categories: memoirs, fiction, relationships, God in creation. Publishes 2-3 titles/yr.; trade paperbacks and e-books. Receives 200 submissions annually. 60% of books from first-time authors. Accepts proposals through agents or authors. No subsidy, print-on-demand, or reprints. Prefers 160-256 pgs. **Royalty 7% on net; sometimes offers a small advance.** Average first printing 1,000. Publication within 1 yr. Considers simultaneous submissions. Responds in 3-6 mos. Prefers NIV, NRSV. Guidelines on website ("For Authors"); catalog online.

Nonfiction: Query letter only first (we're very selective); e-query OK.

Fiction: Query letter only first (1-2 pgs.); e-query OK (copied into message). For adults. "Prefers gripping stories depicting inner struggles and real-life issues; well crafted. Interested in frontier fiction set in Colorado."

Tips: "We want writing that shows God active in our world and that helps readers experience His presence and power in their lives. Check out our website for current guidelines and published books to see whether your book is a fit for Cladach." Unsolicited mss are returned unopened.

CLC PUBLICATIONS, PO Box 1449, Fort Washington PA 19034. (215) 542-1242. E-mail: submissions@clcpublications.com. Website: www.clcpublications.com. CLC Ministries Intl. David Almack, pub.; Tracey Lewis-Giggetts, mng. ed. Books that reflect a passion for the topic and a depth of spirituality—a book that grows out of a fervent relationship with Christ. Publishes 12 titles/yr.; hardcover, trade paperbacks, mass-market paperbacks, e-books. Receives 200+ submissions annually. 80% of books from first-time authors. Accepts mss through agents or authors. Reprints books. Prefers under 60,000 wds. or under 300 pgs. **Royalty 10-12% of net; pays an advance.** Average first printing 3,000. Publication within 1 yr. Considers simultaneous submissions. Responds in 2-5 days.

Requires accepted mss on disk or by e-mail. Prefers NKJV. Guidelines by mail/e-mail/website (at top "Writers Guidelines"); catalog for 9 x 12 SAE/2 stamps.

Nonfiction: Query first; proposal/2-3 chapters; e-query OK. Books for the deeper life.

Special Needs: A fresh approach to deepening one's relationship with God.

This publisher serviced by ChristianManuscriptSubmissions.com and The Writer's Edge.

***COMFORT PUBLISHING,** PO Box 6265, Concord NC 28027. (704) 782-2353. Fax (704) 782-2393. E-mail: khuddle@comfortpublishing.com. Website: www.comfortpublishing.com. Comfort Publishing Services, LLC. Pamilla S. Tolen, sr. vp; Kristy Huddle, acq. mg. Submit to Kristy Huddle (khuddle@comfortpublishing.com). To promote Christian literature in a manner that is easy to read and understand, with a message that either teaches a principle or supports the truth of Christian faith. Nonfiction, self-help, true stories. Publishes 10 titles/yr.; hardcover, trade paperbacks, digital. Receives 3,000 submissions annually. 65% of books from first-time authors. Prefers mss through agents; will accept from authors. No subsidy or print-on-demand. No reprints. Prefers 75,000 wds. or 200 pgs. **Royalty 8-15% on retail; some advances; e-books 50% of net.** Average first printing 2,500. Publication within 12 mos. Considers simultaneous submissions. Responds in 18 mos. Accepts requested mss by e-mail. Guidelines by mail/e-mail/website ("Submission Guidelines"); digital catalog. Accepts freelance photos. Prefers NKJV.

Nonfiction: Proposal/3 chapters or complete ms; e-query preferred.

Fiction: For teens & adults. Submit complete ms.

Special Needs: Adventure, romance, mystery romance, suspense, teen/YA fiction, adult.

Also Does: E-books.

Photos: Accepts freelance photos for book covers.

Tips: "Desire to break away from traditional Christian literature. Readers are looking for more modern stories that deal with current dilemmas. Through our books we want to provide entertainment but also present books that represent good moral judgment within the Christian experience."

***CONARI PRESS,** 665 Third St., Ste. 400, San Francisco CA 94107. E-mail: submissions@rwwbooks.com. Website: www.redwheelweiser.com. An imprint of Red Wheel/Weiser, LLC. Ms. Pat Bryce, acq. ed. Books on spirituality, personal growth, parenting, and social issues. Publishes 30 titles/yr. Responds in up to 3 mos. Guidelines and catalog on website ("Submission Guidelines"). Incomplete topical listings.

CONCILIAR PRESS, Ben Lomond CA. E-mail for adult submissions: khyde@conciliarmedia.com (for children's submissions: jmeyer@conciliarmedia.com). Website: www.conciliarpress.com. Antiochian Orthodox Christian Archdiocese of N.A. Katherine Hyde, acq. ed. Jane Meyer, children's ed. Publishes 8-18 adult, 2-4 children's titles/yr. Receives 100 submissions annually. 20% of books from first-time authors. Accepts mss through agents or authors. Reprints books. **Royalty; no or small advance.** Average first printing 2,000. Accepts simultaneous submissions. E-mail submissions only. Responds in 1-3 mos. Prefers NKJV. Guidelines on website (scroll to bottom "Submissions"); catalog on website.

Nonfiction: E-query only. Accepts Eastern Orthodox material from Eastern Orthodox authors only.

Children's Books: E-query only. Send full manuscript for picture books under 2,000 wds. Accepts Eastern Orthodox material from Eastern Orthodox authors only.

Photos: Accepts freelance photos for book covers.

Tips: "Please explore our website before submitting and carefully follow posted guidelines. We accept only material by Eastern Orthodox Christians with specifically Orthodox content. We reserve the right not to respond to inappropriate submissions."

CONCORDIA PUBLISHING HOUSE, 3558 S. Jefferson Ave., St. Louis MO 63118-3968. (314) 268-1080. E-mail: ed.engelbrecht@cph.org. Website: www.cph.org. Lutheran Church/Missouri Synod.

Rev. Edward A. Engelbrecht, STM, sr. ed. Bible resources. Publication within 2 yrs. Responds in 6 wks. Guidelines on website (at bottom under "Popular Resources"/"Manuscript Submissions").

Nonfiction: Proposal/sample chapters.

Tips: "Freelance submissions for academic publications in biblical studies are welcome. Prospective authors should consult the peer review guidelines on the website for an author prospectus and submission guidelines."

This publisher serviced by The Writer's Edge.

CONTEMPORARY DRAMA SERVICE, Meriwether Publishing Ltd., 885 Elkton Dr., Colorado Springs CO 80907. E-mail: editor@meriwether.com. Website: www.ChristianPlaysandMusicals.com. Publishes Christian plays for mainline churches. Also supplemental textbooks on theatrical subjects. Prefers comedy but does publish some serious works. Accepts full-length or one-act plays—comedy or musical. General and Christian. Publishes 30 plays/yr. Responds in 4-6 wks. See the Meriwether Publishing listing or website for additional details ("Author's Corner" at top of list).

***DAVID C. COOK,** 4050 Lee Vance View, Colorado Springs CO 80918. (719) 536-0100. Fax (719) 536-3269. Website: www.davidccook.com. Don Pape, publisher, print and media; Terry Behimer, ed. dir. and assoc. publisher; Ingrid Beck, mng. ed. Discipleship is foundational; everything we publish needs to move the reader one step closer to maturity in Christ. Brands: David C. Cook (for teachers or program leaders who want Bible-based discipleship resources; Bible and study resources for serious Bible students; books for Christian families seeking biblical answers to life problems; books to equip kids—birth to age 12—for life); and fiction (inspiring fiction for mature believers). Publishes 85 titles/yr.; hardcover, trade paperbacks. 10% of books from first-time authors. Requires mss through agents. Publication within 1-2 yrs. Considers simultaneous submissions. Responds in 3-6 mos. Prefers requested ms by e-mail. Prefers NIV. Guidelines by mail/e-mail/website ("Contact Information"/"Writers Guidelines" on left).

Nonfiction/Fiction: Accepts submissions only through agents or on request of one of their editors at a writers' conference.

This publisher serviced by ChristianManuscriptSubmissions.com.

CROSSLINK PUBLISHING, PO Box 1232, Rapid City SD 57709. Toll-free (888) 697-4851. Toll-free fax (800) 934-6762. E-mail: publisher@crosslink.org. Website: www.crosslinkpublishing.com. Christian Church/Church of Christ. Rick Bates, dir. Focused on providing valuable resources to authors as well as bringing vibrant and helpful resources to the Christian community. Estab. 2008. Publishes 15-20 titles/yr.; trade paperbacks. Receives 150 submissions annually. 25% of books from first-time authors. No subsidy; does print-on-demand. No reprints. Prefers 200-300 pgs. **Royalty 10% of retail; no advance.** Publication within 4 mos. Considers simultaneous submissions. Responds in 7 days. Requires ms submission on website. Guidelines on website ("Authors").

Nonfiction: Complete ms; e-query OK.

Special Needs: Devotionals and small group studies.

Photos/Artwork: Accepts freelance photos for book covers; open to queries from freelance artists.

Tips: "We are particularly interested in providing books that help Christians succeed in their daily walk (inspirational, devotional, small groups, etc.)."

This publisher serviced by The Writer's Edge.

CROSSWAY, 1300 Crescent St., Wheaton IL 60174. (630) 682-4300. Fax (630) 682-4785. E-mail: submissions@crossway.org. Website: www.crossway.org. A publishing ministry of Good News Publishers. Allan Fisher, sr. vp for book publishing; submit to Jill Carter, editorial administrator, or www.submissions.org. Publishes books that combine the truth of God's Word with a passion to live it out, with unique and compelling Christian content. Publishes 70 titles/yr.; hardcover, trade paperbacks. Receives 1,000 submissions annually. 1% of books from first-time authors. Accepts mss through agents or authors. No reprints. Prefers 25,000 wds. & up. **Royalty 10-21% of net; advance varies.** Average first printing 5,000-10,000. Publication within 18 mos. Considers simultaneous submissions. Responds in 6-8 wks. Prefers ESV. Guidelines on website; free catalog.

Nonfiction: Currently not accepting unsolicited submissions.

Also Does: Tracts (Good News Publishers).

This publisher serviced by ChristianManuscriptSubmissions.com and The Writer's Edge.

***CSS PUBLISHING GROUP INC.,** 5450 N. Dixie Hwy., Lima OH 45807-9559. (419) 227-1818. Fax (419) 228-9184. E-mail: david@csspub.com, or through website: www.csspub.com. Serves the needs of pastors, worship leaders, and parish program planners in the broad Christian mainline of the American church. Imprints: Fairway Press (subsidy—see separate listing); B.O.D. (Books On Demand); FaithWalk Books. Publishes 30-40 titles/yr.; trade paperbacks, digital. Receives 500-1,000 submissions annually. 50% of books from first-time authors. Subsidy publishes 50-60% through Fairway Press; does print-on-demand. Reprints books. Prefers 100-125 pgs. **No royalty or advance.** Average first printing 1,000. Publication within 12-24 mos. Considers simultaneous submissions. Responds in 3 wks. to 3 mos.; final decision within 12 mos. Requires requested ms on disk and in hard copy. Prefers NRSV. Guidelines by e-mail/website ("Contact Us"/"Submissions Guidelines"); no catalog.

Nonfiction: Query or proposal/3 chapters; phone/e-query OK; complete ms for short works. "Looking for pastoral resources for ministry; lectionary sermons. Our material is practical in nature."

Fiction: Complete ms. Easy-to-perform dramas and pageants for all age groups. "Our drama interest primarily includes Advent, Christmas, Epiphany, Lent, and Easter. We do not publish long plays." Subsidy-only for fiction.

Tips: "We're looking for authors who will help with the marketing of their books."

CUPOLA PRESS, 3284 Withers Avenue, Lafayette CA 94549. (925) 285-7754. E-mail: info@cupolapress.com. Website: www.cupolapress.com. Gail Johnston, ed. Publishes 3 titles/yr. 50% by first-time authors. Does some POD. Publication in 1 year. Considers simultaneous submissions. Writer guidelines not available.

Nonfiction: Query letter only first. Query by e-mail. Inspirational nonfiction; how-to books with an enjoyable tone.

Tips: "Light reading for intentional living."

***DAWN PUBLICATIONS,** 12402 Bitney Springs Rd., Nevada City CA 95959. (530) 274-7775. Fax (530) 274-7778. E-mail: submission@dawnpub.com. Website: www.dawnpub.com. Glenn Hovemann, acq. ed. Dedicated to inspiring in children a sense of appreciation for all of life on earth. Publishes 6 titles/yr.; hardcover, trade paperbacks. Receives 2,500 submissions annually. 35% of titles are by new authors. Accepts mss through agents or authors. No reprints. **Royalty on net; pays an advance.** Publication within 1-2 yrs. Considers simultaneous submissions. Responds in 2 mos. Guidelines/catalog on website ("Submissions").

Nonfiction: Complete manuscript by mail or e-mail.

Artwork: Open to queries from freelance artists (send sample c/o Muffy Weaver).

Tips: "Most open to creative nonfiction. We look for nature awareness and appreciation titles that promote a relationship with the natural world and specific habitats, usually through inspiring treatment and nonfiction."

DESERT BREEZE PUBLISHING, E-mail: submissions@desertbreezepublishing.com. Website: www.desertbreezepublishing.com. Gail Delaney, ed. Goal is to publish exceptionally crafted and captivating romance novels in multiple genres. Accepts 50,000 wds. or over 100,000 wds. (prefers 75,000-100,000). No simultaneous submissions. Guidelines on website (click on "Submissions"); catalog online.

Fiction: See guidelines. Now accepting women's fiction with either secondary or no romantic elements required.

Special Needs: Seeking single-title works in all sub-genres. Will consider series. See guidelines for other specific genres.

Tips: "If you have questions about the guidelines, e-mail us at submissionsquestions@desert breezepublishing.com."

DISCOVERY HOUSE PUBLISHERS, PO Box 3566, Grand Rapids MI 49501. Toll-free (800) 653-8333. (616) 942-9218. Fax (616) 974-2224. E-mail: dhptc@rbc.org. Website: www.dhp.org. RBC Ministries. Carol Holquist, pub.; submit to Manuscript Review Editor. Publishes nonfiction books that foster Christian growth and godliness. Publishes 12-18 titles/yr.; hardcover, trade paperbacks, mass-market paperbacks. Accepts mss through agents or authors. Reprints books. **Royalty 10-14% on net; no advance.** Publication within 12-18 mos. Considers simultaneous submissions. Prefers e-mail submissions. Responds in 4-6 wks. Guidelines by mail/e-mail/website (FAQ #4); free catalog.

Nonfiction: Ms proposals preferred. If by e-mail, "Attn: Ms Review Editor" in subject line.

This publisher serviced by ChristianManuscriptSubmissions.com and The Writer's Edge.

DOUBLEDAY RELIGIOUS PUBLISHING, 1745 Broadway, New York NY 10019. (212) 782-9000. Fax (212) 782-8338. E-mail: tmurphy@randomhouse.com. Website: www.randomhouse.com. Imprint of Random House, Inc. Trace Murphy, editorial dir. Imprints: Image, Galilee, New Jerusalem Bible, Three Leaves Press, Anchor Bible Commentaries, Anchor Bible Reference Library. Publishes 45-50 titles/yr.; hardcover, trade paperbacks. Receives 1,500 submissions annually. 10% of books from first-time authors. Requires mss through agents. Reprints books. **Royalty 7.5-15% on retail; pays an advance.** Average first printing varies. Publication within 8 mos. Considers simultaneous submissions. Responds in 4 mos. No disk. Guidelines on website ("About Random House"/"Manuscript Submissions"); catalog for 9 x 12 SASE/3 stamps.

Nonfiction: Agented submissions only. Proposal/3 chapters; no phone query.

Fiction: Religious fiction. Agented submissions only.

Ethnic Books: African American; Hispanic.

Tips: "Most open to a book that has a big and well-defined audience. Have a clear proposal, lucid thesis, and specified audience."

This publisher serviced by ChristianManuscriptSubmissions.com.

DOVE INSPIRATIONAL PRESS, 1000 Burmaster St., Gretna LA 70053. (504) 368-1175. Fax (504) 368-1195. E-mail: editorial@pelicanpub.com. Website: www.pelicanpub.com. Nina Kooij, ed-in-chief. To publish books of quality and permanence that enrich the lives of those who read them. Imprint of Pelican Publishing. Publishes 1 title/yr.; hardcover, trade paperbacks. Receives 250 submissions annually. No books from first-time authors. Accepts mss through agents or authors. Reprints books. Prefers 200+ pgs. **Royalty; some advances.** Publication within 9-18 mos. No simultaneous submissions. Responds in 1 mo. on queries. Requires accepted ms on disk. Prefers KJV. Guidelines on website ("About Us"/"Submissions").

Nonfiction: Proposal/2 chapters; no phone/fax/e-query.

Fiction: Children's picture books only.

Artwork: Open to queries from freelance artists.

***EARTHEN VESSEL PUBLISHING,** 9 Sunny Oaks Dr., San Raphael CA 94903. (415) 302-1199. Fax (415) 499-8199. E-mail: kentphilpott@comcast.net. Website: www.earthenvessel.net. Evangelical/Baptist. Kent & Katie Philpott, eds. Our goal is to preach Jesus Christ and Him crucified. Imprint: Siloam Springs Press. Publishes 3 titles/yr.; trade paperbacks. Receives 15 submissions annually. 50% of books from first-time authors. Prefers mss through agents; accepts through author. Reprints books. No subsidy or POD for now. Any length. **Royalty on retail price; no advance.** Average first printing varies. Publication within 6 mos. Considers simultaneous submissions. Accepted mss by disk or e-mail. Responds in 1 wk. to 1 mo. Guidelines on website; no catalog.

Nonfiction: Query first by phone or e-mail; proposal/1 chapter.

Fiction: Query first by phone or e-mail; proposal/1 chapter.

Special Needs: Books of a solid biblical nature, Christ centered, perhaps of a Reformed nature, but not limited to this theology. Special interest in awakenings and a special interest in pastors of small churches and their congregations.

Photos/Artwork: Accepts freelance photos for book covers; open to queries from freelance artists.

Tips: "Well-written and edited work is best. Not able to do major rewriting or editing. Lean toward, but not exclusively, Reformed thought. Our goal is to present the gospel to unbelievers and the Scriptures to believers. We are small and can do very little, but we look forward to working with the print-on-demand format."

EERDMANS BOOKS FOR YOUNG READERS, 2140 Oak Industrial Dr. N.E., Grand Rapids MI 49505. Toll-free (800) 253-7521. (616) 459-4591. Fax (616) 459-6540. E-mail: youngreaders @eerdmans.com or info@eerdmans.com. Website: www.eerdmans.com/youngreaders. Wm. B. Eerdmans Publishing. Submit to Acquisitions Editor. Produces books for general trade, school, and library markets. Publishes 12-15 titles/yr.; hardcover, trade paperbacks. Receives 5,000 submissions annually. 3% of books from first-time authors. Prefers mss through agents. Age-appropriate length. **Royalty & advance vary.** Average first printing varies. Publication within 36 mos. Responds within 3 mos. only if interested. Guidelines by mail/e-mail/website ("Submission Guidelines"); catalog for 9 x 12 SAE/4 stamps.

Fiction: Proposal/3 chapters for book length; complete ms for picture books. For children and teens. No e-mail or fax submissions.

Artwork: Please do not send illustrations with picture-book manuscripts unless you are a professional illustrator. When submitting artwork, send color copies, not originals. Send illustrations sample to Gayle Brown, art dir.

Tips: "Most open to thoughtful submissions that address needs in children's literature. We are not looking for Christmas stories at this time."

This publisher serviced by The Writer's Edge.

***WM. B. EERDMANS PUBLISHING CO.,** 2140 Oak Industrial Dr. N.E., Grand Rapids MI 49505. Toll-free (800) 253-7521. (616) 459-4591. Fax (616) 459-6540. E-mail: info@eerdmans.com. Website: www.eerdmans.com. Protestant/Academic/Theological. Jon Pott, ed-in-chief. Imprint: Eerdmans Books for Young Readers (see separate listing). Publishes 120-130 titles/yr.; hardcover, trade paperbacks. Receives 3,000-4,000 submissions annually. 10% of books from first-time authors. Accepts mss through agents or authors. Reprints books. **Royalty; occasional advance.** Average first printing 4,000. Publication within 1 yr. Considers simultaneous submissions. Responds in 4 wks. to query; several months for mss. Guidelines by mail/website (www.eerdmans.com/submit.htm); free catalog.

Nonfiction: Proposal/2-3 chapters; no fax/e-query. "Looking for religious approaches to contemporary issues, spiritual growth, scholarly works."

Fiction: Proposal/chapter; no fax/e-query. For all ages. "We are looking for adult novels with high literary merit."

Tips: "Most open to material with general appeal, but well-researched, cutting-edge material that bridges the gap between evangelical and mainline worlds. Please include e-mail and/or SASE for a response."

EVERGREEN PRESS, 5601-D Nevius Rd., Mobile AL 36619. (251) 861-2525. Fax: (251) 287-2222. E-mail: brian@evergreenpress.com. Website: www.evergreenpress.com. Genesis Communications. Brian Banashak, pub.; Kathy Banashak, ed-in-chief. Publishes books that empower people for breakthrough living by being practical, biblical, and engaging. Imprints: Evergreen Press, Gazelle Press, Axiom Press (print-on-demand). Publishes 30 titles/yr. Receives 250 submissions annually. 40% of books from first-time authors. Accepts mss through agents or authors. Subsidy publishes 35%. Does print-on-demand. No reprints. Prefers 96-160 pgs. **Royalty on net; no advance.** Average first printing 4,000. Publication within 6 mos. Considers simultaneous submissions. Requires requested ms on disk or by e-mail. Responds in 4-6 wks. Guidelines on website ("Get Published"/"Book Submissions"); free catalog.

Nonfiction: Complete ms; fax/e-query OK. Submission form on website.

Fiction: For all ages. Complete ms; phone/fax/e-query OK. Submission form on website.

Special Needs: Business, finance, personal growth, women's issues, family/parenting, relationships, prayer, humor, and angels.

Also Does: Booklets.

Tips: "Most open to books with a specific market (targeted, not general) that the author is qualified to write for and that is relevant to today's believers and seekers. Author must also be open to editorial direction."

FAITHWORDS/HACHETTE BOOK GROUP, 10 Cadillac Dr., Ste. 220, Brentwood TN 37027. (615) 221-0996, ext. 221. Fax (615) 221-0962. Website: www.faithwords.com. Hachette Book Group USA. Anne Horch, ed. Publishes 35 titles/yr.; hardcover, trade paperbacks, mass-market paperbacks. Few books from first-time authors. Requires mss through agents. Prefers 60,000-90,000 wds. **Royalty on retail; pays an advance.** Publication within 12 mos. Considers simultaneous submissions. Prefers proposals & accepted ms by e-mail. Guidelines on website ("Manuscript submissions" on right side).

Nonfiction: Proposal with table of contents & 3 chapters from agents only. No phone/fax query; e-query OK.

Fiction: For teens and adults. Proposal/3 chapters.

This publisher serviced by ChristianManuscriptSubmissions.com.

FOCUS ON THE FAMILY BOOK PUBLISHING AND RESOURCE DEVELOPMENT, (street address not required), Colorado Springs CO 80995. (719) 531-3400. Fax (719) 531-3448. E-mail through website: www.focusonthefamily.com. Exists to support the family; all our products are about topics pertaining to families. Publishes 30-40 titles/yr.; hardcover, trade paperbacks, mass-market paperbacks (rarely). 12% of books from first-time authors. Rarely reprints books. Length depends on genre. **Royalty or work-for-hire; advance varies.** Average first printing varies. Publication within 18 mos. No longer considers unsolicited submissions. Responds in 1-3 mos. Prefers NIV (but accepts 10 others). Guidelines by e-mail/website; no catalog.

Nonfiction: Query letter only through an agent or writers' conference contact with a Focus editor. "Most open to family advice topics. We look for excellent writing and topics that haven't been done to death—or that have a unique angle."

Fiction: Query letter only through an agent or writers' conference contact with a Focus editor. Stories must incorporate traditional family values or family issues; from 1900 to present day. Also does Mom Lit.

Artwork: Open to queries from freelance artists (but not for specific projects).

This publisher serviced by ChristianManuscriptSubmissions.com and The Writer's Edge.

FRANCISCAN MEDIA (formerly St. Anthony Messenger Press) 28 West Liberty Street, Cincinnati OH 45202. Toll-free (800) 488-0488; (513) 241-5615. Fax (513) 241-0399. E-mail: samamin@FranciscanMedia.org. Websites: www.FranciscanMedia.org, www.Catalog.FranciscanMedia.org, www.AmericanCatholic.org. Director of Product Development for Franciscan Media Books: MCKendzia@FranciscanMedia.org. Directors of Product Development, Servant Books: Louise Paré (LPare@FranciscanMedia.org) and Claudia Volkman (CVolkman@FranciscanMedia.org). Managing Editor, Book Department: Katie Carroll (KCarroll@FranciscanMedia.org). Seeks to publish affordable resources for living a Catholic-Christian lifestyle. Imprints: Franciscan Media Books, Servant Books,

Fischer Video Productions, Catholic Update Video, Franciscan Communications, Ikonographics (videos). Servant Books is dedicated to spreading the gospel of Jesus Christ, helping Catholics live in accordance with that gospel, and promoting renewal in the Church. Publishes on Christian living, the sacraments, Scripture, prayer, spirituality, popular apologetics, Church teaching, Mary, the saints, charismatic renewal, marriage and family life, and popular psychology. Catalog.FranciscanMedia.org/ServantBooks. Guidelines on website: www.AmericanCatholic.org. ("Contact Us"/"Writer's Guidelines"). Publishes 15-20 titles/yr; trade paperbacks (mostly). Receives 450 submissions annually. 5% of books from first-time authors. Accepts mss through agents or authors. Reprints books (seldom). Prefers 25,000-50,000 wds or 100-250 pgs. **Royalty 10-14% on net; advance $1,000-3,000.** Average first printing 4,000. Publication within 18 mos. No simultaneous submissions. Accepts requested mss by e-mail. Responds in 5-9 wks. Prefers NRSV. Catalog for 9 x 12 SAE/4 stamps. Nonfiction: proposal/outline/1-2 chapters; fax/e-query OK. Franciscan Media seeks manuscripts that inform and inspire adult Catholic Christians, that identify trends surfacing in the Catholic world, and that help Catholics and those who want to be Catholic understand their faith better. Publishes for those who want to connect to the world around them in the context of the Catholic faith and for those who minister to adult Catholics in the parish and in religious institutions and schools. Catalog.FranciscanMedia.org/FranciscanMediaBooks. Guidelines on website www.AmericanCatholic.org ("Contact Us"/"Writer's Guidelines"). Publishes 20-30 titles/yr.; trade paperbacks (mostly). Receives 450 submissions annually. 5% of books from first-time authors. Accepts mss through agents or authors.

Nonfiction: proposal/outline/1-2 chapters; fax/e-query OK.

This publisher serviced by The Writer's Edge.

***GOSPEL LIGHT,** 1957 Eastman Ave., Ventura CA 93003. Toll-free (800) 4-GOSPEL. (805) 644-9721, ext. 1223. Website: www.gospellight.com. Anita Griggs, ed. Accepts proposals for Sunday school and Vacation Bible School curriculum and related resources for children from birth through the preteen years; also teacher resources. Guidelines on website (scroll to bottom "Submissions").

Also Does: Sometimes has openings for readers of new curriculum projects. See website for how to apply.

Tips: "All our curriculum is written and field-tested by experienced teachers; most of our writers are on staff."

This publisher serviced by ChristianManuscriptSubmissions.com.

GRACE PUBLISHING, PO Box 1233, Broken Arrow OK 74011-1233. (918) 346-7960. E-mail: editorial@grace-publishing.com. Website: www.grace-publishing.com. Publishes 5-10 titles/yr. Receives 250 submissions/yr. 50% first-time authors. Accepts books submitted by agents. Does print-on-demand. Trade, mass-market, digital. Does reprints. Preferred book length 140-240 pages. **Royalty varies based on net. Outright purchase varies.** First run varies. Responds in 6-12 mo. Considers simultaneous submissions. Responds to freelance submission in 3-6 mo. Guidelines on website. Accepts freelance photos for book covers. Preferred Bible version NIV/NKJV/KJV. Looking for Christian living, Christian fiction, leaders' resources, children's.

Nonfiction: Query letter only first. Proposal with 3 sample chapters. Complete manuscript. E-mail queries. Requires mss on disk or e-mail.

Fiction: Query letter only first. Book proposal with 3 sample chapters. Complete manuscript by e-mail.

Photos/Artwork: Open to queries from freelance artists.

Tips: "Well written with a unique approach. Our intent is to make Christian authors and their works easily accessible to the Christian body around the world in every form of media possible; to develop and distribute—with integrity and excellence—biblically based resources that challenge, encourage, teach, equip, and entertain Christians young and old in their personal journeys."

GROUP PUBLISHING INC., Attn: Submissions, 1515 Cascade Ave., Loveland CO 80539-0481. Toll-free (800) 447-1070. (970) 292-4243. Fax (970) 622-4370. E-mail: PuorgBus@group.com. Website: www.group.com. Nondenominational. Kerri Loesche, contract & copyright administrator. Imprint: Group Books. To equip churches to help children, youth, and adults grow in their relationship with Jesus. Publishes 65 titles/yr.; trade paperbacks. Receives 1,000+ submissions annually. 5% of books from first-time authors. Accepts mss through agents or authors. Some subsidy. No reprints. Prefers 128-250 pgs. **Outright purchases of $25-3,000 or royalty of 8-10% of net; advance $3,000.** Average first printing 5,000. Publication within 12-18 mos. Considers simultaneous submissions. Responds in 6 mos. Requires requested ms in Word or by e-mail. Prefers NLT. Guidelines by mail (2 stamps)/e-mail/website; catalog.

Nonfiction: Query or proposal/2 chapters/intro/cover letter/SASE; no phone/fax query; e-query OK. "Looking for practical ministry tools for youth workers, C.E. directors, and teachers with an emphasis on active learning."

Artwork: Open to queries from freelance artists.

Tips: "Most open to a practical resource that will help church leaders change lives; innovative, active/interactive learning. Tell our readers something they don't already know, in a way that they've not seen before."

This publisher serviced by The Writer's Edge.

GUARDIAN ANGEL PUBLISHING INC., 12430 Tesson Ferry Rd., #186, St. Louis MO 63128. (314) 276-8482. E-mail: editorial_staff@guardianangelpublishing.com. Website: www.guardianangelpublishing.com. Lynda S. Burch, pub. Goal is to inspire children to learn and grow and develop character skills to instill a Christian and healthy attitude of learning, caring, and sharing. Imprints: Wings of Faith, Angel to Angel, Angelic Harmony, Littlest Angels, Academic Wings, Guardian Angel Animals & Pets, Spanish Editions, Guardian Angel Health & Hygiene. Publishes 60-70 titles/yr.; trade paperbacks, some hardcover. Receives 600-800 submissions annually. 25% of books from first-time authors. No subsidy; does print-on-demand. Prefers 500-5,000 wds. or 32 pgs. **Royalty 30-50% on download; no advance.** Average first printing 50-100. Print books are wholesaled and distributed; e-books are sold through many distribution networks. Publication within 12-18 mos. No simultaneous submissions. Responds in 1 wk.-1 mo. Accepted mss by e-mail only. Guidelines on website ("Submissions" on left side); catalog as e-book PDF. **Submissions are only open May 1 to September 1, 2014.**

Nonfiction: Complete ms; no phone/fax query; e-query OK. "Looking for all kinds of kids' books."

Fiction: Complete ms; no phone/fax query; e-query OK.

Also Does: E-books.

Photos/Artwork: Accepts freelance photos for book covers; open to queries from freelance artists.

Contest: Sponsors children's writing contest for schools.

Tips: "Most open to books that teach children to read and love books; to learn or grow from books."

GUIDEPOSTS BOOKS, 16 E. 34th St., 12th Fl., New York NY 10016-4397. (212) 251-8100. E-mail: bookeditors@guideposts.org. Website: www.guideposts.org. "Discovering God's presence in our everyday lives." Keren Baltzer, nonfiction ed.; Jessica Barnes, fiction ed.

Nonfiction: Inspirational memoir and Christian living.

Fiction: Contemporary women's fiction focusing on faith, family, and friendships.

Tips: Accepts mss through agents only. Publishes 20 titles/yr.

***HANNIBAL BOOKS,** 313 S. 11th Street, Suite A, Garland TX 75040. Toll-free (800) 747-0738. Toll-free fax (888) 252-3022. E-mail: hannibalbooks@earthlink.net. Website: www.hannibalbooks.com. KLMK Communications Inc. Louis Moore, pub. Evangelical Christian publisher specializing in missions, marriage and family, critical issues, and Bible-study curriculum. Publishes 4-8 titles/yr.; trade paperbacks, mass-market paperbacks. Receives 300 submissions annually. 80% of books from first-time authors. Accepts mss from authors only. Some print-on-demand. Prefers 50,000-60,000 wds. **Royalty on net or outright purchase; no advance.** Average first printing 2,000-10,000. Publication within 3 mos. No simultaneous submissions. Responds in 1 mo. Prefers NIV. Guidelines on website ("Become an Author"/"Writer's Guidelines"); free catalog by mail.

Nonfiction: Book proposal/1-3 chapters; no phone/fax/e-query. "Looking for missionary, marriage restoration, homeschooling, and devotionals."

Fiction: Book proposal/1-3 chapters; accept e-mail inquiries as long as they are not impersonal, simultaneous submissions. Nothing we dislike more than seeing "Dear Publisher" with (a) no indication in the letter or e-mail that the person has any familiarity with our company and (b) that gives every indication that the e-mail has been sent generically to dozens of publishers at the same time.

Tips: "We are looking for go-get-'em new authors with a passion to be published. Most open to missionary life and Bible studies. Obtain our guidelines and answer each question thoroughly."

HARBOURLIGHT BOOKS, PO Box 1738, Aztec NM 87410. E-mail: inquiry@harbourlightbooks.com. Website: www.pelicanbookgroup.com. Division of Pelican Ventures, LLC. Nicola Martinez, editor-in-chief. Christian fiction 25,000-80,000 wds. Limited-edition hardback, trade paperbacks, and e-book. **Royalty 40% on download; 7% on print. Pays nominal advance.** Accepts unagented submissions. Responds to queries in 30 days, full ms in 90 days. Considers reprints but accepts few. E-mail submissions only; see website for submission form and procedure.

Fiction: Query via submission form on website. Interested in series ideas.

***HARPERONE,** 353 Sacramento St., #500, San Francisco CA 94111-3653. (415) 477-4400. Fax (415) 477-4444. E-mail: hcsanfrancisco@harpercollins.com. Website: www.harpercollins.com. Religious division of HarperCollins. Michael G. Maudlin, ed. dir. Strives to be the preeminent publisher of the most important books across the full spectrum of religion and spiritual literature, adding to the wealth of the world's wisdom by respecting all traditions and favoring none; emphasis on quality Christian spirituality and literary fiction. Publishes 75 titles/yr.; hardcover, trade paperbacks. Receives 10,000 submissions annually. 5% of books from first-time authors. Requires mss through agents. No reprints. Prefers 160-256 pgs. **Royalty 7.5-15% on retail; advance $20,000-100,000.** Average first printing 10,000. Publication within 18 mos. Considers simultaneous submissions. Responds in 3 mos. Requires requested ms on disk. Guidelines on website ("About Us"/"Manuscript Submissions"); catalog.

Nonfiction: Proposal/1 chapter; fax query OK.

Fiction: Complete ms; contemporary adult fiction, literary, fables & parables, spiritual.

Tips: "Agented proposals only."

***HARRISON HOUSE PUBLISHERS,** Box 35035, Tulsa OK 74153. Toll-free (800) 888-4126. (918) 523-5400. E-mail: customerservice@harrisonhouse.com. Website: www.harrisonhouse.com. Evangelical/charismatic. Julie Lechlider, mng. ed. To challenge Christians to live victoriously, grow spiritually, and know God intimately. Publishes 20 titles/yr.; hardcover, trade paperbacks, mass-market paperbacks. 5% of books from first-time authors. No mss through agents. No reprints. **Royalty on net or retail; no advance.** Average first printing 5,000. Publication within 12-24 mos. Responds in 6 mos. Accepts requested ms by e-mail. No guidelines or catalog. Not currently accepting any proposals or manuscripts.

Nonfiction: Query first; then proposal/table of contents/1 chapter; no phone/fax query; e-query OK.

This publisher serviced by ChristianManuscriptSubmissions.com.

HAY HOUSE INC., PO Box 5100, Carlsbad CA 92018-5100. (760) 431-7695. E-mail: editorial@hayhouse.com. Website: www.hayhouse.com. Alex Freemon, submissions ed. Books to help heal the planet. Publishes 1 religious title/yr.; hardcover, trade paperbacks and e-books/print-on-demand paperbacks. Receives 50 religious submissions annually. 5% of books from first-time authors. Accepts mss through agents only. Prefers 70,000 wds. or 250 pgs. **Royalty.** Average first printing 5,000. Publication within 12-15 mos. Considers simultaneous submissions. Responds in 1-2 mos. Guidelines (www.hayhouse.com/guides.php).

Nonfiction: Proposal/3 chapters. "Looking for self-help/spiritual with a unique ecumenical angle."

Tips: "We are looking for books with a unique slant, ecumenical, but not overly religious. We want an open-minded approach." Includes a broad range of religious titles, including New Age.

***HENSLEY PUBLISHING,** 6116 E. 32nd St., Tulsa OK 74135. (918) 664-8520. Fax (918) 664-8562. E-mail: editorial@hensleypublishing.com. Website: www.hensleypublishing.com. Terri Kalfas, dir. of publishing. Goal is to get people studying the Bible instead of just reading books about the Bible; Bible study only. Publishes 5-10 titles/yr.; trade paperbacks. Receives 800 submissions annually. 50% of books from first-time authors. **Royalty on net; some outright purchases; no advance.** Average first printing varies. Publication within 12-18 mos. Considers simultaneous submissions. Requires requested ms in MAC format. Responds in 4 mos. Guidelines ("Writers' Corner") & catalog on website.

Nonfiction: Query first, then proposal/first 3 chapters; no phone/fax query. "Looking for Bible studies of varying length for use by small or large groups, or individuals."

This publisher serviced by The Writer's Edge.

HIGHER LIFE PUBLISHING AND MARKETING, 400 Fontana Cir., Bldg. 1, Ste. 105, Oviedo FL 32765. (407) 563-4806. E-mail: info@ahigherlife.com. Website: www.ahigherlife.com. Estab. 2006. Recognized in the industry. Full-service publishing (books, e-books, mobile apps), marketing strategy, and services, trade sales distribution, curriculum development, author development, and coaching. Open to unpublished authors and new clients. Handles religious/inspirational novels and nonfiction for all ages, picture books, crossover books. Open to simultaneous submissions; responds in 2 wks.

HOPE PUBLISHING HOUSE, PO Box 60008, Pasadena CA 91106. (626) 792-6123. Fax (626) 792-2121. E-mail: hopepublishinghouse@gmail.com. Website: www.hope-pub.com. Southern California Ecumenical Council. Faith A. Sand, pub. Produces thinking books that challenge the faith community to be serious about their pilgrimage of faith. Imprint: New Paradigm Books. Publishes 6 titles/yr. Receives 40 submissions annually. 30% of books from first-time authors. No mss through agents. Reprints books. Prefers 200 pgs. **Royalty 10% on net; no advance.** Average first printing 3,000. Publication within 6 mos. No simultaneous submissions. Accepts mss by disk or e-mail. Responds in 3 mos. Prefers NRSV. No guidelines; catalog for 7 x 10 SAE/4 stamps.

Nonfiction: Query only first; no phone/fax query; e-query OK.

Tips: "Most open to a well-written manuscript, with correct grammar, that is provocative, original, challenging, and informative."

***HOWARD BOOKS,** 216 Centreville Dr., Ste. 303, Brentwood TN 37027-3226. (615) 873-2080. E-mail through website: http://imprints.simonandschuster.biz/howard. Becky Nesbitt, vp & ed-in-chief; submit to Manuscript Review Committee. A division of Simon & Schuster Inc. Publishes 65 titles/yr.; hardcover, trade paperbacks. Receives 1,000 submissions annually. 5% of books from first-time authors. Prefers 200-250 pgs. **Negotiable royalty & advance.** Average first printing 10,000. Publication within 16 mos. Considers simultaneous submissions. Accepted ms by e-mail. Responds in 6-8 mos. No disk. Prefers NIV. Guidelines on website (click on "Author Resources"/"Manuscript Submission"); catalog.

Nonfiction: Accepting queries by e-mail from agents only.

Fiction: Proposal/3 chapters from agents only. Adult.

Tips: "Our authors must first be Christ-centered in their lives and writing, then qualified to write on the subject of choice. Public name recognition is a plus. Authors who are also public speakers usually have a ready-made audience."

This publisher serviced by ChristianManuscriptSubmissions.com and The Writer's Edge.

IDEALS PUBLICATIONS, ATTN: Submissions Editor, 2630 Elm Hill Pike, Ste. 100, Nashville TN 37214. E-mail: idealsinfo@guideposts.org. Website: www.idealsbooks.com. Ideals Publications, a Guideposts company. Peggy Schaefer, pub.; Melinda Rumbaugh, ed. Imprints: Ideals Children's Books, CandyCane Press, Ideals Magazine. Publishes 20 new children's titles/yr under various imprints. Receives 1,000 unsolicited submissions annually. Fewer than 5% will be published. Response time for submissions ranges from 3 to 6 months. Due to the large volume of unsolicited submissions, editors are unable to provide specific feedback and critiques. Queries not accepted. Manuscripts for Ideals Children's Books (picture books) should be 800-1,000 words. Manuscripts for CandyCane Press (board books) should be no more than 250 words. E-mail submissions not accepted. Ideals Publications reviews uplifting, optimistic, and inspirational poetry and prose for possible use in our Easter and Christmas magazine.

Tip: Please familiarize yourself with the magazine before submitting. Sample issues are available. Consult submission guidelines on website.

***INHERITANCE PRESS, LLC,** PO Box 950477, Lake Mary FL 32795. (407) 474-0483. E-mail: submissions@inheritancepress.com. Website: www.inheritancepress.com. Independent publisher. Monique Donahue, ed. **No advance.** Responds in 60 days. Guidelines on website ("Submissions"). Incomplete topical listings.

Nonfiction: Proposal by mail or e-mail; no phone query.

***INKLING BOOKS,** 6528 Phinney Ave. N., Seattle WA 98103. (206) 365-1624. E-mail: editor@inklingbooks.com. Website: www.InklingBooks.com. Michael W. Perry, pub. Publishes 6 titles/yr.; hardcover, trade paperbacks. No mss through agents. Reprints books. Prefers 150-400 pgs. **No advance.** Print-on-demand. Publication within 2 mos. No guidelines or catalog. Not currently accepting submissions.

***INTERVARSITY PRESS,** Box 1400, Downers Grove IL 60515-1426. Receptionist: (630) 734-4000. Fax (630) 734-4200. E-mail: email@ivpress.com. Website: www.ivpress.com. InterVarsity Christian Fellowship. Andrew T. LePeau, ed. dir.; submit to General Book Editor or Academic Editor. IVP books are characterized by a thoughtful, biblical approach to the Christian life that transforms the hearts, souls, and minds of readers in the university, church, and the world, on topics ranging from spiritual disciplines to apologetics, to current issues, to theology. Imprints: IVP Academic (Gary Deddo, ed.), IVP Connect (Cindy Bunch, ed.), IVP Books (Al Hsu, ed.). Publishes 110-120 titles/yr.; hardcover, trade paperbacks, mass-market paperbacks. Receives 1,300 submissions annually. 15% of books from first-time authors. Accepts mss through agents or authors. Reprints books. Prefers 50,000 wds. or 200 pgs. **Negotiable royalty on retail or outright purchase; negotiable advance.** Average first printing 5,000. Publication within 12 mos. Considers simultaneous submissions. Responds in 3 mos. Prefers NIV, NRSV. Accepts e-mail submissions after acceptance. Guidelines on website (scroll to bottom "Submissions"); catalog for 9 x 12 SAE/5 stamps.

Nonfiction: Query only first, with detailed letter according to submissions guidelines, then proposal with 2 chapters; no phone/fax/e-query.

Ethnic Books: Especially looking for ethnic writers (African American, Hispanic, Asian American).

Also Does: Booklets, 5,000 wds.; e-books.

Blogs: www.ivpress.com/blogs/behindthebooks; www.ivpress.com/blogs/andyunedited; www.ivpress.com/blogs/addenda-errata.

Tips: "Most open to books written by pastors (though not collections of sermons) or other church staff, by professors, by leaders in Christian organizations. Authors need to bring resources for publicizing and selling their own books, such as a website, an organization they are part of that will promote their books, speaking engagements, well-known people they know personally who will endorse and promote their book, writing articles for national publication, etc."

This publisher serviced by ChristianManuscriptSubmissions.com and The Writer's Edge.

***JOURNEYFORTH/BJU PRESS,** 1700 Wade Hampton Blvd., Greenville SC 29614. (864) 370-1800, ext. 4350. Fax (864) 298-0268. E-mail to: jb@bju.edu. Website: www.bjupress.com or www.journey forth.com. Nancy Lohr, acquisitions ed. Our goal is to publish engaging books for children with a biblical worldview as well as Bible studies and Christian-living titles for teens and adults. Publishes 8-12 titles/yr.; trade paperbacks. Receives 400 submissions annually (50 Christian living/350 youth novels). 10% of books from first-time authors. Accepts mss through agents or authors. **Royalty.** Average first printing varies. Publication within 12-18 mos. Considers simultaneous submissions but not multiple submissions. Accepts submissions by US mail or e-mail. Responds in 8-12 wks. Requires KJV. Guidelines online, by mail, or by e-mail; free catalog.

Nonfiction: Proposal/3-5 chapters; e-query OK.

Fiction: Proposal/5 chapters or complete ms. For children & teens. "Fiction must have a Christian worldview."

Artwork: Open to queries from freelance artists.

Tips: "The pre-college, homeschool market welcomes print-rich, well-written novels. No picture books, please, but compelling novels for early readers are always good for us, as are biographies on the lives of Christian heroes and statesmen. We focus on books for all ages that will help to both develop skill with the written word as well as discernment as a believer; we complement the educational goals of BJU Press, our K-12 textbook division."

This publisher serviced by The Writer's Edge.

JUDSON PRESS, PO Box 851, Valley Forge PA 19482-0851. Toll-free (800) 458-3766. Fax (610) 768-2107. E-mail: acquisitions@judsonpress.com. Website: www.judsonpress.com. American Baptist Churches USA/American Baptist Home Mission Societies. Rebecca Irwin-Diehl, ed. We are theologically moderate, historically Baptist, and in ministry to empower, enrich, and equip disciples of Jesus and leaders in Christ's church. Publishes 10-12 titles/yr.; hardcover, trade paperbacks. Receives 800 submissions annually. 25% of books from first-time authors. Accepts mss through agents or authors. No subsidy; rarely does print-on-demand or reprints. Prefers 100-200 pgs. or 30,000-75,000 wds. **Royalty 10-15% on net; some work-for-hire agreements or outright purchases; occasional advance $300.** Average first printing 3,000. Publication within 18 mos. Considers simultaneous submissions. Requires accepted submissions on disk or by e-mail. Responds in 4-6 mos. Prefers NRSV or CEB. Guidelines on website (under "Contact Us"); catalog online.

Nonfiction: Query or proposal/2 chapters; e-query OK. Practical books for today's church and leaders.

Ethnic Books: African American, Asian North American, and Hispanic.

Tips: "Most open to practical books that are unique and compelling, for a clearly defined niche audience. Theologically and socially we are a moderate publisher. And we like to see a detailed marketing plan from an author committed to partnering with us."

This publisher serviced by The Writer's Edge.

***KIRK HOUSE PUBLISHERS,** PO Box 390759, Minneapolis MN 55439. (952) 835-1828. Toll-free (888) 696-1828. Fax (952) 835-2613. E-mail: publisher@kirkhouse.com. Website: www.kirkhouse .com. Leonard Flachman, pub. Imprints: Lutheran University Press, Quill House Publishers. Publishes 10-15 titles/yr.; hardcover, trade paperbacks, coffee table books. Receives hundreds of submissions annually. 95% of books from first-time authors. No mss through agents. No reprints. **Royalty 10-15%**

on net; no advance. Average first printing 500-3,000. Publication within 6 mos. No simultaneous submissions. Initial inquiry only via e-mail. Requires hard copy and electronic submission. Responds in 2-3 wks. Guidelines by e-mail/website ("Submissions").

Nonfiction: Inquiries and author bio.

Tips: "Our catalog is eclectic; send a query. Our imprint, Quill House Publishers, accepts adult fiction."

KREGEL PUBLICATIONS, PO Box 2607, Grand Rapids MI 49501-2607. (616) 451-4775. Fax (616) 451-9330. E-mail: kregelbooks@kregel.com. Website: www.kregel.com. Blog: www.kregel .com/news. Evangelical/conservative. Dennis R. Hillman, pub.; Dr. Fred Mabie, dir., academic & ministry books; submissions policy on website. Publishes for both the Christian trade and academic markets. Imprints: Kregel Publications (trade), Kregel Academic and Professional, Kregel Classics, and Kregel Children's. Publishes 75 titles/yr.; hardcover, trade paperbacks. 20% of books from first-time authors. Prefers mss through agents. Reprints limited number of previously published books. **Royalty 14-20% of net; some outright purchases; pays advances.** Average first printing 4,000. Publication within 12-18 mos. Considers simultaneous submissions. Responds in 2-3 mos. Does not review unsolicited queries, proposals, or manuscripts, except through agents, Kregel author referrals, or ChristianManuscriptSubmissions.com.

Nonfiction: "Always looking for contemporary issues, Christian living, ministry, or academic works for the classroom."

Fiction: Some YA. "Looking for high-quality contemporary and Amish fiction with strong Christian themes and characters."

Tips: "In fiction we are very selective. Strong story lines with an evident spiritual emphasis are required. Visit our website to get a sense of the category we publish."

This publisher serviced by ChristianManuscriptSubmissions.com and The Writer's Edge.

LANGMARC PUBLISHING, PO Box 90488, Austin TX 78709-0488. (512) 394-0989. Fax (512) 394-0829. E-mail: langmarc@booksails.com. Website: www.langmarc.com. Lutheran. Lois Qualben, pub. Focuses on spiritual growth of readers. Publishes 3-5 titles/yr.; hardcover, trade paperbacks. Receives 230 submissions annually. 60% of books from first-time authors. Accepts mss through agents or authors. No reprints. Prefers 150-300 pgs. **Royalty 10-14% on net; no advance.** Average first printing varies. Publication usually within 18 mos. Considers simultaneous submissions. Responds in 3 mos. Requires requested ms on disk. Prefers NIV. Guidelines on website ("Guidelines for Nonfiction Authors"); free catalog.

Nonfiction: Proposal/3 chapters; no phone query. "Most open to inspirational books."

***LEGACY PRESS,** PO Box 261129, San Diego CA 92196. Toll-free (800) 323-7337. Toll-free fax (800) 331-0297. E-mail: editor@rainbowpublishers.com. Website: www.LegacyPressKids.com. Rainbow Publishers. Submit to Manuscript Submissions. Publishes nondenominational nonfiction and fiction for children in the evangelical Christian market. Publishes 15 titles/yr. Receives 250 submissions annually. 50% of books from first-time authors. Reprints books. Prefers 150 pgs. & up. Average first printing 5,000. Publication within 2 yrs. Considers simultaneous submissions. Prefers requested ms on disk. Responds in 2-8 wks. Prefers NIV. Guidelines (go to bottom "Submissions") & catalog on website.

Nonfiction: Proposal/3-5 chapters; no e-queries. "Looking for nonfiction for girls and boys ages 2-12."

Fiction: Proposal/3 chapters. For ages 2-12 only. Must include an additional component beyond fiction (e.g., devotional, Bible activities, etc.).

Special Needs: Nonfiction for ages 10-12, particularly Christian twists on current favorites, such as cooking, jewelry making, games, etc.

Artwork: Open to queries from freelance artists.

Tips: "All books must offer solid Bible teaching in a fun, meaningful way that appeals to kids. Research popular nonfiction for kids in the general market, then figure out how to present those fun ideas in ways that teach the Bible. As a smaller publisher, we seek to publish unique niche books that stand out in the market."

***LIFE CYCLE BOOKS,** 1085 Bellamy Rd. N #20, Toronto ON M1H 3C7 Canada. (416) 690-5860. E-mail: paulb@lifecyclebooks.com. Website: www.lifecyclebooks.com. Paul Broughton, gen. mngr.; submit to Attention: The Editor. Canadian office: 1149 Bellamy Rd. N., Unit 20, Toronto ON M1H 1H7 Canada. Toll-free (866) 880-5860. Toll-free fax (866) 690-8532. Attn: The Editor. Specializes in pro-life material. Publishes 6 titles/yr.; trade paperbacks. Receives 100 submissions annually. No mss through agents. 50% of books from first-time authors. Reprints books. **Royalty 8-10% of net; outright purchase of brochure material, $250+; advance $250-1,000.** Subsidy publishes 10%. Publication within 1 yr. No simultaneous submissions. Responds in 3-5 wks. Catalog on website.

Nonfiction: Query or complete ms. "Our emphasis is on pro-life and pro-family titles."

Tips: "We are most involved in publishing leaflets of about 1,500 wds., and we welcome submissions of manuscripts of this length." No fiction or poetry.

LIFE SENTENCE PUBLISHING, 404 N. 5th St., Abbotsford WI 54405. (715) 223-3013. E-mail: info@lifesentencepublishing.com. Website: www.lifesentencepublishing.com. Jeremiah Zeiset, acct. mgr. Imprints: Life Sentence Publishing, ANEKO Press, Launch! We especially wish to publish books for ministries/missionaries. Publishes 36-48 titles/yr. Receives 75 proposals/yr. 60% first-time authors. Accepts books submitted by agents. 25% SUBSIDY PUBLISHER. 50% print-on-demand. Hardcover, trade, mass-market, coffee table books, digital. Reprints out-of-print books. Prefers 100,000 wds. or 150-200 pgs. **ROYALTY 25-40% based on net. E-books 25% based on net.** No advance. Average first printing 1,000 offset or 50 POD. Publishes within 3 mos. Considers simultaneous submissions. Responds quarterly. Charges for catalog. Guidelines by mail. Accepts freelance photos for covers. Open to queries from freelance artists.

Nonfiction: Complete mss. Accepts phone queries.

Fiction: Christian or Christian themed only. All ages. Complete mss.

Tips: "Seeing a lot of submissions about the gospel (explaining salvation or the Bible). We publish all books, provided they aren't contrary to our knowledge of salvation by faith, and they must be well written. It's preferable that the author has an existing platform. Our Christian authors know from the moment they hand over their manuscript, we'll bring glory to God by paying attention to each and every detail of the publishing process, because we do more than simply put books in print. Our authors are sharing the gospel worldwide."

***LIFT EVERY VOICE BOOKS,** 820 N. LaSalle Blvd., Chicago IL 60610. (312) 329-2140. Fax (312) 329-4157. E-mail: lifteveryvoice@moody.edu. Website: www.lifteveryvoicebooks.com. African American imprint of Moody Publishers. Moody Bible Institute. Cynthia Ballenger, acq. ed. To publish culturally relevant books and promote other resources that will help millions of African Americans experience the power and amazement of a fresh encounter with Jesus Christ. Publishes 10 titles/yr. Receives 50-75 submissions annually. 98% of books from first-time authors. Accepts mss through agents or authors. No subsidy. Reprints books. Prefers minimum of 50,000 wds. or 250 pgs. **Royalty on retail; pays an advance.** Average first printing 5,000. Publication within 12 mos. Considers simultaneous submissions. Responds quarterly. Accepts requested ms by e-mail. Prefers KJV, NASB, NKJV. Guidelines by e-mail; free catalog.

Nonfiction: Proposal/3 chapters; e-query OK.

Fiction: Proposal/3 chapters; e-query OK. For all ages. Send for fiction writers' guidelines.

Special Needs: Children's fiction, especially for boys; nonfiction & fiction for teen girls; also marriage books.

Ethnic Books: African American imprint.

Photos: Accepts freelance photos for book covers.

Tips: "Looking for quality fiction and nonfiction. LEVB is looking for good, strong, and focused writing that is Christ-centered and speaks to the African American community."

LIGHTHOUSE PUBLISHING, 754 Roxholly Walk, Buford GA 30518. E-mail: info@lighthousechristian publishing.com. Website: www.lighthousechristianpublishing.com. Nondenominational. Andy Overett, ed.; submit to Sylvia Charvet, sr. ed. To distribute a wide variety of Christian media to vast parts of the globe so people can hear about the gospel for free or very inexpensively (e-books, comics, movies, and online radio). Imprints: Lighthouse Publishing, Lighthouse Music Publishing. Publishes 30-40 titles/yr.; hardcover, trade paperbacks, mass-market paperbacks. Receives 100-150 submissions annually. 60% of books from first-time authors. Accepts mss through agents or authors. Subsidy publishes 35-40%. Does print-on-demand. Reprints books. Any length. **Royalty on net; no advance.** Publication within 6 to 8 mos. Considers simultaneous submissions. Prefers submissions by e-mail. Responds in 6-8 wks. Prefers NAS. Guidelines on website ("Submissions"); catalog $5.

Nonfiction: Complete ms by e-mail only (info@lighthousechristianpublishing.com). Any topic. "Looking for children's books, Intelligent Design, and science."

Fiction: Complete ms by e-mail only. Any genre, for all ages.

Ethnic Books: Publishes books for almost all foreign-language markets.

Also Does: Comics, animation on CD, music CDs, plans to do Christian computer games in the future. E-books.

Photos/Artwork: Accepts freelance photos for book covers; open to queries from freelance artists.

Tips: "Most open to children's books, comics, and graphic novels; scientific and academic works with a Christian perspective."

LIGHTHOUSE PUBLISHING OF THE CAROLINAS, 2333 Barton Oaks Dr., Raleigh NC. E-mail: light housepublishingcarolinas@gmail.com. Website: http://lighthousepublishingofthecarolinas.com. LPC is an approved ACFW, royalty-paying publisher of e-books and print-on-demand (POD) paperbacks. Fiction, nonfiction, and niche devotional compilations considered. To pitch your book, meet with us at a writer's conference. Unsolicited manuscripts returned unread.

LIGHTHOUSE TRAILS PUBLISHING LLC PO Box 908, Eureka MT 59917. (406) 889-3610. Fax (406) 889-3633. E-mail: editors@lighthousetrails.com. Website: www.lighthousetrails.com. Blog: www.lighthousetrailsresearch.com/blog. David Dombrowski, acq. ed. We publish books that bring clarity and light to areas of spiritual darkness or deception, and we seek to preserve the integrity of God's Word in all our books. Publishes 4 titles/yr. Receives 100-150 submissions annually. 35% of books from first-time authors. Accepts mss through agents or authors. No subsidy or print-on-demand. Reprints books. Prefers 160-300 pgs. **Royalty 12-17% of net or 20% of retail.** Publication within 9-12 mos. Considers simultaneous submissions. Requires accepted ms on disk or by e-mail. Responds in 8 wks. Prefers KJV. Guidelines on website ("Publishing Info"/"Author Guidelines" on right); free catalog by mail.

Nonfiction: Proposal/2 chapters; no phone/fax query; e-query OK.

Fiction: Proposal/2-3 chapters. For all ages. "We are looking for a fiction book or fiction series that would include elements from our nonfiction books exposing the emerging church and mystical/New Age spirituality; Bible prophecy/eschatological."

Special Needs: Will look at autobiographies or biographies about people who have courageously endured through overwhelming circumstances (Holocaust survivors, child-abuse survivors, etc.) with a definite emphasis on the Lord's grace and faithfulness and his Word.

Artwork: Open to queries from freelance artists.

Tips: "No poetry at this time. Any book we consider will not only challenge the more scholarly reader, but also be able to reach those who may have less experience and comprehension. Our books will include human interest and personal experience scenarios as a means of getting the point across. Read a couple of our books to better understand the style of writing we are looking for. Also check our research website for an in-depth look at who we are (www.lighthousetrails research.com). We also have a doctrinal statement on our website that helps to define us."

LOVE INSPIRED (formerly Steeple Hill), 233 Broadway, Ste. 1001, New York NY 10279-0001. (212) 553-4200. Fax (212) 277-8969. E-mail: giselle_regus@harlequin.ca. Website: www.harlequin.com. Harlequin Enterprises. Submit to any of the following: Joan Marlow Golan, exec. ed.; Melissa Endlich, sr. ed.; Tina James, sr. ed.; Emily Rodmell, ed.; Elizabeth Mazer, assoc. ed.; Shana Smith, assoc. ed.; Giselle Regus, asst. ed.; Emily Brown, ed. asst. Mass-market Christian romance novels. Imprints: Love Inspired, Love Inspired Historical, Love Inspired Suspense. Publishes 168 titles/yr.; mass-market paperbacks. Receives 500-1,000 submissions annually. 15% of books from first-time authors. Accepts mss through agents or authors. No reprints. Prefers 55,000-60,000 wds. **Royalty on retail; competitive advance.** Publication within 12-24 mos. Requires ms on disk/hard copy. Responds in 3 mos. Prefers KJV. Guidelines by mail/website; no catalog.

Fiction: Query letter or 3 chapters and up to 5-page synopsis; no phone/fax/e-query.

Tips: "We want character-driven romance with an author voice that inspires."

This publisher serviced by ChristianManuscriptSubmissions.com.

***LOYOLA PRESS,** 3441 N. Ashland Ave., Chicago IL 60657. (773) 281-1818. Toll-free (800) 621-1008. Fax (773) 281-0152. E-mail: editorial@loyolapress.com. Website: www.loyolabooks.org. Catholic. Joseph Durepos, acq. ed. (durepos@loyolapress.com). Publishes in the Jesuit and Ignatian Spirituality tradition. Publishes 20-30 titles/yr.; hardcover, trade paperbacks. Receives 500 submissions annually. Accepts mss through agents or authors. Prefers 25,000-75,000 wds. or 150-300 pgs. **Standard royalty; reasonable advance.** Average first printing 7,500-10,000. Considers simultaneous submissions and first-time authors without agents. Responds in 10-12 wks. Prefers NRSV (Catholic Edition). Guidelines/catalog on website (under "Contact Us"/"Submissions").

Nonfiction: E-query first; proposal/sample chapters; no phone query.

Tips: "Looking for books and authors that help make Catholic faith relevant and offer practical tools for the well-lived spiritual life."

This publisher serviced by The Writer's Edge.

***LUTHERAN UNIVERSITY PRESS,** PO Box 390759, Minneapolis MN 55439. (952) 835-1828. Toll-free (888) 696-1828. Fax (952) 835-2613. E-mail: publisher@lutheranupress.org. Website: www.lutheranupress.org. Leonard Flachman, pub.; Karen Walhof, ed. Publishes 8-10 titles/yr.; hardcover, trade paperbacks, coffee table books. Receives dozens of submissions annually. Subsidy publishes 25%. No print-on-demand or reprints. **Royalty 10-15% of net; no advance.** Average first printing 500-2,000. Publication within 6 mos. No simultaneous submissions. Responds in 3 wks. Guidelines by e-mail/website ("Submissions"); free catalog by mail.

Nonfiction: Proposal/sample chapters in electronic format.

Photos: Accepts freelance photos for book covers.

Tips: "We accept manuscripts only from faculty of Lutheran colleges, universities, seminaries, and Lutheran faculty from other institutions."

MAGNUS PRESS, 1647 Shire Ave., Oceanside CA 92057. (760) 806-3743. Fax (760) 806-3689. E-mail: magnuspres@aol.com. Website: www.magnuspress.com. Warren Angel, ed. dir. All books must reflect a strong belief in Christ, solid biblical understanding, and the author's ability to relate to the average person. Imprint: Canticle Books. Publishes 3 titles/yr.; trade paperbacks. Receives 60 submissions annually. 50% of books from first-time authors. Accepts mss through agents or authors. Reprints books. Prefers 105-300 pgs. **Graduated royalty on retail; no advance.** Average first printing 2,500. Publication within 1 yr. Considers simultaneous submissions. Accepts requested ms on disk. Responds in 1 mo. Guidelines by mail/e-mail/website ("Magnus Press Submissions"); free catalog by mail.

Nonfiction: Query or proposal/3 chapters; fax query OK. "Looking for spirituality, thematic biblical studies, unique inspirational/devotional books, e.g., *Adventures of an Alaskan Preacher*."

Tips: "Our writers need solid knowledge of the Bible and a mature spirituality that reflects a profound relationship with Jesus Christ. Most open to a popularly written biblical study that addresses a real concern/issue in the church at large today; or a unique inspirational book. Study the market; know what we do and don't publish."

MARCHER LORD PRESS, 3846 Constitution Avenue, Colorado Springs CO 80909. (719) 266-8874. E-mail: Jeff@marcherlordpress.com. Website: www.marcherlordpress.com. Jeff Gerke, pub. The premier publisher of Christian speculative fiction—it's all we do. Publisher of multiple Christy, Carol, EPIC, and Indie award winners. Publishes 8-15 titles/yr.; trade paperbacks. Receives 200 submissions annually. 70% of books from first-time authors. Accepts mss through agents or authors. No subsidy; does print-on-demand. No reprints. Prefers 65,000+ wds. **Author receives 50% after development costs are recouped; advance.** Publication within 12 mos. Considers simultaneous submissions. Responds in 9-18 mos. Guidelines/catalog on website ("For writers" link).

Fiction: Submit only through acquisitions form on website.

Special Needs: Full-length, Christian speculative fiction for an adult and older YA audience (11 and up).

Photos/Artwork: Accepts freelance photos and artwork for book covers; open to queries from freelance artists.

Tips: "I'm most open to high fiction craftsmanship and a story that sweeps me away."

MERIWETHER PUBLISHING LTD./CONTEMPORARY DRAMA SERVICE, 885 Elkton Dr., Colorado Springs CO 80907. (719) 594-4422. Fax (719) 594-9916. E-mail: editor@meriwether.com. Website: www.ChristianPlaysandMusicals.com. Nondenominational. Arthur L. Zapel, exec. ed.; submit to Rhonda Wray, assoc. ed. Publishes 30-45 plays & books/yr. Primarily a publisher of plays for Christian and general markets; must be acceptable for use in a wide variety of Christian denominations. Imprint: Contemporary Drama Service. Publishes 3 bks./25 plays/yr. Receives 1,200 submissions annually (mostly plays). 75% of submissions from first-time authors. Accepts mss through agents or authors. No reprints. Prefers 225 pgs. **Royalty 10% of net or retail; no advance.** Average first printing of books 1,500-2,500, plays 500. Publication within 6 mos. Considers simultaneous submissions. No e-mail submissions. Responds in up to 3 mos. Any Bible version. Guidelines by mail/e-mail/website ("Writers Guidelines"); catalog for 9 x 12 SASE.

Nonfiction: Table of contents/1 chapter; fax/e-query OK. "Looking for creative worship books, i.e., drama, using the arts in worship, how-to books with ideas for Christian education." Submit books to Meriwether.

Fiction: Complete ms for plays. Plays only, for all ages. Always looking for Christmas and Easter plays (1 hr. maximum). Submit plays to Contemporary Drama.

Special Needs: Religious drama—or religious plays—mainstream theology. We prefer plays that can be staged during a worship service.

Tips: "Our books are on drama or any creative, artistic area that can be a part of worship. Writers should familiarize themselves with our catalog before submitting to ensure that their manuscript fits with the list we've already published." Contemporary Drama Service wants easy-to-stage comedies, skits, one-act plays, large-cast musicals, and full-length comedies for schools (junior high through college), and churches (including chancel dramas for Christmas and Easter). Most open to anything drama-related. "Study our catalog so you'll know what we publish and what would fit our list."

***MOODY PUBLISHERS,** 820 N. LaSalle Blvd., Chicago IL 60610. Fax (312) 329-2144. Email: acquisitions@moody.edu. Website: www.moodypublishers.com/. Imprints: Moody Publishers, Northfield Publishing, Lift Every Voice (African American). Moody Publishers exists to help our readers know, love, and serve Jesus Christ. Publishes 60-70 titles per year; hardcover, trade paperbacks, mass-market paperbacks, e-books. Receives 3,500 submissions annually; 10% of books from first-time authors. Does not accept unsolicited manuscripts in any category unless submitted via: literary agent; an author who has published with us; a Moody Bible Institute employee; a personal contact at a writers conference. **Royalty paid on net; advances begin at $500.** Average first printing 10,000. Publication within 1 year. Manuscripts submitted electronically. Responds in 1-2 mos. Prefers NAS, ESV, NKJV, NIV (1984). Guidelines (also on website at www.moodypublishers.com/pub_main.aspx?id=46381): Moody Publishers titles are designed to glorify God in content and style. Titles are selected for publication based upon fit with this goal, quality of writing, and potential for market success. Please do not call our offices with manuscript ideas. Rather, for submissions meeting the criteria detailed above, have your query sent to: Acquisitions Coordinator, Moody Publishers, 820 North LaSalle Blvd., Chicago, IL 60610. Responds in 1 month. Catalog for 9 x 12 SAE/$2.38 postage (mark "Media Mail").

Nonfiction Categories & Audiences: Academic & Bible reference; spiritual growth; Millennials (18- to 30-year-olds); women; urban; family & relationships

Fiction: "We are looking for stories that glorify God both in content and style. Featured categories include mystery, contemporary, historical, young adult.

Ethnic Books: African American.

Tips: "Most open to books where the writer is a recognized expert with a platform to promote the book."

This publisher serviced by ChristianManuscriptSubmissions.com and The Writer's Edge.

***MOPS INTERNATIONAL,** 2370 S. Trenton Way, Denver CO 80231-3822. (303) 733-5353. Fax (303) 733-5770. E-mail: jblackmer@MOPS.org. Website: www.MOPS.org. Jean Blackmer, pub. mngr.; Carla Foote, dir. of media. Publishes books dealing with the needs and interests of mothers with young children, who may or may not be Christians. Publishes 2-3 titles/yr. Catalog on website.

Nonfiction: Query or proposal/3 chapters; by mail, fax, or e-mail.

Tips: "Review existing titles on our website to avoid duplication."

MORGAN JAMES PUBLISHING, 5 Penn Plaza, 23rd Floor, New York City NY 10001. (212) 655-5470. Fax (516) 908-4496. Morgan James, LLC. E-mail: terry@morganjamespublishing.com. Website: www.morganjamespublishing.com. W. Terry Whalin, acq. ed. Imprints: Guerrilla Marketing Press, Koehler Books (fiction), Morgan James Faith, Morgan James Kids, Sports Professor. Religious titles/yr 45-50. Receives 5,000 proposals/yr. 10-15% first-time authors. Accept books submitted by agents. Reprints. Preferred book length 40-60,000 wds. or 200 pgs. **Royalty 20-30% of net. 50% on e-books.** Offer an advance. Avg. first printing 1800-2200. Publication 4 months. Consider simultaneous submissions. Catalog free on request. Writer's guidelines by e-mail. Accept freelance photos for covers.

Nonfiction: Query letter, proposal with 3 sample chapters, or complete mss. Accept e-mail queries. Require mss by e-mail.

Fiction: Accept for children, teens, adults. Query letter, proposal with 3 sample chapters, or complete manuscript.

***MOUNTAINVIEW PUBLISHING,** 1284 Overlook Dr., Sierra Vista AZ 85635-5512. (520) 458-5602. Fax (520) 459-0162. E-mail: leeemory@earthlink.net. Website: www.trebleheartbooks.com. Christian division of Treble Heart Books. Ms. Lee Emory, ed./pub. Online Christian publisher; books never have to go out of print as long as they're being marketed and are selling. Imprints: Treble Heart (see separate listing), Sundowners, Whoodo Mysteries. Publishes 12-24 titles/yr; trade paperbacks. Receives 350 submissions annually. 70% of books from first-time authors. Accepts mss through agents or authors. No reprints. No word-length preference. **Royalty 35% of net on most sales; no advance.** Books are published electronically; average first printing 30-500. Publication usually within 1 yr. No simultaneous submissions (a 90-day exclusive is required on all submissions, plus a marketing plan). Responds in 90 days to submissions, 1-2 wks. to queries. Guidelines on website ("Submissions Guidelines" right side).

Nonfiction: Send query (by e-mail) to: leeemory@earthlink.net. Submissions of full ms by invitation only. Excellent nonfiction, inspirational books are highly desired here.

Fiction: Complete ms (by e-mail only). Genres: historical romances; contemporary romances; novellas; mainstream and traditional inspirations in most categories; also Christian mysteries, Christian horror, and Christian westerns, and some outstanding short stories.

Photos: Accepts high-quality freelance photos for book covers.

Tips: "All inspirational fiction should contain faith elements. Challenge the reader to think, to look at things through different eyes. Avoid point-of-view head hopping and clichés; avoid heavy-handed preaching. No dark angel stories, hardcore science fiction/fantasy, though will consider futuristic Christian works. Send consecutive chapters, not random. A well-developed marketing plan must accompany all submissions, and no submissions will be accepted for consideration unless guidelines are followed. Actively seeking more nonfiction at this time."

***MULTNOMAH BOOKS,** 12265 Oracle Blvd., Ste. 200, Colorado Springs CO 80921. (719) 590-4999. Fax (719) 590-8977. E-mail: info@waterbrookmultnomah.com. Website: www.waterbrookmultnomah.com. Part of WaterBrook Multnomah, a division of Random House Inc. Ken Petersen, VP/pub.dir. Imprint information listed below. Publishes 75 titles/yr.; hardcover, trade paperbacks. **Royalty on net; advance.** Multnomah is currently not accepting unsolicited manuscripts, proposals, or queries; no proposals for biographies, poetry, or children's books. Queries will be accepted through literary agents and at writers' conferences at which a Multnomah representative is present. Catalog on website.

Multnomah Books: Christian living and popular theology books.

Multnomah Fiction: Well-crafted fiction that uses truth to change lives.

This publisher serviced by The Writer's Edge.

MY HEALTHY CHURCH, 1445 N. Boonville Ave., Springfield MO 65802. Toll-free (800) 641-4310. (417) 831-8000. E-mail: newproducts@myhealthychurch.com. Website: www.myhealthychurch.com. Assemblies of God/Pentecostal. Steve Blount, VP publishing. We do not accept unsolicited manuscripts unless represented by a professional literary agent. For a listing of the unsolicited manuscripts we are accepting, please visit the website.

***NAVPRESS,** 3820 N. 30th Street, Colorado Springs CO 80904. E-mail: editorial.submissions@navpress.com. Website: www.navpress.com. Imprint: TH1NK. Publishes 45 titles/yr. Hardcover, trade paperbacks, digital. Reprints. **Royalties. Advance.** Publication in 12-18 mos. Considers simultaneous submissions. Responds in 6-12 wks. Catalog free on request. Guidelines on website. Need books for TH1NK, 16- to 21-yr-olds, inc. Bible studies, nonfiction, YA fiction.

Nonfiction: proposal with 2-3 chap. E-mail queries OK. Require mss by e-mail.

Fiction: Teen/YA fiction. No adult at this time. Proposal with 2-3 sample chap.

Special Needs: Transforming, life-changing nonfiction and Bible studies, as well as YA fiction.

This publisher serviced by The Writer's Edge.

THOMAS NELSON & ZONDERVAN FICTION, the combined division under HarperCollins Christian Publishers, PO Box 141000, Nashville TN 37215. (615) 889-9000. Website: www.harpercollinschristian.com. Thomas Nelson Inc. Ami McConnell, sr. acq. ed.; Amanda Bostic, acq. ed. Zondervan: Sue Browers, exec. ed.; Becky Philpott, assist. acq. ed. Fiction from a Christian worldview. Publishes fewer than 100 titles/yr.; hardcover, trade. Requires mss through agents; does not accept unsolicited manuscripts. Prefers 80,000-100,000 wds. **Royalty on net; pays an advance.** Publication within 12 mos. Accepts simultaneous submissions. Responds in about 60 days. No guidelines; catalog available online at www.harpercollinschristian.com/media/.

Fiction: Proposal/3 chapters. For teens and adults. Submissions will be considered simultaneously for both imprints. Unsolicited queries are not considered or returned.

This publisher serviced by The Writer's Edge.

THOMAS NELSON PUBLISHERS, PO Box 141000, Nashville TN 37214-1000. (615) 889-9000. Fax (615) 902-2745. Website: www.thomasnelson.com. Does not accept or review any unsolicited queries, proposals, or manuscripts.

This publisher serviced by ChristianManuscriptSubmissions.com and The Writer's Edge.

TOMMY NELSON. See Thomas Nelson Publishers above.

NEW HOPE PUBLISHERS, PO Box 12065, Birmingham AL 35202-2065. (205) 991-8100. Fax (205) 991-4015. Website: www.newhopedigital.com. Division of WMU. Imprints: Fiction (contemporary issues); New Hope Impact (missional community, social, personal-commitment, church-growth, and leadership issues); New Hope Arise (inspiring women, changing lives); New Hope Grow (Bible-study & teaching resources). Publishes 24-28 titles/yr.; hardcover, trade paperbacks. No unsolicited queries, proposals, or manuscripts.

This publisher serviced by ChristianManuscriptSubmissions.com and The Writer's Edge.

NEW LEAF PUBLISHING GROUP, PO Box 726, Green Forest AR 72638-0726. (870) 438-5288. Fax (870) 438-5120. E-mail: submissions@newleafpress.net or through website: www.nlpg.com. Craig Froman, acq. ed. The world's largest creation-based publisher. Imprints: New Leaf Press, Master Books, Attic Books. Publishes 25-30 titles/yr.; hardcover, trade paperbacks, occasionally high-end gift titles, digital. Receives 1,000 submissions annually. 10% of books from first-time authors. Accepts mss through agents or authors. No subsidy, print-on-demand, or reprints. No length preference. **Variable royalty on net; no advance.** Average first printing varies. Publication within 8 mos. Considers simultaneous submissions. Responds within 3 mos. Requires accepted ms on disk. Guidelines by mail/e-mail/website; free catalog by mail.

Nonfiction: Must complete Author's Proposal form; no phone/fax query; e-query OK. Accepts mss by e-mail. "Looking for books for the homeschool market, especially grades 1-8."

Special Needs: Stewardship of the earth; ancient man technology, inventions, etc.; educational products for grades K-12.

Contest: Master Books Scholarship Essay Contest; $3,000 college scholarship; www.nlpg.com.

Tips: "Accepts submissions only with Author's Proposal form available by e-mail or on our website."

This publisher serviced by The Writer's Edge.

OAKTARA PUBLISHERS, PO Box 8, Waterford VA 20197. (540) 882-9062. Fax (540) 882-3719. E-mail: jnesbit@oaktara.com or rtucker@oaktara.com. Website: www.oaktara.com. Jeff Nesbit, mng. dir. (jnesbit@oaktara.com); Ramona Tucker, ed. dir. (rtucker@oaktara.com). To create opportunities for new, talented Christian writers in both fiction and nonfiction and to promote leading-edge fiction and nonfiction by established Christian authors. Does print-on-demand. Will consider reprinted books. **Royalty; no advance.** Guidelines on website ("Writers' Corner/Writers' Guidelines").

Fiction and Nonfiction: Submit by e-mail (attached file) in one Word file. Fiction for ages 8 and up.

This publisher serviced by The Writer's Edge.

ON MY OWN NOW MINISTRIES (formerly The Quilldriver), PO Box 573, Clarksville AR 72830. Phone/fax (479) 497-0321. E-mail: donna@onmyownnow.com. Website: www.onmyownnow.com. Donna Lee Schillinger, pub. Inspirational nonfiction directed at young adults (17-25). Imprint: Two-Faced Books. Publishes 3 titles/yr. Receives 12 submissions annually. 67% of books from first-time authors. No mss through agents. Would consider reprinting books. Prefers 200 pgs. **Royalties; $500 advance.** Average first printing 2,000. Publication within 18 mos. Considers simultaneous submissions. Responds in 8 wks. Prefers NIV. Guidelines by e-mail; catalog for #10 SAE/1 stamp.

Nonfiction: Query first; or proposal/2 chapters; e-query OK.

Tips: "Most open to books that are hip and biblically sound—must resonate with young adults."

***OUR SUNDAY VISITOR INC.,** 200 Noll Plaza, Huntington IN 46750-4303. (260) 356-8400. Toll-free (800) 348-2440. Fax (260) 356-8472. E-mail: booksed@osv.com. Website: www.osv.com. Catholic. Submit to Acquisitions Editor. To assist Catholics to be more aware and secure in their faith and capable of relating their faith to others. Publishes 30-40 titles/yr.; hardcover, trade paperbacks. Receives 500+ submissions annually. 10% of books from first-time authors. Prefers not to work through agents. Reprints books. **Royalty 10-12% of net; average advance $1,500.** Average first printing 5,000. Publication within 1-2 yrs. No simultaneous submissions. Responds in 3 mos. Requires requested ms on disk. Guidelines on website ("About Us"/"Writer's Guidelines"); catalog for 9 x 12 SASE.

Nonfiction: Proposal/2 chapters; e-query OK. "Most open to devotional books (not first person), church history, heritage and saints, the parish, prayer, and family."
Also Does: Pamphlets, booklets.
Photos: Occasionally accepts freelance photos for book covers.
Tips: "All books published must relate to the Catholic Church; unique books aimed at our audience. Give as much background information as possible on author qualification, why the topic was chosen, and unique aspects of the project. Follow our guidelines. We are expanding our religious education product line and programs."

PACIFIC PRESS PUBLISHING ASSN., PO Box 5353, Nampa ID 83653-5353. (208) 465-2500. Fax (208) 465-2531. E-mail: booksubmissions@pacificpress.com. Website: www.pacificpress.com. Seventh-day Adventist. David Jarnes, book ed.; submit to Scott Cady, acq. ed. Books of interest and importance to Seventh-day Adventists and other Christians of all ages. Publishes 35-40 titles/yr.; hardcover, trade paperbacks. Receives 500 submissions annually. 5% of books from first-time authors. Accepts mss through agents or authors. No reprints. Prefers 50,000-130,000 wds. or 160-400 pgs. **Royalty 12-15% of net; advance $1,500.** Average first printing 5,000. Publication within 6 mos. Considers simultaneous submissions. Responds in 1 mo. Requires requested ms on disk or by e-mail. Guidelines at www.pacificpress.com/index/php?pgName=newsSubGuides; no catalog.

Nonfiction: Query only; e-query OK.
Fiction: Query only; almost none accepted; mainly biblical. Children's books: "Must be on a uniquely Seventh-day Adventist topic. No talking animals or fantasy."
Ethnic Books: Hispanic.
Also Does: Booklets.
Tips: "Most open to spirituality, inspirational, and Christian living. Our website has the most up-to-date information, including samples of recent publications. For more information, see www.adventistbookcenter.com. Do not send full manuscript unless we request it after reviewing your proposal."

P&R PUBLISHING CO., PO Box 817, Phillipsburg NJ 08865. (908) 454-0505. Fax (908) 859-2390. E-mail: editorial@prpbooks.com. Website: www.prpbooks.com. Devoted to stating, defending, and furthering the gospel in the modern world. Publishes 40 titles/yr.; hardcover and trade paperbacks. Receives 400 submissions annually. Fewer than 10% of books from first-time authors. Accepts mss through agents. Reprints books. Prefers 140-240 pgs. **Royalty 10-15% of net; advance.** Average first printing 3,500. Publication within 10-12 mos. Considers simultaneous submissions. Responds in 1-4 mos. Guidelines on website.

Nonfiction: Proposal/2-3 chapters. E-mail only.
Fiction: Proposal/2-3 chapters. E-mail only. For children or teens.
Tips: "Direct biblical/Reformed content. Clear, engaging, and insightful applications of Reformed theology to life. Offer us fully developed proposals and polished sample chapters. Check our website to see the categories we publish."

***PARAGON HOUSE,** 1925 Oakcrest Ave., Ste. 7, St. Paul MN 55113-2619. (651) 644-3087. Fax (651) 644-0997. E-mail: submissions@paragonhouse.com. Website: www.paragonhouse.com. Gordon Anderson, acq. ed. Serious nonfiction and texts with an emphasis on religion, philosophy, and society. Imprints: Omega, Vision of . . . . Publishes 12-15 titles/yr.; hardcover, trade paperbacks, e-books. Receives 1,200 submissions annually. 20% of books from first-time authors. Accepts mss through agents or author. Prefers average 250 pgs. **Royalty 7-10% of net; advance $1,000.** Average first printing 1,500-3,000. Publication within 12-18 mos. Considers few simultaneous submissions. Accepts e-mail submissions (attached file). Responds in 1-2 mos. Guidelines/catalog on website ("Help"/"Authors Guidelines" on left).

Nonfiction: Query; proposal/2-3 chapters or complete ms; no phone/fax query. Endorsements are helpful. "Looking for scholarly overviews of topics in religion and society; textbooks in philosophy; ecumenical subjects; and reference books."

PARSON PLACE PRESS LLC, PO Box 8277, Mobile AL 36689-0277. (251) 643-6985. E-mail: info@parsonplacepress.com. Website: www.parsonplacepress.com. Michael L. White, mng. ed. Devoted to giving both Christian authors and Christian readers a fair deal. Publishes 2-5 titles/yr.; hardcover, trade paperbacks, e-books. Receives ca. 25 submissions annually. 80% of books from first-time authors. Accepts mss through agents or authors. Does print-on-demand. Prefers 100-220 pgs. **Royalty on net; no advance.** Average first printing 50. Publication within 3 mos. No simultaneous submissions. Responds in 4-6 wks. Requested mss by e-mail (attached file). Prefers NKJV or NASB. Guidelines on website ("Author Guidelines"); electronic catalog on website.

Nonfiction: Proposal/2 chapters; e-query OK. Christian topic/content only.

Fiction: Proposal/2 chapters; e-query OK. For middle school through adult.

Special Needs: In nonfiction: end-times prophecy, evangelism, and Bible studies. In fiction: mystery, romance, historical.

Photos/Artwork: Accepts freelance photos for book covers; open to queries from freelance artists.

Tips: "Most open to conservative, biblically based content that ministers to Christians. Write intelligently, clearly, sincerely, and engagingly."

***PARSONS PUBLISHING HOUSE,** PO Box 488, Stafford VA 22554. (850) 867-3061. Fax (540) 659-9043. E-mail: info@parsonspublishinghouse.com. Website: www.parsonspublishinghouse.com. Nondenominational. Diane Parsons, chief ed. Exists to partner with authors to release their voice into their world. Publishes 5 titles/yr.; hardcover, trade paperbacks. Receives 40 submissions annually. 85% of books from first-time authors. No mss through agents; accepts from authors. Reprints books. Prefers 120-160 pgs. **Royalty 10% on net; no advance.** Average first printing 300. Publication within 9 mos. Considers simultaneous submissions. Responds in 60 days. Prefers accepted mss by e-mail. Guidelines by e-mail/website ("Submissions"); no catalog.

Nonfiction: Query; e-query OK.

Fiction: Query; proposal/3 chapters; e-query OK. For teens & adults.

Ethnic Books: Hispanic.

Artwork: Open to queries from freelance artists.

Tips: "Most open to Christian living and worship."

PAULINE BOOKS & MEDIA, Daughters of St. Paul, 50 Saint Pauls Ave., Jamaica Plain MA 02130-3491. (617) 522-8911. E-mail: editorial@paulinemedia.com. Website: www.pauline.org. Catholic/Daughters of St. Paul. Christina Wegendt, FSP, and Sr. Sean Mayer, FSP, acq. eds. Submit to Brittany Schlorff, ed. asst. Responds to the hopes and needs of their readers with the Word of God and in the spirit of St. Paul, utilizing all available forms of media so others can find and develop faith in Jesus within the current culture. Publishes 20 titles/yr.; hardcover & trade paperbacks. Receives 350-400 submissions annually. 10% of books from first-time authors. Accepts mss through agents or authors. No subsidy or print-on-demand. Reprints books. Prefers 10,000-60,000 wds. **Royalty 5-10% on net; offers an advance.** Average first printing 2,000-5,000. Publication within 24 mos. Considers simultaneous submissions. Responds in 2-3 mos. Prefers requested ms by e-mail. Prefers NRSV. Guidelines by mail/e-mail/website (scroll to bottom "Manuscript Submissions"); free catalog by mail.

Nonfiction: Proposal/2 chapters; complete ms; e-query OK.

Fiction: See entry for Pauline Kids and Teens; no adult fiction.

Special Needs: "Spirituality (prayer/holiness of life/seasonal titles), faith formation (religious instruction/catechesis), family life (marriage/parenting issues), biographies of the saints, prayer books. Of particular interest is our faith and culture line, which includes titles that show how Christ is present and may be more fully embraced and proclaimed within our media culture."

Tips: "Submissions are evaluated on adherence to gospel values, harmony with the Catholic tradition, relevance of topic, and quality of writing."

This publisher serviced by The Writer's Edge.

PAULINE KIDS AND TEEN, 50 St. Paul's Ave., Boston MA 02130. (617) 522-8911. Fax (617) 524-9805. E-mail: editorial@paulinemedia.com. Website: www.pauline.org. Pauline Books & Media/ Catholic. Marilyn Monge, FSP, and Jaymie Stuart Wolfe, eds.; submit to Brittany Schlorff, ed. asst. Seeks to provide wholesome and entertaining reading that can help children and teens develop strong Christian values. Publishes 20-25 titles/yr.; hardcover, trade paperbacks. Receives 300-450 submissions annually. 10% of books from first-time authors. Accepts mss through agents or authors. Reprints books. **Royalty 5-10% on net; pays an advance.** Average first printing 2,000-5,000. Publication within 24 mos. Considers simultaneous submissions. Responds in 2-3 mos. Prefers accepted ms by e-mail. Prefers NRSV. Guidelines by mail/e-mail/website (scroll to bottom "Manuscript Submissions"); free catalog by mail.

Nonfiction/Fiction: Proposal/2 chapters for easy-to-read, middle-grade readers, and teen; complete ms for board and picture books; e-query OK.

Special Needs: Easy-to-read fiction, middle-grade nonfiction.

Photos/Artwork: Accepts freelance photos for book covers; open to queries from freelance artists. Send illustration queries to Sr. Mary Joseph Peterson, Design Dept., Pauline Books & Media, 50 St. Paul's Ave., Jamaica Plain MA 02130.

PELICAN PUBLISHING CO. INC., 1000 Burmaster St., Gretna LA 70053. (504) 368-1175. Fax (504) 368-1195. E-mail: editorial@pelicanpub.com. Website: www.pelicanpub.com. Nina Kooij, ed-in-chief. To publish books of quality and permanence that enrich the lives of those who read them. Imprints: Firebird Press, Jackson Square Press, Dove Inspirational Press (see separate listing). Publishes 1 title/yr.; hardcover, trade paperbacks. Receives 250 submissions annually. No books from first-time authors. Accepts mss through agents or authors. Reprints books. Prefers 200+ pgs. **Royalty; pays some advances.** Publication within 9-18 mos. No simultaneous submissions. Responds in 1 mo. on queries. Requires accepted ms on disk. Prefers KJV. Guidelines on website ("About Us"/"Submissions").

Nonfiction: Proposal/2 chapters; no phone/fax/e-query. Children's picture books to 1,100 wds. (send complete ms); middle readers about Louisiana (ages 8-12) at least 25,000 wds.; cookbooks at least 200 recipes.

Fiction: Complete ms. Children's picture books only. For ages 5-8 only.

Artwork: Open to queries from freelance artists.

Tips: "On inspirational titles we need a high-profile author who already has an established speaking circuit so books can be sold at these appearances."

PLAYERS PRESS INC., PO Box 1132, Studio City CA 91614-0132. (818) 789-4980. E-mail: players press@att.net. Website: www.ppeps.com. (New website is under construction.) Robert W. Gordon, ed. To create is to live life's purpose. Publishes mostly dramatic works; prides themselves on high-quality titles. Imprints: Players Press, Brown Son Fergusson, Phantom Publications, and Showcase. Publishes 1-6 religious titles/yr.; hardcover, trade paperbacks, acting editions, workbooks, paperbacks, coffee table books. Receives 50-80 religious submissions annually. 90% of books from first-time authors. Accepts mss through agents or authors. No subsidy publishing. Does print-on-demand with older titles. Sometimes reprints quality theater titles and costume books. Variable length. **Royalty 10% on net; pays advances on some titles.** Average first printing 1,000-10,000. Publication within 12 mos. No simultaneous submissions. No submissions by e-mail. Responds in 1-3 wks. on query; 3-12 mos. on ms. Guidelines by mail; catalog for 9 x 12 SAE/11 stamps or $4.50.

Nonfiction/Plays: Query letter only; no phone/fax/e-query. "Always looking for plays and musicals, books on theater, film, and/or television. Good plays; all categories. For all ages." Likes religious, romantic, comic, and/or children's plays. New classic translations and musicals are important to them.

Contests: Sometimes sponsors a contest.

Photos/Artwork: Accepts freelance photos for book and play covers; open to queries from freelance artists.

Tips: "Most open to plays, musicals, books on theater, film, television, and supporting areas: cameras, lighting, costumes, etc."

PORT YONDER PRESS, 6332—33rd Ave. Dr., Shellsburg IA 52332. (319) 436-3015. E-mail: contact@portyonderpress.com. Website: www.PortYonderPress.com. Chila Woychik, ed-in-chief. Imprints: SharksFinn, SkySail, Sea Beast, and Port Yonder Books. Crossover publisher of both Christian and general market books. Publishes 6-8 titles/yr. Receives 500 submissions annually. 30% of books from first-time authors. Accepts mss through agents or authors. Prefers 150-300 pgs. **Royalty 40-50% on net; small advance.** An award-winning trade publisher primarily using print-on-demand digital printing. Publication within 12-18 mos. No simultaneous queries or submissions. Accepts submissions only during our reading months (varies) or at conferences where publisher/editor attends. Requires accepted mss by e-mail and hard copy. Responds in 2 mos. Guidelines on website (click on "Getting Published"). Not included in topical listings.

Poetry, Nonfiction & Fiction: Query only during reading months, listed on website.

Tips: "Only the highest quality manuscripts will be accepted. Current needs: Crossover speculative fiction, mystery, spy thrillers, contemporary poetry, some western fiction, creative nonfiction, slipstream, and experimental. *Crossover—that which appeals to Christians and non-Christians alike. Our goal is to publish award-winning books of literary merit. Anything for our Christian imprints must be extremely non-preachy."

PRAEGER PUBLISHERS, 130 Cremona Dr., Santa Barbara CA 93117. (805) 968-1911. E-mail: achiffolo@abc-clio.com. Website: www.abc-clio.com. Imprint of ABC-CLIO. Anthony Chiffolo, acq. ed. Primary market is public and university libraries worldwide; no bookstore distribution. Publishes 5-10 titles/yr. in religion; hardcover and e-book; nonfiction only. Receives 50-100 submissions annually. Accepts mss through agents or authors. No subsidy or reprints. Minimum length: 100,000 wds. **Variable royalty on net; pays minor advances.** Average first printing 450. Publication within 12-18 mos. Considers simultaneous submissions. Responds in 2-4 mos. Guidelines on website; catalog on website.

Nonfiction: Thorough book proposal/1-3 chapters or all chapters available; e-query preferred.

Special Needs: Religion and society/culture; religious controversies/issues; paranormal; neuro-religion.

Ethnic Books: African American religion; Native American religion; Hispanic/Latino religion; Asian American religion.

Tips: "Most open to books on 'headline' issues and controversies; books on 'religion and culture' are needed; must be written for general, nonspecialist readership. No monographs/no dissertations. No self-help or how-to books. No scriptural studies or Bible scholarship. No fiction or poetry."

RAINBOW PUBLISHERS, PO Box 261129, San Diego CA 92196. Toll-free (800) 323-7337. Toll-free fax (800) 331-0297. E-mail: editor@rainbowpublishers.com. Website: www.rainbowpublishers.com. Tony Bonds, ed. Submit to The Editor. Publishes Bible-teaching, reproducible books for children's teachers. Publishes 20 titles/yr. Receives 250 submissions annually. 50% of books from first-time authors. Reprints books. Prefers 96 pgs. **Outright purchases $640 & up.** Average first printing 2,500. Publication within 2 yrs. Considers simultaneous submissions. Responds in 3 mos. No disk or e-mail submissions. Prefers NIV. Guidelines/catalog on website ("Submissions" at bottom).

Nonfiction: Proposal/2-5 chapters; no phone/e-query. "Looking for fun and easy ways to teach Bible concepts to kids, ages 2-12."
Special Needs: Creative puzzles and unique games.
Artwork: Open to queries from freelance artists.
Tips: "Visit your Christian bookstore or our website to see what we have already published. We have over 100 titles and do not like to repeat topics, so a proposal needs to be unique for us but not necessarily unique in the market. Most open to writing that appeals to teachers who work with kids and Bible activities that have been tried and tested on today's kids."

***RANDALL HOUSE DIGITAL,** 114 Bush Rd., PO Box 17306, Nashville TN 37217. Toll-free (800) 877-7030. (615) 361-1221. Fax (615) 367-0535. E-mail through website: www.randallhouse.com. National Assn. of Free Will Baptists. Alan Clagg, dir. Produces curriculum-on-demand via the Internet, and electronic resources to supplement existing printed curriculum. Guidelines on website (click on "Contact Us"/"Book Proposal Guide").
Nonfiction: Query first; e-query OK.
Special Needs: Teacher-training material (personal or group), elective Bible studies for adults, children's curriculum (other than Sunday school), and elective materials for teens.
Also Does: Digital books.
Tips: "We are looking for writers with vision for worldwide ministry who would like to see their works help a greater section of the Body of Christ than served by the conventionally printed products."

***RANDALL HOUSE PUBLICATIONS,** 114 Bush Rd., Nashville TN 37217. Toll-free (800) 877-7030. (615) 361-1221. Fax (615) 367-0535. E-mail: michelle.orr@randallhouse.com. Website: www.randallhouse.com. Free Will Baptist. Michelle Orr, sr. acq. ed. Publishes Sunday school and Christian education materials to make Christ known, from a conservative perspective. Publishes 10-15 titles/yr.; hardcover, trade paperbacks, digital. Receives 300-500 submissions annually. 40% of books from first-time authors. Accepts mss through agents or authors. No subsidy or reprints. Prefers 40,000 wds. **Royalty 12-18% on net; pays an advance.** Average first printing 5,000. Publication within 18 mos. Considers simultaneous submissions. Accepts requested mss by e-mail. Responds in 10-12 wks. Guidelines by e-mail/website ("Contact"/click on "Book Proposal Guide" in text); no catalog.
Nonfiction: Query; e-query OK; proposal/2 chapters. Must fill out book proposal form they provide.
Artwork: Open to queries from freelance artists (andrea.young@randallhouse.com).
Tips: "We are expanding our book division with a conservative perspective. We have a very conservative view as a publisher."
This publisher serviced by ChristianManuscriptSubmissions.com.

***RAVENHAWK BOOKS,** 7739 E. Broadway Blvd., #95, Tucson AZ 85710. E-mail: ravenhawk6dof@yahoo.com. Website: www.6dofsolutions.com. Blog: see website. The 6DOF Group. Karl Lasky, pub.; Shelly Geraci, submissions ed. Publishes variable number of titles/yr.; hardcover, trade paperbacks. Receives 1,000-1,500 submissions annually. 70% of books from first-time authors. Print-on-demand. Reprints books. **Royalty 40-50% on gross profits; no advance.** Average first printing 2,500. Publication in up to 18 mos. Considers simultaneous submissions. Responds in 6 wks., if interested. Catalog on website.
Nonfiction: Query first; e-query OK. "Looking for profitable books from talented writers."
Fiction: Query first. For all ages. Unsolicited full mss returned unopened.
Special Needs: Looking for books from young authors, 16-22 years old.
Photos/Artwork: Accepts freelance photos for book covers; open to queries from freelance artists.

Tips: "Most open to crisp, creative, entertaining writing that also informs and educates. Writing, as any creative art, is a gift from God. Not everyone has the innate talent to do it well. We are author-oriented. We don't play games with the numbers."

REFERENCE SERVICE PRESS, 5000 Windplay Dr., Ste. 4, El Dorado Hills CA 95762. (916) 939-9620. Fax (916) 939-9626. E-mail: info@rspfunding.com. Website: www.rspfunding.com. R. David Weber, ed. Books related to financial aid and Christian higher education. Publishes 1 title/yr.; hardcover, trade paperbacks. Receives 3-5 submissions annually. Most books from first-time authors. No reprints. **Royalty 10% of net; usually no advance.** Publication within 5 mos. May consider simultaneous submissions. No guidelines; free catalog for 2 stamps.

Nonfiction: Proposal/several chapters.

Special Needs: Financial aid directories for Christian college students.

REVELL BOOKS, 6030 E. Fulton Rd., Ada MI 49301. (616) 676-9185. Fax (616) 676-2315. Website: www.revellbooks.com. Imprint of Baker Publishing Group. Publishes inspirational fiction and nonfiction for the broadest Christian market. Catalog on website. No unsolicited proposals. Submit only through an agent, Authonomy.com, The Writer's Edge Service, or ChristianManuscriptSubmissions.com.

***STANDARD PUBLISHING,** 8805 Governor's Hill Dr., Ste. 400, Cincinnati OH 45249. (513) 931-4050. Fax (513) 931-0950. Website: www.standardpub.com. CFM Religion Publishing Group LLC. Provides true-to-the-Bible resources that inspire, educate, and motivate Christians to a growing relationship with Jesus Christ. Accepts mss through agents or authors. Hardcover & trade paperbacks. No reprints. **Royalty or outright purchase; advance.** No simultaneous submissions. Responds in 3-6 mos. Prefers NIV/KJV. Guidelines on website (www.standardpub.com/writers).

Nonfiction: Query only; e-query OK.

Fiction: Query only; e-query OK. Children's picture or board books; juvenile novels.

Special Needs: Adult and youth ministry resources; children's ministry resources.

This publisher serviced by ChristianManuscriptSubmissions.com and The Writer's Edge.

ST. ANTHONY MESSENGER PRESS (see FRANCISCAN MEDIA)

SUMMERSIDE PRESS/GUIDEPOSTS, 16 E. 34th St., 12th Floor, New York NY 10016. (212) 251-8100. E-mail: info@summersidepress.com. Website: www.summersidepress.com. Rachel Meisel, ed. dir. Inspirational romance fiction series. Accepts mss through agents only. Publishes 12 titles/yr. Prefers 80,000-100,000 wds. Guidelines on website ("Submissions").

Fiction: Agents send paragraph overview plus a 2-3 page synopsis and 3 sample chapters by e-mail (attached files).

SUNPENNY PUBLISHING, 10 Aspen Close, Harriseahead Staffordshire ST7 4HD, United Kingdom. E-mail: writers@sunpenny.com. Website: www.sunpenny.com. Jo Holloway, ed. Publishes 15-20 titles/yr.; hardcover, trade paperbacks, mass-market paperbacks, electronic originals (e-books). 50% of books from first-time authors. Accepts mss through agents or authors. **Royalty on sliding scale beginning at 15% of margin.** Considers simultaneous submissions. Responds in 1-2 wks. to queries; 1-2 mos. to proposals; 2-3 mos. to manuscripts. Guidelines ("Submissions") & catalog on website.

Nonfiction: Query, proposal, or complete ms. Boating, sailing, travel, knowledge, how-to, self-help, and Christian/inspirational books.

Fiction: Query, proposal, or complete ms. Children's, general fiction, romance, and Christian/inspirational books.

Photos/Artwork: Accepts freelance photos for book covers; open to queries from freelance artists.

TATE PUBLISHING & ENTERPRISES LLC, Tate Publishing Bldg., 127 E. Trade Center Ter., Mustang OK 73064-4421. Toll-free (888) 361-9473. Fax (405) 376-4401. E-mail: publish@tatepublishing

.com. Website: www.tatepublishing.com. Dr. Richard Tate, founder and chairman of the board. Owns and operates a state-of-the-art printing plant facility. Hardcover, trade paperbacks, mass-market paperbacks. All work is done by professional in-house staff of over 200 full-time employees. Tate is a traditional publisher and absorbs 100% of the cost of production, manufacturing, marketing, and distribution of the few works that are selected. No production work is outsourced for any project. Receives 60,000-75,000 unsolicited contacts annually. 60% of books from first-time authors. Accepts mss through agents. Some first-time unpublished authors may be asked to contribute a refundable $3,990 if they cannot provide legitimate marketing and publicist staff. The retainer is refunded to the author once the book sells 1,000 copies in distribution. Not print-on-demand. Accepts reprints. Prefers 115,000 wds. **Royalty 15-40% of net; negotiable author cash advances and no refundable retainer if the author meets minimum requirements.** Average first print budget is 5,000. Publication within 90 days is an option if certain criteria met. Considers simultaneous submissions. Responds in 3-6 wks. Accepts submissions by e-mail or US mail. Any Bible version. Guidelines by mail/e-mail/website; free catalog.

Nonfiction: Proposal with synopsis & any number of chapters, or complete ms; phone/fax/e-query OK. Any topic. "Looking for books that sell."

Fiction: Proposal with synopsis & any number of chapters or complete ms; phone/fax/e-query OK. For all ages. Any genre.

Ethnic Books: For all ethnic markets.

Artwork: Has full-time artists on staff; open to queries from freelance artists.

Tips: "We invest resources in every work we accept, and accept first-time authors."

TRAIL MEDIA, 1320 Ynez Place #181306, Coronado CA 92118. (619) 701-8737. E-mail: Admin@Chisholm-TrailMedia.com. Website: www.Chisholm-TrailMedia.com. Dana S. Chisholm, pub. Publishes 20 mss/yr. Receives 100 mss/yr. 100% first-time authors. Does not accept books submitted by agents. No subsidy. Paperbacks, Digital. **Royalty 15-30% of retail price.** POD/ePub. Publication within 6 mos. Will consider simultaneous submissions. Guidelines on website.

Nonfiction: Submit proposal with one chapter. E-mail queries only.

Fiction: Adult, children, teen. Most interested in YA, children's illustrated, historical fiction, adult/general. Query letter first by e-mail.

Tips: We are a new publishing house specifically established to help new authors refine their work and publish, with professional editors and graphic artists, no up-front fees. We are looking for nonfiction inspirational life experiences, YA fiction, children's illustrated books, and Americana (getting back to the founders' intent). The industry is flooded with self-publishing options, or authors can submit to big publishing houses and face rejection after rejection. Trail Media is called to meet writers in the gap.

THE TRINITY FOUNDATION, PO Box 68, Unicoi TN 37692. (423) 743-0199. Fax (423) 743-2005. E-mail: tjtrinityfound@aol.com. Website: www.trinityfoundation.org. Thomas W. Juodaitis, ed. To promote the logical system of truth found in the Bible. Publishes 5 titles/yr.; hardcover, trade paperbacks. Receives 3 submissions annually. No books from first-time authors. No mss through agents. Reprints books. Prefers 200 pgs. **Outright purchases up to $1,500; free books; no advance.** Average first printing 2,000. Publication within 9 mos. No simultaneous submissions. Requires requested ms in electronic editable format. Responds in 2-3 mos. No guidelines; catalog on website.

Nonfiction: Query letter only. Open to Calvinist/Clarkian books, Christian philosophy, economics, and politics.

Also Does: Pamphlets, booklets, tracts.

Photos: Accepts freelance photos for book covers.

Tips: "Most open to doctrinal books that conform to the Westminster Confession of Faith; nonfiction, biblical, and well-reasoned books, theologically sound, clearly written, and well organized."

TYNDALE ESPAÑOL, 351 Executive Dr., Carol Stream IL 60188. (630) 784-5272. Fax (630) 344-0943. E-mail: andresschwartz@tyndale.com. Website: www.tyndale.com. Andres Schwartz, publisher—Spanish division of Tyndale House Publishers.

TYNDALE HOUSE PUBLISHERS, INC. 351 Executive Dr., Carol Stream IL 60188. Toll-free (800) 323-9400. (630) 668-8300. Toll-free fax (800) 684-0247. E-mail through website: www.tyndale.com. Submit to Manuscript Review Committee. Practical Christian books for home and family. Imprints: Tyndale Español (Spanish imprint). Publishes 150-200 titles/yr.; hardcover, trade paperbacks. 5% of books from first-time authors. Requires mss through agents. Average first printing 5,000-10,000. Publication within 9 mos. Considers simultaneous submissions. Responds in 3-6 mos. Prefers NLT. No unsolicited mss. Guidelines/catalog on website (under "Site Map"/"Authors"/"Manuscript Policy").

Nonfiction: Query from agents or published authors only; no phone/fax query. No unsolicited mss (they will not be acknowledged or returned).

Fiction: "We accept queries only from agents, Tyndale authors, authors known to us from other publishers, or other people in the publishing industry. Novels 75,000-100,000 wds. All must have an evangelical Christian message."

Also Does: E-books.

This publisher serviced by ChristianManuscriptSubmissions.com and The Writer's Edge.

VBC PUBLISHING, PO Box 9101, Vallejo CA 94591. (707) 315-1219. Fax (707) 648-2169. E-mail: akgordon1991@att.net. Vallejo Bible College. Kevin Gordon, pres. To glorify the Lord through Christian literature; to provide the Christian community with material to aid them in their personal studies and to help in their life and ministry. New publisher; plans 1-5 titles/yr.; hardcover, trade paperbacks. Receives 10 submissions annually. Plans to publish 50% of books from first-time authors. Accepts mss through agents or authors. Print-on-demand publisher. No reprints. Prefers 100+ pgs. **Royalty 8-12% on net; no advance.** Publication within 8 mos. Considers simultaneous submissions. Responds in 2-6 wks. Accepted mss on disk. Prefers KJV, NKJV, NASB, NIV. Guidelines by mail; no catalog.

Nonfiction: Proposal/2 chapters or complete ms; phone/e-query OK; no fax query.

Special Needs: Biblical theology, Bible study, and Christian living.

Artwork: Open to queries from freelance artists.

Tips: "Most open to doctrinally sound and relevant manuscripts. Have a well-written manuscript and a plan to market your book. Follow guidelines when submitting and trust in the Lord!"

***THE VISION FORUM,** 4719 Blanco Rd., San Antonio TX 78212. (210) 340-5250. Fax (210) 340-8577. Website: www.visionforum.com. Douglas W. Phillips, pres. Dedicated to the restoration of the biblical family. Historical fiction, practical Christian living.

WARNER PRESS INC., 1201 E. 5th St., Anderson IN 46012. Fax (765) 640-8005. E-mail: rfogle@warnerpress.org. Website: www.warnerpress.org. Church of God. Karen Rhodes, sr. ed.; submit to Robin Fogle, asst. product ed. Committed to excellence in developing and marketing products and services based on scriptural truths to energize, educate, nurture, inspire, and unite the whole people of God. Hardcover, paperback, and e-books. Receives 100+ submissions annually. Rarely accepts mss through agents. No subsidy. No reprints. Not presently publishing kids' picture books. 250-350 pgs. for teen books. **Royalty & advance based on the author and type of book.** Publication within 12 mos. Considers simultaneous submissions. Responds in 6-8 wks. Prefers KJV or NIV. Guidelines on website (scroll to bottom "Submissions Guidelines"); no catalog.

Nonfiction: Complete ms; fax/e-query OK. Accepts e-mail submissions. We are currently accepting mss for adult Bible studies (personal and small group) and personal spiritual growth, as well as short instructional booklets (32-64 pgs.) dealing with various aspects of ministry and leadership.

Fiction: Query first, then complete ms; fax/e-query OK. Accepts e-mail submissions. Also producing chapter books (120-150 pages) for ages 8-12. "We want our books to be biblically sound with a nondenominational viewpoint."

Artwork: Send to Curtis Corzine, Creative Art Director (curtis@warnerpress.org).

Tips: "We primarily create books for ages 6-10 and 8-12 (fantasy fiction but open to other genres as well). We are looking for books that are not preachy but do contain a biblical or moral foundation. Well-written, creative books by writers who have done their market research. We are also looking for Bible studies for kids and adults, and leadership materials for those in ministry. To see other products we produce, visit our website."

***WATERBROOK PRESS,** 12265 Oracle Blvd., Ste. 200, Colorado Springs CO 80921. (719) 590-4999. Fax (719) 590-8977. E-mail: info@waterbrookmultnomah.com. Website: www.waterbrookmultnomah.com. Part of WaterBrook Multnomah, a division of Random House Inc. Ken Petersen, VP/ed-in-chief; Laura Barker, ed. dir. Publishes 75 titles/yr.; hardcover, trade paperbacks. **Royalty on net; advance.** WaterBrook is currently not accepting unsolicited manuscripts, proposals, or queries; no proposals for biographies or poetry. Queries will be accepted though literary agents and at writers' conferences at which a WaterBrook representative is present. Catalog on website.

Nonfiction/Fiction: Agented submissions only.

This publisher serviced by The Writer's Edge.

WATERSHED BOOKS, PO Box 1738, Aztec NM 87410. E-mail: customer@pelicanbookgroup.com. Website: www.pelicanbookgroup.com. Division of Pelican Ventures, LLC. Nicola Martinez, editor-in-chief. Christian fiction 25,000-60,000 wds. Limited-edition hardback, trade paperbacks, and e-book. **Royalty 40% on download; 7% on print.** Pays nominal advance. Accepts unagented submissions. Responds to queries in 30 days, full ms in 90 days. Considers reprints but accepts few. E-mail submissions only; see website for submission form and procedure.

Fiction: Query via submission form on website. Interested in series ideas. Submissions must be Young Adult fiction that features young adult characters.

***WESLEYAN PUBLISHING HOUSE,** PO Box 50434, Indianapolis IN 46250-0434. (317) 774-7900. E-mail: wph@wesleyan.org. Website: www.wesleyan.org/wph. The Wesleyan Church. Attn: Editorial Director. Communicates the life-transforming message of holiness to the world. Publishes 30 titles/yr.; hardcover, trade paperbacks. Receives 150 submissions annually. 25% of books from first-time authors. Accepts mss through agents or authors. No reprints. Prefers 25,000-40,000 wds. **Royalty and advance.** Average first printing 4,000. Publication within 9-12 mos. Considers simultaneous submissions. Prefers ms by e-mail (submissions@wesleyan.org). Responds within 60-90 days. Prefers NIV. Guidelines by e-mail/website (www.wesleyan.org/wg). Free online catalog.

Nonfiction: Proposal/3-5 chapters; no phone/fax/e-query. "Looking for books that help Christians understand the faith and apply it to their lives."

This publisher serviced by ChristianManuscriptSubmissions.com and The Writer's Edge.

WHITAKER HOUSE, 1030 Hunt Valley Cir., New Kensington PA 15068. (724) 334-7000. (724) 334-1200. E-mail: publisher@whitakerhouse.com. Website: www.whitakerhouse.com. Whitaker Corp. Tom Cox, sr. ed. To advance God's Kingdom by providing biblically based products that proclaim the power of the gospel and minister to the spiritual needs of people around the world. Publishes 30-40 titles/yr.; hardcover, trade paperbacks, mass-market paperbacks. Receives 500 submissions annually. 15% of books from first-time authors. Accepts mss through agents or authors. No subsidy, print-on-demand, or reprints. Prefers 50,000 wds. **Royalty 6-15% on net; some variable advances.** Average first printing 5,000. Publication within 10 mos. Considers simultaneous submissions. Prefers accepted ms by e-mail. Responds in 4 mos. Prefers NIV. Guidelines on website ("Submissions Guidelines" center); no catalog.

Nonfiction/Fiction: Query only first; no phone/fax query; e-query OK.

Special Needs: Charismatic nonfiction, Christian historical romance, Amish romance, Christian African American romance.

Ethnic Books: Spanish translations of current English titles.

Tips: "Looking for quality nonfiction and fiction by authors with a national marketing platform. Most open to high-quality, well-thought-out, compelling pieces of work. Review the guidelines and submit details as thoroughly as possible for publication consideration."

***WHITE FIRE PUBLISHING,** (866) 245-2211. Fax: (410) 571-0292. E-mail: info@whitefire-publishing.com. Website: www.whitefire-publishing.com. Roseanna White, ed. Publishes 4-10 titles/yr. Receives 100 submissions annually. 60% of books from first-time authors. Prefers mss through agents. Prefers 60,000-150,000 wds. Publishes trade paperbacks and digital. **Royalty 10-15%. Pay for e-books 50% on net. Offers advance.** Average first run 1,000. Publication in 6-12 months. Accepts simultaneous submissions. Responds to proposals within 3 months. Guidelines on website.

Nonfiction: Query letter only first. Query by e-mail. Narrative nonfiction. Must meet our motto of "Where Spirit Meets the Page." Send to Wendy Chorot, Nonfiction Editor at w.chorot@whitefire-publishing.com.

Fiction: Query letter only first. Query by e-mail. Accepts fiction for teens and adults. Likes historical, especially with exotic settings and with romance threads.

Tips: "Where Spirit Meets the Page." Looking for unique voices and settings others shy away from. Fiction editors Dina Sleiman, d.sleiman@whitefire-publishing.com, and Roseanna White, r.white@whitefire-publishing.com.

WHITE ROSE PUBLISHING, PO Box 1738, Aztec NM 87410. E-mail: customer@pelicanbookgroup.com. Website: www.pelicanbookgroup.com. A division of Pelican Ventures, LLC. Nicola Martinez, ed.-in-chief. Christian romance 10,000-80,000 wds. Limited-edition hardback, trade paperbacks, and e-book. **Royalty 40% on download; 7% on print. Pays nominal advance.** Accepts unagented submissions. Responds to queries in 30 days, full ms in 90 days. Considers reprints but accepts few. E-mail submissions only; see website for submission form and procedure.

Fiction: Query via submission form on website. Interested in series ideas. Submissions must be Christian romance.

WINGSPREAD PUBLISHERS, 2020 State Road, Camp Hill PA 17011. (717) 761-7047. Fax: (717) 761-7273. Facebook: WingSpread Publishers. Website: www.echurchdepot.com. Parent company: Zur Ltd. Pamela Brossman, ed. Publishes 5 titles/yr. Receives 50 proposals/yr. 75% from first-time authors. Accepts books submitted by agents. Does print-on-demand. Prefers 200 pages. **Royalty 10% based on retail.** E-books 25%. Average first printing 1,000. Publication in 18 mos. Considers simultaneous submissions. Responds to proposals in 6 mos. Catalog free on request, guidelines by e-mail. Accepts freelance photos for book covers. Looking for Christian living, spiritual growth.

Nonfiction: Query letter only first. Accepts fax/e-mail queries. Requires mss by e-mail.

Tips: "We are the authorized publisher and copyright owner of books by A. W. Tozer. We prefer to carry on this tradition by publishing books of deeper Christian life."

WORTHY PUBLISHING GROUP, 134 Franklin Road, Ste 200, Brentwood TN 37027. (615) 932-7600. Website: http://www.worthypublishing.com. Imprints: Worthy Publishing, Freeman-Smith, Ellie Claire. Publishes 36 titles/yr. Requires submission by agents. Hardcover, trade paperbacks, digital. Offers advance. Guidelines on website. Unsolicited mss returned unopened.

Fiction: Adult

WRITE INTEGRITY PRESS, 130 Prominence Point Pkwy., #130-330, Canton GA 30114. (678) 493-9330. E-mail: editor@writeintegrity.com. Websites: www.WriteIntegrity.com and www.PixNPens.com. Tracy Ruckman, ed. Imprints: Write Integrity Press, Pix-N-Pens Publishing. Publishes 10-18 titles/yr. Receives 300+ proposals/yr. 80% from first-time authors. Accepts books submitted by agents. Does print-on-demand. Trade, mass-market, digital. Does reprint out-of-print books. **Royalty based on net.** Publication in 6 mos. Responds in 6 wks. Guidelines on website.

Nonfiction: Query letter only first. E-mail queries only.

Fiction: Strong preference for contemporary fiction, mystery/suspense, others that don't fit a formula. We don't publish traditional historical novels, but we are open to novels set from the 1940s to present. Query letter only first.

Tips: "Be professional. Be courteous. Have a website and social media presence. Write Integrity Press publishes clean, wholesome entertainment. Pix-N-Pens Publishing is our evangelical imprint, and each book will carry a strong gospel message."

WRITE NOW PUBLICATIONS, PO Box 110390, Nashville TN 37222. Toll-free (800) 21-WRITE. E-mail: RegAForder@aol.com. Website: www.writenowpublications.com. Reg A. Forder, exec. ed. To train and develop quality Christian writers; books on writing and speaking for writers and speakers. Royalty division of ACW Press. Publishes 1-2 titles/yr.; trade paperbacks. Receives 6 submissions annually. 0% from first-time authors. Accepts mss through agents or authors. Reprints books. **Royalty 10% of net.** Average first printing 2,000. Publication within 12 mos. Considers simultaneous submissions. Requires requested ms on disk. No guidelines/catalog.

Nonfiction: Writing how-to only. Query letter only; e-query OK.

YALE UNIVERSITY PRESS, PO Box 209040, New Haven CT 06520-9040. (203) 432-6807. Fax (203) 436-1064. E-mail: jennifer.banks@yale.edu. Website: www.yalebooks.com. Jennifer Banks, ed. Publishes scholarly and general-interest books, including religion. Publishes 15 religious titles/yr.; hardcover, trade paperbacks. Receives 1,000 submissions annually. 10% of books from first-time authors. Accepts mss through agents or authors. **Royalty from 0% to standard trade royalties; advance $0-100,000.** Publication within 1 yr. Considers simultaneous submissions. Requires requested ms on hard copy; no e-mail submissions. Responds in 2 mos. Guidelines/catalog on website (www.yalebooks.com).

Nonfiction: Query or proposal/sample chapters; fax query OK; no e-query. "Excellent and salable scholarly books."

***ZONDERKIDZ,** 5300 Patterson S.E., Grand Rapids MI 49530-0002. (616) 698-6900. Fax (616) 698-3578. E-mail: zpub@zondervan.com. Website: www.zonderkidz.com. Zondervan/ HarperCollins. Children's book line of Zondervan; ages 12 & under. Not currently accepting proposals.

This publisher serviced by ChristianManuscriptSubmissions.com.

***ZONDERVAN,** General Trade Books; Academic and Professional Books, 5300 Patterson S.E., Grand Rapids MI 49530-0002. (616) 698-6900. Manuscript submission line: (616) 698-3447. E-mail through website: www.zondervan.com. HarperCollins Publishers. Mission is to be the leading Christian communications company meeting the needs of people with resources that glorify Jesus Christ and promote biblical principles. Publishes 120 trade titles/yr.; hardcover, trade paperbacks, mass-market paperbacks. Few books from first-time authors. Accepts mss through agents or authors. No subsidy or reprints. **Royalty 12-14% of net; variable advance.** Publication within 12-18 mos. Considers simultaneous submissions. Requires requested ms by e-mail. Prefers NIV. Guidelines on website (under "About Us"/"Manuscript Submissions"); catalog online.

Nonfiction: Submissions only by e-mail and only certain types of mss. See website for e-mail address and submission guidelines.

Fiction: No fiction at this time; refer to website for updates.

Special Needs: Currently accepting unsolicited book proposals in academic, reference, or ministry resources only (see guidelines).

Children's Lines: ZonderKidz and Faithgirlz (not currently accepting new products).

Ethnic Books: Vida Publishers division: Spanish and Portuguese.

Tips: "Almost no unsolicited manuscripts are published. Book proposals should be single-spaced with one-inch margins on all sides."

This publisher serviced by ChristianManuscriptSubmissions.com and The Writer's Edge.

3

Subsidy Publishers

A subsidy publisher requires that the author pay for any part of the publishing costs. They may call themselves by a variety of names, such as book packager, cooperative publisher, self-publisher, or simply someone who helps authors get their books printed. Print-on-demand (POD) businesses print books in quantities as few as one at a time and usually much faster than traditional publishers. Custom publishers develop new authors to eventually work with royalty publishers.

My own Christian Writers Guild has added subsidy publishing to our services (see our listing), but we require an education component—a course called *Published*. There are cheaper ways to get your book published, so you'll want to evaluate whether you want to go to the expense of getting the best, top-quality help at every stage of the process.

To my knowledge the following subsidy publishers are legitimate (as opposed to simply being out to take your money and offering little in return), but I cannot guarantee that. Any time you pay for any part of the production of your book, you are entering into a nontraditional relationship. Some subsidy publishers do some royalty publishing, so you could approach them as a royalty publisher. They are likely to offer you a subsidy deal, so if you are interested only in a royalty arrangement, indicate that in your cover letter.

Some subsidy publishers will publish any book, as long as the author is willing to pay for it. Others are as selective about what they publish as a royalty publisher would be. As subsidy publishers become more selective, the professional quality of subsidy books is improving.

It has been my experience that for every complaint I get about a publisher, several other authors sing the praises of the same publisher. All I can do is give a brief overview of what to expect from a subsidy publisher and what terms should raise a red flag.

If you are unsuccessful placing your book with a royalty publisher but feel strongly about seeing it published, a subsidy publisher can make printing your book easier and often less expensive than doing it yourself.

Get more than one bid to determine whether the terms you are being offered are competitive. A legitimate subsidy publisher will provide a list of former clients as references. Get a catalog of the publisher's books to check the quality of their work, the covers, bindings, etc. See if their books are available through Amazon.com or similar online services. Get answers before committing yourself. Also have someone in the book publishing industry review your contract before you sign it. Some experts listed in the Editorial Services section of this book review contracts. The listings that follow include printers who could help you complete the printing process yourself.

The more copies of a book printed, the lower the cost per copy. But never let a publisher talk you into more copies than you think is reasonable. Also, some subsidy publishers will do as much promotion as a royalty publisher; others do none at all. If the publisher is not doing promotion and you don't have any means of distribution, you may prefer print-on-demand so you don't end up with a garage full of books you can't sell.

Definitions of different types of publishers:

Commercial/Mainstream/Traditional Publisher: One who takes all the risks and pays all the costs of producing and promoting your book (see previous book section).

Vanity Publisher: Prints at the author's expense. Will print any book the author is willing to pay for. May offer marketing help, warehousing, editing, or promotion of some sort at the author's expense.

Subsidy Publisher: Shares the cost of printing and binding a book. Often more selective, but the completed books belong to the publisher, not the author. Author may buy books from the publisher and may also collect a royalty for books the publisher sells.

Self-Publishing: Author pays all the costs of publishing the book and is responsible for all the marketing, distribution, promotion, etc. Author may select a service package that defines the cost and services. The books belong to the author and he/she keeps all the income from sales. Following this section I include the names and addresses of Christian book distributors. Some will consider distributing a subsidy-published book. You may want to contact them to determine their interest before you sign a contract with a subsidy publisher. For more help on self-publishing, go to: www.bookmarket.com/index.html.

(*) before a listing indicates unconfirmed information or no information update.

ACW PRESS, American Christian Writers, PO Box 110390, Nashville TN 37222. Toll-free (800) 21-WRITE. E-mail: Jim@JamesWatkins.com. Website: www.acwpress.com. Reg A. Forder, owner; James Watkins, editorial advisor. A self-publishing book packager. Imprint: Write Now Publications (see separate listing). Publishes 40 titles/yr.; hardcover, trade paperbacks, mass-market paperbacks, coffee table books. Reprints books. SUBSIDY PUBLISHES 95%; does print-on-demand. Average first printing 200+. Publication within 2-4 mos. Responds within 8 hrs. Request estimate by sending number of words in ms to Jim@JamesWatkins.com. Not in topical listings; will consider any nonfiction, fiction, or poetry. Guidelines on website.

Nonfiction/Fiction/Poetry: All types considered.

Tips: "We offer a high-quality publishing alternative to help Christian authors get their material into print. High standards, high quality. If authors have a built-in audience, they have the best chance to make self-publishing a success." Has a marketing program available to authors.

This publisher serviced by ChristianManuscriptSubmissions.com.

***AMERICAN BINDING & PUBLISHING CO.,** PO Box 60049, Corpus Christi TX 78466-0049. Toll-free (800) 863-3708. (361) 658-4221. E-mail: rmagner@grandecom.net. Website: www.americanbindingpublishing.com. Rose Magner, pub. E-book publishing. Downloads only.

AMPELOS PRESS, 951 Anders Rd., Lansdale PA 19446. Phone/fax (484) 991-8581. E-mail: mbagnull@aol.com. Website: www.writehisanswer.com. Marlene Bagnull, LittD, pub./ed. Services (depending on what is needed) include critiquing, editing, proofreading, typesetting, and cover design. Publishes 1-3 titles/yr. SUBSIDY PUBLISHES 100%. Query only. Not included in topical listings (see Tips).

Special Needs: Books about missions and meeting the needs of children both at home and abroad.

Tips: "Our vision statement reads: 'Strongly, unashamedly, uncompromisingly Christ-centered. Exalting the name of Jesus Christ. Seeking to teach His ways through holding up the Word of God as the Standard.' (*Ampelos* is the Greek word for 'vine' in John 15:5.)"

***BELIEVERSPRESS,** 6820 W. 115th St., Bloomington MN 55438. Toll-free (866) 794-8774. E-mail: info@believerspress.com. Website: www.believerspress.com. A division of Bethany Press International. Submit through website. Funds global missions training with proceeds. Provides authors with a Christian team of A-list industry professionals to help them achieve their publishing goals. Offers professional packages and a la carte services to fit every budget. Authors are in full control and pay only for services they need. All work is work-for-hire. Includes editorial, typesetting, cover design, digital/conventional book printing and production, e-books, POD, distribution to trade, marketing/publicity, author e-store book sales, social media, and blog articles by industry professionals.

***BIOGRAPHICAL PUBLISHING CO.,** 95 Sycamore Dr., Prospect CT 06712-1493. (203) 758-3661. Fax (305) 768-0261. E-mail: biopub@aol.com. Website: www.biopub.co.cc. John R. Guevin, ed. Provides services to get books published and to help market and sell them. Publishes 1-4 religious titles/yr.; hardcover, trade paperbacks, digital. Receives 200 submissions annually. 75% of books from first-time authors. Accepts mss through agents. No print-on-demand. Reprints books. Prefers 50-500 pgs. **Author receives 95% of sales amount after expenses; no advance.** Average first printing 100-1,000. Publication within 2 mos. Considers simultaneous submissions. Responds in 1 wk. Guidelines by mail/e-mail/website; free catalog.

Nonfiction: Query letter only first. Most open to topical issues.

Fiction: Query letter only first. Any genre.

Photos/Artwork: Accepts freelance photos for book covers; open to queries from freelance artists.

BK ROYSTON PUBLISHING LLC, PO Box 43321, Jeffersonville IN 47131. (502) 802-5385. E-mail: bkroystonpublishing@gmail.com. Website: www.bkroystonpublishing.com. Julia A. Royston, ed. The focus of the BK Royston Publishing LLC are books that inform, inspire, and entertain. Imprints: Everyday Miracles, Frontline Worshipper, How Hot Is Your Love Life, 30 Lessons That the Student Taught the Teacher, Yield, All New Season in Word. Publishes 5-10 titles/yr. Receives 20 mss/yr. 95% first-time authors. Prefers books submitted by agents. SUBSIDY PUBLISHES 10%. Print-on-demand. Hardcover, trade, mass-market, digital. **Royalty 30-50% based on net. Pays for e-books.** First printing 50. Publishes in 6-10 mos. Considers simultaneous submissions. Responds in 1 mo. Guideline by e-mail. Accepts freelance photos for covers. Open to queries from freelance artists. Prefers KJV.

Nonfiction: Query letter only first. Accepts phone queries and e-mail queries. Mss by e-mail.

Fiction: All genres. Query letter only first.

Tips: Need children's books.

BOOKLOCKER.COM INC., 5726 Cortez Road W. #349, Bradenton FL 34210. (305) 768-0261. fax (305) 768-0261. E-mail: angela@booklocker.com. Website: www.booklocker.com. Angela Hoy, pub. We seek unique, eclectic, and different manuscripts. Publishes 400 titles/yr.; hardcover, trade paperbacks, e-books. 70% of books from first-time authors. No mss through agents. SUBSIDY PUBLISHES 100%; does print-on-demand. Reprints books. Prefers 48-1050 pgs.; less for children's books. **Royalty 35% on retail (15% on wholesale orders; 35% on booklocker.com orders; 50-70% for e-books); no advance.** Publication within 4-6 wks. Considers simultaneous submissions. Responds in less than a week. Bible version is author's choice. Guidelines on website; no catalog.

Nonfiction: Complete ms; e-query OK. "We're open to all unique ideas."

Fiction: Complete ms; e-query OK. All genres for all ages.

Ethnic Books: Publishes for all ethnic groups.

Photos/Artwork: Uses stock photos or author-supplied photos/artwork.

Contest: The WritersWeekly.com 24-Hour Short Story Contest is held quarterly.

***BROWN BOOKS PUBLISHING GROUP,** 16250 Knoll Trail Dr., Ste. 205, Dallas TX 75248. (972) 381-0009. Fax (972) 248-4336. E-mail: publishing@brownbooks.com. Website: www.brownbooks.com. Publishes books in the areas of self-help, religion/inspirational, relationships, business, mind/body/spirit, and women's issues; we build relationships with our authors. Imprints: Personal Profiles, The P3 Press. Publishes 150 titles/yr.; hardcover, trade paperbacks, coffee table books. Receives 4,000 submissions annually. 70% of books from first-time authors. No mss through agents. SUBSIDY PUBLISHES 100% through Personal Profiles & P3 imprints. **Royalty 100% of retail; no advance.** Authors retain rights to their work. Average first printing 3,000-5,000. Publication in 6 mos. Accepts simultaneous submissions. Responds in 2 wks. Requires mss on disk or by e-mail. Responds in 2 wks. Guidelines on website.

Nonfiction: Complete ms; phone/e-query preferred.

Fiction: Complete ms; phone/e-query OK. For all ages.

Tips: "We publish all genres with an emphasis on business, self-help, children's, and general Christian topics."

CARPENTER'S SON PUBLISHING, 307 Verde Meadow Drive, Franklin TN 37067. (615) 472-1128. Fax (615) 472-1128. E-mail: larry@christianbookservices.com. Website: www.carpentersson publishing.com. Parent Co: Christian Book Services, LLC. Imprint: Carpenter's Son Publishing. Larry Carpenter, pres./CEO, ed. Publishes 100 mss/yr. Receives 300 mss/yr. 90% first-time authors. Accepts books submitted by agents. SUBSIDY PUBLISHER. 100% subsidy. Print-on-demand. Hardcover, trade, mass-market, digital. Does reprint. All sizes mss. **Author receives 63% of net revenue.** Avg. first print 1,000-10,000. Publication within 9 mos. Considers simultaneous submissions. Responds in 1 week. Ads: charge $350 for half-page ad/$600 for full-page ad. Guidelines by mail or e-mail. Accepts freelance photo for book cover. Accepts all topics. Open to queries from freelance artists.

Nonfiction: Complete mss. Phone/e-mail queries. Accepts mss by e-mail.

Fiction: Complete mss. Phone/e-mail queries. Accepts mss by e-mail.

This publisher serviced by ChristianManuscriptSubmissions.com

CHRISTIAN SMALL PUBLISHERS ASSOCIATION (CSPA), PO Box 481022, Charlotte NC 28269. (704) 277-7194. Email: cspa@christianpublishers.net. Website: www.christianpublishers.net. CSPA is an organization for small publishers producing materials for the Christian marketplace. We help small publishers (including those who self-publish) market their books.

CHRISTIAN WRITERS GUILD PUBLISHING, 5525 N. Union, Ste. 101, Colorado Springs CO 80918. (719) 495-5177. Fax: (719) 495-5181. E-mail: contactus@ChristianWritersGuild.com. Website: http://www.CWGPublishing.com. Imprint: CWGP. Offers print-on-demand. Trade, digital. Does reprint out-of-print books. Prefers up to 75,000 wds. Offers service packages and a la carte services. No minimum number of books. No markup costs. Packages: http://cwgpublishing.com/publishing-packages/. Publishes e-books. Distributes books. No royalties. Offers discounted payment plans. Publishes in 6 mos. Responds in one week. Guidelines on website. Prefers proposal with first 5 pages for fiction and nonfiction. Accepts phone, fax, e-mail queries. Requires mss via e-mail. No freelance artists. We match you with a published author who will come alongside and walk you through our Published course, showing you how to turn your manuscript into a book that will keep readers turning the pages. In addition, our team of publishing veterans will edit, proof, design, cover, and produce your book to the highest quality standards.

CREATION HOUSE, 600 Rinehart Rd., Lake Mary FL 32746-4872. (407) 333-0600. Fax (407) 333-7100. E-mail: creationhouse@charismamedia.com. Website: www.creationhouse.com. Charisma Media. Submit to Acquisitions Editor. To inspire and equip people to live a Spirit-led life and to walk in the divine purpose for which they were created. Publishes 125 titles/yr.; hardcover, trade paperbacks, mass-market paperbacks, coffee table books. Receives 1,500 submissions annually. 80% of books from first-time authors. Accepts mss through agents. Reprints books. Prefers 25,000+ wds. or 100-200 pgs. **Royalty 12-15% of net; no advance.** Average first printing 2,000. Publication within 2-4 mos. Considers simultaneous submissions. Responds in 10-12 wks. Open to submissions on disk or by e-mail. Guidelines by mail/e-mail; free catalog.

Nonfiction: Proposal/complete ms; no phone/fax query; e-query OK. "Open to any books that are well written and glorify Jesus Christ."

Fiction: Proposal/complete ms; no phone/fax query; e-query OK. For all ages. "Fiction must have a biblical worldview and point the reader to Christ."

Photos: Accepts freelance photos for book covers.

Tips: "We use the term copublishing to describe a hybrid between conventional royalty publishing and self- or subsidy publishing, utilizing the best of both worlds. We produce a high-quality book for our own inventory, market it, distribute it, and pay the author a royalty on every copy sold. In return, the author agrees to buy, at a deep discount, a portion of the first print run."

CREDO HOUSE PUBLISHERS, 3148 Plainfield Ave. NE, Ste. 111, Grand Rapids MI 49525-3285. (616) 363-2686. E-mail: connect@credocommunications.net. Website: www.credohousepublishers .com. A division of Credo Communications LLC. Timothy J. Beals, pres. Works with Christian ministry leaders and organizations to develop life-changing books, Bible-related products, and other Christian resources. CUSTOM PUBLISHER. Publishes 10-12 titles/yr. Publication within 60-90 days. Average first printing 1,000. Guidelines on website. Not included in topical listings.

Nonfiction/Fiction: Complete online author survey.

***CROSSHOUSE PUBLISHING,** 2844 S. FM 549, Suite A, Rockwall TX 75032. Toll-free (877) 212-0933. Fax (877) 212-0933. E-mail: sales@crosshousepublishing.org or through website: www.cross housepublishing.org. Self-publishing branch of KLMK Communications. Dr. Katie Welch, pub. To achieve excellence in Christian self-publishing without sacrificing personal interest and care for customers. Publishes hardcover, trade paperbacks. No mss through agents. SUBSIDY PUBLISHER. **Royalty 25% on net; no advance.** Publication within 3 mos. Guidelines on website (under "Downloads").

Nonfiction/Fiction: Accepts fiction for all ages.

Photos: Accepts freelance photos for book covers.

Tips: "We provide authors the opportunity to have their books distributed through a wide array of Christian and general bookstores. We aspire to offer the marketplace superior Christian literature that will impact readers' lives."

***DCTS PUBLISHING,** PO Box 40276, Santa Barbara CA 93140. (805) 570-3168. E-mail: dennis@ dctspub.com. Website: www.dctspub.com. "For authors who want quality low-cost publishing, we will partner with you in producing a fantastic marketable book that will sell anywhere in the world. Please contact me for more details." Dennis Stephen Hamilton, ed. Books are designed to enrich the mind, encourage the heart, and empower the spirit. Publishes 5 titles/yr. Receives 25 submissions annually. 35% of books from first-time authors. No mss through agents. SUBSIDY PUBLISHES 70%. No reprints. Prefers 100-300 pgs. **Royalty 17% of retail; no advance.** Average first printing 3,500. Publication within 6-8 mos. No simultaneous submissions. Prefers KJV. Guidelines by mail; free catalog/brochure.

Nonfiction: Query or proposal/2-3 chapters; e-query OK.

***DEEP RIVER BOOKS** (formerly VMI Publishers), 26306 Metolius Meadows Dr., Camp Sherman OR 97730. E-mail: bill@deepriverbooks.com, nancie@deepriverbooks.com. Website: www.deepriver books.com. Bill and Nancie Carmichael, pubs. Partnering with new authors. Publishes 35 titles/yr.; hardback, trade paperbacks, coffee table books. Receives hundreds of submissions annually. 90% of books from first-time authors. Accepts mss through agents. No reprints. Prefers 45,000+ wds. or 192-400 pgs. **Royalty 12-18% of net; no advance.** CUSTOM PUBLISHER; see website for details. Average first printing 2,500+. Publication within 9-12 mos. Considers simultaneous submissions. Requires accepted ms by e-mail. Responds in 2 mos. Guidelines on website.

Nonfiction: Query first by e-mail only; proposal/2-3 chapters.

Fiction: Query first by e-mail only; proposal/2-3 chapters. For all ages. "Anything Christian or inspirational that is well written, especially from new authors."

Tips: "Go to our website first, and read how we partner with new authors. Then, if you feel Deep River Books would be a good fit for you, e-mail your proposal."

This publisher serviced by ChristianManuscriptSubmissions.com.

DESTINY IMAGE PUBLISHERS, PO Box 310, Shippensburg PA 17257. Toll-free (800) 722-6774. (717) 532-3040. Fax (717) 532-9291. E-mail: rrr@destinyimage.com or through website: www .destinyimage.com. Mykela Krieg, exec. acq. asst. To help people grow deeper in their relationship with God and others. Accepts mss through agents or authors. Prefers 40,000-60,000 wds. Publication within 12 mos. Considers simultaneous submissions. Send unsolicited mss via book proposal and listed e-mail address. Guidelines on website.

Tips: "Most open to books on the deeper life, or of charismatic interest."

EKKLESIA PRESS, 1401 S. 64th Ave., Omaha NE 68106. Cell(402) 416-4068. E-mail: tim@ekklesiapress.com or through website: http://ekklesiapress.com. Timothy L. Price, ed. Imprint: Trestle Press. Publishes 10+ titles/yr. Receives 25+ mss/yr. 75% from first-time authors. Accepts books submitted by agents. Does publish from freelance authors. Hardcover, trade, digital. Reprints out-of-print books. Prefers 25,000-70,000 wds for nonfiction. Can print 48-720 pgs per volume. Payment a la carte, accepts payments, determined by author's needs/wants. No minimum number of books. Add markup costs to printing, less than industry standard. Publishes e-books. Does not distribute yet. Author receives 78% of distribution royalties, paid quarterly. Services offered: editing, dynamic cover design, marketing/branding, typesetting, screenplay conversion, e-book conversion, audiobook production, limited run, four-color separation printing, exclusive viral promotion, printing and distribution on three continents, consulting, video production, video interviews of authors edited and hosted on YouTube, and payment plans. Response time 2-6 mos. Responds in 15 days. All books entered into Ingram Advance. Guidelines: http://ekklesiapress.com/submission-requirements. Accepts photos for book covers. Looking for Kingdom of God and church as a counterculture books. Query letter, submissions of complete mss. E-mail queries. Require mss by e-mail. Story should challenge reader's perspective of reality and normative religious acceptabilities. Open to queries from freelance artists. We publish disconcerting works that challenge religious lethargy and establishment perspectives, in order for believers to become ambassadors (non-belonging people) who can realize their giftings and callings and be able to have them refined and watered in fellowships where everyone is ministering and working alongside variations in voicing and capability equal effectiveness and inclusion.

ESSENCE PUBLISHING CO. INC., 20 Hanna Ct., Belleville ON K8P 5J2, Canada. Toll-free (800) 238-6376, ext. 7110. (613) 962-2360. Fax (613) 962-3055. E-mail: info@essence-publishing.com. Website: www.essence-publishing.com. David Visser, mng. ed.; Sherrill Brunton, publishing mgr., (s.brunton@essence-publishing.com). Provides affordable, short-run book publishing to mainly the Christian community; dedicated to furthering the work of Christ through the written word. Imprints: Essence Publishing, Guardian Books, Epic Press. Epic Press is reserved for non-Christian books such as biographies, cookbooks, text books, history books, etc.). Publishes 100-150+ titles/yr.; hardcover, trade paperbacks, mass-market paperbacks, coffee table books. Receives 250+ submissions annually. 75% of books from first-time authors. Accepts mss from agents or authors. SUBSIDY PUBLISHES 100%. Does print-on-demand. Reprints books. Any length. Completes books in other languages. **Royalty. 50% from bookstore and e-books, no advance.** Average first printing 500-1,000. Publication within 3 mos. Considers simultaneous submissions. Responds in 2 wks. Prefers requested ms on disk or by e-mail. Bible version is author's choice. Free publishing guide by mail/e-mail; catalog online (www.essencebookstore.com); and international distribution available. E-books available with listings on Kindle, Apple, and KOBO.

Nonfiction: Complete ms; phone/fax/e-query OK. Accepts all topics.

Fiction: Complete ms. All genres for all ages. Including full-color children's picture books.

Also Does: Pamphlets, booklets, tracts, and posters.

Photos/Artwork: Accepts freelance photos for book covers; open to queries from freelance artists.

***FAIRWAY PRESS,** subsidy division for CSS Publishing Company, 5450 N. Dixie Hwy., Lima OH 45807-9559. Toll-free (800) 241-4056. (419) 227-1818. E-mail: david@csspub.com or through website: www.fairwaypress.com. David Runk, ed. (david@csspub.com); submit to Attn: Sales Representative. Imprint: Express Press. Publishes 30-50 titles/yr. Receives 200-300 submissions annually. 80% of books from first-time authors. Reprints books. SUBSIDY PUBLISHES 100%. **Royalty to 50%; no advance.** Average first printing 500-1,000. Publication within 6-9 mos. Considers simultaneous submissions. Responds in up to 1 mo. Prefers requested ms on disk; no e-mail submissions. Prefers NRSV. Guidelines on website ("Submit Your Manuscript"); catalog for 9 x 12 SAE.

Nonfiction: Complete ms; phone/fax/e-query OK. All types. "Looking for manuscripts with a Christian theme, and seasonal material."

Fiction: Complete ms. For adults, teens, or children; all types. No longer producing anything in full color or with four-color illustrations.

***FAITH BOOKS & MORE,** 3255 Lawrenceville-Suwanee Rd., Ste. P250, Suwanee GA 30024. (678) 232-6156. E-mail: publishing@faithbooksandmore.com. Website: www.faithbooksandmore.com. 100% custom publishing. Nicole Smith, mng. ed. Imprints: Faith Books & More; Friends of Faith, Corporate Connoisseur, or custom imprint for author branding. Publishes 100 titles/yr; hardcover, trade paperbacks, and e-books. Receives 200 submissions annually. 90% of books from first-time authors. Accepts mss through agents or authors. SUBSIDY PUBLISHES 50%; does print-on-demand and offset. Reprints books. Any length; no less than 4 pages. **Royalty; no advance.** Publication within 2 mos. Considers simultaneous submissions. Responds in 1 mo. Prefers NKJV or NIV. Guidelines by e-mail/website; no catalog.

Nonfiction: Complete ms; phone/e-query OK. Any topic.

Fiction: Complete ms; phone/e-query OK. Any genre, for all ages.

Photos/Artwork: Accepts freelance photos for book covers; considers queries from freelance artists.

FOR THE MASTER PUBLICATIONS, 400 Mission Ct., St Louis MO 63130. (314) 608-6489. E-mail: inquiry@forthemaster.com. Website: www.ForTheMaster.com. Van Sharpley, pub. Self-publishing. Adviser for first-time authors regarding budget and marketing. Full service pre-publication (editing and formatting) through printing and distribution. *FTM gives the author a voice in every major decision.* See website for list of manuscripts we accept and statement of theological review. Response within 24 hours.

Printer: Dickinson Press, Inc.

Distributor: Advocate Distribution Solutions

FRUITBEARER PUBLISHING LLC, PO Box 777, Georgetown DE 19947. (302) 856-6649. Fax (302) 856-7742. E-mail: cfa@candyabbott.com or through website: www.fruitbearer.com. Candy Abbott, mng. partner. Offers editing services and advice for self-publishers. Publishes 5-10 titles/yr.; hardcover, picture books. Receives 10-20 submissions annually. 90% of books from first-time authors. SUBSIDY PUBLISHES 100%. No reprints. Average first printing 500-5,000. Publication within 1-6 mos. Responds in 3 mos. Guidelines by mail/e-mail; brochure for #10 SAE/1 stamp.

Nonfiction: Proposal/2 chapters; phone/fax/e-query OK.

Fiction: For all ages.

Also Does: Pamphlets, booklets, tracts.

Photos: Accepts freelance photos for book covers.

Tips: "Accepting limited submissions."

***GRACE ACRES PRESS,** PO Box 22, Larkspur CO 80118. (303) 681-9995. Fax (303) 681-9996. E-mail: info@GraceAcresPress.com. Website: www.GraceAcresPress.com. Grace Acres, Inc. Anne R. Fenske, ed./pub. A conservative publisher with an emphasis on dispensational theology. Publishes 4-6 titles/yr.; hardcover, trade paperbacks, digital. Receives 50-100 submissions annually. 80-90% of books from first-time authors. Accepts mss through agents or authors. SUBSIDY PUBLISHER. Reprints books. **Royalty 10-15% on net; no advance.** Average first printing 1,500-2,500. Publication within 6 mos. Considers simultaneous submissions. Responds in 3 mos. Guidelines by e-mail; free catalog.

Nonfiction: Query first; e-query OK. Requires accepted mss on disk.

Artwork: Open to queries from freelance artists.

Tips: "Most open to a book with a built-in audience/buyer; i.e., speaker, textbook."

HALO PUBLISHING INTL., 1031 Cherry Spring, AP #726, Houston TX 77038. (877) 705-9647. E-mail: contact@halopublishing.com. Website: www.halopublishing.com. www.facebook.com

/HaloPublishing. Twitter: @halopublishing. V. S. Grenier, chief ed. Publishes unique subject matter. Publishes 200 titles/yr.; hardcover, trade paperbacks. Receives 600-1,000 submissions annually. 89% of books from first-time authors. **Royalty 95%; no advance.** Publication within 2 mos. Considers simultaneous submissions. Responds in 3 wks. Guidelines by e-mail/website; no catalog.

Nonfiction: Proposal/3 chapters; phone/e-query OK.

Fiction: Proposal/3 chapters; phone/e-query OK. For all ages.

Special Needs: Educational books.

Artwork: Open to queries from freelance artists.

HEALTHY LIFE PRESS, 2603 Drake Drive, Orlando FL 32810. E-mail: HealthyLifePress@aol.com. Website: www.HealthyLifePress.com. Blog: www.davebiebel.com. Evangelical, nondenominational. David Biebel, pub. Imprint: Healthy Life Press. We see health as a verb . . . a dynamic sum of one's wellness in all areas at any given time. Helping people toward greater is our goal. Helping previously unpublished authors with something important to contribute to this field to market brings significant satisfaction to us. Keeping worthy books that fit our focus in print is also important to us. Publishes 6-10 titles/yr. Receives 20 mss/yr. 80% first-time authors. Accepts books submitted by agent. SUBSIDY PUBLISHER. 60% subsidy. Print-on-demand EXCLUSIVELY. Trade, mass-market, digital. Does reprint out-of-print books. Prefers 120-220 pgs. **Royalty of 50% based on net. E-books 50% of net.** Outright purchase option. Author purchase: 50-60% off retail (plus S&H), depending on contract terms. Print-on-demand, shipped direct from distributor. Publishes in 6-8 mos. Responds in 1 month. Catalog free on request. Guidelines on website. Accepts freelance photos for book covers. Always looking for books in the interface of the Christian faith and health, as viewed from a holistic perspective (physical, emotional, relational, spiritual).

Nonfiction: Query letter first. Book proposal with 3 sample chapters. E-mail queries. Require mss by e-mail.

Fiction: Prefers romance, mystery, allegory. Query letter first. Book proposal with 3 sample chapters.

Tips: "Well-written, edited, and ready for design manuscripts on a topic within our purview that the author is passionate about, and about which he/she is able to provide a new, different, unique, original perspective."

LIFE SENTENCE PUBLISHING, 404 N. 5th St., Abbotsford WI 54405. (715) 223-3013. E-mail: info@lifesentencepublishing.com. Website: www.lifesentencepublishing.com. Jeremiah Zeiset, acct. mgr. Imprints: Life Sentence Publishing, ANEKO Press, Launch! We especially wish to publish books for ministries/missionaries. Publishes 36-48 titles/yr. Receives 75 proposals/yr. 60% first-time authors. Accepts books submitted by agents. 25% SUBSIDY PUBLISHER. 50% print-on-demand. Hardcover, trade, mass-market, coffee table books, digital. Reprints out-of-print books. Prefers 100,000 wds or 150-200 pgs. **ROYALTY 25-40% based on net. E-books 25% based on net.** No advance. Average first printing 1,000 offset or 50 POD. Publishes within 3 mo. Considers simultaneous submissions. Responds quarterly. Charges for catalog. Guidelines by mail. Accepts freelance photos for covers. Open to queries from freelance artists.

Nonfiction: Complete mss. Accepts phone queries.

Fiction: Christian or Christian themed only. All ages. Complete mss.

Tips: "Seeing a lot of submissions about the gospel (explaining salvation or the Bible). We publish all books, provided they aren't contrary to our knowledge of salvation by faith, and they must be well written. It's preferable that the author has an existing platform. Our Christian authors know from the moment they hand over their manuscript, we'll bring glory to God by paying attention to each and every detail of the publishing process, because we do more than simply put books in print. Our authors are sharing the gospel worldwide."

***MARKETINGNEWAUTHORS.COM,** 2910 E. Eisenhower Pkwy., Ann Arbor MI 48108. Toll-free (800) 431-1579. (734) 975-0028. Fax (734) 973-9475. E-mail: info@marketingnewauthors.com or MarketingNewAuth@aol.com. Website: www.MarketingNewAuthors.com. Imprint of Robbie Dean Press. To primarily serve authors who wish to self-publish. Dr. Fairy C. Hayes-Scott, owner. 100% of books from first-time authors. Accepts mss through agents. SUBSIDY PUBLISHES 100%. Reprints books. Length flexible. Publication within 6 mos. Considers simultaneous submissions. Responds in 2-6 wks. Guidelines by e-mail/website (under "Self-Publishing with MANA"). Offers 7 different marketing plans; see website.

MYSTICAL ROSE, PO Box 13, Warrenton VA 20188. (540) 364-2841. Fax 1-888-965-7955. E-mail: query@mysticalroseinspirations.com. Website: www.mysticalroseinspirations.com. Blog: www.mysticalroseinspirations.com/blog-preludes-to-peace.html. Tamara Amos/CEO, ed. Mystical Rose specializes in presenting fresh perspectives and new solutions that pertain to our present time and culture using inspirational, humorous, and creative methodology. Accepts books submitted by agents. SUBSIDY PUBLISHER. Print-on-demand. Hardcover, trade, mass-market, coffee table books, digital. Reprints out-of-print books. Considers simultaneous submissions. Responds in 1 mo. Guidelines on website. Accepts freelance photos for covers. Open to queries from freelance artists.

Nonfiction: Proposal with 2 sample chapters. E-mail queries. Accepts mss by e-mail.

Fiction: Proposal with 2 sample chapters. We are looking for fresh voices that bring new perspectives to modern issues, convey wisdom without being preachy, and use creative, humorous, inspiring, and entertaining methods. We are also looking for fiction pertaining to ADD/ADHD and learning disabilities.

Also Does: Educational materials, greeting cards, inspirational, and humorous merchandise.

Tips: "Multidimensional educational resources, right-brained educational resources; books and resources pertaining to ADD/ADHD; insightful books that are well written and entertaining."

***PORT HOLE PUBLICATIONS,** 179 Laurel St., Florence OR 97439. (541) 902-9091. E-mail: info@ellentraylor.com. Website: www.portholepublications.com. Ellen Traylor, ed./pub. A COOPERATIVE PUBLISHER requiring a financial investment on the part of the author, along with a standard contract and optional marketing package.

Nonfiction/Fiction: Query first.

Tips: "We are open to publishing family-friendly and/or Christian content books of any length or genre. We are especially open to thought-provoking books on being a Christian in this difficult world, terrific fiction, Christian philosophy, short-story collections, and poetry (no sermons, please)."

RECOVERY COMMUNICATIONS INC., PO Box 19910, Baltimore MD 21211. (410) 243-8352. Fax (410) 243-8558. E-mail: tdrews3879@aol.com. Website: www.GettingThemSober.com. Toby R. Drews, ed. Publishes 4-6 titles/yr. No mss through agents. SUBSIDY PUBLISHER. Prefers 110 pgs. **Co-op projects; no royalty or advance.** Average first printing 5,000. Publication within 9 mos. Excellent nationwide distribution and marketing in bookstores. Send for their free information packet.

Nonfiction: Query only.

Tips: "Although technically we are a subsidy publisher, we are more of a hybrid publisher in that we give the author enough free books to sell in the back of the room to totally recoup all the money they have paid; plus we share 50/50 on net sales at bookstores. Over half of our authors have gotten their money back and made a great profit. We are also aggressive in our pursuit of catalog sales and foreign rights sales (we recently sold to a German publisher). We also individually coach all of our authors, at no cost to them, to help them successfully obtain speaking engagements."

***THE SALT WORKS,** PO Box 37, Roseville CA 95678. (916) 784-0500. Fax (916) 773-7421. E-mail: books@publishersdesign.com. Website: www.publishersdesign.com. Division of Publishers Design Group Inc. Robert Brekke, pub.; submit to Project Manager. Seeks to demonstrate through books that God is sovereign, just, and merciful in all he does. Imprint: Salty's Books (children's—see separate listing), PDG, Humpback Books. Publishes 7-10 titles/yr.; hardcover, trade paperbacks, coffee table books. Receives 100+ submissions annually. 90% of Christian books from first-time authors. No mss through agents. SUBSIDY PUBLISHES 95%. Offset and print-on-demand. Reprints books. Prefers 95,000-150,000 wds. **Rarely pays royalty of 7-12% on net; occasional advance.** Average first printing 1,500-5,000. Publication within 4-12 mos. Considers simultaneous submissions. Responds within 45 days. Prefers ESV/NASB/NKJV/NIV (in that order). Prospects must study publisher's website labeled "Custom Publishing" along with all five case studies before contacting. After preliminary screening, prospect will be sent a Project Questionnaire and a Project Assessment will be performed for projects with strong concepts.

Nonfiction: E-query only first; after query & phone meeting, send proposal. Unsolicited mss returned unopened.

Fiction: E-query only first; after query & phone meeting, send proposal. Unsolicited mss returned unopened. For adults and children. "Looking for titles that help believers in exploring and facing common issues surrounding God's sovereignty, his grace and forgiveness, their own sin and idolatry, and the areas where pop culture has influenced the church. Characters are blatantly human."

Special Needs: Looking for titles that communicate a biblical Christian worldview without promoting overly simplistic, idealistic, or theoretical solutions to life's biggest questions; books that honestly show no timidity in addressing our humanness. Looking for manuscripts that demonstrate that society's problems are rooted in the personal and spiritual, not in the political, educational, moral, and financial realms.

Also Does: Board games and other specialty products: fitness products, art projects and products, interactive projects for children. Specializes in projects designed to build a person or organization into a brand in the marketplace. See publisher's "MarketByPublishing.com" division for details.

Photos/Artwork: Rarely accepts freelance photos for book covers; open to queries from freelance artists.

Tips: "Most open to books that look at the Christian experience through a realistic biblical and Reformed perspective. Books that address the Christian's real problems as a 'heart' problem—not a theological problem; not from a victim mind-set, not a mental or logical one; not from a perspective of merely needing another program, pep talk, or the latest rehash of formulas for victorious living. Books that show the author understands that unless God changes the heart and brings a person to repentance, there are no real and lasting answers."

This publisher serviced by ChristianManuscriptSubmissions.com.

***SALVATION PUBLISHER AND MARKETING GROUP,** PO Box 40860, Santa Barbara CA 93140. (805) 682-0316. Fax (call first). E-mail: opalmaedailey@aol.com. Wisdom Today Ministries. Opal Mae Dailey, ed-in-chief. We encourage, inspire, and educate; author has the choice to be involved as much or little as desired—which gives the opportunity to control income; personal coaching and collective marketing available. Publishes 5-7 titles/yr.; hardcover, trade paperbacks, mass-market paperbacks. 60% of books from first-time authors. No mss through agents. SUBSIDY PUBLISHES 80%; does print-on-demand. Reprints books. Prefers 96-224 pgs. Average first printing 1,000. Publication within 3-4 mos. No simultaneous submissions. Accepts requested ms on disk or by e-mail (not attachments). Responds in 1 mo. Prefers KJV. Guidelines (also by e-mail).

Nonfiction: Query only first; phone/fax/e-query OK.

Tips: "Turning taped messages into book form for pastors is a specialty of ours. We do not accept any manuscript that we would be ashamed to put our name on."

***STONEHOUSE INK,** (208) 514-6631. E-mail: stonehousepress@hotmail.com. Website: www.stonehouseink.net. Clean-fiction imprint of Ampelon Press (www.ampelonpublishing.com). Aaron

Patterson, ed./pub. Specializing in thrillers, mystery, young adult, paranormal, and out-of-print titles. Find on Facebook and Twitter @StoneHouseInk.

***STRONG TOWER PUBLISHING,** PO Box 973, Milesburg PA 16853. E-mail: strongtowerpubs@aol .com. Website: www.strongtowerpublishing.com. Heidi L. Nigro, pub. Specializes in eschatology and books that challenge readers to think more deeply about their faith and scriptural truths; must be biblically responsible, doctrinally defensible, and consistent with their statement of faith. Publishes 1-2 titles/yr.; trade paperbacks. 50% of books from first-time authors. No mss through agents. Reprints books. PRINT-ON-DEMAND 100%. **Royalty 25% of net; no advance.** Average first printing 50. Publication within 3-4 mos. Guidelines/information/prices on website.

Nonfiction: Query. Eschatology.

Tips: "We recommend that all first-time authors have their manuscripts professionally edited. We will consider putting first-time authors into print, but by invitation only. That invitation comes only after the manuscript has been thoroughly evaluated and we have discussed the pros and cons of our unique on-demand publishing model with the author."

TRESTLE PRESS, 1401 S. 64th Ave., Omaha NE 68106. Cell (402) 416-4068. E-mail: TPSubmissions@outlook.com. Website: http://trestlepress.net/. Parent Company: Ekklesia Press. Timothy L. Price, ed. Publishes 14+ titles/yr. Receives 75+ titles/yr. 35+ first-time authors. Accepts books submitted by agents. Publishes books from freelance authors. Hardcover, trade, coffee table books, digital. Reprints out-of-print books. Prefers 25,000-75,000 wds. for nonfiction. 60,000-110,000 wds. for fiction. Can print from 48 pgs. to 720 pgs. per volume. Payment: a la carte, and we accept payments. Tailor programs to author's needs/wants. No minimum number of books with package. Does add markup costs, less than industry standard. Publishes e-books, does not distribute yet. Author receives 78% of distribution royalties, paid quarterly. Services offered: editing, dynamic cover design, marketing/branding, typesetting, screenplay conversion, e-book conversion, audiobook production, limited run, four-color separation printing, exclusive viral promotion, printing and distribution on three continents, consulting, video production, video interviews of authors edited and hosted on YouTube, and payment plans.

TRUTH BOOK PUBLISHERS, 824 Bills Rd., Franklin IL 62638. (217) 675-2191. (217) 675-2050. E-mail: truthbookpublishers@yahoo.com. Website: www.truthbookpublishers.com. JaNell Lyle, ed. Publishes 75 titles/yr. Receives 100 submissions annually. 75% of books from first-time authors. Accepts mss through agents. Prefers 360 pgs. Average first run 100-500. Publication within 2 mo. Responds within 2 weeks. Guidelines by e-mail/website.

Nonfiction: Send book proposal with 3 sample chapters.

Fiction: Send book proposal with 3 sample chapters.

Tips: "We are missionary minded and desire to help the body of Christ mature."

WESTBOW PRESS, 1663 Liberty Dr., Bloomington IN 47403. Toll-free (866) 928-1240. Website: www.westbowpress.com. Subsidy division of Thomas Nelson Publishers. Kevin A. Gray, news media contact. Estab. 2009. A Christian self-publishing company that provides author services to help them fulfill their dream of becoming a published author. Fill out online form to receive information on their publishing program. Guidelines on website (click on "FAQ").

WINEPRESS PUBLISHING, 1730 Railroad St., Enumclaw WA 98022. Toll-free (800) 326-4674. (360) 802-9758. Fax (360) 802-9992. E-mail: acquisitions@winepresspublishing.com. Website: www.winepresspublishing.com. Blog: http://blog.winepresspublishing.com. Follow us: facebook .com/winepresspublishing, twitter.com/WinepressPub. Produces both print-on-demand and offset books, with distribution and marketing services. Publishes all family-friendly and/or biblically oriented material and genres, spanning all ages. Also offers these services: audiobooks, e-books, multimedia, website design and hosting, blogs, DVD production, CD/book packages, manuals, genuine-leather Bibles, full-color children's books, board books, full publicity and marketing campaigns, book trailers, marketing consultation, blog and social network consultations, and advertising campaigns. 100% net profit on print-on-demand sales. 80% net royalty on offset and e-books.

Tips: "WinePress reviews and provides free feedback on manuscripts prior to acceptance and welcomes your submission."

***WORD ALIVE PRESS,** 131 Cordite Rd., Winnipeg MB R3W 1S1, Canada. Toll-free (866) 967-3782. (204) 777-7100. Toll-free fax (800) 352-9272. (204) 669-0947. E-mail: publishing@wordalivepress.ca. Website: www.wordalivepress.ca. C. Schmidt, publishing consultant. SUBSIDY PUBLISHER. Offset printing, print-on-demand, editing services, sales, marketing and distribution services, website development, professional custom cover design, Adobe and Kindle e-books, audiobooks, and MP3 book files. Guidelines and price list available. Request their "Free Guide to Publishing" brochure from their website.

Nonfiction/Fiction: All genres. Fiction for all ages.

***ZOË LIFE PUBLISHING,** 9282 General Dr., Suite 150, Plymouth MI 48170. (734) 254-1043. Fax (734) 254-1063. E-mail: info@zoelifepub.com. Website: www.zoelifepub.com. Zoë Life Industries LLC. Sabrina Adams, ed. Books that help people live better, more productive lives while growing closer to God. Imprints: Pen of a Ready Writer, Titus, Business Builders. Publishes 40 titles/yr.; hardcover, trade paperbacks, mass-market paperbacks, coffee table books, digital. 50+% of books from first-time authors. Accepts mss through authors or agents. SUBSIDY PUBLISHES 50%; no print-on-demand or reprints. Length open. **Royalty 10-25% of net; usually no advance.** Average first printing 3,000. Publication within 12 mos. Responds in 21-40 days. Open on Bible version. Guidelines by e-mail/website; free catalog.

Nonfiction: Proposal/ 3 chapters + final chapter; phone/fax/e-query OK.

Fiction: Proposal/ 3 chapters + final chapter; phone/fax/e-query OK. For all ages; all genres. Complete mss for picture books.

Special Needs: Children's books, tweens, women's issues, Bible studies, and Christian living.

Photos: Accepts freelance photos for book covers.

SUPPLIERS TO SELF-PUBLISHING AUTHORS

***BOOK COVER & INTERIOR DESIGN SERVICES,** PO Box 1382, Running Springs CA 92382. (909) 939-0311. E-mail: info@lionsgatebookdesign.com. Website: www.lionsgatebookdesign.com. Call/e-mail. Has 35 yrs exp. in prof. graphic design, art direction, and advertising. Works with new and seasoned authors, providing personal attention and custom design. Book cover packages range from $395-$650. Custom interior designs compliment book cover designs and range from $3-$5/pg. See portfolios on website. Free consultation.

***BOOK PROMOTION & MARKETING MATERIALS,** PO Box 1382, Running Springs CA 92382. (909) 939-0311. E-mail: info@lionsgatebookdesign.com. Portfolio: www.lionsgatebookdesign.com. Call/e-mail. Has 35 yrs exp. in prof. graphic design, art direction, and advertising for national accounts. Products designed, printed, and delivered include bookmarks, postcards, promotional business cards, posters, banners, retractable signs for book signings, conferences, and events, and more. Logo design and website design are also available. Free consultation.

Note: Please see chapter 10: Editorial Services for your editorial needs.

4

Distributors

CHRISTIAN BOOK/MUSIC/GIFT DISTRIBUTORS

AMAZON ADVANTAGE PROGRAM, Go to Amazon.com, scroll down to "Features & Services," click on "Selling with Amazon," and on the drop-down menu, click on "Advantage Program" in left-hand column. This is the site to contact if you want Amazon to distribute your book.

***B. BROUGHTON CO., LTD.,** 322 Consumers Rd., North York ON M2J 1P8, Canada. Toll-free (800) 268-4449 (Canada only). (416) 690-4777. Fax (416) 690-5357. E-mail: sales@bbroughton.com. Website: www.bbroughton.com. Brian Broughton, owner. Canadian distributor. Distributes books, DVDs, gifts, greeting cards. Does not distribute self-published books.

CBA MAILING LISTS OF CHRISTIAN BOOKSTORES, 9240 Explorer Dr., Ste. 200, Colorado Springs CO 80920. (719) 265-9895. Fax (719) 272-3510. E-mail: info@cbaonline.org. Website: www.cbaonline.org. Contact: info@cbaonline.org. Available for rental. Three different lists available, including nonmember stores, 4,700 addresses ($249); member stores, 1,275 addresses ($599); or a combined list of all stores, 5,800 addresses ($699). Prices and numbers available subject to change. Call toll-free (800) 252-1950 for full details.

CHRISTIAN BOOK DISTRIBUTORS, PO Box 7000, Peabody MA 01961-7000. Toll-free (800) 247-4784. (978) 977-5000. Fax (978) 977-5010. E-mail through website: www.christianbooks.com. Does not distribute self-published books.

MCBETH CORP., Fulfillment and Distribution Headquarters, PO Box 400, Chambersburg PA 17201. Toll-free (800) 876-5112. (717) 263-5600. Fax (717) 263-5909. E-mail: mcbethcorp@supernet .com. Distributes Christian gifts, boxed cards, and napkins.

***QUALITY BOOKS,** 1003 W. Pines Rd., Oregon IL 61061. Toll-free (800) 323-4241. (815) 732-4450. Fax (815) 732-4499. E-mail: publisher.relations@quality-books.com. Website: www.quality books.com. Distributes small press books, audios, DVDs, CD-ROMs, and Blu-ray to public libraries. Distributes self-published books; asks for 1 copy of your book.

***WORD ALIVE, INC.,** 131 Cordite Rd., Winnipeg MB R3W 1S1, Canada. Toll-free (800) 665-1468. (204) 667-1400. Toll-free fax (800) 352-9272. (204) 669-0947. E-mail: orderdesk@wordalive.ca. Website: www.wordalive.ca. Distributor of Christian books and products into the Canadian market. Contact: Rosa Peters. Contact by e-mail.

BONUS SECTION

Writer's Helps

Discipline

Debunking a Myth

by Jerry B. Jenkins

NAYSAYERS WILL TELL YOU that if you want to get rich, do something other than write.

It may seem disingenuous for one who has, in essence, hit the lottery to tell you why you should buy a ticket.

But forget 63 million copies of Left Behind series titles sold in a decade. Before that tidal wave rolled in, I was already making a good living as a full-time freelance writer. My annual income was in six figures, and my wife and I were going to be able to pay off our home and put our three sons through college.

Why? Because I was never one to be cowed by statistics, bleak as they might be. Nielsen BookScan says the average book published in the United States currently sells fewer than 250 copies a year and fewer than 3,000 overall. Of the 1.2 million titles BookScan tracked in 2004 (during publishing's heyday), 950,000 sold fewer than 99 copies. Only 25,000 sold more than 5,000 copies.

If those numbers set you back on your heels, freelance writing may not be the game for you. But if you're the type who hunkers down and works, who reads and studies and grows, determined to hone your craft and defy the odds, you can be among the few who make more than a living at writing.

If you were drawn to writing partly because so few succeed at it, you can be the one who excels. Give yourself wholly to your art, and be the one. Be the one.

This originally appeared in the September 2010 issue of *Writer's Digest*.

Your Own Writing Miracle

by Sandra P. Aldrich

I'M LESS THAN TWO CHAPTERS from finishing my latest project. Though this is my nineteenth book, it feels as though I'm trying to pull my own wisdom teeth.

I want the scenes to flow easily from my brain, through my fingers, and onto the computer screen. I want the transitions to appear without my creating them. I want the historical details to be precise without having to double check.

In other words, I want a miracle. I want this book to write itself. There! That whine felt good.

Needing Help

Of course, I invite the Lord into each work—page by page. But it also helps to remember the healing of the ten lepers in Luke 17. As Jesus encountered the lepers "at a distance," they called to him, "Jesus, Master, have mercy on us!" (vs. 12-13, NLT)

Jesus said, "Go show yourselves to the priests" (vs. 14, NLT)

If I had been one of those lepers, I would have raised my hand. "Uh, Lord, I know how this is supposed to work. First, you heal me, *and then* I go show myself to the priests."

I'm glad none of the lepers had my mind-set. The rest of verse 14 contains seven powerful words: "And as they went, they were healed." They didn't hang around and debate healing. They didn't take two steps and say, "Well, that didn't work." They just started their journey and were healed.

Step by Step

Books are written as we write. Words appear as we type. As we check historical details, new scenes present themselves. We can't take one course, attend one conference, and then—because we don't see the six-figure royalty check—give up. Keep on the journey.

I wish writing were as easy as my relatives think it is. I wish I could find a computer to read my mind, write the scenes, then edit them. I wish I could sleep late, stroll into my office, and miraculously produce five thousand words before the morning news is over.

But just as the lepers had to take action, so must I.

This previously appeared on the Christian Writers Guild blog: www.christianwritersguild.com/blog/your-own-writing-miracle/.

What Are You Waiting For?

by Lindsey A. Frederick

"Success depends upon previous preparation. Without such preparation there is sure to be failure."—CONFUCIUS

FOR ONCE MY FORTUNE COOKIE GOT IT RIGHT.

What are you doing to prepare for success? Honing your skills? Building relationships? Researching markets?

Or are you, as I was, waiting for something? Perhaps inspiration, or opportunity, or confidence? I needed accountability. So I enrolled in the Christian Writers Guild course *Articles that Sell.* For six months, every two weeks, I had a deadline. Discipline? Check! Here are a few things I learned.

Show Up

Some days, scrubbing toilets or changing your car's oil may seem more exciting than sitting down to write. You may be tempted to succumb to distraction or even declare "writer's block." Whether or not the words come easily, writing is like any other job: you don't get paid unless you show up.

Set Goals

Author Jack London followed a strict regimen of one thousand words a day. Set manageable yet still challenging goals. If it helps, make your goals visible. Find a word, phrase, or picture that represents your goal and put it in your workstation as a reminder.

Fill Your Tank

The only thing created in a vacuum is a pile of lint. So look outside yourself. What inspires you? Maybe it's a walk in the park, a chat with a friend, or a brainstorming session with your writers group. I find help in my inspiration box. I've filled it with quotes, stories, ideas, chocolates, and teas—all of which inspire and motivate me. When I'm running on empty, I peek in my box.

Stay a Student

You've put every dot and dash into place and released your baby into the world. Now you're anxious. What will your work look like when your editor gets to it? My Christian Writers Guild mentor splashed my pages with highlighter and comments and helped me improve my skills. She never told me I was *wrong*; she told me how I could be *better*. In the process, she taught me to work with an editor.

Surround Yourself

At some point you will hear something you don't like. Maybe it's tough criticism. Maybe it's rejection. You might get discouraged and question your commitment. Combat this by surrounding yourself with people who know you well. They will remind you who you are and what God created you to do.

You can have all the ideas and ambitions in the world, but unless you sit down to develop them, they're just floating dreams. Don't wait.

This previously appeared on the Christian Writers Guild blog: www.christianwritersguild.com/blog/what-are-you-waiting-for/.

What to Feed a Writer

by Virelle Kidder

I RECENTLY ASKED A NEW WRITER, "What do you read?"

"Read?" she said. "There's no time! I barely have time to write."

I read every day for two hours before I go to bed. I read my Bible first, then something else, usually a novel. If you don't read, you're starving yourself as a writer.

Necessity

Words are my food. After writing all day, I look forward to a smorgasbord of great books. As the Bible feeds my soul, good literature feeds my mind and heart. I can't live without either.

Variety of Diet

I have a friend who creates an annual list of books he wants to read: classics and children's books he missed growing up, current literature in various genres, theology, biographies, and selections from the *New York Times* Best Sellers List. On a cardboard bookmark he lists around seventy books a year. He reads only about half of them, but he has a list. I average a book a week.

Acquired Tastes

Stories teach, mold our thinking, and impart language styles and emotions we may never otherwise experience. Reading makes me hunger to learn more. It even alters my path.

Over the years, I've switched from reading mainly nonfiction to mostly fiction. How I wish I'd done that sooner! What I once considered made-up stories now widen my vision from the flat screen to 3-D—complete with surround sound.

Soon I hungered to write a murder mystery of my own. Now it's nearing completion. The experience has recharged me as a writer and opened dreams for more novels.

My new writer friend has also caught the hunger for well-seasoned words and has begun to nibble; she's looking healthier already.

This previously appeared on the Christian Writers Guild blog: www.christianwritersguild.com/blog/what-to-feed-a-writer/.

Just Write: Building Stories out of Writer's Block

by Matthew Koceich

HAVE YOU EVER BEEN SITTING THERE, waiting for the perfect *New York Times* bestseller idea—but your muse is silent and your well of creativity is drier than the Sahara?

I learned a great lesson during my Christian Writers Guild *Craftsman* residency. Jerry B. Jenkins reminded us that as writers we are not called to make excuses. Especially, the biggie: writer's block. I'm a schoolteacher. What would my principal say if I called in one day and said, "I'm not coming to work today because I have teacher's block!"?

Where Do I Begin?

That blank pad of paper or computer screen can be intimidating. But I need to just jump in and write. I pick one of my characters and begin writing a paragraph where they are doing something related to the plot.

Where Do I Go?

I must admit, I have AWD: Attention Writing Disorder. When I finally get started on my day's writing, my brain starts coming unglued. I check e-mail, Facebook, even the dog's food bowl. All while the cursor blinks and blinks. But, "I will not make excuses. I will just write and make stories!"

I found a strategy that works for me. I grab a legal pad and a pen. Let's say my writing goal is 1,000 words. I write the number 100 on the first line, another 100 on the second line, and so on until I have 10 lines numbered with 100. Next to each 100, I make a note about what I will write about. I repeat until my mini-outline is complete. Then I write the first hundred and reward myself by crossing out the first line. This helps me stay on task, and I get quick satisfaction as I meet the mini-goals.

Where Do I End?

Don't look for your worth in the outcome. Write the story God has placed in your heart. Enjoy the journey. As you write, remember that your real identity is who you are in Christ. His grace is enough—not a published novel.

If you ever find yourself on the corner of Writer's Block and Main, take a write. From there, you'll be well on your way to building a great story!

This previously appeared on the Christian Writers Guild blog: www.christianwritersguild.com/blog/just-write-building-stories-out-of-writers-blocks/.

Overcoming Writer's Isolation

by Jennifer E. Lindsay

A WRITER FRIEND AND I were corresponding. She was struggling with her current manuscript and finding it difficult to continue. She'd been getting in some productive writing time, but was feeling discouraged. I recognized her symptoms. It wasn't writer's block; she was wrestling with something far worse. I call it writer's isolation.

Writing is largely a solitary pursuit. We lock ourselves away in our offices, turn on our favorite playlist, and cut ourselves off from this world. This comes with a price. Writing requires focus, dedication, passion, and a dream that those who aren't writers cannot fully understand. While family and friends may offer tremendous support, they struggle to relate to the frustrations that come from hours alone at the keyboard.

Finding Colleagues

I've met many of my writing companions during my time as a Christian Writers Guild Craftsman and at various Writing for the Soul Conferences. I belong to a local critique group. I've also found a community of writers through Twitter and Facebook. We rarely, if ever, meet in person. But just knowing we're on similar journeys goes a long way in forming a bond. We encourage each other, brainstorm, applaud accomplishments, and swap stories about our real lives, which reminds us why we chose this path: to inspire others and ourselves.

Scripture affirms that Christians, regardless of their craft, are never meant to undertake life's journey alone. "Two are better than one, because they have a good return for their work: If one falls down, his friend can help him up. But pity the man who falls and has no one to help him up!" (Ecclesiastes 4:9-10, NIV).

If you're struggling with writer's isolation, don't drop your pen in despair. Seek out a fellow writer who can help you through whatever is dragging you down. But most importantly, remember God's greatest promise: "I am with you always" (Matthew 28:20, NLT).

You are never alone.

This previously appeared on the Christian Writers Guild blog: www.christianwritersguild.com/blog/overcoming-writer%E2%80%99s-isolation/.

Day-to-Day Writing

by Bill Myers

In America, few writers make a full-time living. Many don't because they lack the discipline to write every day.

My schedule may sound luxurious, but it works for me. See what you can apply to your writing.

Get in the Groove

After reading the Bible and praying for a while (usually forty-five minutes), I begin writing—hopefully by 9 a.m. Actually, I begin rewriting. The scene that was brilliant yesterday reeks today.

Rewriting is how I sneak up on actual writing. Staring at a blank screen terrifies me. If I tell myself I'm just going to tinker with what already exists, it's easier to start.

Get It Written, No Matter What

After a couple of hours I take a break, sometimes a walk, sometimes a junk food raid. Once my head has cleared (or my waistline grown), I return for another two-hour session.

The hard work comes after rewriting yesterday's work. Now it's time to create from scratch. I liken original writing to hoisting a lump of clay onto a potter's wheel. It's gross, clumsy, and ugly. But each time that critical voice inside screams I'm a failure, I tell it, "Leave me alone, I'm just getting it on the wheel. I'll fix it tomorrow."

Next is another break, lunch, and maybe a twenty-minute power nap.

Get It Perfect

Finally, my last two hours. I polish and rewrite what I wrote the day before and thought I'd fixed in today's first session. This is where the work finally starts to look fit for human consumption.

Get It to Work for You

You may not have the luxury of being a full-time writer. Regardless, the key is discipline. For five years my pal Frank Peretti worked in a ski factory by day and carved out time in the evenings to write. Frank didn't just dream about writing—he sucked it up and did it. He disciplined himself and created a schedule. He found what worked for him, stuck to it, and wrote.

You can too.

This previously appeared on the Christian Writers Guild blog: www.christianwritersguild.com/blog/day-to-day-writing/.

The Quality Time Myth

by Jerry B. Jenkins

MY WIFE AND I LONG AGO set a policy that prohibited me from bringing home any work from the office and from doing any writing from the time I got home from work until the time the kids went to bed. (Of course, sometimes we put them to bed at four thirty in the afternoon.)

Bottom line: no writing when the kids were at home and awake. This pushed my only available freelance writing time to late at night.

I had to rise early every day to get from the suburbs into Chicago, so I had to be in bed no later than midnight. That meant that during my three sons' early years, my writing window was roughly nine to midnight.

I'm not a night person, but I had no choice. It's amazing how much you can get done when you have only three-hour blocks.

Unexpected Benefits

I was more productive during those years, in terms of the number of pages produced and books published, than any time since—even after going freelance full time.

The major benefit to me as a writer? No guilt. I told my kids they were my top priority, and if I had made that a lie by always being busy when they were around, I'd have written under a burden of guilt.

Kids—and spouses—may hear what you say, but they believe what you do.

Maintain your priorities, and your work will benefit.

Too many parents fall for the myth of quality time. It goes like this: If you can't spend a lot of time with your kids, make sure the time you do spend is quality time.

But to kids, quality *is* quantity.

Invest the time, and they all get what they need.

Writing needs to be a high priority. But for as long as you have a family, writing should never be number one.

This previously appeared on Jerry Jenkins's personal blog: http://jerry-jenkins.com/2013/05/20/the-quality-time-myth-2/.

Tell (and Sell) Your Story in Five Hundred Words

by Karen O'Connor

"Write without pay until somebody offers to pay; if nobody offers within three years, sawing wood is what you were intended for."—MARK TWAIN

I STARTED THE PATH to publication more than thirty years ago, sure of one thing: I'd never make it as a woodcutter. My writing had to pay.

Within two years, I had collected checks for forty articles. There's no mystery to it. I simply lived, looked at life in a creative way, then wrote about what I saw, what I experienced, what I learned. Most of those pieces were shorter than five hundred words, what editors call fillers because they fill out a page in a magazine or a space on a website.

Finding Topics at Home

The most effective ideas come from my family, friends, and experiences. I jot down bits of dialogue, names, dates, places, lone facts that intrigue me, snappy titles, whatever catches my attention, no matter how unrelated it sounds.

Then I play with them until something clicks. One year my family decided to save money by having a staycation, a vacation at home. Each day we did something special that was fun and relaxing. I wrote about this in under five hundred words and sold it to the *Focus on the Family* online magazine.

Other fillers covered topics such as:

- the gift of a second chance after I wounded a neighbor with a thoughtless gesture
- my experience hiking to the top of Half Dome in Yosemite
- how my husband and I celebrate Thanksgiving all year long

Your Turn

Think about the life experiences you'd like to share. How about:

- something on prayer
- a lesson you learned through parenting
- overcoming grief
- the joy of simple living

I've written on all these, but that doesn't mean you can't also.

Start with a short anecdote and end with a take-away the reader can apply. Write and sell fillers and you'll never have to saw wood—unless you want to!

This previously appeared on the Christian Writers Guild blog: www.christianwritersguild.com/blog/tell-and-sell-your-story-in-500-words-or-fewer/.

Six Ways to Keep Writing (When You Feel like Quitting)

by Karen O'Connor

COOKIES. CANDY. COFFEE. Do you reach for them as easily as a paper clip, pen, or your style guide?

What you eat, how you exercise, and how long you sleep affect your ability to think, write, meet deadlines, and sustain a writing career. You may have the necessary office equipment, but be sure you don't neglect the most important piece—your health.

Wellness expert Solveig (soul-vay) Fuentes says we can achieve health "and hold onto it by taking care of ourselves in basic ways." Fuentes's "Simple Six" can make a difference in your creative life.

1. **Water.** Drink a tall glass (not tea, coffee, or juice) when you wake to lubricate your system. Then drink at least four ounces every hour. Keep a glass on your desk as a reminder.
2. **Exercise.** Choose one activity daily, such as walking, running, biking, or swimming. "Do what you enjoy!" Fuentes says.
3. **Food.** Select living foods—an apple or orange off the tree—when possible. Crunchy carrots from a farm stand. Fresh salads. Skip the chips and dip. They put you down when you want to be up.
4. **Affirmations.** Personalize your favorite Scriptures and recite those. "For God so loved me that he . . ."
5. **Supplements.** "Unfortunately our food doesn't deliver all the nutrients we need," Fuentes says. "We can all use help from quality supplements."
6. **Sleep.** It's underrated! Fuentes claims a short nap can do wonders to refresh your mind. Many people are chronically tired—even too tired to enjoy time off.

Six simple suggestions can lead to healthy results in your life and in your writing career.

This previously appeared on the Christian Writers Guild blog: www.christianwritersguild.com/blog/six-ways-to-keep-writing-when-you-feel-like-quitting/.

Just Write It

by Andy Scheer

HAVE YOU WRITTEN ANYTHING TODAY? Will you?

Late science fiction writer Ray Bradbury said, "Quantity produces quality. If you only write a few things, you're doomed."

Trumpeter Lu Watters, who sparked a revolution in jazz in the 1940s, saw his career deferred when he answered his country's call to arms. But he did what he could during the war to prepare to launch a reconstituted band in peacetime.

Serving aboard a slow transport, the SS *Antigua,* bound for Hawaii, he forced himself to engage in what became his most productive period as a composer.

> Every day, just to get away from everything . . . I went to the bow of the ship . . . and I wrote a tune a day. Some of them weren't very good, and . . . of course I knew this. . . . Once in a while you get a wild inspiration and you outline a tune, and if you have any sense after that initial stage you'll play around with it a little bit, but anyway I wrote one a day.

And thanks to Watters's postwar band and other bands, many of those tunes became traditional jazz standards.

Notice the consecutive dates that Watters, at the bow of the SS *Antigua,* wrote these tunes:

"Annie Street Rock"—September 10, 1944
"Sage Hen Strut"—September 11, 1944
"Antigua Blues"—September 12, 1944
"Big Bear Stomp"—September 13, 1944
"Hambone Kelly"—September 14, 1944

To write something good, you have to write something. To avoid mistakes, false starts, and material you'll have to discard, don't write anything.

Post this acronym in your work space: FOKSIC

Fingers on keyboard, seat in chair.

This previously appeared on the Christian Writers Guild blog: www.christianwritersguild.com/blog/just-write-it/.

Maybe I Can Do This

by Andy Scheer

THE ASSIGNMENT CAME OUT of the blue. Would I write a week's worth of devotions?

I'd never written any, let alone seven. But the editor said the Scripture passages had already been selected. And I'd have nine weeks.

So I said yes. I took the provided template, pasted in each day's Scripture portion, then read and reread each one—looking for verses to serve as daily springboards. At last I highlighted seven verses and generated seven catchy titles. Then I set it aside in the face of more comfortable projects.

Get Started

Time ran out. Before noon on Tuesday, I sent the publisher the novel I'd just finished editing. After lunch I'd have to start writing devotions.

So I did. I reviewed the samples and the outlines I'd sketched. For the first devotion, I'd clipped a newspaper article to serve as a starter. I struggled through the piece, a constant eye toward the word count.

Now the second one: What will I write? But as I set my fingers to the keyboard, the ideas and the words came—like the oil from the widow's cruse as long as she kept pouring. By suppertime, I had two completed devotions. *I think I can do this.*

Expect Interruptions

Wednesday I planned to complete two in the morning and two more after lunch. But that morning the phone rang. A client wanted me to write an article for her by tomorrow afternoon. Several e-mails later, I got an extension until late next week.

Nearly 10 a.m. Could I write two devotions before lunch? By the grace of God I did. Then one after lunch, even with some errands. I planned to stop, but decided to peek at the next key verse. *Of course! That's what I'll write.* Almost before I knew it, I had another 205 words polished and saved.

The Words Will Come

This morning I had just one more to write. Again an illustration popped into mind—one I'd been reflecting on without realizing its connection to this passage. Done!

Until now I've seen Luke 12:11-12 as applying only to believers who face persecution: "Do not worry about how you will defend yourselves or what you will say, for the Holy Spirit will teach you at that time what you should say" (NIV).

I'll be the last one to claim inspiration for my work. But I'm learning that when I admit my inadequacies, then apply myself to the writing opportunities God brings, the words will come.

This previously appeared in the December 2012 Christian Writers Guild *WordSmith* newsletter.

Writer's Block vs. Submission Block

by PeggySue Wells

AFTER PITCHING their beloved projects to editors and agents at a writers conference, many writers leave their appointments thrilled to have been told, "Send that to me. I'd like to take a look at it." But editors report that many times, they never see the projects they invite writers to send.

There are writers who submit their work for sale—and those who don't. The difference between pros and pretenders is determined by who takes the next step.

Opportunities Missed

While some claim writer's block, professionals insist it doesn't really exist.

"A professional writer doesn't wait for inspiration any more than a professional plumber does," says John Erickson, author of over sixty *Hank the Cowdog* books. "A professional plumber knows you don't lay a pipe uphill or in frozen ground, but he lays that pipe. Professional writers write. I write four hours a day, seven days a week because I'm fanatical. It's what I do."

Batter Up

Are your projects stuffed in a drawer or stored in a computer? Submission block is like a batter who refuses to swing. Opportunities zip past.

What are you afraid of? Rejection? Success? Both?

Even a rejection proves you are in the game. A "no, thank you," is not the same as someone calling your baby ugly. It is a step closer to connecting with the agent or publisher who shares your passion for the project. It is valuable feedback. Behind a "no" are generally three plays:

- The piece does not fit the purpose of the publisher. If you've mistakenly tried to sell your novel to a publisher of nonfiction books, that's on you.
- The publisher has similar projects already in store. That's just an issue of timing.
- Your writing needs improvement. That's also on you.

Get in the Game

If submission block is keeping you out of the game:

- Tell a friend you will submit on or before a specific date, then follow through. No excuses.
- Submit only your best work after studying the publisher's guidelines.
- Express eagerness to be a team player. Be coachable, willing to revise.
- Like athletes, writers improve with practice. Every time you submit, you take a swing at the ball.
- If you receive a "send it to me" from an editor, don't sit on it. Submit it as soon as you can. Don't let the opportunity zip by.

This previously appeared on the Christian Writers Guild blog: www.christianwritersguild.com/blog/writer%E2%80%99s-block-vs-submission-block/.

PART 2

Periodical Publishers

5

Topical Listings of Periodicals

Study the periodicals in the primary/alphabetical listings (as well as their writer's guidelines and sample copies) and select the most likely targets for the piece you are writing.

Most ideas can be written for more than one periodical if you slant them to the needs of different audiences. Have a target periodical and audience in mind before you start writing. Each topic is divided by age group/audience.

If the magazine requires a query letter, write that first, and then follow their suggestions if they give you a go-ahead to write the article.

APOLOGETICS

ADULT/GENERAL

Bible Advocate
Brink Magazine
CBN.com
Celebrate Life
Christianity Today
Christian Online
Christian Ranchman
Christian Research
Christian Standard
Columbia
Halo Magazine
Live
Lookout
Manna
Movieguide
On Mission
Our Sunday Visitor
Perspectives
Priscilla Papers
Seek

CHILDREN

SHINE brightly

DAILY DEVOTIONALS

Brink Magazine
Penned from the Heart

MISSIONS

Studio

PASTORS/LEADERS

Christian Century
Enrichment
Small Groups.com

TEEN/YOUNG ADULT

Boundless Webzine
Young Salvationist

ARTS/ENTERTAINMENT

ADULT/GENERAL

Genuine Motivation
Guide

CHILDREN

Guide

PASTORS/LEADERS

Brink Magazine

TEEN/YOUNG ADULT

Genuine Motivation
Single! Young Christian Woman
Sisterhood

WOMEN

Single! Young Christian Woman

BEAUTY/FASHION

ADULT/GENERAL

Genuine Motivation
Guide
Halo Magazine

CHILDREN

Guide

TEEN/YOUNG ADULT

Genuine Motivation
Single! Young Christian Woman
Sisterhood

WOMEN

Single! Young Christian Woman

BIBLE STUDIES

ADULT/GENERAL

CBN.com
Christian Online
Christian Ranchman
Christian Research
Christian Standard
Church Herald & Holiness
Columbia
Eternal Ink
Gem
Halo Magazine
Highway News
Kyria
Lutheran Journal
Mature Years
Our Sunday Visitor
Perspectives
Priscilla Papers
Seek
War Cry

CHILDREN

SHINE brightly

PASTORS/LEADERS

Group Magazine
Sharing the Practice
SmallGroups.com

WOMEN

Virtuous Woman

BOOK EXCERPTS

ADULT/GENERAL

CBN.com
Charisma
Chicken Soup Books
Christianity Today
Christian Retailing
Columbia
Genuine Motivation
Indian Life
New Heart
Power for Living
Priscilla Papers

CHRISTIAN EDUCATION/ LIBRARY

Journal/Adventist Ed.

PASTORS/LEADERS

Christian Century
Ministry Today

TEEN/YOUNG ADULT

Boundless Webzine
Genuine Motivation
Single! Young Christian Woman

WOMEN

Share
Single! Young Christian Woman
Virtuous Woman

WRITERS

Freelance Writer's Report
Writer

BOOK REVIEWS

ADULT/GENERAL

America
Brink Magazine
CBN.com
Charisma
Christian Courier/ Canada
Christianity Today
Christian Journal
Christian Ranchman
Christian Research
Christian Retailing
Eternal Ink
Faith Today
Genuine Motivation
Home Times
Indian Life
Movieguide
New Frontier
Our Sunday Visitor
Ozark
Penwood Review
Prairie Messenger
Priscilla Papers
Studio
Testimony
Time of Singing
Weavings

CHILDREN

SHINE brightly
Sparkle

CHRISTIAN EDUCATION/ LIBRARY

Church Libraries
Journal/Adventist Ed.

MISSIONS

Operation Reveille

PASTORS/LEADERS

Christian Century
Diocesan Dialogue
Enrichment
Leadership
Ministry Today
Sharing the Practice

TEEN/YOUNG ADULT

Boundless Webzine
Genuine Motivation
Single! Young Christian Woman

WOMEN

Christian Homeschool Moms
Dabbling Mum
Share
Single! Young Christian Woman
Virtuous Woman

WRITERS

Adv. Christian Writer
Christian Communicator
Fellowscript
Writer

CANADIAN/FOREIGN MARKETS

ADULT/GENERAL

Canada Lutheran
Canadian Lutheran
Christian Courier/ Canada
Creation
Faith Today
Indian Life
Living Light
Messenger
Prairie Messenger
Studio
Testimony

DAILY DEVOTIONALS

Rejoice!

WRITERS

Fellowscript

CELEBRITY PIECES

ADULT/GENERAL

Angels on Earth
Brink Magazine
CBN.com
Celebrate Life
Christian Journal
Christian Online
Christian Ranchman
Genuine Motivation
Guideposts
Home Times
Indian Life
Kindred Spirit
Living Light
Movieguide
Our Sunday Visitor
Power for Living
Priority!
War Cry

CHILDREN

SHINE brightly
Sparkle

PASTORS/LEADERS

Ministry Today

TEEN/YOUNG ADULT

Genuine Motivation
Single! Young Christian Woman
Young Salvationist

WOMEN

Single! Young Christian Woman
Virtuous Woman

WRITERS

Writer's Chronicle

CHRISTIAN BUSINESS

ADULT/GENERAL

Angels on Earth
Brink Magazine
CBA Retailers
CBN.com
Christian Courier/Canada
Christian News NW
Christian Online
Christian Ranchman
Christian Retailing
Evangel
Faith Today
Gem
Genuine Motivation
Guideposts
Home Times
Lookout
Manna
Our Sunday Visitor
Power for Living
War Cry

PASTORS/LEADERS

InSite

TEEN/YOUNG ADULT

Boundless Webzine
Genuine Motivation
Single! Young Christian Woman

WOMEN

Dabbling Mum
Single! Young Christian Woman
Virtuous Woman

CHRISTIAN EDUCATION

ADULT/GENERAL

America
Animal Trails
Celebrate Life
Christian Courier/Canada
Christian Examiner
Christian Home & School
Christianity Today
Christian News NW
Christian Online
Christian Ranchman
Christian Retailing
Christian Standard
Columbia
Eternal Ink
Faith Today
Gem
Genuine Motivation
Guide
Home Times
Live
Lookout
Manna
Movieguide
Our Sunday Visitor
Penned from the Heart
Perspectives
Presbyterians Today
RevWriter Resource
Seek
Testimony
War Cry

CHILDREN

Guide
JuniorWay
Sparkle

CHRISTIAN EDUCATION/LIBRARY

Journal/Adventist Ed.

PASTORS/LEADERS

Christian Century
Enrichment
Ministry Today
RevWriter Resource
SmallGroups.com

TEEN/YOUNG ADULT

Boundless Webzine
Genuine Motivation

WOMEN

Christian Homeschool Moms
Right to the Heart
Share

CHRISTIAN LIVING

ADULT/GENERAL

America
Angels on Earth
Bible Advocate
Brink Magazine
Canada Lutheran
Catholic New York
CBN.com
Celebrate Life
Charisma
Chicken Soup Books
Christian Courier/Canada
Christian Examiner
Christian Home & School
Christian Homeschool Moms
Christianity Today
Christian Journal
Christian Online
Christian Quarterly
Christian Ranchman
Christian Research
Christian Standard
Church Herald & Holiness
Columbia
Eternal Ink
Evangel
Faith Today
Fit Christian
Gem
Gems of Truth
Genuine Motivation
Guide
Guideposts
Halo Magazine
Highway News
Home Times
Indian Life
Keys to Living
Kyria
Leaves
Light & Life
Live

Lookout
Lutheran Digest
Lutheran Journal
Manna
Mature Living
Mature Years
Men of the Cross
New Heart
Our Sunday Visitor
Penned from the Heart
Pentecostal Evangel
Perspectives
Power for Living
Presbyterians Today
RevWriter Resource
Seek
Storyteller
SW Kansas Faith
Testimony
Vision
Vista
War Cry

CHILDREN
Focus/Clubhouse Jr.
Guide
JuniorWay
Pockets

DAILY DEVOTIONALS
Brink Magazine
Penned from the Heart

PASTORS/LEADERS
Christian Century
RevWriter Resource

TEEN/YOUNG ADULT
Boundless Webzine
Genuine Motivation
Single! Young Christian Woman
Young Salvationist

WOMEN
MomSense
P31 Woman
Right to the Heart
Share
Single! Young Christian Woman
Virtuous Woman
Women of the Cross

CHURCH GROWTH

ADULT/GENERAL
America
Christian Examiner
Christian News NW
Christian Online
Christian Quarterly
Christian Standard
Columbia
Evangel
Gem
Genuine Motivation
Live
Lookout
Our Sunday Visitor
Penned from the Heart
Presbyterians Today
Seek
Testimony

MISSIONS
Operation Reveille

PASTORS/LEADERS
Christian Century
Enrichment
Growth Points
Leadership
Ministry Today
Sharing the Practice

TEEN/YOUNG ADULT
Genuine Motivation
Single! Young Christian Woman

WOMEN
Share
Single! Young Christian Woman

CHURCH HISTORY

ADULT/GENERAL
America
CBN.com
Christian Online
Christian Standard
Columbia
Faith Today
Genuine Motivation
Guide
Halo Magazine
Leben
Lookout
Lutheran Journal
Movieguide
Our Sunday Visitor
Presbyterians Today
Priscilla Papers

DAILY DEVOTIONALS
Penned from the Heart

MISSIONS
Operation Reveille

PASTORS/LEADERS
Christian Century
Enrichment
Leadership
Sharing the Practice

TEEN/YOUNG ADULT
Boundless Webzine
Genuine Motivation

WOMEN
Share

CHURCH LIFE

ADULT/GENERAL
America
Bible Advocate
Canada Lutheran
CBN.com
Christian Home & School
Christianity Today
Christian Journal
Christian News NW
Christian Online
Christian Standard
Columbia
Eternal Ink
Evangel
Faith Today
Gem
Home Times
Leaves
Light & Life
Live
Lookout
Lutheran Journal
Our Sunday Visitor
Penned from the Heart
Pentecostal Evangel

Presbyterians Today
Priscilla Papers
RevWriter Resource
Seek
Testimony
War Cry

DAILY DEVOTIONALS
Penned from the Heart

PASTORS/LEADERS
Christian Century
Enrichment
Leadership
L Magazine
Ministry Today
Parish Liturgy
Priest
RevWriter Resource
Sharing the Practice

TEEN/YOUNG ADULT
Boundless Webzine

WOMEN
Share

CHURCH MANAGEMENT
ADULT/GENERAL
America
Canada Lutheran
Christian News NW
Christian Online
Christian Standard
Faith Today
Gem
Lookout
Our Sunday Visitor
Priscilla Papers

DAILY DEVOTIONALS
Penned from the Heart

PASTORS/LEADERS
Enrichment
Group Magazine
Growth Points
Leadership
Ministry Today
RevWriter Resource
Sharing the Practice

WOMEN
Share

CHURCH OUTREACH
ADULT/GENERAL
America
Bible Advocate
Canada Lutheran
CBN.com
Christian Home & School
Christian News NW
Christian Online
Christian Research
Christian Standard
Columbia
Eternal Ink
Evangel
Faith Today
Gem
Home Times
Light & Life
Lookout
On Mission
Our Sunday Visitor
Presbyterians Today
Priority!
Priscilla Papers
Seek
Testimony

CHRISTIAN EDUCATION/ LIBRARY
Journal/Adventist Ed.

PASTORS/LEADERS
Christian Century
Enrichment
Group Magazine
Growth Points
Leadership
Ministry Today
RevWriter Resource
Sharing the Practice
Small Groups.com

WOMEN
Share

CHURCH TRADITIONS
ADULT/GENERAL
America
Brink Magazine
Canada Lutheran
CBN.com
Celebrate Life
Christian Examiner
Christian Online
Christian Research
Christian Standard
Columbia
Eternal Ink
Faith Today
Gem
Halo Magazine
Light & Life
Lutheran Journal
Our Sunday Visitor
Perspectives
Presbyterians Today
Priscilla Papers
Testimony

DAILY DEVOTIONALS
Penned from the Heart

PASTORS/LEADERS
Christian Century
Leadership
L Magazine
Ministry Today
Parish Liturgy
Sharing the Practice

WOMEN
Share

CONTROVERSIAL ISSUES
ADULT/GENERAL
Animal Trails
Bible Advocate
Brink Magazine
Canada Lutheran
CBN.com
Celebrate Life
Christian Courier/Canada
Christian Examiner
Christian Home & School
Christianity Today
Christian Online
Christian Standard
Columbia
Eternal Ink
Faith Today
Genuine Motivation
Home Times
Indian Life
Light & Life
Live

Lookout
Manna
Movieguide
Now What?
Our Sunday Visitor
Perspectives
Prairie Messenger
Priscilla Papers
War Cry

CHILDREN

Skipping Stones

MISSIONS

Operation Reveille

PASTORS/LEADERS

Christian Century
Enrichment
InSite
L Magazine
Ministry Today

TEEN/YOUNG ADULT

Boundless Webzine
Genuine Motivation
Single! Young Christian Woman
Young Salvationist

WOMEN

Single! Young Christian Woman

CRAFTS

ADULT/GENERAL

Christian Online
Guide
Indian Life
Mature Living

CHILDREN

Focus/Clubhouse
Focus/Clubhouse Jr.
Guide
JuniorWay
Pockets
SHINE brightly
Sparkle

WOMEN

MomSense
P31 Woman
Virtuous Woman

CREATION SCIENCE

ADULT/GENERAL

Answers Magazine
Bible Advocate
CBN.com
Christian Courier/Canada
Christian Examiner
Christian Research
Creation Illust.
Guide
Home Times
Indian Life
Light & Life
Live
Lookout
Sparkle
War Cry

CHILDREN

Guide
Nature Friend
Sparkle

CHRISTIAN EDUCATION/LIBRARY

Journal/Adventist Ed.

TEEN/YOUNG ADULT

Boundless Webzine
Young Salvationist

CULTS/OCCULT

ADULT/GENERAL

Bible Advocate
CBN.com
Christian Examiner
Christian Research
Guide
Light & Life
Lookout
New Heart
Now What?

CHILDREN

Guide

PASTORS/LEADERS

Ministry Today

TEEN/YOUNG ADULT

Boundless Webzine
Young Salvationist

CURRENT/SOCIAL ISSUES

ADULT/GENERAL

Bible Advocate
Brink Magazine
Canada Lutheran
Catholic New York
CBN.com
Christian Courier/Canada
Christian Examiner
Christian Home & School
Christianity Today
Christian Journal
Christian Online
Christian Ranchman
Christian Research
Christian Standard
Columbia
Evangel
Faith Today
Gem
Genuine Motivation
Guide
Halo Magazine
Home Times
Indian Life
Light & Life
Live
Lookout
Manna
Movieguide
New Heart
Now What?
Our Sunday Visitor
Perspectives
Prairie Messenger
Priority!
Priscilla Papers
Seek
Storyteller
War Cry

CHILDREN

Guide
JuniorWay
SHINE brightly
Skipping Stones
Sparkle

CHRISTIAN EDUCATION/DAILY DEVOTIONALS

Brink Magazine
Penned from the Heart

MISSIONS
Operation Reveille

PASTORS/LEADERS
Christian Century
Enrichment
Group Magazine
InSite
Leadership
Ministry Today

TEEN/YOUNG ADULT
Boundless Webzine
Genuine Motivation
Single! Young Christian Woman
Young Salvationist

WOMEN
Single! Young Christian Woman
Virtuous Woman

DEATH/DYING

ADULT/GENERAL
America
Bible Advocate
Brink Magazine
CBN.com
Celebrate Life
Chicken Soup Books
Christianity Today
Christian Online
Christian Quarterly
Christian Ranchman
Columbia
Gem
Genuine Motivation
Guide
Guideposts
Indian Life
Light & Life
Live
Lookout
New Heart
Now What?
Our Sunday Visitor
Prairie Messenger
Presbyterians Today
Seek
Storyteller
Testimony
War Cry

CHILDREN
Guide
Skipping Stones
Sparkle

DAILY DEVOTIONALS
Penned from the Heart

PASTORS/LEADERS
Christian Century
Enrichment
InSite
Leadership
L Magazine
RevWriter Resource
Sharing the Practice

TEEN/YOUNG ADULT
Boundless Webzine
Genuine Motivation
Single! Young Christian Woman

WOMEN
Single! Young Christian Woman
Virtuous Woman

DEPRESSION

ADULT/GENERAL
Bible Advocate
Genuine Motivation
Now What?

WOMEN
Brink Magazine
Single! Young Christian Woman

DEVOTIONALS/ MEDITATIONS

ADULT/GENERAL
America
CBN.com
Chicken Soup Books
Christian Home & School
Christian Journal
Christian Online
Christian Quarterly
Christian Ranchman
Columbia
Eternal Ink
Evangel
Gem
Genuine Motivation
Halo Magazine
Highway News
Keys to Living
Kyria
Leaves
Live
Lutheran Digest
Mature Living
New Heart
Penned from the Heart
Pentecostal Evangel
Perspectives
Vision
War Cry
Weavings
WorshipMinistry Devotions.com

CHILDREN
Keys for Kids
Pockets
Sparkle

DAILY DEVOTIONALS
Brink Magazine
Christian Devotions
Daily Dev. for Deaf
Light from the Word
Mustard Seed
Penned from the Heart
Quiet Hour
Rejoice!
Secret Place
Upper Room
Word in Season

PASTORS/LEADERS
Group Magazine
Ministry Today
RevWriter Resource

TEEN/YOUNG ADULT
Single! Young Christian Woman
Take Five Plus

WOMEN
Dabbling Mum
Single! Young Christian Woman
Virtuous Woman

WRITERS
Fellowscript

DISCIPLESHIP
ADULT/GENERAL
Bible Advocate
Canada Lutheran
CBN.com
Christian Journal
Christian Online
Christian Ranchman
Christian Research
Christian Standard
Columbia
Eternal Ink
Evangel
Faith Today
Gem
Genuine Motivation
Guide
Halo Magazine
Highway News
Kyria
Light & Life
Live
Lookout
Manna
Men of the Cross
Movieguide
Penned from the Heart
Perspectives
Seek
War Cry

CHILDREN
Guide
SHINE brightly
Sparkle

DAILY DEVOTIONALS
Brink Magazine
Penned from the Heart

PASTORS/LEADERS
Christian Century
Enrichment
Group Magazine
Growth Points
InSite
Leadership
RevWriter Resource
SmallGroups.com

TEEN/YOUNG ADULT
Boundless Webzine
Single! Young Christian Woman
Young Salvationist

WOMEN
P31 Woman
Single! Young Christian Woman
Virtuous Woman
Women of the Cross

DIVORCE
ADULT/GENERAL
Angels on Earth
Bible Advocate
CBN.com
Christian Examiner
Christian Online
Christian Quarterly
Christian Ranchman
Columbia
Gem
Guide
Guideposts
Home Times
Kyria
Light & Life
Live
Lookout
Manna
New Heart
Our Sunday Visitor
Perspectives
Priscilla Papers
Seek
Storyteller
War Cry

CHILDREN
Guide

PASTORS/LEADERS
Christian Century

TEEN/YOUNG ADULT
Young Salvationist

DOCTRINAL
ADULT/GENERAL
Bible Advocate
CBN.com
Christian Online
Christian Research
Christian Standard
Guide
Movieguide
Our Sunday Visitor
Perspectives
Priscilla Papers

CHILDREN
Guide

PASTORS/LEADERS
L Magazine
Sharing the Practice

DVD REVIEWS
ADULT/GENERAL
Genuine Motivation

WOMEN
Brink Magazine
Single! Young Christian Woman

ECONOMICS
ADULT/GENERAL
America
CBA Retailers
CBN.com
Christian Online
Christian Quarterly
Christian Ranchman
Christian Retailing
Genuine Motivation
Halo Magazine
Home Times
Light & Life
Live
Movieguide
Our Sunday Visitor
Perspectives

TEEN/YOUNG ADULT
Boundless Webzine
Single! Young Christian Woman

WOMEN
Single! Young Christian Woman

ENCOURAGEMENT

ADULT/GENERAL

Adoptee Search
Bible Advocate
Brink Magazine
CBN.com
Christian Home & School
Christian Journal
Christian Online
Christian Quarterly
Christian Ranchman
Christian Standard
Evangel
Gems of Truth
Genuine Motivation
Highway News
Home Times
Indian Life
Keys to Living
Kyria
Leaves
Light & Life
Live
Lookout
Lutheran Digest
Manna
Mature Living
Men of the Cross
New Heart
Penned from the Heart
Seek
Storyteller
Vision
Vista

CHILDREN

SHINE brightly
Skipping Stones
Sparkle

DAILY DEVOTIONALS

Brink Magazine
Penned from the Heart

TEEN/YOUNG ADULT

Boundless Webzine
Genuine Motivation
Single! Young Christian Woman
Young Salvationist

WOMEN

P31 Woman
Single! Young Christian Woman
Virtuous Woman
Women of the Cross

WRITERS

Christian Communicator
Fellowscript

ENVIRONMENTAL ISSUES

ADULT/GENERAL

America
Animal Trails
Bible Advocate
Brink Magazine
Christian Courier/Canada
Christian Online
Creation Illust.
Faith Today
Genuine Motivation
Guide
Light & Life
Lookout
Our Sunday Visitor
Perspectives
Prairie Messenger
Seek
War Cry

CHILDREN

Guide
Pockets
SHINE brightly
Skipping Stones
Sparkle

PASTORS/LEADERS

Christian Century
InSite

TEEN/YOUNG ADULT

Boundless Webzine
Single! Young Christian Woman
Young Salvationist

WOMEN

Share
Single! Young Christian Woman

ESSAYS

ADULT/GENERAL

America
Chicken Soup Books
Christian Courier/Canada
Christianity Today
Christian Online
Columbia
Faith Today
Gem
Genuine Motivation
Lutheran Digest
Our Sunday Visitor
Penwood Review
Seek
Storyteller
War Cry

CHILDREN

Nature Friend
Skipping Stones

CHRISTIAN EDUCATION/LIBRARY

Journal/Adventist Ed.

PASTORS/LEADERS

Christian Century
Priest
RevWriter Resource

TEEN/YOUNG ADULT

Genuine Motivation
Single! Young Christian Woman

WOMEN

Dabbling Mum
Single! Young Christian Woman

WRITERS

Adv. Christian Writer
Christian Communicator
Writer
Writer's Chronicle
Writer's Digest

ETHICS

ADULT/GENERAL

America
Angels on Earth
Brink Magazine

CBN.com
Celebrate Life
Christian Courier/Canada
Christian Examiner
Christian Online
Christian Ranchman
Christian Research
Christian Standard
Columbia
Faith Today
Genuine Motivation
Light & Life
Live
Lookout
Manna
Movieguide
New Heart
Our Sunday Visitor
Perspectives
Prairie Messenger
Priscilla Papers
Seek
War Cry

CHILDREN

Skipping Stones

DAILY DEVOTIONALS

Brink Magazine
Penned from the Heart

PASTORS/LEADERS

Christian Century
Enrichment
L Magazine
Ministry Today
Sharing the Practice

TEEN/YOUNG ADULT

Boundless Webzine
Genuine Motivation
Single! Young Christian Woman
Young Salvationist

WOMEN

Single! Young Christian Woman

ETHNIC/CULTURAL PIECES

ADULT/GENERAL

America
Brink Magazine
Canada Lutheran
CBA Retailers
CBN.com
Celebrate Life
Christian Courier/Canada
Christian Home & School
Christian Online
Columbia
Faith Today
Gem
Genuine Motivation
Guide
Indian Life
Light & Life
Live
Lookout
Manna
Movieguide
Our Sunday Visitor
Penned from the Heart
Prairie Messenger
Priscilla Papers
Seek
War Cry

CHILDREN

Guide
Skipping Stones
Sparkle

DAILY DEVOTIONALS

Brink Magazine
Penned from the Heart

MISSIONS

Operation Reveille

PASTORS/LEADERS

Christian Century
Enrichment
Ministry Today

TEEN/YOUNG ADULT

Boundless Webzine
Genuine Motivation
Single! Young Christian Woman
Young Salvationist

WOMEN

Single! Young Christian Woman

EVANGELISM/WITNESSING

ADULT/GENERAL

America
Bible Advocate
Brink Magazine
CBN.com
Christian Home & School
Christianity Today
Christian Online
Christian Ranchman
Christian Research
Christian Standard
Columbia
Evangel
Faith Today
Gem
Genuine Motivation
Guide
Halo Magazine
Highway News
Leaves
Light & Life
Live
Lookout
Lutheran Journal
Manna
New Heart
On Mission
Our Sunday Visitor
Penned from the Heart
Power for Living
Priority!
Seek
Testimony
War Cry

CHILDREN

Focus/Clubhouse Jr.
Guide
JuniorWay
Sparkle

DAILY DEVOTIONALS

Brink Magazine
Penned from the Heart

MISSIONS

Operation Reveille

PASTORS/LEADERS

Cook Partners
Enrichment

Group Magazine
Growth Points
Leadership
Ministry Today
RevWriter Resource
SmallGroups.com

TEEN/YOUNG ADULT
Boundless Webzine
Genuine Motivation
Single! Young Christian Woman
Young Salvationist

WOMEN
P31 Woman
Share
Single! Young Christian Woman

EXEGESIS

ADULT/GENERAL
Bible Advocate
CBN.com
Christian Ranchman
Christian Standard
Our Sunday Visitor
Perspectives
Priscilla Papers

PASTORS/LEADERS
Enrichment

TEEN/YOUNG ADULT
Boundless Webzine

FAITH

ADULT/GENERAL
America
Believers Bay
Bible Advocate
Brink Magazine
Canada Lutheran
CBN.com
Christian Courier/Canada
Christian Home & School
Christianity Today
Christian Journal
Christian Online
Christian Quarterly
Christian Research
Christian Retailing
Christian Standard
Church Herald & Holiness
Columbia
Eternal Ink
Gem
Genuine Motivation
Guide
Highway News
Home Times
Indian Life
Kyria
Light & Life
Live
Lookout
Lutheran Digest
Lutheran Journal
Manna
New Heart
Now What?
Our Sunday Visitor
Penned from the Heart
Prairie Messenger
Priscilla Papers
Seek
SW Kansas Faith
Testimony
Vista
Weavings

CHILDREN
Focus/Clubhouse Jr.
Guide
JuniorWay
SHINE brightly
Sparkle

DAILY DEVOTIONALS
Brink Magazine
Penned from the Heart

PASTORS/LEADERS
Ministry Today
Plugged In
RevWriter Resource
SmallGroups.com

TEEN/YOUNG ADULT
Boundless Webzine
Genuine Motivation
Single! Young Christian Woman
Young Salvationist

WOMEN
Christian Homeschool Moms
P31 Woman
Single! Young Christian Woman
Virtuous Woman
Women of the Cross

FAMILY LIFE

ADULT/GENERAL
Adoptee Search
America
Angels on Earth
Believers Bay
Brink Magazine
Canada Lutheran
CBN.com
Chicken Soup Books
Christian Courier/Canada
Christian Home & School
Christian Journal
Christian Online
Christian Quarterly
Christian Ranchman
Church Herald & Holiness
Columbia
Eternal Ink
Gem
Guide
Guideposts
Halo Magazine
Highway News
Home Times
Indian Life
Keys to Living
Kyria
Live
Living Light
Lookout
Lutheran Digest
Manna
Mature Years
Men of the Cross
Our Sunday Visitor
Penned from the Heart
Pentecostal Evangel
Power for Living
Prairie Messenger
Priscilla Papers
Seek

Storyteller
SW Kansas Faith
Testimony
Thriving Family
Vision
Vista
War Cry

CHILDREN
Focus/Clubhouse
Focus/Clubhouse Jr.
Guide
JuniorWay
Pockets
Sparkle

DAILY DEVOTIONALS
Penned from the Heart

PASTORS/LEADERS
Enrichment
InSite
Ministry Today
RevWriter Resource

TEEN/YOUNG ADULT
Young Salvationist

WOMEN
Christian Homeschool Moms
Dabbling Mum
MomSense
P31 Woman
Share
Virtuous Woman
Women of the Cross

FEATURE ARTICLES

ADULT/GENERAL
Animal Trails
Bible Advocate
Canada Lutheran
Columbia
Faith Today

CHILDREN
Sparkle

CHRISTIAN EDUCATION/ LIBRARY
Seek

PASTORS/LEADERS
Group Magazine

WOMEN
Brink Magazine

FILLERS: ANECDOTES

ADULT/GENERAL
Angels on Earth
Animal Trails
Christian Journal
Christian Quarterly
Christian Ranchman
Church Herald & Holiness
Eternal Ink
Gem
Home Times
Lutheran Digest
Manna
Movieguide
Pentecostal Evangel
Vista
War Cry

CHILDREN
Skipping Stones

PASTORS/LEADERS
Enrichment
Leadership
Sharing the Practice

TEEN/YOUNG ADULT
Genuine Motivation
Single! Young Christian Woman
Young Salvationist

WOMEN
Right to the Heart
Single! Young Christian Woman
Virtuous Woman

WRITERS
Fellowscript
New Writer's Mag.

FILLERS: CARTOONS

ADULT/GENERAL
Angels on Earth
Animal Trails
Christian Journal
Christian Quarterly
Christian Ranchman
Evangel
Gem
Guide
Home Times
Lutheran Digest
Mature Years
Movieguide
New Heart
Power for Living
Presbyterians Today
Storyteller

CHILDREN
Guide
SHINE brightly
Skipping Stones

CHRISTIAN EDUCATION/ LIBRARY
Journal/Adventist Ed.

PASTORS/LEADERS
Christian Century
Diocesan Dialogue
Enrichment
Leadership
Priest
Sharing the Practice
SmallGroups.com

TEEN/YOUNG ADULT
Young Salvationist

WRITERS
New Writer's Mag.
Writer

FILLERS: FACTS

ADULT/GENERAL
Animal Trails
Christian Ranchman
Gem
Home Times
Lutheran Digest
Lutheran Journal
Movieguide
Pentecostal Evangel
Vista

CHILDREN
Nature Friend

MISSIONS
Boundless Webzine
Operation Reveille

PASTORS/LEADERS
Enrichment

TEEN/YOUNG ADULT
Young Salvationist

WOMEN
Virtuous Woman

WRITERS
New Writer's Mag.

FILLERS: GAMES
ADULT/GENERAL
Christian Ranchman
Gem
Guide
Lutheran Journal
Movieguide

CHILDREN
Guide
Pockets
SHINE brightly

TEEN/YOUNG ADULT
Young Salvationist

FILLERS: IDEAS
ADULT/GENERAL
Animal Trails
Christian Home & School
Christian Quarterly
Christian Ranchman
Gem
Home Times
Manna
Movieguide
Seek

PASTORS/LEADERS
Small Groups.com

WOMEN
P31 Woman
Right to the Heart
Virtuous Woman

FILLERS: JOKES
ADULT/GENERAL
Christian Journal
Christian Ranchman
Eternal Ink
Gem
Home Times
Lutheran Digest
Mature Years
Movieguide
New Heart

PASTORS/LEADERS
RevWriter Resource
Sharing the Practice

WOMEN
Virtuous Woman

FILLERS: KID QUOTES
ADULT/GENERAL
Animal Trails
Christian Journal
Eternal Ink
Home Times
Indian Life
Movieguide

FILLERS: NEWSBREAKS
ADULT/GENERAL
Christian Journal
Christian Ranchman
Gem
Home Times
Movieguide
Vista

MISSIONS
Operation Reveille

WRITERS
New Writer's Mag.

FILLERS: PARTY IDEAS
ADULT/GENERAL
Animal Trails
Christian Ranchman
Manna
Movieguide

CHILDREN
Sparkle

WOMEN
P31 Woman
Right to the Heart
Virtuous Woman

FILLERS: PRAYERS
ADULT/GENERAL
Angels on Earth
Animal Trails
Christian Journal
Christian Online
Christian Ranchman
Eternal Ink
Gem
Home Times
Mature Years
Movieguide
Vista

CHILDREN
SHINE brightly

DAILY DEVOTIONALS
Word in Season

TEEN/YOUNG ADULT
Young Salvationist

WOMEN
Right to the Heart
Virtuous Woman

FILLERS: PROSE
ADULT/GENERAL
Bible Advocate
Christian Online
Christian Ranchman
Eternal Ink
Gem
Movieguide
Pentecostal Evangel

CHILDREN
Sparkle

WRITERS
Freelance Writer's Report
Writer

FILLERS: QUIZZES
ADULT/GENERAL
Animal Trails
Christian Online
Christian Ranchman
Church Herald & Holiness
Gem
Guide
Lutheran Journal
Movieguide

CHILDREN
Focus/Clubhouse
Guide
Nature Friend
SHINE brightly
Skipping Stones
Sparkle

CHRISTIAN EDUCATION/ LIBRARY
Ministry Today

TEEN/YOUNG ADULT
Young Salvationist

WOMEN
Virtuous Woman

FILLERS: QUOTES
ADULT/GENERAL
Animal Trails
Christian Journal
Christian Quarterly
Christian Ranchman
Gem
Home Times
Indian Life
Lutheran Journal
Movieguide
Seek
Storyteller
Vista

CHILDREN
Skipping Stones

WOMEN
Right to the Heart

WRITERS
Fellowscript

FILLERS: SERMON ILLUSTRATIONS
PASTORS/LEADERS
RevWriter Resource

FILLERS: SHORT HUMOR
ADULT/GENERAL
Angels on Earth
Animal Trails
Christian Journal
Christian Online
Christian Quarterly
Christian Ranchman
Eternal Ink
Gem
Home Times
Indian Life
Leben
Lutheran Digest
Manna
Mature Living
Movieguide
New Heart
Presbyterians Today
Seek

CHILDREN
SHINE brightly

PASTORS/LEADERS
Enrichment
Leadership
Sharing the Practice

TEEN/YOUNG ADULT
Young Salvationist

WRITERS
Christian Communicator
Fellowscript
New Writer's Mag.

FILLERS: TIPS
ADULT/GENERAL
Animal Trails
Christian Ranchman
Home Times
Manna
Movieguide
Storyteller

PASTORS/LEADERS
Enrichment

WOMEN
MomSense
Virtuous Woman

WRITERS
Fellowscript
Freelance Writer's Report

FILLERS: WORD PUZZLES
ADULT/GENERAL
Animal Trails
Christian Journal
Christian Quarterly
Christian Ranchman
Evangel
Gem
Guide
Mature Years
Movieguide
Power for Living

CHILDREN
Focus/Clubhouse
Guide
Nature Friend
Pockets
SHINE brightly
Skipping Stones

TEEN/YOUNG ADULT
Young Salvationist

FOOD/RECIPES
ADULT/GENERAL
Animal Trails
CBN.com
Christian Online
Christian Quarterly
Indian Life
Mature Living

CHILDREN
Focus/Clubhouse
Focus/Clubhouse Jr.
Pockets
SHINE brightly
Sparkle

TEEN/YOUNG ADULT
Boundless Webzine

WOMEN
Dabbling Mum
Virtuous Woman

GRANDPARENTING
ADULT/GENERAL
Christian Standard
Columbia
Seek

WOMEN
Brink Magazine

HEALING

ADULT/GENERAL

America
Angels on Earth
CBN.com
Celebrate Life
Christian Home & School
Christian Online
Christian Quarterly
Christian Ranchman
Gem
Guideposts
Home Times
Light & Life
Live
New Heart
Our Sunday Visitor
Perspectives
Seek
Testimony

CHILDREN

Skipping Stones

DAILY DEVOTIONALS

Penned from the Heart

TEEN/YOUNG ADULT

Boundless Webzine

WOMEN

Share
Virtuous Woman

HEALTH

ADULT/GENERAL

Angels on Earth
Brink Magazine
CBN.com
Celebrate Life
Christian Courier/Canada
Christian Home & School
Christian Online
Christian Quarterly
Christian Ranchman
Fit Christian
Genuine Motivation
Guide
Guideposts
Halo Magazine
Highway News
Home Times
Light & Life
Live
Lookout
Mature Years
Our Sunday Visitor
Penned from the Heart
Pentecostal Evangel
Testimony
Vista
War Cry

CHILDREN

Guide
Skipping Stones
Sparkle

DAILY DEVOTIONALS

Penned from the Heart

PASTORS/LEADERS

Christian Century
InSite

TEEN/YOUNG ADULT

Boundless Webzine
Genuine Motivation
Single! Young Christian Woman

WOMEN

Dabbling Mum
Share
Single! Young Christian Woman
Virtuous Woman

HISTORICAL

ADULT/GENERAL

Angels on Earth
Capper's
CBN.com
Celebrate Life
Christian Courier/Canada
Christian Online
Columbia
Faith Today
Guide
Halo Magazine
Home Times
Indian Life
Leben
Light & Life
Lutheran Digest
Our Sunday Visitor
Perspectives
Power for Living
Priscilla Papers
Storyteller

CHILDREN

Focus/Clubhouse Jr.
Guide
Sparkle

PASTORS/LEADERS

Leadership
Ministry Today
Priest

TEEN/YOUNG ADULT

Boundless Webzine

HOLIDAY/SEASONAL

ADULT/GENERAL

Angels on Earth
Animal Trails
Brink Magazine
Capper's
Catholic New York
CBN.com
Chicken Soup Books
Christian Courier/Canada
Christian Home & School
Christian Journal
Christian Online
Christian Retailing
Columbia
Eternal Ink
Evangel
Gem
Gems of Truth
Genuine Motivation
Guide
Guideposts
Highway News
Home Times
Light & Life
Live
Living Light
Lookout
Manna
Mature Living
Mature Years

On Mission
Our Sunday Visitor
Penned from the Heart
Power for Living
Prairie Messenger
Seek
Vista
War Cry

CHILDREN

Focus/Clubhouse
Focus/Clubhouse Jr.
Guide
JuniorWay
Nature Friend
Pockets
SHINE brightly
Skipping Stones
Sparkle

DAILY DEVOTIONALS

Brink Magazine
Penned from the Heart

TEEN/YOUNG ADULT

Boundless Webzine
Genuine Motivation
Single! Young Christian Woman
Young Salvationist

WOMEN

P31 Woman
Virtuous Woman

HOLY SPIRIT

ADULT/GENERAL

Columbia
Genuine Motivation
Kyria
Single! Young Christian Woman

PASTORS/LEADERS

Brink Magazine

HOMESCHOOLING

ADULT/GENERAL

Animal Trails
Columbia
Guide
Home Times
Our Sunday Visitor

CHILDREN

Guide
Skipping Stones

TEEN/YOUNG ADULT

Boundless Webzine

WOMEN

Christian Homeschool Moms
Virtuous Woman

HOMILETICS

ADULT/GENERAL

CBN.com
Christian Ranchman
Columbia
Perspectives
Priscilla Papers
Testimony

PASTORS/LEADERS

Christian Century
Enrichment
Preaching
Priest

HOW-TO

ADULT/GENERAL

Animal Trails
Brink Magazine
Canada Lutheran
CBA Retailers
CBN.com
Celebrate Life
Christian Online
Christian Retailing
Faith Today
Home Times
Live
On Mission
Presbyterians Today
Testimony
Vista

CHRISTIAN EDUCATION/ LIBRARY

Church Libraries
Journal/Adventist Ed.

PASTORS/LEADERS

Ministry Today
Newsletter Newsletter
RevWriter Resource

WOMEN

Christian Homeschool Moms
Dabbling Mum
Virtuous Woman

WRITERS

Adv. Christian Writer
Fellowscript
Freelance Writer's Report
Poets & Writers
Writer's Digest

HOW-TO ACTIVITIES (JUV.)

ADULT/GENERAL

Animal Trails
Christian Home & School
Christian Online
Keys to Living
On Mission

CHILDREN

Focus/Clubhouse
Focus/Clubhouse Jr.
Guide
JuniorWay
Nature Friend
Pockets
SHINE brightly
Sparkle

WOMEN

Christian Homeschool Moms

HUMOR

ADULT/GENERAL

Angels on Earth
Brink Magazine
CBN.com
Chicken Soup Books
Christian Courier/Canada
Christian Home & School
Christianity Today
Christian Journal
Christian Online
Christian Quarterly
Christian Ranchman
Eternal Ink
Gem
Genuine Motivation
Guide
Halo Magazine

Home Times
Indian Life
Living Light
Lookout
Manna
Mature Living
Our Sunday Visitor
Penned from the Heart
Seek
Storyteller
Testimony
Thriving Family
Vista
War Cry
Weavings

CHILDREN
Focus/Clubhouse Jr.
Guide
SHINE brightly
Sparkle

DAILY DEVOTIONALS
Penned from the Heart

PASTORS/LEADERS
Enrichment
Leadership
L Magazine
Priest

TEEN/YOUNG ADULT
Boundless Webzine
Genuine Motivation
Single! Young Christian Woman
Young Salvationist

WOMEN
MomSense
Single! Young Christian Woman

WRITERS
Christian Communicator
New Writer's Mag.

INNER LIFE

ADULT/GENERAL
Canada Lutheran
CBN.com
Christian Journal
Christian Ranchman
Genuine Motivation
Kyria
Light & Life
Live
Mature Years
Our Sunday Visitor
Penned from the Heart
Presbyterians Today
Seek
Testimony
Weavings

TEEN/YOUNG ADULT
Boundless Webzine
Single! Young Christian Woman
Young Salvationist

WOMEN
Single! Young Christian Woman

INSPIRATIONAL

ADULT/GENERAL
Adoptee Search
Angels on Earth
Animal Trails
Brink Magazine
Capper's
CBN.com
Celebrate Life
Chicken Soup Books
Christian Home & School
Christian Journal
Christian Online
Christian Quarterly
Christian Ranchman
Columbia
Eternal Ink
Evangel
Gem
Genuine Motivation
Guideposts
Highway News
Home Times
Indian Life
Keys to Living
Leaves
Live
Lookout
Lutheran Digest
Mature Living
New Heart
Penned from the Heart
Power for Living
Prairie Messenger
Presbyterians Today
Priority!
Seek
Storyteller
SW Kansas Faith
Testimony
Vista
War Cry

CHILDREN
SHINE brightly
Sparkle

DAILY DEVOTIONALS
Brink Magazine
Penned from the Heart
Rejoice!

MISSIONS
Operation Reveille

PASTORS/LEADERS
Ministry Today
Priest

TEEN/YOUNG ADULT
Boundless Webzine
Genuine Motivation
Single! Young Christian Woman
Young Salvationist

WOMEN
Christian Homeschool Moms
MomSense
P31 Woman
Right to the Heart
Share
Single! Young Christian Woman
Virtuous Woman

WRITERS
Writer's Digest

INTERVIEWS/PROFILES

ADULT/GENERAL
Brink Magazine
Catholic New York
CBN.com

Celebrate Life
Charisma
Christianity Today
Christian Online
Christian Ranchman
Columbia
Eternal Ink
Faith Today
Gem
Guideposts
Highway News
Home Times
Indian Life
Kindred Spirit
Light & Life
Lookout
Manna
New Heart
On Mission
Our Sunday Visitor
Power for Living
Priority!
Testimony
War Cry
Weavings

CHILDREN
Pockets
SHINE brightly
Skipping Stones
Sparkle

CHRISTIAN EDUCATION/ LIBRARY
Church Libraries

MISSIONS
Operation Reveille

PASTORS/LEADERS
Christian Century
Enrichment
InSite
Ministry Today
Priest

TEEN/YOUNG ADULT
Boundless Webzine
Young Salvationist

WOMEN
Christian Homeschool Moms
Virtuous Woman

WRITERS
Adv. Christian Writer
Christian Communicator
Fellowscript
New Writer's Mag.
Poets & Writers
Writer
Writer's Chronicle
Writer's Digest

LEADERSHIP

ADULT/GENERAL
Angels on Earth
CBN.com
Christian Courier/ Canada
Christian Home & School
Christian Retailing
Christian Standard
Columbia
Faith Today
Gem
Kyria
Light & Life
Lookout
Manna
Men of the Cross
Our Sunday Visitor
Priscilla Papers
Testimony
Vista

PASTORS/LEADERS
Christian Century
Enrichment
Group Magazine
Growth Points
InSite
Leadership
L Magazine
Ministry Today
Plugged In
RevWriter Resource
SmallGroups.com

TEEN/YOUNG ADULT
Boundless Webzine

WOMEN
Right to the Heart
Share
Women of the Cross

LIFESTYLE ARTICLES

ADULT/GENERAL
Brink Magazine
Canada Lutheran
CBN.com
Christian Journal
Christian Ranchman
Faith Today
Fit Christian
Genuine Motivation
Home Times
Light & Life
Live
Lookout
Manna
Mature Living
Our Sunday Visitor
Ozark
Priority!
Seek
Share

TEEN/YOUNG ADULT
Boundless Webzine
Genuine Motivation
Single! Young Christian Woman

WOMEN
Single! Young Christian Woman

LITURGICAL

ADULT/GENERAL
Columbia
Lutheran Journal
Our Sunday Visitor
Perspectives
Prairie Messenger
Testimony

PASTORS/LEADERS
Christian Century
Diocesan Dialogue
Parish Liturgy

MARRIAGE

ADULT/GENERAL
Angels on Earth
Bible Advocate
Brink Magazine
CBN.com

Celebrate Life
Christian Courier/ Canada
Christian Examiner
Christian Home & School
Christian Journal
Christian Online
Christian Quarterly
Christian Ranchman
Christian Research
Christian Standard
Church Herald & Holiness
Columbia
Evangel
Gem
Guideposts
Halo Magazine
Highway News
Home Times
Indian Life
Kyria
Light & Life
Live
Living Light
Lookout
Manna
Mature Living
Men of the Cross
Our Sunday Visitor
Penned from the Heart
Perspectives
Prairie Messenger
Priscilla Papers
Seek
Testimony
Thriving Family
Vista
War Cry

DAILY DEVOTIONALS
Penned from the Heart

PASTORS/LEADERS
Christian Century
L Magazine
Ministry Today
SmallGroups.com

TEEN/YOUNG ADULT
Boundless Webzine
Genuine Motivation

WOMEN
Dabbling Mum
MomSense
P31 Woman
Virtuous Woman
Women of the Cross

MEN'S ISSUES

ADULT/GENERAL
Brink Magazine
CBN.com
Chicken Soup Books
Christian Examiner
Christian Journal
Christian News NW
Christian Online
Christian Quarterly
Christian Ranchman
Columbia
Gem
Genuine Motivation
Halo Magazine
Home Times
Indian Life
Light & Life
Live
Lookout
Manna
Men of the Cross
Our Sunday Visitor
Penned from the Heart
Perspectives
Priscilla Papers
Testimony

PASTORS/LEADERS
SmallGroups.com

TEEN/YOUNG ADULT
Boundless Webzine

MIRACLES

ADULT/GENERAL
Angels on Earth
Animal Trails
CBN.com
Chicken Soup Books
Christian Home & School
Christianity Today
Christian Online
Christian Quarterly
Christian Ranchman
Christian Standard
Columbia
Gem
Genuine Motivation
Guide
Guideposts
Home Times
Light & Life
Live
Lookout
Lutheran Journal
New Heart
Now What?
Our Sunday Visitor
Penned from the Heart
Perspectives
Power for Living
Priority!
Priscilla Papers
Seek
Storyteller
Testimony

CHILDREN
Guide
Sparkle

DAILY DEVOTIONALS
Penned from the Heart

PASTORS/LEADERS
Ministry Today

TEEN/YOUNG ADULT
Boundless Webzine
Genuine Motivation
Single! Young Christian Woman
Young Salvationist

WOMEN
Single! Young Christian Woman

MISSIONS

ADULT/GENERAL
Brink Magazine
Canada Lutheran
Christian Home & School
Christian Ranchman
Church Herald & Holiness
Columbia

Faith Today
Genuine Motivation
Guide
Live
On Mission
Our Sunday Visitor

CHILDREN
Guide

DAILY DEVOTIONALS
Brink Magazine

MISSIONS
Operation Reveille

PASTORS/LEADERS
Enrichment
Group Magazine

TEEN/YOUNG ADULT
Genuine Motivation
Single! Young Christian Woman

WOMEN
Christian Homeschool Moms
Single! Young Christian Woman

MONEY MANAGEMENT

ADULT/GENERAL
Brink Magazine
CBA Retailers
CBN.com
Christian Journal
Christian Online
Christian Quarterly
Christian Ranchman
Gem
Genuine Motivation
Highway News
Home Times
Live
Lookout
Manna
Mature Years
Our Sunday Visitor
Penned from the Heart
Testimony
War Cry

CHILDREN
SHINE brightly

DAILY DEVOTIONALS
Penned from the Heart

PASTORS/LEADERS
Enrichment
SmallGroups.com

TEEN/YOUNG ADULT
Boundless Webzine
Genuine Motivation
Single! Young Christian Woman

WOMEN
Single! Young Christian Woman
Virtuous Woman

MOVIE REVIEWS

ADULT/GENERAL
CBN.com
Christian Journal
Genuine Motivation
Home Times
Movieguide
Our Sunday Visitor
Perspectives
Prairie Messenger

TEEN/YOUNG ADULT
Genuine Motivation
Single! Young Christian Woman

WOMEN
Christian Homeschool Moms
Single! Young Christian Woman
Virtuous Woman

MUSIC REVIEWS

ADULT/GENERAL
CBN.com
Charisma
Christian Journal
Christian Retailing
Faith Today
Genuine Motivation
Movieguide
Our Sunday Visitor
Prairie Messenger
Presbyterians Today
Testimony

CHILDREN
Sparkle

CHRISTIAN EDUCATION/LIBRARY
Church Libraries

PASTORS/LEADERS
Christian Century
Ministry Today
Parish Liturgy

TEEN/YOUNG ADULT
Genuine Motivation
Single! Young Christian Woman

WOMEN
Christian Homeschool Moms
Single! Young Christian Woman
Virtuous Woman

NATURE

ADULT/GENERAL
Animal Trails
Brink Magazine
CBN.com
Christian Courier/Canada
Creation
Creation Illust.
Gem
Guide
Keys to Living
Lutheran Digest
Our Sunday Visitor
Penned from the Heart
Seek
Storyteller
Testimony

CHILDREN
Focus/Clubhouse Jr.
Guide
Nature Friend
SHINE brightly
Skipping Stones
Sparkle

TEEN/YOUNG ADULT
Boundless Webzine
Genuine Motivation
Single! Young Christian Woman

WOMEN

Single! Young Christian Woman
Virtuous Woman

NEWS FEATURES

ADULT/GENERAL

Catholic New York
CBN.com
Charisma
Christian Examiner
Christian News NW
Christian Ranchman
Christian Research
Christian Retailing
Faith Today
Genuine Motivation
Home Times
Indian Life
Manna
Movieguide
Our Sunday Visitor
Ozark
Priority!
Testimony
War Cry

CHILDREN

Pockets

MISSIONS

Operation Reveille

PASTORS/LEADERS

Christian Century
Ministry Today

TEEN/YOUNG ADULT

Genuine Motivation
Single! Young Christian Woman

WOMEN

Single! Young Christian Woman

WRITERS

Poets & Writers

NEWSPAPERS/TABLOIDS

Catholic New York
Christian Courier/Canada
Christian Examiner
Christian Journal
Christian News NW
Christian Ranchman
Home Times
Indian Life
Living Light
Manna
New Frontier
Our Sunday Visitor
Prairie Messenger
SW Kansas Faith

NOSTALGIA

ADULT/GENERAL

Home Times
Lutheran Digest
Mature Living
Seek
Storyteller
Testimony

PASTORS/LEADERS

Priest

ONLINE PUBLICATIONS

ADULT/GENERAL

America
Answers Magazine
Believers Bay
Brink Magazine
CBN.com
Charisma
Christian Examiner
Christianity Today
Christian Journal
Christian Online
Christian Standard
Columbia
Eternal Ink
Faith Today
Kyria
Leben
Lookout
Manna
Men of the Cross
Now What?
On Mission
Pentecostal Evangel
Perspectives
Priority!
Testimony

CHILDREN

Focus/Clubhouse
Focus/Clubhouse Jr.
Keys for Kids
Kids' Ark

MISSIONS

Operation Reveille

PASTORS/LEADERS

Cook Partners
InSite
Leadership
Newsletter Newsletter
Preaching
RevWriter Resource
SmallGroups.com

TEEN/YOUNG ADULT

Boundless Webzine
Young Salvationist

WOMEN

Dabbling Mum
Right to the Heart
Virtuous Woman
Women of the Cross

WRITERS

Freelance Writer's Report

OPINION PIECES

ADULT/GENERAL

Brink Magazine
Catholic New York
CBN.com
Christian Courier/Canada
Christian Examiner
Christianity Today
Christian News NW
Christian Research
Home Times
Indian Life
Lookout
Movieguide
Our Sunday Visitor
Perspectives
Prairie Messenger
Testimony

CHILDREN
Skipping Stones

MISSIONS
Operation Reveille

PASTORS/LEADERS
Ministry Today
Priest

WRITERS
Adv. Christian Writer
New Writer's Mag.

PARENTING
ADULT/GENERAL
Angels on Earth
Canada Lutheran
CBN.com
Celebrate Life
Chicken Soup Books
Christian Courier/Canada
Christian Home & School
Christian Quarterly
Christian Ranchman
Christian Research
Columbia
Gem
Home Times
Indian Life
Light & Life
Live
Living Light
Lookout
Lutheran Journal
Manna
Movieguide
Our Sunday Visitor
Penned from the Heart
Pentecostal Evangel
Power for Living
Prairie Messenger
Seek
SW Kansas Faith
Testimony
Thriving Family
Vista
War Cry

DAILY DEVOTIONALS
Penned from the Heart

PASTORS/LEADERS
Plugged In

WOMEN
Christian Homeschool Moms
Dabbling Mum
MomSense
P31 Woman
Virtuous Woman

PASTORS' HELPS
PASTORS/LEADERS
Christian Century
Cook Partners
Diocesan Dialogue
Enrichment
Growth Points
InSite
Leadership
Ministry Today
Newsletter Newsletter
Parish Liturgy
Plugged In
Preaching
Sharing the Practice
SmallGroups.com

PEACE ISSUES
ADULT/GENERAL
CBN.com
Columbia
Genuine Motivation
Lookout
Our Sunday Visitor
Penned from the Heart
Perspectives
Seek
Testimony

CHILDREN
Pockets
Skipping Stones

PASTORS/LEADERS
Christian Century

TEEN/YOUNG ADULT
Genuine Motivation
Single! Young Christian Woman

WOMEN
Single! Young Christian Woman

PERSONAL EXPERIENCE
ADULT/GENERAL
Adoptee Search
Angels on Earth
Bible Advocate
Brink Magazine
Catholic New York
CBN.com
Celebrate Life
Chicken Soup Books
Christian Courier/Canada
Christianity Today
Christian Journal
Christian Online
Christian Quarterly
Columbia
Evangel
Gem
Genuine Motivation
Guide
Guideposts
Highway News
Home Times
Keys to Living
Kyria
Leaves
Light & Life
Live
Lookout
Lutheran Journal
Mature Living
New Heart
Now What?
On Mission
Penned from the Heart
Power for Living
Seek
Storyteller
Testimony
Vision
War Cry

CHILDREN
Guide
Skipping Stones
Sparkle

CHRISTIAN EDUCATION/ LIBRARY
Journal/Adventist Ed.

DAILY DEVOTIONALS
Penned from the Heart
Rejoice!

PASTORS/LEADERS
Priest

TEEN/YOUNG ADULT
Boundless Webzine
Genuine Motivation
Single! Young Christian Woman
Young Salvationist

WOMEN
MomSense
Single! Young Christian Woman
Virtuous Woman

WRITERS
New Writer's Mag.

PERSONAL GROWTH

ADULT/GENERAL
Bible Advocate
CBN.com
Christian Courier/Canada
Christian Journal
Christian Online
Christian Quarterly
Christian Ranchman
Columbia
Evangel
Gem
Genuine Motivation
Guide
Halo Magazine
Home Times
Indian Life
Keys to Living
Kyria
Leaves
Light & Life
Live
Lookout
Lutheran Digest
Manna
Mature Living
Mature Years
New Heart
Now What?
Penned from the Heart
Prairie Messenger
Seek
Share
Testimony
War Cry

CHILDREN
Guide
Skipping Stones
Sparkle

DAILY DEVOTIONALS
Penned from the Heart

PASTORS/LEADERS
Group Magazine
Ministry Today

TEEN/YOUNG ADULT
Boundless Webzine
Genuine Motivation
Single! Young Christian Woman
Young Salvationist

WOMEN
Dabbling Mum
MomSense
P31 Woman
Single! Young Christian Woman
Virtuous Woman

PHOTO ESSAYS

ADULT/GENERAL
Genuine Motivation
Our Sunday Visitor
Priority!

CHILDREN
Skipping Stones

CHRISTIAN EDUCATION/ LIBRARY
Journal/Adventist Ed.

PASTORS/LEADERS
Priest

TEEN/YOUNG ADULT
Genuine Motivation
Single! Young Christian Woman

WOMEN
Single! Young Christian Woman

PHOTOGRAPHS

Note: "Reprint" indicators (R) have been deleted from this section and "B" for black & white glossy prints or "C" for color transparencies inserted. An asterisk (*) before a listing indicates they buy photos with articles only.

ADULT/GENERAL
*Animal Trails—B/C
Bible Advocate—C
Canada Lutheran—B
Catholic New York—B
CBA Retailers—C
Celebrate Life—C
*Charisma—C
*Christian Courier/ Canada—B
*Christian Examiner—C
Christian Home & School—C
*Christianity Today—C
*Christian Online
Christian Retailing—C
*Christian Standard—B/C
*Evangel—B
*Guideposts—B/C
Halo Magazine—C
*Home Times—B/C
Indian Life—B/C
Leaves—B/C
*Leben—C
Light & Life—B/C
*Live—B/C
*Living Light—B/C
*Lookout—B/C
*Lutheran Journal—C
*Manna—C
*Mature Living
*Mature Years—C
*New Heart—C
On Mission—B/C
Our Sunday Visitor—B/C
Pentecostal Evangel—B/C
*Perspectives—B
Power for Living—B

*Presbyterians Today—B/C
*Seek—C
*Storyteller—B
*Testimony—B/C
Vision—B/C
*War Cry—B/C

CHILDREN

*Focus/Clubhouse—C
*Focus/Clubhouse Jr.—C
Nature Friend—B/C
*Pockets—C
SHINE brightly—C
Skipping Stones

CHRISTIAN EDUCATION/ LIBRARY

*Church Libraries—B/C
Journal/Adventist Ed.—B

DAILY DEVOTIONALS

Secret Place—B
Upper Room

MISSIONS

Operation Reveille—B/C

PASTORS/LEADERS

Christian Century—B/C
*InSite—C
*Leadership—B
Priest

TEEN/YOUNG ADULT

Take Five Plus—B/C

WOMEN

Right to the Heart

WRITERS

Best New Writing—C
*New Writer's Mag.
*Poets & Writers
*Writer's Chronicle—B
*Writer's Digest—B

POETRY

ADULT/GENERAL

America
Bible Advocate
Christian Courier/ Canada
Christian Journal
Christian Research
Creation Illust.
Eternal Ink
Evangel
Gem
Home Times
Indian Life
Keys to Living
Leaves
Light & Life
Live
Lutheran Digest
Lutheran Journal
Mature Living
Mature Years
Men of the Cross
New Heart
Penned from the Heart
Penwood Review
Perspectives
Prairie Messenger
Priscilla Papers
Relief Journal
Storyteller
Studio
Testimony
Time of Singing
Vision
Weavings

CHILDREN

Focus/Clubhouse Jr.
Pockets
SHINE brightly
Skipping Stones

DAILY DEVOTIONALS

Christian Devotions
God's Word for Today
Penned from the Heart
Secret Place

PASTORS/LEADERS

Christian Century
Sharing the Practice

TEEN/YOUNG ADULT

Take Five Plus
Young Salvationist

WOMEN

MomSense
Virtuous Woman

WRITERS

Best New Writing
Christian Communicator
New Writer's Mag.
Writer's Digest

POLITICS

ADULT/GENERAL

Brink Magazine
CBN.com
Christian Courier/Canada
Christian Examiner
Christianity Today
Faith Today
Home Times
Light & Life
Movieguide
Our Sunday Visitor
Perspectives
Testimony

PASTORS/LEADERS

Christian Century

TEEN/YOUNG ADULT

Boundless Webzine

PRAISE

ADULT/GENERAL

Evangel
Genuine Motivation
Highway News
Kyria

WOMEN

Brink Magazine
Single! Young Christian Woman

PRAYER

ADULT/GENERAL

Angels on Earth
Believers Bay
Bible Advocate
Brink Magazine
CBN.com
Celebrate Life
Christian Home & School
Christianity Today
Christian Journal
Christian Online
Christian Quarterly

Christian Ranchman
Christian Research
Christian Standard
Columbia
Gem
Genuine Motivation
Guide
Halo Magazine
Highway News
Home Times
Kyria
Leaves
Light & Life
Live
Lookout
Lutheran Digest
Lutheran Journal
Manna
Mature Years
Our Sunday Visitor
Penned from the Heart
Pentecostal Evangel
Perspectives
Presbyterians Today
Priority!
Seek
Testimony
War Cry

CHILDREN

Guide
Sparkle

DAILY DEVOTIONALS

Brink Magazine
Penned from the Heart

PASTORS/LEADERS

Diocesan Dialogue
Leadership
Ministry Today
SmallGroups.com

TEEN/YOUNG ADULT

Boundless Webzine
Single! Young Christian Woman
Young Salvationist

WOMEN

P31 Woman
Right to the Heart
Single! Young Christian Woman
Virtuous Woman

PROPHECY

ADULT/GENERAL

Believers Bay
Bible Advocate
CBN.com
Christian Online
Christian Quarterly
Christian Research
Light & Life
Live
Our Sunday Visitor
Testimony

PASTORS/LEADERS

Ministry Today

TEEN/YOUNG ADULT

Young Salvationist

PSYCHOLOGY

ADULT/GENERAL

CBN.com
Christian Courier/ Canada
Christian Online
Gem
Light & Life
Our Sunday Visitor
Testimony

RACISM

ADULT/GENERAL

Brink Magazine
CBN.com
Christianity Today
Columbia
Faith Today
Genuine Motivation
Guide
Light & Life
Live
Lookout
Manna
Our Sunday Visitor
Perspectives
Priscilla Papers
Testimony

CHILDREN

Guide
Skipping Stones
Sparkle

PASTORS/LEADERS

Ministry Today

TEEN/YOUNG ADULT

Boundless Webzine
Genuine Motivation
Single! Young Christian Woman
Young Salvationist

WOMEN

Single! Young Christian Woman

RECOVERY

ADULT/GENERAL

Bible Advocate
CBN.com
Christian Journal
Home Times
Kyria
Light & Life
Live
Lookout
Manna
Our Sunday Visitor
Priority!
Seek

PASTORS/LEADERS

Ministry Today

TEEN/YOUNG ADULT

Boundless Webzine

WOMEN

Right to the Heart

RELATIONSHIPS

ADULT/GENERAL

Angels on Earth
Brink Magazine
Canada Lutheran
CBN.com
Celebrate Life
Chicken Soup Books
Christian Home & School
Christian Journal

Christian Online
Christian Quarterly
Christian Ranchman
Eternal Ink
Evangel
Faith Today
Gem
Gems of Truth
Genuine Motivation
Guideposts
Home Times
Keys to Living
Kyria
Light & Life
Live
Lookout
Manna
Mature Years
Men of the Cross
New Heart
Our Sunday Visitor
Ozark
Penned from the Heart
Pentecostal Evangel
Perspectives
Priscilla Papers
Seek
Storyteller
Testimony
Vision
Vista
War Cry

CHILDREN

SHINE brightly
Skipping Stones
Sparkle

PASTORS/LEADERS

Leadership
SmallGroups.com

TEEN/YOUNG ADULT

Boundless Webzine
Genuine Motivation
Single! Young Christian Woman
Young Salvationist

WOMEN

Dabbling Mum
MomSense
P31 Woman
Single! Young Christian Woman
Virtuous Woman

RELIGIOUS FREEDOM

ADULT/GENERAL

Brink Magazine
CBN.com
Christian Examiner
Christian Home & School
Christianity Today
Christian Online
Christian Ranchman
Columbia
Faith Today
Gem
Genuine Motivation
Guide
Home Times
Light & Life
Live
Lookout
Manna
Our Sunday Visitor
Perspectives
Prairie Messenger
Seek
Testimony

CHILDREN

Guide
Skipping Stones

MISSIONS

Operation Reveille

PASTORS/LEADERS

Christian Century

TEEN/YOUNG ADULT

Boundless Webzine
Genuine Motivation
Single! Young Christian Woman

WOMEN

Single! Young Christian Woman

RELIGIOUS TOLERANCE

ADULT/GENERAL

Brink Magazine
CBN.com
Christian Examiner
Christian Home & School
Christianity Today
Christian Online
Columbia
Faith Today
Genuine Motivation
Light & Life
Live
Lookout
Manna
Our Sunday Visitor
Perspectives
Prairie Messenger
Seek
Testimony

CHILDREN

Skipping Stones

MISSIONS

Operation Reveille

PASTORS/LEADERS

Christian Century

TEEN/YOUNG ADULT

Boundless Webzine
Genuine Motivation
Single! Young Christian Woman

WOMEN

Single! Young Christian Woman

REVIVAL

ADULT/GENERAL

Bible Advocate
CBN.com
Christian Home & School
Christian Quarterly
Christian Ranchman
Columbia
Evangel
Home Times
Light & Life
Live
Lookout
Manna

PASTORS/LEADERS

Ministry Today

TEEN/YOUNG ADULT
Boundless Webzine

SALVATION TESTIMONIES

ADULT/GENERAL
Believers Bay
CBN.com
Christian Home & School
Christian Journal
Christian Online
Christian Quarterly
Christian Ranchman
Christian Research
Columbia
Gem
Guide
Guideposts
Halo Magazine
Highway News
Home Times
Leaves
Light & Life
Live
New Heart
Now What?
On Mission
Power for Living
Priority!
Seek
Testimony
War Cry

CHILDREN
Guide
Sparkle

TEEN/YOUNG ADULT
Boundless Webzine

SCIENCE

ADULT/GENERAL
Answers Magazine
CBN.com
Christian Courier/Canada
Creation
Creation Illust.
Faith Today
Guide
Home Times
Light & Life
Our Sunday Visitor
Perspectives
Testimony

CHILDREN
Guide
Nature Friend
Skipping Stones
Sparkle

SELF-HELP

ADULT/GENERAL
CBN.com
Home Times
Light & Life
Lookout
Manna
Men of the Cross
Seek
Testimony

CHILDREN
Skipping Stones

WOMEN
Women of the Cross

SENIOR ADULT ISSUES

ADULT/GENERAL
Angels on Earth
CBN.com
Christian Quarterly
Christian Ranchman
Christian Standard
Columbia
Evangel
Faith Today
Gem
Home Times
Light & Life
Live
Mature Living
Mature Years
Our Sunday Visitor
Penned from the Heart
Power for Living
Seek
Testimony
War Cry

DAILY DEVOTIONALS
Penned from the Heart

PASTORS/LEADERS
Diocesan Dialogue

SERMONS

ADULT/GENERAL
Lutheran Journal
Testimony
Weavings

PASTORS/LEADERS
Ministry Today
Preaching
Sharing the Practice

SHORT STORY: ADULT/GENERAL

Best New Writing
CBN.com
Evangel
Lutheran Journal
New Writer's Mag.
Perspectives
Seek

SHORT STORY: ADULT/RELIGIOUS

Angels on Earth
CBN.com
Christian Century
Christian Courier/Canada
Christian Home1 & School
Christian Journal
Christian Online
Christian Ranchman
Christian Research
Evangel
Gem
Gems of Truth
Halo Magazine
Home Times
Indian Life
Live
On Mission
Perspectives
Relief Journal
Seek
Studio
Testimony
Vision
Vista

SHORT STORY: ADVENTURE

ADULT

Angels on Earth
Animal Trails
Best New Writing
CBN.com
Gem
Indian Life
Storyteller
Studio
Vision
Weavings

CHILDREN

Eternal Ink
Focus/Clubhouse Jr.
Kids' Ark
SHINE brightly
Skipping Stones
Sparkle

TEEN/YOUNG ADULT

SHINE brightly
Storyteller

SHORT STORY: ALLEGORY

ADULT

Animal Trails
CBN.com
Christian Journal
Gem
Home Times
Indian Life
Men of the Cross
Studio
Vision
Women of the Cross

CHILDREN

Nature Friend

TEEN/YOUNG ADULT

Home Times

SHORT STORY: BIBLICAL

ADULT

Animal Trails
CBN.com
Christian Journal
Christian Online
Christian Ranchman
Evangel
Gem
Lutheran Journal
Kindred Spirit
Seek
Studio
Vista

CHILDREN

Christian Ranchman
Eternal Ink
Focus/Clubhouse
Nature Friend
Pockets
Sparkle

TEEN/YOUNG ADULT

Christian Ranchman
Home Times

SHORT STORY: CONTEMPORARY

ADULT

Animal Trails
Angels on Earth
CBN.com
Christian Century
Christian Courier/Canada
Christian Home & School
Evangel
Gem
Indian Life
Mature Living
New Writer's Mag.
Perspectives
Relief Journal
Seek
Storyteller
Studio
Vision

CHILDREN

Focus/Clubhouse
Focus/Clubhouse Jr.
Kids' Ark
Pockets
SHINE brightly

TEEN/YOUNG ADULT

Home Times
Storyteller

SHORT STORY: ETHNIC

ADULT

Animal Trails
Gem
Indian Life
Relief Journal
Seek
Studio

CHILDREN

Focus/Clubhouse
Kids' Ark
Skipping Stones
Sparkle

TEEN/YOUNG ADULT

SHINE brightly

SHORT STORY: FANTASY

ADULT

Animal Trails
Gem
Storyteller
Studio

CHILDREN

Focus/Clubhouse
SHINE brightly

TEEN/YOUNG ADULT

SHINE brightly
Storyteller

SHORT STORY: FRONTIER

ADULT

Gem
Indian Life
Storyteller
Studio

CHILDREN

Eternal Ink
Kids' Ark
SHINE brightly

TEEN/YOUNG ADULT

Home Times
Storyteller

SHORT STORY: FRONTIER/ROMANCE

Gem
Studio

SHORT STORY: HISTORICAL
ADULT
Animal Trails
CBN.com
Gem
Home Times
Indian Life
New Writer's Mag.
Seek
Storyteller
Studio

CHILDREN
Christian Ranchman
Focus/Clubhouse
Focus/Clubhouse Jr.
Home Times
Kids' Ark
Nature Friend
SHINE brightly
Sparkle

TEEN/YOUNG ADULT
Christian Ranchman
Home Times
SHINE brightly
Storyteller

SHORT STORY: HISTORICAL/ROMANCE
CBN.com
Gem
Studio

SHORT STORY: HUMOROUS
ADULT
Animal Trails
CBN.com
Christian Courier/Canada
Christian Journal
Gem
Home Times
Mature Living
Mature Years
Men of the Cross
New Writer's Mag.
Seek
Storyteller
Studio
Vista

CHILDREN
Christian Ranchman
Eternal Ink
Focus/Clubhouse
Home Times
SHINE brightly
Skipping Stones
Sparkle

TEEN/YOUNG ADULT
Christian Ranchman
Home Times
Storyteller

SHORT STORY: JUVENILE
CBN.com
Church Herald & Holiness
Focus/Clubhouse
Focus/Clubhouse Jr.
Keys for Kids
Kids' Ark
Pockets
Seek
SHINE brightly
Skipping Stones
Sparkle

SHORT STORY: LITERARY
ADULT
Christian Courier/Canada
Gem
Perspectives
Relief Journal
Seek
Storyteller
Studio

CHILDREN
Skipping Stones

TEEN/YOUNG ADULT
Home Times
Storyteller

SHORT STORY: MYSTERY/ROMANCE
Gem
Studio

SHORT STORY: MYSTERY/SUSPENSE
ADULT
Animal Trails
Best New Writing
CBN.com
Gem
Relief Journal
Storyteller
Studio

CHILDREN
Kids' Ark
SHINE brightly
Sparkle

TEEN/YOUNG ADULT
SHINE brightly
Storyteller

SHORT STORY: PARABLES
ADULT
Animal Trails
Christian Courier/Canada
Christian Journal
Gem
Lutheran Journal
Perspectives
Seek
Studio
Testimony

CHILDREN
Eternal Ink
Focus/Clubhouse Jr.

TEEN/YOUNG ADULT
Home Times
SHINE brightly
Testimony

SHORT STORY: PLAYS
SHINE brightly
Studio

SHORT STORY: ROMANCE
ADULT
CBN.com
Gem
Storyteller
Studio

SHORT STORY: SCIENCE FICTION

ADULT

Gem
Storyteller
Studio

CHILDREN

Kids' Ark
SHINE brightly
Sparkle

TEEN/YOUNG ADULT

Home Times
SHINE brightly
Storyteller

SHORT STORY: SENIOR ADULT FICTION

ADULT

Live
Mature Living
Mature Years
Seek
Vista

SHORT STORY: SKITS

CHILDREN

Focus/Clubhouse Jr.
SHINE brightly

TEEN/YOUNG ADULT

SHINE brightly

SHORT STORY: SPECULATIVE

ADULT

Relief Journal
Studio

TEEN/YOUNG ADULT

Home Times

SHORT STORY: TEEN/YOUNG ADULT

Animal Trails
CBN.com
Seek
Skipping Stones
Storyteller
Testimony

SHORT STORY: WESTERNS

ADULT

Animal Trails
Storyteller
Studio

CHILDREN

Christian Ranchman
Kids' Ark
Sparkle

TEEN/YOUNG ADULT

Christian Ranchman
Storyteller

SINGLES' ISSUES

ADULT/GENERAL

Brink Magazine
CBN.com
Christian Examiner
Christian Online
Christian Ranchman
Columbia
Evangel
Faith Today
Gem
Genuine Motivation
Halo Magazine
Home Times
Kyria
Light & Life
Live
Lookout
Our Sunday Visitor
Penned from the Heart
Power for Living
Priscilla Papers
Seek
Testimony
War Cry

DAILY DEVOTIONALS

Brink Magazine
Penned from the Heart

PASTORS/LEADERS

Ministry Today

TEEN/YOUNG ADULT

Boundless Webzine
Genuine Motivation
Single! Young Christian Woman
Young Salvationist

WOMEN

Single! Young Christian Woman
Women of the Cross

SMALL-GROUP HELPS

ADULT/GENERAL

Kyria
Ministry Today
SmallGroups.com

PASTORS/LEADERS

RevWriter Resource

SOCIAL JUSTICE

ADULT/GENERAL

Brink Magazine
Canada Lutheran
CBN.com
Christian Courier/Canada
Christianity Today
Christian Online
Christian Standard
Columbia
Faith Today
Gem
Genuine Motivation
Guide
Indian Life
Kyria
Light & Life
Lookout
Our Sunday Visitor
Penned from the Heart
Perspectives
Prairie Messenger
Priscilla Papers
Seek
Testimony

CHILDREN

Guide
Pockets
Skipping Stones

CHRISTIAN EDUCATION/LIBRARY

Journal/Adventist Ed.

PASTORS/LEADERS

Christian Century
Group Magazine
L Magazine
Sharing the Practice

TEEN/YOUNG ADULT

Boundless Webzine
Genuine Motivation
Single! Young Christian Woman
Young Salvationist

WOMEN

Single! Young Christian Woman

SOCIOLOGY

ADULT/GENERAL

Christian Courier/Canada
Christian Online
Gem
Light & Life
Our Sunday Visitor
Perspectives
Priscilla Papers
Testimony

TEEN/YOUNG ADULT

Boundless Webzine

WOMEN

Women of the Cross

SPIRITUAL GIFTS

ADULT/GENERAL

Bible Advocate
Brink Magazine
CBN.com
Christian Home & School
Christianity Today
Christian Online
Christian Quarterly
Christian Ranchman
Christian Standard
Columbia
Guide
Home Times
Kyria
Light & Life
Live
Mature Years
Penned from the Heart
Priscilla Papers
Seek
Testimony
Vista

CHILDREN

Guide
Sparkle

DAILY DEVOTIONALS

Penned from the Heart

PASTORS/LEADERS

Ministry Today
RevWriter Resource

WOMEN

P31 Woman
Virtuous Woman

SPIRITUALITY

ADULT/GENERAL

Angels on Earth
Bible Advocate
Brink Magazine
CBN.com
Christian Courier/Canada
Christianity Today
Christian Journal
Christian Online
Columbia
Faith Today
Gem
Genuine Motivation
Guideposts
Halo Magazine
Indian Life
Leaves
Light & Life
Live
Lookout
Mature Years
New Heart
Our Sunday Visitor
Penned from the Heart
Penwood Review
Prairie Messenger
Presbyterians Today
Priscilla Papers
Seek
Testimony
Vista
War Cry
Weavings

CHILDREN

Skipping Stones

DAILY DEVOTIONALS

Penned from the Heart

PASTORS/LEADERS

Christian Century
Diocesan Dialogue
Group Magazine
Leadership
L Magazine
Ministry Today
RevWriter Resource
Sharing the Practice

TEEN/YOUNG ADULT

Boundless Webzine
Genuine Motivation
Single! Young Christian Woman

WOMEN

Single! Young Christian Woman
Women of the Cross

SPIRITUAL LIFE

ADULT/GENERAL

Bible Advocate
Brink Magazine
CBN.com
Christian Examiner
Christian Home & School
Christian Journal
Christian Online
Christian Quarterly
Christian Ranchman
Christian Research
Columbia
Eternal Ink
Faith Today
Guide
Highway News
Home Times
Light & Life
Live
Lookout
Lutheran Journal
Mature Living
New Heart
Our Sunday Visitor
Penned from the Heart
Perspectives
Presbyterians Today

Priscilla Papers
Seek
Testimony
Weavings

CHILDREN
Guide
Sparkle

DAILY DEVOTIONALS
Brink Magazine
Penned from the Heart

PASTORS/LEADERS
Group Magazine
Leadership
L Magazine
Ministry Today
SmallGroups.com

TEEN/YOUNG ADULT
Boundless Webzine
Genuine Motivation
Single! Young Christian Woman
Young Salvationist

WOMEN
P31 Woman
Right to the Heart
Single! Young Christian Woman

SPIRITUAL RENEWAL
ADULT/GENERAL
Bible Advocate
Brink Magazine
Canada Lutheran
CBN.com
Christian Home & School
Christian Online
Christian Quarterly
Christian Ranchman
Columbia
Eternal Ink
Evangel
Faith Today
Genuine Motivation
Home Times
Light & Life
Live
Lookout
Manna
Pentecostal Evangel
Seek
Testimony

PASTORS/LEADERS
Christian Century
Group Magazine
Leadership
L Magazine
Ministry Today

TEEN/YOUNG ADULT
Boundless Webzine
Genuine Motivation
Single! Young Christian Woman
Young Salvationist

WOMEN
Right to the Heart
Single! Young Christian Woman
Virtuous Woman

SPIRITUAL WARFARE
ADULT/GENERAL
Angels on Earth
Believers Bay
Bible Advocate
Brink Magazine
CBN.com
Celebrate Life
Christian Home & School
Christianity Today
Christian Online
Christian Quarterly
Christian Ranchman
Christian Research
Columbia
Gem
Leaves
Light & Life
Live
Lookout
Manna
New Heart
Penned from the Heart
Seek
Testimony

DAILY DEVOTIONALS
Penned from the Heart

MISSIONS
Operation Reveille

PASTORS/LEADERS
Group Magazine
Growth Points
Ministry Today
Small Groups.com

TEEN/YOUNG ADULT
Young Salvationist

SPORTS/RECREATION
ADULT/GENERAL
Angels on Earth
CBN.com
Gem
Guide
Guideposts
Home Times
Living Light
Lookout
Our Sunday Visitor
Storyteller
Testimony

CHILDREN
Guide
SHINE brightly
Sparkle

TEEN/YOUNG ADULT
Boundless Webzine
Young Salvationist

STEWARDSHIP
ADULT/GENERAL
Angels on Earth
Bible Advocate
Canada Lutheran
CBN.com
Celebrate Life
Christian Courier/Canada
Christian News NW
Christian Online
Christian Ranchman
Christian Standard
Columbia
Evangel
Faith Today
Gem
Genuine Motivation
Guide

Home Times
Light & Life
Live
Lookout
Lutheran Journal
Manna
Our Sunday Visitor
Penned from the Heart
Perspectives
Power for Living
Seek
Testimony

CHILDREN
Guide
SHINE brightly
Sparkle

DAILY DEVOTIONALS
Penned from the Heart

PASTORS/LEADERS
InSite
Ministry Today
RevWriter Resource
Sharing the Practice

TEEN/YOUNG ADULT
Boundless Webzine
Genuine Motivation
Single! Young Christian Woman
Young Salvationist

WOMEN
P31 Woman
Single! Young Christian Woman

TAKE-HOME PAPERS
ADULT/GENERAL
Evangel
Gem
Gems of Truth
Live
Power for Living
Seek
Vision
Vista

CHILDREN
Guide
JuniorWay

THEOLOGICAL
ADULT/GENERAL
America
Bible Advocate
Brink Magazine
CBN.com
Christian Courier/Canada
Christianity Today
Christian Online
Christian Ranchman
Christian Research
Christian Standard
Faith Today
Light & Life
Lookout
Movieguide
Our Sunday Visitor
Perspectives
Prairie Messenger
Priscilla Papers
Testimony

DAILY DEVOTIONALS
Brink Magazine
Penned from the Heart

PASTORS/LEADERS
Christian Century
Diocesan Dialogue
Group Magazine
Growth Points
RevWriter Resource
Sharing the Practice
SmallGroups.com

TEEN/YOUNG ADULT
Boundless Webzine
Young Salvationist

THINK PIECES
ADULT/GENERAL
Brink Magazine
Christian Courier/Canada
Christianity Today
Christian Online
Faith Today
Gem
Genuine Motivation
Light & Life
Lookout
Manna
Men of the Cross
Our Sunday Visitor
Penned from the Heart
Penwood Review
Seek
Testimony

CHILDREN
Skipping Stones

PASTORS/LEADERS
Enrichment
Ministry Today

TEEN/YOUNG ADULT
Boundless Webzine
Genuine Motivation
Single! Young Christian Woman
Young Salvationist

WOMEN
MomSense
Single! Young Christian Woman
Women of the Cross

TIME MANAGEMENT
ADULT/GENERAL
Brink Magazine
CBA Retailers
CBN.com
Christian Online
Gem
Genuine Motivation
Home Times
Light & Life
Live
Living Light
Lookout
Men of the Cross
Penned from the Heart
Testimony

DAILY DEVOTIONALS
Brink Magazine
Penned from the Heart

PASTORS/LEADERS
Enrichment

TEEN/YOUNG ADULT
Boundless Webzine
Genuine Motivation
Single! Young Christian Woman

WOMEN

P31 Woman
Single! Young Christian Woman
Virtuous Woman

WRITERS

Adv. Christian Writer
Christian Communicator
Fellowscript
Writer

TRAVEL

ADULT/GENERAL

Angels on Earth
Brink Magazine
Capper's
CBN.com
Gem
Genuine Motivation
Mature Living
Mature Years
Movieguide
Seek
Testimony

CHILDREN

SHINE brightly
Skipping Stones
Sparkle

TEEN/YOUNG ADULT

Boundless Webzine
Genuine Motivation
Single! Young Christian Woman

WOMEN

Christian Homeschool Moms
Single! Young Christian Woman

TRUE STORIES

ADULT/GENERAL

Adoptee Search
Angels on Earth
Brink Magazine
CBN.com
Celebrate Life
Christian Online
Christian Quarterly
Christian Ranchman
Columbia
Eternal Ink
Evangel
Gem
Gems of Truth
Genuine Motivation
Guide
Guideposts
Halo Magazine
Highway News
Home Times
Indian Life
Kyria
Light & Life
Live
Lutheran Digest
Mature Living
Men of the Cross
New Heart
Now What?
On Mission
Penned from the Heart
Pentecostal Evangel
Power for Living
Priority!
Seek
Storyteller
Testimony
Vision
Vista
War Cry

CHILDREN

Focus/Clubhouse Jr.
Guide
Pockets
SHINE brightly
Skipping Stones
Sparkle

MISSIONS

Operation Reveille

PASTORS/LEADERS

Leadership
Sharing the Practice

TEEN/YOUNG ADULT

Boundless Webzine
Genuine Motivation
Single! Young Christian Woman
Young Salvationist

WOMEN

MomSense
Single! Young Christian Woman

VIDEO REVIEWS

ADULT/GENERAL

CBN.com
Eternal Ink
Genuine Motivation
Home Times
Movieguide
Our Sunday Visitor
Presbyterians Today
Testimony

CHRISTIAN EDUCATION/LIBRARY

Church Libraries

PASTORS/LEADERS

Christian Century
Ministry Today

TEEN/YOUNG ADULT

Genuine Motivation
Single! Young Christian Woman

WOMEN

Dabbling Mum
Single! Young Christian Woman
Virtuous Woman

WEBSITE REVIEWS

ADULT/GENERAL

CBN.com
Christianity Today
Eternal Ink
On Mission
Our Sunday Visitor

MISSIONS

Operation Reveille

WOMEN'S ISSUES

ADULT/GENERAL

Brink Magazine
CBA Retailers
CBN.com
Celebrate Life
Chicken Soup Books
Christian Courier/Canada

Christian Examiner
Christian Journal
Christian News NW
Christian Online
Christian Quarterly
Christian Ranchman
Columbia
Evangel
Faith Today
Gem
Halo Magazine
Indian Life
Kyria
Light & Life
Live
Lookout
Manna
Our Sunday Visitor
Penned from the Heart
Perspectives
Prairie Messenger
Priscilla Papers
Seek
Share
Single! Young Christian Woman
Storyteller
Testimony
War Cry

CHILDREN

Skipping Stones

DAILY DEVOTIONALS

Penned from the Heart

PASTORS/LEADERS

SmallGroups.com

TEEN/YOUNG ADULT

Boundless Webzine

WOMEN

Dabbling Mum
MomSense
P31 Woman
Right to the Heart
Share
Single! Young Christian Woman
Virtuous Woman
Women of the Cross

WORKPLACE ISSUES

ADULT/GENERAL

CBN.com
Christian Examiner
Christian Online
Christian Ranchman
Christian Retailing
Evangel
Faith Today
Light & Life
Live
Lookout
Manna
New Heart
Our Sunday Visitor
Penned from the Heart
Perspectives
Seek
Testimony

MISSIONS

Operation Reveille

TEEN/YOUNG ADULT

Boundless Webzine

WRITERS

Adv. Christian Writer

WORLD ISSUES

ADULT/GENERAL

Brink Magazine
CBN.com
Christian Examiner
Christian Online
Columbia
Evangel
Faith Today
Gem
Genuine Motivation
Guide
Home Times
Indian Life
Light & Life
Lookout
Movieguide
Our Sunday Visitor
Penned from the Heart
Perspectives
Seek
Testimony
War Cry

CHILDREN

Guide
Skipping Stones

MISSIONS

Operation Reveille

PASTORS/LEADERS

Christian Century
L Magazine
Ministry Today

TEEN/YOUNG ADULT

Boundless Webzine
Genuine Motivation
Single! Young Christian Woman

WOMEN

Single! Young Christian Woman

WORSHIP

ADULT/GENERAL

Angels on Earth
Bible Advocate
Brink Magazine
Canada Lutheran
CBN.com
Christian Examiner
Christianity Today
Christian Online
Christian Ranchman
Christian Standard
Columbia
Eternal Ink
Evangel
Halo Magazine
Highway News
Kyria
Light & Life
Live
Lookout
Lutheran Journal
Manna
Penned from the Heart
Perspectives
Power for Living
Presbyterians Today
Priscilla Papers
Seek
Testimony

Time of Singing
Vista
War Cry

CHILDREN

Keys for Kids
Sparkle

DAILY DEVOTIONALS

Brink Magazine
Penned from the Heart

PASTORS/LEADERS

Enrichment
Group Magazine
Growth Points
Leadership
L Magazine
Ministry Today
Parish Liturgy
Preaching
RevWriter Resource
Sharing the Practice

TEEN/YOUNG ADULT

Boundless Webzine

WOMEN

Virtuous Woman

WRITING HOW-TO

ADULT/GENERAL

Canada Lutheran
CBA Retailers
CBN.com
Christian Online
Home Times
Penwood Review

CHILDREN

Skipping Stones

PASTORS/LEADERS

Newsletter Newsletter

TEEN/YOUNG ADULT

Boundless Webzine

WOMEN

Dabbling Mum
Right to the Heart

WRITERS

Adv. Christian Writer
Best New Writing
Christian Communicator
Fellowscript
Freelance Writer's Report
New Writer's Mag.
Poets & Writers
Writer
Writer's Chronicle
Writer's Digest

YOUNG-WRITER MARKETS

Note: These publications have indicated they will accept submissions from children or teens (C or T).

ADULT/GENERAL

Animal Trails
CBN.com (T)
Celebrate Life (C or T)
Christian Home & School (C or T)
Christian Journal (C or T)
Christian Online (C or T)
Church Herald & Holiness (C or T)
Eternal Ink (C or T)
Home Times (T)
Indian Life (C or T)
Leben (T)
Light & Life (C or T)
Lutheran Journal (C or T)
Manna (C or T)
Men of the Cross (T)
Penned from the Heart (C or T)
Priority! (C or T)
Storyteller (C or T)
Vista (C or T)

CHILDREN

Focus/Clubhouse (C)
Kids' Ark (C or T)
Pockets (C)

DAILY DEVOTIONALS

Penned from the Heart (C or T)

TEEN/YOUNG ADULT

Boundless Webzine (T)
Take Five Plus (T)

WOMEN

Dabbling Mum (T)
Women of the Cross (T)

WRITERS

Fellowscript (T)

YOUTH ISSUES

ADULT/GENERAL

Canada Lutheran
CBN.com
Chicken Soup Books
Christian Examiner
Christian Home & School
Christian News NW
Christian Online
Christian Ranchman
Columbia
Guide
Home Times
Indian Life
Lookout
Manna
Our Sunday Visitor
Penned from the Heart
Seek
Testimony

CHILDREN

Guide
Keys for Kids
SHINE brightly
Skipping Stones
Sparkle

CHRISTIAN EDUCATION/LIBRARY

Journal/Adventist Ed.

PASTORS/LEADERS

Group Magazine
InSite
L Magazine
Plugged In

TEEN/YOUNG ADULT

Boundless Webzine
Sisterhood
Young Salvationist

WOMEN

P31 Woman

BONUS SECTION

Writer's Helps

Professionalism

Writing What You Want

by Jerry B. Jenkins

WHEN DO YOU get to the point you can write anything you want—and not have to write for the marketplace? If I ever get there I'll let you know.

In case you think I can simply write what I want, with no eye toward editors, publishers, and readers, let me pull back the curtain on some of the market-driven changes I made to the fiction project that occupied me much of last year.

In May 2012 I told an interviewer I was writing the first of a two-volume epic novel based on the life of the apostle Paul. I saw this as a natural place to go after having written the Jesus Chronicles (*Matthew's Story, Mark's Story, Luke's Story, John's Story*) for Penguin. Much of *Luke's Story* especially dealt with the early church and Paul's place in it.

My publisher had agreed with my plans for two 150,000-word accounts, *I, Saul* and *I, Paul*, fleshing out the stories hinted at in the Bible. For example, a few verses indicate that Paul's nephew overheard a murder plot against Paul and was able to help thwart it. That begs for a few chapters about the nephew: who he was and how he heard this.

A few months later, my publisher brought into the process a top New York editor. On June 29 I wrote this in an e-mail:

> I've been in touch with the famous editor I mentioned and am brimming with new angles and ideas for Paul. This will likely push my deadline from August to October. The upside is that I couldn't have imagined my enthusiasm for the project growing—but it is.
>
> August 17:
>
> New deadline for *I, Saul* is November 1. I'm on pace and loving the task.
>
> August 31:
>
> The Tim LaHaye on this project, James MacDonald of Harvest Bible Chapel, has finally gotten a chance to see what I've written so far. He seems thrilled, which is a great encouragement to me.
>
> October 12:
>
> It's great to be back behind the keyboard, especially after a momentous trip to New York to meet with my editor. The result was a great idea: switch from two 150,000-word books to one of about 100,000. The biggest complication with that—despite that the publisher and my agent and I agree it will make the project better—is that it so significantly impacts the pacing. With 75,000 words behind me, I had been setting up many situations that would be resolved in book two. Instead everything will have to be included in the one novel.
>
> Now I'm back to the stage of writing that I love: rewriting, recasting, re-pacing. And I have until the end of the year to do it.
>
> November 14:
>
> A thorny plot point finally came together, as such always do. I needed just the right location for a pivotal scene, and for weeks it eluded me. In the shower the other day, with

the stream of water massaging my brain, it came to me in a flash . . . and it's an exotic locale Dianna and I have visited. It was the last piece of the puzzle that will allow me to just speed to the end of the writing without wondering where to set everything.

The scheduled release date for the novel is August 13, 2013. Once I've delivered the manuscript, it's going to be hard to wait that long, but such is publishing life.

November 21:

I submitted the first 250 pages of the novel (about 70 percent of the total) to my New York editor.

November 27:

If your editor is happy, it makes your day. If she's also the legendary editor of Clancy, Cornwell, Cussler . . . safe to say my week is made.

Keep your eye on the marketplace and keep listening to your readers and your editors. It works for me.

This first appeared in the March 2013 issue of *Christian Communicator*.

The Myth of the Part-Time Writer

by Deborah Dee Harper

WE CAN BE SURE OF ONE THING: the part-time writer does not exist. If you're a writer, you work every hour of every day of the year. You are the ultimate full-time employee.

Never Closed

The "part-time writer" myth has its roots in the number of hours a writer spends in front of her computer. If she's not sitting there eight hours a day, five days a week—or if she works at another job—she must be a part-timer. That's how it's defined in the rest of the working world.

But much of our work is not done at a computer. While others punch out or lock the office door at the end of their workday, writers toil from dawn to dawn. Our desk and computer comprise just one of our branch offices. Others include the bathroom, kitchen, waiting rooms, checkout lines, the car, even our paying job.

A writer's main office is her brain—and it never closes. Behind those doors, deep in the busy hallways of our imagination and creativity, we do our best work. We refine that work while visiting one of our branch offices, but those locations change at a moment's notice. So we take our files with us.

Stocking Up

Because many of our ideas live only as long as it takes them to escape, we work hard to capture them with notebooks, digital recorders, or Post-it Notes. In our line of work, respectful eavesdropping and unobtrusive observation are not rude; they're work-related. Observing people—noting their behavior and appearance, capturing dialogue and imagining what might be going on in their lives—is corporate espionage, except we're not doing it for our gain, but for the Kingdom of God.

Our brains are multitasking, mental tape recorders of unlimited magnitude that store the continuous array of sights, sounds, smells, tastes, and tactile experiences of our daily lives. Close your eyes, recall a situation, and let the sensory images flow. We retain more than we think and we never stop processing that information.

Yes, taking notes helps, but written down or not, the information is tucked away in our cerebral office—our ultimate backup system. We can reach into the supply room of our mobile workplace (open twenty-four hours a day) and pull what we need from the wide array of stock accumulated over the years. Every experience, encounter, and environment we've known is available for recall and use.

So while you're never off the clock, enjoy the discovery and creativity. Then write it down!

This previously appeared on the Christian Writers Guild blog: www.christianwritersguild.com/blog/the-myth-of-the-part-time-writer/.

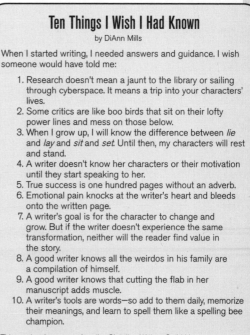

Ten Things I Wish I Had Known

by DiAnn Mills

When I started writing, I needed answers and guidance. I wish someone would have told me:

1. Research doesn't mean a jaunt to the library or sailing through cyberspace. It means a trip into your characters' lives.
2. Some critics are like boo birds that sit on their lofty power lines and mess on those below.
3. When I grow up, I will know the difference between *lie* and *lay* and *sit* and *set.* Until then, my characters will rest and stand.
4. A writer doesn't know her characters or their motivation until they start speaking to her.
5. True success is one hundred pages without an adverb.
6. Emotional pain knocks at the writer's heart and bleeds onto the written page.
7. A writer's goal is for the character to change and grow. But if the writer doesn't experience the same transformation, neither will the reader find value in the story.
8. A good writer knows all the weirdos in his family are a compilation of himself.
9. A good writer knows that cutting the flab in her manuscript adds muscle.
10. A writer's tools are words—so add to them daily, memorize their meanings, and learn to spell them like a spelling bee champion.

This previously appeared on the Christian Writers Guild blog: www.christianwritersguild.com/blog/10-things-i-wish-i-had-known/.

Writers' Guidelines: Your Directions to Publication

by Jeanette Gardner Littleton

I OFTEN USE GOOGLE MAPS. Anytime I go somewhere I haven't been, I map the place, print the directions, and head out. Usually, I arrive right where I want to be.

Don't you wish editors had similar mapping guides to help you reach your publication goal? "Take a right at the illustration, go left at the Bible verse . . . travel five paragraphs until you reach a satisfying conclusion" and you're there! You've sold your writing.

Editors' Maps Point the Way

Fortunately they do. Editors' maps are called writers' guidelines. Editors create them to let writers know exactly what kind of materials they want to see. The guidelines tell, among other things, who the target audience is, how long the articles should be, what kind of tone, and what genres they don't want.

Guidelines give writers other helpful facts as well, such as editor contact information, how to submit your manuscript (snail mail or e-mail), and sometimes a theme list. Often, guidelines will provide specific formatting and other tips that help.

Where to Find Them

You'll often find writers' guidelines at writers conferences, such as the Guild's Writing for the Soul. Alternately, you can often find them on a publisher's website. The annual *Christian Writer's Market Guide* provides information on what specific publishers are looking for, where to find guidelines, or how to contact the publisher to request their guidelines.

Unlike online maps, writers' guidelines never steer you in the wrong direction. Look for them and use them. They're a road map to your destination of publication.

This previously appeared on the Christian Writers Guild blog: www.christianwritersguild.com/blog/writers%E2%80%99-guidelines-your-directions-to-publication/.

Formatting–and More–for Success

by PeggySue Wells

TO WIN EDITORS AND INFLUENCE PUBLISHERS you need to write like a professional. Here are some essential formatting and style secrets that spell the difference.

Formatting

- Use 12-point Times New Roman.
- Double-space unless a publisher states otherwise.
- Write with verbs and nouns. Adverbs and adjectives should be rare.
- Use an exclamation point only if the house is on fire.
- People don't speak in parentheses, so don't use them in your fiction.
- Write short paragraphs.
- Use spell-check, but also be careful of the wrong word spelled correctly, like *their* for there or *to* for too.
- Names of books, publications, and titles of songs are italicized, not underlined.

More Easy Fixes

Omit needless words like:

Very. *It was very large.* How large? The size of a South Carolina palmetto bug? As big as a beluga whale? Be specific.

Just. Just is just not needed.

Really. *It was really sweet.* How sweet? Like southern tea? Like sugared breakfast cereal that makes your teeth hurt just looking at the box? Describe how sweet, or even better, show it through a character's reaction.

Some. *Some children went to the beach.* How many? The grandmother's seven grandchildren? A first grade class?

All. *They all arrived at the battle.* Remove *all* and the sentence reads better.

Literally. *Anne's hair was literally green.* It was either green or it wasn't. Literally is literally not needed.

Other Suggestions:

- Avoid excessive stage direction every time your character moves. *He got up from his chair and made his way into the kitchen. From the refrigerator he pulled bread.* Just say, *He made a sandwich.*
- Vary the length and structure of your sentences.
- Avoid repetition.
- Read your manuscript aloud to catch overused words.
- Be concise.

This previously appeared on the Christian Writers Guild blog: www.christianwritersguild.com/blog/formatting%E2%80%94and-more%E2%80%94for-success/.

Please Follow the Directions

by Andy Scheer

THIS MORNING I rejected three inquiries from people who wanted me to be their agent. They made my choices easy. None gave more than a hint of having read and followed the directions.

The literary agency's website lists what we want to see from a potential client. It also spells out the elements of a book proposal. There's a reason for that. Without a complete picture, we can't correctly assess a project's potential—and neither can a publisher's acquisitions editor.

I recently attended the convention of a literary group. In five years with them, I've gotten to know the members. Some I can count on to do the right thing. I enjoy being around them and try to help them if I can. Others think they deserve special privileges. I try to be polite, but . . .

I reflected on that experience as I reviewed this morning's e-mails.

- The first writer concluded her query by asking if I'd like to review her full manuscript. (Nope. If I were interested, I'd like to study her proposal.)
- The next (a retired CIA agent working on a spy novel) sent his resume in the hope I'd take him on as a client. (I told him to wait until he'd finished his novel, then send a proposal.)
- The third, who'd written a combination memoir/devotional, sent three attachments: a table of contents, three chapters, and a sample devotion. All important elements, but lacking key ingredients of a full proposal.

Identify Yourself to Editors

by Andy Scheer

Imagine a magazine or anthology editor wants to publish something you've written, but isn't sure who you are, how to reach you, or where to send payment.

That really happens. "Once I had two authors with the same name," says a compilation editor who works with hundreds of contributors, "and neither put their contact information on the manuscripts. I didn't realize it was two authors and sent a contract to the wrong person.

"I recently had an author who submitted to me under two different names and e-mail addresses and didn't put contact information on her manuscript," she says. "I had to send an e-mail to make sure the other submission was also hers."

The solution? Apply what you learned in kindergarten: Put your name on your paper. And also your e-mail address, conventional address, and a phone number. (Single-space this at the top of the first page of any article.)

Customize your e-mail settings so each time you send a message, it automatically inserts a "signature." Many writers create a signature block that gives their full name, a line about their specialty (such as Author/Conference Speaker), the title of their most recent book, and a link to their blog or website.

"I prefer when the e-mail address matches the person's name," the compilation editor says. "If Susan Longfellow has SLongfellow or SusanLongfellow in her address, it's easier to reach her. If she goes by *kiteflyermom@smith.net*, I have to spend precious time searching for her."

Clearly identifying yourself marks you as a professional.

This previously appeared in the May 2013 Christian Writers Guild newsletter *WordSmith*.

Maybe they were fantastic potential clients—just too new to writing to know the expectations. So in my responses, I tried to educate them. But I'll choose to work with writers who come across as serious professionals.

This previously appeared on the Christian Writers Guild blog: www.christianwritersguild.com/blog/please-follow-the-directions/.

Five Must-Dos Before You Submit

by Michele Huey

After months, even years, your book is done. The next step is to find a publisher. Isn't it? Maybe not. In today's highly competitive market, sending your manuscript off as soon as you think it's done won't wash.

Before you click *Send*, make certain your manuscript is ready:

1. **Revise Again.** You get only one opportunity with a publisher or agent—don't blow it. Read *Revision and Self-editing for Publication* by James Scott Bell and find ways to improve your draft. Work through Donald Maass's *Writing the Breakout Novel Workbook*.
2. **Get Critiqued.** Submit your manuscript to an editor or a critique service. Check the list of editorial services in *The Christian Writer's Market Guide*. Good critiques cost, but are worth every cent.
3. **Develop a Book Proposal.** Most publishers want to see a proposal. Then, if they're interested, they will ask to see your entire manuscript. W. Terry Whalin's *Book Proposals that Sell* walks you through this vital step. Read Kevin Scott's article in the *Market Guide* about nonfiction proposals and the evaluation process.
4. **Become a Contestant.** Enter your manuscript in a contest, such as Operation First Novel, the ACFW Genesis, or Amazon's Breakthrough Novel. *The Christian Writer's Market Guide* lists more contests.
5. **Confer with Professionals.** Attend a writer's conference to meet agents and editors, plus fellow writers. Networking is vital.

Pursuing your dream of publication takes persistence. Send only your best.

This previously appeared on the Christian Writers Guild blog: www.christianwritersguild.com/blog/5-must-dos-before-you-submit/.

Make Your Words Do the Work

by Angela Hunt

I DANCED WITH MY DADDY at my debutante ball in 1975. Being Baptists, we didn't do much more than step on each other's feet.

If I were a *beginning* writer, I might write this about that evening:

> The night was a beginning and an end!!! A farewell to childhood, a welcoming of new horizons! An occasion to put on my best, invest in a few formal manners, learn how to curtsy!! If I'd been a little less giddy, I might have appreciated these things!!!

Nothing exposes a beginning writer faster than an overdose of punctuation, specifically exclamation points. Take them out and your content is improved 100 percent.

Choose Carefully

Consider exclamation points like a president's ability to launch an air strike; use them with the same deliberation and reserve. Be sure the effect will be worth the big guns. Words are supposed to do the work of evoking emotion, not punctuation (!), ALL CAPITAL LETTERS, or bold and colored fonts.

No Props

When you choose words, choose hunky ones. Don't opt for spindly verbs that require an adverb to prop them up. You might need adverbs on occasion, but they should, like calling in the military, be used reluctantly. I teach my writing classes to say "Boo, hiss" every time I say "adverb."

In one of my favorite *Seinfeld* episodes, Elaine is dating and editing an author named Jake Jarmel. When he takes a phone message about a friend having a baby and doesn't use an exclamation point, Elaine is peeved that he doesn't appreciate how important the baby is to women everywhere. To demonstrate her displeasure, she peppers his manuscript with exclamation points. Her boss and Jake Jarmel are not amused. And neither will your editor be if you follow Elaine's example.

Search and Destroy

So do yourself—and your editor—a favor. Pore over your work in progress and eliminate every exclamation point, unless it's the rare, appropriate one. Your manuscript will begin to have that professional polish.

This previously appeared on the Christian Writers Guild blog: www.christianwriters guild.com/blog/make-your-words-do-the -work/.

Triple-D Writers

by Julie-Allyson Ieron

Editors have pages to fill. You want to fill those pages, but your words will never get there if you can't meet the Triple-D: the drop dead deadline. In publishing, the deadline rules.

If your article doesn't arrive on time, the editor's pages will still be filled. Just not by you. They'll be filled by someone who can meet or beat a delivery date.

You want a reputation for meeting the Triple-D, but it takes planning—and sometimes Olympic-level gymnastics.

Your Reputation, Your Promise

As one business professor taught me, it's about integrity—always delivering what you promise and never promising more than you can deliver. Once you agree to a date, do whatever it takes to meet it, or drop dead trying.

Whatever It Takes

The tightest deadline I've undertaken was a three-books-in-three-months contract. Yes, that was nuts! But I got the manuscripts to the editor on time. I wrote in airports, waiting rooms, even the cancer ward as my dozing friend received a transfusion. I met my promise—the deadline.

An editor was depending on me. Will editors see you as a Triple-D writer? It's up to you.

This previously appeared on the Christian Writers Guild blog: www .christianwritersguild.com/blog/triple-d/.

First Rights Means First

by Roger Palms

WE WERE THRILLED to receive a well-known author's article. Our magazine always paid more for first rights so we could be the first to publish this strong piece.

After we published that article, another magazine editor called. This same author had sold that same article to him—also on a first rights basis. He said another editor had called him saying that he, too, had purchased the article with the same understanding.

I called the writer. "Oh," she said, "I didn't know that's what 'first rights' means."

Any writer who has been in the business very long must learn and understand the various rights publications purchase. Buying first rights means an editor doesn't have to worry about the "me too" syndrome.

Know What You're Selling

There are other forms of first rights. A writer could sell first rights in a limited geographic area: first North American rights or European or Australian. The writer can also sell first electronic rights.

Once an article is published and a period of time has passed, the writer can sell other rights to the same article to a different publication—but naturally not first rights. When selling second rights or second serial rights or even reprint rights, it's ethical to tell the new editor where the article first appeared.

For definitions of terms such as all rights, electronic rights, first rights, and reprint rights, check the Glossary in the back of this Market Guide.

Protect Your Integrity

As far as I know, that woman never published another article with any of us. What she didn't realize—but you should—is that editors know each other and read one another's publications. Her reputation was tarnished. She may have earned a few extra dollars at the time, but she wouldn't earn any more money from any of us.

Your honesty and professionalism are valuable. Editors respect writers who conduct their business ethically.

This previously appeared on the Christian Writers Guild blog: www.christianwritersguild.com/blog/first-rights-means-first/

What Not to Say to an Editor

by PeggySue Wells

Query letters and elevator pitches are designed to get an editor to look at your project. What not to say is every bit as important as what to include.

Use the Guidelines

Lin Johnson, editor of the *Christian Communicator, Advanced Christian Writer*, and *Church Libraries*, runs each query she receives through a well-defined litmus test.

"Don't propose a topic that doesn't fit the periodical," Johnson says. "That tells me you haven't studied my magazine (or guidelines). That's a guaranteed rejection."

Do Your Homework

Publishers market to targeted readers. While most writers know not to send a children's book manuscript to a publisher that doesn't produce projects for young people, there are other areas to steer clear of.

"I cringe whenever I see 'there's nothing else like it on the market,'" says Nick Harrison, Harvest House editor. "First, if there's truly nothing else like it, there's probably a reason. Second, there usually *is* something else out there like it, and the author is showing his or her ignorance by not being aware of the competition."

Watch What You Say

Ann Parrish, an editor at Bethany House Publishers, loses interest when a writer claims, "The Lord told me your company is the one to publish my book."

Other statements that do not make friends and influence editors:

"It's an instant bestseller."
"This is the next Left Behind series."
"This is the Christian Harry Potter (or Twilight)."
"My mom (spouse, children, critique group, parrot) loves this, so I know you will too."

Integrity Is Critical

Don't put words in an endorser's mouth. "My pet peeve is when someone writes, 'Doc Hensley thought it was wonderful,'" says Dennis E. Hensley, director of the Professional Writing Department at Taylor University. "In fact, I said it had potential but needed a lot of copyediting and revision."

Errors like these flag you as an amateur. Editors and publishers are drawn to writers who present their ideas—and themselves—professionally.

This previously appeared on the Christian Writers Guild blog: www.christianwritersguild.com/blog/what-not-to-say-to-an-editor/.

The Good News about Rejection

by Virelle Kidder

AFTER TWENTY-FIVE YEARS, it was time to clean out my editorial files. Each held treasured letters and years of correspondence with editors who have shaped my writing.

Then I reached the last file, "Rejection Letters." Feelings of failure crept back. I chucked it in the garbage, then retrieved it. Most of the personalized form letters and handwritten notes said my work did not match their current publishing needs.

Offering a Target

But I hadn't remembered the compliments: "I love your writing," "We were inspired by your piece and found it well written," and "Please send us more ideas."

Those rejection letters pushed me to write better. To grow. If I didn't hit the mark, I determined to nail it the next time. I studied issues of the publication and their guidelines more carefully. If I was too wordy or unfocused, that meant I hadn't done my best self-editing.

I Needed That

One of the toughest editors I ever worked with made me cry when she called my work "fluffy." I'd seen myself as gut-level honest. When she pointed out the dreaded fluff, she helped me write my most authentic book to that date (***Donkeys Still Talk***, NavPress, 2004).

Does my writing still get rejected? Yes. It's less often now, but it still hurts. But once the sting has passed, I look at the editor's comments, swallow my pride, and start over.

Now I realize my rejection letters are too valuable for the junk heap. I've put them back in my file drawer, this time in front.

This previously appeared on the Christian Writers Guild blog: www.christianwritersguild.com/blog/the-good-news-about-rejection/.

Nailing Down Your Professional Status

by Gary A. Hensley

IN THE OLD TELEVISION SHOW *Sanford and Son,* Fred Sanford asks a man, "Who says you're an attorney?"

"I do," the man says.

Fred says, "Who says you're not?"

The man mumbles, "The State of California."

You don't want to be on the wrong end of this punch line with the Internal Revenue Service if you're audited.

Who Says You're a Professional?

If you're an undocumented writer (the IRS term for someone who writes only as a hobby), you have nothing to prove. You need only to report your writing income on Form 1040 as other income, and your writing expenses on Schedule A, if you itemize deductions.

But if you reported your writing income and expenses on Schedule C as a professional writer, you must be able to substantiate that your writing career is "an activity engaged in for profit."

All income you receive from your writing efforts is taxable, whether you represent yourself as a professional or a hobbyist. The benefit of *professional* status comes on the expense (or deduction) side of the ledger. Professional writers can deduct all "reasonable and ordinary" business expenses, even if this results in a business loss.

Your Intention

Key in determining if your writing is a business or a hobby is whether you write with the intention of making a profit. The IRS limits deductions related to an activity not engaged in for profit (a hobby).

How Intent Is Determined

The IRS considers nine factors to evaluate the profit motive of a business activity, so be prepared to discuss these and provide documentation if you're audited:

- businesslike manner
- expertise
- time and effort devoted to the activity
- expected appreciation
- taxpayer's success with other activities
- history of income and losses of the activity
- amount of occasional profits earned
- financial status
- personal pleasure or recreation

Professional writers should consider a one- or two-hour appointment with a professional tax adviser to help set up their financial books, including a day planner for documentation of business activities, a business mileage log book, and the documentation needed for other travel, education, and entertainment expenses.

This will be money well spent, and it's tax deductible.

This previously appeared on the Christian Writers Guild blog: www.christianwritersguild.com/blog/nailing-down-your-professional-status/.

6

Alphabetical Listings of Periodicals

Request writer's guidelines and a recent sample copy or visit a periodical's website before submitting.

If you do not find the publication you are looking for, look in the General Index (see page 375).

For a detailed explanation of how to get the most out of these listings, as well as marketing tips, see "How to Use This Book" (see pages xv-xvii). Unfamiliar terms are explained in the Glossary (see pages 365-370).

(*) before a listing indicates unconfirmed information or no information update.

ADULT/GENERAL MARKETS

ADOPTEE SEARCH, E-mail: piecesoftymes@yahoo.com. This publication is devoted to finding biological families for adoptees. Writers are encouraged to share their stories of how Christ played a role in their own adoption reunions. Quarterly mag. 90% unsolicited. Send complete mss. E-mail queries w/cover letter. **Pay on publication.** One-time rights. Prefers KJV. 500-1,000 wds. Responds in 3 wks. Seasonal 3-6 mos. in adv. Accepts simultaneous or prevs published submissions (when & where). No kill fee. Regular sidebars. Always inc. bio on feature article. Photos. Accept submissions from teens.

***AMERICA,** 106 W. 56th St., New York NY 10019-3893. (212) 581-4640. Fax (212) 399-3596. E-mail: articles@americamagazine.org. Website: www.americamagazine.org. Catholic. Submit to Editor-in-Chief. For thinking Catholics and those who want to know what Catholics are thinking. Weekly mag. & online version; 32+ pgs.; circ. 46,000. Subscription $56. 100% unsolicited freelance. Complete ms/cover letter; fax/e-query OK. **Pays $150-300** on acceptance. Articles 1,500-2,000 wds. Responds in 6 wks. Seasonal 3 mos. ahead. Does not use sidebars. Guidelines by mail/website; copy for 9 x 12 SAE. Incomplete topical listings. (Ads)

Poetry: Buys avant-garde, free verse, light verse, traditional; 20-35 lines; $2-3/line.

A NEW HEART, PO Box 4004, San Clemente CA 92674-4004. (949) 496-7655. Fax (949) 496-8465. E-mail: HCFUSA@gmail.com. Website: www.HCFUSA.com. Aubrey Beauchamp, ed. For Christian healthcare givers; information regarding medical/Christian issues. Quarterly mag.; 16 pgs.; circ. 5,000. Subscription $25. 20% unsolicited freelance; 10% assigned. Complete ms/cover letter; phone/fax/e-query OK. **PAYS 2 COPIES** for onetime rts. Not copyrighted. Articles 600-1,800 wds. (20-25/yr.). Responds in 2-3 wks. Accepts simultaneous submissions & reprints. Accepts e-mail submission. Does not use sidebars. Guidelines by mail/fax; copy for 9 x 12 SAE/3 stamps. (Ads)

Poetry: Accepts 1-2/yr. Submit max. 1-3 poems.

Fillers: Accepts 3-4/yr. Anecdotes, cartoons, facts, jokes, short humor; 100-120 wds.

Columns/Departments: Accepts 20-25/yr. Chaplain's Corner, 200-250 wds. Physician's Corner, 200-250 wds.

Tips: "Most open to real-life situations which may benefit and encourage healthcare givers and patients. True stories with medical and evangelical emphasis."

***ANGELS ON EARTH,** 16 E. 34th St., New York NY 10016. (212) 251-8100. Fax (212) 684-1311. E-mail: submissions@angelsonearth.com. Website: www.angelsonearth.com. Guideposts. Colleen

Hughes, ed-in-chief; Meg Belviso, depts. ed. for features and fillers. Presents true stories about God's angels and humans who have played angelic roles on earth. Bimonthly mag.; 75 pgs.; circ. 550,000. Subscription $19.95. 90% unsolicited freelance. Complete ms/cover letter; no phone/fax/e-query. **Pays $25-400** on publication for all rts. Articles 100-2,000 wds. (100/yr.); all stories must be true. Responds in 13 wks. Seasonal 6 mos. ahead. E-mail submissions from website. Guidelines on website (www.angelsonearth.com/writers_Guidelines.asp); copy for 7 x 10 SAE/4 stamps.

Fillers: Buys many. Anecdotal shorts of similar nature (angelic); 50-250 wds. $50-100.

Columns/Departments: Buys 50/yr. Messages (brief, mysterious happenings), $25. Earning Their Wings (good deeds), 150 wds. $50. Only Human? (human or angel?/mystery), 350 wds. $100. Complete ms.

Tips: "We are not limited to stories about heavenly angels. We also accept stories about human beings doing heavenly duties."

ANIMAL TRAILS, E-mail: animaltrails@yahoo.com. Website: http://animaltrailsmagazine.doodlekit.com. Tellstar Publishing. Shannon Bridget Murphy, ed. Keeping animal memories alive through education and homeschooling. Quarterly mag. 85% unsolicited freelance. Complete ms/cover letter; e-query OK. **Pays .02-.05/wd.** on acceptance for 1st, onetime, reprint, or simultaneous rts. Articles to 2,000 wds.; fiction to 2,000 wds. Responds in 2-8 wks. Accepts simultaneous submissions & reprints (tell when/where appeared). Accepts disk or e-mail submissions (attached or copied into message). No kill fee. Regularly uses sidebars. Prefers KJV. Guidelines by e-mail. (No ads)

Poetry: Buys variable number. Avant-garde, free verse, haiku, light verse, traditional; any length. Pays variable rates. Submit any number.

Fillers: Buys most types, to 1,000 wds.

Tips: "Most open to articles, stories, poetry, and fillers that explain the value of animals and their relationship with God. The value of animals is the mission of Animal Trails. Include a Scripture reference." Picture books are being accepted for publication.

***ANSWERS MAGAZINE & ANSWERSMAGAZINE.COM,** PO Box 510, Hebron KY 41048. (859) 727-2222. Fax (859) 727-4888. E-mail: nationaleditor@answersmagazine.com. Website: www.answersmagazine.com. Answers in Genesis. Mike Matthews, exec. ed-in-chief. Bible-affirming, creation-based. Quarterly mag. Subscription $24. Articles 300-600 wds. Responds in 30 days. Details on website ("Contact"/"Write for Answers Magazine"/"Writers Guidelines").

**2010 EPA Award of Merit: General.

BELIEVERS BAY, 1202 S. Pennsylvania St., Marion IN 46953. (765) 997-1736. E-mail: editor@BelieversBay.com. Website: www.BelieversBay.com. Tim Russ, pub. To share the love of God with common sense. Monthly online mag. Mostly freelance. Submission process found at www.believersbay.com/submissions/. **NO PAYMENT** for 1st & electronic rts. (permanently archives pieces). Articles 500-1,000 wds. Guidelines listed at www.believersbay.com/submissions.

Columns/Departments: Columns 300-500 wds.

Special needs: Living in Responsible Grace.

Tips: "Only accepts on-site submissions."

BIBLE ADVOCATE, PO Box 33677, Denver CO 80233. (303) 452-7973. Fax (303) 452-0657. E-mail: bibleadvocate@cog7.org. Website: http://baonline.org. Church of God (Seventh Day). Calvin Burrell, ed.; Sherri Langton, assoc. ed. Adult readers; 50% not members of the denomination. Bimonthly (6X) mag.; 32 pgs.; circ. 13,000. Subscription free. 25-35% unsolicited freelance. Complete ms/cover letter; no phone/fax/e-query. **Pays $25-55** on publication for 1st, reprint, electronic, simultaneous rts. Articles 600-1,200 wds. (10-20/yr.). Responds in 4-10 wks. Seasonal 9 mos. ahead (no Christmas or Easter pieces). Accepts simultaneous submissions & reprints (tell when/where appeared). Accepts requested ms by e-mail (attached). Prefers e-mail. Regularly uses sidebars. Prefers NIV1984, NKJV. Guidelines/theme list by mail/website ("Write for Us," top); copy for 9 x 12 SAE/3 stamps. (No ads)

Poetry: Buys 6-8/yr. Free verse, traditional; 5-20 lines; $20. Submit max. 5 poems.
Special needs: Articles centering on upcoming themes (see website).
Tips: "If you write well, all areas are open to freelance. Articles that run no more than 1,100 words are more likely to get in. Also, fresh writing with keen insight is most readily accepted."

THE BRINK MAGAZINE, 114 Bush Rd., Nashville TN 37217. Toll-free (800) 877-7030. (615) 361-1221. Fax (615) 367-0535. E-mail: thebrink@randallhouse.com or through the website: www.thebrinkonline.com. Randall House. David Jones, ed. Devotional magazine for young adults; focusing on Bible studies, life situations, discernment of culture, and relevant feature articles. Quarterly & online mag.; 64 pgs.; circ. 8,000. Subscription $6.99. Estab. 2008. 30% unsolicited freelance; 70% assigned. Query, query/clips; prefers e-query. Accepts full mss by e-mail. **Pays $50-150** on acceptance for all rts. Articles 500-2,000 wds. (10-15/yr.). Responds in 1-2 wks. Seasonal 6 mos. ahead. Accepts simultaneous submissions & reprints (tell when/where appeared). Requires accepted articles by e-mail (attached file). No kill fee. Regularly uses sidebars. Does not accept freelance devotions. Guidelines/theme list on website (under "The Magazine"/"Write for the Brink"). (No ads)
Fillers: Buys 4/yr. Ideas, newsbreaks, book reviews, app reviews, quizzes; 50-100 wds. Pays $50-100.
Tips: "Pitch articles that are specific and relevant to young adults."

CANADA LUTHERAN, 600—177 Lombard Ave., Winnipeg MB R3B 0W5, Canada. Toll-free (888) 786-6707, ext. 172. (204) 984-9172. Fax (204) 984-9185. E-mail: editor@elcic.ca. Website: www.elcic.ca/clweb. Evangelical Lutheran Church in Canada. Provides information and inspiration to help our readers relate their faith to everyday life and foster a connection with their congregation, synods, and national office. Trina Gallop, ed. dir. (tgallop@elcic.ca); Susan McIlveen, ed. Denominational. Monthly (8X) mag.; 32 pgs.; circ. 14,000. Subscription $22.60 Cdn.; $49.89 US. E-query or complete ms. **Pays $.20/wd. Cdn.** on publication for 1st rts. Articles 700-1,200 wds. Responds in 1-2 wks. Seasonal 6 mos. ahead. No simultaneous submissions; prefers first publication; very occasionally accepts reprints (tell when/where appeared). Prefers e-mail submission (attached file). Sometimes pays kill fee. Regularly uses sidebars. Prefers NRSV. Guidelines on website ("Contribute"/"Writing Guide"); no copy. (Ads)
Columns/Departments: Buys 8/yr. Practicing Our Faith (how-to piece to help readers deepen or live out their faith); 600 wds. Pays .20/wd.
Tips: "Canadians/Lutherans receive priority here; others considered but rarely used. Want material that is clear, concise, and fresh. Primarily looking for how-to articles."

THE CANADIAN LUTHERAN, 3074 Portage Ave., Winnipeg MB R3K 0Y2, Canada. Toll-free (800) 588-4226. (204) 895-3433. Fax (204) 897-4319. E-mail: communications@lutheranchurch.ca or through website: www.lutheranchurch.ca. Lutheran Church—Canada. Matthew Block, ed. Bimonthly (6X) mag. Subscription $20. Open to unsolicited freelance. Not in topical listings. (Ads)

***CAPPER'S,** 1503 S.W. 42nd St., Topeka KS 66609. (785) 274-4300. Fax (785) 274-4305. E-mail: cappers@cappers.com or through website: www.cappers.com. Ogden Publications. K. C. Compton, ed-in-chief. Timely news-oriented features with positive messages. Monthly mag.; 40-56 pgs.; circ. 150,000. Subscription $18.95. 40% unsolicited freelance. Complete ms/cover letter by mail only. **Pays about $2.50/printed inch for nonfiction** on publication. Articles to 1,000 wds. (50/yr.). Responds in 2-6 mos. Seasonal 6 mos. ahead. No simultaneous submissions or reprints. Prefers requested ms by e-mail. Uses some sidebars. Guidelines by mail/website; copy $4/9 x 12 SAE/4 stamps. (Ads)
Columns/Departments: Buys 12/yr. Garden Path (gardens/gardening), 500-1,000 wds. Payment varies. This column most open.
Tips: "Our publication is all original material either written by our readers/freelancers or occasionally by our staff. Every department, every article is open. Break in by reading at least 6 months of issues to know our special audience. Most open to nonfiction features and garden stories." Submissions are not acknowledged or status reports given.

***CATHOLIC NEW YORK,** 1011 First Ave., Ste. 1721, New York NY 10022. (212) 688-2399. Fax (212) 688-2642. E-mail: cny@cny.org. Website: www.cny.org. Catholic. John Woods, ed-in-chief. To inform New York Catholics. Biweekly newspaper; 40 pgs.; circ. 132,680. Subscription $26. 2% unsolicited freelance. Query or complete ms/cover letter. **Pays $15-100** on publication for onetime rts. Articles 500-800 wds. Responds in 5 wks. Copy $3.

Tips: "Most open to columns about specific seasons of the Catholic Church, such as Advent, Christmas, Lent, and Easter."

CBA RETAILERS + RESOURCES, 9240 Explorer Dr., Colorado Springs CO 80920. Toll-free (800) 252-1950. (719) 272-3555. Fax (719) 272-3510. E-mail: ksamuelson@cbaonline.org. Website: www.cbaonline.org. Christian Booksellers Assn. Submit queries to Kathleen Samuelson, publications dir. To provide Christian retail store owners and managers with professional retail skills, product information, and industry news. Monthly trade journal (also in digital edition); 48-100 pgs.; circ. 5,000. Subscription $59.95 (for nonmembers). 10% unsolicited freelance; 80% assigned. Query/clips; fax/e-query OK. **Pays .30/wd.** on publication for all rts. Articles 800-2,000 wds. (30/yr. assigned); book/music/video reviews, 150 wds. ($35). Responds in 8 wks. Seasonal 4-5 mos. ahead. Prefers requested ms e-mailed in MS Word file. Regularly uses sidebars. Accepts any modern Bible version. (Ads/Dunn & Dunn/856-582-0690)

Special needs: Trends in retail, consumer buying habits, market profiles. By assignment only.

Tips: "Looking for writers who have been owners/managers/buyers/sales staff in Christian retail stores. Most of our articles are by assignment and focus on producing and selling Christian products or conducting retail business. We also assign reviews of books, music, videos, giftware, kids products, and software to our regular reviewers."

***CBN.COM (CHRISTIAN BROADCASTING NETWORK),** 977 Centerville Turnpike, Virginia Beach VA 23463. (757) 226-3557. Fax (757) 226-3575. E-mail: chris.carpenter@cbn.org or through website: www.CBN.com. Christian Broadcasting Network. Chris Carpenter, dir. of internal programming; Belinda Elliott, books ed. Online mag.; 1.6 million users/mo. Free online. Open to unsolicited freelance. E-mail submissions (attached as a Word document). Query/clips; e-query OK. **NO PAYMENT.** Devotions 500-700 wds. Spiritual Life Teaching, 700-1,500 wds. Living Features (Family, Entertainment, Health, Finance), 700-1,500 wds. Movie/TV/Music Reviews, 500-1,000 wds. Hard News, 300-700 wds. News Features, 700-1,500 wds. News Interviews, 1,000-2,000 words; fiction. Accepts reprints (tell when/where appeared). Also accepts submissions from teens. Prefers NLT/NAS/NKJV. Guidelines by e-mail; copy online. (No ads)

Special needs: Adoption stories/references, world religions from Judeo-Christian perspective.

Tips: "In lieu of payment, we link to author's website and provide a link for people to purchase the author's materials in our Web store."

CELEBRATE LIFE MAGAZINE, PO Box 1350, Stafford VA 22555. Phone (540) 659-4171; fax (540) 659-2586. E-mail: clmag@all.org. Website: www.clmagazine.org. Published by American Life League (www.all.org). Bonnie Seers, mng. ed. Quarterly full-color mag.; 32 pgs.; circ. 35,000; subscription $12.95. Covers all respect-for-life matters according to the Catholic Church's teaching. **Pays on publication**, according to quality of article, for 1st rights or work-for-hire assignments; rarely accepts reprints. No kill fee. Article length 600-1,800 wds. Seasonal 6 mos. ahead. Prefers Jerusalem Bible or New American Bible (Catholic) translations. Guidelines/theme list on website (see "Writers Guidelines"). Prefers e-mail for queries and submissions. Accepts paid ads (see website).

Ongoing needs: Personal experience with abortion, post-abortion trauma/healing, adoption, pro-life activism/young people's involvement, disability, elder care, death/dying, euthanasia, eugenics, special-needs children, human personhood, chastity, large families, stem-cell science, and other respect-for-life topics.

Tips: "We are pro-life, with no exceptions, in keeping with Catholic teaching. Looking for interviews with pro-life leaders and pro-life public figures, and nonfiction stories about pro-life activities and people who live according to pro-life ethics despite adversity. Photos are preferred for personal stories. No fiction, songs, art, or poetry. Break in by submitting work."

CGA WORLD, PO Box 249, Olyphant PA 18447. Toll-free (800) 836-5699. (570) 586-1091. Fax (570) 586-7721. E-mail: cgaemail@aol.com. Website: www.catholicgoldenage.org. Catholic Golden Age. Barbara Pegula, mng. ed. For Catholics 50+. Quarterly newsletter. Subscription/membership $12. Uses little freelance. Query. Pays .10/wd. on publication for 1st, onetime, or reprint rts. Articles 600-1,000 wds.; fiction 600-1,000 wds. Responds in 6 wks. Seasonal 6 mos. ahead. Accepts reprints (tell when/where appeared). Accepts requested ms on disk. Guidelines by mail; copy for 9 x 12 SAE/3 stamps. (Ads)

***CHARISMA,** 600 Rinehart Rd., Lake Mary FL 32746. (407) 333-0600. Fax (407) 333-7100. E-mail: charisma@charismamedia.com. Website: www.charismamag.com. Communications. Marcus Yoars, ed.; Jimmy Stewart, mng. ed.; Felicia Mann, online ed.; submit to J. Lee Grady. Primarily for the Pentecostal and Charismatic Christian community. Monthly & online mag.; 100+ pgs.; circ. 250,000. Subscription $14.97. 80% assigned freelance. Query only; no phone query, e-query OK. **Pays up to $1,000** (for assigned) on publication for all rts. Articles 2,000-3,000 wds. (40/yr.); book/music reviews, 200 wds. ($20-35). Responds in 8-12 wks. Seasonal 5 mos. ahead. Kill fee $50. Prefers accepted ms by e-mail. Regularly uses sidebars. Guidelines on website (click on "Writers Guidelines" at the bottom of home page); copy $4. (Ads)

Tips: "Most open to news section, reviews, or features. Query (published clips help a lot)."

CHICKEN SOUP FOR THE SOUL BOOK SERIES, PO Box 700, Cos Cob CT 06807. Fax (203) 861-7194. E-mail: webmaster@chickensoupforthesoul.com. Website: www.chickensoup.com. Chicken Soup for the Soul Publishing, LLC. Submit questions/requests to Web master's e-mail. *No submissions to Web master's e-mail.* A world leader in self-improvement, helps real people share real stories of hope, courage, inspiration, and love that is open to all ages, races, etc. Quarterly trade paperback books; 385 pgs.; circ. 60 million. $14.95/book. 98% unsolicited freelance. Make submissions via website only. **Pays $200 (plus 10 free copies of the book, worth more than $110)** on publication for reprint, electronic, and nonexclusive rts. Articles 300-1,200 wds. Seasonal anytime. Accepts simultaneous submissions & sometimes reprints (tell when/where appeared). Submissions only through the website: Go to www.chickensoupforthesoul.com and click on "Submit Your Story" on the left toolbar. No kill fee. Accepts submissions from children & teens. Guidelines/themes on website; free sample. (No ads)

Special needs: See website for a list of upcoming titles.

Contest: See website for list of current contests.

Tips: "Visit our website and be familiar with our book series. Send in stories via our website, complete with contact information. Submit story typed, double-spaced, max. 1,200 words, in a Word document."

CHRISTIAN COURIER (Canada), 5 Joanna Dr., St. Catherines ON L2N 1V1, Canada. (US address: PO Box 110, Lewiston NY 14092-0110.) Toll-free (800) 969-4838. (905) 682-8311. Toll-free fax (800) 969-4838. (905) 682-8313. E-mail: editor@christiancourier.ca or through website: www.christiancourier.ca. Reformed Faith Witness. Angela Reitsma Bick, ed.; Cathy Smith, features ed. Mission: To present Canadian and international news, both religious and general, from a Reformed Christian perspective. Biweekly newspaper; 20-24 pgs.; circ. 2,500. Subscription $58 Cdn.; 20% unsolicited freelance; 80% assigned. Send queries to editor@christiancourier.ca. **Pays $75-120 ms., up to .10/wd.** for assigned; 30 days after publication for onetime, reprint, or simultaneous rts. Not copyrighted. Articles 700-1,200 wds. (40/yr.); fiction to 1,200-2,500 wds. (6/yr.); book reviews 750 wds. Responds in 1-2 wks. Seasonal 3 mos. ahead. Accepts simultaneous submissions & reprints (tell when/where appeared). Prefers accepted ms by e-mail (attached file). No kill fee. Uses some sidebars. Prefers NIV. Guidelines/deadlines on website (under "Writers"); no copy. (Ads)

Poetry: Buys 12/yr. Avant-garde, free verse, light verse, traditional; 10-30 lines; $20-30. Submit max. 5 poems.

Tips: "Suggest an aspect of the theme which you believe you could cover well, have insight into, could treat humorously, etc. Show that you think clearly, write clearly, and have something to say that we should want to read. Have a strong biblical worldview and avoid moralism and sentimentality." Responds only if material is accepted.

CHRISTIAN EXAMINER, PO Box 2606, El Cajon CA 92021. (619) 668-5100. Fax (619) 668-1115. E-mail: info@christianexaminer.com. Website: www.christianexaminer.com. Selah Media Group. Lori Arnold and Scott Noble, eds. Reports on current events from an evangelical Christian perspective, inspirational articles, and church trends. Focus is on ministries in S. California and Minneapolis. Monthly & online newspaper; 24-36 pgs.; circ. 150,000. Subscription $19.95. 5% assigned. Query/clips. **Pays .10/wd.,** on publication for 1st & electronic rts. Articles 600-900 wds. Responds in 4-5 wks. Seasonal 2 mos. ahead. No simultaneous submissions or reprints. Prefers e-mail submissions (copied into message). No kill fee. Uses some sidebars. Guidelines by e-mail; copy $1.50/9 x 12 SAE. (Ads)

Tips: "We prefer news stories."

** 2010 EPA Award of Merit: Online; 2010, 2011 EPA Award of Excellence: Newspaper; 2012 EPA Award of Excellence: Online; 2012 EPA Award of Merit: Newspaper. Member of Association of Christian Newspapers (ACN).

CHRISTIAN HOME & SCHOOL, 3350 East Paris Ave. S.E., Grand Rapids MI 49512. Toll-free (800) 635-8288. (616) 957-1070, ext. 240. Fax (616) 957-5022. E-mail: rheyboer@csionline.org. Website: www.csionline.org/christian_home_and_school. Christian Schools Intl. Rachael Heyboer, mng. ed. Promotes and explains the concept of Christian education. Encourages Christian parents in their daily walk and helps them improve their parenting skills as a form of discipleship. Please note this is NOT a homeschooling magazine. Biannual mag.; 40 pgs.; circ. 66,000. Subscription $13.95. 25% unsolicited; 75% assigned. Complete ms or e-query. Accepts full mss by e-mail. **Pays $50-250** on publication for 1st rts. Articles 1,000-2,000 wds. (30/yr.); book reviews $25 (assigned). Responds in 4 wks. Seasonal 6 mos. ahead (no Christmas or summer). Accepts simultaneous query. Prefers mss by e-mail (attached). Regularly uses sidebars. Accepts submissions from children/teens. Prefers NIV. For guidelines/theme list/sample issues, check website ("What We Do"/"Member Resources"/"Christian Home & School"). (Ads)

Tips: "Writers can break in by submitting articles based on the CH&S editorial calendar, geared from a Christian perspective and current with the times." Check out website for updated editorial calendar: www.csionline.org/christian_home_and_school.

** 2007 EPA Award of Merit: Organizational. This periodical was #46 on the 2010 Top 50 Christian Publishers list (#41 in 2009, #36 in 2008, #44 in 2007, #32 in 2006).

CHRISTIANITY TODAY, 465 Gundersen Dr., Carol Stream IL 60188-2498. (630) 260-6200. Fax (630) 260-9401. E-mail: cteditor@christianitytoday.com. Website: www.christianitytoday.com. Mark Galli, ed. For intentional Christians who seek to thoughtfully integrate their faith with responsible action in the church and world. 10X/year & online mag.; 65-120 pgs. Circ. 130,000. Subscription $24.95. Prefers e-query. **Pays .25-.35/wd.** on publication for print 1st rts.; less for online. Articles 1,000-4,000 wds. (50/yr.); book reviews 800-1,200 wds. (pays per-page rate). Responds in 6 wks. Seasonal 6 mos. ahead. Accepts reprints (tell when/where appeared—payment 25% of regular rate). Kill fee 50%. Does not use sidebars. Prefers NIV. Guidelines on website ("Contact Us"/"Writers Guidelines"); much prefer online submissions. (Ads)

Tips: "Read the magazine." Does not return unsolicited manuscripts.

** Various and sundry journalism awards through EPA and other professional associations.

THE CHRISTIAN JOURNAL, 1032 W. Main, Medford OR 97501. (541) 773-4004. Fax (541) 773-9917. E-mail: info@thechristianjournal.org. Website: www.TheChristianJournal.org. Chad McComas, ed. Dedicated to sharing encouragement and inspiration with the body of Christ in Southern Oregon and Northern California. Monthly & online newspaper; 16-24 pgs.; circ. 12,000. Subscription $20; most copies distributed free. Paper is sent to inmates across the country free. 50% unsolicited freelance; 50% assigned. Complete ms; phone/fax query OK. **NO PAYMENT** for onetime rts. Articles & fiction to 500 words; reviews to 500 wds.; children's stories 500 wds. Prefers articles by e-mail to info@thechristian journal.org (attached file). Also accepts submissions from children/teens. Guidelines/theme list located on the website or by e-mail ("Writer's Info"); copy online. (Ads)

Poetry: Accepts 12-20/yr. Free verse, haiku, light verse, traditional; 4-12 lines. Submit max. 2 poems.

Fillers: Accepts 50/yr. Anecdotes, cartoons, jokes, kid quotes, newsbreaks, prayers, quotes, short humor, or word puzzles; 100-300 wds.

Columns/Departments: Accepts 6/yr. Youth; Seniors; Children's stories; all to 500 wds.

Tips: "Send articles on themes; each issue has a theme. Theme articles get first choice."

** This periodical was #40 on the 2010 Top 50 Christian Publishers list.

CHRISTIAN NEWS NORTHWEST, PO Box 974, Newberg OR 97132. Phone/fax (503) 537-9220. E-mail: cnnw@cnnw.com. Website: www.cnnw.com. John Fortmeyer, ed./pub. News of ministry in the evangelical Christian community in western and central Oregon and southwest Washington; distributed primarily through evangelical churches. Monthly newspaper; 24-32 pgs.; circ. 29,000. Subscription $22. 10% unsolicited freelance; 5% assigned. Query; phone/fax/e-query OK. **NO PAYMENT.** Not copyrighted. Articles 300-400 wds. (100/yr.). Responds in 4 wks. Seasonal 3 mos. ahead. Accepts reprints (tell when/where appeared). Accepts e-mail submissions. Regularly uses sidebars. Guidelines by mail/e-mail; copy $1.50. (Ads)

Tips: "Most open to ministry-oriented features. Our space is always tight, but stories on lesser-known, Northwest-based ministries are encouraged. Keep it very concise. Since we focus on the Pacific Northwest, it would probably be difficult for anyone outside the region to break into our publication."

** 2006 EPA Award of Merit: Newspaper.

CHRISTIAN ONLINE MAGAZINE, PO Box 262, Wolford VA 24658. E-mail: submissions@ christianmagazine.org. Website: www.ChristianMagazine.org. Darlene Osborne, pub. (darlene@ christianmagazine.org). Strictly founded on the Word of God, this magazine endeavors to bring you the best Christian information on the net. Monthly e-zine. Subscription free. 10% unsolicited freelance; 90% assigned. E-query. Articles 500-700 wds. Responds in 1 wk. Seasonal 2 mos. ahead. Prefers accepted ms by e-mail (attached file). **NO PAYMENT.** Regularly uses sidebars. Also accepts submissions from children/teens. Prefers KJV. Guidelines on website ("Submit an Article: Writer's Guidelines"). (Ads)

Fillers: Accepts 50/yr. Prayers, prose, quizzes, short humor; 500 wds.

Columns/Departments: Variety Column, 700-1,000 wds. Query.

Tips: "Most open to solid Christian articles founded on the Word of God."

CHRISTIAN QUARTERLY, PO Box 311, Palo Cedro CA 97073. Phone/fax (530) 247-7500. E-mail: ChristQtly@aol.com. Nondenominational. Cathy Jansen, pub. E-mail: cathy@christianquarterly.org or christianquarterly@aol.com. Uplifting and encouraging articles. Quarterly magazine; circ. 15,000. Subscription free. 100% unsolicited freelance. Phone or e-query. Accepts full mss by e-mail. **NO PAYMENT.** Not copyrighted. Articles 400-700 wds. Responds immediately. Accepts reprints (tell when/where appeared). Accepts e-mail (attached or copied into message). Use Microsoft Word format or file saved in text format. Never uses sidebars. Also accepts submissions from children/teens. Guidelines by e-mail; copy for 10 x 13 SAE/$2 postage. (Ads)

Poetry: Accepts 6-10/yr. Free verse, traditional.

Fillers: Accepts anecdotes, cartoons, ideas, quotes, short humor, and word puzzles.

Columns/Departments: Uses many. Marriage & Family; Health; Financial; Testimonies.

Special needs: "Looking for articles that inspire and encourage, not too preachy or not coming off like a Bible study. Content that stimulates readers to ponder on the good things of God."

THE CHRISTIAN RANCHMAN/COWBOYS FOR CHRIST, 3011 FM 718, Newark TX 76071, or PO Box 7557, Fort Worth TX 76111. (817) 236-0023. Fax (817) 236-0024. E-mail: cwb4christ@cowboysforchrist.net, or CFCmail@cowboysforchrist.net, or through website: www.CowboysforChrist.net. Interdenominational. Dave Harvey, ed. Monthly tabloid; 16 pgs.; circ. 15,000. No subscription. 85% unsolicited freelance. Complete ms/cover letter. **NO PAYMENT** for all rts. Articles 350-1,000 wds.; book/video reviews (length open). Does not use sidebars. Guidelines on website ("Contact Us"/ "Submit an Article"); sample copy.

Poetry: Accepts 40/yr. Free verse. Submit max. 3 poems.

Fillers: Accepts all types.

Tips: "We're most open to true-life Christian stories, Christian testimonies, and Christian or livestock news. Contact us with your ideas first."

***CHRISTIAN RESEARCH JOURNAL,** PO Box 8500, Charlotte NC 28271-8500. (704) 887-8200. Fax (704) 887-8299. E-mail: submissions@equip.org. Website: www.equip.org. Christian Research Institute. Elliot Miller, ed-in-chief; Melanie Cogdill, ed. Probing today's religious movements, promoting doctrinal discernment and critical thinking, and providing reasons for Christian faith and ethics. Quarterly mag.; 64 pgs.; circ. 30,000. Subscription $39.50. 75% freelance. Query or complete ms/cover letter; fax query OK; e-query & submissions OK. **Pays .16/wd.** on publication for 1st rts. Articles to 4,200 wds. (25/yr.); book reviews 1,100-2,500 wds. Responds in 4 mos. Accepts simultaneous submissions. Kill fee to 50%. Guidelines by mail/e-mail (guidelines@equip.org); copy $6. (Ads)

Columns/Departments: Effective Evangelism, 1,700 wds. Viewpoint, 875 wds. News Watch, to 2,500 wds.

Special needs: Viewpoint on Christian faith and ethics, 1,700 wds.; news pieces, 800-1,200 wds.

Tips: "Be familiar with the *Journal* in order to know what we are looking for. We accept freelance articles in all sections (features and departments). E-mail for writer's guidelines."

CHRISTIAN RETAILING, 600 Rinehart Rd., Lake Mary FL 32746. (407) 333-0600. Fax (407) 333-7133. E-mail: Christian.Retailing@charismamedia.com. Website: www.christianretailing.com. Charisma Media (formerly Strang Communications). Christine D. Johnson, ed. (chris.johnson@charismamedia.com). For Christian product industry manufacturers, distributors, retailers. Trade & online journal published monthly; circ. 6,200 (print), 9,000 (digital). Subscription $40 print/free digital/free print to authors and Christian retailers. 10% assigned. E-query with clips; no phone/fax query. **Pays .25/wd.** on publication for articles (various lengths). No simultaneous submissions. Accepts requested mss by e-mail (attached file). Kill fee. Prefers NIV. Guidelines by e-mail. (Ads)

Tips: "Notify the editor, Christine D. Johnson (chris.johnson@charismamedia.com), of your expertise in the Christian products industry." Also publishes *Inspirational Gift Mart*, four times/yr.

CHRISTIAN STANDARD, 8805 Governor's Hill Dr., Ste. 400, Cincinnati OH 45249. (513) 931-4050. Fax (513) 931-0950. E-mail: christianstandard@standardpub.com. Website: www.christianstandard.com. Standard Publishing/Christian Churches/Churches of Christ. Mark A. Taylor, ed. Devoted to the restoration of New Testament Christianity, its doctrines, its ordinances, and its fruits. Monthly & online mag.; 68 pgs.; circ. 25,000 (print). Subscription $37.99. 40% unsolicited freelance; 60% assigned. Complete ms; no phone/fax/e-query. **Pays $20-200** on publication for onetime, reprint, & electronic rts. Articles 800-1,600 wds. (200/yr.). Responds in 9 wks. Seasonal 8-12 mos. ahead. Accepts reprints (tell when/where appeared). Guidelines/copy on website. (Ads)

Tips: "We would like to hear ministers and elders tell about the efforts made in their churches. Has the church grown? developed spiritually? overcome adversity? succeeded in missions?"

***CHURCH HERALD AND HOLINESS BANNER,** 7407 Metcalf, Overland Park KS 66212. Fax (913) 722-0351. E-mail: HBeditor@juno.com. Website: www.heraldandbanner.com. Church of God (Holiness)/Herald and Banner Press. Mark D. Avery, ed. Offers the conservative holiness movement a positive outlook on their church, doctrine, future ministry, and movement. Monthly mag.; 24 pgs.; circ. 1,100. Subscription $12.50. 5% unsolicited freelance; 50% assigned. Query; e-query OK. Accepts full mss by e-mail. **NO PAYMENT** for onetime, reprint, or simultaneous rts. Not copyrighted. Articles 600-1,200 wds. (3-5/yr.). Responds in 9 wks. Seasonal 6 mos. ahead. Accepts simultaneous submissions & reprints (tell when/where appeared). Accepts requested ms on disk or by e-mail (attached file). Uses some sidebars. Prefers KJV. Also accepts submissions from children/teens. No guidelines; copy for 9 x 12 SAE/2 stamps. (No ads)

Fillers: Anecdotes, quizzes; 150-400 wds.

Tips: "Most open to short inspirational/devotional articles. Must be concise, well written, and get one main point across; 200-600 wds. Be well acquainted with the Wesleyan/Holiness doctrine and tradition. Articles which are well written and express this conviction are very likely to be used."

***COLUMBIA,** 1 Columbus Plaza, New Haven CT 06510-3326. (203) 752-4398. Fax (203) 752-4109. E-mail: columbia@kofc.org. Website: www.kofc.org/columbia. Knights of Columbus. Alton Pelowski, mng. ed. Geared to a general Catholic family audience; most stories must have a Knights of Columbus connection. Monthly & online mag.; 32 pgs.; circ. 1.5 million. Subscription $6; foreign $8. 25% unsolicited freelance; 75% assigned. Query; e-query OK. Accepts full mss by e-mail. **Pays $250-1,000** on acceptance for 1st & electronic rts. Articles 500-1,500 wds. (12/yr.). Responds in 4-6 wks. Seasonal 4 mos. ahead. Accepts e-mail submission (attachment preferred). Sometimes pays kill fee. Regularly uses sidebars. Prefers NAS. Guidelines by mail/e-mail; free copy. (No ads)

Special needs: Essays on spirituality, personal conversion. Catholic preferred. Query first.

Tips: "We welcome contributions from freelancers in all subject areas. An interesting or different approach to a topic will get the writer at least a second look from an editor. Most open to feature writers who can handle church issues, social issues from an orthodox Roman Catholic perspective. Must be aggressive, fact-centered writers for these features."

** This periodical was #45 on the 2006 & 2007 Top 50 Christian Publishers list.

CONVERGE MAGAZINE, (888) 899-3777. E-mail: info@convergemagazine.com. Website: www.convergemagazine.com.

CREATION, PO Box 4545, Eight Mile Plains QLD 4113, Australia. 61-07 3340 9888. Fax 61-07 3840 9889. E-mail: mail@creation.info. Website: www.creation.com. Creation Ministries Intl. Carl Wieland, managing dir. A family, nature, science magazine focusing on creation/evolution issues. Quarterly mag.; 56 pgs.; circ. 46,000. Subscription $28. 10% unsolicited freelance. Query; phone/fax/e-query OK. **NO PAYMENT** for all rts. Articles to 1,500 wds. (20/yr.). Responds in 2-3 wks. Prefers requested ms on disk or by e-mail (attached file). Regularly uses sidebars. For guidelines, see creation.com/creation-magazine-writing-guidelines. (No ads)

Tips: "Get to know the basic content/style of the magazine and emulate. Send us a copy of your article, or contact us by phone."

CREATION ILLUSTRATED, PO Box 7955, Auburn CA 95604. (530) 269-1424. Fax (888) 415-1989. E-mail: ci@creationillustrated.com. Website: www.creationillustrated.com. Tom Ish, ed./pub. An uplifting, Bible-based Christian nature magazine that glorifies God; for ages 9-99. Quarterly mag.; 68 pgs.; circ. 20,000. Subscription $19.95. 60% unsolicited freelance; 40% assigned. Query or query/clips; fax/e-query OK (put query submission in subject line). **Pays $75-125** within 30 days of publication for 1st rts. (holds North American Serial Rights, Archival Rights, and Internet Duplication of the Magazine in PDF Format). Articles 1,000-2,000 wds. (20/yr.). Response time varies. Seasonal 6 mos. ahead. Accepts simultaneous submissions & reprints (tell when/where appeared). Prefers e-mail submission (attached file or copied into message). Kill fee 25%. Uses some sidebars. Prefers NKJV. Guidelines/theme list on website or by e-mail; copy $3/9 x 12 SAE/$3 postage. (Some ads)

Columns/Departments: Creation Up Close feature, 1,500-2,000 wds. $100; Re-Creation and Restoration Through Outdoor Adventure, 1,500-2,000 wds. $100; Creatures Near and Dear to Us, 1,500-2,000 wds. $100; Children's Story, 500-1,000 wds. $50-75; My Walk with God, 1,000-1,500 wds. $75; Gardens from Eden Around the World, 1,000-1,500 wds., $75; Creation Day (a repeating series), 1,500-2,000 wds. $100.

Poetry: Short, usually 4 verses. Needs to have both nature and spiritual thoughts. Pays about $15.

Tips: "Most open to an experience with nature/creation that brought you closer to God and will inspire the reader to do the same. Include spiritual lessons and supporting Scriptures—at least 3 or 4 of each."

***ETERNAL INK,** 4706 Fantasy Ln., Alton IL 62002. E-mail: eternallyours8@yahoo.com. Nondenominational. E-mail publication; open to any serious effort or submission. Mary-Ellen Grisham, ed. (meginrose@gmail.com); Ivie Bozeman, features ed. (ivie@rose.net); Pat Earl, devotions ed. Biweekly e-zine; 1 pg.; circ. 450. Subscription free. 25% unsolicited freelance; 75% assigned. Complete ms/cover letter by e-mail only. **NO PAYMENT** for onetime rts. Not copyrighted. Articles/devotions 300-500 wds. (26/yr.); reviews 300-500 wds. Responds in 6 wks. Seasonal 2 mos. ahead. Accepts simultaneous submissions & reprints. Accepts e-mail submissions (copied into message). No kill fee or sidebars. Prefers NIV. Occasionally accepts submissions from children/teens. Guidelines/copy by e-mail. (No ads)

Poetry: Elizabeth Pearson, poetry ed. (roybet@comcast.net). Accepts 24-30/yr. Free verse, traditional, inspirational; to 30 lines. Submit max. 3 poems.

Fillers: Ivie Bozeman, features and fillers ed. (ivie@rose.net). Accepts 24-30/yr. Anecdotes, jokes, kid quotes, prayers, prose, short humor; 150-250 wds.

Columns/Departments: Accepts many/yr. See information in e-zine. Query.

Contest: Annual Prose/Poetry Contest in November-December, with 1st, 2nd, and 3rd-place winners in each category. Book awards for first-place winners.

Tips: "Please contact Mary-Ellen Grisham by e-mail with questions."

EVANGEL, 770 N. High School Rd., Indianapolis IN 46214. (800) 342-5531. E-mail: evangeleditor@fmcusa.org. Submit to: Julie Innes, ed. Printed quarterly. SS take home paper. 8 pgs. Send complete mss with cover letter. Accepts full mss by e-mail. **Pays $10 min. for articles or .06/wd.** Pay on publication, one-time rights. Copyrighted. Prefers NIV. Responds in 6-8 wks. Seasonal 9 mos. in adv. Accepts simultaneous or prev. published submissions by e-mail. No kill fee. Sometimes sidebars. Writer's guidelines available by e-mail. Sample copy #10 env. .46 or .92 postage. Photos with articles only. Accepts teen submissions. (No ads)

Nonfiction: Send complete manuscript.

Fiction: For adults.

Poetry: Free verse, light verse, traditional. Max 5 at a time. Pays $10 max.

Fillers: Cartoons, word puzzles. Pays $10-20.

***FAITH TODAY: To Connect, Equip and Inform Evangelical Christians in Canada,** PO Box 5885, West Beaver Creek, Richmond Hill, ON L4B 0B8, Canada. (905) 479-5885. Fax (905) 479-4742. E-mail: editor@faithtoday.ca. Website: www.faithtoday.ca. Evangelical Fellowship of Canada. Gail Reid, mng. ed.; Bill Fledderus, sr. ed.; Karen Stiller, assoc. ed. A general-interest publication for Christians in Canada; almost exclusively about Canadians, including Canadians abroad. Bimonthly & online mag.; 56 pgs.; circ. 18,000. US print subscription $35.99, online free. 20% unsolicited freelance; 80% assigned. Query only; fax/e-query preferred. **Pays $80-500 (.20-.25 Cdn./wd.)** on publication for 1st & electronic rts.; reprints .15/wd. Features 800-1,700 words; cover stories 2,000 wds.; essays 650-1,200 wds.; profiles 900 words; reviews 300 wds. (75-100/yr.). Responds in 6 wks. Prefers e-mail submission. Kill fee 30-50%. Regularly uses sidebars. Any Bible version. Guidelines at www.faithtoday.ca/writers; copy at www.faithtoday.ca/digital. (Ads)

Columns/Departments: Guest column (a kind of essay/Canadian focus), 650 wds. Buys 2/yr. Pays $150.

Special needs: Canadian-related content.

Tips: "Most open to short, colorful items, statistics, stories, profiles for Kingdom Matters department. Content (not author) must have a Canadian connection." All issues since Jan. 2008 now available free online at www.faithtoday.ca/digital. Unsolicited manuscripts will not be returned.

** This periodical was #42 on the 2006 Top 50 Christian Publishers list.

***THE FIT CHRISTIAN MAGAZINE,** PO Box 563, Ward Cove AK 99928. (206) 274-8474. Fax (614) 388-0664. E-mail: editor@fitchristian.com. Website: www.fitchristian.com. His Work Christian Publishing. Angela J. Willard Perez, ed. A Christian rendering health and fitness. Bimonthly mag. Subscription free. Open to unsolicited freelance. Guidelines online at www.fitchristian.com/jobs.html. Features and Articles in the magazine and online. Topics on health, fitness, diet, nutrition, family, faith.

GEM, 700 E. Melrose Ave., Box 926, Findlay OH 45839-0926. (419) 424-1961. Fax (419) 424-3433. E-mail: communications@cggc.org, or through website: www.cggc.org. Churches of God, General Conference. Rachel L. Foreman, ed. To encourage and motivate people in their Christian walk. Monthly (13X) take-home paper for adults; 8 pgs.; circ. 6,000. Subscription $14. 95% unsolicited freelance; 5% assigned. Complete ms/cover letter; phone/fax/e-query OK. **Pays $5-15** after publication for one-time rts. Articles 300-1,200 wds. (125/yr.); fiction 1,200 wds. (125/yr.). Responds in 12 wks. Seasonal 3 mos. ahead. Accepts simultaneous submissions & reprints (tell when/where appeared). Prefers submissions by e-mail. Uses some sidebars. Prefers NIV. Guidelines on website ("Ministries"/"Denominational Communications"/"The Gem" on the right sidebar); copy for #10 SAE/2 stamps. (No ads)

Poetry: Buys 100/yr. Any type, 3-40 lines; $5-15. Submit max. 3 poems.

Fillers: Buys 25/yr. All types except party ideas; 25-100 words; $5-10.

Special needs: Missions and true stories. Be sure that fiction has a clearly religious/ Christian theme.

Tips: "Most open to real-life experiences where you have clearly been led by God. Make the story interesting and Christian."

** This periodical was #13 on the 2010 Top 50 Christian Publishers list (#9 in 2009, #7 in 2008, #9 in 2007, #37 in 2006).

***GEMS OF TRUTH,** PO Box 4060, 7407-7415 Metcalf Ave., Overland Park KS 66204. (913) 432-0331. Fax (913) 722-0351. E-mail: sseditor1@juno.com. Website: www.heraldandbanner.com. Church of God (Holiness)/Herald & Banner Press. Arlene McGehee, Sunday school ed. Denominational. Weekly adult take-home paper; 8 pgs.; circ. 14,000. Subscription $2.45. Complete ms/cover letter; phone/ fax/e-query OK (prefers mail or e-mail). **Pays .005/wd.** on publication for 1st rts. Fiction 1,000-2,000 wds. Seasonal 6-8 mos. ahead. Accepts simultaneous submissions & reprints (tell when/where appeared). Prefers KJV. Guidelines/theme list/copy by mail. Not in topical listings. (No ads)

GENUINE MOTIVATION: YOUNG CHRISTIAN MAN, PO Box 573, Clarksville AR 72830. (479) 439-4891. E-mail: thebeami@juno.com; Website: www.onmyownnow.com; On My Own Ministries, Inc. Rob Beames, ed. Christian alternative to the men's magazine. For young, single men ages 17-23 who are sincerely seeking to be disciples of Christ. Monthly e-zine; 18 pgs; circ. 1,000. Free subscription. Estab. 2009; 40% unsolicited. 60% assigned. Complete manuscript by e-mail. E-mail query OK. **NO PAYMENT, nonexclusive rights.** Prefer NIV. 800-1200 wds. Accepts 24 nonfiction mss/yr. Responds in 2 weeks. Seasonal 2 mo ahead. Accepts simultaneous and previously published submissions. (Tell when/where appeared). Require articles by e-mail. No kill fee. Always inc. bio on feature article. Guidelines on website. Book, Music, Video review 800 wds. Accept submissions from teens. Column: Tool Box (resources for young adult men) 450-550 wds; Faith and Finance (good and godly stewardship) 700-1000 wds; The Recap (review of books, movies, music, etc) 600-1000 wds; Election Year (where faith and politics intersect) 800-1200 wds. Accepts 18 mss/yr. Query, send complete manuscript.

Tips: "Looking for guest columnists for Faith and Finance, Tool Box, and The Recap. Also seek new writers for feature articles." (No ads)

GUIDEPOSTS, (212) 251-8100. E-mail: submissions@guideposts.org. Website: www.guideposts.org. Interfaith. Submit to Articles Editor. Personal faith stories showing how faith in God helps each person cope with life in some particular way. Monthly mag.; 68 pgs.; circ. 2 million. Subscription $16.97. 40% unsolicited freelance; 20% assigned. Complete ms/cover letter by e-mail (attached or copy into message). **Pays $100-500** on publication for all rts. Articles 750-1,500 wds. (40-60/yr.), shorter pieces 250-750 words ($100-250). Responds only to mss accepted for publication in 2 mos. Seasonal 3 mos. ahead. Accepts simultaneous submissions & reprints. Kill fee 20%. Uses some sidebars. Free guidelines on website: www.guideposts.org/tellusyourstory; copy. (Ads)

Columns/Departments: Mysterious Ways (divine intervention), 250 wds. What Prayer Can Do, 250 wds. Divine Touch (tangible evidence of God's help), 400 wds.

Contest: Writers Workshop Contest held on even years with a late June deadline. Winners attend a weeklong seminar (all expenses paid) on how to write for *Guideposts*.

Tips: "Be able to tell a good story, with drama, suspense, description, and dialog. The point of the story should be some practical spiritual help that the subject learns through his or her experience. Use unique spiritual insights, strong and unusual dramatic details. We rarely present stories about deceased or professional religious people." First person only.

HALO MAGAZINE, 148 Banks Dr., Winchester VA 22602. (540) 877-3568. Fax (540) 877-3535. E-mail: halomag@aol.com. Website: www.halomag.com. Submit to: Ms. Marian Newman Braxton, sr. ed. Halo is a magazine in which Christian writers of any or no experience in writing can submit what God has placed in their hearts. Quarterly pub. 80 pgs. 97% freelance. Send complete manuscript by e-mail. First rights purchased. Copyrighted. Prefer NIV, KJV, NAS. Fiction articles 500-1500 wds. Accepts 4 nonfiction/yr. Respond in 2 weeks. Submit seasonal 6 mos. in adv. Accepts simultaneous/prev. published submissions (when/where). Accepts articles by e-mail in attached file. No kill fee. Always inc. bio notes on writer of feature article. Guidelines on website. Sample copy avail. Accepts color photos. Send contributor 1 copy. Book reviews 300 wds., music reviews 300 wds., video reviews 300 wds. Accept submissions from children/teens. (Ads)

Nonfiction: Delbert Teachout, mg. ed.

Columns/Depts: Just for Men, Christian Living. 500 wds. 20/yr. Send complete ms.

Fiction: Adult, biblical, historical, send complete ms.

Poetry: Light verse. Accepts 12/yr. Max submit at one time—2. Line length 24.

Fillers: Facts, games, prayers, quotes, short humor, word puzzles. Accept 20/yr. 50-200 wds.

Tips: Send article by e-mail. Use *The Christian Writer's Manual of Style* for guidelines; if not followed, article will be rejected. All areas are open to freelance. Send your article; if we like it, we'll use it. *Halo* is a good place for new writers to get published. Use Times New Roman 12 pt. font; do not justify margins.

Contest: Max. 1,000 wds. on topic of "How I Found Jesus." Deadline is July 31. $25 entry fee. 1st prize $150, 2nd prize $100, 3rd prize $50. All participants receive a one year subscription. Send submissions to Halo Magazine Writing Contest, 1643 Pinnacle Dr. SW, Wyoming MI 49519. All entries become property of *Halo Magazine* and may be used in future issues.

HIGHWAY NEWS AND GOOD NEWS, PO Box 117, Marietta PA 17547-0117. For UPS or FedEx: 1525 River Rd., Marietta PA 17547. (717) 426-9977. Fax (717) 426-9980. E-mail: editor@transportforchrist.org. Website: www.transportforchrist.org. Transport for Christ. Inge Koenig, ed. For truck drivers and their families; evangelistic, with articles for Christian growth. Monthly mag.; 16 pgs.; circ. 25,000. Subscription $35 tax-deductible donation. 25% unsolicited freelance. Complete ms/cover letter; e-query preferred. **Pays in copies** for rights offered. Articles 600 to 800 wds. Seasonal 4 mos. ahead. Accepts simultaneous submissions & reprints (tell when/where appeared). Prefers requested ms by e-mail (attached or copied into message). Uses some sidebars. Prefers NIV. Guidelines/idea list by mail; free copy mailed upon request. (No ads)

Poetry: Accepts 2/yr. 3-20 lines. Submit max. 1 poem. Rarely uses poetry; should be related to the trucking life, with a Christian focus.

Fillers: None

Tips: "As a magazine with truckers as its primary audience, we especially look for articles dealing with issues of interest to truckers (not necessarily Christian—for example, we may publish an article addressing new DOT rulings); also experiences and testimonies that address or are related to the trucking life, its challenges, problems, rewards, etc."

***HOME TIMES FAMILY NEWSPAPER,** PO Box 22547, West Palm Beach FL 33416-2547. (561) 439-3509. Fax (561) 908-6701. E-mail: hometimes2@aol.com. Website: www.hometimes.org. Neighbor News, Inc. Dennis Lombard, ed./pub. Conservative, pro-Christian community newspaper. Monthly tabloid; 12-20 pgs.; circ. 4,000. Subscription $24, 12 issues. 15% unsolicited freelance; 25% assigned. Complete ms only/cover letter; no phone/fax/e-query. **Pays $5-25** on acceptance for onetime rts. Articles 100-1,000 wds. (15/yr.); fiction 300-1,500 wds. (1-2/yr.). Responds in 2-3 wks. Seasonal 2 mos. ahead. Accepts simultaneous submissions & reprints (tell when/where appeared). No kill fee. Regularly uses sidebars. Also accepts submissions from teens. Any Bible version. Guidelines SASE; 3 issues $3. (Ads)

Poetry: Buys almost none. Free verse, traditional; 2-16 lines; $5. Submit max. 3 poems.

Fillers: Uses a few/yr. Anecdotes, cartoons, facts, ideas, jokes, kid quotes, newsbreaks, prayers, quotes, short humor, tips; to 100 wds. pays 3-6 copies, if requested.

Columns/Departments: Buys 30/yr. See guidelines for departments, to 800 wds. $5-15.

Special needs: Good short stories (creative nonfiction or fiction). Home & Family, parenting, education, etc. More faith, miracles, personal experiences, local people stories.

Tips: "Most open to personal stories or home/family pieces. Very open to new writers, but study guidelines and sample first; we are different. Published by Christians, but not 'religious.' Looking for more positive articles and stories. Occasionally seeks stringers to write local people features with photos. Journalism experience is preferred. E-mail query for more info with your name, background, and address to hometimes2@aol.com. We strongly suggest you read *Home Times*. Also consider our manual for writers: *101 Reasons Why I Reject Your Manuscript* (reduced to $12, reg. $19)."

** This periodical was #47 on the 2010 Top 50 Christian Publishers list.

***INDIAN LIFE,** PO Box 3765, Redwood Post Office, Winnipeg MB R2W 3R6, Canada. US address: PO Box 32, Pembina ND 58271. (204) 661-9333. Fax (204) 661-3982. E-mail: ilm.editor@indianlife.org or through website: www.indianlife.org. Indian Life Ministries/nondenominational. Jim Uttley, ed. An evangelistic publication for English-speaking aboriginal people in North America. Bimonthly tabloid newspaper; 20 pgs.; circ. 14,500. Subscription $18. 5% unsolicited freelance; 5% assigned. Query (query or complete ms for fiction); phone/fax/e-query OK. **Pays .15/wd (to $200)** on publication for 1st rts. Articles 150-2,500 wds. (20/yr.); fiction 500-2,000 wds. (8/yr.); reviews, 250 wds. ($40). Responds in 6 wks. Seasonal 4 mos. ahead. Accepts simultaneous submissions & reprints (tell when/where appeared). Accepts requested ms by e-mail (copied into message preferred). Some kill fees 50%. Uses some sidebars. Accepts submissions from children/teens. Prefers New Life Version, NIV. Guidelines by mail/e-mail/website; copy for 9 x 12 SAE/$2 postage (check or money order). (Ads)

Poetry: Buys 4 poems/yr.; free verse, light verse, traditional, 10-100 wds. pays $40. Submit max. 5 poems.

Fillers: Kid quotes, quotes, short humor, 50-200 wds. $10-25.

Special needs: Celebrity pieces must be aboriginal only. Looking for legends.

Tips: "Most open to testimonies from Native Americans/Canadians—either first person or third person—news features, or historical fiction with strong and accurate portrayal of Native American life from the Indian perspective. A writer should have understanding of some Native American history and culture. We suggest reading some Native American authors. Native authors preferred, but some others are published. Aim at a 10th-grade reading level; short paragraphs; avoid multisyllable words and long sentences."

**2010 EPA Award of Merit: Newspaper. This periodical was #6 on the 2010 Top 50 Christian Publishers list (#30 in 2009).

JOBTOJOY.US, 5042 E. Cherry Hills Blvd., Springfield MO 65809. (417) 832-8409. Fax (508) 632-8409. E-mail: editor@JobToJoy.us, e-mail submissions only (attachment formats are fine in Word, WordPerfect, Works, or the free OpenOffice word processor; not PDF files). Also attach a brief author's bio, and digital photo if available. E-query OK. Open to 80% unsolicited freelance! Reprints fine, electronic rights. Future selection for inclusion in a book is a possibility. Get in on the ground floor. We are a startup with a small staff; if your writing requires edits, it will delay posting it online. J. R. Chrystie, managing director. All submissions should have a positive focus. **NO PAYMENT.** In lieu of payment, accepted authors will be featured on Our Authors page with their bio, photo, and link to their website or blog. Devotions 300-500 words; include Scripture and ending prayer. Book reviews (query first) 400-800 words; books about careers, change, moving, retirement, job-related issues. Inspiring testimonials (successful job change, career change, new retirement years' career transition into ministry or volunteerism) 600-1000 words. Keep it positive. Some poetry, any form.

Fillers: Inspiring quotations 20-75 words; humorous short stories about a job change 70-150 words; positive job change how-to tips 50-150 words; review of a helpful job-related website 30-50 words; a Bible verse and how it helped you through a job change 20-50 words; cartoons should be attached as a .jpg file (remember this is a Christian site).

Special Needs: Feature articles (query first) such as how to know when God wants you elsewhere, what is the difference between a job and a ministry, and relevant interviews. Read our online mission statement and be creative.

THE JOURNAL OF ADVENTIST EDUCATION, 12501 Old Columbia Pike, Silver Spring MD 20904-6600. (301) 680-5069. Fax (301) 622-9627. Email: goffc@gc.adventist.org. Website: http://jae.adventist.org. General Conference of Seventh-day Adventists. Beverly J. Robinson-Rumble, ed. For Seventh-day teachers teaching in the church's school system, kindergarten to university and educational administrators. Bimonthly (5X) jour.; peer reviewed; 48 pgs.; circ. 13,500. Selected articles are translated into French, Spanish, and Portuguese for a twice-yearly international edition. Subscription $18.25 (add $3 outside US). Percentage of freelance varies. Query or complete ms; phone/fax/e-query OK. **Pays $25-300** on publication for 1st North American and translation rts., and permission to post on website. Articles 1,000-2,000 wds. (2-20/yr.). Responds in 6-17 wks. Seasonal 6 mos. ahead. Accepts reprints (tell when/where appeared). Accepts requested ms on disk. All manuscripts must be submitted in electronic form. Regularly uses sidebars. Guidelines on website ("For Authors"); copy for 10 x 12 SAE/5 stamps.

Fillers: Cartoons only, no payment.

Special needs: "All articles in the context of parochial schools (not Sunday school tips); professional enrichment and teaching tips for Christian teachers. Need feature articles and articles on the integration of faith and learning."

KEYS TO LIVING, 105 Steffens Rd., Danville PA 17821. (570) 437-2891. E-mail: owcam@verizon.net. Website: http://keystoliving.homestead.com. Connie Mertz, ed./pub. Educates, encourages, and challenges readers through devotional and inspirational writings; also nature articles, focusing primarily on wildlife in eastern US. Quarterly newsletter; 12 pgs. Subscription $10. 30% unsolicited freelance (needs freelance). Complete ms/cover letter; prefers e-mail submissions; no phone query. **Pays 2 copies** for onetime or reprint rts. Articles 350-500 wds. Responds in 4 wks. Accepts reprints. No disk; e-mail submission OK (copied into message). Prefers NIV. Guidelines/theme list on website ("Guidelines/Subscription"); copy for 7 x 10 SAE/2 stamps. (No ads)

Poetry: Accepts if geared to family, nature, personal living, or current theme. Traditional with an obvious message.

Special needs: More freelance submissions on themes only.

Tips: "We are a Christ-centered family publication. Seldom is freelance material used unless it pertains to a current theme. No holiday material accepted. Stay within word count."

***KINDRED SPIRIT,** 3909 Swiss Ave., Dallas TX 75204. (214) 841-3556. Fax (972) 222-1544. E-mail: sglahn@dts.edu. Website: www.dts.edu/ks. Dallas Theological Seminary. Sandra Glahn, ed-in-chief. Publication of Dallas Theological Seminary. Tri-annual & online mag.; 16-20 pgs.; circ. 30,000. Subscription free. 75% unsolicited freelance. Query/clips; fax/e-query OK. **Pays $300 flat fee** on publication for 1st & electronic rts. Articles 1,100 wds.; also accepts biblical fiction. Responds in 6 wks. Seasonal 8 mos. ahead. No simultaneous submissions; accepts reprints. Requires accepted mss by e-mail (attached or copied into message). Regularly uses sidebars. Prefers NIV. Guidelines on website ("Submissions"); copy by mail. (No ads)

Special needs: Profiles/interviews of DTS grads and faculty are open to anyone.

Tips: "Any news or profiles or expositions of Scripture with a link to DTS will receive top consideration; all topics other than interviews need to come from DTS graduates."

** 2010 Award of Merit: Cause of the Year.

LEAVES, PO Box 87, Dearborn MI 48121-0087. (313) 561-2330. Fax (313) 561-9486. E-mail: leaves-mag@juno.com. Website: www.mariannhill.us. Catholic/Mariannhill Fathers of Michigan. Jacquelyn M. Lindsey, ed. For all Catholics; promotes devotion to God and his saints and publishes readers' spiritual experiences, petitions, and thanksgivings. Bimonthly mag.; 24 pgs.; circ. 25,000. Subscription free. 50% unsolicited freelance. Complete ms/cover letter; phone/fax/e-query OK. **NO PAYMENT** for 1st or reprint rts. Not copyrighted. Articles 500 wds. (6-12/yr.). Responds in 4 wks. Seasonal 4 mos. ahead. Accepts reprints. Accepts e-mail submissions (copied into message). Does not use sidebars. Prefers NAB, RSV (Catholic edition). No guidelines or copy. (No ads)

Poetry: Accepts 6-12/yr. Traditional; 8-20 lines. Submit max. 4 poems.

Special needs: Testimonies of conversion or reversion to Catholicism.

Tips: "Besides being interestingly and attractively written, an article should be confidently and reverently grounded in traditional Catholic doctrine and spirituality. The purpose of our magazine is to edify our readers."

LEBEN, 2150 River Plaza Dr., Ste. 150, Sacramento CA 95833. (916) 473-8866, ext. 4. E-mail: editor@leben.us or through website: www.leben.us. City Seminary Press. Wayne Johnson, ed. Focuses on Protestant Christian history and biography. Quarterly & online mag.; 24 pgs.; circ. 5,000. Subscription $19.95. 20% unsolicited freelance; 80% assigned. Complete ms; e-query OK. Accepts full mss by e-mail. **Pays .05/wd.** (copies & subscription) on acceptance for 1st & electronic rts. Articles 500-2,500 wds. (4/yr.). Responds in 2 wks. Accepts simultaneous submissions & reprints (tell when/where appeared). Prefers e-mail submissions (attached file). Uses some sidebars. Also accepts submissions from teens. Prefers KJV. Guidelines on website ("Write for Leben"); copy for 9 x 12 SAE/$2 postage. (Ads)

Fillers: Buys 4-6/yr. Short humor. Pays $5-10.

Special needs: Reprints from old publications; historical, humor, etc.

Tips: "We feature stories that are biographical, historically accurate, and interesting—about Protestant martyrs, patriots, missionaries, etc., with a 'Reformed' slant."

LIGHT & LIFE, Box 535002, Indianapolis IN 46253-5002. (317) 244-3660. Fax (317) 244-1247. E-mail: LLMAuthors@fmcna.org. Website: http://llcomm.org/writersguidelines. Free Methodist Church of North America. Jeff Finley, ed. Interactive magazine for maturing Christians; contemporary-issues oriented, thought-provoking; emphasizes spiritual growth, discipline, holiness as a lifestyle.

Bimonthly mag.; 32 pgs. (plus pullouts); circ. 13,000. Subscription $16. 95% unsolicited freelance. Query first; e-query OK. **Pays .15/wd.** on acceptance for 1st rts. Articles 800-1,500 wds. (24/yr.). Responds in 8-12 wks. Seasonal 12 mos. ahead. No simultaneous submissions. Prefers e-mail submission (attached file) after acceptance. No kill fee. Uses some sidebars. Prefers NIV. Also accepts submissions from children/teens. Guidelines on website ("Writer's Guides"); copy $4. (Ads)

Tips: "Best to write a query letter. We are emphasizing contemporary issues articles, well researched. Ask the question, 'What topics are not receiving adequate coverage in the church and Christian periodicals?' Seeking unique angles on everyday topics."

LIVE, 1445 N. Boonville Ave., Springfield MO 65802-1894. (417) 862-2781. Fax (417) 863-1874. E-mail: rl-live@gph.org. Website: www.gospelpublishing.com. Assemblies of God/Gospel Publishing House. Wade Quick, ed. Inspiration and encouragement for adults. Weekly take-home paper; 8 pgs.; circ. 31,000. Subscription $14.40. 100% unsolicited freelance. Complete ms/cover letter; no phone/fax query; e-query OK. **Pays .10/wd. (.07/wd. for reprints)** on acceptance for onetime or reprint rts. Articles 400-1,100 wds. (80-90/yr.); fiction 400-1,100 wds. (20/yr.). Responds in 4-6 wks. Seasonal 18 mos. ahead. Accepts simultaneous submissions & reprints (tell when/where appeared). Accepts e-mail submissions (attached file). No kill fees. Few sidebars. Prefers NIV. Guidelines by mail/e-mail/website ("Writer's Guides"); copy for #10 SAE/1 stamp. (No ads)

Poetry: Buys 12-18/yr. Free verse, light verse, traditional; 8-25 lines; $60 (payment for reprints varies) when scheduled. Submit max. 3 poems.

Tips: "We are often in need of good shorter stories (400-600 wds.), especially true stories or based on true stories. Often need holiday stories that are not 'how-to' stories, particularly for patriotic or nonreligious holidays. All areas open to freelance—human interest, inspirational, and difficulties overcome with God's help. Fiction must be especially good with biblical application. Follow our guidelines. Most open to well-written personal experience with biblical application. Send no more than two articles in the same envelope and send a SASE."

** This periodical was #10 on the 2010 Top 50 Christian Publishers list (#3 in 2009, #5 in 2008, #1 in 2007, #8 in 2006).

LIVING LIGHT NEWS, #200, 5306—89th St., Edmonton AB T6E 5P9, Canada. (780) 468-6397. Fax (780) 468-6872. E-mail: shine@livinglightnews.com. Website: www.livinglightnews.com. Living Light Ministries. Jeff Caporale, ed. To inspire and encourage Christians; witnessing tool to the lost. Bimonthly tabloid; 28 pgs.; circ. 80,000. Subscription $24.95 US. 30% unsolicited freelance; 70% assigned. Query; e-query OK. **Pays $20-125** (.10/wd. Cdn. or .10/wd. US) on publication for all, 1st, onetime, simultaneous, or reprint rts. Articles 350-700 wds. (75/yr.). Responds in 4 wks. Accepts simultaneous submissions & reprints (tell when/where appeared). Guidelines by e-mail/website ("More"/"Writing Guidelines" left side); copy for 9 x 12 SAE/$4.50 Cdn. postage or IRCs (no US postage). (Ads)

Columns/Departments: Buys 20/yr., 450-600 wds. $10-30 Cdn. Parenting; relationships. Query.

Special needs: Celebrity interviews/testimonials of well-known personalities.

Tips: "Most open to a timely article about someone who is well known in North America, in sports or entertainment, and has a strong Christian walk."

** This periodical was #34 on the 2007 Top 50 Christian Publishers list (#38 in 2006).

***THE LOOKOUT,** 8805 Governor's Hill Dr., Ste. 400, Cincinnati OH 45249. (513) 931-4050. Fax (513) 931-0950. E-mail: lookout@standardpub.com. Website: www.lookoutmag.com. Standard Publishing. Shawn McMullen, ed. For adults who are interested in learning more about applying the gospel to their lives. Weekly & online mag.; 16 pgs.; circ. 52,000. Subscription $45. 40% unsolicited freelance; 60% assigned. Query for theme articles; e-query OK. **Pays $145-225** on acceptance (after contract is signed), for 1st rts. Articles 1,000-1,600 wds. Responds in 10 wks. Seasonal 9-12 mos. ahead. Accepts simultaneous submissions; no reprints. No disks or e-mail submissions. Kill fee 50%.

Regularly uses sidebars. Prefers NIV. Guidelines/theme list by e-mail/website: www.lookoutmag.com /write/default.asp); copy for #10 SAE/$1. (Ads)

Tips: "Open to feature articles according to our theme list. Get a copy of our theme list and query about a theme-related article at least six months in advance. Request sample copies of our magazine to familiarize yourself with our publishing needs (also available online)."

** This periodical was #22 on the 2010 Top 50 Christian Publishers list (#10 in 2009, #17 in 2008, #10 in 2007, #30 in 2006).

***THE LUTHERAN DIGEST,** 6160 Carmen Ave. E., Inver Grove MN 55076. (651) 451-9945. E-mail: editor@lutherandigest.com. Website: www.lutherandigest.com. The Lutheran Digest, Nick Skapyak, ed. Blend of general and light theological material used to win nonbelievers to the Lutheran faith. Quarterly literary mag.; 64 pgs.; circ. 60,000. Subscription $16. 100% unsolicited freelance. Query or complete ms/cover letter; phone/fax/e-query OK. **Pays $35-100+ ($25-50 for reprints)** on publication for onetime & reprint rts. Articles to 1,000 wds. or no more than 7,000 characters—3,000 preferred (25-30/yr.). Prefers full mss by e-mail. Responds in 4-9 wks. Seasonal 6-9 mos. ahead. Accepts simultaneous submissions & reprints (tell when/where appeared). Accepts e-mail submissions (attached). No kill fee. Uses some sidebars. Rarely accepts submissions from children/teens. Guidelines by mail/website ("Write for Us"); copy $3.50/6 x 9 SAE. (Ads)

Poetry: Accepts 20+/yr. Light verse, traditional; short/varies; no payment. Submit max. 3 poems/mo.

Fillers: Anecdotes, facts, short humor, tips; length varies; no payment.

Tips: "We want our readers to feel uplifted after reading our magazine. Therefore, short, hopeful pieces are encouraged. We need well-written short articles that would be of interest to middle-aged and senior Christians—and also acceptable to Lutheran Church pastors. We prefer real-life stories over theoretical essays. Personal tributes and testimony articles are discouraged. Please read sample articles and follow our writers' guidelines prior to submission—a little research goes a long way. Too much inappropriate and irrelevant material received."

**This periodical was #31 on the 2010 Top 50 Christian Publishers list (#24 in 2009).

THE LUTHERAN JOURNAL, PO Box 28158, Oakdale MN 55128. (651) 702-0086. Fax (651) 702-0074. E-mail: christianad2@msn.com. Vance Lichty, pub.; Roger S. Jensen, ed.; submit to Editorial Assistant. Family magazine for, by, and about Lutherans, and God at work in the Lutheran world. Annual mag.; 48 pgs.; circ. 200,000. Subscription $6. 60% unsolicited freelance; 40% assigned. Complete ms/cover letter; fax query OK. **Pays .01-.04/wd.** on publication for all or 1st rts. Articles 750-1,500 wds. (25-30/yr.); fiction 1,000-1,500 wds. Response time varies. Seasonal 4-5 mos. ahead. Accepts reprints. Uses some sidebars. Prefers NIV, NAS, KJV. Accepts requested ms on disk. Also accepts submissions from children/teens. Guidelines by mail; copy for 9 x 12 SAE/2 stamps. (Ads)

Poetry: Buys 4-6/yr. Light verse, traditional; 50-150 wds. $10-30. Submit max. 3 poems.

Fillers: Buys 5-10/yr. Anecdotes, facts, prayers, quotes; 50-300 wds. $5-30.

Columns/Departments: Buys 1st time rights only.

Tips: "Most open to Lutheran lifestyles or Lutherans in action." Does not return rejected manuscripts.

***THE MANNA,** PO Box 130, Princess Anne MD 21853. (410) 543-9652. Fax (410) 651-9652. E-mail: wolc@wolc.org. Website: www.wolc.org. Maranatha Inc. Debbie Byrd, ed-in-chief. A free monthly tabloid featuring evangelical articles, and distributed in the marketplace in Delaware, Maryland, and Virginia. Digital online tabloid; 32-40 pgs; circ. 42,000. Subscription free. 10-15% unsolicited freelance; 15% assigned. Query/clips; e-query OK. No full mss by e-mail. **Pays $30-50** on publication for 1st, onetime, or reprint rts. Articles 1,000-1,200 wds. Responds in 1-2 wks. Seasonal 3-4 mos. ahead. No simultaneous submissions. Accepts reprints (tell when/where appeared). Accepted articles on disk or by e-mail (copied into message). Uses some sidebars. Also accepts submissions from children/teens. No guidelines; copy for 9 x 12 SAE/2 stamps. (Ads)

Fillers: Anecdotes, ideas, party ideas, short humor, and tips. No payment.

Columns/Departments: Accepts up to 12/yr. Finances (business or personal); Counseling (Q & A); Personal Integrity (scriptural); all 800 wds. No payment.

Special needs: Themes: marital fidelity, conquering fear, hypocrites, heaven, showing compassion, and What Is Your Hope? Most open to these theme pieces.

Tips: "E-mail your query."

** 2010 Award of Merit: Newspaper; 2009 Award of Excellence: Newspaper.

***MATURE LIVING,** One Lifeway Plaza, MSN 175, Nashville TN 37234-0175. (615) 251-5677. E-mail: matureliving@lifeway.com. Website: www.lifeway.com. LifeWay Christian Resources/Southern Baptist. Rene Holt, content ed. Christian leisure reading for 55+ adults, characterized by human interest and Christian warmth. Monthly mag.; 60 pgs.; circ. 318,000. Subscription $22.50. 90% unsolicited freelance; 10% assigned. Complete ms/cover letter; no phone/fax/e-query. Accepts full mss by e-mail (attached or copied into message). **Pays $85-115** for feature articles ($105-115 for fiction) on acceptance for all rts. Articles 400-1,200 wds. (85/yr.); senior adult fiction 900-1,200 wds. (12/yr.). Responds in 6-8 wks. Seasonal 6-8 mos. ahead. No simultaneous submissions or reprints. No kill fee. Uses some sidebars. Prefers KJV, HCSB. Guidelines by mail/e-mail (rene.holt@lifeway.com); to see sample, www.lifeway.com/matureliving.

Fillers: Accepts 144/yr. Grandchildren stories, 50-100 wds. No payment.

Columns/Departments: Buys 300+/yr. Cracker Barrel, 4-line verse, $15; Grandparents' Brag Board, 50-100 wds.; Over the Garden Fence (gardening), 300-350 wds.; Communing with God (devotional), 125-200 wds.; Fun 'n Games (wordsearch/crossword puzzles), 300-350 wds.; Crafts; Recipes; $15-50. Complete ms. See guidelines for full list.

Tips: "Almost all areas open to freelancers except medical and financial matters. Study the magazine for its style. Write for our readers' pleasure and inspiration. Fiction for 55+ adults needs to underscore a biblical truth."

** This periodical was #12 on the 2010 Top 50 Christian Publishers list (#22 in 2009, #44 in 2008, #13 in 2007, #10 in 2006).

MATURE YEARS, PO Box 801, Nashville TN 37202. (615) 749-6292. Fax (615) 749-6512. E-mail: matureyears@umpublishing.org. United Methodist. Marvin W. Cropsey, ed. To help persons in and nearing retirement years understand and appropriate the resources of the Christian faith in dealing with specific problems and opportunities related to aging. Quarterly mag.; 112 pgs.; circ. 55,000. Subscription $24. 60% unsolicited freelance; 40% assigned. Complete ms/cover letter; fax/e-query OK. **Pays .07/wd.** on acceptance for onetime rts. Articles 900-2,000 wds. (60/yr.). Responds in 9 wks. Seasonal 14 mos. ahead. Accepts reprints. Prefers accepted ms by e-mail (copied into message). Regularly uses sidebars. Prefers NRSV, NIV, and CEB. Guidelines by mail/e-mail; copy $5. (No ads)

Poetry: Buys 24/yr. Free verse, haiku, light verse, traditional; 4-16 lines; .50-1.00/line. Submit max. 6 poems.

Fillers: Buys 20/yr. Anecdotes (to 300 wds.), cartoons, jokes, prayers, word puzzles (religious only); to 30 wds. $5-25.

Columns/Departments: Buys 20/yr. Health Hints, 900-1,200 wds. Modern Revelations (inspirational), 900-1,100 wds. Fragments of Life (true-life inspirational), 250-600 wds. Going Places (travel), 1,000-1,500 wds. Money Matters, 1,200-1,800 wds.

Special needs: Articles on crafts and pets. All areas open except Bible studies.

** This periodical was #36 on the 2010 Top 50 Christian Publishers list (#30 in 2007, #35 in 2006).

MEN OF THE CROSS, 920 Sweetgum Creek, Plano TX 75023. (972) 517-8553. E-mail: info@menofthecross.com. Website: www.menofthecross.com. Greg Paskal, content mngr. (greg@

gregpaskal.com). Encouraging men in their walk with the Lord; strong emphasis on discipleship and relationship. Online community. 50% unsolicited freelance. Query by e-mail. **NO PAYMENT.** Not copyrighted. Articles 500-1,500 wds. (10/yr.). Responds in 2-4 wks. Seasonal 3 mos. ahead. Accepts simultaneous submissions; no reprints. Prefers e-mail submissions (attached or copied into message). Uses some sidebars. Prefers NIV, NKJV, NAS. Also accepts submissions from teens. Guidelines by e-mail; copy online. (No ads)

Poetry: Accepts 1/yr. Avant-garde, free verse; 50-250 lines. Submit max. 1 poem.

Special needs: Christian living in the workplace.

Tips: "Appropriate topic could be a real, firsthand account of how God worked in the author's life. We are looking for humble honesty in hopes it will minister to those in similar circumstances. View online forums for specific topics."

***THE MESSENGER,** 440 Main St., Steinbach MB R5G 1Z5, Canada. (204) 326-6401. Fax (204) 326-1613. E-mail: messenger@emconf.ca or through website: www.emconf.ca/Messenger. Evangelical Mennonite Conference. Terry M. Smith, ed.; Rebecca Roman, asst. ed. Serves Evangelical Mennonite Conference members and general readers. Monthly mag.; 36 pgs. Subscription $24. Uses little freelance, but open. Query preferred; phone/fax/e-query OK. Accepts full mss by e-mail. **Pays $50-135** on publication for 1st rts. only. Articles. Brief guidelines on website ("Subscriptions, Article Submission Information"). Not included in topical listings.

THE MESSIANIC TIMES, PO Box 2096, Niagara Falls NY 14302. (951) 249-8134. Fax (951) 677-7353. E-mail: editor.messianictimes@gmail.com or through website: www.messianictimes.com. Times of the Messiah Ministries. Eric Tokajer, publisher; Karen S. Meissner, managing editor. To unify the International Messianic Jewish community to serve as an evangelistic tool to the Jewish community, and to educate Christians about the Jewish roots of their faith. Bimonthly newspaper; circ. 35,000. Subscription based. $29.99. Accepts freelance. Query preferred. Articles and reviews. Not in topical listings. (Ads)

***MOVIEGUIDE,** 1151 Avenida Acaso, Camarillo CA 93012. Toll-free (800) 577-6684. (770) 825-0084. Fax (805) 383-4089. E-mail through website: www.movieguide.org. Good News Communications/Christian Film & Television Commission. Dr. Theodore Baehr, pub. Family guide to media entertainment from a biblical perspective. 10% unsolicited freelance. Query/clips. **Pays in copies** for all rts. Articles 1,000 wds. (100/yr.); book/music/video/movie reviews, 750-1,000 wds. Responds in 6 wks. Seasonal 6 mos. ahead. Accepts requested ms on disk. Regularly uses sidebars. Guidelines/theme list; copy for SAE/4 stamps. (Ads)

Fillers: Accepts 1,000/yr.; all types; 20-150 wds.

Columns/Departments: Movieguide; Travelguide; Videoguide; CDguide, etc.; 1,000 wds.

Contest: Scriptwriting contest for movies with positive Christian content. Go to www.kairos prize.com.

Tips: "Most open to articles on movies and entertainment, especially trends, media literacy, historical, and hot topics."

NEW FRONTIER, 180 E. Ocean Blvd., 4th Fl., Long Beach CA 90802. (562) 491-8723. Fax (562) 491-8791. Email: new.frontier@usw.salvationarmy.org. www.newfrontierpublications.org. The Salvation Army Western Territory. Robert L. Docter, ed. News of The Salvation Army in the Western United States and from 126 countries where the Army is at work. Biweekly newspaper; circ. 25,000. Subscription $15. Open to freelance. Prefers query. **NO PAYMENT.** Articles & reviews; no fiction. Not in topical listings. (Ads)

***NOW WHAT?,** PO Box 33677, Denver CO 80233. (303) 452-7973. Fax (303) 452-0657. E-mail: nowwhat@cog7.org. Website: http://nowwhat.cog7.org. Church of God (Seventh Day). Sherri Langton, assoc. ed. Articles on salvation, Jesus, social issues, life problems, that are seeker sensitive. Monthly online mag.; available only online. 100% unsolicited freelance. Complete ms/cover letter;

no query. **Pays $25-55** on publication for first, electronic, simultaneous, or reprint rts. Articles 1,000-1,500 wds. (10/yr.). Responds in 4-10 wks. Accepts simultaneous submissions & reprints (tell when/where appeared). Accepts requested ms by e-mail. E-mail preferred. Regularly uses sidebars. Prefers NIV 1984. Guidelines by mail/website ("Send Us Your Story").

Special needs: "Personal experiences must show a person's struggle that either brought him/her to Christ or deepened faith in God. The entire *Now What?* site is built around a personal experience each month."

Tips: "The whole e-zine is open to freelance. Think how you can explain your faith, or how you overcame a problem, to a non-Christian. It's a real plus for writers submitting a personal experience to also submit an objective article related to their story. Or they can contact Sherri Langton for upcoming personal experiences that need related articles. No Christmas or Easter pieces."

OCACW NEWSLETTER, 5042 E. Cherry Hills Blvd., Springfield MO 65809. (417) 832-8409. Fax (508) 632-8409. E-mail: OzarksACW@yahoo.com. E-mail submissions only. Guidelines on website: www.ozarksacw.org/columns.php. Ozarks Chapter of American Christian Writers, bimonthly print newsletter, 8 pages. Jeanetta Chrystie, pres., James Cole-Rous, newsletter ed. **NO $ PAYMENT**, pays in copies & publicity. Also attach a brief author's bio and digital photo. E-query OK. Open to 90% unsolicited freelance! Reprints welcome, electronic rights requested.

Tips: Writing-related topics only, writing basics, grammar, advanced how-to, inspiration.

Special needs: Articles, shorts & fillers, writing book reviews (not market guides), some devotions, some poetry.

***ON MISSION,** 4200 North Point Pkwy., Alpharetta GA 30022-4176. (770) 410-6382. Fax (770) 410-6105. E-mail: onmission@namb.net. Website: www.onmission.com. North American Mission Board, Southern Baptist. Carol Pipes, ed. Helping readers share Christ in the real world. Quarterly & online mag.; 48 pgs.; circ. 230,000. Subscription free. 1-5% unsolicited freelance; 50-60% assigned. Query (complete ms for fiction); no phone/fax query; e-query OK. Accepts full mss by e-mail. **Pays .25/wd.** on acceptance for 1st rts. Articles 500-1,000 wds. (20/yr.). Responds in 8 wks. Seasonal 8 mos. ahead. No simultaneous submissions or reprints. Accepts e-mail submissions (attached or copied into message). Kill fee. Regularly uses sidebars. Prefers HCSB. Guidelines by mail/e-mail/website (put "Writers Guidelines" in search box); copy for 9 x 12 SAE/$2.38 postage. (Ads)

Columns/Departments: Buys 4-8/yr. The Pulse (outreach/missions ideas); 500 wds. Query.

Special needs: Needs articles on these topics: sharing your faith, interviews/profiles of missionaries, starting churches, volunteering in missions, sending missionaries.

Tips: "We are primarily a Southern Baptist publication reaching out to Southern Baptist pastors and laypeople, equipping them to share Christ, start churches, volunteer in missions, and impact the culture. Write a solid, 750-word, how-to article geared to 20- to 40-year-old men and women who want fresh ideas and insight into sharing Christ in the real world in which they live, work, and play. Send a résumé, along with your best writing samples. We are an on-assignment magazine, but occasionally a well-written manuscript gets published."

** 2010, 2007, 2006 EPA Award of Merit: Missionary.

***OUR SUNDAY VISITOR,** 200 Noll Plaza, Huntington IN 46750. Toll-free (800) 348-2440. (260) 356-8400. Fax (260) 356-8472. E-mail: oursunvis@osv.com. Website: www.osv.com. Catholic. John Norton, ed.; Sarah Hayes, article ed. Vital news analysis, perspective, spirituality for today's Catholic. Weekly newspaper; 24 pgs.; circ. 68,000. 10% unsolicited freelance; 90% assigned. Query or complete ms; fax/e-query OK. **Pays $100-800** within 4 wks. of acceptance for 1st & electronic rts. Articles 500-3,500 wds. (25/yr.). Responds in 4-6 wks. Seasonal 2 mos. ahead. No simultaneous submissions; rarely accepts reprints (tell when/where appeared). Kill fee. Regularly uses sidebars. Prefers RSV. Guidelines by mail/e-mail/website (click on "About Us"/"Writers' Guidelines" in left column); copy for $2/10 x 13 SAE/$1 postage. (Ads)

Columns/Departments: Faith; Family; Trends; Profile; Heritage; Media; Q & A. See guidelines for details.

Tips: "Our mission is to examine the news, culture, and trends of the day from a faithful and sound Catholic perspective—to see the world through the eyes of faith. Especially interested in writers able to do news analysis (with a minimum of 3 sources) or news features."

** This periodical was #11 on the 2009 Top 50 Christian Publishers list (#48 in 2006).

THE OZARKS CHRISTIAN NEWS, PO Box 336, Rockaway Beach MO 65740. Phone/fax (417) 336-3636. E-mail: editor@ozarkschristiannews.com. Website: www.ozarkschristiannews.com. John Sacoulas, ed. Celebrating the common ground in the body of Christ. Monthly newspaper; circ. 20,000. Subscription $30. Open to unsolicited freelance. Complete ms. Articles & reviews. (Ads)

***PENTECOSTAL EVANGEL** (formerly *Today's Pentecostal Evangel*), 1445 N. Boonville, Springfield MO 65802-1894. (417) 862-2781. Fax (417) 862-0416. E-mail: pe@ag.org. Website: www.pe.ag .org. Assemblies of God. Ken Horn, ed.; submit to Scott Harrup, sr. assoc. ed. Assemblies of God. Weekly & online mag.; 32 pgs.; circ. 170,000. Subscription $28.99. 5% unsolicited freelance; 95% assigned. Complete ms/cover letter; no phone/fax/e-query. Accepts full mss by e-mail. **Pays .06/wd. (.04/wd. for reprints)** on acceptance for 1st & electronic rts. Articles 500-1,200 wds. (10-15/yr.); testimonies 200-300 wds. Responds in 6-8 wks. Seasonal 6-8 mos. ahead. No simultaneous submissions; accepts reprints (tell when/where appeared). Kill fee 100%. Prefers e-mail submissions (attached file). Uses some sidebars. Prefers NIV, KJV. Guidelines on website (click on "Writer's Guidelines" just under "Customer Service" & "Media"); copy for 9 x 12 SAE/$1.39 postage. (Ads)

Fillers: Anecdotes, facts, personal experience, testimonies; 250-500 wds. Practical, how-to pieces on family life, devotions, evangelism, seasonal, current issues, Christian living; 250 wds. Pays about $25.

Special needs: "The *Pentecostal Evangel* offers a free e-mail/online devotional, *Daily Boost*. Contributors are not paid, but a number of these writers have been published in the magazine."

Tips: "True, first-person inspirational material is the best bet for a first-time contributor. We reserve any controversial subjects for writers we're familiar with. Positive family-life articles work well near Father's Day, Mother's Day, and holidays."

**2010 EPA Award of Excellence: Denominational.

THE PENWOOD REVIEW, PO Box 862, Los Alamitos CA 90720-0862. E-mail: submissions@ penwoodreview.com. Website: www.penwoodreview.com. Lori Cameron, ed. Poetry, plus thought-provoking essays on poetry, literature, and the role of spirituality and religion in the literary arts. Biannual jour.; 40+ pgs.; circ. 80-100. Subscription $12. 100% unsolicited freelance. Complete ms; no e-query. **NO PAYMENT** ($2 off subscription & 1 free copy), for one time and electronic rts. Articles 1 pg. (single spaced). Responds in 9-12 wks. Accepts requested ms by e-mail (copied into message). Guidelines (also by e-mail/website); copy $6.

Poetry: Accepts 120-160/yr. Any type, including formalist; to 2 pgs. Submit max. 5 poems.

Special Needs: Faith and the literary arts; religion and literature. Needs essays (up to 2 pgs., single spaced).

Tips: We publish poetry almost exclusively and are looking for well-crafted, disciplined poetry, not doggerel or greeting-card-style poetry. Poets should study poetry, read it extensively, and send us their best, most original work. Visit our website or buy a copy for an idea of what we publish.

***PERSPECTIVES: A Journal of Reformed Thought,** 4500—60th Ave. S.E., Grand Rapids MI 49512. (616) 392-8555, ext. 131. Fax (616) 392-7717. E-mail: perspectives@rca.org. Website: www.perspectivesjournal.org. Reformed Church Press. Steve Mathonnet-VanderWell and Arika

Theule-Van Dam, eds. To express the Reformed faith theologically; to engage issues that Reformed Christians meet in personal, ecclesiastical, and societal life; and thus to contribute to the mission of the church of Jesus Christ. Monthly (10X) & online mag.; 24 pgs.; circ. 3,000. Subscription $30. 75% unsolicited freelance; 25% assigned. Complete ms/cover letter or query; fax/e-query OK. **Pays 6 copies** for 1st rts. Articles (10/yr.) and fiction (3/yr.), 2,500-3,000 wds.; reviews 1,000 wds. Responds in 20 wks. Seasonal 10 mos. ahead. Accepts reprints (tell when/where appeared). Prefers requested ms by e-mail (attached file). Uses some sidebars. Prefers NRSV. Guidelines on website ("About Us"/"Writer's Guidelines"); no copy. (Ads)

Poetry: Accepts 2-3/yr. Traditional. Submit max. 3 poems.

Columns/Departments: Accepts 12/yr. As We See It (editorial/opinion), 750-1,000 wds. Inside Out (biblical exegesis), 750 wds. Complete ms.

Tips: "Most open to feature-length articles. Must be theologically informed, whatever the topic. Avoid party-line thinking and culture-war approaches. I would say that a reading of past issues and a desire to join in a contemporary conversation on the Christian faith would help you break in here. Also the 'As We See It' column is a good place to start."

***POWER FOR LIVING,** #104—Manuscript Submission, 4050 Lee Vance View, Colorado Springs CO 80918. Toll-free (800) 708-5550. (719) 536-0100. Fax (719) 535-2928. Website: www.cookministries.org. Cook Communications/Scripture Press Publications. Catherine Devries, ed. mgr. To expressly demonstrate the relevance of specific biblical teachings to everyday life via reader-captivating profiles of exceptional Christians. Weekly take-home paper; 8 pgs.; circ. 375,000. Subscription $3.99/quarter. 50% unsolicited freelance; 50% assigned. Complete ms; no phone/fax/e-query. **Pays up to .15/wd. (reprints up to .10/wd.)** on acceptance for onetime rts. Profiles 700-1,500 wds. (20/yr.). Responds in 10 wks. Seasonal 1 yr. ahead. Accepts simultaneous submissions & reprints (tell when/where appeared). Accepts requested ms on disk. Kill fee. Requires NIV or KJV. Guidelines on website (click on "About David C. Cook"/"Writers Guidelines"); copy for #10 SAE/1 stamp (use address above, but change to MS #205—Sample Request). (No ads)

Special needs: "Third-person profiles of truly out-of-the-ordinary Christians who express their faith uniquely. We use very little of anything else."

Tips: "Most open to vignettes, 450-1,500 wds. of prominent Christians with solid testimonies or profiles from church history. Focus on the unusual. Signed releases required." Not currently open to freelance submissions; check website for any changes.

***PRAIRIE MESSENGER: Catholic Journal,** PO Box 190, Muenster SK S0K 2Y0, Canada. (306) 682-1772. Fax (306) 682-5285. E-mail: pm.canadian@stpeterspress.ca. Website: www.prairiemessenger.ca. Catholic/Benedictine Monks of St. Peter's Abbey. Peter Novecosky, OSB, ed.; Maureen Weber, assoc. ed. For Catholics in Saskatchewan and Manitoba, and Christians in other faith communities. Weekly tabloid (46X); 16-20 pgs.; circ. 5,100. Subscription $35 Cdn. 10% unsolicited freelance; 90% assigned. Complete ms/cover letter; phone/fax/e-query OK. **Pays $55 Cdn. ($2.75/column inch for news items)** on publication for 1st, onetime, simultaneous, reprint rts. Not copyrighted. Articles 800-900 wds. (15/yr.). Responds in 9 wks. Seasonal 3 mos. ahead. Accepts simultaneous submissions & reprints. Regularly uses sidebars. Guidelines by e-mail/website (scroll down left side to "Writers' Guidelines"); copy for 9 x 12 SAE/$1 Cdn./$1.39 US postage. (Ads)

Poetry: Accepts 15/yr. Avant-garde, free verse, haiku, light verse; 3-30 lines. Pays $25 Cdn.

Columns/Departments: Accepts 5/yr. Pays $60 Cdn.

Special needs: Ecumenism; social justice; native concerns.

Tips: "Comment/feature section is most open; send good reflection column of about 800 words; topic of concern or interest to Prairie readership. It's difficult to break into our publication. Piety not welcome." This publication is limited pretty much to Canadian writers only.

***PRESBYTERIANS TODAY,** 100 Witherspoon St., Louisville KY 40202-1396. Toll-free (800) 728-7228. (502) 569-5520. (502) 569-8632. E-mail: today@pcusa.org. Website: www.pcusa.org/today.

Presbyterian Church (USA). Eva Stimson, ed. Denominational; not as conservative or evangelical as some. Primary focus on mission and ministry of the Presbyterian Church (USA)'s General Assembly Mission Council. Monthly (10X) mag.; 52 pgs.; circ. 40,000. Subscription $24.95. 25% freelance. Query or complete ms/cover letter; phone/fax/e-query OK to eva.stimson@pcusa.org. (502) 569-5635. **Pays $100-300** on acceptance for 1st rts. Articles 800-2,000 wds. (prefers 1,000-1,500); (20/yr.). Also uses short features 250-600 wds. Responds in 2-5 wks. Seasonal 3 mos. ahead. Few reprints. Accepts requested ms by postal mail, on disk, or by e-mail. Kill fee 50%. Prefers NRSV. Guidelines on website: www.presbyterianmission.org/ministries/today/writers-guidelines.

Tips: "Most open to feature articles about Presbyterians—individuals, churches with special outreach, creative programs, or mission work. Do not often use inspirational or testimony-type articles."

** This periodical was #40 on the 2006 Top 50 Christian Publishers list and won a "Best in Class" award (2012) from the Associated Church Press.

***PRIORITY!** 440 W. Nyack Rd., West Nyack NY 10994. (845) 620-7450. Fax (845) 620-7723. E-mail: linda_johnson@use.salvationarmy.org. Website: www.prioritypeople.org. The Salvation Army. Linda D. Johnson, ed.; Robert Mitchell, assoc. ed. Quarterly & online mag.; 48-56 pgs.; circ. 28,000. Subscription $8.95. 50% assigned. Query/clips; e-query OK. **Pays $200-800** on acceptance for 1st rts. Articles 400-1,700 wds. (8-10/yr.). All articles assigned. Responds in 2 wks. Occasionally buys reprints (tell when/where appeared). Prefers accepted ms by e-mail (in Word or copied into message). Kill fee 50%. Regularly uses sidebars. Prefers NIV. Occasionally buys submissions from children/teens. Guidelines/theme list by e-mail; copy $1/9 x 12 SAE. (Ads)

Columns/Departments: Buys 5-10/yr. Prayer Power (stories about answered prayer, or harnessing prayer power); Who's News (calling attention to specific accomplishments or missions); My Take (opinion essay); all 400-700 wds. $200-400. Query.

Special needs: All articles must have a connection to The Salvation Army. Can be from any part of the US. Looking especially for freelancers with Salvation Army connections; Christmas recollections (by August 1); people/program features.

Tips: "Most open to features on people. Every article, whether about people or programs, tells a story and must feature the Salvation Army. Stories focus on evangelism, holiness, prayer. The more a writer knows about the Salvation Army, the better."

**This publication was #11 on the 2010 Top 50 Christian Publishers List.

***PRISCILLA PAPERS,** 122 W. Franklin Ave., Ste. 218, Minneapolis MN 55404-2451. Send submissions to editor at: 130 Essex St., Gordon-Conwell Theological Seminary, S. Hamilton MA 01982. (612) 872-6898. Fax (612) 872-6891. E-mail: debbeattymel@aol.com. Website: www.cbeinternational.org. Christians for Biblical Equality. William David Spencer, ed.; Deb Beatty Mel, assoc. ed. Addresses biblical interpretation and its relationship to women and men sharing authority and ministering together equally, not according to gender, ethnicity, or class but according to God's gifting. Quarterly jour.; 32 pgs.; circ. 2,000. Subscription $40 (includes subscription to *Mutuality*). 85% unsolicited freelance; 15% assigned. Query preferred; e-query OK. **Pays 3 copies, plus a gift certificate at cbe's ministry** for 1st & electronic rts. Articles 600-5,000 wds. (1/yr.); no fiction; book reviews 600 wds. (free book). Slow and careful response. No reprints. Seasonal 12 mos. ahead. Prefers proposed ms on disk or by e-mail (attached file) with hard copy. No kill fee. Uses some sidebars. Guidelines on website; copy for 9 x 12 SAE/$2.07 postage. (Ads)

Poetry: Accepts 1/yr. Avant-garde, free verse, traditional (on biblical gender equality themes); pays a free book.

Tips: "P.P. is the academic voice of CBE. Our target is the informed lay reader. All sections are open to freelancers. Any well-written, single-theme article (no potpourri) presenting a solid exegetical and hermeneutical approach to biblical equality from a high view of Scripture will be considered for publication." Seeks original cover artwork. Use *Chicago Manual of Style*.

PURPOSE, 718 N. Main St., Newton KS 67114. (316) 281-4412. Fax (316) 283-0454. E-mail: PurposeEditor@mpn.net. Website: www.mpn.net. Mennonite Publishing Network/Agency of Mennonite Church USA & Canada. Carol Duerksen, ed. Denominational, for older youth & adults. Monthly take-home paper; 32 pgs.; circ. 8,900. Subscription $22.65; $23.78 Cdn. 80% unsolicited freelance; 20% assigned. Complete ms (only)/cover letter; e-mail submissions preferred. **Pays $10-42 or .06-.07/wd.** on acceptance (or when editor chooses) for onetime rts. Articles & fiction, 400-600 wds. (95/yr.). Responds in 6 mos. Seasonal 1 yr. ahead. Accepts simultaneous submissions & reprints (tell when/where appeared). Regularly uses sidebars. Guidelines on website (click on "Periodicals"/"Writers Guidelines"); copy $2/6 x 9 SAE/2 stamps. (No ads)

Poetry: Buys 120/yr. Free verse, haiku, traditional; 3-12 lines; up to $2/line ($7.50-20). Submit max. 5 poems.

Fillers: Buys 25/yr. Anecdotes, prose; up to 300 wds., up to .06/wd.

Tips: "Read our guidelines. All areas are open. Articles must carry a strong story line. First person is preferred. Don't exceed maximum word length, send no more than 3 works at a time."

** This periodical was #44 on the 2010 Top 50 Christian Publishers list (#25 in 2009, #19 in 2008, #38 in 2007, #43 in 2006).

RELIEF JOURNAL A Christian Literary Expression, 8933 Forestview, Evanston IL 60203. E-mail: editor@reliefjournal.com. Website: www.reliefjournal.com. CC Publishing, NFP. Brad Fruhauff, ed-in-chief; Brady Clark, nonfiction ed.; Joshua Hren, fiction ed.; Tania Runyan, poetry ed. Semiannual mag.; 140 pgs.; circ. 300. Subscription $23. 90% unsolicited freelance; 10% assigned. Online submission: e-mail submissions. Complete ms. **Pays in copies** for 1st rts. Creative nonfiction to 5,000 wds (10/yr); fiction to 8,000 wds. (12/yr.). Poetry to 5 poems (50/yr); images to 5 pieces (8/yr). Responds in 16 wks. Accepts simultaneous submissions & reprints (only when solicited). Any Bible version. Guidelines on website ("Submit Your Work"). Incomplete topical listings. (Ads)

Poetry: Tania Runyan, poetry ed. Accepts 50-60/yr. Poetry that is well-written, concrete, and grounded and makes sense; to 1,000 wds. Submit max. 5 poems.

CNF: Brady Clark, cnf ed. Accepts 6-10/yr. Personal essays, nonfiction with a narrative and/or emotional arc; to 5,000 wds.

Fiction: Joshua Hren, fiction ed. Accepts 9-12/yr. Fiction unafraid of the tough questions and willing to live in the ambiguity that requires faith; to 8,000 wds.

Images: Brad Fruhauff, image ed. Accepts 6-10/yr. B/W photos, drawings, or paintings that strike the eye and engage the imagination; to 5 images.

SEEK, 8805 Governor's Hill Dr., Ste. 400, Cincinnati OH 45249. E-mail: seek@standardpub.com. Website: www.Standardpub.com. Standard Publishing. Margaret K. Williams, ed. Light, inspirational, take-home reading for young and middle-aged adults. Weekly take-home paper; 8 pgs.; circ. 29,000. Subscriptions $18.49 (sold only in sets of 5). 75% unsolicited freelance; 25% assigned. Complete ms; no phone/fax/e-query. **Pays .07/wd.** on acceptance for 1st rts., **.05/wd. for reprints**. Articles 750-1,000 wds. (150-200/yr.); fiction 500-1,200 wds. Responds in 18 wks. Seasonal 1 yr. ahead. Accepts reprints (tell when/where appeared). Prefers submissions by e-mail (attached file). Uses some sidebars. Guidelines/theme list by mail/website ("About Standard Publishing"/"View Writer's Guidelines" left side); copy for 6 x 9 SAE/2 stamps. (No ads)

Fillers: Buys 50/yr. Ideas, short humor per word count.

Tips: "We now work with a theme list. Only articles tied to these themes will be considered for publication. Check website for theme list and revised guidelines."

** This periodical was #19 on the 2010 Top 50 Christian Publishers list (#19 in 2009, #11 in 2008, #7 in 2007, #26 in 2006).

***SOUTHWEST KANSAS FAITH AND FAMILY,** PO Box 1454, Dodge City KS 67801. (620) 225-4677. Fax (620) 225-4625. E-mail: info@swkfaithandfamily.org. Website: www.swkfaithandfamily

.org. Independent. Stan Wilson, pub. Dedicated to sharing the Word of God and news and information that honors Christian beliefs, family traditions, and values that are the cornerstone of our nation. Monthly newspaper; circ. 9,000. Subscription $25. Accepts freelance. Prefers e-query; complete ms OK. Articles; no reviews. Guidelines on website ("Submit Articles"). Incomplete topical listings. (Ads)

***ST. ANTHONY MESSENGER,** 28 W. Liberty St., Cincinnati OH 45202-6498. (513) 241-5615. Fax (513) 241-0399. E-mail: StAnthony@AmericanCatholic.org. Website: www.AmericanCatholic.org. John Feister, ed. For Catholic adults & families. Monthly & online mag.; 64 pgs.; circ. 180,000. Subscription $28. 55% unsolicited freelance. Query/clips (complete ms for fiction); e-query OK. **Pays .20/wd.** on acceptance for 1st, reprint (right to reprint), and electronic rts. Articles 1,500-3,000 wds., prefers 1,500-2,500 (35-50/yr.); fiction 1,500-2,500 wds. (12/yr.); book reviews 500 wds. $50. Responds in 3-9 wks. Seasonal 6 mos. ahead. Kill fee. Uses some sidebars. Prefers NAB. Guidelines on website ("Contact Us"/"Writer's Guidelines"); copy for 9 x 12 SAE/4 stamps. (Ads)

Poetry: Christopher Heffron, poetry ed. Buys 20/yr. Free verse, haiku, traditional; 3-25 lines; $2/line ($20 min.). Submit max. 2 poems.

Fillers: Cartoons.

Tips: "Many submissions suggest that the writer has not read our guidelines or sample articles. Most open to articles, fiction, profiles, interviews of Catholic personalities, personal experiences, and prayer. Writing must be professional; use Catholic terminology and vocabulary. Writing must be faithful to Catholic belief and teaching, life, and experience. Our online writers' guidelines indicate the seven categories of articles. Texts of articles reflecting each category are linked to the online writers' guidelines for nonfiction articles."

** This periodical was #28 on the 2009 Top 50 Christian Publishers list (#25 in 2008, #22 in 2007, #33 in 2006).

***THE STORYTELLER,** 2441 Washington Rd., Maynard AR 72444. (870) 647-2137. E-mail: story tellermag1@yahoo.com. Website: www.thestorytellermagazine.com. Fossil Creek Publishing. Regina Cook Williams, ed./pub.; Ruthan Riney, review ed. Family audience. Quarterly jour.; 72 pgs.; circ. 850. Subscription $24. 100% unsolicited freelance. Complete ms/cover letter; phone/e-query OK. **NO PAYMENT.** Articles 2,500 wds. (60/yr.); fiction 2,500 wds. (100-125/yr.). Responds in 1 wk. Seasonal 3 mos. ahead. Accepts simultaneous submissions & reprints (tell when/where appeared). Responds in 1-2 wks. No disk or e-mail submissions; does not use sidebars. Also accepts submissions from children/teens (not children's stories). Guidelines by mail/website ("Guidelines"); copy $6/9 x 12 SAE/5 stamps. (Ads)

Poetry: Jamie Johnson, poetry ed. Accepts 100/yr. Free verse, haiku, light verse, traditional; 5-40 lines. Submit max. 3 poems. Pays $1/poem.

Fillers: Accepts 10-20/yr. Cartoons, quotes, tips; 25-50 wds. Writing-related only.

Special needs: Original artwork. Funny or serious stories about growing up as a pastor's child or being a pastor's wife. Also westerns and mysteries.

Contest: Offers 1 or 2 paying contests per year, along with People's Choice Awards, and Pushcart Prize nominations. Go to www.thestorytellermagazine.com for announcements of all forthcoming contests for the year.

Tips: "We look for stories that are written well, flow well, have believable dialogue, and good endings. So many writers write a good story but fizzle at the ending. All sections of the magazine are open except how-to articles. Study the craft of writing. Learn all you can before you send anything out. Pay attention to detail, make sure manuscripts are as free of mistakes as possible. Follow the guidelines—they aren't hard." Always looking for B & W photos for front cover.

** This periodical was #42 on the 2007 Top 50 Christian Publishers list.

***STUDIO: A Journal of Christians Writing,** 727 Peel St., Albury NSW 2640, Australia. Phone/fax +61 2 6021 1135. E-mail: studio00@bigpond.net.au. Website: http://web.me.com /pdgrover?StudioJournal. Submit to Studio Editor. Quarterly jour.; 36 pgs.; circ. 300. Subscription

$60 AUS. 90% unsolicited freelance; 10% assigned. Query. **Pays in copies** for onetime rts. Articles 3,000 wds. (15/yr.); fiction 3,000 wds. (50/yr.); book reviews 300 wds. Responds in 3 wks. Accepts simultaneous submissions & reprints (tell when/where appeared). No disks; e-mail submissions OK. Does not use sidebars. Guidelines by mail (send IRC); copy for $10 AUS. (Ads)

Poetry: Accepts 200/yr. Any type; 4-100 lines. Submit max. 3 poems.

Contest: See copy of journal for details.

Tips: "We accept all types of fiction and literary article themes."

***SUCCESS/VICTORY NEWS,** Franklin Publishing Company, 2723 Steamboat Circle, Arlington TX 76006. (817) 548-1124. E-mail: ludwigotto@sbcglobal.net. Website: www.franklinpublishing.net. Submit to Dr. Ludwig Otto, publisher. Bimonthly journal. 170 pgs; circ. 8,000. Subscription $80. **NO PAYMENT.** 100% unsolicited. Responds in 3 wks. E-mail queries. Send submissions by e-mail attachment. No writer's guidelines. Book reviews 3 pgs. Audience general public with a Christian message.

***TESTIMONY,** 2450 Milltower Ct., Mississauga ON L5N 5Z6, Canada. (905) 542-7400. Fax (905) 542-7313. E-mail: testimony@paoc.org. Website: www.testimonymag.ca. The Pentecostal Assemblies of Canada. Stephen Kennedy, ed. To encourage a Christian response to a wide range of issues and topics, including those that are peculiar to Pentecostals. Monthly & online mag.; 24 pgs.; circ. 8,000. Subscription $30 US/$24 Cdn. (includes GST). 10% unsolicited freelance; 90% assigned. Query; fax/e-query OK. **Pays $100** on publication for 1st rts. (no pay for reprint rts.). Articles 700-900 wds. Responds in 6-8 wks. Seasonal 4 mos. ahead. Accepts reprints (tell when/where appeared). Prefers e-mail submission (copied into message). Regularly uses sidebars. Prefers NIV. Guidelines/theme list by mail/e-mail/website (click on "Fellowship Services"/ "Publications"/"Testimony"/scroll down to "View our Submission Guidelines Here"); $3 US or $2.50 Cdn./copy 9 x 12 SAE. (Ads)

Tips: "View theme list on our website and query us about a potential article regarding one of our themes. Our readership is 98% Canadian. We prefer Canadian writers or at least writers who understand that Canadians are not Americans in long underwear. We also give preference to members of this denomination, since this is related to issues concerning our fellowship."

THRIVING FAMILY, 8605 Explorer Dr., Colorado Springs CO 80920. E-mail: thrivingfamily submissions@family.org. Website: www.thrivingfamily.com. Focus on the Family. Submit to The Editor. Focuses on marriage and parenting from a biblical perspective; mostly for families with 4- to 12-year-old children. Monthly & online mag. Open to unsolicited freelance. Complete ms or query; e-query OK (no attachments). **Pays .25/wd.** Feature articles 1,200-2,000 wds.; online articles 800-1,200 wds. Guidelines/theme list; copy online. Incomplete topical listings.

Columns/Departments: Family Stages (practical tips), 50-200 wds. For Him (male perspective), 400 wds. For Her (female perspective), 400 wds. Blended Family (concerns of blended families), 400 wds. Single Parents (issues related to single parenting), 400 wds.

TIME OF SINGING: A Magazine of Christian Poetry, PO Box 149, Conneaut Lake PA 16316. E-mail: timesing@zoominternet.net. Website: www.timeofsinging.com. Lora Homan Zill, ed. We try to appeal to all poets and lovers of poetry. Quarterly booklet; 44 pgs.; circ. 250. Subscription $17. 95% unsolicited freelance; 5% assigned. Complete ms; e-query OK. **Pays in copies** for 1st, onetime, or reprint rts. Poetry only (some book reviews by assignment). Responds in 12 wks. Seasonal 6 mos. ahead. Accepts simultaneous submissions & reprints (tell when/where appeared). Accepts e-mail submission (attached file). Guidelines by mail/e-mail/website ("Guidelines"); copy $4 ea. or 2/$7 (Checks, money orders payable to Wind & Water Press.)

Poetry: Accepts 150-200/yr. Free verse, haiku, light verse, traditional; 3-60 lines. Submit max. 5 poems. Always need form poems (sonnets, villanelles, triolets, etc.) with Christian themes. Fresh rhyme. "Cover letter not needed; your work speaks for itself."

Contest: Sponsors 1-2 annual poetry contests on specific themes or forms ($3 entry fee/poem) with cash prizes (see website or send SASE for rules).

Tips: "Study poetry, read widely—both Christian and non-Christian. Work at the craft. Be open to suggestions and critique. If I have taken time to comment on your work, it is close to publication. If you don't agree, submit elsewhere. I appreciate poets who take chances and a fresh look at abstract, but substantive, Christian concepts like grace, faith, etc. *Time of Singing* is a literary poetry magazine, so I'm not looking for greeting card verse or sermons that rhyme."

THE VISION, 8855 Dunn Rd., Hazelwood MO 63042-2299. (314) 837-7300. Fax (314) 336-1803. E-mail: WAP@upci.org. Website: www.wordaflame.org. United Pentecostal Church. Richard M. Davis, ed.; submit to Karen Myers, administrative aide. Denominational. Weekly take-home paper; 4 pgs.; circ. 4,000. Subscription $3.49/quarter. 95% unsolicited freelance. Complete ms/cover letter; no e-query. **Pays $8-25** on publication. Articles 500-1,600 wds. (to 120/yr.); fiction 1,200-1,600 wds. (to 120/yr.); devotionals 350-400 wds. Seasonal 9 months ahead. Accepts simultaneous submissions & reprints. Guidelines by mail/e-mail/website ("Writer's Guidelines" left side); free copy/#10 SASE. (No ads)

Poetry: Buys 30/yr.; traditional; $3-12.

Columns/Departments: Devotionals 350-400 wds. Requires KJV.

Tips: "Most open to fiction short stories, real-life experiences, and short poems. Whether fiction or nonfiction, we are looking for stories depicting everyday life situations and how Christian principles are used to solve problems, resolve issues, or enhance one's spiritual growth. Be sure manuscript has a pertinent, spiritual application. Best way to break into our publication is to send a well-written article that meets our specifications."

VISTA, PO Box 50434, Indianapolis IN 46250-0434. (317) 774-7900. E-mail: submissions@wesleyan.org. Website: www.wesleyan.org/wg. Wesleyan Publishing House. Jim Watkins, ed. Weekly take-home paper; 8 pgs. 60% unsolicited freelance; 40% assigned. Accepts full mss by e-mail only. **Pays $15-35** on publication for onetime and reprint rts. Articles 500-550 wds.; fiction 500-550 wds.; humor 250 wds. Seasonal 9 mos. ahead. Theme based. E-mail to request theme list. No simultaneous submissions. Requires e-mail submissions (no attachments). No kill fee. Also accepts submissions from children/teens. Prefers NIV. Guidelines on website (www.wesleyan.org/wg).

Tips: "Great market for beginning writers. Any subject related to Christian growth."

WAR CRY, 615 Slaters Ln., Alexandria VA 22314. (703) 684-5500. Fax (703) 684-5539. E-mail: war_cry@usn.salvationarmy.org. Website: www.thewarcry.org. The Salvation Army. Maj. Allen Satterlee, ed-in-chief; Jeff McDonald, mng. ed. Pluralistic readership reached primarily by Salvation Army units across the country, including distribution in institutions. 15 issues/yr including special Easter & Christmas issues. 36 pgs., circ. 288,000. Prefers full mss by e-mail (attached or copied into message); e-query OK. **Pays .25/wd.** upon publication and .15/wd. for reprints. Publishes 45 nonfiction articles per year, limited fiction. New *Intersection* insert accepts features geared for nonreligious audience. Articles 500-1,200 wds.; fillers 100-400 wds. Limited poetry. Responds in 3-4 wks. Submit material 3 mos. in adv. for monthly issues, 6 mos. for special issues/holidays. Accepts simultaneous submissions or reprints. Guidelines on website/by mail/e-mail; copy of sample issue provided with a 9 x 12 SASE. Copies available online as flipbook. Accepts ads.

WEAVINGS, 1908 Grand Ave., PO Box 340004, Nashville TN 37203-0004. (615) 340-7254. E-mail: weavings@upperroom.org. Website: www.weavings.org. Publisher: The Upper Room. Submit to The Editor. For clergy, lay leaders, and all thoughtful seekers who want to deepen their understanding of, and response to, how God's life and human lives are being woven together. Quarterly mag. Subscription $29.95. Open to freelance that relates to a specific upcoming theme. Complete ms. **Pays .12/wd. & up** on acceptance. Articles, sermons, meditations, stories 1,500-2,000 wds. maximum; poetry (pays $75 and up on acceptance); book reviews 750 wds. Responds within 13 wks. Accepts reprints. Accepts requested ms on disk or by e-mail. Guidelines/theme list on website (click on the "About" tab on the home page); sample copy for 6.5 x 9.5 SAE/5 stamps. Incomplete topical listings.

Tips: Note that this publication is transitioning as we go to press and will likely be changing format, as well as other aspects of this listing. Check their website for current information.

***WORD & WAY,** 3236 Emerald Ln., Ste. 400, Jefferson City MO 65109-3700. (573) 635-5939, ext. 205. Fax (573) 635-1774. E-mail: wordandway@wordandway.org. Website: www.wordandway.org. Baptist. Bill Webb, ed. (bwebb@wordandway.org). Contact: Vicki Brown, Assoc. ed. (vbrown@wordandway.org). Biweekly. Subscription $17.50. To share the stories of God at work through Baptists in Missouri and surrounding areas.

CHILDREN'S MARKETS

CADET QUEST, PO Box 7259, Grand Rapids MI 49510. (616) 241-5616. Fax (616) 241-5558. E-mail: submissions@CalvinistCadets.org. Website: www.CalvinistCadets.org. Calvinist Cadet Corps. G. Richard Broene, ed. To show boys ages 9-14 how God is at work in their lives and in the world around them. Mag. published 7X/yr.; 24 pgs.; circ. 7,500. Subscription $16.10. 35% unsolicited freelance. Complete ms/cover letter. **Pays .04-.06/wd.** on acceptance for 1st, onetime, or reprint rts. Articles 800-1,500 wds. (12/yr.); fiction 1,000-1,300 wds. (14/yr.). Responds in 4-6 wks. Accepts simultaneous submissions & reprints (tell when/where appeared). Accepts ms by e-mail (copied into message). Uses some sidebars. Prefers NIV. Guidelines/theme list by mail/website ("Submissions/Help"/"Cadet Quest Author's Info"); copy for 9 x 12 SAE/3 stamps. (Ads—limited)

Fillers: Buys several/yr. Quizzes, tips, puzzles; 20-200 wds. $5 & up.

Tips: "Most open to fiction or fillers tied to themes; request new theme list in January of each year (best to submit between February and April each year). Also looking for simple projects/crafts, and puzzles (word, logic)."

FOCUS ON THE FAMILY CLUBHOUSE, 8605 Explorer Dr., Colorado Springs CO 80920. (719) 531-3400. Website: www.clubhousemagazine.com. Focus on the Family. Jesse Florea, ed.; submit to Stephen O'Rear, asst. ed. For children 8-12 years who desire to know more about God and the Bible. Monthly & online mag.; 32 pgs.; circ. 64,000. Subscription $19.99. 25% unsolicited freelance; 40% assigned. Complete ms/cover letter; no phone/fax/e-query. **Pays .15-.25/wd.** for articles, **up to $300 for fiction** on acceptance for nonexclusive license. Articles to 800 wds. (5/yr.); fiction 500-1,800 wds. (30/yr.). Responds within 3 mos. Seasonal 9 mos. ahead. Accepts simultaneous submissions; no reprints. No disk or e-mail submissions. Kill fee. Uses some sidebars. Prefers HCSB. Guidelines online; copy (call 800-232-6459). (Minimal ads accepted)

Fillers: Buys 6-8/yr. Quizzes, crafts, word puzzles, recipes; 200-800 wds., .15-.25/wd.

Tips: "Most open to fiction, personality stories, quizzes, and how-to pieces with a theme. Avoid stories dealing with boy-girl relationships, poetry, and contemporary, middle-class family settings. We look for fiction in exciting settings with ethnic characters. True stories of ordinary kids doing extraordinary things and historical fiction are good ways to break in. Send manuscripts with list of credentials. Read past issues."

** 2012, 2011, 2010, 2009, 2008, 2007, 2006 EPA Award of Merit: Youth.

FOCUS ON THE FAMILY CLUBHOUSE JR., 8605 Explorer Dr., Colorado Springs CO 80920. (719) 531-3400. Fax (719) 531-3499. Website: www.clubhousejr.com. Focus on the Family. Jesse Florea, ed. Submit to Joanna Echols, sr. assoc. ed. For 3- to 7-year-olds. Monthly & online mag.; 32 pgs.; circ. 54,000. Subscription $19.99. 30% unsolicited freelance; 30% assigned. Complete ms/cover letter; no phone/fax/e-query. **Pays $25-200 ($50-200 for fiction)** on acceptance for nonexclusive rts. Articles 100-500 wds. (1-2/yr.); fiction 250-1,000 wds. (10/yr.); Bible stories 250-800 wds.; one-page rebus stories to 350 wds. Responds within 3 mos. Seasonal 9 mos. ahead. Kill fee. Prefers NIrV. Uses some sidebars. Guidelines online; copy (call 800-232-6459). (No ads)

Poetry: Buys 4-8/yr. Traditional; 10-25 lines (to 250 wds.); $50-100.

Fillers: Buys 4-8/yr. Recipes/crafts; 100-500 wds. $30-100.

Special needs: Bible stories, rebus, fiction, and crafts.

Tips: "Most open to short, nonpreachy fiction, beginning reader stories, and read-to-me. Looking for true stories of ordinary kids doing extraordinary things. Be knowledgeable of our style and try it out on kids first. Looking for stories set in exotic places; nonwhite, middle-class characters; historical pieces; humorous quizzes; and craft and recipe features are most readily accepted."

** 2010 EPA Award of Excellence: Youth; 2012, 2011, 2007 EPA Award of Merit: Youth.

***GUIDE,** 55 W. Oak Ridge Dr., Hagerstown MD 21740. (301) 393-4037. Fax (301) 393-4055. E-mail: Guide@rhpa.org. Website: www.guidemagazine.org. Seventh-day Adventist/Review and Herald Publishing. Randy Fishell, ed. A Christian journal for 10- to 14-yr.-olds, presenting true stories relevant to their needs. Weekly mag.; 32 pgs.; circ. 26,000. Subscription $54.95/yr. 75% unsolicited freelance; 20% assigned. Complete ms/cover letter; fax/e-query OK. **Pays .07-.10/wd. ($25-140)** on acceptance for 1st, reprint, simultaneous, and electronic rts. True stories only, 500-1,300 wds. (200/yr.). Responds in 4-6 wks. Seasonal 8 mos. ahead. Accepts simultaneous submissions & reprints (tell when/where appeared; pays 50% of standard rate). Prefers requested ms by e-mail (attached or copied into message). Kill fee 20-50%. Regularly uses sidebars. Accepts submissions from children/teens. Prefers NIV. Guidelines on website (link on home page) or by mail; copy for 6 x 9 SAE/2 stamps. (Ads)

Fillers: Buys 40-50/yr. Cartoons, games, quizzes, word puzzles on a spiritual theme; 20-50 wds. $20-40. Accepting very few games, only the most unusual concepts.

Columns/Departments: All are assigned.

Special needs: "Most open to true action/adventure, Christian humor, and true stories showing God at work in a 10- to 14-year-old's life. Stories must have energy and a high level of intrinsic interest to kids. Put it together with dialog and a spiritual slant, and you're on the 'write' track for our readers. School life."

Tips: "We are very open to freelancers. Use your best short-story techniques (dialogue, scenes, a sense of 'plot') to tell a true story starring a kid ages 10-14. Bring out a clear spiritual/biblical message. We publish multipart true stories regularly; 3-12 chapters, 1,200 words each. We can no longer accept nature or historical stories without documentation. All topics indicated need to be addressed within the context of a true story."

** This periodical was #17 on the 2010 Top 50 Christian Publishers list (#23 in 2009, #24 in 2008, #27 in 2007, #44 in 2006).

***JUNIORWAY,** PO Box 436987, Chicago IL 60643. Fax (708) 868-6759. Website: www.urbanministries.com. Urban Ministries, Inc. K. Steward, ed. (ksteward@urbanministries.com). Sunday school magazine with accompanying teacher's guide and activity booklet for 4th-6th graders. Open to freelance queries; 100% assigned. Query and/or e-query with writing sample and/or clips; no phone queries. **Pays $150** for curriculum, 120 days after acceptance for all rts. Articles 1,200 wds. (4/yr.), pays $80. Responds in 4 wks. No simultaneous submissions. Requires requested material by e-mail (attached file). Guidelines by e-mail. Incomplete topical listings. (No ads)

Poetry: Buys 8/yr.; 200-400 wds. Pays $40.

Tips: "*Juniorway* principally serves an African American audience; editorial content addresses broad Christian issues. Looking for those with educational or Sunday school teaching experience who can actually explain Scriptures in an insightful and engaging way and apply those Scriptures to the lives of children 9-11 years old."

KEYS FOR KIDS, PO Box 1001, Grand Rapids MI 49501-1001. (616) 647-4971. Fax (616) 647-4950. E-mail: Hazel@cbhministries.org or geri@cbhministries.org. Website: www.cbhministries.org. CBH Ministries. Hazel Marett, ed.; Geri Walcott, ed. A daily devotional booklet for children (8-14) or for family devotions. Quarterly booklet & online version; 112 pgs.; circ. 70,000. Subscription free. 100%

unsolicited freelance. Complete ms; e-query OK. Accepts full mss by e-mail. **Pays $25** on acceptance for 1st, reprint, or simultaneous rts. Devotionals (includes short fiction story) 375-425 wds. (30-40/yr.). Responds in 4-8 wks. Seasonal 4-5 mos. ahead. Accepts simultaneous submissions & reprints. Prefers NKJV. Guidelines by mail/e-mail; copy for $1.50 postage/handling. (No ads)

Tips: "We want children's devotions. If you are rejected, go back to the sample and study it some more. We use only devotionals, but they include a short fiction story. Any appropriate topic is fine."

***THE KIDS' ARK CHILDREN'S CHRISTIAN MAGAZINE,** PO Box 3160, Victoria TX 77903. Toll-free (800) 455-1770. (361) 485-1770. E-mail for queries: editor@thekidsark.com. Website: http://thekidsark.com. Interdenominational. Submit to: Joy Mygrants, sr. ed., at thekidsarksubmissions@yahoo.com. To give kids, 6-12, a biblical foundation on which to base their choices in life. Quarterly & online mag.; 36 pgs.; circ. 8,000. 100% unsolicited freelance. Complete ms; e-query OK. Accepts full ms by e-mail. **Pays $100 max.** on publication for 1st, reprint ($25), electronic, worldwide rts. Fiction 600 wds. (Buys 4 stories/issue—16/yr., must match issue's theme); no articles. Responds in 3-4 wks. No reprints. Prefers accepted submissions by e-mail (attached file). Kill fee 15%. Uses some sidebars. Also accepts submissions from children/teens. Prefers NIV. Guidelines/theme list on website ("Writer's Guidelines"); paper copy for $1 postage. Sample magazine on website. (Ads—limited)

Tips: "Open to fiction only (any time period). Think outside the box! Must catch children's attention and hold it; be biblically based and related to theme. We want to teach God's principles in an exciting format. Every issue contains the Ten Commandments and the plan of salvation."

NATURE FRIEND: Helping Children Explore the Wonders of God's Creation, 4253 Woodcock Ln., Dayton VA 22821. (540) 867-0764. Fax (540) 867-9516. E-mail: editor@naturefriendmagazine.com. Website: www.naturefriendmagazine.com. Dogwood Ridge Outdoors. Kevin Shank, ed. For ages 6-16. Monthly mag.; 28 pgs; circ. 10,000. Subscription $38. 50-80% freelance written. Complete ms/cover letter; no phone/fax/e-query. **Pays .05/wd.** on publication for 1st rts. Articles 250-900 wds. (50/yr.); or fiction 500-750 wds. (40/yr.). Seasonal 4 mos. ahead. Accepts simultaneous submissions and reprints. Submit accepted articles on disk (Word format) or by e-mail. Uses some sidebars. KJV only. Guidelines $5 (www.naturefriendmagazine.com/index.pl?linkid=12;class=gen); copy $5/SAE/$2 postage. (No ads)

Fillers: Buys 12/yr. Quizzes, word puzzles; 100-500 wds. $10-15.

Columns/Departments: "Month" Nature Trails (seasonal, nature activity for each month); 100-450 wds. Write up as something you do each year, such as mushroom hunting, wildflower walk, snowshoeing, Christmas bird count, viewing a specific meteor shower, etc.

Tips: "We want to bring joy and knowledge to children by opening the world of God's creation to them. We endeavor to create a sense of awe about nature's Creator and a respect for His creation. I'd like to see more submissions of hands-on things to do with a nature theme. The best way to learn about the content we use is to be a current, active subscriber."

***POCKETS,** PO Box 340004, Nashville TN 37203-0004. (615) 340-7333. Fax (615) 340-7267. E-mail: pockets@upperroom.org or through website: pockets.upperroom.org. United Methodist/The Upper Room. Submit to Lynn W. Gilliam, ed. Devotional magazine for children (6-11 yrs.). Monthly (11X) mag.; 48 pgs.; circ. 67,000. Subscription $21.95. 75% unsolicited freelance. Complete ms/brief cover letter; no phone/fax/e-query. **Pays .14/wd.** on acceptance for onetime rts. Articles 400-800 wds. (10/yr.) & fiction 600-1,400 wds. (40/yr.). Responds in 8 wks. Seasonal 1 yr. ahead. Accepts simultaneous submissions & reprints (tell when/where appeared). No mss by e-mail. Uses some sidebars. Prefers NRSV. Also accepts submissions from children through age 12. Guidelines/theme list by mail/e-mail/website (click on "Print Magazine"/"Write for Pockets"); copy for 9 x 12 SAE/4 stamps. (No ads)

Poetry: Buys 25/yr. Free verse, haiku, light verse, traditional; to 25 lines; $25-48. Submit max. 7 poems.

Fillers: Buys 50/yr. Games, word puzzles; $25-50.

Columns/Departments: Buys 20/yr. Complete ms. Kids Cook; Pocketsful of Love (ways to show love in your family), 200-300 wds. Peacemakers at Work (children involved in environmental, community, and peace/justice issues; include action photos and name of photographer), to 600 wds. Pocketsful of Prayer, 400-600 wds. Someone You'd Like to Know (preferably a child whose lifestyle demonstrates a strong faith perspective), 600 wds. Pays .14/wd.

Special needs: Two-page stories for ages 5-7, 600 words max. Need role model stories, retold biblical stories, Someone You'd Like to Know, and Peacemakers at Work.

Contest: Fiction-writing contest; submit between March 1 & August 15 every year. Prize $1,000 and publication in *Pockets*. Length 1,000-1,600 wds. Must be unpublished and not historical fiction. Previous winners not eligible. Send to Pockets Fiction Contest at above address, and include an SASE for return of manuscript and response. Write "Fiction Contest" on envelope and on title/first page of manuscript.

Tips: "Well-written fiction that fits our themes is always needed. Make stories relevant to the lives of today's children and show faith as a natural part of everyday life. All areas open to freelance. Nonfiction probably easiest to sell for columns (we get fewer submissions for those). Read, read, read, and study. Be attentive to guidelines, themes, and study past issues."

** This periodical was #8 on the 2010 Top 50 Christian Publishers list (#6 in 2009, #8 in 2008, #11 in 2007, #12 in 2006).

SHINE BRIGHTLY, PO Box 7259, Grand Rapids MI 49510. (616) 241-5616, ext. 3034. Fax (616) 241-5558. E-mail: kelli@gemsgc.org. Website: www.gemsgc.org. GEMS Girls Clubs. Kelli Gilmore, mng. ed. (616) 334-6059; kelli@gemsgc.org. To show girls ages 9-14 that God is at work in their lives and in the world around them and they have the potential to be world changers. Monthly (9X) mag.; 24 pgs.; circ. 16,000. Subscription $13.95. 80% unsolicited freelance; 20% assigned. Complete ms; e-mail queries. **Pays .03-.05/wd.** on publication for 1st or reprint rts. Articles 100-400 wds. (35/yr.); fiction 400-900 wds. (30/yr.). Responds in 4-6 wks. Seasonal 10 mos. ahead. Accepts simultaneous submissions & reprints. Accepts requested ms on disk. Regularly uses sidebars. Prefers NIV. Guidelines/theme list on website (click on "Girls" tab/"Shine Brightly"/Magazine cover for SB in the right-hand column/"Writers"); copy $1/9 x 12 SAE/3 stamps. (No ads)

Fillers: Buys 10/yr. Cartoons, games, party ideas, prayers, quizzes, short humor, word puzzles; 50-200 wds. $5-10.

Special needs: Craft ideas that can be used to help others. Articles on how words can help build others up or tear people down.

Tips: "Be realistic—we get a lot of fluffy stories with Pollyanna endings. We are looking for real-life-type stories that girls relate to. We mostly publish short stories but are open to short reflective articles. Know what girls face today and how they cope in their daily lives. We need angles from home life and friendships, peer pressure, and the normal growing-up challenges girls deal with."

***SKIPPING STONES: A Multicultural Literary Magazine,** PO Box 3939, Eugene OR 97403. (541) 342-4956. E-mail: editor@skippingstones.org. Website: www.skippingstones.org. Interfaith/multicultural. Arun N. Toké, exec. ed. A multicultural awareness and nature appreciation magazine for young people 7-17, worldwide. In 24th year. Bimonthly (5X) mag.; 36 pgs.; circ. 2,000. Subscription $25. 85% unsolicited freelance; 15% assigned. Query or complete ms/cover letter; no phone query; e-query/submissions OK. **Pays in copies** (2-4) (40% discount on extra issues) for 1st, electronic, and nonexclusive reprint rts. Articles (15-25/yr.) 750-1,000 wds.; fiction for teens, 750-1,000 wds. Responds in 9-13 wks. Seasonal 2-4 mos. ahead. Accepts simultaneous submissions. Accepts ms on disk or by e-mail. Regularly uses sidebars. Guidelines/theme list by mail/e-mail/website ("Submissions/For Adults" on left side); copy $6. (No ads) Winner of many awards.

Poetry: Only from kids under 18. Accepts 100/yr. Any type; 3-30 lines. Submit max. 4-5 poems.

Fillers: Accepts 10-20/yr. Anecdotes, cartoons, games, quizzes, short humor, word puzzles; to 250 wds.

Columns/Departments: Accepts 10/yr. Noteworthy News (multicultural/nature/international/social, appropriate for youth), 200 wds.

Special needs: Stories and articles on your community and country, peace, nonviolent communication, compassion, kindness, spirituality, tolerance, and giving.

Contest: Annual Book Awards for published books and authors (deadline February 1); Annual Youth Honor Awards for students 7-17 (deadline June 20). Send SASE for guidelines, or check the website.

Tips: "Most of the magazine is open to freelance. We're seeking submissions by minority, multicultural, international, and/or youth writers. Do not be judgmental or preachy; be open or receptive to diverse opinions."

SPARKLE, PO Box 7259, Grand Rapids MI 49510. (616) 241-5616. Fax (616) 241-5558. E-mail: amy@gemsgc.org; elli@gemsgc.org; servicecenter@gemsgc.org; sparkle@gemsgc.org. Website: www.gemsgc.org. GEMS Girls' Clubs (nondenominational). Kelli Gilmore, (616) 241-5616. To prepare girls, grades 1-3, to discover who God is and how He works in His world and their lives; to help girls sparkle Jesus' light into the world. Published 6x/yr. (October-March). Subscription $10.70. 80% unsolicited freelance; 20% assigned. Complete ms; no e-query. **Pays .03/wd.** on publication for 1st, reprint, or simultaneous rts. Articles 200-400 wds. (10/yr.); fiction 200-400 words (6/yr.). Responds in 6 wks. Seasonal 10 mos. ahead. Accepts simultaneous submissions & reprints. Accepts requested ms on disk. Regularly uses sidebars. Prefers NIV. Guidelines/theme list by mail/e-mail/website (click on "Girls" tab/"Sparkle"/Magazine cover for Sparkle in right-hand column/"Writers"); copy $1/9 x 12 SAE/3 stamps. (No ads)

Fillers: Buys 10/yr. Games, party ideas, prayers, quizzes, short humor; 50-200 wds. $5-15.

Tips: "Send in pieces that teach girls how to be world changers for Christ, or that fit our annual theme. We also are always looking for games, crafts, and recipes. Keep the writing simple. Keep activities short. Engage a 3rd grader, while being easy enough for a 1st grader to understand."

CHRISTIAN EDUCATION/LIBRARY MARKETS

CHURCH LIBRARIES, 9118 W. Elmwood Dr., Ste. 1G, Niles IL 60714-5820. (847) 296-3964. Fax (847) 296-0754. E-mail: linjohnson@ECLAlibraries.org. Website: www.ECLAlibraries.org. Evangelical Church Library Assn. Lin Johnson, mng ed. To assist church librarians in setting up, maintaining, and promoting church libraries and media centers. Quarterly mag.; 28-32 pgs.; circ. 300. Subscription $40. 25% unsolicited freelance. Complete ms or queries by e-mail only. **Pays .05/wd.** on acceptance for 1st or reprint rts. Articles 500-1,000 wds. (24/yr.). Responds in 8-10 wks. Seasonal 6 mos. ahead. Accepts reprints (tell when/where appeared). Requires e-mail submission. Regularly uses sidebars. Prefers NIV. Guidelines by e-mail/website; sample copy on the website. (Ads)

Tips: "Talk to church librarians or get involved in library or reading programs. Most open to training articles, promotional ideas, and profiles of church libraries."

DAILY DEVOTIONAL MARKETS

Due to the nature of the daily devotional market, the following market listings give a limited amount of information. Because most of these markets assign all material, they do not wish to be listed in the usual way.

If you are interested in writing daily devotionals, send to the following markets for guidelines and sample copies, write up sample devotionals to fit each one's particular format, and send to the editor with a request for an assignment. **DO NOT** submit any other type of material to these markets unless indicated.

***CHRISTIAN DEVOTIONS,** PO Box 6494, Kingsport TN 37663. E-mail: cindy@christiandevotions.us. Website: www.christiandevotions.us. Cindy Sproles & Eddie Jones, eds. Prefers completed devotions; 300-400 wds. Accepts poetry. Accepts reprints & e-mail submissions. Guidelines on website under "Write for Us."

DAILY DEVOTIONS FOR THE DEAF, 21199 Greenview Rd., Council Bluffs IA 51503-4190. (712) 322-5493. Fax (712) 322-7792. E-mail: JoKrueger@deafmissions.com. Website: www.deafmissions.com. Jo Krueger, ed. Published 3 times/yr. Circ. 26,000. Prefers to see completed devotionals; 225-250 wds. **NO PAYMENT.** E-mail submissions OK.

FORWARD DAY BY DAY, 412 Sycamore St. #2, Cincinnati OH 45202-4110. Toll-free (800) 543-1813. (513) 721-6659. Fax (513) 721-0729. E-mail: nseiferth@forwardmovement.org. Website: www.forwardmovement.org. Nicole Seiferth, mg. ed. Also online version. Send three sample devotions according to guidelines posted on website. Likes author to complete an entire month's worth of devotions. Subscription $13. Accepts e-mail submissions. Length: 215 wds. **Pays $300 for a month of devotions.** No reprints. Guidelines on website. ("About Us"/"Writers Guidelines"). (No ads)

GOD'S WORD FOR TODAY, 1445 N. Boonville Ave., Springfield MO 65802. E-mail: rl-gwft@gph.org. Website: www.GospelPublishing.com. Assemblies of God. No freelance submissions. Contact to see if they are accepting new writers. New writers will need to write two assigned sample devotions. **Pays $25.** Accepts poetry and e-mail submissions. No reprints.

LIGHT FROM THE WORD, PO Box 50434, Indianapolis IN 46250-0434. (317) 774-7900. E-mail: submissions@wesleyan.org. Website: www.wesleyan.org/wg. Wesleyan. Craig A. Bubeck, ed. dir. Devotions 220-250 wds. **Pays $100 for seven devotions.** Electronic submissions only. Send a couple of sample devotions to fit their format and request an assignment. Accepts e-mail submissions. No reprints.

MUSTARD SEED MINISTRIES DEVOTIONAL, PO Box 501, Bluffton IN 46714. E-mail: devotionals@mustardseedministries.org. Website: www.mustardseedministries.org. Devotional mag. 100% unsolicited freelance. Complete ms; e-mail submissions preferred. Devotions 225-275 wds. Guidelines on website.

Tips: "We do not return any submissions and prefer that they are e-mailed to us. We are looking for submissions that are biblically based. Sincerity is as important as your writing skills. Most of us have a story to tell about how Christ touched our life in some situation that others in this world would benefit from; please send this to us."

PENNED FROM THE HEART, Marilyn Nutter, 437 Woodward Ridge Drive, Mount Holly NC 28120 E-mail: nutter4penned@gmail.com. Website: www.marilynnutter.com. Son-Rise Publications (toll-free 800-358-0777). Annual daily devotional book; about 240 pgs.; 5,000 copies/yr. 100% unsolicited freelance. Complete ms/cover letter; phone/e-query OK. **Pays one copy of the book**; opportunity to purchase books at a discount.

***THE QUIET HOUR,** David C Cook, 4050 Lee Vance View, Colorado Springs CO 80918. Scott Stewart, ed. E-mail: scott.stewart@DavidCCook.com. Quarterly subscription. To be considered for paid assignment on seven preselected passages, send short bio and a sample devotional encouraging a life of faith from a truth in a Scripture passage of your choice. Limit 201 wds. Use anecdotal launch, bring biblical insight as a companion in faith.

***REFLECTING GOD,** 2923 Troost Ave., Kansas City MO 64109. (816) 931-1900. Fax: (816) 412-8306. E-mail: dcbrush@wordaction.com. Website: www.reflectinggod.com. Duane Brush, ed. E-mail for writer's guidelines and application. Daily devotional guide published quarterly.

***REJOICE!** 35094 Laburnum Ave., Abbotsford BC V2S 8K3, Canada. (778) 549-8544. E-mail: RejoiceEditor@MennoMedia.org. Website: www.faithandliferesources.org/periodicals/rejoice.

Faith & Life Resources/MennoMedia. Jonathan Janzen, ed. Daily devotional magazine grounded in Anabaptist theology. Quarterly mag.; 112 pgs.; circ. 12,000. Subscription $29.40. 5% unsolicited freelance; 95% assigned. **Pays $100-125 for 7-day assigned meditations,** 250-300 wds. each; on publication for 1st rts. Also accepts testimonies 500-600 wds. (8/yr.). Prefers that you send a couple of sample devotions and inquire about assignment procedures; fax/e-query OK. Accepts assigned mss by e-mail (attached). Responds in 4 wks. Seasonal 8 mos. ahead. No simultaneous submissions or reprints. Some kill fees 50%. No sidebars. Prefers NRSV. Guidelines by e-mail/website (scroll down to "Writing for Rejoice!" center).

Poetry: Buys 8/yr. Free verse, light verse; 60 characters. Pays $25. Submit max. 3 poems.

Tips: "Don't apply for assignment unless you are familiar with the publication and Anabaptist theology."

THE SECRET PLACE, PO Box 851, Valley Forge PA 19482-0851. (610) 768-2434. Fax (610) 768-2441. E-mail: thesecretplace@abc-usa.org. Website: www.judsonpress.com. Ingrid and Dave Dvirnak, eds. Prefers to see completed devotionals, 200 wds. (use unfamiliar Scripture passages). 64 pgs. Circ. 250,000. 100% freelance. **Pays $20** for 1st rts. Accepts poetry. Prefers e-mail submissions. No reprints. Guidelines by mail, e-mail, or website.

THESE DAYS, 7969 Burntwood Cove, Germantown TN 38138. (901) 752-0770. Fax (901) 759-0788. E-mail: donmckim@comcast.net. Website: www.ppcpub.com. Presbyterian Publishing Corp. Dr. Donald K. McKim, ed. Quarterly booklet; circ. 200,000. Subscription $7.95. Query/samples. 95% unsolicited freelance. Open to submissions from members of The Cumberland Presbyterian Church, the Presbyterian Church (USA), the United Church of Canada, or The United Church of Christ. **Pays $14.25/devotion** on acceptance for 1st and nonexclusive reprint rts. (makes work-for-hire assignments); 200 wds. (including key verse and short prayer). Wants short, contemporary poetry ($15) on church holidays and seasons of the year—overtly religious (15 lines, 33-character/line maximum). Query for their two feature segments (short articles): "These Moments" and "These Times." Guidelines by mail; copy for 6 x 9 SAE/3 stamps.

Poetry: Accepts poetry.

Photos: Buys digital photos for the cover.

***THE UPPER ROOM,** PO Box 340004, Nashville TN 37203-0004. (615) 340-7252. Fax (615) 340-7267. E-mail: TheUpperRoomMagazine@upperroom.org. Website: www.upperroom.org. Mary Lou Redding, ed. dir. 95% unsolicited freelance. **Pays $30/devotional** on publication. 72 pgs. This publication wants freelance submissions and does not make assignments. Phone/fax/e-query OK. Send devotionals up to 250 wds. Buys explicitly religious art, in various media, for use on covers only (transparencies/slides requested); buys onetime, worldwide publishing rts. Accepts e-mail submissions (copied into message). Guidelines by mail/website ("Writers"); copy for 5x7 SAE/2 stamps. (No ads)

Tips: "We do not return submissions. Accepted submissions will be notified in 6-9 wks. Follow guidelines. Need meditations from men." Always include postal address with e-mail submissions.

THE WORD IN SEASON, PO Box 1209, Minneapolis MN 55440-1209. Fax (612) 330-3215. E-mail: dancingturtle@sbcglobal.net. Website: www.augsburgfortress.org. Augsburg Fortress. Rev. Rochelle Y. Melander, ed./mngr. 96 pgs. Devotions to 200 wds. **Pays $20/devotion; $75 for prayers.** Accepts e-mail submissions (copied into message) after reading guidelines. Guidelines at www.augsburg fortress.org, type "The Word in Season" in search box.

Tips: "We prefer that you write for guidelines. We will send instructions for preparing sample devotions. We accept new writers based on the sample devotions we request and make assignments after acceptance."

WORSHIPMINISTRYDEVOTIONS.COM, 65 Shepherds Way, Hillsboro MO 63050-2605. (636) 789-4522. E-mail: staff@training-resources.org. Website: www.worshipministrydevotions.com. Tom

Kraeuter, ed. Prefer to see completed devotions, 500-750 wds. **Pays $50 or more.** Accepts submissions by e-mail.

Tips: "Please check the website and follow guidelines. We won't consider any submission that does not follow our guidelines."

MISSIONS MARKETS

OPERATION REVEILLE E-JOURNAL, PO Box 3488, Monument CO 80132-3488. (800) 334-0359. Fax (775) 248-8147. E-mail: bside@oprev.org. Website: www.oprev.org. Mission To Unreached Peoples. Bruce T. Sidebotham, dir. Provides information to equip US military Christians for cross-cultural ministry. Bimonthly e-zine. Subscription free. 20% unsolicited freelance; 80% assigned. Query; e-query OK. Accepts full mss by e-mail. **Pays in copies or up to $99** for electronic, reprint, or nonexclusive rights (negotiable). Articles 500-2,500 wds. (2/yr.); book reviews 700 wds. Responds in 2 wks. Accepts simultaneous submissions & reprints (tell when/where appeared). Accepts requested ms by e-mail (attached file). Uses some sidebars. Prefers NIV. No guidelines; copy online. (Ads)

Fillers: Accepts 4/yr. Facts; newsbreaks; commentary, to 150 wds.

Columns/Departments: Accepts 4/yr. Agency Profile (describes a mission agency's history and work), 200-300 wds. Area Profile (describes spiritual landscape of a military theater of operations), 300-750 wds. Resource Review (describes a cross-cultural ministry tool), 100-200 wds. Query.

Special needs: Commentary on service personnel in cross-cultural ministry situations and relationships.

Tips: "We need insights for military personnel on understanding and relating the gospel to Muslims."

PASTOR/LEADERSHIP MARKETS

THE CHRISTIAN CENTURY, 104 S. Michigan Ave., Ste. 1100, Chicago IL 60603. (312) 263-7510 (no phone calls). Website: http://christiancentury.org. Christian Century Foundation. Submit queries by e-mail to: submissions@christiancentury.org. For ministers, educators, and church leaders interested in events and theological issues of concern to the ecumenical church. Biweekly mag.; 48 pgs.; circ. 30,000. Subscription $59. 10% unsolicited freelance; 90% assigned. **Pays $150** on publication for all or onetime rts. Articles 1,500-3,000 wds. (150/yr.); book reviews, 800-1,500 wds.; music or film reviews 1,000 wds.; pays $0-75. No fiction submissions. Responds in 2-6 wks. Seasonal 4 mos. ahead. No simultaneous submissions. Accepts reprints (tell when/where appeared). No kill fee. Regularly uses sidebars. Prefers NRSV. Guidelines/theme list by e-mail/website (scroll to bottom & click on "Contact Us"); copy $10. (Ads)

Poetry: Poetry Editor (poetry@christiancentury.org). Buys 50/yr. Any type (religious but not sentimental); to 20 lines; $50. Submit max. 10 poems.

Special needs: Film, popular-culture commentary; news topics and analysis.

Tips: "Keep in mind our audience of sophisticated readers, eager for analysis and critical perspective that goes beyond the obvious. We are open to all topics if written with appropriate style for our readers."

CHRISTIAN EDUCATION JOURNAL, 13800 Biola Ave., La Mirada CA 90639. (562) 903-6000, ext. 5528. Fax (562) 906-4502. E-mail: editor.cej@biola.edu. Website: www.biola.edu/cej. Talbot School of Theology, Biola University. Kevin E. Lawson, ed. Academic journal on the practice of Christian education; for students, professors, and thoughtful ministry leaders in Christian education. Semiannual jour.; 200-250 pgs.; circ. 750. Subscription $32. Open to freelance. Query; e-query OK. Accepts full mss by e-mail. **NO PAYMENT** for 1st rts. Articles 3,000-6,000 wds. (20/yr.); book reviews 2-5 pgs. Responds in 4-6 wks. No seasonal. Might accept simultaneous submissions & reprints (tell when/where appeared). Requires e-mail submissions (attached file in Word format). Does not use sidebars.

Any Bible version. Guidelines on website ("Publications Policy"/ "Guidelines for writing and reviewing articles"); no copy. (Ads)

Tips: "Focus on foundations and/or research with implications for the conception and practice of Christian education." Book reviews must be preassigned and approved by the editor; guidelines on website.

***COOK PARTNERS,** 4050 Lee Vance View, Colorado Springs CO 80918. (719) 536-0100. Fax (719) 536-3266. E-mail: Marie.Chavez@davidccook.org. Website: www.cookinternational.org. Cook International. Submit to Marie Chavez. Seeks to encourage self-sufficient, effective indigenous Christian publishing worldwide to spread the life-giving message of the gospel. Bimonthly online publication; circ. 2,000. Subscription free. Open to unsolicited freelance. Query or complete ms. Articles & reviews 400-1,500 wds. Responds in 1-4 wks. **Most writers donate their work, but will negotiate for payment if asked.** Wants all rts. Incomplete topical listings. (No ads)

***DIOCESAN DIALOGUE,** 16565 S. State St., South Holland IL 60473. (708) 331-5485. Fax (708) 331-5484. E-mail: acp@acpress.org. Website: www.americancatholicpress.org. American Catholic Press. Father Michael Gilligan, editorial dir. Targets Latin-Rite dioceses in the US that sponsor a Mass broadcast on TV or radio. Annual newsletter; 8 pgs.; circ. 750. Free. 20% unsolicited freelance. Complete ms/cover letter; no phone/fax/e-query. Articles 200-1,000 wds. **Pays variable rates** on publication for all rts. Responds in 10 wks. Accepts simultaneous submissions & reprints. Uses some sidebars. Prefers NAB (Confraternity). No guidelines; copy $3/9 x 12 SAE/2 stamps. (No ads)

Fillers: Cartoons, 2/yr.

Tips: "Writers should be familiar with TV production of the Mass and/or the needs of senior citizens, especially shut-ins."

***ENRICHMENT: A Journal for Pentecostal Ministry,** 1445 N. Boonville Ave., Springfield MO 65802. (417) 862-2781, ext. 4095. Fax (417) 862-0416. E-mail: enrichmentjournal@ag.org. Website: www.enrichmentjournal.ag.org. Assemblies of God. George P. Wood, exec. ed.; Rick Knoth, mng. ed. (rknoth@ag.org). Quarterly jour.; 128-144 pgs.; circ. 33,000. Subscription $24; foreign add $30. 15% unsolicited freelance. Complete ms/cover letter. **Pays up to .15/wd. ($75-350)** on acceptance for 1st rts. Articles 1,000-2,800 wds. (25/yr.); book reviews, 250 wds. ($25). Responds in 8-12 wks. Seasonal 1 yr. ahead. Accepts simultaneous submissions & reprints (tell when/ where appeared). Requires requested ms by e-mail (copied into message or attached). Kill fee up to 50%. Regularly uses sidebars. Prefers NIV. Guidelines on website; copy for $7/10 x 13 SAE. (Ads)

Fillers: Buys over 100/yr. Anecdotes, cartoons, facts, short humor, tips; $25-40, or .10-.20/wd.

Columns/Departments: Buys 40/yr. for Women in Ministry (leadership ideas), Associate Ministers (related issues), Managing Your Ministry (how-to), Financial Concepts (church stewardship issues), Family Life (minister's family), When Pews Are Few (ministry in smaller congregation), Worship in the Church, Leader's Edge, Preaching That Connects, Ministry & Medical Ethics; all 1,200-2,500 wds. $75-275. Query or complete ms.

Tips: "Most open to EShorts: short, 150-250 word, think pieces covering a wide range of topics related to ministry and church life, such as culture, worship, generational issues, church/community, trends, evangelism, surveys, time management, and humor."

** 2010, 2009 Award of Merit: Christian Ministries. 2008, 2007 EPA Award of Excellence: Christian Ministry. This periodical was #16 on the 2010 Top 50 Christian Publishers list (#15 in 2009, #43 in 2008, #47 in 2006).

GROUP MAGAZINE, 1515 Cascade Ave, Loveland CO 80538. (970) 669-3836. Fax (970) 622-4243/(970) 292-4374. E-mail: puorgbus@group.com. Website: http://group.com/customer-support /submissions. Submit to Proposal Review Team. We equip churches to help children, youth, and adults grow in their relationship with Jesus. Bimonthly Mag/Ezine. 90pg. Circ. 15,000. Sub $24.95. 60% unsolicited freelance; 20% assigned. Send complete ms. Query fax/e-mail. Cover letter. Accepts full mss by e-mail. **Pays $50-200** for articles. Pay on acceptance/publication. Rights purchased:

exclusive, first, onetime, electronic. Preferred Bible version: NLT. Articles up to 2,000 wds. Accept 300 nonfiction mss/yr. from freelancers. Responds 1-12 wks. Submit holiday 8 mos. in adv. Accepts simultaneous submissions. Accepts articles on disk or e-mail (attached file). No kill fee. Regular sidebars. Sometimes inc. bio notes on writer of feature articles. Guidelines on website. No photos. Sends contributor copies upon request. (ads to breynolds@group.com/970-292-4675)

Fillers: Games, ideas, tips. (6/yr) 150-200 wds. Pays $25-50.

Tips: Try this one!

***GROWTH POINTS,** PO Box 892589, Temecula CA 92589-2589. Phone/fax (951) 506-3086. E-mail: cgnet@earthlink.net. Website: www.churchgrowthnetwork.com. Dr. Gary L. McIntosh, ed. For pastors and church leaders interested in church growth. Monthly newsletter; 2 pgs.; circ. 8,000. Subscription $16. 10% unsolicited freelance; 90% assigned. Query; fax/e-query OK. **Pays $25** for onetime rts. Not copyrighted. Articles 1,000-2,000 wds. (2/yr.). Responds in 4 wks. Accepts simultaneous submissions & reprints. Accepts requested ms on disk. Does not use sidebars. Guidelines by mail; copy for #10 SAE/1 stamp. (No ads)

Tips: "Write articles that are short (1,200 words), crisp, clear, with very practical ideas that church leaders can put to use immediately. All articles must have a pro-church-growth slant, be very practical, have how-to material, and be very tightly written with bullets, etc."

***INSITE,** PO Box 62189, Colorado Springs CO 80962-2189. (719) 260-9400. Fax (719) 260-6398. E-mail: editor@ccca.org, or info@ccca.org. Website: www.ccca.org. Christian Camp and Conference Assn. Jackie M. Johnson, ed. To inform and inspire professionals serving in the Christian camp and conference center community. Bimonthly mag.; 52 pgs.; circ. 8,200. Subscription $29.95. 15% unsolicited freelance; 85% assigned. Query; e-query OK. **Pays .20/wd.** on publication for 1st and electronic rts. Cover articles 1,500-2,000 wds. (12/yr.); features 1,200-1,500 wds. (30/yr.); sidebars 250-500 wds. (15-20/yr.). Responds in 4 wks. Seasonal 6 mos. ahead. Accepts simultaneous submissions & reprints (tell when/where appeared). Prefers e-mail submission (attached file). Kill fee. Regularly uses sidebars. Prefers NIV. Guidelines on website; copy $4.99/9 x 12 SAE/$1.73 postage. (Ads)

Special needs: Outdoor setting; purpose and objectives; administration and organization; leadership; personnel development; camper/guest needs; programming; health and safety; food service; site/facilities maintenance; business/operations; marketing and PR; relevant spiritual issues; and fund-raising.

Tips: "Most open to how-to pieces; get guidelines, then query first. Don't send general camping-related articles. We print stories specifically related to Christian camp and conference facilities; innovative programs or policies; how a Christian camp or conference experience affected a present-day leader; spiritual renewal and leadership articles. Review several issues so you know what we're looking for." ** 2010, 2008, 2006 EPA Award of Merit: Christian Ministries; 2007 EPA Award of Excellence: Christian Ministries; 2006 EPA Award of Merit: Most Improved Publication.

***LEADERSHIP,** 465 Gundersen Dr., Carol Stream IL 60188. (630) 260-6200. Fax (630) 260-0451. E-mail: LJEditor@LeadershipJournal.net. Website: www.leadershipjournal.net. Christianity Today Intl. Marshall Shelley, ed-in-chief. Practical help for pastors/church leaders, covering the spectrum of subjects from personal needs to professional skills. Quarterly & online jour.; 104 pgs.; circ. 48,000. Subscription $24.95. 20% unsolicited freelance; 80% assigned. Query or complete ms/cover letter; fax/e-query OK. Accepts full mss by e-mail. **Pays .15-.20/wd.** on acceptance for 1st & electronic rts. Articles 500-3,000 wds. (10/yr.); book reviews 100 wds. (pays $25-50). Responds in 6 wks. Seasonal 6 mos. ahead. Accepts reprints (tell when/where appeared). Accepts requested ms by e-mail (copied into message or attached Word doc). Kill fee 30%. Regularly uses sidebars. Prefers NLT. Guidelines on website; copy for 9 x 12 SAE/$2 postage. (Ads)

Fillers: Buys 80/yr. Cartoons, short humor; to 150 wds. $25-50.

Columns/Departments: Skye Jethani, mng. ed. Buys 12/yr. Tool Kit (practical stories or resources for preaching, worship, outreach, pastoral care, spiritual formation, and administration); 100-700 wds. Complete ms. Pays $50-250.

Tips: "*Leadership* is a practical journal for pastors. Tell real-life stories of church life—defining moments—dramatic events. What was learned the hard way—by experience. We look for articles that provide practical help for problems church leaders face, not essays expounding on a topic, editorials arguing a position, or homilies explaining biblical principles. We want 'how-to' articles based on first-person accounts of real-life experiences in ministry in the local church."

** 2010, 2006 EPA Award of Excellence: Christian Ministries; 2008 EPA Award of Merit: General; 2007 EPA Award of Merit: Christian Ministries. This periodical was #21 on the 2010 Top 50 Christian Publishers list (#21 in 2009, #18 in 2008, #15 in 2007, #14 in 2006).

L MAGAZINE, 9764 Gares Avenue, Cleveland OH 44105-6055. (888) 317-7270. Fax (888) 317-0342. E-mail: tstaveteig@myliterarycoach.com. Website: www.LMagazine.net. Online magazine. Empowering ELCA (Evangelical Lutheran Church in America) leaders. Rev. Timothy Staveteig, exec. ed. Aimed at ordained and lay ministers in the Evangelical Lutheran Church in America (ELCA). Bimonthly magazine 32-36 pgs. Circulation 16,000. Free. 50% unsolicited, 50% assigned. Writers should query. Prefer cover letter, full mss by e-mail up to 1,500 wds. **Pay $100-200** on publication. Purchase one-time rights. Copyrighted. Prefer NRSV. Articles 750, lead articles 1,500 wds. Responds in 2 wks. Submit holiday/seasonal 4 mos. in advance. Accepts simultaneous and reprints (tell when and where). Require ms by e-mail in attached file. Regularly uses sidebars. No kill fee. Inc. writer bio of feature article. Send contributor 1 copy. Accepts ads.

Columns/Depts: Accepts 30 mss/yr. Query for columns. Pays $100.

***MINISTRY TODAY,** 600 Rinehart Rd., Lake Mary FL 32746. (407) 333-0600. Fax (407) 333-7133. E-mail: ministrytoday@charismamedia.com. Website: www.ministrytodaymag.com. Charisma Media. Submit to The Editor. Helps for pastors and church leaders, primarily in Pentecostal/Charismatic churches. Quarterly & online mag.; 112 pgs.; circ. 30,000. Subscription $14.97. 60-80% freelance. Query; fax/e-query preferred. **Pays $50 or $500-800** on publication for all rts. Articles 1,800-2,500 wds. (25/yr.); book/music/video reviews, 300 wds. $25. Responds in 4 wks. Prefers accepted ms by e-mail. Kill fee. Regularly uses sidebars. Prefers NIV. Guidelines on website (scroll to bottom of home page & click on "Writers' Guidelines"); copy $6/9 x 12 SAE. For free subscription to online version go to: ministrytodaymag.com/index.php/ministry-today-digital. (Ads)

Tips: "Most open to columns. Study guidelines and the magazine. Please correspond with editor before sending an article proposal."

***THE NEWSLETTER NEWSLETTER,** PO Box 36269, Canton OH 44735. Toll-free (800) 992-2144. E-mail: service@newsletternewsletter.com or through website: www.newsletternewsletter.com. Communication Resources. Stephanie Martin, ed. To help church secretaries and church newsletter editors prepare high-quality publications. Monthly & online newsletter; 14 pgs. Subscription $71.80. 100% assigned. Complete ms; e-query OK. **Pays $50-150** on acceptance for all rts. Articles 800-1,000 wds. (12/yr.). Responds in 4 wks. Seasonal 4 mos. ahead. Requires requested ms by e-mail. Guidelines by e-mail.

Tips: "Most open to how-to articles on various aspects of producing newsletters and e-newsletters—writing, layout and design, distribution, etc."

***PARISH LITURGY,** 16565 S. State St., South Holland IL 60473. (708) 331-5485. Fax (708) 331-5484. E-mail: acp@acpress.org. Website: www.americancatholicpress.org. American Catholic Press. Father Michael Gilligan, exec. dir. A planning tool for Sunday and holy day liturgy. Quarterly mag.; 40 pgs.; circ. 1,200. Subscription $24. 5% unsolicited freelance. Query; no phone/e-query. **Pays variable rates** for all rts. Articles 400 wds. Responds in 4 wks. Seasonal 4 mos. ahead. Accepts simultaneous submissions & reprints (tell when/where appeared). Uses some sidebars. Prefers NAB. No guidelines; copy available. (No ads)

Tips: "We only use articles on the liturgy—period. Send us well-informed articles on the liturgy."

PLUGGED IN ONLINE, Colorado Springs CO 80920 (no street address needed). Toll-free (800) 232-6459. (719) 531-3400. Fax (719) 548-5823. E-mail: waliszrs@fotf.org, or pluggedin@family.org. Website: www.pluggedin.com. Focus on the Family. Steven Isaac, online ed.; Bob Smithhouser, sr. ed. To assist parents and youth leaders in better navigating popular entertainment and equip them to impart principles of discernment in young people. Online newsletter. Open to queries only. Articles. Incomplete topical listings. (No ads)

**2010 EPA Award of Excellence: Online, 2013 NRB Award for Best Website.

***PREACHING, PREACHING ONLINE & PREACHING NOW,** 402 BNA Dr., Ste. 400, Nashville TN 37217. (615) 386-3011. Fax (615) 312-4277. E-mail: Alee@SalemPublishing.com. Salem Communications. Dr. Michael Duduit, ed. Bimonthly; circ. 9,000. Subscription $24.95/2 yrs. 50% unsolicited freelance; 50% assigned. Query; fax/e-query OK. **Pays a subscription** for onetime & electronic rts. Responds in 1-2 days. Seasonal 10-12 mos. ahead. Reprints from books only. Prefers requested ms by e-mail (attached file). Uses some sidebars. Guidelines on website; copy online. (ads). *Preaching Online* is a professional resource for pastors that supplements *Preaching* magazine. Includes all content from magazine, plus additional articles and sermons. Feature articles, 2,000-2,500, **$50**. Sermons 1,500-2,000 wds. **$35**. *Preaching Now* is a weekly e-mail/e-zine; circ. 43,500. Subscription $39.95. Accepts books for review. Guidelines on website (scroll down to bottom of home page and click on "Site Map"/scroll down to "Help"/ "Writing for Us"); Copy $8. (Ads)

***THE PRIEST,** 200 Noll Plaza, Huntington IN 46750-4304. Toll-free (800) 348-2440. (260) 356-8400. Fax (260) 359-9117. E-mail: tpriest@osv.com. Website: www.osv.com. Catholic/Our Sunday Visitor Inc. Msgr. Owen F. Campion, ed.; submit to Murray Hubley, assoc. ed. For Catholic priests, deacons, and seminarians; to help in all aspects of ministry. Monthly jour.; 56 pgs.; circ. 6,500. Subscription $43.95. 40% unsolicited freelance. Query (preferred) or complete ms/cover letter; phone/fax/e-query OK. **Pays $50-250** on acceptance for 1st rts. Not copyrighted. Articles to 1,500 wds. (96/yr.); some 2-parts. Responds in 5-13 wks. Seasonal 3 mos. ahead. Uses some sidebars. Prefers disk or e-mail submissions (attached file). Prefers NAB. Guidelines on website (click on "About Us"/"The Priest Writers' Guidelines"; free copy. (Ads)

Fillers: Murray Hubley, fillers ed. Cartoons; $35.

Columns/Departments: Buys 36/yr. Viewpoint, to 1,000 wds. $75.

Tips: "Write to the point, with interest. Most open to nuts-and-bolts issues for priests, or features. Keep the audience in mind; need articles or topics important to priests and parish life. Include Social Security number."

Special needs: Anglican and Episcopal theology, religion, history, doctrine, ethics, homiletics, liturgies, hermeneutics, biography, prayer, practice.

THE REVWRITER RESOURCE, PO Box 81, Perkasie PA 18944. Phone/fax (215) 453-8128. E-mail: editor@revwriter.com. Website: www.revwriter.com. Nondenominational/RevWriter Resources LLC. Rev. Susan M. Lang, ed. An electronic newsletter for busy lay and clergy congregational leaders. Monthly e-zine; circ. 750. Subscription free. 90% unsolicited freelance; 10% assigned. Query; e-query preferred. **Pays $20 on publication for 1st electronic rts; $10 for devotions.** Articles 1,500 wds.; questions or exercises for group use, 250-500 wds. No simultaneous submissions or reprints. Also accepts submissions from teens. Guidelines by e-mail/website; copy online.

Fillers: Buys 10/yr. Ministry ideas; ministry resources. List to accompany article; 250-400 wds. They are usually written by the feature-article writer.

Tips: "Be sure to read archived issues for previous formats and ministry resources already covered. Looking for a new approach to stewardship. Most open to devotion writing in Lent and Advent, and the monthly articles and discussion questions. Send me an e-query detailing the article you'd like to write and include your expertise in this area. The material must be practical and applicable to life as a busy congregational leader. They want information they can use."

***SHARING THE PRACTICE,** c/o Central Woodward Christian Church, 3955 W. Big Beaver Rd., Troy MI 48084-2610. (248) 644-0512. Website: www.apclergy.org. Academy of Parish Clergy/Ecumenical/

Interfaith. Rev. Dr. Robert Cornwall, ed-in-chief (drbobcornwall@msn.com); (s.spade@att.net). Growth toward excellence through sharing the practice of parish ministry. Quarterly international jour.; 40 pgs.; circ. 250 (includes 80 seminary libraries & publishers). Subscription $30/yr. (send to APC, 2249 Florinda St., Sarasota FL 34231-1414). 100% unsolicited freelance. Complete ms/cover letter; e-query OK; query/clips for fiction. **NO PAYMENT** for 1st, reprint, simultaneous, or electronic rts. Articles 500-2,500 wds. (25/yr.); reviews 500-1,000 wds. Responds in 2 wks. Seasonal 6 mos. ahead. Accepts simultaneous submissions & reprints (tell when/where appeared). Prefers e-mail submissions (copied into message). Uses some sidebars. Prefers NRSV. Guidelines/theme list by mail/e-mail; free copy. (No ads)

Poetry: Accepts 12/yr. Any type; 25-35 lines. Submit max. 2 poems.

Fillers: Accepts 6/yr. Anecdotes, cartoons, jokes, short humor; 50-100 wds.

Columns/Departments: Academy News; President's.

Contest: Book of the Year Award ($100+), Top Ten Books of the Year list, Parish Pastor of the Year Award ($200+). Inquire by e-mail to DIELPADRE@aol.com.

Tips: "We desire articles and poetry by practicing clergy of all kinds who wish to share their practice of ministry. Join the Academy."

***SMALLGROUPS.COM,** 465 Gundersen Dr., Carol Stream IL 60188. (630) 260-6200. Fax (630) 260-0451. E-mail: smallgroups@christianitytoday.com. Website: www.smallgroups.com. Christianity Today. Amy Jackson, assoc. ed. Serves small-group leaders and churches and provides training and curriculum that is easy to use. Weekly e-newsletter; circ. 50,000. Subscription $99. 10% unsolicited freelance; 50% assigned. Complete ms/cover letter; e-query OK. Accepts full mss by e-mail. **Pays $75-150 for articles; $350-750 for curriculum;** on acceptance for electronic & nonexclusive rts. Articles 750-1,500 wds. (50/yr.). Responds in 2 wks. Seasonal 2 mos. ahead. Accepts simultaneous submissions & reprints (tell when/where appeared). Prefers requested ms by e-mail (attached file). Some kill fees 50%. No sidebars. Accepts reprints. Prefers NIV. Guidelines/copy by e-mail. (Ads)

Fillers: Icebreakers and other small-group learning activities.

Special needs: Creative, practical ideas for small-group ministry, esp. from experience.

Tips: "It's best to submit articles that you have used to train and support small groups and leaders in your own church."

**2010 EPA Award of Merit: Online; 2012 EPA Award of Excellence: Online Newsletter.

***YOUTHWORKER JOURNAL,** c/o Salem Publishing, 402 BNA Drive, Suite 400, Nashville TN 37217-2509. (615) 386-3011. Fax (615) 386-3380. E-mail: proposals@youthworker.com. Website: www.Youthworker.com. Salem Communications. Steve & Lois Rabey, eds. For youth workers/church and parachurch. Bimonthly & online jour.; 72 pgs.; circ. 15,000. Subscription $39.95. 100% unsolicited freelance. Query or complete ms (only if already written); e-query preferred. **Pays $50-300** on publication for 1st/perpetual rts. Articles 250-3,000 wds. (30/yr.); length may vary. Responds in 26 wks. Seasonal 6 mos. ahead. No reprints. Kill fee $50. Guidelines/theme list on website: www.youthworker.com/editorial_guidelines.php; copy $5/10 x 13 SAE. (Ads)

Columns/Departments: Buys 10/yr. International Youth Ministry, and Technology in Youth Ministry.

Tips: "Read *YouthWorker*; imbibe its tone (professional, though not academic; conversational, though not chatty). Query me with specific, focused ideas that conform to our editorial style. It helps if the writer is a youth minister, but it's not required. Check website for additional info, upcoming themes, etc. WorldView column on mission activities and trips is about the only one open to outsiders."

TEEN/YOUNG-ADULT MARKETS

BOUNDLESS, Focus on the Family, Colorado Springs CO 80995 (no street address needed). (719) 531-3419. Fax (719) 548-4599. E-mail: editor@boundless.org. Website: www.boundless.org. Focus on the Family. Martha Krienke, ed., producer. For Christian singles up to their mid-30s. Weekly e-zine; 300,000 visitors/mo.; 130 page views/mo. on blog. Free online. 5% unsolicited freelance; 95% assigned. Query/clips; e-query OK. Accepts full ms by e-mail. **Pays** on acceptance for nonexclusive rts. Articles 1,200-1,800 wds. (52/yr.). Responds in 4 wks. Seasonal 4 mos. ahead. Accepts simultaneous submissions & reprints (tell when/where appeared). Requires e-mail submission (attached—preferred—or copied into message). No kill fee. Does not use sidebars. Prefers ESV. Guidelines by mail/website (click on "About Us"/scroll down to "Write for Us"/"Writers' Guidelines"); copy online. (Ads)

Tips: "See author guidelines on our website. Most open to conversational, winsome, descriptive, and biblical."

** This periodical was #15 on the 2010 Top 50 Christian Publishers list (#18 in 2009, #12 in 2008, #25 in 2007, #24 in 2006).

DIRECTION MAGAZINE, PO Box 17306, Nashville TN 37217. (615) 361-1221. Fax (615) 367-0535. E-mail: direction@d6family.com. Website: www.randallhouse.com. Randall House. Jonathan Yandell, ed.; submit to Derek Lewis, ed. asst. Bringing junior high students to a closer relationship with Christ through devotionals, relevant articles, and pertinent topics. Quarterly mag.; 56 pgs.; circ. 5,300. Open to freelance. Complete ms/cover letter; query for fiction. Accepts full mss by e-mail. **Pays $35-150 for nonfiction; $35-150 for fiction;** on publication for 1st rts. Articles 600-1,500 wds. (35/yr.); book reviews 500-600 wds. ($35). Responds in 6 wks. Seasonal 6 mos. ahead. Accepts simultaneous submissions; no reprints. Prefers e-mail submissions (attached file). No kill fee. Regularly uses sidebars. Also accepts submissions from teens. Guidelines by e-mail/website; copy for 9 x 12 SAE. (No ads)

Columns/Departments: Buys 10/yr. Changing Lanes (describe how God is changing you; teens only), 500-1000 wds. Between the Lines (review of book approved by Randall House), 500-600 wds. $35-50. Missions (describe a personal opportunity to serve others), 500-1000 wds.

Tips: "We are open to freelancers by way of articles and submissions to 'Changing Lanes,' 'Between the Lines,' 'Missions,' and feature articles/interviews. All articles should be about an aspect of the Christian life or contain a spiritual element, as the purpose of this magazine is to bring junior high students closer to Christ. We are happy to accept personal testimonies or knowledgeable articles on current hot topics and how they compare to biblical standards."

***SISTERHOOD: Magazine for Teen Girls,** (888) 817-8743. E-mail: susieshell@comcast.net. Susie Shellenberger, editor. A publication appealing and relevant for today's teen girl. Estab. 2009. Bimonthly mag. Open to unsolicited freelance. E-mail complete manuscripts labeled "Free Freelance." **NO PAYMENT.** Nonfiction & fiction. Not included in topical listings.

***TAKE FIVE PLUS YOUTH DEVOTIONAL GUIDE,** 1445 N. Boonville Ave., Springfield MO 65802-1894. (417) 862-2781, ext. 4357. Fax (417) 862-6059. E-mail: rl-take5plus@gph.org. Assemblies of God. Wade Quick, ed. Devotional for teens. By assignment only. Query. Accepts e-mail submissions. **Pays $25/devotion.** Devotions may range from 210 to 235 wds. (max.). Guidelines on request.

Poetry: Accepts poetry from teens; no more than 25 lines.

Tips: "The sample devotions need to be based on a Scripture reference available by query. You will not be paid for the sample devotions." Also accepts digital photos, and artwork from teens.

YOUNG SALVATIONIST, PO Box 269, Alexandria VA 22313-0269. (703) 684-5500. Fax (703) 684-5539. E-mail: ys@usn.salvationarmy.org. Website: http://publications.salvationarmyusa.org. The Salvation Army. Amy Reardon, ed. For teens and young adults in the Salvation Army. Monthly (10X) & online mag.; 24 pgs.; circ. 48,000. Subscription $4.50. 20% unsolicited freelance; 80% assigned. Complete ms preferred; e-query OK. **Pays .25/wd.** on acceptance for 1st, onetime, or reprint rts. Articles (60/yr.); short evangelistic pieces, 350-600 wds. No fiction. Responds in 9 wks. Seasonal 6 mos. ahead. Accepts reprints (tell when/where appeared). Accepts requested ms on disk or by e-mail. Uses some sidebars. Prefers NIV. Guidelines/theme list by mail/website; copy for 9 x 12 SAE/3 stamps. (No ads)

** This periodical was #2 on the 2010 Top 50 Christian Publishers list (#4 in 2009, #9 in 2008, #5 in 2007, #3 in 2006).

WOMEN'S MARKETS

CHRISTIAN HOMESCHOOL MOMS, PO Box 6004, Monterrey CA 93944. Website: www.christian homeschoolmoms.com. Demetria Zinga, pub./ed. Online digital magazine and blog which provides practical education advice and spiritual encouragement, helps moms to homeschool with a spirit of joy. Online, updated 3-4 times/week. Ezine, blog. Circ. 3,708. Est. 2012. 5% unsolicited, 95% assigned. Query with published clips. **NO PAYMENT.** Byline/credits given to authors. First rights, copyrighted. 500-1,000 wds. Responds in 2 wks. Submit holiday 3 mos. adv. Accepts simultaneous submissions. Prefers articles on disk. No kill fee. Always inc. bios on feature articles. Guidelines by e-mail. Accepts photos, color, with articles only. Book reviews 200-500 wds., video reviews 200-500 wds. Accepts submissions from children/teens.

CHRISTIAN WORK AT HOME MINISTRIES, PO Box 974, Bellevue NE 68005. E-mail: jill@cwahm .com Website: www.cwahm.com. Christian Work at Home Inc. Jill Hart, pres. Primary audience is moms looking for information and advice about working from home. Weekly online mag.; 2,000 pgs. sitewide; circ. 30,000-35,000 unique visitors/mo. Subscription free online. 50% unsolicited freelance; 50% assigned. Query or complete ms; e-query OK. Accepts full mss by e-mail. **NO PAYMENT** for nonexclusive rts. Articles 600 wds. & up (50-75/yr.); reviews 300 wds. Responds in 2 wks. Seasonal 2 mos. ahead. Accepts reprints. Requires accepted mss by e-mail (copied into message). Uses some sidebars. (Ads)

Special needs: Turning writing into a career from home. Advice on treating writing like a business.

Tips: "We are always looking for how-to articles related to running a home business, and profiles of successful work-at-home people."

THE DABBLING MUM, 508 W. Main St., Beresford SD 57004. (866) 548-9327. E-mail: dm@ thedabblingmum.com. Website: www.thedabblingmum.com. Alyice Edrich, ed. The Dabbling Mum is an inspirational eMagazine featuring how-to articles, step-by-step craft tutorials, creative writing tips, and business coaching articles for busy, creative entrepreneurs who work out of their home offices. Weekly blog; monthly e-zine; circ. 30,000-40,000. Subscription free online. 90% unsolicited freelance; 10% assigned. Complete ms submitted online; e-query OK. Accepts full mss by e-mail. **Pays $20 to $40 on acceptance** for 1st rts., and exclusive indefinite archival rts. $10 for reprint rts. Accepts guest posts (donated material). Articles 500-1,500 wds. (48-96/yr.); book & video reviews 500 wds. (no payment). Responds in 4-12 wks. Seasonal 1 mo. ahead. No simultaneous submissions; accepts reprints (tell when/where appeared). Accepts e-mail submissions (copied into message). No kill fee or sidebars. Also accepts submissions from teens. Prefers KJV or NAS. Guidelines/editorial calendar/copy on website ("E-Magazine"/ "Women"). (Ads)

Special needs: Small-business ideas; grammar and style tips; do-it-yourself tutorials and arts and crafts projects

Tips: "Please use e-mail and submissions forms when contacting us. We're looking for material that is not readily available on the Internet. When adding a personal twist to your how-to piece, make sure you write in a way that is universal. In other words, it's not enough to say how you did it; we want you to teach others how to do it too. Write in a conversational tone so that readers feel as though you're speaking to them over the kitchen table, but keep it professional."

** This periodical was #29 on the 2010 Top 50 Christian Publishers list (#49 in 2008, #39 in 2007).

***KYRIA,** 465 Gundersen Dr., Carol Stream IL 60188. (630) 260-6200. Fax (630) 260-0114. E-mail: Kyria@christianitytoday.com. Website: www.kyria.com. Christianity Today Intl. Submit to Acquisitions Editor. To equip and encourage women to use their gifts, take responsibility for their spiritual formation, and fulfill the work God has called them to—through the power of the life-transforming and life-sustaining Spirit. Women's online digizine. Subscription $14.95. Estab. 2009. Open to unsolicited freelance. Query; e-query OK. Does not accept full mss by e-mail. **Pays $50-150** on acceptance for 1st or reprint rts. Articles 600-1,500 wds. Responds in 8-10 wks. Seasonal 4 mos. ahead. Accepts simultaneous submissions & reprints (tell when/where appeared). No kill fee. Uses some sidebars. Prefers NLT. Guidelines/theme list on website ("Help & Info"/"FAQs"/"Kyria Writer's Guidelines"); no copy. (Ads)

Fillers: Buys 12/yr. Devotions, 150-200 wds. pays $25-50.

Special needs: Spiritual disciplines.

Tips: "See our website for more specifics: kyria.com/help/writersguidelines/kyriawriters guidelines.html."

***MOMSENSE (MomSense),** 2370 S. Trenton Way, Denver CO 80231. (303) 733-5353. Fax (303) 733-5770. E-mail: MomSense@mops.org or info@mops.org. Website: www.MomSense.org, or www.MOPS.org. MOPS Intl. Inc. (Mothers of Preschoolers). Mary Darr, ed. Nurtures mothers of preschoolers and school-age kids from a Christian perspective with articles that both inform and inspire on issues relating to womanhood and motherhood. Bimonthly mag.; 32 pgs.; circ. 100,000. Subscription $23.95. 35% unsolicited freelance; 65% assigned. Complete ms/cover letter & bio; e-query OK. Accepts full mss by e-mail. **Pays .15/wd.** on publication for 1st & reprint rts. Articles 450-650 wds. (15-20/yr.). Responds in 12 wks. Seasonal 6 mos. ahead. Accepts simultaneous submissions & reprints (tell when/where appeared). Prefers requested ms by e-mail (attached file or copied into message). Some kill fees 10%. Uses some sidebars. Prefers NIV. Guidelines/theme list by mail/e-mail/or at www.MOPS.org/write; copy for 9 x 12 SAE/$1.39 postage. (Ads)

Special needs: "We always need practical articles to the woman as a woman, and to the woman as a mom."

Contest: Sponsors several contests per year for writing and photography. Check website for details on current contests.

Tips: "Most open to theme-specific features. Writers are more seriously considered if they are a mother with some connection to MOPS (but not required). Looking for original content ideas that appeal to Christian and non-Christian readers."

P31 WOMAN, 630 Team Rd., #100, Matthews NC 28105. (704) 849-2270. Fax (704) 849-7267. E-mail: editor@proverbs31.org. Website: www.proverbs31.org. Proverbs 31 Ministries. Glynnis Whitwer, ed.; submit to Janet Burke, asst. ed. (janet@proverbs31.org). Seeks to offer a godly woman's perspective on life with an emphasis on practical application. Bimonthly mag.; 24 pgs.; circ. 15,000. Subscription for donation. 50% unsolicited freelance; 50% assigned. Complete ms; e-query OK. **Pays in copies** for onetime rts. Not copyrighted. Articles 200-1,000 wds. (40/yr.). Responds in 4-6 wks. Seasonal 3 mos. ahead. Accepts simultaneous submissions & reprints (tell when/where appeared). Prefers accepted ms by e-mail (attached file or copied into message). Uses some sidebars. Prefers NIV. Guidelines/theme list on website. (No ads)

Tips: "Looking for articles that equip women with practical advice in every area of their lives. We enjoy personal stories integrated in the piece, but welcome all submissions."

RIGHT TO THE HEART OF WOMEN E-ZINE, PO Box 6421, Longmont CO 80501. (303) 772-2035. Fax (303) 678-0260. E-mail: righttotheheart@aol.com. Website: www.righttotheheartofwomen.com. Linda Shepherd, ed. Encouragement and helps for women in ministry. Weekly online e-zine; 5 pgs.; circ. 20,000. Subscription free. 10% unsolicited freelance; 90% assigned. Query; e-query OK. **NO PAYMENT** for nonexclusive rts. Articles 100-800 wds. (20/yr.). Responds in 2 wks. Seasonal 2 mos. ahead. Accepts simultaneous submissions & reprints (tell when/where appeared). Requires accepted mss by e-mail (copied into message). Does not use sidebars. No guidelines; copy on website. (Ads)

Columns/Departments: Accepts 10/yr. Women Bible Teachers; Profiles of Women in Ministry; Women's Ministry Tips; Author's and Speaker's Tips; 100 wds. Query.

Special needs: Book reviews must be in first person, by the author. Looking for women's ministry event ideas. Topics related to women and women's ministries.

New department: Articles needed for helps for hurting or suicidal. 500 wds. $10 on acceptance. See www.thinkingaboutsuicide.com to see existing article format and topics.

Tips: "For free subscription, subscribe at website above; also view e-zine. We want to hear from those involved in women's ministry or leadership. Also accepts manuscripts from AWSAs (see www.awsawomen.com). Query with your ideas."

***SHARE,** 10 W. 71st St., New York NY 10023-4201. (212) 877-3041. Fax (212) 724-5923. E-mail: CDofANatl@aol.com. Website: www.catholicdaughters.org. Catholic Daughters of the Americas. Peggy O'Brien, exec. dir.; submit to Peggy Eastman, ed. For Catholic women. Quarterly mag.; circ. 85,000. Free with membership. Most articles come from membership, but is open. **NO PAYMENT.** Buys color photos & covers. Guidelines/copy by mail. (Ads)

Tips: "We use very little freelance material unless it is written by Catholic Daughters."

SINGLE! YOUNG CHRISTIAN WOMAN, PO Box 573, Clarksville AR 72830. (479) 439-4891. E-mail: donna@onmyownnow.com. Website: www.onmyownnow.com. On My Own Now Ministries, Inc. Donna Lee Schillinger, ed. Christian alternative to the fashion magazine. For young, single women ages 17-23. Monthly e-zine. 18 pgs.; circ. 1,000. Free subscription. Est. 2009. 40% unsolicited, 60% assigned. Query or send complete manuscript by e-mail. **NO PAYMENT.** Nonexclusive rights. Copyrighted. Prefers NIV. 800-1200 wds. Accept 24 nonfiction mss/yr. Responds in 2 wks. Submit holiday 2 mos. in advance. Accepts simultaneous submissions/prev. published (tell when/where published). Require articles on disk or in e-mail (attached). No kill fee. Some sidebars. Inc. bio on feature articles. Sample copy online. No photos. Book, music, video reviews 800 wds. Accept submissions from teens.

Columns: Just What You Need (resources for young adult women), 450-550 wds; Fashion DIVinA (how to look good and remain godly), 700-1000 wds.; The Recap (reviews of books, movies, music, etc.), 600-1,000; Accepts 18 mss/yr. Query/send complete manuscript.

Tips: Looking for guest columnists for Fashion DIVinA, Just What You Need, and The Recap. Also seek new writers for feature articles. (No ads)

TREASURE, PO Box 5002, Antioch TN 37011. Toll-free (877) 767-7662. (615) 731-6812. Fax (615) 727-1157. E-mail: treasure@wnac.org. Website: www.wnac.org. Women Nationally Active for Christ of National Assn. of Free Will Baptists. Sarah Fletcher, mng. ed. A women's Bible study guide with emphasis on missions and mentoring. Quarterly publication; 48 pgs.; circ. 4,500. Subscription $12. Estab. 2011. 25% unsolicited freelance; 75% assigned. Complete ms/cover letter. Accepts full ms by e-mail. **Pays in copies** for 1st rts. Articles 750-1,200 wds. (10/yr.). Responds in 8 wks. Seasonal 12 mos. ahead. No simultaneous submissions; accepts reprints (tell when/where appeared). Prefers e-mail submissions (attached file). Regularly uses sidebars. Also accepts submissions from teens. Prefers KJV. Guidelines/theme list by e-mail; copy for 5.35 x 8.5 SAE/$1. (No ads)

Columns/Departments: What Works (practical tips/lists about women's health, homes, fitness, fashion, or finances).

Special needs: Spiritual formation, family issues, life coaching/mentoring, church life, community outreach and global evangelism.

Tips: "Most open to articles. Bulk of material comes from Women Active for Christ or Free Will Baptist writers."

***A VIRTUOUS WOMAN,** 594 Ivy Hill, Harlan KY 40831. (606) 573-6506. E-mail: submissions@avirtuouswoman.org. Website: www.avirtuouswoman.org. Independent Seventh-day Adventist ministry. Melissa Ringstaff, dir./ed. Strives to provide practical articles for women ages 20-60 years; based on Proverbs 31. Monthly e-zine; circ. 20,000+ online. 80% unsolicited freelance; 20% assigned.

Complete ms/cover letter; e-query OK. Accepts full mss by e-mail. **NO PAYMENT** for first, reprint, electronic, anthology rts. Articles 500-2,000 wds. (150+/yr.); reviews 500-1,000 wds. Responds in 6-8 wks. Seasonal 6 mos. ahead. No simultaneous submissions; accepts reprints (tell when/where appeared). Accepts e-mail submissions (attached file in .doc or .txt or copied into message). Uses some sidebars. Prefers KJV, NIV, NLT. Guidelines/theme list on website (click on "Main"/"Writers' Guidelines"); copy for 9 x 12 SAE/$2.02 postage plus $3.50. (Ads)

Poetry: Accepts 5/yr. Free verse, traditional. Submit max. 2 poems.

Fillers: Accepts 12/yr. Anecdotes, facts, ideas, jokes, party ideas, prayers, quizzes, and tips; to 200 wds.

Tips: "Write practical articles that appeal to the average woman—articles that women can identify with. Do not preach. Read our writer's helps for ideas."

WOMEN OF THE CROSS, 920 Sweetgum Creek, Plano TX 75023. (972) 517-8553. Website: www.womenofthecross.com. Greg Paskal, content mngr. (greg@gregpaskal.com). Encouraging women in their walk with the Lord; strong emphasis on discipleship and relationship. Online community. 50% unsolicited freelance. Complete ms by e-mail; e-query OK. **NO PAYMENT.** Articles 500-1,500 wds. (10/yr.). Responds in 2-4 wks. Seasonal 3 mos. ahead. Accepts simultaneous submissions; no reprints. Prefers e-mail submissions (attached or copied into message). Uses some sidebars. Prefers NIV, NKJV, NAS. Also accepts submissions from teens. Guidelines by e-mail. (No ads)

Poetry: Accepts 2/yr. Avant-garde, free verse, haiku, or light verse; 50-250 lines. Submit max. 1 poem.

Columns/Departments: Accepts 10/yr. Features (Christian living, encouragement); article (to other women); all 500-1,500 wds.

Special needs: Personal stories of growing in the Lord; faith-stretching stories about international adoption.

Tips: "Appropriate topics could be firsthand accounts of how God worked in the author's life through a personal or family experience. View online forum for specific topics."

WRITERS' MARKETS

ADVANCED CHRISTIAN WRITER, 9118 W. Elmwood Dr., Ste. 1G, Niles IL 60714-5820. (847) 296-3964. Fax (847) 296-0754. E-mail: ljohnson@wordprocommunications.com. Website: www.ACWriters.com or call (800) 21-WRITE. American Christian Writers/Reg Forder, PO Box 110390, Nashville TN 37222. E-mail: ACWriters@aol.com (for samples, advertising, and subscriptions). Lin Johnson, mng. ed. A professional newsletter for published writers. Bimonthly e-mail newsletter; 8 pgs.; circ. 500. Subscription $19.95. 50% unsolicited freelance. Query or complete ms, correspondence, & mss by e-mail only. **Pays $20** on publication for 1st or reprint rts. Articles 700-1,000 wds. (24/yr.). Responds in 6-8 wks. Seasonal 6 mos. ahead. No simultaneous submissions. Accepts reprints (tell when/where appeared). Uses some sidebars. Requires e-mail submission (attached or copied into message). No kill fee. Prefers NIV. Guidelines by e-mail. (Ads)

Special needs: How to market your writing and grow your freelance career; time management; workplace issues.

Tips: "We accept articles only from well-published writers and from editors. We need manuscripts about all aspects of building a freelance career and how to increase sales and professionalism; on the advanced level; looking for depth beyond the basics."

***BEST NEW WRITING,** PO Box 11, Titusville NJ 08560. E-mail: cklim@bestnewwriting.com. Website: www.bestnewwriting.com. Christopher Klim, exec. ed.; Robert Gover, ed. This annual anthology carries the results of the Eric Hoffer Award for Books and Prose and the Gover Prize for short-short writing. Submit books via mail; no queries. Submit prose online. The prose category is for creative fiction and nonfiction less than 10,000 wds. (Hoffer Award) and less than 500 wds (Gover Prize).

Annual award for books features 18 categories, including self-help and spiritual. **Pays $250 for winning prose; $2,000 for winning book; $250 for short-short prose; $75 for cover art.** Guidelines at www.HofferAward.com and www.BestNewWriting.com.

CHRISTIAN COMMUNICATOR, 9118 W. Elmwood Dr., Ste. 1G, Niles IL 60714-5820. (847) 296-3964. Fax (847) 296-0754. E-mail: ljohnson@wordprocommunications.com. Website: www.ACWriters.com. American Christian Writers/Reg Forder, P.O. Box 110390, Nashville TN 37222. E-mail: ACWriters@aol.com (for samples, advertising, or subscriptions). Lin Johnson, mng. ed.; Sally Miller, poetry ed. For Christian writers/speakers who want to improve their writing craft and speaking ability, stay informed about writing markets, and be encouraged in their ministries. Monthly (11X) mag.; 20 pgs.; circ. 1,500. Subscription $29.95. 50% unsolicited freelance. Complete ms/queries by e-mail only. **Pays $5-10** on publication for 1st or reprint rts. Articles 650-1,000 wds. (90-100/yr.). Responds in 6-8 wks. Seasonal 6 mos. ahead. Accepts reprints (tell when/where appeared). Requires e-mail submission. Guidelines by e-mail; copy for 9 x 12 SAE/3 stamps to Nashville address. (Ads)

Poetry: Buys 22/yr. Free verse, haiku, light verse, traditional; to 20 lines. Poems on writing or speaking only; $5. Send to Sally Miller: sallymiller@ameritech.net.

Columns/Departments: Buys 35/yr. A Funny Thing Happened on the Way to Becoming a Communicator (humor), 75-300 wds. Interviews (well-published authors with unique angle or editors), 650-1,000 wds. Speaking (techniques for speakers), 650-1,000 wds.

Tips: "I need anecdotes for the 'Funny Thing Happened' column and articles on research, creativity, and writing nonfiction."

***FELLOWSCRIPT,** Canada. E-mail: fellowscript@gmail.com. Website: www.inscribe.org/fellowscript. Bonnie Way, acq. ed. Writer's quarterly newsletter for, by, and about writers/writing. 32 pgs.; circ. 200. Subscription with InScribe membership. Submit complete ms. by e-mail. **Pays 2.5 cents per word** (Canadian funds) for onetime rights, or 1.5 cents per word for reprint rights, paid by PayPal on publication; an extra half cent paid for publication (with author's permission) on our website for a period of no more than three months. 750-2,000 wds. Responds in 4 weeks. Plans 6 months ahead. Guidelines on website.

Tips: "We always prefer material specifically slanted toward the needs and interests of Canadian Christian writers. We do not publish poetry except as part of an instructional article, nor do we publish testimonials. We give preference to members and to Canadian writers."

***FREELANCE WRITER'S REPORT,** 45 Main St., PO Box A, North Stratford NH 03590-0167. (603) 922-8338. E-mail: editor@writers-editors.com. Website: www.writers-editors.com. General/CNW Publishing Inc. Dana K. Cassell, ed. Covers marketing and running a freelance writing business. Monthly newsletter; 8 pgs. 25% freelance. Complete ms via e-mail (attached or copied into message). **Pays .10/wd.** on publication for onetime rts. Articles to 900 wds. (50/yr.). Responds within 1 wk. Seasonal 2 mos. ahead. Accepts simultaneous submissions & reprints (tell when/where appeared). Does not use sidebars. Guidelines on website; copy for 6 x 9 SAE/2 stamps (for back copy); $4 for current copy.

Fillers: Prose fillers to 400 wds.

Contest: Open to all writers. Deadline March 15, 2013 (annual). Nonfiction, fiction, children's, poetry. Prizes: $100, $75, $50. Details on website.

Tips: "No articles on the basics of freelancing; our readers are established freelancers. Looking for marketing and business building for freelance writers/editors/book authors."

***NEW WRITER'S MAGAZINE,** PO Box 5976, Sarasota FL 34277-5976. (941) 953-7903. E-mail: newriters@aol.com. General/Sarasota Bay Publishing. George S. Haborak, ed. Bimonthly mag.; circ. 5,000. 95% freelance. Query or complete ms by mail. **Pays $10-50 ($20-40 for fiction)** on publication for 1st rts. Articles 700-1,000 wds. (50/yr.); fiction 700-800 wds. (2-6/yr.). Responds in 5 wks. Guidelines by mail; copy $3.

Poetry: Buys 10-20/yr. Free verse, light verse; 8-20 lines. Pays $5 min. Submit max. 3 poems.
Fillers: Buys 25-45/yr. Writing-related cartoons; buys 20-30/yr.; pays $10 max. Anecdotes, facts, newsbreaks, short humor; 20-100 wds. Buys 5-15/yr. Pays $5 max.
Tips: "We like interview articles with successful writers."

***POETS & WRITERS MAGAZINE,** 90 Broad St., Ste. 2100, New York NY 10004-2272. (212) 226-3586. Fax (212) 226-3963. E-mail: editor@pw.org. Website: www.pw.org. General. Submit to The Editors. Professional trade journal for poetry, fiction, and nonfiction writers. Subscription $19.95. Bimonthly mag.; circ. 60,000. Query/clips by mail; e-query OK. **Pays $150-500** on acceptance for 1st & nonexclusive rts. Articles 500-3,000 wds. (35/yr.). Responds in 4-6 wks. Seasonal 4 mos. ahead. Some kill fees 25%. Guidelines on website; copy $5.95. (Ads)
Tips: "Most open to News & Trends, The Literary Life, and The Practical Writer (columns)."

***THE WRITER,** 21027 Crossroads Cir., Waukesha WI 53187. (262) 796-8776. Fax (262) 798-6468. E-mail: queries@writermag.com. Website: www.writermag.com. General. Jeff Reich, ed.; Ron Kovach, sr. ed. (rkovach@writermag.com); Sarah Lange, assoc. ed. (slange@writermag.com). How-to for writers; lists religious markets on website. Monthly mag.; 60-68 pgs.; circ. 30,000. Subscription $32.95. 80% unsolicited freelance. Query; no phone/fax query (prefers hard copy or e-query). **Pays $250-400** for feature articles; book reviews ($40-80, varies); on acceptance for 1st rts. Features 600-3,500 wds. (60/yr.). Responds in 4-8 wks. Uses some sidebars. Guidelines on website ("The Magazine"/"Submissions"). (Ads)
Fillers: Prose; writer-related cartoons $50. Send cartoons to slange@writermag.com.
Columns/Departments: Buys 24+/yr. Freelance Success (shorter pieces on the business of writing); Off the Cuff (personal essays about writing; avoid writer's block stories). All 600-1,600 wds. Pays $100-300 for columns; $25-75 for Take Note. Query 4 months ahead. See guidelines for full list of columns.
Special needs: How-to on the craft of writing only.
Contests: Currently running two to three contests a year, generally in personal-essay or short-story categories.
Tips: "Get familiar first with our general mission, approach, tone, and the types of articles we do and don't do. Then, if you feel you have an article that is fresh and well suited to our mission, send us a query. Personal essays must provide takeaway advice and benefits for writers; we shun the 'navel-gazing' type of essay. Include plenty of how-to, advice, and tips on techniques. Be specific. Query for features six months ahead. All topics indicated must relate to writing."
** This periodical was #42 on the 2010 Top 50 Christian Publishers list (#17 in 2009, #45 in 2008).

***THE WRITER'S CHRONICLE: The Magazine for Serious Writers,** The Association of Writers & Writing Programs, George Mason University, MSN 1E3, 4400 University Dr., Fairfax VA 22030-4444. (703) 993-4301. Fax (703) 993-4302. E-mail: awp@awpwriter.org. Website: www.awpwriter.org. Supriya Bhatnagar, ed. Magazine for serious writers; articles used as teaching tools. Mag. published 6X during academic yr.; 96 pgs.; circ. 35,000. Subscription $20/yr.; $34.2/yr. 90% unsolicited freelance; 10% assigned. Query; phone/fax/e-query OK. No full mss by e-mail. **Pays .11/wd.** on publication for 1st rts. Articles 3,000-6,000. Responds in 12 wks. Accepts simultaneous submissions. No reprints. No articles on disk or by e-mail. No kill fee. Uses some sidebars. Guidelines/theme list on website ("Magazine"/"Editorial Guidelines"); copy for 10 x 13 SAE/first-class postage. (Ads)
Special needs: Articles on the craft of writing and interviews with established writers from all over the world. Essays, trends, and literary controversies. No poetry or fiction.
Contests: Grace Paley Prize for Short Fiction, $6,000 & publication; AWP Prize for Creative Nonfiction, $3,000 & publication; Donald Hall Prize for Poetry, $6,000 & publication; AWP Prize for the Novel, $3,000 & publication. Website: www.awpwriter.org.

***WRITER'S DIGEST,** 4700 E. Galbraith Rd., Cincinnati OH 45236. (513) 531-2690, ext. 11483. Fax (513) 891-7153. E-mail: wordsubmissions@fwmedia.com. Website: www.writersdigest.com. General/F & W. Submit to Acquisitions Editor. To inform, instruct, or inspire the freelancer and author. Media (8X) mag.; 84-92 pgs.; circ. 110,000. Subscription $24.96. 20% unsolicited; 60% assigned. E-mail submissions only. Responds in 8-16 wks. **Pays .30-.50/wd.** on acceptance for 1st & electronic rts. Articles 800-1,500 wds. (75/yr.). Seasonal 8 mos. ahead. Requires requested ms by e-mail (copied into message). Kill fee 25%. Regularly uses sidebars. Guidelines/editorial calendar on website; no copy. (Ads)

Contests: Sponsors annual contest for articles, short stories, poetry, and scripts. Also The International Self-Published Book Awards. Send SASE for rules.

Tips: "We're looking for technique pieces by published authors. The Inkwell section is the best place to break in."

** This periodical was #45 on the 2010 Top 50 Christian Publishers list (#49 in 2009, #38 in 2008).

THE WRITER'S MONTHLY REVIEW, 106 Fletcher Dr., Logansport LA 71049. (318) 469-5481. Marcella Simmons, pub./ed. E-mail: writersmonthlyreview@gmail.com or marcies04@yahoo.com. Website: http://writersmonthlyreview.homestead.com. Monthly mag where creative writers of every genre can come together and learn, hone their crafts, and interact with others who share their passion of writing. US sub. $35/Can $40. Features 550-1,000 wds./essay 550-1,000/humor 50-500. All accepted submissions will receive one copy of magazine.

Poetry: Well-crafted in any style and on the subject of writing. Max. 20 lines. Poetry-related features about the elements of craft, marketing, form poetry, poetics, or influence of specific poets. 1500-1800 wds. Poetry book review 500 wds.

BONUS SECTION

Writer's Helps

Writing Tips

It's Time to Write Nonfiction

by Roger Palms

"IF I AM GOING to make money as a writer, I have to learn to write fiction." Where did that idea come from?

Tell that to nonfiction writers Philip Yancey and Os Guinness and David Jeremiah. Tell that to Kay Arthur and Lee Strobel. Did anybody tell Thomas Friedman or Stephen Covey they needed to write fiction if they were going to be successful? C. S. Lewis didn't simply write The Chronicles of Narnia. He also wrote *Mere Christianity*.

People who help change their world are often nonfiction writers who influence minds and hearts in a way that fiction can't. Jerry B. Jenkins may be most known for his fiction, but he has written almost as much nonfiction. He is a successful writer who knows how to do both. Why be a bird trying to fly with only one wing?

Each of my own fifteen books is nonfiction. Even the ones long out of print are still being read and passed along. I hear from people who have read my books years after they were published. Nonfiction isn't a read-once-and-give-it-away project. Nonfiction speaks to people who understand the value of the transformed mind. Fiction as entertainment is fun; fiction can even make a culture-altering point, such as Harriet Beecher Stowe's *Uncle Tom's Cabin*. But year in and year out, nonfiction is the genre that makes the greatest and longest-lasting impact on people's lives.

Is Your Ship Listing?

If a writer's ship is listing to one side—the fiction side—the ship won't move as well. We need writers who are balanced, who can write fiction and nonfiction. It takes research, accuracy, attribution, and substantiation to write strong nonfiction. But most of those skills are also part of the fiction writer's life. So the fiction writer can also craft nonfiction. And, by the guidance of God, the next powerful, life-changing nonfiction writer may be you.

Nobel Prize-winning fiction writer Toni Morrison says, "If there is a book you really want to read, but it hasn't been written yet, then you must write it." Apply that quote to nonfiction. What is your burden? What do you feel passionate about? What is burning inside that has to come out? You don't have to turn to fiction to write that book. Look at the great-ideas people in our history and see how many made a difference through writing nonfiction.

If you feel God is calling you to expand your ministry of writing to include nonfiction, pay attention to the disciplines writers apply to their fiction:

- Am I writing only from my emotions?
- Where is the substantiation for what I am writing?
- Where is the careful thought?

I've read manuscripts in which the writer hammers hard at something terrible he believes is happening in our country. It must be changed, he writes. But then I examine the basis for what that writer has stated—and I find it isn't true. A bit of research shows that the "facts" the author is so upset about were based on propaganda, not fact. His information came from commentators who don't mind publishing what is known as "managed news." A writer who hasn't researched the source of his material will soon be dismissed as silly, or worse, as a liar.

But if your idea is based on truth, often a nonfiction article or book can be far more powerful than what you might communicate on that same subject through fiction.

Writing for People Who Think

Christian apologist and author Ravi Zacharias tells us, "Let my people think." Where are the new writers who will think, who will research, analyze, and study—and then write articles and books that will turn others around in their own thinking?

How many people may come to saving faith because of the nonfiction book you will write? And how many believers who need to become serious, thinking Christians will find the help they need in your strong, clear nonfiction writing?

People need what God has put into your heart to write. The time for writing nonfiction is now.

This previously appeared on the Christian Writers Guild blog:www.christianwritersguild.com/blog/its-time-to-write-nonfiction/.

Gleaning Writing Ideas from the Ten Commandments

by Deborah Christensen

The Ten Commandments not only set the standard for how God wants us to worship him and treat others, but in them you can also find a wealth of writing ideas.

The first four commandments focus on our relationship with God.

No Gods before Me

How do you keep God first? What happens to your relationship with God when your life gets out of balance? How do you maintain a vibrant relationship with God? These are just a few ideas you could pursue for the anecdotal articles readers enjoy.

No Carved Image

What competes with God for your attention? Share with readers how, with God's help, you overcame those distractions—TV, work, money, possessions, relationships. What are the signs another god is taking over your life? How have you learned to put those carved images in their proper perspective?

Don't Take the Lord's Name in Vain

Share with readers ways to make sure their speech honors God. What are some productive ways to respond when other people use the Lord's name in vain? How can we teach our children to honor God with their speech?

Keep the Sabbath Holy

What are some unique ways to keep the Sabbath? What priorities have you set in that regard? What obstacles have you encountered and how have you overcome them?

If you struggle in these areas, other people do too. When you write about your struggles, they will know they're not alone.

What if you write fiction? Your experiences may provide the perfect theme for a novel or a children's book.

The last six commandments guide us in our relationships with others. They, too, provide a wealth of writing ideas.

Honor Your Father and Your Mother

What is your relationship with your parents like? Easy? Difficult? How did you—or are you—dealing with the issues? What lessons did they teach you? What did you learn about parenting or marriage from them? Have you learned to forgive them for something, or do you need to apologize for something?

Don't Murder

Jesus told us this command goes beyond actual murder and includes hatred. How do you handle conflict? What role does forgiveness play? What about respect? What joys have you celebrated with others? What pain have you worked through? How do you build stronger relationships to avoid "murdering" someone?

Don't Commit Adultery

Many people struggle in their marriages—even Christians. How do you protect your marriage? If you're single, how do you avoid compromising situations and maintain purity? What are some ways to treat members of the opposite sex with respect? What about temptation? Pornography? How do you keep your mind pure?

Don't Steal

Have you ever taken credit for someone else's ideas? How do you deal with the temptation to take something that doesn't belong to you? What about borrowing music from the library and downloading it? Is that stealing? How about right-clicking on a web image and using it on *your* blog? What is stealing online?

Don't Bear False Witness

What is your opinion of the so-called "little white lie"? Has one of your lies destroyed a relationship? Made a bad situation worse? What about the lie you told that never was found out—what do you do with that guilt? How do you choose to tell the truth, even when it's difficult?

Don't Covet

Has jealousy over someone else's belongings (or writing contract) caused a break in your relationship with him or her? Do you rejoice when good things happen to others? Have you ever gone into debt to get something you want? What was the result? What are your secrets for being content in all circumstances?

This previously appeared as a two-part article on the Christian Writers Guild blog: www.christianwritersguild.com/blog/gleaning-writing-ideas-from-the-10-commandments-part-1/.

Capture Your Ideas

by Heather Kreke

IN THE MIDDLE OF THE NIGHT, you realize you have just dreamt the perfect scene for your novel. As you drift back to sleep, you repeat the scene to yourself in an attempt to remember every detail. But in the morning, all you remember is that you had a great idea. The gist of it is gone.

No More Lost Scenes

It's time to embrace technology: use your cell phone. Most give you the ability to take notes, so learn this feature and start a new note for each idea when you're away from your computer. Use labels so you can easily find the note later. Set your phone to "silent" mode while you sleep.

If your phone has e-mail, send your notes to yourself so they'll be there when you're back at your computer.

If you have a brainstorm while driving, pull over and leave yourself a voice mail message. Or take a handheld recorder with you. This works great wherever you are. If you get strange looks, just nod and smile.

No Excuses

There's also the old-fashioned way of keeping a small notebook near your bed, in your car, or in your pocket or purse. Leave a blank page after each idea to give yourself room to add to it.

Find the method that works for you.

This previously appeared on the Christian Writers Guild blog: www.christianwritersguild.com/blog/capture-your-ideas/.

Write Book Reviews

by Danielle Grandinetti

WANT A FUN WAY to keep up with the latest books in your genre—and maybe get paid? Try writing book reviews.

Opportunities to publish reviews range from Amazon.com to national magazines. Make a list of the reviews you usually read, then search those places for submission guidelines. Check the *Market Guide* topical listings of periodicals for additional possibilities.

Before you attempt landing a deal with a leading newspaper, build your repertoire by writing free reviews for booksellers such as Barnes and Noble, Christianbook.com, or BookSneeze.com (a branch of Thomas Nelson). Through research and practice, learn how to write a well-crafted review so readers begin to see you as a trusted source.

Write a Review Readers Want to Read

Do your homework. Read to see how others do it. Discover what you appreciate most, emulate that, and avoid the rest.

Read the *entire* book. This may seem like a given, but don't overlook it. Take notes so you're not hunting for that plot twist or fantastic quote later.

Aim for 250 words. Long reviews are tedious. Leave readers where they feel they must buy the book (or avoid it).

Don't give away the story. This is difficult in reviewing fiction, but readers want to experience the story on their own. Study back covers and note how the copy lures readers without giving away the story.

Be honest, be sincere, and be respectful, even when you don't like a book. It's okay to give your opinion about the material, but don't discredit the author. As a Christian book reviewer, be gracious and remember to write unto others as you'd like to be written about.

This previously appeared on the Christian Writers Guild blog: www.christianwritersguild.com/blog/write-book-reviews-and-maybe-get-paid/.

Become a Temporary Expert

by Karen O'Connor

EARLY IN MY WRITING CAREER I met a woman who had written and published hundreds of articles on subjects ranging from laying a wood floor to managing anxiety. When I asked her about her broad base of knowledge, she joked, "I'm a temporary expert. I learn enough to write about a topic and then move on to the next one."

Her joke was good advice. I have followed my friend's five-step plan with good results (sales!) for more than thirty years. You can too.

Step 1: Select Topics of Interest

Don't be fooled by the obvious simplicity of this step. My list included grandparenting, refugees, money addictions, gratitude, classical Christian literature, and more. Notice how diverse the subjects are. That doesn't matter. You can learn and write about anything.

Step 2: Contact Professionals

While researching and writing *When Spending Takes the Place of Feeling* (Thomas Nelson), I interviewed professionals in the field of compulsive behavior, attended a twelve-step program for debtors, and consulted with therapists who treated people with addictions. My temporary expertise resulted in the book being nominated for a Gold Medallion Award by the Evangelical Christian Publishers Association.

Step 3: Meet the Real Experts

While researching my chapter on extraterrestrial trash for my book *Garbage,* I read a magazine interview with Don Kessler, a space debris expert with the Johnson Space Center. The next day when I called to speak with him, he answered my questions, put me in touch with appropriate literature on the subject, and sent me free photographs. Voilà! I became a temporary expert.

Step 4: Conduct Your Own Research

A friend traveled to Stockholm to research her book on women who have won the Nobel Prize. If you cannot find an original source such as this, look for a reliable secondary source. For my children's book on Vietnam I spoke with a Vietnamese family now living in the United States. They helped with the pronunciation guide, recipes, folk tales, and details on daily life only they could provide.

Learn to Interview Well

by Estee B. Wells

Conducting a great interview is an art. But you must engage sound disciplines as you learn the craft.

This may sound obvious, but always verify the time of the interview—especially if it's in another time zone. My first interview was with a person on the other side of the country. I forgot to confirm his time zone. He was gracious, but that was embarrassing.

I learned to do my homework.

Interviewing Tips

- Know your subject's name and how he spells it. What sounds like "John Smith" could easily be "Jon Smythe."
- Google the interviewee so you can develop an angle and ask intelligent and unique questions.
- Talk slowly.
- Play the fool. Ask your interviewee to explain what you don't understand, then repeat what you heard to be sure you have it right.
- Never assume. Confirm dates, names, and abbreviations, especially if you found them on the Internet.

I find it helpful, when interviewing by phone, to have a photo of the subject handy as we talk. This helps me personalize the conversation.

I survived that embarrassing first interview and learned from my mistakes. You can too.

This previously appeared on the Christian Writers Guild blog: www.christianwritersguild.com/blog/learn-to-interview-well/.

Step 5: Make the Experience Real

Experience is a writer's best friend. Bake a loaf of bread and then write up the history of this food staple, including a recipe. Spend a day at the zoo, as I did for my book *Maybe You Belong in a Zoo: Careers with Animals,* and learn all you can firsthand.

Don't shy away from asking questions and participating in person, when possible. Get your feet wet, your hands dirty, your mind engaged, your heart beating. Look, listen, taste, touch, and smell. Then write about it because you know what you're talking about. You're an expert—at least temporarily.

This previously appeared on the Christian Writers Guild blog: www.christianwritersguild.com/blog/become-a-temporary-expert/.

Atomic-Powered Titles

by James N. Watkins

AS YOU PREPARE TO present your articles and book proposals to agents and editors, keep in mind the importance of a first impression.

As an editor, what first impresses me is a great title. Unfortunately, I find most titles are trite, cliché, or plain boring. So, how do you create a powerful title? Here's how I brainstorm titles. It looks like atomic fission.

I start with the subject in a circle in the middle of a blank page, then start adding circles all around it for synonyms, antonyms, homonyms, rhyming words, associated nouns and verbs, biblical phrases, etc. Let the atomic reaction begin.

Find the Relationships

Once I have brainstormed and fission has slowed down, then I start looking for relationships among the various circles.

I was asked to write an article for a funeral director on the importance of showing emotion. I wrote *grief* in the middle circle and fission-ed out to topics such as *emotions, feeling, funeral home, cemetery, burial plot*, etc. I then made the connection between *feelings* and *burial* and came up with *Don't bury your feelings*.

Favorite Examples

Here are some of my favorite titles that came from similar atomic reactions:

Synonyms on a lack of follow-up in evangelism: *Losing the found.*
Antonyms on faith healing: *Healing: faith or fake?*
On irritations in staff ministry: *Staff or staph?*
On the importance of healthy touches: *Mood altering hugs* (rhymes with drugs).
Familiar phrases on the importance of encouragement: *Affirmative action.*
On the message of Christmas: *The 365 days of Christmas.*
On assurance: *Are you eternally in-secure?*
On treating Scripture honestly: *The rest of the Bible story*.
Book titles: *Seven Habits of the Purpose-Driven Writer*, or *The Papoose-Driven Life.*
Song titles: *Looking for love in all the right places*, *Lord, I lift Your name in vain*, and *I can hear you snore*.

Have fun—and let the reaction begin.

This previously appeared on the Christian Writers Guild blog: www.christianwritersguild.com/blog/atomic-powered-titles/.

Have You Hooked Your Readers?

by Andy Scheer

REMEMBER THE LAST TIME you glanced at a magazine article—then flipped the page.

Now remember that piece you couldn't put down. You e-mailed copies and told friends about it. That's the kind of writing editors seek.

An article has perhaps ten seconds to grab a reader's attention. Editors want articles that grab readers—and hold them to the end. Great topics aren't enough. Ask yourself, "Would I read my article if someone else had written it?" Sure, your mom, your spouse, or your best friend would. Editors want articles everyone else wants to read.

Old Topic, New Treatment

Editors want writing that breathes life into a topic—not that rehashes material they've already seen. Proposing an article about Christmas? Make it different than the "Let's Put Christ Back into Christmas" article that you, the editor, and her readers have seen countless times.

The same for other important but perennial topics such as supporting missionaries, opposing abortion, or strengthening marriage. Take a fresh approach. Make the lead paragraph surprising.

Some years back, *Focus on the Family* printed "When Feathers Fly" by Janet E. Pratt, which examined principles couples could use to resolve conflicts.

The application points were standard. But Pratt hooked readers with an anecdotal lead in which she described needing to cooperate with her husband (to whom she wasn't speaking) to haul off the carcass of a dead ostrich. (Maybe a ho-hum lead for *Today's Ostrich Rancher*, but for *Focus*, it was arresting.)

As Pratt concludes her anecdote, readers stick with her as she turns the corner: "Immediately afterward, as I showered off the dead bird smell, it occurred to me that the principles of handling conflicts in a marriage are a lot like the mechanics of dealing with a dead ostrich."

If your topic is worth reading about, find a fresh way to approach it. Include a dramatic quote from a neighbor or an expert. Perhaps you have a memory of an argument with a coworker that prompted you to see a Scripture verse in a fresh way.

After They're Hooked

Once you've hooked a reader, maintain her interest with good writing: concrete nouns, vivid verbs, sentence variety, specific examples, and consistent, logical development. You don't need gimmicks.

Christian editors (and readers) look for accounts that find a topic's human dimension, apply God's living Word, then convey that information in simple, straightforward language.

Earn a reputation for that kind of writing, and editors will welcome your next article.

This previously appeared on the Christian Writers Guild blog: www.christianwritersguild.com/blog/have-you-hooked-your-readers/.

From the First Line

by Karen O'Connor

HAVE YOU EVER MOVED on to the next article in your favorite magazine because the first sentence didn't grab you? I'm with you. I only have so much time for reading, and I want to spend it on something terrific.

Be the writer who hooks readers immediately by trying these five tips for your lead.

1. **Clever dialogue:** *Never tell a child, "Go clean your room!"* With an opening like that, it would be difficult for a reader to set the article aside without finding out more.
2. **Surprising information:** *In a culture where the divorce rate is about 50 percent, according to divorcerate.org, there is still a large population of married couples who love one another and are actually happy.* This surprised me, since I was once divorced and wondered if anyone could have a truly happy marriage, so I used it to open "Advice from Happily Married Couples," published in *The Lookout* magazine.
3. **Intriguing question:** *Is money driving you crazy?* This lead, for an article in a local newspaper, hooked readers who wanted help as overspenders. Use questions like these to tap into felt needs.
4. **Startling statement:** *My stepchildren love me!* There's a first line to cause a reader to sit up and notice. Many articles are written about how to navigate the difficult waters of a blended family, but I wanted to encourage stepparents with this article in *Living with Teenagers*.
5. **Unusual circumstance:** *I looked around my beautiful new house and then sat down and cried!* I hoped it would seem unusual for a woman to feel sad about moving to a lovely new home. Apparently it did, because I sold this article to numerous magazines and book compilations.

What hooks have you used to entice readers?

This previously appeared on the Christian Writers Guild blog: www.christianwritersguild.com/blog/hook-your-reader-from-the-first-line/.

Earn Those Quarters

by Angela Hunt

THIS IS A TRIBUTE TO the best English teacher I ever had: Janet Williams. She is in heaven now, but I hope she knows I still use a trick she taught me.

Just this once, feel free to copy off my paper.

One of Mrs. Williams's pearls of wisdom: After you write, go through your piece and pay yourself a quarter for every word you cut. This is something I now do with every draft.

Search and Destroy

I don't cut important words or hunky verbs. Adverbs bite the dust, as do fillers like *rather, just, that,* and *very*. Gone also are *was* and *were*, as these signal passive voice.

Watch out for unnecessary words. "She stood to her feet." (What else would she stand to?) "He scratched his forehead with his hand." (What else? If he used a felt-tip pen that might be worth mentioning—particularly if the cap was off.)

Be Active

We are children of the video age. If I write, "The cat was on the table," the movie screen in my mind is blank. Instead I write, "The cat was yawning on the table." But I earn a quarter if I write, "The cat on the table yawned." There! Active voice—and I can see it.

I cut backstory from the first fifty pages. Readers want to move forward, not backward. I carve out exclamation points and explanations, because my purpose is to grab the reader. I also delete paragraphs of description, as I can describe what I need to as my characters move through the story.

Practice Makes Perfect

One of my publishers reissued a book I wrote years ago. Without changing the plot, I cut 6,000 words.

Learn and practice the skill of self-editing. Imagine what you can do with all those quarters. . . .

This previously appeared on the Christian Writers Guild blog: www.christianwritersguild.com/blog/earn-those-quarters/.

Potentially Tense Canaries: Why Spell-Check Is for the Birds

by Andy Scheer

PERHAPS THEIR EXPERIENCE with spell-check had made the canaries tense. They flew at me off the page, daring me to discover their sentence's original meaning, before spell-check and its minion, "suggest word replacement," had scrambled the sentence.

The sentence taunted me; what could it mean? Nothing in the manuscript I'd been editing hinted at the problems posed by question 5:

> What potential tensions canaries from a transition in mower, authority, responsibility, and promise as we see with Abraham and Isaac?

I pored over the sentence, my curiosity piqued. What had spell-check wrought? I started with "mower." Context suggested the author meant "power."

But canaries? What potentially could make them tense? I noted the problem and moved on, hoping my subconscious would solve the computer-induced quandary.

Spell-check is wonderful. But I always give each document a line-by-line, word-by-word reading. Otherwise you end up with a paragraph like this, from a nonfiction proposal that once came my way:

> I remember at the age of twenty-one thinking surly marriage was eminent and my prince charming was right around the corner. With each passing birthday I would try to quite the ache in my heart with the thought "maybe this year."

Perhaps if she didn't want a marriage that stood out so much, she wouldn't be feeling surly. But I decided to "quite" my objections. Maybe I was the one being surly, condemning a writer for three correctly spelled typos in one short paragraph, not counting the lack of capitalization.

Then I turned the page and saw this:

> I was like many eighteen year old girls when I graduated from high school. When I walked down the isle with my diploma in hand, my sights were set on the next exciting chapter of my life, college.

Aisle not read further, I thought. It's no good atoll.

A half-hour later, my subconscious did its job and I returned to the canaries. With my editing knife, I cut them in two, then switched the order of two letters. Canaries = can arise.

> What potential tensions can arise from a transition in power, authority, responsibility, and promise, as we see with Abraham and Isaac?

The sentence now made sense, even if spell-check didn't care.

This previously appeared in the August 2012 issue of the Christian Writers Guild newsletter *WordSmith*.

Resources for You if You Want to Write Movies

by Dallas Jenkins

Note: Several resources listed below contain foul language or mature content—refer to these with that in mind. These represent my recommendations and not necessarily those of the Christian Writers Guild.

Books*

"Behind the scenes" industry titles:

Hello, He Lied
You'll Never Eat Lunch in This Town Again
*Adventures in the Screen Trade**
*Hollywood Animal**
*The Devil's Guide to Hollywood**
High Concept
Down and Dirty Pictures
Keys to the Kingdom

"How-to" titles:

Making Movies
Directors Close Up
Wannabe
Conversations with Directors
Thinking in Pictures
Rebel with a Camera (documentary)

"Making of" titles:

*Sex, Lies, and Videotape** (film)
*Do the Right Thing** (film)
*The Screenwriter's Problem Solver**
*Story**
*Save the Cat**

I recommend any book on the craft by K. Callan.

Best title on working with actors (nothing else comes close):

I'll Be in My Trailer

Magazines

Entertainment Weekly
Script Magazine
Moviemaker

*Best books and resources for screenwriters

Online Sites

Film Threat
Indiewire
Variety
IMDbPro

Movies

American Film Institute's list of the top 100 movies ever made
Best Picture nominees each year
Always watch commentaries, especially from writers/directors

Movies That Most Influenced Me

One Flew Over the Cuckoo's Nest
Jerry Maguire
It's a Wonderful Life
Erin Brockovich
Traffic
Magnolia

Filmmaking

With the technology available today, making a film is easier than ever. Start small and work your way up, getting something—anything—made. Festivals like "168" provide opportunities like that. If you can make something remarkable, it will break through and get attention. Talk to your pastor about doing a short film for a special service or holiday event.

PART 3
Specialty Markets

7

Greeting Card/Gift/Specialty Markets

This list contains both Christian/religious card publishers and secular publishers that have religious lines or produce some religious or inspirational cards. Secular companies may produce other lines of cards that are not consistent with your beliefs, and for a secular company, inspirational cards usually do not include religious imagery. Support groups for greeting card writers can be found at http://groups.yahoo.com/group/GreetingCardWriters.

CARD PUBLISHERS

***BLUE MOUNTAIN ARTS INC.,** PO Box 4549, Boulder CO 80306. (303) 449-0536. Fax (303) 447-0939. E-mail: editorial@sps.com. Website: www.sps.com. Submit to Editorial Department. General card publisher that does a few inspirational cards. Open to freelance; buys 50-100 ideas/yr. Prefers outright submissions. Pays $300 for all rts. for use on a greeting card, or $50 for onetime use in a book, on publication. No royalties. Responds in 12-16 wks. Uses unrhymed or traditional poetry; short or long, but no one-liners. Produces inspirational and sensitivity. Needs anniversary, birthday, Christmas, congratulations, Easter, Father's Day, friendship, get well, graduation, keep in touch, love, miss you, Mother's Day, new baby, please write, reaching for dreams, relatives, sympathy, thank you, valentines, wedding. Holiday/seasonal 6 mos. ahead. Open to ideas for new card lines. Send any number of ideas (1 per pg.). Open to ideas for gift books. Guidelines; no catalog.

Contest: Sponsors a poetry card contest online. Details on website.

Tips: "We are interested in reviewing poetry and writings for greeting cards, and expanding our field of freelance poetry writers."

***DAYSPRING CARDS INC.,** Editorial Department, PO Box 1010, 21154 Hwy. 16 East, Siloam Springs AR 72761. Fax (479) 524-9477. E-mail: info@dayspring.com (type "write" in message or subject line). Website: www.dayspring.com. Attn: Freelance Editor. Christian/religious card publisher. Please read guidelines before submitting. Prefers outright submission. Pays $60/idea on acceptance for all rts. No royalty. Responds in 4-8 wks. Uses unrhymed, traditional, light verse, conversational, contemporary; various lengths. Looking for inspirational cards for all occasions, including anniversary, birthday, relative birthday, congratulations, encouragement, friendship, get well, new baby, sympathy, thank you, wedding. Also needs seasonal cards for friends and family members for Christmas, Valentine's Day, Easter, Mother's Day, Father's Day, Thanksgiving, graduation, and Clergy Appreciation Day. Include Scripture verse with each submission. Send 10 ideas or less. Guidelines by phone or e-mail; no catalog.

Tips: Prefers submissions on 8.5 x 11 inch sheets, not 3x5 cards (one idea per sheet).

WARNER PRESS INC., 1201 E. 5th St., PO Box 2499, Anderson IN 46018-9988. (765) 644-7721. Fax (765) 640-8005. E-mail: rfogle@warnerpress.org. Website: www.warnerpress.org. Karen Rhodes, sr. ed.; Robin Fogle, ed. Producer of church, ministry, and kids' resources (greeting cards, bulletins, color/activity books, puzzle books). 30% freelance; buys 30-50 ideas/yr. Guidelines on website. Pays $30-35 on acceptance (for bulletins and greeting card copy). No royalties. Responds in 6-8 wks. Uses unrhymed, traditional verse, and devotionals for bulletins; 16-24 lines. Accepts 10 ideas/submission. Guidelines for bulletins; no catalog.

Also Does: We are in need of teaching resources for children's Sunday school or children's church. We are also interested in children's Bible studies (personal and small group) and

materials geared toward family ministry, Sunday school teachers' leadership and training, and children's ministry. Payment varies based on project.
Photos/Artwork: Accepts freelance photos and queries from freelance artists. E-mail curtis@warnerpress.org, Curtis Corzine, creative director.

GIFT/SPECIALTY-ITEM MARKETS

LORENZ CORP., PO Box 802, Dayton OH 45401. Toll-free (800) 444-1144, ext. 1. (937) 228-6118. Fax (937) 223-2042. E-mail: submit@lorenz.com or through website: www.lorenz.com. Piano, organ, choral, handbell, instrumental, and more. Guidelines online for music submissions; click on "Submissions."

BONUS SECTION

Writer's Helps

Fiction

Without a Sermon

by Gayle Roper

As a new writer, I felt I had to preach the gospel in every book. I've learned that any book can illustrate a spiritual truth, but not every book must be a salvation story.

How can you say what needs to be said spiritually but make it organic to your story?

Let Your Characters Speak

When you intrude as the author, your story suffers. But if your character struggles with integrity, when *he* realizes the truth that your sin will find you out and that sin has consequences, *bingo*, it resonates.

Readers are intelligent. You don't have to yell at them.

Example: Overkill

Sean watched Jerry being helped into the backseat of the police cruiser. That could have been him being shamed before the whole neighborhood. It *would* have been him sitting there if he'd stuck his foot over the line. His skin prickled at how close he'd come. No one'll know, Jerry'd said. And Sean had almost fallen for that lie. It was like the verse said, "Be sure your sin will find you out."

"Oh, Lord, you saved me from falling. Thank you!"

He looked at his wife and saw her disappointment in him. She knew how close he'd been skating to moral disaster.

"Marie, I'm sorry."

She gave him a sad smile and walked to the house. How could he prove to her that he loved her as Christ loved the church? That he regretted even tiptoeing near sin? Shoulders slumped, he watched the cops drive Jerry away.

Example: Less Is More

Sean watched Jerry being helped into the backseat of the police cruiser. That could have been him, shamed before the whole neighborhood. It would have been him if he'd stuck his foot over the line. His skin prickled at how close he'd come. No one'll know, Jerry'd said. And Sean had almost fallen for the lie.

He looked at his wife and saw her disappointment. In him. She understood much more than he'd realized.

"Marie." His voice cracked on the plea for understanding, forgiveness.

She gave a sad smile and walked back to the house.

He watched the police drive Jerry away.

In scene 2, I didn't spell out how conflicted Sean is, as I did in scene 1. We can tell without the words.

Truth Reveals Itself Over Time

Realization of truth may seem like it comes in one great burst of insight—but it doesn't. When we look back, we see a series of incidents led us to the decisive moment. So it needs to be with your characters.

This previously appeared on the Christian Writers Guild blog: www.christianwritersguild.com/blog/creating-a-spiritual-arc-without-a-sermon/.

Characters That Rival Scarlett and Rhett

by DiAnn Mills

WHO ARE YOUR FAVORITE CHARACTERS? Scarlett O'Hara and Rhett Butler from *Gone with the Wind*? Luke Skywalker and Princess Leia from *Star Wars*? Sam and Frodo? Ahab and the whale? The Lone Ranger and Tonto?

Why do such characters live on in our imaginations? What about them causes us to laugh and cry and wonder if they are all right?

The key is that the writer defined the characters with believable traits and clear motivations. They created characters we can care about.

How Can You Create Memorable Characters?

Firmly establish the wants and needs foundational for your character's critical motivation.

If I asked you to write down all the things you wanted, you might fill a book. But if I asked you to compile a list of what you need, the project becomes more difficult. We don't always know what we need, and finding out may require soul-searching.

When we create realistic needs for our characters—and those needs become their most sought after goals—suddenly we've motivated them to seek those things vital to their survival.

The Real Roots of Motivation

How *unmet* needs are fulfilled depends on your character's integrity, established over time through life experiences, heredity, culture, setting, and environment. No wonder we humans are flawed!

No protagonist should be perfect. No antagonist or villain should be completely evil. But some characters have more flaws than others—and out of those flaws come weaknesses and room for growth. Out of the admirable traits come our heroes and heroines, who have the stuff that gives us hope and helps us believe again in the goodness of flawed humans.

Weaknesses and Struggle

We all need relationships, significance, and security. We are supposed to allow God to meet these critical needs, but we are all flawed and often look for fulfillment in other areas. Those areas become our weaknesses.

Examine your character's struggle. Does he have a need for material goods, power, work, education? How are those weaknesses manifest? Does your character seek to satisfy his basic needs in ways that honor God?

Reaction and Response

Study your characters from every angle to determine the underlying factors that shove them out of bed each morning. Interview your characters. Live with them. Go to dinner with them. Place them in settings unlike those in previous scenes.

Their reactions and responses determine who they are. Steer away from predictable behavior, but stay within the bounds of the traits you've assigned to each.

Discover

The next time you read a dynamic novel or watch a movie that has you on the edge of your chair, try to determine why the characters gripped you. Discover who they are by examining their wants and needs, motivation, weaknesses, and reactions.

This previously appeared on the Christian Writers Guild blog: www.christianwritersguild.com/blog/memorable-characters-that-rival-scarlett-and-rhett/.

Is Anything Original?

by Deborah Raney

AFTER DISCOVERING I'd already written a book with a premise she thought was original to her work-in-progress, an aspiring novelist asked me, "Is anything original?"

That's an age-old question, one every writer has asked—even King Solomon (Ecclesiastes 1:9-10):

What has been will be again,
  what has been done will be done again;
  there is nothing new under the sun.
Is there anything of which one can say,
  "Look! This is something new"?
It was here already, long ago;
  it was here before our time. (NIV)

When a review for my novel *In the Still of Night*—about a woman who becomes pregnant as a result of rape—appeared in *Library Journal*, it followed a review of Francine Rivers's wonderful book *The Atonement Child*, about, of course, a woman who becomes pregnant as a result of rape. I could not believe it!

I know every story has been done before. But *no one*—not even Francine Rivers—could tell my story the way I did. Did mine sell as many copies as hers? Not even a fraction. But God used that book to touch lives—including the life of a real young woman who gave birth to a baby conceived through rape. Maybe my book was for her. It doesn't matter. I wrote the story God gave me, and that's all I could do.

If God has given you a story, tell it as only you can. God created you with a distinctive voice, unique life circumstances, and a way of telling the story that will resonate with certain readers. Your story will be as individual as a snowflake, as different from mine as you and I are from each other.

Don't be discouraged if your idea shows up in a book with someone else's name on the cover. Write your story anyway. There really is nothing new under the sun—except you!

This previously appeared on the Christian Writers Guild blog: www.christianwritersguild.com/blog/is-anything-original/.

Is Your Plot Believable?

by Sandra Byrd

YOU'RE BUILDING a world entirely from your own imagination. But to reach the hearts and minds of readers, you must base your fiction on the real world.

Weaving an unquestioningly believable plot is tough. You never want a reader to think, *I don't buy that* or *Too many coincidences*. To create believability, write scenes that are probable, possible, and plausible.

Probable: Likely; More Evidence for Than Against

Probable events raise no flags, and the reader continues without doubt. As long as they make sense within your story, there is no limit to the number of probable events you can use.

Possible: May or Can Be; Chance

More than a few possible events, especially at the beginning, signal the reader your story is contrived.

Plausible: Seemingly Worthy of Approval or Acceptance

What if, for the sake of your story, you need a *possible* circumstance to become *probable*? You make it plausible. Like a lawyer, you show evidence—and you do so without fanfare.

In my current manuscript, I needed someone to die of the plague. But this couldn't come out of the blue, so early on I mentioned that the plague had been on the increase. I even had a minor character die of the plague.

Later, when I killed someone off by plague, I'd already made it plausible.

This previously appeared on the Christian Writers Guild blog: www.christianwritersguild.com/blog/is-your-plot-believable/.

Writing as a Process of Discovery

by Jerry B. Jenkins

ABOUT HALF THE NOVELISTS I know are outliners, and half are not. Some need the safety net of an outline. Some outline so completely that the writing becomes filling in the blanks, yet somehow it works.

I prefer to write as a process of discovery.

I try to put interesting characters in difficult situations and write to find out what happens. If the story surprises and delights or shocks and scares me, it should have the same effect on the reader.

The last thing a novelist wants to be is predictable, and if you're not sure what's going to happen until it does, the reader sure won't be either.

Just Add Conflict

If a scene seems to stall, I remind myself that conflict is the soul of fiction. Say you write a conversation designed to give the reader important information. If it feels flat, have one character suddenly disagree or even insult the other.

"Of course you'd say that; that's the way you've always felt. If it were up to you, you'd let her get away with murder."

The other character will respond defensively, maybe with anger. And suddenly the scene is alive.

Give your characters opposing goals or opinions, and let the consequences play out in your mind, recording them as you go.

How much better to follow the story than to contrive it.

Sometimes I make a note or two to remind myself to finish a thought or a puzzle so I don't wind up with loose ends, but that's as close as I come to an outline.

Immediate Conflict

I began *Left Behind* with the line, "Rayford Steele's mind was on a woman he had never touched." I then immediately established that he is piloting a 747, has a wife and kids, and yet is daydreaming about a possible affair. That's on the edge of risqué for a novel in the inspirational market, and while I did not pursue any graphic details, you can see how that juxtaposition alone gave the reader enough to stay curious—and seemed to help the novel succeed. As novel structure guru James Scott Bell would say, it upset the *status quo*.

Trust Your Reader

Above all, give the reader credit and let him figure some things out for himself.

Show, don't tell, but don't show everything.

A Hemingway novel begins with a woman cutting bread and a boy delivering the *Paris Review* on cobblestone streets. Papa H. didn't have to come right out and say where the story was set.

Avoid clunky exposition; strive for subtlety. And write as a process of discovery.

It's a lot of fun—like reading and writing at the same time.

This previously appeared at Jerry Jenkins's personal blog: http://jerry-jenkins.com/2013/02/18/writing-as-a-process-of-discovery-3/.

Add Fireworks to Your Fiction

by James Scott Bell

> The only people for me are the mad ones, the ones who are mad to live, mad to talk, mad to be saved, desirous of everything at the same time, the ones who never yawn or say a commonplace thing, but burn, burn, burn like fabulous yellow roman candles exploding like spiders across the stars and in the middle you see the blue centerlight pop and everybody goes "Awww!"

Not only is that clip, from *On the Road* by Jack Kerouac, about fireworks, but it also demonstrates the power of fireworks in fiction. It's the heat and heart that produces an unforgettable reading experience.

Indefinable Power

This is the elusive concept called *voice*. It's something agents and editors talk about but no one seems able to define. They just know it when they see it. So do readers. It's the kind of writing that makes them all go, "Awww!"

How can you get that into your fiction? As Red Smith, the famous sportswriter, said, "There's nothing to writing. You just sit down at a typewriter and open a vein."

It means having skin in the game—having a heart for your material. If you don't feel it, the reader won't.

Craft Your Message

But you also must add craft. Sometimes writers think that because they have a message they believe in, or a concept that excites them, that's enough. It's not.

You must translate that into a story readers can relate to, and that's what the craft—fashioning plot, structure, characters, dialogue, description—is about.

Put it all together to get the spark that ignites fireworks.

Let the show begin.

This previously appeared on the Christian Writers Guild blog: www.christianwritersguild.com/blog/add-fireworks-to-your-fiction/.

Add Extra Dimension to Your Writing

by Bill Myers

RESEARCH IS THE BEST PART OF WRITING. What other job allows you to explore any topic you want while getting paid?

Follow a Paper Trail

For background in my novels, I read thirty to eighty books. Not always the entire book, but parts I find interesting or that will help ground my work in reality. I underline those sections, then catalog them by topic in my computer.

My novel *The Judas Gospel* involves a cop and a young prophetess who track down a serial killer. So one of my topics is "Police Procedure." Under that I type:

Title of research book

Page 53—forensic tests
Page 64—rookie mistakes
Page 76—smells at a murder site

Now I know exactly where to go as I'm writing to review the details and give the story depth and authenticity.

Go to the Source

The best tool—which many writers are too shy to pursue—is the personal interview. People love to talk about their work and experiences, even important people.

If you're too intimidated to call, ask a friend to be your assistant. I did this when I contacted the head of the CIA psychic research division. My friend called and said he was "Bill Myers's research assistant." He asked if we could schedule a time to talk—and it worked. By now I've interviewed serial killers, demoniacs, UFO abductees, professors, scientists, doctors, politicians, and the list goes on.

Go on Location

Yes, there's Google Earth, but it doesn't yet come with the sights, smells, and sounds that give your work that extra pop of authenticity. Visit the actual locations whenever possible. (Remember, your research expenses are tax deductible.)

Research provides added depth to your work. Details draw the reader in. So, what are you researching today?

This previously appeared on the Christian Writers Guild blog: www.christianwritersguild.com/blog/adding-extra-dimension-to-your-writing/.

Put Dialogue to Work

by Karen O'Connor

DIALOGUE PULLS READERS IN and keeps them reading. Make it obvious who said what without a bunch of *he saids* and *she saids*.

A much more interesting way to tell readers who is speaking is to have your characters do something as they speak.

Tag, You're It

Try replacing dialogue tags (attribution) with action that puts your character on stage. These are called *action tags* or *beats*. Example:

> **Dialogue tag:** "Papa, can you hear me?" Charlie said. "Is it Christmas in heaven, too?"
>
> **Action tag:** Charlie looked into the early morning sky. "Papa, can you hear me? Is it Christmas in heaven, too?" He blinked back tears. "I miss you."

The second example more completely captures the reader. The actions show rather than tell, and they keep the story moving.

The Name Game

Some writers clutter dialogue by repeating characters' names too frequently. When only two people populate a scene, this is unnecessary.

> "Charlie, is that you?" Mama said as she stood in the doorway in a frayed bathrobe.
>
> "Yes, Mama, it's me," Charlie said.
>
> "Charlie, I know you're sad. I am too." She opened her arms. "It's our first Christmas without your father."
>
> "I really miss him," Charlie said. "Mama," he added, as he ran to his mother, "Christmas isn't the same without Papa."

> "Charlie, is that you?" Mama said, standing in the doorway in a frayed bathrobe.
>
> "Yes, it's me." He blinked back tears.
>
> "I'm sad too." She opened her arms. "It's our first Christmas without your father."
>
> Charlie ran to her. "I really miss him. Christmas isn't the same without him."

Try these options to quickly improve your dialogue.

This previously appeared on the Christian Writers Guild blog: www.christianwritersguild.com/blog/put-dialogue-to-work/.

What's in a Name?

by Andy Scheer

DO YOU PUT AS MUCH EFFORT INTO naming your characters as you do titling your novel?

My experience at a recent writers conference, plus a novel I read en route, prompts me to ponder what's in a character's name.

Boys Named Sue

As expected, the writers whose work I reviewed ran the gamut from veterans to first-timers. But the name of one novel's protagonist cast a cloud over the entire work.

The name was Shamrock. A winsome Irish lass with a lilting brogue and long auburn locks floating over the heather, right?

Wrong. Shamrock was a guy. In contemporary New York City. With conventionally named parents who had given their other child a normal name. What was going on?

I should have seen it coming. The writer had targeted twentysomething readers and used an edgy style. That's one euphemism for first-person, present-tense with random punctuation. But a guy named Shamrock? Shades of that old Johnny Cash song.

Edwina's Insights

Talking to another novelist reassured me some writers remain dedicated to getting character names right. She mentioned how her parents came to name her Edwina. I'd never have expected her to carry that name. But as I got to know her, the name fit perfectly.

She mentioned she never gave two major characters names that began with the same initial. Why risk confusing the reader? We talked about how names reflect time and culture. And she pointed to a great source for names for people of a given place and generation: high school yearbooks.

Shane Quintana

Flying home from the conference, I enjoyed John Dunning's 1995 *New York Times* "notable book of the year," *The Bookman's Wake,* a mystery that explores the dark side of book collecting.

The woman who holds the key to the book's MacGuffin was born in 1969. Her family name is Rigby. Her parents named her Eleanor.

Through much of the novel, cop-turned-rare-book-dealer Cliff Janeway tries to evade a determined Seattle police officer identified only as Quintana. The name suggests a man at odds with expectations. A scene near the end—when Janeway finally meets Quintana—reinforces that impression.

> I asked if he had a first name.
>
> "Shane," he said, daring me not to like it.
>
> But I couldn't play it straight. "Shane *Quintana?*" . . .
>
> "I was named after Alan Ladd. Kids today don't even know who . . . Alan Ladd was."

Dunning needed these characters to resolve their differences, and he needed to show another side of the Seattle cop. Revealing an unexpected first name and the story behind it helped accomplish those goals.

What's in a character name? Potentially a lot.

This previously appeared on the Christian Writers Guild blog: www.christianwritersguild.com/blog/whats-in-a-name-2/.

Bonding through Backstory

by James Scott Bell

SOME WRITING TEACHERS argue there should be no backstory in your opening chapters because backstory has happened before your narrative begins. They suggest establishing the action first to get readers locked in.

Create a Connection

But I advocate that in your opening your strategy is to bond your character with the reader. Without that, readers won't care about the action. Properly used, backstory can create this emotional attachment. Fiction is, after all, an emotional experience.

I also stress *properly used*. That means the backstory is marbled within the action, not standing alone demanding to be read. Two guys who do this really well also happen to be two of the bestselling novelists of our time: Stephen King and Dean Koontz.

Start with Action

Let readers see a character in motion, doing something. Make sure there's trouble, even minor, and then give them bite-sized bits, or several paragraphs (if written well) of backstory.

An early Koontz novel (when he was using the pseudonym Leigh Nichols), *The Servants of Twilight,* opens with a mother and her six-year-old son at a shopping mall (after an opening line that portends trouble, of course). On page one Koontz drops this in:

> To Christine, Joey sometimes seemed to be a little old man in a six-year-old boy's small body. Occasionally he said the most amazingly grown-up things, and he usually had the patience of an adult, and he was often wiser than his years.
>
> But at other times, especially when he asked where his daddy was or why his daddy had gone away—or even when he *didn't* ask but just stood there with the question shimmering in his eyes—he looked so innocent, fragile, so heartbreakingly vulnerable that she just had to grab him and hug him.

Koontz bonds us with this lead character through sympathy. We don't know why the boy's father isn't there, but we don't have to know right away, do we? In this way Koontz also creates a little mystery that makes us want to keep on reading. But then he gets right back to the action, which is key.

Some time ago I interviewed Laura Caldwell, author of the Izzy McNeil series. She said:

> I wish I'd known how to weave in background information instead of dumping it in big chunks. It's still something I struggle with, although I think I've improved a lot. It's a skill that has to constantly be refined so the background information which gets delivered reads and feels organic at that point in the story.

If you can master this skill, you will be well on your way to creating that all-important emotional bond between your reader and your character.

This previously appeared on the Christian Writers Guild blog: www.christianwritersguild.com/blog/bonding-through-backstory/.

Pointers from My Dogs

by Angela Hunt

I'VE SPENT HOURS agonizing over whether to use the term *slacks* or *dress pants* in a sentence, and my two dogs have served as a welcome distraction. I live with a couple of two-hundred-pound mastiffs. Charley Gansky, the seven-year-old, is a big wimp, but he's smart. Babe, our six-year-old, is territorial and thick as a brick.

If you throw a bone to Charley, he'll catch it. Babe? She goes cross-eyed as it hits her on the nose.

Babe likes to throw herself at our windows and front door when a stranger approaches. She's broken so many, I've taken to setting a dining room chair in front of the door. She could move it with one swipe of her massive paw, but doesn't.

But Charley lets nothing stand in his way. When he wants something, he moves chairs, pushes fences, and opens doors. Fortunately, he has sense enough not to throw himself at glass partitions.

Pointing at What?

How did I determine their IQs? Simple. When I point to something in the other room, Charley looks in the other room. Babe looks at my hand.

So while playing with them, I had a writing epiphany: To train a dog to look where you're pointing, *you have to make the object being pointed out more interesting than your hand.*

In my fiction, if I focus on pretty words, flowing language, or musical metaphors, the reader will look at my hand. It's not that my reader is as dense as Babe; it's that I'm intruding. Maybe even showing off.

The trick is to make the object in the distance—the message of the story—more arresting than my language. If I pull it off, I have a happier reader.

Now, *slacks* or *dress pants*. Which draws attention to my hand?

This previously appeared on the Christian Writers Guild blog: www.christianwritersguild.com/blog/schooled-by-my-dogs/.

Learning from Tom Sawyer

by Jerry B. Jenkins

No, not that Tom Sawyer. Thomas B. Sawyer was head writer and producer of the hit TV series *Murder, She Wrote*. He has written nine network series pilots, a hundred episode scripts, and has worked on fifteen series.

He's been nominated for both an Edgar and an Emmy and was cocreator of Plots Unlimited software and its successor, Storybase. But for now let me exult about Tom's book *Fiction Writing Demystified: Techniques That Will Make You a More Successful Writer*.

I read every writing book I can find, and this is easily the best I've seen since Dean Koontz's *How to Write Bestselling Fiction* in 1981. My enthusiasm for Koontz's book has been corroborated by the fact it has been selling for several hundred dollars per first edition at used-book stores and online.

On vacation shortly before tackling a deadline, I took *Fiction Writing Demystified* with me and nearly beat it to death. The cover is curled; chlorine from the pool stains the pages whose dog-eared corners mark many *aha!* moments.

I let Tom know how thrilled I was with his book and that I would be urging writers at every stage of their careers to check it out. [Caution: it contains some earthy language.]

Gems from Tom Sawyer's Book

Perhaps, like Tom, you'll find you seem to instinctively know more than you thought you did, "the result, I suspect, of an almost universal, close-to-saturation exposure—by the time we reach adulthood—to stories, of our having read or viewed or otherwise absorbed hundreds or even thousands of them—from the classic children's tales to countless episodes of *I Love Lucy* and other shows, to movies, novels, and so on."

Do you need to be reminded, as I do, that as writers we are entertainers? Sawyer writes, "No matter how lofty our literary intentions, [we] want an audience, or we *hope* to find one . . . and we want to hold its attention. Strike that: we *must* hold its attention. . . . To accomplish that, we *must* entertain. It's an obligation. This is true whether we're poets, peddlers, or preachers."

Never forget that your novel needs what Sawyer calls "the money scene," which he describes as "the facedown on the dusty Western street, the big emotional moment between two of your characters, the climactic battle, or the solitary protagonist's instant of revelation."

This previously appeared at Jerry Jenkins's personal blog: http://jerry-jenkins.com/2013/06/03/learning-from-tom-sawyer-2/.

Stopping Stop-itis in Fiction

by Les Stobbe

MANY READERS CAN DEVELOP *STOP-ITIS*, a deadly malady to your novel. Here are five tips to create fiction immune to stop-itis.

1. Who's the Good Guy?

A lack of clarity about who to root for can make readers stop reading. If readers do not fall in love with the protagonist in the first chapter and develop a distaste for the antagonist (or admiration for her or his genius), stop-itis is likely.

2. Too Much Backstory

I see this in too many fiction proposals. Don't be so intent on setting the story in context that you forget today's readers want action and conflict now—right now. Don't make them wait.

3. Lack of Clarity

If your readers ask, "Why is this happening?" or "What's going on here?" they can succumb to stop-itis. But if you have a clear plot outline and remind yourself of it at the start of every chapter, your readers will not want to stop reading.

4. Offended Sensibilities

If readers develop moral outrage at what one of your characters does or says, stop-itis can occur. Suppose the interaction between a couple offends a reader's perception of how a man should treat a woman. Even if your story has a compelling plot that requires the interaction, the reader may set aside your novel.

I'm not advocating milquetoast characters, but be aware of the possibility of offense so you can mitigate the problem before it occurs.

5. Overuse of Scripture

I believe the Bible is inspired and useful for reproof, correction, and inspiration—but beginning fiction writers often overwhelm readers with truth. They insert Scripture in and out of context and slow the story so much that stop-itis occurs.

This previously appeared on the Christian Writers Guild blog: www.christianwritersguild.com/blog/stopping-stop-itis-in-fiction/.

Self-Editing Tips for Fiction Writers

by Danielle Grandinetti

THE FIRST DRAFT of your story is complete. Now it's time to refine your work through self-editing. I approach this task through three layers.

Layer 1: Overall Story Structure

Where is the true beginning of your story? For many novelists, it's hidden in chapter two. Does the plot flow seamlessly in ever-intensifying fashion—or are there holes to fill and scenes to cut? Does each scene begin in the middle of the action and end before it dies? Are the main characters living, breathing people with flaws and strengths? Does the setting evoke a vivid picture? Is point of view established immediately in every scene? Does your dialogue carry tension? Will the ending leave your reader satisfied?

Don't be afraid to delete whole sections or rewrite entire chapters. If a scene doesn't feel right, read it aloud. Your ear will catch a lot of what your eye misses. If you have trouble killing your darlings (deleting favorite passages), put them in a separate document, but if they don't fit in your manuscript, let them go.

Layer 2: Mechanics

Take out your fine-tooth comb, highlight every adverb and adjective, then ask whether a stronger verb or noun would do the job better. When in doubt, delete the adverb or adjective.

Next, search your manuscript for the word *was*. These usually signify passive sentences, so you'll want to rewrite those. Also search for weaselly words like *that* and *very*—most can be deleted. Short sentences and paragraphs give the appearance of faster action. Double-check your spelling and grammar because spell-check doesn't catch everything.

Layer 3: Whole Document

Print out your story, double spaced, and read it carefully in one sitting, if possible. Some writers catch more this way than by editing on a computer screen.

Instead of stopping to fix a mistake or smooth a passage, make a note in the margin and return to it later. Look for anything that will jerk the reader from the story world.

Self-editing is a powerful tool. Trust your instincts. If it sounds off, fix it. The Delete button is your friend.

This previously appeared on the Christian Writers Guild blog: www.christianwritersguild.com/blog/self-editing-tips-for-fiction-writers/.

What Makes Fiction Christian

by Gayle Roper

Too much fiction today fails to consider spiritual issues. That men and women would actually ponder God and his place in their lives doesn't seem to occur to most writers, or if it does, they don't let these knotty issues bleed into their writing.

Christians, on the other hand, bring certain assumptions and convictions to our characters and our plots because we are believers in Jesus. We assume underlying truths:

- The depravity of man affects even our heroes and heroines.
- The grace of God transforms lives, even the lives of our villains.
- The heart of man is either in rebellion against God (and therefore our characters are capable of any evil) or in submission to him (and therefore our believing characters are capable of any strength).
- Our characters have a vacuum that can be filled only by the presence of Christ.
- Our characters can't self-actualize, but they can grow and become more than they were because of a developing relationship with God.
- The love of God is a legitimate motive for action, and the power of God is a reasonable cause for change.

God's Story in Your Story

The trick is translating our beliefs into logical stories with characters who live and breathe. Everyone likes a good story, and we recognize Scripture as God's story. We teach our children about the adventures of Bible characters and encourage them to visit story worlds like Narnia. And we devour by the score adventures, romances, mysteries, and speculative books.

Story doesn't lecture. Story doesn't point fingers. Story shows.

Readers invest in our characters—these imagined people who work out the complications in their lives. In so doing, readers—real people with real complications—find patterns they can apply in their lives. No sermons. No harangues. Patterns based in Truth. Patterns offering hope.

And, because it's a story, the patterns are bound in a tale so rich and lively, it keeps them turning the pages.

This previously appeared on the Christian Writers Guild blog: www.christianwritersguild.com/blog/what-makes-fiction-christian%E2%80%94or-not/.

PART 4

Support for Writers

8

Christian Writers' Conferences and Workshops

(*) before a listing indicates unconfirmed or no information update.

ALABAMA

SOUTHERN CHRISTIAN WRITERS CONFERENCE. Tuscaloosa/First Baptist Church; early June. Contact: Joanne Sloan, SCWC, PO Box 1106, Northport AL 35476. (205) 333-8603. E-mail: SCWCworkshop@bellsouth.net. Website: www.scwconference.com. Editors/agents in attendance. Attendance: 200+.

ARIZONA

AMERICAN CHRISTIAN WRITERS MENTORING RETREAT. Phoenix, Grace Inn; October 31–November 1, 2014. Contact: Reg A. Forder, PO Box 110390, Nashville TN 37222. Toll-free (800) 21-WRITE. E-mail: ACWriters@aol.com. Website: www.ACWriters.com. Attendance: 40-80.

ARKANSAS

SILOAM SPRINGS WRITERS WORKSHOP. Siloam Springs; October 2014. Director: Rachel Kulp. E-mail: Rachelck@centurylink.net.

CALIFORNIA

***ACT ONE: WRITING PROGRAM.** Hollywood. Contact: Terence Berry, 2690 N. Beachwood Dr., Hollywood CA 90068. (323) 464-0815. Fax (323) 468-0315. E-mail: information@actoneprogram.com. Website: www.ActOneProgram.com. Act One offers an intensive training program for screenwriters, taught by professionals working in Hollywood. We also offer a Script Consulting service and run a Screenplay Competition with a $5,000 cash prize. Speakers: Barbara Nicolosi, David McFadzean, Karen Hall, Ron Austin, Bill Marsilli, and more. See website for bios.

CASTRO VALLEY CHRISTIAN WRITERS SEMINAR. Castro Valley; February 21–22, 2014. Contact: Pastor Jon Drury, 19300 Redwood Rd., Castro Valley CA 94546-3465. (510) 886-6300. E-mail: jdrury@redwoodchapel.org. Website: www.christianwriter.org. No editors/agents in attendance. Speaker: Susy Flory. Offers full or partial scholarships. We offer 40 writing workshops. Written critiques available for fee if website guidelines are followed. CDs of all workshops available after seminar (see list on website).

CHAIRS (The Christian Authors, Illustrators, and Readers Society). Contact: Nancy I. Sanders, 6361 Prescott Court, Chino CA 91710. (909) 590-0226. E-mail: jeffandnancys@gmail.com. Website: www.nancyisanders.com. Occasional writer's mentor groups and classes for children's writers. Some events are free and some require registration and a fee. Contact for more information.

MOUNT HERMON CHRISTIAN WRITERS CONFERENCE. Mount Hermon (near Santa Cruz); April 11–15, 2014. Website: www.mounthermon.org/writers. (888) MH-CAMPS. Keynote speaker: Glenna Salsbury. Offering instruction for all levels of writers, professional to beginner (including special track for teen writers). Many well-known editors and agents in attendance. Offers partial scholarships *on tuition only*. Awards for a variety of writing genres. Mentoring Clinic two days before Writers Conference, April 9–11. All details on website November 1 (no brochure). Faculty: 50. Writers: 400. Director: Rachel A. Williams.

***MOUNT HERMON HEAD-START MENTORING CLINIC.** Mount Hermon; April 9–11, 2014. This mentoring session is held the two days prior to the regular spring conference. See the listing for Mount Hermon Christian Writers Conference for details or www.mounthermon.org.

NATIONAL CHRISTIAN WRITERS CONFERENCE. San Diego; March 2014. Contact: Antonio L. Crawford, PO Box 1458, National City CA 91951-1458. (619) 791-5810. E-mail: ncwcsd@yahoo.com. Website: nationalchristianwritersconference.com.

***ORANGE COUNTY CHRISTIAN WRITERS FELLOWSHIP SPRING WRITERS DAY.** Orange County. Contact: John DeSimone, dir.; PO Box 1173, Orange CA 92856. (714) 244-0554. E-mail: john@occwf.org. Website: www.occwf.org. Consult with editors, agents, published authors. Offers full and partial scholarships. See website for list of faculty and conference details. Attendance: 150+.

SAN DIEGO CHRISTIAN WRITER'S GUILD FALL CONFERENCE. San Diego; October. Contact: Jennie Gillespie, PO Box 270403, San Diego CA 92198. (760) 294-3269. E-mail: info@sandiegocwg.org. Website: www.sandiegocwg.org. Offers an advanced track. Editors/agents in attendance. Offers some scholarships. Attendance: 200.

***SANTA BARBARA CHRISTIAN WRITERS CONFERENCE.** Westmont College. Contact: Opal Mae Dailey, PO Box 40860, Santa Barbara CA 93140. Phone/fax (805) 682-0316 (call first for fax). E-mail: opalmaedailey@aol.com. Website: www.CWGSB.com. Offers scholarships to students.

SOCIETY OF CHILDREN'S BOOK WRITERS & ILLUSTRATORS CONFERENCE IN CHILDREN'S LITERATURE. Los Angeles; early August. Society of Children's Book Writers & Illustrators. Contact: Lin Oliver, 8271 Beverly Blvd., Los Angeles CA 90048. (323) 782-1010. Fax (323) 782-1892. E-mail: scbwi@scbwi.org. Website: www.scbwi.org. Includes a track for professionals. Editors/agents in attendance. Attendance: 900.

WRITER'S SYMPOSIUM BY THE SEA. San Diego/Point Loma Nazarene University; February 25–27, 2014. Contact: Dean Nelson, Professor, Journalism Dept., PLNU, 3900 Lomaland Dr., San Diego CA 92106. (619) 849-2592. Fax (619) 849-2566. E-mail: deannelson@pointloma.edu. Website: www.pointloma.edu/writers. Speakers, interviews, and workshops. No scholarships. Attendance: 500.

***WRITE TO INSPIRE.** Elk Grove. Contact: Elizabeth M. Thompson, PO Box 276794, Sacramento CA 95827-6794. (916) 607-7796. E-mail: inspiregroup@comcast.net. Website: www.InspireWriters.com. Contests: Fiction and Nonfiction—limited to writers unpublished by traditional publishers, or published only in anthologies, compilations, or periodicals. May have 3rd contest for one sheet (check website). Information about the contests is available at www.InspireWriters.com. Offers full scholarships (pay half the hotel and lunch on Saturday is included. Limited by availability and meeting requirements on website).

COLORADO

COLORADO CHRISTIAN WRITERS CONFERENCE. Estes Park; May 14–17, 2014, at the YMCA of the Rockies, Estes Park Center. Director: Marlene Bagnull, LittD, 951 Anders Rd., Lansdale PA 19446. Phone/fax (484) 991-8581. E-mail: mbagnull@aol.com. Website: www.writehisanswer.com/Colorado. Conferees choose 6 hour-long workshops from 42 offered or a clinic—fiction, nonfiction, and speakers—by application) plus one six-hour continuing session from 8 offered. Four 15-minute one-on-one appointments, paid critiques, editors' panels, and general sessions. Early bird workshops Wednesday afternoon. Teens Write all day Saturday, plus teens are welcome to attend the entire conference at 60% off. Contest for published and not-yet-published writers (only open to conferees) awards two 50% discounts off 2014 conference registration fee. Faculty of 50 authors, editors, and agents. Attendance: 225. Offers partial scholarships.

JERRY B. JENKINS CHRISTIAN WRITERS GUILD WRITING FOR THE SOUL CONFERENCE. The Broadmoor, Colorado Springs; February 13–16, 2014. Sponsored by the Jerry B. Jenkins Christian Writers Guild. Host: Jerry B. Jenkins. Speakers/Teachers: James Scott Bell, Brandilyn Collins, Dennis E. Hensley, Angela Hunt, Sammy Tippit, C. McNair Wilson. Payment plans available. General sessions with national keynote speakers and in-depth workshops. Contact: Christian Writers Guild, 5525 N. Union Blvd., Ste. 101, Colorado Springs CO 80918. Toll-free (866) 495-5177. Fax (719) 495-5181. E-mail: ContactUs@christianwritersguild.com. Website: www.ChristianWritersGuild.com. Attendance: 300.

DISTRICT OF COLUMBIA

NATIONAL CHRISTIAN WRITERS CONFERENCE. Washington DC; October 2014. Contact: Antonio L. Crawford, PO Box 1458, National City CA 91951-1458. (619) 791-5810. E-mail: ncwcsd@yahoo.com. Website: www.nationalchristianwritersconference.com.

FLORIDA

AMERICAN CHRISTIAN WRITERS MENTORING RETREAT. Orlando, Ramada Inn Disney; November 21–22, 2014. Contact: Reg A. Forder, PO Box 110390, Nashville TN 37222. Toll-free (800) 21-WRITE. E-mail: ACWriters@aol.com. Website: www.ACWriters.com. Attendance: 40-80.

***DEEP THINKERS RETREAT.** February. Contact: Susan May Warren, PO Box 1290, Grand Marais MN 55604. E-mail: retreats@mybooktherapy.com. Website: http://deepthinkers.mybooktherapy.com. Offers an advanced track. This five-day retreat is for novelists who want to bring their writing to a new level, with deeper characterization, stronger wordsmithing, and a more compelling plot. Speakers: Susan May Warren, Rachel Hauck. No scholarships. Each retreat attendee receives a private consultation about his or her writing. If ready for advanced writing techniques, we teach that. Sponsors the My Book Therapy Frasier Contest. Attendance: 16.

FLORIDA CHRISTIAN WRITERS CONFERENCE. Lake Yale; February 26–March 2, 2014. Contact: Eva Marie Everson/Mark Hancock, 530 Lake Kathryn Circle, Casselberry FL 32707. (407) 414-8188. E-mail: FloridaCWC@aol.com. Website: www.FloridaCWC.net. Special classes for adv writers and teens. Contest (see website). Keynote speakers/editors/agents. Offers scholarships. Attendance: 250. Offers advanced track (15 hours of class time—by application only) and teen track.

GEORGIA

AMERICAN CHRISTIAN WRITERS MENTORING RETREAT. Atlanta, Hotel Indego; July 11–12, 2014. Contact: Reg Forder, Box 110390, Nashville TN 37222. Toll-free (800) 21-WRITE. E-mail: ACWriters@aol.com. Website: www.ACWriters.com. Attendance: 40-80.

***CATCH THE WAVE WRITERS CONFERENCE.** Contact: Cynthia L. Simmons, 322 Homestead Circle, Kennesaw GA 30144. (770) 926-8627. Fax: same number. E-mail: clsimm@comcast.net. Offers well-rounded curriculum. Keynote speakers: Lin Johnson, Tiffany Colter. Editors and agents attend. Full and partial scholarships offered.

***EAST METRO ATLANTA CHRISTIAN WRITERS CONFERENCE.** Meets the second Saturday of each month from 10:00 a.m. to noon at Georgia Piedmont Technical College, 8100 Bob Williams Parkway, Covington GA 30014. Call for information and dates regarding our two-day annual conference and writing contest. (404) 444-7514. Website: www.emacw.org. EMACW is a chapter of the American Christian Writers. Dues $60.00 annually. Our mission is to educate, encourage, and engage the writer.

IDAHO

ANNUAL IDAHOPE WRITERS' CONFERENCE. Boise. PO Box 922, Meridian ID 83680-0922. E-mail: info@idahopewriters.org. Website: http://idahopewriters.org/conference. Keynote speakers multi-published authors, agents, or editors. Contest. Attendance: 40-50.

ILLINOIS

***KARITOS CHRISTIAN ARTS CONFERENCE.** The 20th Annual Karitos Christian Arts Conference. Karitos is unique among conferences for Christian artists in that it brings all of the arts together. In 2012, a 50-person faculty offered workshops in Literary Arts, Music, Dance/Mime, Visual Arts, Film, Theater, and Worship. Three-hour evening celebrations saw the different disciplines coming together on stage for times of extravagant worship, exciting performances, and powerful teaching. More information is available at www.karitos.com.

WRITE-TO-PUBLISH CONFERENCE. Wheaton (Chicago area); June 4–7, 2014. Contact: Lin Johnson, 9118 W. Elmwood Dr., Ste. 1G, Niles IL 60714-5820. (847) 296-3964. Fax (847) 296-0754. E-mail: lin@writetopublish.com. Website: www.writetopublish.com. Offers freelance career track (prerequisite: 1 published book). Majority of faculty are editors and agents. Attendance: 225.

INDIANA

***MIDWEST WRITERS WORKSHOP.** Muncie/Ball State University Alumni Center (always the last Thursday, Friday, and Saturday of July). Our 40th summer workshop! Contact: Dept. of English, Ball State University, Muncie IN 47306-0484. Director: Jama Kehoe Bigger. (765) 282-1055. E-mail: midwest writers@yahoo.com. Website: www.midwestwriters.org. Sponsors a contest. Editors/agents in attendance. Attendance: 150.

IOWA

***CHRISTIAN WRITERS SEMINAR.** Arnolds Park. Contact: Denise Triggs, PO Box 709, Arnolds Park IA 51331. (712) 332-7191. E-mail: waterfalls42@hotmail.com. Website: www.waterfallsretreats.com. No editors/agents in attendance. Scholarships. Attendance: 20-30.

KANSAS

***CALLED TO WRITE.** Pittsburg. Contact: Joyce Love, 1676 Express Rd, Fort Scott KS 66701. (620) 547-2596; E-mail: clove@ckt.net. Website: www.christianwritersfellowship.blogspot.com. Contest for attendees only. Offers full and partial scholarships. Attendance: 75.

KENTUCKY

KENTUCKY CHRISTIAN WRITERS CONFERENCE. Elizabethtown. Director/Contact: Barbara Wells, 4253 Edgewood Ct., Owensboro KY 42303-7609. (270) 683-5920. E-mail: barbara5122@msn.com. Website: www.kychristianwriters.com. June 19–21, 2014. Keynote: Liz Curtis Higgs. Editors/agents in attendance. Offers scholarships. Contest: see website. Attendance 80-100.

MICHIGAN

AMERICAN CHRISTIAN WRITERS MENTORING RETREAT. Grand Rapids, Ramada Plaza Hotel; June 6–7, 2014. Contact: Reg Forder, PO Box 110390, Nashville TN 37222. Toll-free (800) 21-WRITE. E-mail: ACWriters@aol.com. Website: www.ACWriters.com. Attendance: 40-80.

BREATHE CHRISTIAN WRITERS CONFERENCE. Grand Rapids area; October 2014 (exact dates TBD). Contact: Breathe Christian Writers Conference, 3148 Plainfield Ave. NE, Ste. 237, Grand Rapids MI 49525-3285. E-mail: breathewritersconference@gmail.com. Website: www.breatheconference.com. Editors/agents in attendance; limited scholarships. Attendance: 125.

***FAITH WRITERS CONFERENCE.** Faith Writers' 2014 international writing conference is the second weekend in August. Join us for a time of fellowship and teaching from Faith Writers' own skilled members. These conferences are known for being different—as much about support and encouragement as about writing facts and skills. US location to be announced. Check www.faithwriters.com/conference.php for more information.

***FESTIVAL OF FAITH & WRITING.** Grand Rapids; April 2014 (exact dates TBD, held every other year). Contact: Shelly LeMahieu Dunn, 1795 Knollcrest Circle S.E., Grand Rapids MI 49546. (616) 526-6770. E-mail: ffw@calvin.edu. Website: festival.calvin.edu. Editors/agents in attendance; no scholarships. Attendance: 1,800.

MARANATHA CHRISTIAN WRITERS' CONFERENCE. Located on the shore of Lake Michigan. September 24–27, 2014. Contact: Maranatha, 4759 Lake Harbor Rd., Muskegon MI 49441-5299. (231) 798-2161. E-mail: info@writewithpurpose.org. Check website for details and online registration. Website: www.WriteWithPurpose.org. Our experts offer contests, continuing courses, and a wide variety of elective workshops. Focus is on personal attention and up-to-date information to help you meet your goals. Consultations with agents, editors, and publishers included in tuition. Scholarships available. Attendance: 125.

MINNESOTA

AMERICAN CHRISTIAN WRITERS MENTORING RETREAT. Minneapolis, Country Inn & Suites; August 1–2, 2014. Contact: Reg Forder, PO Box 110390, Nashville TN 37222. Toll-free (800) 21-WRITE. Website: www.ACWriters.com. Attendance: 40-80.

***STORYCRAFTERS RETREAT.** Minneapolis. Contact: Susan May Warren, PO Box 1290, Grand Marais MN 55604. (218) 387-2853. E-mail: retreats@mybooktherapy.com. Website: http://storycrafters.mybooktherapy.com. This private coaching retreat is for writers at all levels. We focus on storycrafting—starting with an idea, and leaving with a plotted story. Sponsors the My Book Therapy Frasier Contest (winner attends retreat for free). Limit 16.

MISSOURI

***HEART OF AMERICA CHRISTIAN WRITERS NETWORK CONFERENCES.** Kansas City. Check website for dates of additional events. Contact: Jeanette Littleton, 3706 N.E. Shady Lane Dr., Gladstone MO 64119. Phone/fax (816) 459-8016. E-mail: HACWN@earthlink.net. Website: www.HACWN.org. Offers classes for new and advanced writers. Editors/agents in attendance. Contest details on brochure. Attendance: 125.

NEW HAMPSHIRE

***WRITERS WORKSHOPS FOR ADULTS & YOUNG WRITERS BY MARY EMMA ALLEN.** Taught on request by writers' groups, conferences, schools, and libraries. Topics include Workshops for Young Writers (for schools and home-schooling groups); Writing Your Family Stories; Scrapbooking Your Stories. Contact: Mary Emma Allen (instructor), 55 Binks Hill Rd., Plymouth NH 03264. (603) 536-2641. E-mail: me.allen@juno.com. Blogs: http://maryemmallen.blogspot.com.

NEW MEXICO

CLASS CHRISTIAN WRITERS CONFERENCE. Albuquerque's First Baptist Church; Fall 2014 (see website for date). Editors and agents in attendance. Contact: Linda Gilden, director, PO Box 36551, Albuquerque NM 87176. E-mail: linda@lindagilden.com. Website: www.classeminars.org. Scholarships may be available. Attendance: 150.

SOUTHWEST WRITERS MINI WORKSHOPS. Albuquerque; various times during the year (check website for dates). Contact: Conference Chair, 3200 Carlisle Blvd. NE, Ste. 114, Albuquerque NM

87110. (505) 830-6034. E-mail: swwriters@juno.com. Website: www.southwestwriters.com. General conference. Sponsors the Southwest Writers Contests annually and bimonthly (see website). Agents/editors in attendance. Attendance: 50.

NEW YORK

SOCIETY OF CHILDREN'S BOOK WRITERS & ILLUSTRATORS CONFERENCE IN CHILDREN'S LITERATURE. New York City; early February. Society of Children's Book Writers & Illustrators. Contact: Lin Oliver, 8271 Beverly Blvd., Los Angeles CA 90048. (323) 782-1010. Fax (323) 782-1892. E-mail: scbwi@scbwi.org. Website: www.scbwi.org. Includes a track for professionals. Editors/agents in attendance. Attendance: 900.

NORTH CAROLINA

BLUE RIDGE MOUNTAINS CHRISTIAN WRITERS CONFERENCE. LifeWay Ridgecrest Conference Center; May 18–22, 2014. Contact: Alton Gansky, 4721 W. Princeton Ave., Fresno CA 93722. (760) 220-1075. E-mail: alton@ganskycommunications.com. Website: www.brmcwc.com, or http://ridgecrestconferencecenter.org/event/blueridgemountainchristianwritersconference. Offers an advanced track. Editors and agents in attendance. Sponsors three contests (details at www.brmcwc.com). Offers limited scholarships. Attendance: 350.

WRITE2IGNITE. Conference for Christian Writers of Literature for Children and Young Adults. March 28–29, 2014. Contact: Jean Hall, Director, PO Box 1101, Indian Trail NC 28079. (704) 238-0491. E-mail: write2ignite@jeanmatthewhall.com.

OHIO

NORTHWEST OHIO CHRISTIAN WRITERS. Contact: Shelley R. Lee, Pres. shelleyrlee@gmail.com., Kathy Douglas, VP, mlka@toast.net. Meets 5-6 times a year at St. Mark's Church, Bowling Green OH. Spring retreat and fall seminar with a nationally known author or editor. Meetings are free and open to public. More detail and full schedule found at www.nwocw.org.

PEN TO PAPER LITERARY SYMPOSIUM. Dayton; October 4, 2014. Contact: Valerie J. Lewis Colman, Pen of the Writer, 893 S. Main St., PMB 175, Englewood OH 45322. (888) 802-1802. E-mail: info@penofthewriter.com. Website: www.penofthewriter.com. Editors in attendance. No scholarships. Attendance: 30.

OKLAHOMA

AMERICAN CHRISTIAN WRITERS MENTORING RETREAT. Oklahoma City, LaQuinta Hotel; April 11–12, 2014. Contact: Reg Forder, Box 110390, Nashville TN 37222. Toll-free (800) 21-WRITE. E-mail: ACWriters@aol.com. Website: www.ACWriters.com. Attendance: 40-80.

OREGON

OREGON CHRISTIAN WRITERS SUMMER COACHING CONFERENCE. Portland; August 4–7, 2014. Allen Arnold keynoting. Contact: Lindy Jacobs. E-mail: summerconference@oregonchristianwriters.org. Website: www.OregonChristianWriters.org. Includes about 7 hours of training under a specific coach/topic and more than 30 hour-long afternoon workshops on a variety of writing-related topics. Editors/agents in attendance. Mentoring and manuscript reviews. Offers partial scholarships to members who apply. Attendance: 250. OCW also offers 3 one-day Saturday conferences—winter in Salem, spring in Eugene, and fall in Portland. Check the website for more information on all conferences.

PENNSYLVANIA

GREATER PHILADELPHIA CHRISTIAN WRITERS CONFERENCE. Cairn University (formerly Philadelphia Biblical University), Langhorne; July 30–August 2 or August 6–9, 2014. Founder and director: Marlene Bagnull, LittD, 951 Anders Rd., Lansdale PA 19446. Phone/fax (484) 991-8581. E-mail: mbagnull@aol.com. Website: www.writehisanswer.com/Philadelphia. Conferees choose 6 hour-long workshops from 42 offered or a clinic by application plus one six-hour continuing session from 8 offered. Four 15-minute one-on-one appointments, paid critiques, editors panels, and general sessions. Contest (registered conferees only) awards 50% off 2014 conference registration to a published and not-yet-published conferee. Especially encourages African American writers. Faculty of 50 authors, editors, and agents. Partial scholarships offered. Attendance: 250.

MERCER COUNTY ANNUAL ONE DAY WRITING CONFERENCE. 9 a.m.–4 p.m., Emmanuel Christian Church, Stoneboro. Workshops in fiction, nonfiction, articles, poetry, craft, and writers life. Contests. Lunch included. Website: www.writingsuccess.info or contact Gloria Clover at glowworm@certainty.net.

MONTROSE CHRISTIAN WRITERS CONFERENCE. Montrose; July 20–25, 2014. Patti Souder, dir. Contact: Donna Kosik, Montrose Bible Conference, 218 Locust St., Montrose PA 18801-1473. (570) 278-1001. Fax (570) 278-3061. E-mail: mbc@montrosebible.org. Website: www.montrosebible.org. Tracks for beginners, advanced writers, and teens (some years). Editors/agents in attendance. Attendance: 100. Provides a few partial scholarships.

ST. DAVIDS CHRISTIAN WRITERS' CONFERENCE. Grove City College, Grove City; June 2014. Lora Zill, director. Contact: Audrey Stallsmith, registrar, 87 Pines Rd. E., Hadley PA 16130-1019. (724) 253-2738. E-mail: registrar@stdavidswriters.com. Website: www.stdavidswriters.com. Offers tracks for beginning and advanced writers, fiction, nonfiction, children's, poetry, and more. Contests for participants; information on website. Editors in attendance. Offers partial scholarships. See website for information on their Writers' Colony. Attendance: 60-70.

***SUSQUEHANNA VALLEY WRITERS WORKSHOP.** Lewisburg. Contact: Marsha Hubler, 1833 Dock Hill Rd., Middleburg PA 17842. (570) 837-0002. (570) 374-8700. E-mail: marshahubler@wildblue.net. Website: www.susquehannavalleywritersworkshop.wordpress.com.

SOUTH CAROLINA

CAROLINA CHRISTIAN WRITERS CONFERENCE. Spartanburg, First Baptist Church, 250 East Main Street, Spartanburg SC 29306; March 21–22, 2014. Editors and agents in attendance. Contact: Linda Gilden, director, PO Box 2928, Spartanburg SC 29304. E-mail: linda@lindagilden.com. Website: www.fbs.org/writersconference. Scholarships available. Attendance: 100.

CHRISTIAN COMMUNICATORS CONFERENCE. The Billy Graham Training Center at The Cove; Fall 2014 and more. Contact: Vonda Skelton, 205 White Meadow Court, Simpsonville SC 29681. (864) 906-2256. E-mail: vondaskelton@gmail.com. Website: http://christiancommunicators.com. Christian Communicators Conference's mission is to educate, validate, and launch women in their speaking ministry. Fourteen classes/breakouts, high tea, professional videotape of attendee presentations. Scholarships. Space is limited.

TENNESSEE

AMERICAN CHRISTIAN WRITERS MENTORING RETREAT. Nashville, Opryland Guest House; April 4–5, 2014. Contact: Reg Forder, PO Box 110390, Nashville TN 37222. Toll-free (800) 21-WRITE. E-mail: ACWriters@aol.com. Website: www.ACWriters.com. Attendance: 40-80.

TEXAS

***EAST TEXAS CHRISTIAN WRITERS CONFERENCE.** Marshall; last weekend of October annually. Contact: Dr. Jerry Hopkins, East Texas Baptist University, One Tiger Drive, Marshall TX 75670. (903) 923-2083. Fax (903) 923-2077. E-mail: jhopkins@etbu.edu. Website: www.etbu.edu/news/CWC. Offers an advanced & teen track. Sponsors a Writers Contest in three categories—Short Story, Poetry, Essay (Grand prize, 1st–3rd Place winners; cash awards). Speakers: Bill Keith, Becca Anderson, Conn

Taylor, Terry Burns, Lexie Smith, and others. Editors/agents in attendance. Partial scholarships for students only. Attendance: 200+.

NORTH TEXAS CHRISTIAN WRITERS MENTORING WORKSHOPS. Ft. Worth; June 2014. Contact: NTCW Conference, PO Box 820802, Fort Worth TX 76182. (817) 715-2597. E-mail: info@NTChristianWriters.com. Website: www.NTChristianWriters.com. Offers track for advanced writers. No editors or agents in attendance. Offers partial scholarships. Sponsors a contest for conference registrants only. Attendance: 150.

WASHINGTON

AMERICAN CHRISTIAN WRITERS MENTORING RETREAT. Spokane, Ramada Airport; September 26–27, 2014. Contact: Reg Forder, PO Box 110390, Nashville TN 37222. Toll-free (800) 21-WRITE. E-mail: ACWriters@aol.com. Website: www.ACWriters.com. Attendance: 40-80.

NORTHWEST CHRISTIAN WRITERS RENEWAL CONFERENCE. Overlake Christian Church, Redmond; April 11–12, 2014. Contact: Judy Bodmer. E-mail: renewal@nwchristianwriters.org. Website: www.nwchristianwriters.org. Keynote speaker, Davis Bunn. Editors/agents in attendance. Offers 3 scholarships. Attendance: 175.

WASHINGTON DC

NATIONAL CHRISTIAN WRITERS CONFERENCE. Washington DC. Contact: Antonio L. Crawford, PO Box 1458, National City CA 91951-1458. (619) 791-5810. E-mail: ncwcsd@yahoo.com. Website: www.nationalchristianwritersconference.com.

WISCONSIN

GREEN LAKE CHRISTIAN WRITERS CONFERENCE. Green Lake; August 2014. Contact: Jan Moon, W2511 State Rd., Green Lake WI 54941-9300. (920) 294-3323. Fax (920) 294-3686. E-mail: Janet.P.White@gmail.com. Website: www.glcc.org. Contest: Choice of 5 topics/$5 entry fee/top 3 winners asked to read submissions to conference group. Editors in attendance. Partial scholarships. Attendance: 30-40.

WRITING WORKSHOPS & RETREATS. La Crosse; check our website for dates. Contact: Franciscan Spirituality Center, 920 Market St., La Crosse WI 54601. E-mail: FSCenter@fspa.org. Website: www.FSCenter.org.

CANADA/FOREIGN

***COMIX35 CHRISTIAN COMICS TRAINING SEMINAR.** Various international locations & dates. Contact: Nate Butler, PO Box 27470, Albuquerque NM 87125-7470. E-mail: comix35@comix35.org. Website: www.comix35.org/comix35_home.html. Speakers: Nate Butler and others. Sometimes has editors/agents in attendance. Attendance: 15-20. Sponsors contests (details at www.comix35.org/competitions.html).

INSCRIBE CHRISTIAN WRITERS' FELLOWSHIP FALL CONFERENCE. Wetaskiwin AB, Canada; last weekend of September 2014. Contact: Gwen Mathieu, PO Box 6201, Wetaskiwin, AB T9A 2E9. (780) 352-4006. E-mail: mathieug@xplornet.com. Website: www.inscribe.org/events/fall-conference/. Some editors in attendance. No agents. Hosted by Inscribe Christian Writer's Fellowship, a Canada-wide organization for Christians who write. Contests for members (see www.inscribe.org/contests/inscribe-fall-competition for details). Attendance: 100.

***WRITE! CANADA.** Guelph, Ontario; Contact: N. J. Linddquist, The Word Guild, PO Box 1243, Trenton ON K8V 5R9, Canada. E-mail: info@thewordguild.com. Website: www.writecanada.org. Hosted by The Word Guild, an association of Canadian writers and editors who are Christian. Offers an advanced track. Editors/agents in attendance. God Uses Ink Contest. No scholarships offered. Attendance: 250.

CONFERENCES THAT CHANGE LOCATIONS

***ACT ONE: SCREENWRITING WEEKENDS.** Two-day workshops; see website for dates and locations. Contact: Conference Coordinator, 2690 Beachwood Dr., Lower Fl., Hollywood CA 90068. (323) 464-0815. Fax (323) 468-0315. E-mail: info@ActOneProgram.com. Website: www.ActOneProgram.com. Open to anyone who is interested in learning more about the craft of screenwriting. No editors/agents in attendance. Attendance: 75.

***AMERICAN CHRISTIAN FICTION WRITERS CONFERENCE.** Rotates cities. Contact: Robin Miller, conf. dir., PO Box 101066, Palm Bay FL 32910-1066. E-mail: cd@acfw.com. Website: www.ACFW.com. Offers varied skill-level tracks for published and unpublished writers. Editors/agents in attendance. Sponsors 3 contests (details on website). Offers scholarships each year to ACFW members only.

AMERICAN CHRISTIAN WRITERS CONFERENCES. Various dates and locations (see individual states where held). Contact: Reg A. Forder, PO Box 110390, Nashville TN 37222. Toll-free (800) 21-WRITE. E-mail: ACWriters@aol.com. Website: www.ACWriters.com. Attendance 30-40.

***AUTHORIZEME.** Various locations and dates. Contact: Sharon Norris Elliott, PO Box 1519, Inglewood CA 90308-1519. (310) 508-9860. Fax (323) 567-8557. E-mail: AuthorizeMe@sbcglobal.net. Website: www.AuthorizeMe.net. AuthorizeMe is a 12-hour, hands-on seminar that helps writers get their book ideas out of their heads, down onto paper, and into a professional book proposal format ready to submit to an acquisitions editor. Seminars offered nationwide. For a list of scheduled seminars, or to sponsor a seminar in your area, check website. No editors or agents in attendance. Attendance: 10-50.

***CHRISTIAN LEADERS AND SPEAKERS SEMINARS (The CLASSeminar).** PO Box 36551, Albuquerque NM 87176. (702) 882-0638. Website: www.classeminars.org. Sponsors several seminars across the country each year. Check website for CLASSeminar dates and locations. For anyone who wants to improve his or her communication skills for either the spoken or written word, for professional or personal reasons. Speakers: Florence Littauer and others. Attendance: 75-100.

EVANGELICAL PRESS ASSOCIATION CONVENTION. Various locations. Anaheim; May 4–6, 2014. Contact: Lamar Keener, Conv. Chairperson, PO Box 20198, El Cajon CA 92021. (888) 311-1731. E-mail: business@evangelicalpress.com. Website: www.evangelicalpress.com. Attendance: 175. Annual convention for editors of evangelical periodicals; freelance communicators welcome. Editors in attendance. Contest open to members only.

INTERNATIONAL CHRISTIAN RETAIL SHOW. (Held in a different location each year.) Contact: Scott Graham. Colorado Springs CO 80962-2000. Toll-free (800) 252-1950. (719) 265-9895. Fax (719) 272-3510. E-mail: info@cbaonline.org. Website: www.christianretailshow.com. Entrance badges available through book publishers. Attendance: 5,000.

***THE SCRIMMAGE (PROPOSAL, PROMOTION, PITCH) SEMINAR.** Before the ACFW conference. Contact: Susan May Warren, PO Box 1290, Grand Marais MN 55604. (218) 387-2853. E-mail: scrimmage@mybooktherapy.com. Website: http://scrimmage.mybooktherapy.com. This one-day seminar, hosted right before the annual ACFW conference, helps authors plan their pitch during the conference, hone their proposal, and create a marketing plan for their book. Sponsors the My Book Therapy Frasier Contest (winner attends conference free). Attendance: 25.

"WRITE HIS ANSWER" SEMINARS & RETREATS. Various locations around US; dates throughout the year; a choice of focus on periodicals or books (includes indie publishing or mastering the craft). Contact: Marlene Bagnull, LittD, 951 Anders Rd., Lansdale PA 19446. (484) 991-8581. E-mail: mbagnull@aol.com. Website: www.writehisanswer.com/seminars. Attendance: 20-60. One- and two-day seminars by the author of *Write His Answer: A Bible Study for Christian Writers*.

9

Area Christian Writers' Clubs, Fellowship Groups, and Critique Groups

(*) before a listing indicates unconfirmed or no information update.

ALABAMA

***CHRISTIAN FREELANCERS.** Tuscaloosa. Contact: Joanne Sloan, 4195 Waldort Dr., Northport AL 35473. (205) 333-8603. E-mail: cjosloan@bellsouth.net. Membership (30-40) open.

ARIZONA

CHANDLER WRITERS GROUP. Chandler. Contact: Jenne Acevedo. (480) 510-0419. E-mail: jenneacevedo@cox.net. http://chandlerwriters.wordpress.com. ACW Chapter.

EAST VALLEY CHRISTIAN WRITERS (EVCW). Mesa. Contact: Brenda Jackson. (480) 510-0419. E-mail: brendaatheranch@yahoo.com. Membership (3) open.

FOUNTAIN HILLS CHRISTIAN WRITERS' GROUP. Contact: Jewell Johnson, 14223 N. Westminster Pl., Fountain Hills AZ 85268. (480) 836-8968. E-mail: tykeJ@juno.com. Membership (10-20). ACW chapter.

WORD WEAVERS NORTHERN ARIZONA. Cottonwood. Contact: Joy Gage, chapter president. E-mail: jnkwriters@swiftaz.net. Website: www.word-weavers.com. Membership (30+) open. Meeting time: Second Saturday, 9:30–noon. Meeting address: Spirit of Joy Lutheran Church, 330 Scenic Drive, Clarkdale AZ.

ARKANSAS

***LITTLE ROCK CHAPTER AMERICAN CHRISTIAN WRITERS/LRACW.** Little Rock. Contact: Carole Geckle, 5800 Ranch Dr., Little Rock AR 72223. (501) 228-2477. E-mail: cgeckle@familylife.com. Membership open.

SILOAM SPRINGS WRITERS. Siloam Springs. Contact: Margaret Weathers, 716 University St., Siloam Springs AR 72761. (479) 524-6598. Members (21) open. Sponsors contest, open to non-members.

CALIFORNIA

***AMADOR FICTION WRITERS CRITIQUE GROUP.** Four groups meet every other week in Ione. Contact: Kathy Boyd Fellure, PO Box 1209, Ione CA 95640-1209. (209) 274-0205. E-mail: kathyfellure2@juno.com. Website: www.amadorfictionwriters.com. Membership (16); open to readers. Sponsors an annual Literary Read and an annual Children's Read.

***BAY AREA WRITERS CRITIQUE GROUP.** Fremont. Contact: Carol Hall, PO Box 290, Fremont CA 94537. (510) 565-0619. E-mail: info@CarolLeeHall.com. Website: www.amadorfictionwriters.com. Membership (10) open to experienced writers only.

CASTRO VALLEY CHRISTIAN WRITERS GROUP. Contact: Pastor Jon Drury, 19300 Redwood Rd., Castro Valley CA 94546-3465. (510) 886-6300. E-mail: jdrury@redwoodchapel.org. Website: www.christianwriter.org. Membership (8-12) open. Sponsors the Christian Writers Seminar, February 21–22, 2014. Susy Flory, keynoter, and 40 writing workshops.

***INSPIRE CHRISTIAN WRITERS: Equipping Writers to Inspire the World.** Meetings in Auburn, El Dorado Hills, Elk Grove, Fair Oaks, Sacramento, & Roseville, and now in Reno NV. Contact: Elizabeth Thompson, PO Box 276794, Elk Grove CA 95827. (916) 670-7796. E-mail: elizabeth mthompson@comcast.net. Group e-mail: inspiregroup@comcast.net. Website: www.inspirewriters .com. Membership (90) open. Hosts annual Write to Inspire Conference and frequent workshops. Check website for details.

***SACRAMENTO CHRISTIAN WRITERS.** Citrus Heights. Contact: Beth Miller Self, 2012 Rushing River Ct., Elverta CA 95626-9756. (916) 992-8709. E-mail: cwbself@msn.com. Website: www .scwriters.org. Membership (32) open. Sponsors a contest for members. Next seminar 2015.

***SAN DIEGO COUNTY CHRISTIAN WRITERS GUILD.** Contact: Jennie & Bob Gillespie, PO Box 270403, San Diego CA 92198. Phone/fax (760) 294-3269. E-mail: info@sandiegocwg.org. Website: www.sandiegocwg.org. Membership (200) open. To join their Internet newsgroup, e-mail your name and address to info@sandiegocwg.com. Sponsors 10 critique groups, fall seminar, and spring fellowship brunch.

TEMECULA CHRISTIAN WRITERS CRITIQUE GROUP. Contact: Rebecca Farnbach, 41403 Bitter Creek Ct., Temecula CA 92591-1545. (951) 699-5148. Fax (951) 699-4208. E-mail: sunbrook@ hotmail.com. Membership (18) open. Part of San Diego Christian Writers Guild.

***THE WRITE BUNCH.** Stockton. Contact: Shirley Cook, 3123 Sheridan Way, Stockton CA 95219-3724. (209) 477-8375. E-mail: shirleymcp@sbcglobal.net. Membership (8) not currently open.

COLORADO

ACFW COLORADO GROUP & 4 CHAPTERS. Website: www.acfwcolorado.com. Sponsors Inkwell blog, retreats, contests, and miniconferences, plus the following 4 chapters: HIS Writers, North Denver; www.HisWriters.acfwcolorado.com. Mile High Scribes, South Denver; www.MileHighScribes .acfwcolorado.com. Worship! Write! Witness!, Colorado Springs; www.worshipwritewitness.acfw colorado.com. Spunk and Spirit Writers, Ft. Morgan; www.spunkandspirit.acfwcolorado.com.

***SPRING WRITERS.** Woodmen Valley Chapel/Colorado Springs. Contact: Scoti Domeij. E-mail: scoti domeij@gmail.com. Offers free monthly workshop; boot camps (2/yr.), critique group training. Membership open.

CONNECTICUT

WORD WEAVERS BERKSHIRES. Contact: Carol Barnier, chapter president. E-mail: carol@carol barnier.com. Website: www.word-weavers.com. Membership (15+) open. Additional information: Meeting time: Third Saturday, 9:00 a.m.–noon. Meeting address: Sherman Congregational, 6 Church Road, Sherman CT 06784.

DELAWARE

DELMARVA CHRISTIAN WRITERS' FELLOWSHIP. Georgetown. Contact: Candy Abbott, PO Box 777, Georgetown DE 19947-0777. (302) 856-6649. Fax (302) 856-7742. E-mail: cfa@candyabbott .com. Website: www.delmarvawriters.com. Membership (20+) open.

FLORIDA

BRANDON CHRISTIAN WRITERS/ACW CHAPTER #3029. Contact: Cheryl Johnston, President, 1317 Juniper Circle, Plant City FL 33563. (813) 763-3154. E-mail: info@brandonchristianwriters .com or cherylbethjohnston@mac.com Membership (35) open. Meets 4th Thursdays monthly.

***HOBE SOUND WRITERS GROUP/ACW CHAPTER.** Hobe Sound. Contact: Faith Tofte, 9342 Bethel Way, Hobe Sound FL 33455. (772) 545-4023. E-mail: faithtofte@bellsouth.net. Membership (5) open.

PALM BEACH AMERICAN CHRISTIAN WRITERS. Contact: Natalie Kim Rodriguez, 11231 US Highway 1, #231, North Palm Beach FL 33408. (561) 293-5725. E-mail: Natalie@Platform-Power.com. Website: http://PalmBeachACW.wordpress.com. Membership open. Meeting dates, times, and locations are available on the website.

PLATFORM-POWER LLC. Contact: Natalie Kim Rodriguez/Aria Dunham. 11231 US Highway 1, #231, North Palm Beach FL 33408. (561) 293-5725 or (561) 707-0757. E-mail: Natalie@Platform-Power.com. Website: http://Platform-Power.com. Meeting dates, times, and locations are available on the website.

***SUNCOAST CHRISTIAN WRITERS.** Seminole. Contact: Elaine Creasman, 13014—106th Ave. N., Largo FL 33774-5602. Phone/fax (727) 595-8963. E-mail: emcreasman@aol.com. Membership (10-15) open.

WORD WEAVERS FIRST COAST. Contact: Samantha Koivistoe, chapter copresident. E-mail: koitoes@gmail.com or Richard New, chapter copresident. E-mail: loco7mo@yahoo.com. Website: www.word-weavers.com. Membership (15+) open. Additional information: Meeting time is second Saturday each month, 10:00 a.m.–1:00 p.m. Meeting address: St. Augustine. Contact either chapter president for address details.

WORD WEAVERS GAINESVILLE. Contact: Lori Roberts, chapter president. E-mail: llwroberts@cox.net. Website: www.word-weavers.com. Membership (10+) open.

WORD WEAVERS ORLANDO. Contact: Edwina Perkins, chapter president. E-mail: perkster6@earthlink.net. Website: www.word-weavers.com. Membership (80+) open.

WORD WEAVERS PALM BEACH. Contact: Natalie Rodriguez, chapter president. (561) 293-5725. E-mail: Natalie@Platform-Power.com. Website: www.word-weavers.com. Membership (20+) open. Additional information: Meeting time: Second Saturday, 9:30 a.m.–noon. Meeting address: 1417 Villa Juno Drive, South Juno Beach FL 33408.

WORD WEAVERS SOUTH FLORIDA. Contact: Laura Ann Miller, chapter president. E-mail: LauraAnnMiller05@gmail.com. Website: www.word-weavers.com. Membership (25+) open.

WORD WEAVERS SPACE COAST. Contact: Evelyn Miracle, chapter president. E-mail: everymiracle@gmail.com. Website: www.word-weavers.com. Membership (20+) open. Additional information: Meeting time: Second Sunday, 2:30-5 p.m. Meeting address: Ma'gen Da'vid Messianic Synagogue, 3815 N US 1, Suite 123 in the Cocoa Commercial Center, Cocoa FL.

WORD WEAVERS TAMPA. Contact: Janet Rockey, chapter president. E-mail: rockeyjanet@yahoo.com. Website: www.word-weavers.com. Membership (20+) open.

WORD WEAVERS TREASURE COAST. Contact: Marene Graham, chapter president. E-mail: MTGTorch@aol.com. Website: www.word-weavers.com. Membership (20+) open.

WORD WEAVERS VOLUSIA COUNTY. Contact: Donna Tinsley, chapter president. E-mail: ThornRose7@aol.com. Website: www.word-weavers.com. Membership (15+) open. Additional information: Meeting time: First Monday, 7:00–9:00 p.m. Meeting address: Java Jungle, 4606 Clyde Morris Ave., Port Orange FL 32129.

GEORGIA

CHRISTIAN AUTHORS GUILD. Meets at Prayer and Praise Christian Fellowship, 6409 Bells Ferry Rd., Woodstock GA 30188. First and third Mondays, 7 p.m. with critique groups at 8:15 p.m. Website: www.christianauthorsguild.org. In the spring we also have a Saturday meeting called Coffee and Quill, and in August CAG hosts the "Catch the Wave" Writers Conference. Yearly dues $30.

CONNEXUS WRITER'S GROUP. Atlanta. Contact: Ricardo Jolly, 2055 Mount Paran Road, Atlanta GA 30327. 678-371-6194. E-mail: ric.jolly@gmail.com. Website: www.connexuswritersgroup.wordpress.com. Membership open. Meets first and third Saturdays of month at Mount Paran Church of God, Walker Center, Rm. 105, Atlanta GA.

***EAST METRO ATLANTA CHRISTIAN WRITERS/ACW CHAPTER.** Covington. Contact: Colleen Jackson, PO Box 2896, Covington GA 30015. (404) 444-7514. E-mail: colleenjackson@charter.net. Website: www.emacw.org. Membership (40) open. Check website for monthly meetings and speakers.

WORD WEAVERS GREATER ATLANTA. Contact: Jorja Davis, chapter president. E-mail: jorja.davis@gmail.com. Website: www.word-weavers.com. Membership (10+) open. Additional information: Meeting time: First Saturday, 9:30 a.m.–noon. Meeting address: 2315 Rocky Mountain Road NE, Atlanta GA 30066-2113.

ILLINOIS

WORD WEAVERS AURORA. Contact: Cindy Huff, chapter pres. E-mail: cindyshuff@comcast.net. Website: www.word-weavers.com. Membership (10+) open. Additional information: Meeting time: Second Saturday, 1-3 p.m. Meeting address: Hope Fellowship Church, 221 Locust St., Aurora IL 60506.

WORD WEAVERS LAND OF LINCOLN. Contact: Sarah Tierney, chapter president. E-mail: mpcc.counseling@gmail.com. Website: www.word-weavers.com. Membership (15+) open.

WORD WEAVERS NAPERVILLE. Contact: Kristina Cowan, chapter president. E-mail: kristina.cowan@gmail.com. Website: www.word-weavers.com. Membership (15+) open. Additional information: Meeting time: Third Saturday, 1:00–4:00 p.m. Meeting address: Naperville Community Christian Church, 1635 Emerson Lane, Naperville IL 60540.

IOWA

CEDAR RAPIDS CHRISTIAN WRITER'S GROUP. Contact: Susan Fletcher, 513 Knollwood Dr. S.E., Cedar Rapids IA 52403. (319) 365-9844. E-mail: skmcfate@msn.com. Membership (4) open.

***IOWA SCRIBES.** Contact: Ed Dickerson, 1764 62nd St., Garrison IA 52229-9628. (319) 477-3011. E-mail: edickers@netins.net. Facebook: www.facebook.com/KimnGollnick#!/groups/215400341881935/. Website: www.kimn.net/scribes.htm. Membership (6-10) open.

LOUISIANA

SOUTHERN CHRISTIAN WRITERS GUILD. Mandeville City Hall, 3101 E Causeway Approach, Mandeville LA 70448. Contact chairman: Marlaine Peachey, 419 Juliette Ln., Mandeville LA 70448. (985) 630-1798. Website: www.southernchristianwritersguild.com.Meets second Saturday of month at 10:00 a.m.-noon. Dues $25/year. Educational classes, critiquing, retreats, conference and speaker training. Has monthly speakers. Membership (25-30) open.

TOLEDO BEND AMERICAN CHRISTIAN WRITER'S GROUP. Calvary Abundant Life Tabernacle, 2413 Bethel Rd., Logansport LA. Contact: Marcella Simmons, 106 Fletcher Dr., Logansport LA 71049. (318) 697-5649. E-mail: writersmonthlyreview@gmail.com or marcies04@yahoo.com. Website: writersgroups.homestead.com. Membership (5). Open. ACW Chapter. Sponsors contest and annual writer's conference.

MARYLAND

BALTIMORE AREA CHRISTIAN WRITERS. Owings Mills. Contact: Theresa V. Wilson, MEd, PO Box 47182, Windsor Mill MD 21244-3571. (443) 622-4907. E-mail: writerseminar@aol.com. Website: www.writersinthemarketplace.org. Social networking sites: www.twitter.com/WritersCoach21; www.facebook.com/writersinthemarketplaceupdates. Webinar conferencing. Focused on building author platform and publishing support. Membership (50) open.

MICHIGAN

***FIRST FRIDAY'S WRITERS GROUP.** Critique group meets the first Friday of each month. Davison Free Methodist Church, 502 Church Street, Davison MI 48423. Contact Arlene Knickerbocker for details. (810) 793-0316 or writer@thewritespot.org.

WORD WEAVERS KALAMAZOO. Kalamazoo. Peter DeHaan, chapter president. E-mail: Peter@PeterDeHaan.com. Website: www.word-weavers.com.

WORD WEAVERS KENTWOOD. Kentwood. Tim Burns, chapter president. E-mail: TB@TimothyBurns.com. Website: www.word-weavers.com.

WORD WEAVERS SPRING LAKE. Spring Lake. Tim Burns, chapter president. E-mail: TB@TimothyBurns.com. Website: www.word-weavers.com.

WORD WEAVERS WALKER. Walker. Tim Burns, chapter president. E-mail: TB@TimothyBurns.com. Website: www.word-weavers.com.

WORD WEAVERS WEST MICHIGAN. Contact: Tim Burns, chapter president. E-mail: TB@TimothyBurns.com. Website: www.word-weavers.com. Membership (60+) open.

MISSISSIPPI

***BYHALIA CHRISTIAN WRITERS/ACW CHAPTER.** Contact: Marylane Wade Koch, Byhalia MS. E-mail: bcwriters@gmail.com. Has a BCW online Yahoo group. Has on-ground, online Yahoo group, and Facebook group. Membership (60) open.

MISSOURI

HEART OF AMERICA CHRISTIAN WRITERS NETWORK. Kansas City metro area. Contact: Mark and Jeanette Littleton, 3706 N.E. Shady Lane Dr., Gladstone MO 64119. Phone/fax (816) 459-8016. E-mail: HACWN@earthlink.net. Website: www.HACWN.org. Membership (150) open. Sponsors monthly meetings, weekly critique groups, professional writers' fellowships, a contest (open to nonmembers), a newsletter, marketing e-mails, and a conference in November.

OZARKS CHAPTER OF AMERICAN CHRISTIAN WRITERS. Springfield. Meets monthly, Sept. to May. Contact: Jeanetta Chrystie, pres., OCACW, 5042 E. Cherry Hills Blvd., Springfield MO 65809-3301. (417) 832-8409. E-mail: DrChrystie@mchsi.com. James Cole-Rous, newsletter ed. Submit articles to OzarksACW@yahoo.com. Guidelines on website: www.OzarksACW.org. Sponsors an annual contest (open to nonmembers); genre, dates, and guidelines on website. See website for other events. Membership (47) open. Newsletter-only subscriptions available.

NEBRASKA

MY THOUGHTS EXACTLY. Fremont. Contact: Cheryl Paden, PO Box 1073, Fremont NE 68025. (402) 727-6508. E-mail: cherylpaden@juno.com. Membership (8) open. Sponsors fall writers retreat. Retreat focuses on individual writing with writing prompts.

NEW YORK

THE SCRIBBLERS/ACW CHAPTER. Riverhead. Contact: Bill Batcher, pres., c/o First Congregational Church, 103 First St., Riverhead NY 11901. E-mail: bbatcher@optonline.net. Membership (12) open. Meets monthly and sponsors annual writing retreat.

SOUTHERN TIER CHRISTIAN WRITERS' FELLOWSHIP. Vestal. Contact: Jean Jenkins, 3 Snow Ave., Binghamton NY 13905-3810. (607) 797-5852. E-mail: jean.d.jenkins@gmail.com. Membership (10) open.

WORD WEAVERS WESTERN NEW YORK. Contact: Janet Erickson, chapter president. E-mail: JanEricks@aol.com. Website: www.word-weavers.com. Membership (10+) open.

NORTH CAROLINA

CAROLINA CHRISTIAN WRITERS, Local chapter of ACFW. SC and NC. Founded 2007. E-mail: carolinaacfw@gmail.com. Website: www.carolinachristianwriters.com. Facebook: www.facebook

.com/CarolinaChristianWriters. Twitter: @carolinacfw. Membership (17). CCW normally meets the second Saturday in even-numbered months, requires an annual membership fee of $10 (in addition to membership in ACFW). Welcomes all ages. Consists of published and unpublished Christian writers in various genres, with the primary focus on writing Christian fiction.

NEW COVENANT WRITERS. Lincolnton. Contact: Robert Redding, 3392 Hwy. 274, Cherryville NC 28021-9634. (704) 445-4962. E-mail: minwriter@yahoo.com. Membership (10) open.

WORD WEAVERS WILMINGTON. Contact: Erica Rizkalla, chapter president. E-mail: RLRizkallah@gmail.com. Website: www.word-weavers.com. Membership (30+) open.

OHIO

DAYTON CHRISTIAN SCRIBES. Kettering. Contact: Lois Pecce, 9909 Stephanie St., Dayton OH 45458-3709. (937) 433-6470. E-mail: epecce@compuserve.com. Membership (30) open. Publish monthly newsletter for local and national membership.

MIDDLETOWN AREA CHRISTIAN WRITERS (MAC WRITERS). Contact: Donna J. Shepherd. (513) 423-1627. E-mail: donna.shepherd@gmail.com. Website: www.middletownwriters.blogspot.com. Healing Word Assembly of God, 5303 S. Dixie Hwy., Franklin OH 45005.

MOVING AHEAD ACW CHAPTER. Marion. Contact: Diana Barnum, 3288 Darby Glen Blvd., Hilliard OH 43026. (614) 529-9459. E-mail: diana@ohiohelp.net. Membership open to inmates of the Marion Correctional Institution (MCI); adult male inmates in a re-entry program for prisoners getting ready to reenter society. May expand group to include those in the community.

NW OHIO CHRISTIAN WRITERS. Bowling Green. Contact: Katherine Douglas, VP, 12407 County Rd. 4, Swanton OH 43558-9568. (419) 825-1376. E-mail: mlka@toast.net. Website: www.NWOCW.org. Members (40) open. ACW Chapter. Sponsor annual conference, October, Holland OH.

OKLAHOMA

OKC CHRISTIAN FICTION WRITERS (ACFW CHAPTER). Edmond/Oklahoma City. Contact: Erin Taylor Young. E-mail: ocfwchapter@gmail.com. Website: www.okcchristianfictionwriters.com. Membership open; includes members-only discussion e-mail loop and discounted special events.

WORDWRIGHTS, OKLAHOMA CITY CHRISTIAN WRITERS. Contact: Milton Smith, 6457 Sterling Dr., Oklahoma City OK 73132-6804. (405) 721-5026. E-mail: HisWordMatters@yahoo.com. Website: www.shadetreecreations.com. Membership (20+) open. Occasional contests for members only. Hosts an annual writers' conference with American Christian Writers, March 22–23, 2013, in Oklahoma City. Send an SASE for information.

OREGON

OREGON CHRISTIAN WRITERS. Contact: president at president@oregonchristianwriters.org or business manager at business@oregonchristianwriters.org or write to 1075 Willow Lake Rd. N., Keizer OR 97303. Website: www.oregonchristianwriters.org. Celebrating our 50th anniversary in 2013. Meets for three all-day Saturday conferences annually: winter in Salem (February 22, 2014—Deborah Raney keynoting); spring in Eugene (May 17, 2014—Jane Kirkpatrick keynoting); and fall in Portland (October 11, 2014—Rachel Hauck keynoting). Print newsletter published the month before each one-day conference, and monthly e-news sent to members. Annual four-day Summer Coaching Conference with editors and agents held mid to late summer (August 4–7, 2014—Allen Arnold keynoting) in Portland metro area. Membership (300) open.

***SALEM I CHRISTIAN WRITERS GROUP (NOVICE WRITERS) & WRITERS ON DEADLINE (ADVANCED WRITERS).** Contact: Sam Hall, 6840 Macleay Rd. S.E., Salem OR 97301. (503) 363-7586. E-mail: samhallarch@msn.com. Membership (9) not currently open.

WORD WEAVERS PORTLAND EAST. Contact: Terry Murphy, chapter president. E-mail: email 4terry@gmail.com. Website: www.word-weavers.com. Membership (10+) open. Additional information: Meeting time: third Tuesday, 9:30-11 a.m. Meeting address: please contact Terry for location.

WORD WEAVERS THE DALLES. The Dalles. Contact: Sheila Parnell, chapter pres. E-mail: nwrsheila@gmail.com. Website: www.word-weavers.com.

***WORDWRIGHTS.** Gresham (near 182nd & Powell). Contact: Susan Thogerson Maas, 27526 S.E. Carl St., Gresham OR 97080-8215. (503) 663-7834. E-mail: susan.maas@frontier.com. Membership (5) possibly open.

PENNSYLVANIA

***FIRST WRITES.** Chambersburg. Contact: Dawn Hamsher. 225 S. Second Street, Chambersburg PA 17201. E-mail: 1stwrites@gmail.com. Website: www.1stwrites.blogspot.com. Membership open.

GREATER PHILADELPHIA CHRISTIAN WRITERS FELLOWSHIP. Contact: Marlene Bagnull, 951 Anders Rd., Lansdale PA 19446-5419. (484) 991-8581. E-mail: Mbagnull@aol.com. Website: http://writehisanswer.com/greaterphillychristianwriters/. Membership open. No application or dues. Meets one Thursday morning a month, September–June in Marlene's Lansdale home. Sponsors annual writers' conference (July 30–August 2, 2014) and contest (open to registered conferees only).

***INSPIRATIONAL WRITERS' FELLOWSHIP.** Brookville. Contact: Patty Zion (814) 648-2672. E-mail: pattyzion@hotmail.com. Membership (15) open. Sometimes sponsors a contest.

JOHNSTOWN CHRISTIAN WRITERS' GUILD. Contact: Betty Rosian, 102 Rustic Ave., Johnstown PA 15904-2122. (814) 255-4351. E-mail: louiserosian@gmail.com. Membership (17) open.

***LANCASTER CHRISTIAN WRITERS/ACW CHAPTER.** Central PA. Contact: Jeanette Windle, 121 E. Woods Dr., Lititz PA 17543. E-mail: jeanette@jeanettewindle.com. Website: www.lancasterchristian writerstoday.blogspot.com. Membership (100+) open. Sponsors a one-day conference in spring.

LANSDALE CHRISTIAN WRITERS FELLOWSHIP/CRITIQUE GROUP. Contact: Marlene Bagnull, 951 Anders Rd., Lansdale PA 19446-5419. (484) 991-8581. E-mail: mbagnull@aol.com. Membership (8) open. Women only.

SOUTH CAROLINA

CAROLINA CHRISTIAN WRITERS, LOCAL CHAPTER OF ACFW. SC AND NC. Founded 2007. E-mail: carolinacfw@gmail.com. Website: www.carolinachristianwriters.com. Facebook: www.face book.com/CarolinaChristianWriters. Twitter: @carolinacfw. Membership (17). CCW normally meets the second Saturday in even-numbered months, requires an annual membership fee of $10 (in addition to membership in ACFW). Welcomes all ages. Consists of published and unpublished Christian authors in various genres, with the primary focus on writing Christian fiction.

PALMETTO CHRISTIAN WRITER'S NETWORK. Lexington/Columbia SC. Contact: Linnette R. Mullin. E-mail: PCWN@live.com; Website: http://pcwn.blogspot.com/. Facebook: www.facebook .com/pages/Palmetto-Christian-Writers-Network/134405679969599. Twitter hashtag: #PCWN. Membership open. PCWN meets monthly. No member fee at this time. Welcomes ages 18 and up. Consists of published and unpublished Christian authors, writers, magazine editors, columnists/ journalists, freelance writers and bloggers in various genres—fiction and nonfiction. We write for the glory of God. Founded March 2011 by Linnette R. Mullin, author and freelance writer at www .LinnetteMullin.com.

WORD WEAVERS SUMMERVILLE. Contact: Kay Colon, chapter president. E-mail: kay_colon@ hotmail.com. Website: www.word-weavers.com. Membership (10+) open. Additional information: Meeting time: First Monday, 8:00-10:00 p.m. Meeting address: Summerville Presbyterian Church, 407 South Laurel St., Summerville SC 29483.

WRITE2IGNITE! TWO-4-ONE CRITIQUES. We offer two simultaneous written critiques from Write2Ignite! team members for one reasonable price. Specialize in manuscripts for children and young adults. Not an editing service. Details at www.write2ignite.com. Contact Jean Hall at write2 ignite@jeanmatthewhall.com.

WRITING 4 HIM. Spartanburg. Contact: Linda Gilden, PO Box 2928, Spartanburg SC 29304. E-mail: linda@lindagilden.com. Meets once a month at Christian Supply. Membership open.

TENNESSEE

***COLLIERVILLE AMERICAN CHRISTIAN WRITERS (CCWriters2)/ACW CHAPTER.** Collierville. Contact: Susan Reichert, 2400 Linkenholt Dr., Collierville TN 38017-8822. (901) 853-4470. E-mail: tnlms44@aol.com. Membership (36) open.

***GERMANTOWN CHRISTIAN WRITERS (ACW).** Contact: Earl Adams, PO Box 750484, Germantown TN 38175-0484. (901) 751-3311. E-mail: erladms@wmconnect.com.

TEXAS

CENTEX CHAPTER, ACFW. Round Rock. Contact: Becky Dean, president, 14905 Fernhill Dr., Austin TX 78717-3969. (512) 567-4251. E-mail: beckydean821@yahoo.com. Website: www.centexacfw .com. Members (20) open.

CENTRAL HOUSTON INSPIRATIONAL WRITERS ALIVE! Houston. Contact: Martha Rogers, 6038 Greenmont, Houston TX 77092-2332. (713) 686-7209. E-mail: marthalrogers@sbcglobal.net. Website: (in progress). Membership open to all writers. Meets second Thursday monthly except July, August, and December.

CHRISTIAN WRITERS GROUP OF GREATER SAN ANTONIO. Universal City/San Antonio area (First Baptist Church of Universal City). Contact: Brenda Blanchard. (210) 945-4163. E-mail: brenda blanchard1@aol.com. Meets every Monday from 6:30-8:30 p.m. at FBCUC in Faith Building, 1401 Pat Booker Rd., Universal City TX. Has quarterly guest speakers. Membership (40-50) open. Sponsors 3 conferences per year. March/June/October at First Baptist Church of Universal City.

CROSS REFERENCE WRITERS. Brazos Valley. E-mail: CrossRefWriters@yahoo.com. Website: http://sites.google.com/site/crossreferencewriters. Membership open.

***DFW READY WRITERS/ACFW BRANCH.** Colleyville. Contact: Janice Olson, president, (214) 415-6967. E-mail: mailto:janice@jkolson.com. Blog: www.dfwreadywriters.blogspot.com. Meeting info on blog. Membership open.

INSPIRATIONAL WRITERS ALIVE! Five chapters statewide in Houston, Amarillo, and Port Neches Grove. Sponsors summer seminar, Texas Christian Writers Conference on August 2, 2014, at Houston's First Baptist Church, a monthly newsletter, and annual contest (January 1–May 15) open to non-members. Contact Danny Woodall. E-mail: dannywoodall500@hotmail.com or at marthalrogers@ sbcglobal.net for more information and registration forms.

***INSPIRATIONAL WRITERS ALIVE!/AMARILLO CHAPTER.** Contact: Jerry McClenagan, pres., 6808 Cloud Crest, Amarillo TX 79124. (806) 674-3504. E-mail: jerrydalemc@sbcglobal.net. Membership open. Sponsors a contest open to members, and a seminar the Saturday after Easter.

NORTH TEXAS CHRISTIAN WRITERS/ACW CHAPTERS. Meetings held in Argyle, Arlington, Burleson, Canton, Cedar Hill, Corinth, Crandall, Dallas, Denton, Double Oak, Flower Mound, Fort Worth, Frisco, Garden Valley, Granbury, Irving, Kilgore, Lake Worth, Lindale, N. Richland Hills, Plainview, and Plano. Contact: NTCW, PO Box 820802, Fort Worth TX 76182-0802. (817) 715-2597. E-mail: info@ntchristianwriters.com. Website: www.NTChristianWriters.com. Membership (250+) open. Sponsors an annual conference in June, evening classes, one-day seminars, and three-day mentoring clinics throughout the year.

ROCKWALL CHRISTIAN WRITERS GROUP. Meets from 7-9:30 p.m. on the fourth Monday of every month (except December) in Room W-214 at LakePointe Church in Rockwall. For more information, visit our website: www.rcwg.blogspot.com or contact Leslie Wilson (214) 505-5336 or at leslieporter wilson@gmail.com.

WORD WEAVERS NORTH TEXAS. Contact: Henry McLaughlin, chapter president. E-mail: henry mclaughlin@att.net. Website: www.word-weavers.com. Membership (25+) open. Additional information: Meeting time: third Tuesday, 6:30-8:30 p.m. Meeting address: Northwood Church, 1870 Rufe Snow Drive, Keller TX 76248.

WORD WEAVERS PINEY WOODS. Contact: Robin Bryce, chapter president. E-mail: robin@robinbryce .com. Website: www.word-weavers.com. Membership (10+) open. Additional information: Meeting time: second Monday, 6:30-9:00 p.m. Meeting address: Target Starbucks, 259 Interstate 45, Huntsville TX 77340.

WORD WEAVERS WEST TEXAS. Big Spring. Contact: Kimberly Long. E-mail: DesignsofHope@ Suddenlink.net. Website: www.word-weavers.com.

WRITERS ON THE STORM. The Woodlands. Chapter of ACFW. Contact: Linda P. Kozar, 7 South Chandler Creek Cir., The Woodlands TX 77381. Prefers cell (832) 797-7522. E-mail: zarcom1@aol .com. Blog: http://acfwwritersonthestorm.blogspot.com. Visitors welcome (e-mail contact).

VIRGINIA

CAPITAL CHRISTIAN WRITERS. Fairfax. Director: Betsy Dill, PO Box 2332, Centreville VA 20122-0873. Phone/fax (703) 803-9447. E-mail: ccwriters@gmail.com. Website: www.CapitalChristianWriters .org. Meets second Monday of odd-numbered months. Speakers, website for authors, blog, occasional workshops.

NEW COVENANT WRITER'S GROUP. Newport News. Contact: Mary Tatem, 451 Summer Dr., Newport News VA 23606-2515. (757) 930-1700. E-mail: rwtatem@juno.com. Membership (8) open.

WASHINGTON

SPOKANE CHRISTIAN WRITERS. Contact: Ruth McHaney Danner, PO Box 18425, Spokane WA 99228-0425. (509) 328-3359. E-mail: ruth@ruthdanner.com. Membership (20) open.

WALLA WALLA CHRISTIAN WRITERS. Walla Walla. Contact: Helen Heavirland, PO Box 146, College Place WA 99324-0146. (541) 938-3838. Fax: (541) 938-3838. E-mail: hlh@bmi.net. Membership (8) open.

WALLA WALLA VALLEY CHRISTIAN SCRIBES. College Place. Contact: Helen Heavirland, PO Box 146, College Place WA 99324-0146. Phone: (541) 938-3838. Fax: (541) 938-3838. E-mail: hlh@ bmi.net. Membership (8) open.

WISCONSIN

LIGHTHOUSE CHRISTIAN WRITERS. Rotating in members' homes. Third Tuesdays, 10 a.m. Contact: Lois Wiederhoeft, 110 Oak St., Apt. #2, Peshtigo WI 54157. (715) 582-1024. E-mail: lois-ann67@hotmail.com. Or, Mary Jansen, PO Box 187, Mountain WI 54149. (715) 276-1706. Membership (5 active) open.

***PENS OF PRAISE CHRISTIAN WRITERS.** Manitowoc. Contact: Cofounders Becky McLafferty, 9225 Carstens Lake Rd., Manitowoc WI 54220. (920) 758-9196; or Sue Kinney, 4516 Laurie Ln., Two Rivers WI 54241. (920) 793-2922. E-mail: mclafferty@lakefield.net, or cal-suek@charter.net. Membership (8-10) open. Meets monthly.

CANADIAN/FOREIGN

NEW ZEALAND CHRISTIAN WRITERS GUILD. Contact: Janet Fleming, PO Box 115, Kaeo 0448, New Zealand. E-mail: mjflamingos@xtra.co.nz. Website: www.nzchristianwritersguild.co.nz.

Workshops, (autumn and spring), biannual weekend retreat, local groups, home study courses, contests for members, and bimonthly magazine.

SWAN VALLEY CHRISTIAN WRITERS GUILD. Swan River. Contact: Addy Oberlin, PO Box 132, Swan River MB R0L 1Z0, Canada. Phone/fax (204) 734-4269. E-mail: waltadio@mymts.net. Membership (8) open. May sponsor a contest open to nonmembers.

***THE WORD GUILD.** An organization of Canadian writers and editors who are Christian. We meet in various cities and online. We sponsor an annual conference in Guelph Ontario, Canada, in June. Write! Canada www.writecanada.org. We sponsor contests open to nonmembers who are Canadian citizens: http://canadianchristianwritingawards.com. Website: www.thewordguild.com. PO Box 1243, Trenton ON K8V 5R9, Canada. E-mail: mailto:info@thewordguild.com.

WORD WEAVERS MISSISSAUGA. Contact: Ann Peachman Stewart, chapter president. E-mail: Peachie01@sympatico.ca. Website: www.word-weavers.com. Membership (15+) open. Additional information: Meeting time: Second Monday, 7:00-9:00 p.m. Meeting address: Portico Community Church Room 212, 1814 Barbertown Rd., Mississauga ON L5M 2M5, Canada.

NATIONAL/INTERNATIONAL GROUPS (NO STATE LOCATION)

AMERICAN CHRISTIAN FICTION WRITERS. PO Box 101066, Palm Bay FL 32910. E-mail: Professional Relations Liaison Cynthia Ruchti, acfwrelations@acfw.com. Website: www.acfw.com. E-mail loop, online courses, critique groups, local chapters, and ACFW *Journal* magazine for members. Send membership inquiries to membership@acfw.com. Membership (2,600+) open. Sponsors contests for published and unpublished writers. Conducts largest fiction conference annually.

AMERICAN CHRISTIAN WRITERS SEMINARS. Sponsors conferences in various locations around the country (see individual states for dates and places). Call or write to be placed on mailing list for any conference. Events are Friday and Saturday unless otherwise noted. Brochures usually mailed three months prior to event. Contact: Reg Forder, PO Box 110390, Nashville TN 37222. Toll-free (800) 21-WRITE. Website: www.ACWriters.com.

JERRY B. JENKINS CHRISTIAN WRITERS GUILD. Contact: Janice Mitchell, 5525 N. Union Blvd., Ste. 101, Colorado Springs CO 80918. Toll-free (866) 495-5177. Fax (719) 495-5181. E-mail: ContactUs@ChristianWritersGuild.com. Website: www.ChristianWritersGuild.com. This international organization offers annual memberships, mentor-guided correspondence courses for adults (Apprentice; advanced one-year Journeyman; and Craftsman) and youth (Pages: ages 9-12, and Squires: 13 and up), a writing contest, a writer's conference, critique service, writers resource books, monthly newsletter, and more. The critique service accepts prose samples of 1-15 pages, as well as full manuscripts. Professional writing assessment covers proper language usage, pacing, presentation, purpose, and persuasiveness.

PEN-SOULS (prayer and support group, not a critique group). Conducted entirely by e-mail. Contact: Janet Ann Collins, Grass Valley CA. E-mail: jan@janetanncollins.com. Membership (12) open by application.

WORD WEAVERS INTERNATIONAL, INC. President, Eva Marie Everson, 530 Lake Kathryn Circle, Casselberry FL. Vice President, Mark T. Hancock. (407) 615-4112. E-mail: WordWeaversInternational@aol.com. Website: www.Word-Weavers.com. Membership (500+) open in over 30 chapters in US and Canada. Sponsors Florida Christian Writers Conference (see conferences) Feb/March annually. Sponsors both face-to-face groups and online groups. Sponsors annual contest for paid members.

WORDWEAVERS ONLINE GROUPS. Contact: Bruce Brady. E-mail: BCBrady01A@gmail.com. Website: www.word-weavers.com.

10

Editorial Services

It is often wise to have a professional editor critique your manuscript before you submit it to an agent or publisher—some agents even require a written evaluation. The following people offer this kind of service. We recommend asking for references or samples of their work.

Abbreviations of work they offer:

- B brochures
- BCE book contract evaluation
- CA coauthoring
- GE general editing/manuscript evaluation
- GH ghostwriting
- LC line editing or copyediting
- NL newsletters
- PP PowerPoint
- SP special projects
- WS website development

Abbreviations of the types of material they evaluate:

- A articles
- BP book proposals
- BS Bible studies
- D devotionals
- E essays
- F fillers
- GB gift books
- JN juvenile novels
- N novels
- NB nonfiction books
- P poetry
- PB picture books
- QL query letter
- S scripts
- SS short stories
- TM technical material
- YA young adults

ACKELSON LIGHTHOUSE EDITING, 13326 Community Rd., #11, Poway CA 92064-4754. (858) 748-9258. Fax (858) 748-7431. E-mail: Isaiah68LA@sbcglobal.net. Website: www.lighthouseedit.com. E-mail/write. GE/LC/GH/CA/B/NL/BCE. Edits: A/SS/N/NB/BP/QL/BS/E/D. Charges $35 for article/short-story critique; $60 for 3-chapter book proposal. Send SASE for full list of fees. Editor since 1981; senior editor 1984–2014.

AMI EDITING/ANNETTE M. IRBY, PO Box 7162, Covington WA 98042-7162. (425) 433-8676. E-mail: editor@AMIediting.com. Website: www.AMIediting.com. E-mail contact. GE/LC/B/NL/critiques. Edits: A/SS/F/N/NB/BS/GB/E/D/website copyedits. Published author; freelance and acquisitions editor. Has been writing for nearly 20 years, has edited manuscripts for well-published and new authors, as well as publishing houses (Summerside Press). See website for testimonials from Susan May Warren, Rachel Meisel, and others. Rates: $25/hr. for general jobs; $35/hr. for rush jobs. Send a $25 deposit with first 15 pages for a job estimate for general job; $35 deposit/15 pages for rush job. Deposit covers first hour in both cases.

ANDY SCHEER EDITORIAL SERVICES, 5074 Plumstead Dr., Colorado Springs CO 80920. (719) 282-3729. E-mail: Andy@AndyScheer.com. Prefers e-mail. GE/LC/GH/CA. Edits: A/SS/N/NB/BP/BS/GB. 25+ years' experience in Christian writing, editing, and publishing. Has served as a judge for national fiction and nonfiction contests. Rates negotiable, depending on size and condition of project.

***ANGAH CREATIVE SERVICES/DANIELLE CAMPBELL-ANGAH,** 961 Taylor Dr., Folcroft PA 19032. (610) 457-8300. E-mail: dcangah@angahcreative.com, or blessingsofgod77@verizon.net. Website: www.angahcreative.com. Ten years' writing experience; 5 years' editing experience.

AMY BOEKE'S EDITING SERVICE, 649 Frances Ave., Loves Park IL 61111-5910. E-mail: abboeke@gmail.com. E-mail contact. GE/LC/CA/B/NL/SP/writing coach. Edits: A/SS/F/N/NB/BP/QL/JN/PB/BS/

GB/E/D. BA English Studies, magna cum laude; M.A.T. (Secondary English Education). Charges $40-100 for articles; $250-750 for books.

A WAY WITH WORDS/RENEE GRAY-WILBURN, 1820 Smoke Ridge Dr., Colorado Springs CO 80919. (719) 271-7076. E-mail: waywords@earthlink.net. Website: www.awaywithwordswriting.wordpress.com. E-mail contact. GE/LC/GH/CA/B/NL/SP. Edits: A/SS/F/N/NB/QL/JN/PB/BS/GB/TM/E/D. Line editing/copyediting: $15-25/hr. & up. Project prices negotiable. 15+ years' experience. Provides editorial services for independent authors, Christian publishers, ministries, and small businesses. Open to coauthoring opportunities. Specializes in children's and nonfiction.

B. K. NELSON EDITORIAL SERVICES/JOHN W. BENSON (editorial director), 1565 Paseo Vida, Palm Springs CA 92264-9508. (760) 778-8800. Fax (760) 778-6242. E-mail: bknelson4@cs.com. Website: www.bknelson.com. E-mail or mail contact. GE/LC/SP/BCE. Edits: A/SS/P/F/N/NB/BP/QL/JN/PB/BS/GB/TM/E/D/S. Has been a literary agent for 22 years and has sold more than 2,000 books to royalty publishers. We do not deal with self-publishing. Contact for rates.

CARLA'S MANUSCRIPT SERVICE/CARLA BRUCE, 10229 W. Andover Ave., Sun City AZ 85351-4509. Phone/fax (623) 876-4648. E-mail: Carlaabruce@cox.net. Call/e-mail. GE/LC/GH/typesetting/PDF files for publishers. Edits: A/SS/P/F/N/NB/BP/QL/BS/GB/TM/E/D. Charges $2/page copyedit, $25/hr., or gives a project estimate after evaluation. Does ghostwriting for pastors and teachers; professional typesetting. Twenty-five years' ghostwriting/editing; 14 years typesetting.

CHRISTIAN COMMUNICATOR MANUSCRIPT CRITIQUE SERVICE/SUSAN TITUS OSBORN, 3133 Puente St., Fullerton CA 92835-1952. (714) 990-1532. E-mail: Susanosb@aol.com. Website: www.christiancommunicator.com. Call/e-mail/write. Staff of 18 editors. GE/LC/GH/CA/SP/BCE. Edits: A/SS/P/F/N/NB/BP/JN/PB/QL/BS/GB/TM/E/D/S/YA screenplays. $100 for short pieces/picture books. Three-chapter book proposal $160 (up to 40 pgs.). Additional editing $40/hr. Prefers e-mail submissions. Can pay electronically through PayPal. Over thirty years' experience.

CHRISTIAN EDITOR NETWORK/KATHY IDE, Brea CA. E-mail: Kathy@kathyide.com. An editorial matchmaking service to connect authors, publishers, and agents with qualified professional editorial freelancers. Free to authors, publishers, and agents. Website: www.christianeditor.com.

CHRISTIAN MANUSCRIPT EDITING SERVICES/LEE WARREN, 4311 S. 38th St., Omaha NE 68107-1236. (402) 884-4074. E-mail: leewarrenjr@outlook.com. Website: www.christianmanuscriptediting.com. Prefer e-mail. GE/LC/GH/writing coach. Edits: A/N/NB/BP/QL/BS/GB/D. Has written 6 royalty books and hundreds of articles in newspapers, magazines, and websites. Also edited more than 30 fiction and nonfiction manuscripts for self-publishing company and edited/critiqued another 50 manuscripts or proposals for a manuscript-critique service. For rates, see www.christianmanuscriptediting.com/p/services.html.

CHRISTIAN MANUSCRIPT SUBMISSIONS.COM, An online manuscript submission service operated by the Evangelical Christian Publishers Association (ECPA). ChristianManuscriptSubmissions.com is the only manuscript service created by the top Christian publishers looking for unsolicited manuscripts in a traditional royalty-based relationship. It allows authors to submit their manuscript proposals in a secure, online format for review by editors from publishing houses that are members of the ECPA. Website: www.ChristianManuscriptSubmissions.com.

CHRISTIAN WRITERS INSTITUTE MANUSCRIPT CRITIQUE SERVICE, PO Box 110390, Nashville TN 37222. Toll-free (800) 21-WRITE. E-mail: ACWriters@aol.com. Website: www.ACWriters.com. Call/write. GE/LC/GH/CA/SP/BCE. Edits: A/SS/P/F/N/NB/BP/JN/PB/BS/TM/E/D/S. Send SASE for rate sheet and submission slip.

***DEDICATED PUBLICATION SERVICES/TAMMY L. HENSEL,** PO Box 382, College Station TX 77841-0382. (979) 204-0674. Fax (979) 823-6252. E-mail: thensel@DedicatedPublicationServices.com. Website: DedicatedPublicationServices.com. E-mail. GE/LC/B/NL/SP/WS/articles, press releases, ads, and other documents, writing coach. Edits: A/SS/F/N/NB/BP/QL/JN/PB/BS/GB/TM/E/D/S/academic books/papers, depending on subject. Bachelor's degree in journalism and history from Baylor University, plus more than 25 years' writing, editing, and public-relations experience in print media. Very strong writing, editing, and communication skills. Experienced in both content and line-by-line editing, page design, manuscript preparation, newsletters, proposals, advertising, and more. Proficient in use of *The Chicago Manual of Style*, *The AP Stylebook*, *APA Publication Manual*, and *The Christian Writer's Manual of Style*. Published works include newspaper and magazine features, devotions, and inspirational articles. Rates are determined by the individual needs of the project and based on those recommended by the Editorial Freelancers Association (www.the-efa.org/res/rates.php). A deposit is required for first project but may be waived on return business. Customary rates from magazine and book publishers are accepted if within industry standards.

EDITOR FOR YOU/MELANIE RIGNEY, 4201 Wilson Blvd., #110328, Arlington VA 22203-1859. (703) 863-3940. E-mail: editor@editorforyou.com. Website: www.editorforyou.com. E-mail contact. GE/LC/writing coach. Edits: SS/N/NB/BP/QL/E/D. Charges $65/hr. for content editing & coaching (provides a binding ceiling on number of hours); fees vary for ms evaluation; generally $200-500 depending on ms length. Eight years of freelance edition and consulting for hundreds of writers, publishers, and agents. Editor of *Writer's Digest* magazine for 5 years; book editor/manager of Writer's Digest Books for 1 year; 3.5 years with Macmillan Computer Publishing and Thomsen Financial Publishing in books; 35 years' editing experience; frequent conference speaker/contest judge.

EDITORIAL SERVICES/BETTY L. WHITWORTH, 11740 S. Hwy. 259, Leitchfield KY 42754. (270) 257-2461. E-mail: Blwhit@bbtel.com. Call/e-mail. Editing for fiction and nonfiction books/articles and short stories. Retired English teacher, currently working as a newspaper columnist/journalist and independent editor. Worked with 50+ writers. Send 20 pages, SASE for return of ms with $25.00. Will give estimate for entire project after viewing those pages.

EDITORIAL SERVICES/DIANE E. ROBERTSON, Bradenton FL. Contact via (941) 928-5302 or by e-mail: pswriter1@netzero.net. Website: www.freelancewritingbydiane.com. E-mail contact is best. GE/GH/SP/writing coach. Edits: A/SS/F/N/NB/BP/QL/JN/PB/BS/E/S. Has written a woman's fiction book, a children's book, a memoir, and 1 book on all types of creative writing, 200+ magazine articles, short stories, and children's stories; previously served as associate editor of 2 magazines; presently teaches Short Story, Novel Writing, Magazine Writing, Writer's Workshops, and Memoir creative writing classes at several colleges and independent living centers. Charges $30/hr.

EDITORIAL SERVICES/JEANETTE HANSCOME, 3071 Tahoe Place, San Ramon CA 94582. (925) 487-7550. E-mail: jeanettehanscome@gmail.com. Website: www.jeanettehanscome.com. E-mail contact. GE/writing coach. Edits: A/SS/F/N/NB/QL/JN/E/D/S/YA novels & nonfiction. Author of 3 YA books with Focus on the Family; editor for almost 10 years; 400+ published articles, devotions, and stories; teaches and critiques online, locally, and at writers' conferences. Charges $35-40/hr; flat fees negotiable.

EDITORIAL SERVICES/KATHY IDE, Brea CA. E-mail: Kathy@kathyide.com. Website: www.KathyIde.com. GE/LC/GH/CA/B/NL/SP/WS, writing coach. Edits: A/SS/F/N/NB/BP/QL/JN/BS/GB/D/S. Charges by the hour (mention this listing and get a $5/hr. discount). Freelance author, editor (full time since 1998), and speaker. Has done proofreading and editing for Moody, Thomas Nelson, Barbour/Heartsong, and other publishers.

***EDITORIAL SERVICES/KELLY KAGAMAS TOMKIES,** 36 N. Cassady Rd., Columbus OH 43209. Phone/fax (614) 732-4860. E-mail: kellytomkies@gmail.com. Call, e-mail, or write. GE/LC/GH/CA/NL writing coach. Edits: A/SS/N/NB/BP/QL/JN/PB/BS/GB/TM/E/D. An author/editor with 20 years' experience. Written and/or edited for individuals, websites, magazines, and publishing houses, such as Barbour Publishing and McGraw-Hill. Prefers to negotiate a flat fee per project.

***EDITORIAL SERVICES/KIM PETERSON,** 1114 Buxton Dr., Knoxville TN 37922. E-mail: petersk@BethelCollege.edu or peterskus@yahoo.com. Write/e-mail. GE/LC/GH/CA/B/NL/SP/PP/mentoring/writing coach. Edits: A/P/F/N/NB/BP/QL/JN/PB/GB/TM/E/D. Freelance writer; college writing instructor; freelance editor; conference speaker. MA in print communication. Charges $25-35/hr.

EDITORIAL SERVICES/LESLIE SANTAMARIA, 1024 Walnut Creek Cove, Winter Springs FL 32708. (407) 497-5365. Call first. E-mail: leslie@lesliesantamaria.com. Website: www.lesliesantamaria.com. Prefers e-mail. GE/LC/WS. Writing coach. Edits: A/QL/JN/PB/GB/TM/E/D/S. Published author and book reviewer with 20+ years' book and magazine editing experience and a BA in English. Specializes in children's materials, as well as fiction and nonfiction for adults. Critiques: $50 for short pieces/picture books; $100 for 3-chapter book proposals. Editing services fee: by the project after free initial consultation.

EDITORIAL SERVICES/LISA HAINLINE, PO Box 1382, Running Springs CA 92382 (909) 939-0311. E-mail: info@lionsgatebookdesign.com Website: www.lionsgatebookdesign.com. Call/e-mail. Edits/evaluates: A/BP/NB/D/GE/GH/LC/NL. Editorial team specializes in nonfiction books by new and self-published authors. We provide manuscript critiques and all levels of editing. Submit 3 chapters for quote.

EDITORIAL SERVICES/MARILYN A. ANDERSON, 127 Sycamore Dr., Louisville KY 40223-2956. (502) 244-0751. Fax (502) 452-9260. E-mail: shelle12@aol.com. Call/e-mail. GE/LC. Edits: A/F/NB/BS/TM/E/D. Charges $15-20/hr. for proofreading, $25/hr. for extensive editing, or negotiable by the job or project. Holds an MA and a BA in English; former high school English teacher; freelance consultant since 1993. References available. Contributing member of The Christian PEN.

EDITORIAL SERVICES/MARION DUCKWORTH, 15917 N.E. 41st St., Vancouver WA 98682-7473. (360) 609-1583. E-mail: mjduck@comcast.net. Website: www.MarionDuckworthMinistries.com. E-mail/write. GE/writing coach. Edits: A/NB/BP/QL/BS; also does consultations. Charges $25/hr. for critique or consultation. Negotiates on longer projects. Author (for over 25 years) of 17 books and 300 articles; writing teacher for over 25 years; extensive experience in general editing and manuscript evaluation.

EDITORIAL SERVICES/MELISSA JUVINALL, 1518 Augusta, Normal IL 61761. (309) 452-8917. E-mail: kangaj1@hotmail.com. Website: www.bearla.com. E-mail contact. GE/LC. Edits: N/NB/JN/PB/BS/GB/TM. Has a BA & MA in English; specializes in children's lit.; more than 10 years' editing experience; judge for Christy Awards. Charges by the page for proofreading and copyediting; by the hour for critiquing.

EDITORIAL SERVICES/SKYLAR HAMILTON BURRIS, Flower Mound TX. (703) 944-1530. E-mail: skylarburris@yahoo.com. Website: www.editorskylar.com. E-mail contact. LC/B/NL/WS. Edits: A/SS/P/F/N/NB/JN/BS/GB/TM/E/D/S. Charges authors $3/double-spaced page for editing. Charges $40/hr. for newsletter editing, writing, and design. Primarily works with authors who are planning either to self-publish or to submit their work to traditional publishing houses and who have completed books that require line-by-line copyediting prior to final proofreading and publication. BA and MA in English. Fourteen years as a magazine editor; 15 years' newsletter editing and design. Free sample edit of 2 pages.

EDITORIAL SERVICES/STERLING DIMMICK, 311 Chemung St., Apt. 5, Waverly NY 14892-1463. (607) 565-4247. E-mail: sterlingdimmick@hotmail.com. Call. GE/LC/GH/CA/SP. Edits: A/SS/P/F/N/NB/BP/QL/JN/PB/BS/GB/TM/E/D/S. Has an AAS in Journalism; BA in Communication Studies. Charges $20/hr. or by the project.

EDITORIAL SERVICES/SUSANNE LAKIN, 219 Double Bogey Dr., Boulder Creek CA 95006. (530) 200-5466. E-mail: cslakin@gmail.com. Website: www.critiquemymanuscript.com. E-mail contact. GE/LC/writing coach. Edits SS/P/N/NB/BP/QL/JN/BS/GB/D. Has years of editing experience for the book publishing industry; member of Christian PEN and CEN (Christian Editor Network); writer of thirteen novels. Specializes in contemporary fiction, fantasy, and nonfiction books, including those on biblical topics. All editing services provided (charged by the hour) and specializing in manuscript critiques (charged by the page). Estimates for editing can be provided, along with current client references.

EDITOR WORLD, Patti Fisher, PO Box 24, Newport VA 24128. (614) 500-3348. E-mail: info@editorworld.com. Website: www.editorworld.com. Submit document online. GE. Edits A/SS/P/F/N/NB/BP/QL/JN/BS/GB/TM/E/D/S. Credentials/experience vary (see site). Charge per word; rates vary depending on turnaround time.

EDIT RESOURCE LLC/ERIC & ELISA STANFORD, 3578-E Hartsel Dr., #387, Colorado Springs CO 80920. (719) 290-0757. E-mail: info@editresource.com. Websites: www.editresource.com, www.inspirationalghostwriting.com. E-mail contact. GE/LC/GH/CA/SP/author coaching/copywriting/proposal development. Edits A/F/N/NB/BP/QL/BS/GB/E/YA/book doctoring. Rates determined after discussion with client. Combined 40+ years of professional editing experience.

EPISTLEWORKS CREATIONS/JOANN RENO WRAY, Helping Writers Reach Their High Call. Cheswick PA. (412) 828-1270 E-mail: epedit@epistleworks.com. Website: http://epistleworks.com. E-mail preferred. GE/LC/GH/CA/B/NL/SP/Research. Edits: A/SS/P/F/N/NB/BP/D. Creates graphic art: covers, logos, cartoons, website design, site content management. PR materials: (static or animated) brochures, booklets, and web ads. Uses signed contracts with clients. Experienced writer, editor, and artist since 1974. Previous editor for two Tulsa OK monthly Christian newspapers, publisher/editor of an online magazine, business columnist, editing clients' work. Edited pastors' and ministers' newsletters, newspapers, and books. Speaker/teacher at national Christian Writers' conferences. Over 3,000 published articles, stories, poem in print, periodicals. Articles in 16 compilation books. Charges start at $25/hr. Required $45 nonrefundable consulting fee (deducted from total). Binding estimates. Detailed time-clock report. Discounts available. Accepts checks, money orders, or PayPal. E-mail or see website for detailed information on services.

FAITHFULLY WRITE EDITING/DAWN KINZER, 25914—188th Ave. S.E., Covington WA 98042-6021. (253) 630-7617. E-mail: dawnkinzer@comcast.net. Website: www.faithfullywriteediting.com. E-mail contact. GE/LC. Edits: A/SS/N/NB/D. Published writer with short stories, articles, and devotions. Experience in editing both fiction and nonfiction. Created and edited department newsletter for national telecommunications corporation. Serves as a judge for contests that award excellence in Christian fiction. Member of The Christian PEN, The Christian Editor Network, and American Christian Fiction Writers. Rates are by page and depend on type of work required. Payment is made in advance of each block of work being completed. Complimentary 2-page sample edit offered with initial contact.

FAITHWORKS EDITORIAL & WRITING, INC./NANETTE THORSEN-SNIPES, PO Box 1596, Buford GA 30515. Phone/fax (770) 945-3093. E-mail: nsnipes@bellsouth.net. Website: www.faithworkseditorial.com. E-mail contact. Freelance editor, copyeditor/line editor, proofreader, work-for-hire projects. Edits juvenile fiction/short stories, picture books/devotions, juvenile or adult nonfiction/articles/business/humor. Author of more than 500 articles/stories; has stories in more than 55 compilation books. Member: The Christian PEN (Proofreaders & Editors Network) and CEN (Christian Editors Network). Proofreader for *Cross & Quill* newsletter (CWFI) for two years. Proofreading corporate newsletters for past 8 years. 25-plus years' writing experience. Eight years' editing experience. Edit for ghostwriters, children's fiction writers, and writers of adult nonfiction.

***FICTION FIX-IT SHOP/MEREDITH EFKEN,** 2885 Sanford Ave. S.W., #17598, Grandville MI 49418. E-mail: editor@fictionfixitshop.com. Website: www.fictionfixitshop.com. E-mail contact. Edit any work of fiction—any genre—that is novella length or longer, either adult fiction or young adult fiction. Provides all levels of editing as well as coaching. Editing based on flat fee estimated on per-project basis, not hourly, and rates or estimates are listed on website. Coaching rates on per-session basis.

ANNA W. FISHEL, 3416 Hunting Creek Dr., Pfafftown NC 27040. E-mail: awfishel@triad.rr.com. Call/write/e-mail. GE/CA/SP. Edits A/SS/P/N/NB/JN/E/D. Charges by the hour. Estimates offered. Two decades of professional editing experience; editor with major Christian publishing house for over 10 years; published author of 6 children's books.

BONNIE C. HARVEY, PhD, 309 Carriage Place Ct., Decatur GA 30033. (404) 299-6149. Cell (404) 580-9431. E-mail: Boncah@aol.com. Website: www.perfectbook.net. Call/e-mail/write to discuss terms and payment. Has doctorate in English; Bible school credits from Montreat NC. Edits academic, theology, and general-interest books and articles. Fifteen years' experience teaching writing and English/college level, especially at Kennesaw University, Georgia; 30 years' editorial experience (including Xulon A +Editor); writing coach, fiction and nonfiction; ghostwrites books and authored 22 books—many available nationwide in schools and libraries. Ghostwrote *The Judge . . . to the Beat of a Different Drummer* (by George W. Trammell, California superior court judge). Also has The Harvey Literary Agency, LLC.

DR. DENNIS E. HENSLEY, 6824 Kanata Ct., Fort Wayne IN 46815-6388. Phone/fax (260) 485-9891. E-mail: dnhensley@hotmail.com. E-mail/write. GE/LC/GH/CA/SP. Edits: A/SS/P/F/N/NB/BP/QL/JN/E/D/comedy/academic articles/editorials/Op-Ed pieces/columns/speeches/interviews. Rate sheet for SASE or by e-mail. Author of 53 books and 3,000 articles and short stories; PhD in English; Taylor University professor of professional writing; columnist for *Metro Business North* and *Advanced Christian Writer*.

***HESTERMAN CREATIVE, V. L. HESTERMAN, PHD,** PO Box 6788, San Diego CA 92166. E-mail: vhes@mac.com (cc to vhes@earthlink.net). E-mail first contact; include phone number if you want follow-up call. Editing, writing, photography. Twenty-five years' experience as book editor, author, writing teacher and coach, journalist, curriculum developer, photographer. Edits/develops nonfiction material, including books, essays, memoirs, and photo books; works with publishers, agents, and writers as coauthor, line editor, or in editorial development. Will do line edits of fiction. Standard industry rates; depends on scope and condition of project. Will give binding quote with sample of writing and query/proposal.

IZZY'S OFFICE/DIANE STORTZ, PO Box 31239, Cincinnati OH 45231. (513) 602-6720. E-mail: diane.stortz@gmail.com. Website: www.dianestortz.com. E-mail contact. GE/LC. Edits: NB/BP/JN/N/PB/BS/GB/D. Former editorial director for a Christian publisher (10 yrs.); published author, experienced children's editor. See website for client list and partial list of projects. Copyediting or substantive editing by the hour per-project basis. One-half payment amount due before work begins.

JOY MEDIA/JULIE-ALLYSON IERON, PO Box 1099, Park Ridge IL 60068. E-mail: j-a@joymediaservices.com. Website: joymediaservices.com. Contact by e-mail. GE/GH/CA/B/NL/SP/PP/ writing coach. Edits: A/NB/BP/BS/GB/D. Master's degree in journalism and 25+ yrs. experience in Christian publishing. Charges $40 per hour; negotiates for larger projects. Half of fee up front.

JRH EDITING/JENNIFER HAMILTON, Coaching, mentoring, in-depth critiques. E-mail me at jennifer@jrhediting.com. To see editing examples visit www.jrhediting.com. JRH EDITING, where "Your Work Is My Heart."

KAREN O'CONNOR COMMUNICATIONS/KAREN O'CONNOR, 10 Pajaro Vista Ct., Watsonville CA 95076. E-mail: karen@karenoconnor.com. Website: www.karenoconnor.com. E-mail. GE/LC. Book proposal commentary/editing. Edits: A/F/NB/BP/QL/D. One-hour free evaluation; $90/hr. or flat fee depending on project. Has 35 years of writing/editing; 25+ years teaching writing; 70 published books and hundreds of magazine articles.

***KMB COMMUNICATIONS INC./LAURAINE SNELLING,** PO Box 1530, Tehachapi CA 93581. (661) 823-0669. Fax (661) 823-9427. E-mail: TLsnelling@yahoo.com. Website: www.LauraineSnelling.com. E-mail contact. GE. Edits: SS/N/JN. Charges $100/hr. with $100 deposit, or by the project after discussion with client. Award-winning author of 70 books (YA and adult fiction, 2 nonfiction); teacher at writing conferences.

LOGOS WORD DESIGNS INC./LINDA L. NATHAN, PO Box 735, Maple Falls WA 98266-0735. (360) 599-3429. Fax (360) 392-0216. E-mail: linda@logosword.com. Website: www.logosword.com. Call/e-mail. GE/LC/GH/CA/B/NL/SP/publishing consultation/writing assistance/writes proposals/manuscript submission services. Edits: A/BP/BS/TM/E/D/F/JN/N/NB/PB/QL/SS/TM/YA/academic/legal/apologetics/conservative political. Over 30 years' experience in wide variety of areas, including publicity, postdoctoral; BA Psychology/some MA. Member: Editorial Freelance Assn.; NW Independent Editors Guild; American Christian Fiction Writers. Quote per project. See website, or e-mail for rates.

NOBLE CREATIVE, LLC/SCOTT NOBLE, PO Box 131402, St. Paul MN 55113. (651) 494-4169. E-mail: snoble@noblecreative.com. Website: www.noblecreative.com. E-mail contact. GE/LC/GH/B/NL/SP/WS. Edits: A/SS/F/N/NB/BP/QL/BS/GB/TM/E/D. More than a decade of experience, including several years as asst. ed. at *Decision* magazine. Masters degree in Theological Studies. Charges by the hour or the project.

PERFECT WORD EDITING SERVICES/LINDA HARRIS, 2617 Montebello Dr. W, Colorado Springs CO 80919-1917. (719) 264-9385. E-mail: lharris@perfectwordediting.com. Website: www.PerfectWordEditing.com. Prefers e-mail contact. GE/LC/GH/CA/B/NL/SP. Edits: A/SS/F/N/NB/BP/QL/BS/E/D. Over 30 yrs. experience. Charges by the page. $2-20 a page. Free evaluation. First 5 pages free for book clients, no obligation.

PICKY, PICKY INK/SUE MIHOLER, 1075 Willow Lake Road N., Keizer OR 97303-5790. (503) 393-3356. E-mail: suemiholer@comcast.net. E-mail contact. LC/B. Edits: A/NB/BS/D. Charges $30 an hour or $50 for first 10 pages of a longer work; writer will receive a firm completed-job quote based on the first 10 pages. Freelance editor for several book publishers since 1998. Will help you get your manuscript ready to submit.

PWC EDITING/PAUL W. CONANT, 527 Bayshore Pl., Dallas TX 75217-7755. (972) 286-2882. Cell (214) 289-3397. E-mail: pwcediting@gmail.com. E-mail contact preferred. LC/NL/SP/PP. Edits: SS/N/NB/BS/TM/E/D/S/Sci-Fi. Writer, editor; proofreader for magazines and book publishers. Member of Christian Editor's Network, The Christian PEN. Terms negotiable for long works. Charges publishers up to $25/hr. Prefers to work up a page rate based on a minimum 5-page sample, giving new clients up to one hour of free editing. Has edited 3 high school science textbooks; technical books on geology, manufacturing, and hypobaric inventions; and numerous books by new or ESL writers.

REVISION EDITING AGENCY/KIMBERLY SHUMATE, PO Box 40974, Eugene OR 97404. E-mail: revisioneditingagency.shumate@gmail.com. Website: www.revisioneditingagency.wordpress.com. E-mail submissions only. Copyediting and critique services for sample chapters, full-length mss, cover letters, book proposals, magazine articles, blog entries, etc. Fiction or nonfiction. Details on website.

RIGHT PRICE EDITING/AMANDA PRICE, 795 CR236, Eureka Springs AR 72631. E-mail: rightpriceediting@gmail.com. Website: www.rightpriceediting.com. GE/LC. Edits: A/SS/N/NB/BP/QL/JN/E/D. Over 6 yrs. experience. See website for details.

SCRIBBLE COMMUNICATIONS/BRAD LEWIS, Colorado Springs CO. (719) 649-4478. Fax (866) 542-5165. E-mail: brad.lewis@scribblecommunications.com. Website: www.scribblecommunications.com. E-mail contact. GE/LC/GH/substantive editing/developmental editing. Edits: A/NB/BP/QL/BS/D/website content. Edited more than 100 nonfiction books; senior editor of the *New Men's Devotional Bible* (Zondervan); content editor for *New Living Translation Study Bible* (Tyndale), contracted publications manager for Association of Gospel Rescue Missions. Charges by project, mutually agreed upon with publisher or author, and stated in editor/author agreement.

***SHIRL'S EDITING SERVICES/SHIRL THOMAS,** 9379 Tanager Ave., Fountain Valley CA 92708-6557. (714) 968-5726. E-mail: Shirlth@verizon.net. Website: shirlthomas.com. E-mail (preferred)/write, and send material with $100 deposit. GE/LC/GH/SP/review/rewriting. Edits: A/SS/P/F/N/NB/BP/

QL/GB/D/greeting cards/synopses. Consultation, $75/hr.; evaluation/critique, $75/hr.; mechanical editing, $65/hr.; content editing/rewriting, $75/hr.

smWORDWORKS, Susan G. Mathis, 945 Rangely Dr., Colorado Springs CO 80921. (719) 331-9352. E-mail: mathis.wordworks@gmail.com. Website: www.SusanGMathis.com. E-mail first, please. GE/LC/GH/CA/SP/BCE. Edits: A/P/F/NB/BP/PB. Published author. Former editor of more than 12 publications. Rates determined after discussion with client. 20+ years' writing/editing experience.

SPREAD THE WORD COMMERCIAL WRITING/KATHERINE SWARTS, Houston TX. (832) 573-9501. E-mail: ks@houstonfreelancewriter.com. Website: www.houstonfreelancewriter.com. Blog: http://strengthfortheweary.wordpress.com; http://newsongsfromtheheart.blogspot.com. E-mail contact preferred. Blogs/articles projects related to Christian encouragement and mental health. Per-project rates. MA in written communications from Wheaton College; over 100 published articles.

SALLY STUART, 15935 S.W. Greens Way, Tigard OR 97224. Phone/fax (503) 642-9844. E-mail: stuartcwmg@aol.com. Website: www.stuartmarket.com. Blog: www.stuartmarket.blogspot.com. Tips for Writers blog: sallystips.blogspot.com. Call/e-mail. GE/BCE/agent contracts. Edits: A/SS/N/NB/BP/GB/JN. No poetry or picture books. Charges $40/hr. for critique; $45/hr. for phone/personal consultations. For books, send a copy of your book proposal: cover letter, chapter-by-chapter synopsis for nonfiction (5-page overall synopsis for fiction), and the first three chapters, double-spaced. Comprehensive publishing contract evaluation $75-200. Author of 37 books (including 26 editions of the *Christian Writer's Market Guide*) and 40+ years' experience as a writer, teacher, marketing expert.

THE CHRISTIAN PEN: PROOFREADERS AND EDITORS NETWORK, Kathy Ide, Brea CA. Website: www.TheChristianPEN.com. Contact: Kathy@KathyIde.com. Provides proofreaders and editors with a venue for "cooperative competition" through mutual support and exchange of information. E-mail discussion loop, online courses, resources and suggestions, tips and tools. Contributing members can post their bios/ads on The Christian PEN website, receive a quarterly e-newsletter, get discounts on online courses, receive active job leads, and more. Open to anyone who is a full-time or part-time proofreader or editor (at any level), is seriously planning to become an editorial freelancer, or is investigating the possibility. If you're a writer looking for an editor or proofreader, contact Kathy Ide at Kathy@KathyIde.com for a referral.

THE WRITE EDITOR/ERIN K. BROWN, E-mail: wordcontract@writeeditor.net or thewriteeditor@gmail.com. Website: www.writeeditor.net. E-mail contact. GE/LC. Edits: A/SS/F/N/NB/BP/QL/JN/BS/E/D/NL/B. Offers e-book conversion, critiques. Has a certificate in editorial practices: graduate school, USDA, Washington DC; Christy Award judge 2006–2013; member of American Christian Fiction Writers; The Christian PEN; coauthor of *The Lost Coin*.

THE WRITE SPOT/ARLENE KNICKERBOCKER, Where Quality and Economy Unite, PO Box 424, Davison MI 48423-9318. (810) 793-0316. E-mail: writer@thewritespot.org. Website: www.thewritespot.org. E-mail/write. GE/LC/GH/CA/B/NL/classes and speaking/writing coach. Edits: A/SS/P/NB/BP/QL/BS/D. Published credits since 1996; references available. Prices on website.

***THE WRITE WAY EDITORIAL SERVICES/JANET K. CREWS/B. KAY COULTER,** 806 Hopi Trl., Temple TX 76504-5008. (254) 778-6490 or (254) 939-1770. E-mails: janetcrews@sbcglobal.net or bkcoulter@sbcglobal.net. Website: www.writewayeditorial.com. Call/e-mail. GE/LC/GH/CA/B/NL/SP/scan to Word document/voice to Word document/graphics. Edits: A/SS/N/NB/BP/QL/JN/BS/GB/D. Published author of 3 books; contributor to 2 books; 14 years' combined experience; certified copyeditor. Free estimate; 50% of estimate as a deposit; $30/hr. Contact for additional details.

***TOPNOTCH WRITING SOLUTIONS/MARYANN DIORIO, PhD,** PO Box 1185, Millville NJ 08109. (856) 488-0366. Fax (856) 488-0291. E-mail: DrMaryAnn@TopNotchWritingSolutions.com. Website: www.TopNotchWritingSolutions.com or www.maryanndiorio.com. E-mail contact. GE/

SP/NL/WS/writing coach (www.TopNotchLifeandCareerCoaching.com). Edits: A/SS/P/F/BP/QL. 25+ years' experience; award winner; 5 published books, contributed to 5 others; hundreds of published articles, short stories, and poems. Rate sheet available on request.

TWEEN WATERS EDITORIAL SERVICES/TERRI KALFAS, PO Box 1233, Broken Arrow OK 74013-1233. (918) 346-7960. E-mail: terri@terrikalfas.com. E-mail contact. GE/LC/GH/CA/B/SP/BCE. Edits: A/N/NB/BP/QL/BS/TM/D/project management/book doctoring. Multiple editorial and freelance writing services. Over 25 years' writing and publishing experience. Writing coach. Available as conference speaker and workshop teacher. Charges $4 per pg./$30 per hr./negotiable on special projects.

JAMES WATKINS/XARISCOM, 729 S. Lenfesty Ave., Marion IN 46952. E-mail: jim@jameswatkins.com. Website: www.jameswatkins.com. E-mail contact. GE/LC/GH/WS. Edits: A/NB/BP/QL/BS/D/S. Award-winning author of 16 books, 2,000+ articles, freelance editor with Wesleyan Publishing House; winner of four editing and 2 book awards. 30+ years' experience. Charge $2/pg. for critique, market suggestions; $5/pg. for content editing; $15/pg. for rewriting/ghosting; $50/hr. for website evaluation/consulting.

BRENDA WILBEE: WRITER, EDITOR & GRAPHIC DESIGNER, (360) 389-6895. E-mail: Brenda@brendawilbee.com. Call/e-mail. GE/LC/B/NL/SP/W/PP. Edits: N/NB. Offers graphic design services for brochures, bookmarks, websites. Has MA in professional writing; BA in creative writing; AA in graphic design; has taught college composition for 7 yrs.; author of 9 CBA books and over 100s of articles; longtime contributor to *Daily Guideposts*; and has freelanced as a writer, editor, and designer for 30 yrs. Will do book design, layout, and covers. Charges can be discussed via e-mail; $50/hr. or flat fee depending on project.

***WINGS UNLIMITED/CRISTINE BOLLEY,** Broken Arrow OK. (918) 250-9239. Fax (918) 250-9597. E-mail: WingsUnlimited@aol.com. Website: www.wingsunlimited.com. E-mail contact. GE/LC/GH/CA/SP. Edits: BP/NB/D. All fees negotiated in advance: developmental edits (format/house-style/clarity) range from $1,500-3,000; 100-250 pgs.; substantive rewrite averages $5,000/250 pgs. Specializes in turning sermon series into books for classic libraries. Author/coauthor/ghostwriter of 30+ titles. Over 25 years' experience in development of bestselling titles for major Christian publishing houses.

WORD PRO/BARBARA WINSLOW ROBIDOUX, 127 Gelinas Dr., Chicopee MA 01020-4813. (413) 594-6567. Fax (413) 594-8375. E-mail: ebwordpro@aol.com. Call/e-mail. GE/LC/writing coach. Edits: A/SS/F/NB/BP/QL/TM/E/D. Fee quoted upon request. BA in English; 18 years as freelancer; book reviewer; on staff of TCC Manuscript Critique Service.

WORDS FOR ALL REASONS/ELIZABETH ROSIAN, 102 Rustic Ave., Johnstown PA 15904-2122. (814) 255-4351. E-mail: louiserosian@gmail.com. Website: www.savingsense2.wordpress.com. GE/LC/GH/CA. Edits A/SS/P/F/N/NB/BP/QL/BS/GB/E/D. More than 35 years' experience writing, teaching, and editing; more than 1,000 published works, plus inspirational novel, how-to book, and 6 chapbooks. Rate sheet on website.

WRITE HIS ANSWER MINISTRIES/MARLENE BAGNULL, LittD, 951 Anders Rd., Lansdale PA 19446. Phone/fax (484) 991-8581. E-mail: mbagnull@aol.com. Website: www.writehisanswer.com. Call/write. GE/LC/typesetting. Edits: A/SS/N/NB/BP/JN/BS/D. Charges $35/hr.; estimates given. Call or write for information on At-Home Writing Workshops, a correspondence study program. Author of 5 books; compiler/editor of 3 books; over 1,000 sales to Christian periodicals.

WRITE NOW SERVICES/KAREN APPOLD, 1554 Red Oak Lane, Macungie PA 18062 (610) 351-5400. Fax (917) 793-8609. E-mail: KAppold@msn.com. Website: www.writenowservices.com. Call/e-mail. GE/LC/GH/CA/B/NL/SP/WS. Edits: A/SS/F/QL/BS/E/D. Professional editor, writer, consultant since 1993 for magazines, journals, and online content. Hundreds of published articles and extensive editing of magazine and newspaper, journal, and website content. Rates determined after free evaluation of project.

WRITER'S EDGE SERVICE, E-mail: info@writersedgeservice.com. Website: www.writersedge service.com. NOTE: We only accept e-mail now. We have no office and no phone number as it is strictly an online service that we provide from freelance editors hired by us to do the evaluations. We no longer accept manuscripts by regular mail. All subscribers must go to the website, click on the "How to Submit a Book" and follow the step-by-step instructions. *For over 20 years, the Writer's Edge Service has been a method of effective communication between writers and major traditional Christian publishers. Writer's Edge, utilizing professional editors with many years of experience in working with major Christian publishers, evaluate, screen, and expose potential books to traditional Christian publishing companies. Because most traditional publishers no longer accept unsolicited manuscripts and no longer sift through what used to be called the "slush" pile, new or relatively unknown writers have little chance to be seen by a traditional publisher unless they have a credible literary agent. Writer's Edge Service, in full cooperation with over 75 traditional royalty-based Christian publishers, gives writers another option. The acquisition editors of these companies have agreed to view relevant manuscripts that "make the cut" at Writer's Edge because they know they have been carefully screened and evaluated before being passed to them for consideration. Over the years, hundreds of authors have been successfully published because of Writer's Edge Service.* Standard Fee is $99. See website for instructions.

WRITER'S RELIEF, INC./RONNIE L. SMITH, 207 Hackensack Street, Wood-Ridge NJ 07075. (866) 405-3003. Fax (201) 641-1253. E-mail: info@wrelief.com. Website: www.WritersRelief.com. Call or e-mail. LC/NL/targeting submissions. Proofs: A/SS/P/F/N/NB/JN/E. Nineteen years' experience as an author's submission service. Subscribe to their e-publication, *Submit Write Now!: Leads & Tips for Creative Writers*. Contact for rates.

WRITE THE FIRST TIME/CAROL E. SCOTT, PO Box 105, Niles OH 44446-0105. (330) 240-2313. E-mail: carolscotte@yahoo.com. Call/e-mail. GE/LC. Edits: A/SS/P/BS/E/D. Retired teacher of 30 years. 8 years' editing experience.

WRITING CAREER COACH, Tiffany Colter, 14665 Fike Rd., Riga MI 49276. (517) 936-5896. E-mail: Tiffany@WritingCareerCoach.com. Website: www.WritingCareerCoach.com. Prefers e-mail. GE/LC/GH/CA/B/NL/WS/live and online seminars/writing coach. Edits: A/SS/F/N/NB/BP/QL/JN/BS/E/D/publishing plans/writing business plan consulting/time management coaching/consulting. I have been a content editor and writing coach for more than 7 years. My clients include award-winning writers, self-published and traditionally published novelists, as well as business consultants, speakers, teachers, and nonwriters with a story to tell. I have judged for top writing contests across the country for published and unpublished writers. I served as judge for ACFW's writing contests for more than five years as well as the top contest in Christian fiction twice. In addition to fiction, I've judged poetry and essay contests. I graduated with my BA in 1998 with a summa cum laude distinction. References available upon request, or simply check my LinkedIn page for a large number of endorsements. I charge a penny per word for content edits or proofreads. $.10 per word for developmental editing. Coaching is $65/hr personalized. Group coaching only $5 per month after a $50 sign-up fee. (All amounts in USD. I work with many intl. clients as well.)

***WRITING COACH/LINDA WINN,** 138 Bluff Dr., Winchester TN 37398. E-mail: lhwinn@comcast .net. Writing coach.

CANADIAN/FOREIGN

AOTEAROA EDITORIAL SERVICES/VENNESSA NG, PO Box 228, Oamaru 9444, New Zealand. +64224346995. (A US-based number is available to clients.) E-mail: editor@aotearoaeditorial.com. Website: www.aotearoaeditorial.com. E-mail contact. GE/LC. Edits: SS/N. Page rates vary depending on project: start from $2/critique, $2/basic proofread, and $4/copyedit. (Rates are in US dollars and can be paid by PayPal or Western Union.) Ten years' critiquing experience.

***AY'S EDIT/ALAN YOSHIOKA, PhD,** 801—21 Maynard Ave., Toronto ON M6K 2Z8, Canada. (416) 531-1857. Fax number upon request. E-mail: ay1@aysedit.com. Website: www.aysedit.com. E-mail contact. GE/LC/PP. Edits: A/NB/TM/E. Certified proofreader and copy editor. Member of Editors' Association of Canada since 1999. In ninth year as freelance editor, writer, and indexer, following four years in-house as medical writer at a major pharmaceutical company. Clients include a large international Christian humanitarian organization. Math degree and PhD in history of science, technology, and medicine. Expertise in orthodox Christian responses to homosexuality. Payment negotiable, starting from basic rate of US $50/hour for clients in US with nonmedical material.

***CHESTNUT LANE CREATIVE/ADELE SIMMONS,** PO Box 116, Whitby ON L1N 5R7, Canada. (905) 263-4211. E-mail: AdeleCLCreative@bell.net. Website: www.AdeleSimmons.WordPress.com. E-mail/write. GE/LC/GH/CA/B/NL/SP/substantive editing/rewriting/writing/writing coach. Edits: A/SS/P/F/NB/PB/BS/GB/TM/E/D/S/songs/speeches. Decades of experience, award-winning, published writer/author. Editor for business, mental health, tourism, marketing, ministry, creative ministry arts, newspaper, television, radio, books, education, nonfiction, how-tos, songs. Freelance and contract work. Member of Editors Association of Canada. Topics mostly nonfiction. Rates negotiated based on project and services required.

DORSCH EDITORIAL/AUDREY DORSCH, 90 Ling Road, PH 302, Toronto ON M1E 4Y3, Canada. (416) 439-4320. E-mail: audrey@dorschedit.ca. Website: www.dorschedit.ca. Audrey Dorsch, ed. Editorial services: substantive editing, copyediting, indexing, proofreading.

EDITORIAL SERVICES/DARLENE OAKLEY, Kemptville ON K0G 1J0, Canada. (613) 816-3277. E-mail: darlene@darscorrections.com. Website: www.darscorrections.com. E-mail contact. GE/LC/GH/B/NL/SP/WS/PP/reviews/critiques/web copy. Edits: A/SS/N/NB/QL/BP/BS/GB/E/D/synopses/web copy. Substantive editor and proofreader with Lachesis Publishing & Glasshouse Publishing. The Word Guild; judge for Silicon Valley Romance Writers of America Gotcha! Contest 2008–2011 (inspirational category). Detailed (substantive) edit $5/pg. or .02/wd. Proofread: .012/wd. Manuscript critique: $1/page. Payment plans negotiable. See website for details.

EDITORIAL SERVICES/AIMEE REID, 1063 King St. W, Suite 301, Hamilton ON L8S 4S3, Canada. (905) 526-8794. E-mail: areid@aimeereid.com. Website: www.aimeereid.com. E-mail or call for contact. GE/CA/SP/(developmental, substantive, stylistic editing). Edits: A/NB/PB/BS/GB/D. Has published nonfiction for youth and adults, both in print and on wiki format. Has done editing for ages 5 to adult; tasks include incorporating reviewer's comments, rewriting as needed, suggesting images and layout, and creating illustration lists. Charges according to individual project depending on length and complexity. Manuscript evaluations are a set fee.

***WENDY SARGEANT,** 4 Lyall Clse, RIVERHILLS, QLD 4074, Australia. E-mail: wordfisher52@gmail.com. Website: www.editorsqld.com/freelance/Wendy_Sargeant.htm. E-mail contact. GE/LC/GH/CA/B/NL/SP/WS(writing & evaluation)/PP/instructional design/writing coach. Edits: A/SS/F/N/NB/BP/QL/JN/PB/BS/GB/TM/E/D/S. Copywriting. Special interests: technical material, business humor, children's books, educational books (primary, secondary, tertiary, and above), fiction, history, legal. Manuscript assessor and instructional designer with The Writing School. Award-winning author published in major newspapers and magazines. Editing educational manuals. Project officer and instructional designer for Global Education Project, United Nationals Assoc. Information specialist for Australian National University. Charges $55/hr. for articles/short stories; .02/wd. for copywriting; $300-400+ for book assessment.

11

Christian Literary Agents

Asking editors and other writers is a great way to find a good, reliable agent. You might also want to visit www.agentresearch.com and www.sfwa.org/beware/agents for tips. For a database of more than 500 agencies, go to www.literaryagent.com.

The site for the Association of Authors' Representatives (www.aaronline.org) carries a list of agents who don't charge fees, except for office expenses. Their website will also provide information on how to receive a list of approved agents. Some listings below indicate which agents belong to the Association of Authors' Representatives, Inc. Those members have subscribed to a code of ethics. Lack of such a designation, however, does not indicate the agent is unethical; most Christian agents are not members. For a full list of member agents, go to www.publishersweekly.com/aar.

(*) before a listing indicates unconfirmed or no information update.

***AGENT RESEARCH & EVALUATION INC.,** 425 N. 20th St., Philadelphia PA 19130. (215) 563-1867. Fax (215) 563-6797. E-mail: info@agentresearch.com. Website: www.agentresearch.info. This is not an agency but a service that tracks the public record of literary agents and helps authors use the data to obtain effective literary representation. Charges fees for this service. Offers a free "agent verification" service at the site. (Answers the question of whether or not the agent has created a public record of sales.) Also offers a newsletter, *Talking Agents E-zine*, free if you send your e-mail address.

***ALIVE COMMUNICATIONS,** 7680 Goddard St., Ste. 200, Colorado Springs CO 80920. (719) 260-7080. Fax (719) 260-8223. E-mail: submissions@alivecom.com. Website: www.alivecom.com. Agents: Rick Christian, president; Lee Hough, Joel Kneedler, Andrea Heinecke. Well known in the industry. Estab. 1989. Represents 175 clients. Not open to unpublished authors. New clients by referral only. Handles adult & teen novels and nonfiction, gift books, and crossover books. Deals in both Christian (70%) and general market (30%). Member Author's Guild & AAR.

Contact: E-mail to: submissions@alivecom.com. Accepts simultaneous submissions. Responds in 6 wks. to referrals only. May not respond to unsolicited submissions.

Commission: 15%

Fees: Only extraordinary costs with client's preapproval; no review/reading fee.

Tips: "If you have a referral, send material by mail, and be sure to mark envelope 'Requested Material.' Unable to return unsolicited materials without postpaid envelope."

***AMBASSADOR AGENCY,** PO Box 50358, Nashville TN 37205. (615) 370-4700, ext. 230. E-mail: Wes@AmbassadorAgency.com. Website: www.AmbassadorAgency.com. Agent: Wes Yoder. Estab. 1973. Recognized in the industry. Represents 25 clients. Open to unpublished authors and new clients. Handles adult nonfiction, crossover books. Also has a Speakers Bureau.

Contact: E-mail.

***BOOKS & SUCH,** 52 Mission Circle #22, PMB 170, Santa Rosa CA 95409. E-mail: representation@booksandsuch.com. Website: www.booksandsuch.com. Agents: Janet Kobobel Grant, Wendy Lawton, Rachelle Gardner, Rachel Kent, Mary Keeley. Well recognized in industry. Estab. 1997. Member of AAR, ACFW, CBA. Represents 250 clients. Open to new or unpublished authors (with recommendation only). Handles fiction and nonfiction for all ages except children's, picture books, speculative fiction, gift books, crossover, and general market books.

Contact: E-mail query (no attachments); no phone query. Accepts simultaneous submissions. Responds in 6-8 wks.

Commission: 15%.

Fees: No fees.

Tips: "Especially looking for narrative nonfiction and memoir."

***CURTIS BROWN LTD.,** 10 Astor Pl., New York NY 10003-6935. (212) 473-5400. Website: www.curtisbrown.com. Agents: Maureen Walters, Laura Blake Peterson, and Ginger Knowlton. Member AAR. General agent; handles religious/inspirational novels for all ages, adult nonfiction, and crossover books.

Contact: Query with SASE; no fax/e-query. Submit outline or sample chapters. Responds in 4 wks. to query; 8 wks. to ms.

Fees: Charges for photocopying & some postage.

***BROWNE & MILLER LITERARY ASSOCIATES,** 410 S. Michigan Ave., Ste. 460, Chicago IL 60605. (312) 922-3063. Fax (312) 922-1905. E-mail: mail@browneandmiller.com. Website: www.browneandmiller.com. Agent: Danielle Egan-Miller. Estab. 1971. Recognized in the industry. Represents 150 clients, mostly general, but also select Christian fiction writers. Open to new clients and talented unpublished authors, but most interested in experienced novelists looking for highly professional, full-service representation including rights management. Handles teen and adult fiction, adult nonfiction, and gift books for the general market; adult Christian fiction only. Member AAR, RWA, MWA, and The Author's Guild.

Contact: E-query to mail@browneandmiller.com, or mailed query letter/SASE. No unsolicited mss. Prefers no simultaneous submissions. Responds in 6 wks.

Commission: 15%, foreign 20%.

PEMA BROWNE LTD., 71 Pine Road, Woodbourne NY 12788. E-mail: ppbltd@optonline.net. Website: www.pemabrowneltd.com. Agent: Pema Browne. Recognized in industry. Estab. 1966. Represents 20 clients (2 religious). Open to unpublished authors; very few new clients at this time. Handles novels and nonfiction for all ages; picture books/novelty books, gift books, crossover books. Only accepts mss not previously sent to publishers; no simultaneous submissions. Responds in 6-8 wks.

Contact: Letter query with credentials; no phone, fax, or e-query. Must include SASE. No simultaneous submissions. No attachments.

Commission: 20% US & foreign; illustrators 30%.

Fees: None.

Tips: "Check at the library in reference section, in *Books in Print*, for books similar to yours. Have good literary skills, neat presentation. Know what has been published and research the genre that interests you."

KEITH CARROLL, AGENT, PO Box 428, Newburg PA 17257. (717) 423-6621. Fax (717) 423-6944. E-mail: keith@christianliteraryagent.com. Website: www.christianliteraryagent.com. Estab. 2009, functioned as an author coach since 2000. Represents 94 clients. New clients welcome. Specializes in helping authors prepare for publication, as a coach. Handles adult and teen nonfiction, adult fiction, picture books, e-books, crossover books. Accepts simultaneous submissions. Responds in 5-8 weeks.

Contact: Phone & e-mail.

Commission: 10%

Fees: Small fee for introductory consultation w/ unpublished authors, which includes a review/analysis of author's material, a two-hour personal phone call to advise and recommend regarding publishability.

CREDO COMMUNICATIONS LLC, 3148 Plainfield Ave. NE, Ste. 111, Grand Rapids MI 49525. (616) 363-2686. Fax (616) 363-7821. E-mail: connect@credocommunications.net. Website: www.credocommunications.net. Agents: Tim Beals, founder and pres.; Ann Byle; Karen Neumair; David Sanford. Recognized and recommended in the industry. Estab. 2005. Represents 60+ clients. Have current contracts with 40+ publishers. New clients by referral only. Handles adult and young-adult and children's religious/inspirational nonfiction and fiction. Other services offered: coaching for self-published authors on production, marketing, sales, and distribution.

Contact: E-mail connect@credocommunications.net. No simultaneous submissions. Responds in one month.

Commission: 15%; foreign 20%.

Fees: No fees or expenses.

Tips: Works with Christian ministry leaders to develop life-changing books, Bible-related products, and other Christian resources. Seeking new voices with thoughtful nonfiction and creative fiction.

THE BLYTHE DANIEL AGENCY INC., PO Box 64197, Colorado Springs CO 80962-4197. (719) 213-3427. E-mail: blythe@theblythedanielagency.com. jessica@theblythedanielagency.com. Website: www.theblythedanielagency.com. Agents: Blythe Daniel, Jessica Kirkland. Managing Editor: Julie Gwinn. Recognized in the industry. Estab. 2005. Represents 65 clients. Open to unpublished authors with an established platform/network and previously published authors. Handles inspirational novels, adult nonfiction, young adult fiction/nonfiction, limited children's books, gift and cookbooks. Represents bestselling authors and ACFW awarded authors. Accepting all fiction except sci-fi, biblical, or mystery. Seeking bloggers with dedicated followers.

Contact: By e-mail or mail. Accepts simultaneous submissions. Responds in 8 weeks.

Commission: 15%.

Fees: None.

Also: Provides publicity and marketing campaigns to clients as a separate service from literary representation.

Tips: "Authors must have a solid proposal on the topic of their book, including research on their audience, comparison to competitor's books, and what the author uniquely brings to the topic. Authors need to have a ready-made marketing plan to promote their book and the ability to promote their own book." See submission guidelines on website.

***DANIEL LITERARY GROUP,** 1701 Kingsbury Dr., Ste. 100, Nashville TN 37215. No phone calls. E-mail: greg@danielliterarygroup.com. Website: www.danielliterarygroup.com. Agent: Greg Daniel. Estab. 2007. Recognized in the industry. Represents 30 clients. Open to unpublished authors and new clients. Handles nonfiction, crossover & secular books.

Contact: E-mail only. Accepts simultaneous submissions. Responds in 3 wks.

Commission: 15%; foreign 20%.

Fees: None.

***JAN DENNIS LITERARY SERVICES,** 19350 Glen Hollow Cir., Monument CO 80132. (719) 559-1711. E-mail: jpdennislit@msn.com. Agent: Jan Dennis. Estab. 1995. Represents 20 clients. Open to unpublished authors and new clients. Handles teen/YA & adult religious/inspirational novels, adult nonfiction, crossover, and general books.

***DYSTEL & GODERICH LITERARY MANAGEMENT INC.,** 1 Union Square W., Ste. 904, New York NY 10003. (212) 627-9100. Fax (212) 627-9313. E-mail: Miriam@dystel.com. Website: www.dystel.com. Agents: Jane Dystel, Miriam Goderich, Stacey Glick, Michael Bourret, Jim McCarthy, Lauren Abramo, Jessica Papin, and John Rudolph. Estab. 1994. Recognized in the industry. Represents 5-10 religious book clients. Open to unpublished authors and new clients. Handles fiction and nonfiction for adults, gift books, general books, crossover books. Member AAR.

Contact: Query letter with bio. Brief e-query; no simultaneous queries. Responds to queries in 3-5 wks.; submissions in 2 mos.
Commission: 15%; foreign 19%.
Fees: Photocopying is author's responsibility.
Tips: "Send a professional, well-written query to a specific agent."

***FINE PRINT LITERARY MANAGEMENT,** 240 W. 35th St., Ste. 500, New York NY 10001. (212) 279-1282. Fax (212) 279-0927. E-mail: peter@fineprintlit.com. Website: www.fineprintlit.com. Agent: Peter Rubie and 7 other agents. Open to unpublished authors and new clients. General agent. Handles adult religion/spirituality nonfiction for teens and adults.
Contact: Query/SASE; accepts e-query. Responds in 2-3 mos.
Commission: 15%; foreign 20%.

GARY D. FOSTER CONSULTING, 733 Virginia Ave., Van Wert OH 45891. (419) 238-4082. E-mail: gary@garydfoster.com. Website: www.garydfoster.com. Agent: Gary Foster. Estab. 1989. Represents 30+ clients. Recognized in the industry. Open to unpublished authors and new clients. Handles adult religious/inspirational novels & nonfiction for all ages and gift books.
Contact: E-mail. Responds in 6 wks.
Commission: 15%.
Fees: Charges a nominal fee upon signing of representation agreement, plus expense reimbursement.

***SAMUEL FRENCH INC.,** 45 W. 25th St., New York NY 10010-2751. (212) 206-8990. Fax (212) 206-1429. E-mail: publications@samuelfrench.com. Website: www.samuelfrench.com, www.bakersplays.com. Agent: Roxane Heinze-Bradshaw. Estab. 1830. Open to new clients. Handles rights to some religious/inspirational stage plays. Owns a subsidiary company that also publishes religious plays.
Contact: Query online or by mail. See website for full submission information. Accepts simultaneous submissions; responds in 10 wks.
Commission: Varies.
Fees: None.

***GLOBAL TALENT REPS, INC./NATIONAL WRITERS LITERARY AGENCY,** 3140 S. Peoria St., #295, Aurora CO 80014. (720) 851-1959. E-mail: Info@globaltalentreps.com. Website: www.globaltalentreps.com. Agent: Andrew J. Whelchel III (a.whelchel@globaltalentreps.com). Estab. 1982. Recognized in the industry. Open to unpublished authors and new clients. Handles religious/inspirational novels for all ages, nonfiction for teens & adults, screenplays, movie scripts, gift books, and crossover/secular books.
Contact: Query by e-mail (use online form). Accepts simultaneous submissions; responds in 8 wks.
Commission: 10% film; 15% books; 5% scouting.
Fees: Postage charged to new, unknown authors.

***SANFORD J. GREENBURGER ASSOCIATES INC.,** 55 Fifth Ave., New York NY 10003. (212) 206-5600. Fax (212) 463-8718. Website: www.greenburger.com. Agents: Heide Lange, Dan Mandel, Matthew Bialer, Brenda Bowen, Faith Hamlin, Michael Harriot, Lisa Gallagher, Courtney Miller-Callihan. Estab. 1945. Represents 500 clients. Open to unpublished authors and new clients. General agent; handles adult religious/inspirational nonfiction. Member of AAR.
Contact: Query/proposal/3 sample chapters to Heide Lange by mail with SASE, or by fax; no e-query. Accepts simultaneous queries. Responds in 6-8 wks. to query; 2 mos. to ms.
Commission: 15%; foreign 20%.
Fees: Charges for photocopying and foreign submissions.

HARTLINE LITERARY AGENCY, 123 Queenston Dr., Pittsburgh PA 15235. (412) 829-2483. Fax (888) 279-6007. E-mail: joyce@hartlineliterary.com. Website: www.hartlineliterary.com. Blog: www

.hartlineliteraryagency.blogspot.com. Agents: Joyce A. Hart, adult novels (romance, mystery/suspense, women's fiction) and nonfiction; Terry Burns, adult fiction & nonfiction, YA, terry@hartlineliterary.com; Diana Flegal, adult novels & nonfiction, diana@hartlineliterary.com. Andy Scheer, adult fiction & nonfiction, andy@hartlineliterary.com; Linda Glaz, adult fiction & nonfiction, linda@hartlineliterary.com. Recognized in industry. Estab. 1992. Represents 150+ clients. Open to new clients. Handles adult nonfiction, gift books. No poetry, children's books, fantasy, or science fiction.

Contact: E-mail/phone/letter; e-mail preferred. Accepts simultaneous submissions; responds in 6-8 wks.

Commission: 15%; foreign 20%; films 20% and 25%.

Fees: No reading fees or expenses.

Tips: "Please look at our website before submitting. Guidelines are listed, along with detailed information about each agent. Be sure to include your biography and publishing history with your proposal. The author/agent relationship is a team effort. Working together we can make sure your manuscript gets the exposure and attention it deserves."

THE HARVEY LITERARY AGENCY, LLC., 309 Carriage Place Ct., Decatur GA 30033. (404) 580-9431. E-mail: BoncaH@aol.com; Website: www.perfectbook.net. Agent: Dr. Bonnie C. Harvey, PhD. Recognized in the industry. Open to unpublished authors and new clients. Handles adult novels—fiction & nonfiction, juvenile & young adult—some children's books.

Contact: E-mail, phone, or letter.

Commission: Standard 15%; foreign negotiable.

Fees: None, except for minor expenses.

JEFF HERMAN AGENCY, PO Box 1522, Stockbridge MA 01262. (413) 298-0077. Fax (413) 298-8188. E-mail: Jeff@jeffherman.com. Website: www.jeffherman.com. Agents: Jeff Herman and Deborah Herman. Estab. 1987. Recognized in the industry. Represents 20+ clients with religious books. Open to unpublished authors and new clients. Handles adult nonfiction (recovery/healing, spirituality), gift books, general books, crossover.

Contact: Query by mail/SASE, or by e-mail or fax. Accepts simultaneous submissions & e-queries.

Commission: 15%; foreign 10%.

Fees: No reading or management fees; just copying and shipping.

Tips: "I love a good book from the heart. Have faith that you will accomplish what has been appointed to you."

***HIDDEN VALUE GROUP,** 1240 E. Ontario Ave., Ste. 102-148, Corona CA 92881. Phone/fax (951) 549-8891. E-mail: bookquery@hiddenvaluegroup.com. Website: www.HiddenValueGroup.com. Agents: Jeff Jernigan & Nancy Jernigan. Estab. 2001. Recognized in the industry. Represents 20+ clients with religious books. Open to previously published authors only. Handles adult fiction and nonfiction, gift books, and crossover books. No poetry, articles, or short stories.

Contact: Letter or e-mail. Accepts simultaneous submissions. Responds in 4-6 wks.

Commission: 15%; foreign 15%.

Fees: None.

Tips: "Looking for romance and suspense fiction projects as well as women's nonfiction. Make sure the proposal includes author bio, 2 sample chapters, and manuscript summary. Marketing plan to promote your project is a must."

***HORNFISCHER LITERARY MANAGEMENT,** PO Box 50544, Austin TX 78763. E-mail: queries@hornfischerlit.com or jim@hornfischerlit.com. Website: www.hornfischerlit.com. Agent: James D. Hornfischer. Estab. 2001. Represents 45 clients. Open to unpublished authors and new clients (with referrals from clients). Considers simultaneous submissions. Responds in 1 mo. General agent; handles adult religious/inspirational nonfiction.

Contact: E-query only for fiction; query or proposal for nonfiction (proposal package, outline, and 2 sample chapters). Considers simultaneous queries. Responds to queries in 5-6 wks.

Commission: 15%; foreign 25%.

D. C. JACOBSON & ASSOCIATES, 3689 Carman Drive, Suite 200 C, Lake Oswego OR 97035. (503) 850-4800. Fax (503) 850-4805. E-mail: submissions@dcjacobson.com. Website: www.dcjacobson.com. Agents: Don Jacobson, Jenni Burke, David Van Diest, Blair Jacobson, Heidi Mitchell, David Jacobsen. Estab. 2006. Represents 100+ clients. Recognized in the industry (former owner of Multnomah Publishers, multiple bestselling books). Open to unpublished authors and new clients. Handles adult & teen religious/inspirational novels & nonfiction, crossover books, children's books.

Contact: Submissions & queries through website form only. Accepts simultaneous submissions; responds in 8 wks.

Commission: 15%.

Fees: No reading fees.

Services: None.

Tips: "Looking for fresh writing that will redeem culture and renew the church. Please review our website thoroughly before submitting your proposal."

***JELLINEK & MURRAY LITERARY AGENCY,** 47—722 Hui Kelu St., Apt. 4, Kaneohe HI 96744. Phone/fax (808) 239-8451. E-mail: rgr.jellinek@gmail.com. Blog: www.hawaiireaders.com. Agent: Roger Jellinek. Estab. 1995. Represents a few Christian clients. Not recognized in the industry. Open to unpublished authors; new clients by personal reference (otherwise only June through December). Handles adult religious/inspirational nonfiction, crossover books, secular books.

Contact: E-mail only. Accepts simultaneous submissions; responds in 6 wks.

Commission: 15%; foreign 20%.

Fees: No, except for unusual travel or Express Mail.

***WILLIAM K. JENSEN LITERARY AGENCY,** 119 Bampton Ct., Eugene OR 97404. Phone/fax (541) 688-1612. E-mail: queries@wkjagency.com. Website: www.wkjagency.com. Agent: William K. Jensen. Estab. 2005. Recognized in the industry. Represents 38 clients. Open to unpublished authors and new clients. Handles adult fiction (no science fiction or fantasy), nonfiction for all ages, picture books, gift books, crossover books.

Contact: E-mail only using online form; no phone queries. Accepts simultaneous submissions. Responds in 12 wks.

Commission: 15%.

Fees: No fees.

***NATASHA KERN LITERARY AGENCY INC.,** PO Box 1069, White Salmon WA 98672. Website: www.natashakern.com. Agent: Natasha Kern. Well-recognized member of Author's Guild, ACFW, RWA. Estab. 1987. Represents 36 religious clients. Open to unpublished authors and new clients. Handles adult religious/inspirational fiction (romance, romantic suspense, women's fiction, historical fiction, mystery, suspense, thrillers, and general market novels).

Contact: Accepts e-queries at queries@natashakern.com only; 3-pg. synopsis & 1 chapter. Responds in 2-4 wks. to queries, if interested. Also meets at conferences or through current clients.

Commission: 15%; 20% foreign (includes foreign-agent commission).

Fees: No reading fee.

Tips: "I have personally sold over 1,000 books, many of them bestsellers and award winners. See submission guidelines on our website before sending a query."

***K J LITERARY SERVICES, LLC,** 1540 Margaret Ave., Grand Rapids MI 49507. (616) 551-9797. E-mail: kim@kjliteraryservices.com. Agent: Kim Zeilstra.

Contact: E-query preferred; phone query OK.
Commission: 15%.
Tips: "Taking new authors by referral only."

***KRIS LITERARY AGENCY,** 34 Oguntona Crescent, Phase 1, Gbagada Estate, Lagos, Nigeria. +2348067628017. E-mail: krisliterary@yahoo.com. Agent: Chris Agada. Estab. 2009. Represents 50 clients. Building recognition in the industry. Open to unpublished authors and new clients. Handles all types of material.
Contact: Query by e-mail or phone. Accepts simultaneous submissions; responds in 2 wks.
Commission: 15%; foreign 15%.
Fees: No fees.

THE STEVE LAUBE AGENCY, 5025 N. Central Ave., #635, Phoenix AZ 85012-1502. (602) 336-8910. E-mail: info@stevelaube.com. Website: www.stevelaube.com. Agents: Steve Laube (pres.), Tamela Hancock Murray, Karen Ball. Estab. 2004. Well recognized in the industry. Represents 170+ clients. Open to new and unpublished authors. Handles adult Christian fiction and nonfiction, theology, how-to, health, Christian living, and selected YA. No children's books, end-times literature, or poetry. Accepts simultaneous submissions. Responds in 6-8 wks.
Contact: Please use guidelines on website: www.stevelaube.com/guidelines. If guidelines are not followed, the proposal will not receive a response.
Commission: 15%; foreign 20%.
Fees: No fees.
Tips: "Looking for fresh and innovative ideas. Make sure your proposal contains an excellent presentation."

***LEVINE GREENBERG LITERARY AGENCY INC.,** 307—7th Ave., Ste. 2407, New York NY 10001. (212) 337-0934. Fax (212) 337-0948. Website: www.levinegreenberg.com. Agent: James Levine. Agent: Arielle Eckstut. Estab. 1989. Represents 250 clients. Open to unpublished authors and new clients. General agent; handles adult religious/inspirational nonfiction. Member AAR.
Contact: See guidelines/submission form on website; requires e-query; does not respond to mailed queries.
Commission: 15%; foreign 20%.
Fees: Office expenses.
Tips: "Our specialties include spirituality and religion."

***THE LITERARY GROUP INTL.,** 14 Penn Plaza, Ste. 925, New York NY 10122. (646) 442-5896. E-mail: js@theliterarygroup.com. Website: www.theliterarygroup.com. Agent: Frank Weimann. Recognized in the industry. Estab. 1986. Represents 300 clients (120 for religious books). Member of AAR. Open to new clients and unpublished authors. Handles adult novels, teen/young adult novels, picture books, adult nonfiction, teen/young adult nonfiction. Children's nonfiction, gift books, e-books, crossover.
Contact: E-mail.
Commission: 15%; foreign 20%.
Fees: Expenses for overseas postage/FedEx/DHL/UPS.
Tips: "Looking for fresh, original spiritual fiction and nonfiction. We offer a written contract which may be canceled after 30 days."

LITERARY MANAGEMENT GROUP INC., PO Box 40965, Nashville TN 37204. (615) 812-4445. E-mail: brucebarbour@literarymanagementgroup.com (for nonfiction); lavonne@literarymanagementgroup.com (for fiction). Website: www.literarymanagementgroup.com. Agents: Bruce R. Barbour (nonfiction), Lavonne Stevens (fiction). Estab. 1995. Well recognized in the industry. Represents 100+ clients. No unpublished authors; open to new clients. Handles adult novels, teen and adult nonfiction, crossover books. Other services offered: book packaging and consulting.

Contact: E-mail preferred. Will review proposals, no unsolicited mss. Accepts simultaneous submissions; responds in 4-6 wks.
Commission: 15%; foreign 20%.
Fees: No fees or expenses on agented books.
Tips: "Follow guidelines, proposal outline, and submissions format on website. Use Microsoft Word. Study the market and know where your book will fit in."

LIVING WORD LITERARY AGENCY/KIMBERLY SHUMATE, PO Box 40974, Eugene OR 97404. E-mail: livingwordliterary@gmail.com. Website: www.livingwordliterary.wordpress.com. Agent: Kimberly Shumate. Estab. 2009. Recognized in the industry as a proud member of the ECPA. Represents 30 clients. Open to unpublished writers as well as established authors. Handles adult fiction and nonfiction (see agency website for genre exclusions).
Contact: E-mail. No simultaneous or hard copy submissions; responds in 1 week.
Commission: 15%; foreign 20%.
Fees: Please refer to the agency website for submission guidelines. No fees.
Tips: "Looking for creative, relevant material. I'm all about the underdog, so don't be shy."

***STERLING LORD LITERISTIC INC.,** 65 Bleecker St., New York NY 10012. (213) 780-6050. Fax (212) 780-6095. E-mail: claudia@sll.com or info@sll.com. Website: www.sll.com. Agent: Claudia Cross. Recognized in the industry. In addition to clients in the general market, she represents 10 clients with Christian/religious books. Open to unpublished clients with referrals and to new clients. Handles adult and teen Christian fiction, including women's fiction, romance novels, adult nonfiction exploring themes of spirituality, gift books, crossover books, general books.
Contact: Letter, fax, or e-query (with referral only). Accepts simultaneous submissions, if informed. Responds in 4-6 wks.
Commission: 15%; foreign 20%.
Fees: "We charge for photocopy costs for manuscripts or any costs above and beyond the usual cost of doing business."

MACGREGOR LITERARY, 2373 N.W. 185th Ave., Ste. 165, Hillsboro OR 97124. E-mail: submissions@macgregorliterary.com. Website: www.MacGregorLiterary.com. Agents: Chip MacGregor, Sandra Bishop, Amanda Luedeke. Estab. 2006. Member of AAR. Recognized in the industry. Rarely open to unpublished authors and taking on few new clients. Handles teen and adult religious/inspirational novels and nonfiction; crossover and secular books.
Contact: E-mail query. Accepts simultaneous submissions. Responds in 4 wks.
Commission: 15%; foreign 20%.
Fees: No fees or expenses.
Tips: "We represent books that make a difference. Working with a list of established authors, we are always looking for strong nonfiction projects in a variety of genres. Please check the website before submitting."

***MANUS & ASSOCIATES LITERARY AGENCY,** 425 Sherman Ave., Ste. 200, Palo Alto CA 94306. (650) 470-5151. Fax (650) 470-5159. E-mail: manuslit@manuslit.com. Website: www.manuslit.com. Agents: Jillian Manus, Penny Nelson, Dena Fischer, and Jandy Nelson. Members AAR. Estab. 1994. Open to unpublished authors and new clients. Handles adult religious/inspirational novels & nonfiction, gift books, crossover & general books.
Contact: Query by mail/fax/e-query (no attachments or phone calls). For fiction, send first 30 pages, bio, and SASE. For nonfiction, send proposal/sample chapters. Responds in 12 weeks, only if interested.
Commission: 15%; foreign 20-25%.

***WILLIAM MORRIS LITERARY AGENCY,** 1325 Avenue of the Americas, New York NY 10019. (212) 586-5100. Fax (212) 246-3583. E-mail: vs@wma.com. Website: www.wma.com. Agent: Valerie

Summers. Recognized in the industry. Estab. 1898. Hundreds of clients with religious books. Not open to unpublished authors or new clients. Handles all types of material. Member AAR.

Contact: Send query/synopsis, publication history by mail/SASE. No fax/e-query. No unsolicited mss.

Commission: 15%; foreign 20%.

Fees: None.

***MORTIMER LITERARY AGENCY,** 43500 Ridge Park Dr., Suite 105-A, Temecula CA 92590. (951) 208-5674. E-mail: kmortimer@mortimerliterary.com. Agent: Kelly Gottuso Mortimer. Estab. 2006. Open to unpublished authors or those not published for 3 yrs. Adult novels, adult nonfiction, cross-over books, secular books. Will not represent writers who are members of Romance Writers of America.

Contact: E-mail only. Accepts simultaneous submissions. Responds in 1 week to queries.

Commission: 20%

Fees: None

Tips: "Check website for current submission guidelines before submitting."

NAPPALAND LITERARY AGENCY, 446 East 29th Street #1674, Loveland CO 80539. (970) 635-0641. Fax (970) 635-9869. E-mail: literary@nappaland.com. Website: www.nappalandliterary.com. Division of Nappaland Communications Inc. Agent: Mike Nappa. Estab. 1995. Recognized in the industry. Represents 10 clients. Prefers published authors; prefers authors who are referred by a current Nappaland author or traditional publishing company professional. Handles literary nonfiction, historical nonfiction, cultural concerns, Christian living, women's issues, suspense fiction, YA fiction, and women's fiction. DOES NOT handle memoirs, children's books, or anything about cats. Submission guidelines and "open submission" periods for unsolicited queries are posted at www.NappalandLiterary.com. Also associated with Author Echo Public Relations (www.AuthorEcho.com), which is available to author clients seeking PR representation in conjunction with literary representation.

Contact: By e-mail. Accepts simultaneous submissions; responds in 2-4 wks. Unsolicited queries are automatically rejected unless sent during "open submission" periods.

Commission: 15% for literary representation; 15% for public-relations representation.

Fees: None.

Tips: "Authors who apply the advice of Mike Nappa's book *77 Reasons Why Your Book Was Rejected* before sending queries will have a much better chance of rising above the slush pile."

***B. K. NELSON LITERARY AGENCY AND LECTURE BUREAU,** 1565 Paseo Vida, Palm Springs CA 92264. (760) 778-8800. Fax (760) 778-6242. NY: 914-741-1322. Fax: 914-741-1324. Websites: www.bknelson.com, bknelsonlecturebureau.com, bknelsoneditorialservices.com. Agent: B. K. Nelson, pres.; ed. asst. dir., John W. Benson. Incorporated in New York, Certificate of Qualification California. Notary Lic., Degree of Bachelors of Laws, Diploma in American Law & Procedure. Sold over 2,000 books. Represents adult & childrens' religious & inspirational fiction & nonfiction, self-help, how-to, movies. Member BBB. 80 clients.

***NUNN COMMUNICATIONS INC.,** 1612 Ginger Dr., Carrollton TX 75007. (972) 394-6866. E-mail: info@nunncommunications.com. Website: www.nunncommunications.com. Agent: Leslie Nunn Reed. Estab. 1995. Represents 20 clients. Recognized in the industry. Not open to unpublished authors. Handles adult nonfiction, gift books, crossover books, and general books.

Contact: By e-mail. Responds in 4-6 wks.

Commission: 15%.

Fees: Charges office expenses if over $100.

***ALLEN O'SHEA LITERARY AGENCY, LLC,** 615 Westover Rd., Stamford CT 06902. (203) 359-9965. E-mail: Marilyn@allenoshea.com. Website: www.allenoshea.com. Agents: Marilyn Allen and

Coleen O'Shea. Estab. 2003. Represents 4 clients with religious books. Recognized in the industry. Open to unpublished authors (with credentials & platform) and new clients. Handles adult nonfiction.

Contact: Query by mail or e-mail. No simultaneous submissions. Responds in 4 wks.

Commission: 15%; foreign 15-25%.

Fees: For overseas mailing.

Tips: "We specifically like practical nonfiction."

KATHI J. PATON LITERARY AGENCY, PO Box 2236, Radio City Station, New York NY 10101-2236. (212) 265-6586. E-mail: KJPLitBiz@optonline.net. Website: www.PatonLiterary.com. Agent: Kathi Paton. Estab. 1987. Handles adult nonfiction: Christian life and issues.

Contact: Prefers e-mail query.

Commission: 15%; foreign 20%.

Fees: For photocopying & postal submissions.

PATRICK-MEDBERRY ASSOCIATES, 567 W. Channel Islands Blvd. #179, Port Hueneme CA 93041. No phone calls please. E-mail: patrickmedberry@sbcglobal.net. Agents: Peggy Patrick & C. J. Medberry. Estab. 2005. Management & production company specializing in Christian writers, directors, and producers, as well as religious and inspirational novels, screenplays, TV/movie scripts, crossover books, general books, and screenplays. Open to unpublished authors and new clients.

Contact: Query by letter, fax, or e-mail; no calls.

Commission: 10%.

Fees: None.

***PELHAM LITERARY AGENCY,** PMB 315, 2650 Jamacha Rd., Ste. 147, El Cajon CA 92019. (619) 447-4468. E-mail: jmeals@pelhamliterary.com. Website: www.pelhamliterary.com. Agents: Howard Pelham & Jim Meals. Estab. 1993. Recognized in the industry. Open to unpublished authors and new clients. Handles adult and teen religious/inspirational novels & nonfiction, crossover books.

Contact: Brief query letter; e-query OK. Provides a list of published clients and titles. Accepts simultaneous submissions; responds in 6 wks.

Commission: 15%; foreign 20%.

Fees: Charges for postage and copying only. Offers an optional extensive critique for $200. Information on website.

Tips: "We are actively seeking writers for the Christian fiction market, but also open to nonfiction. We specialize in genre fiction and enjoy working with new authors."

***THE QUADRIVIUM GROUP,** 7512 Dr. Phillips Blvd., Ste. 50-229, Orlando FL 32819. Website: www.TheQuadriviumGroup.com. Agents: Steve Blount (SteveBlount@TheQuadriviumGroup.com); Susan Blount (SusanBlount@TheQuadriviumGroup.com). Estab. 2006. Represents 20-30 clients. Recognized in the industry. Open to a limited number of unpublished authors (with credentials, platform, compelling story/idea) and to new clients (mostly by referral). General agent. Handles Christian and general fiction and nonfiction for all ages, gift books, crossover books. Other services offered: consulting on book sales and distribution.

Contact: E-mail preferred; responds in 2-4 wks.

Commission: 15%; foreign 20%.

Fees: Only extraordinary costs with client's permission.

RED WRITING HOOD INK, 2075 Attala Rd. 1990, Kosciusko MS 39090. (662) 582-1191. Fax (662) 796-3161. E-mail: redwritinghoodink@gmail.com. Website: redwritinghoodink.net. Agent: Sheri Williams. Estab. 1997. Clients with Christian books: 50%. Recognized in the industry. Open to unpublished authors with strong platform; open to new clients. Handles novels & nonfiction for MG, YA, adult, crossover books. No children's younger than MG.

Contact: E-mail/letter. Accepts simultaneous submissions noted as such; responds in 1-6 weeks to e-mail; no postal submissions accepted or acknowledged.

Commission: 15%; foreign 20%.

Tips: "Beta readers are priceless. Research is essential to a compelling story where readers connect with your characters. Unless specifically stated in our response, we will not accept another query on the same project once we have passed."

***RLR ASSOCIATES, LTD.,** Literary Dept., 7 W. 51st St., New York NY 10019. (212) 541-8641. Fax (212) 262-7084. E-mail: sgould@rlrassociates.net. Website: www.rlrliterary.net. Scott Gould, literary assoc. Estab. 1972. Member AAR. Represents 50 clients. Open to unpublished authors and new clients. General agency; handles adult religious/inspirational nonfiction.

Contact: Query by e-mail, or by mail with SASE. Considers simultaneous submissions. Responds in 4-8 wks.

Commission: 15%; foreign 20%.

ROSS YOON LITERARY AGENCY, 1666 Connecticut Ave. N.W., #500, Washington DC 20009. (202) 328-3282. Fax (202) 328-9162. Website: www.rossyoon.com. Agent: Gail Ross (gail@rossyoon.com). Contact: Anna Sproul (anna@rossyoon.com). Estab. 1988. Represents 200 clients. Open to unpublished authors and new clients (mostly through referrals). General agent; handles adult religious/inspirational nonfiction, history, health, and business books.

Contact: No mailed queries; e-queries only. Accepts simultaneous queries.

Commission: 15%; foreign 25%.

Fees: Office expenses.

SCHIAVONE LITERARY AGENCY INC., 236 Trails End, West Palm Beach FL 33413-2135. Phone/fax (561) 966-9294. E-mail: profschia@aol.com. Website: www.publishersmarketplace.com/members/profschia. Agent: James Schiavone, EdD. Recognized in the industry. Estab. 1997. Represents 6 clients. Open to unpublished and new clients. Handles adult, teen, and children's fiction and nonfiction; celebrity biography; general books; crossover books.

Contact: E-mail only; one-page e-mail query (no attachments).

Commission: 15%; foreign 20%.

Fees: No reading fees; authors pay postage only.

Tips: Works primarily with published authors; will consider first-time authors with excellent material. Actively seeking books on spirituality, major religions, and alternative health. Very selective on first novels.

***SUSAN SCHULMAN LITERARY AGENCY,** 454 W. 44th St., New York NY 10036. (212) 713-1633. Fax (212) 581-8830. E-mail: schulman@aol.com. Agent: Susan Schulman. Estab. 1989. Represents 6 clients. Recognized in the industry. Member of AAR. Open to unpublished authors and new clients. Handles adult & teen/YA religious/inspirational novels, adult nonfiction, picture books.

Contact: Query.

Commission: 15%; foreign 20%.

***SERENDIPITY LITERARY AGENCY, LLC,** 305 Gates Ave., Brooklyn NY 11216. (718) 230-7689. Fax (718) 230-7829. E-mail: rbrooks@serendipitylit.com. Website: www.serendipitylit.com. Agent: Regina Brooks. Member AAR. Estab. 2000. Represents 50 clients; 3 with religious books. Recognized in the industry. Open to unpublished authors and new clients. General agent; handles fiction & nonfiction for all ages, gift books, crossover books, general books. No science fiction. No picture books for now.

Contact: By e-mail or letter; no faxes. Accepts simultaneous submissions. Responds in 8-12 wks.

Commission: 15%; foreign 20%.

Fees: None.

THE SEYMOUR AGENCY, 475 Miner Street Rd., Canton NY 13617. (315) 386-1831. E-mail: marysue@theseymouragency.com. Website: www.theseymouragency.com. Agent: Mary Sue Seymour. Estab. 1992. Member of AAR, ACFW, The Author's Guild, RWS, WGA. Represents 35 religious clients. Open to unpublished authors and new clients (prefers published authors). Handles Christian romance novels, Christian historical romance, and nonfiction for all ages, general books, crossover books. Coagent Nicole Resciniti can be reached at nicole@theseymouragency.com. She handles all types of Christian books, including YA.

Contact: Query letter or e-mail with first 50 pages of ms. For nonfiction, send proposal with chapter 1. Simultaneous query OK. Responds in 1 mo. for queries and 2-3 mos. for mss.
Commission: 15% for unpublished authors.
Fees: None.
Tips: "We have multibook sales to Zondervan, Thomas Nelson, Harvest House, Cook Communications, Abingdon Press, Bethany House, Guideposts, and HarperOne."

KEN SHERMAN & ASSOCIATES, 1275 N. Hayworth, Ste. 103, Los Angeles CA 90046. (310) 273-3840. Fax (310) 271-2875. E-mail: ken@kenshermanassociates.com. Agent: Ken Sherman. Estab. 1989. Represents 50 clients. Open to unpublished authors and new clients. Handles adult religious/inspirational novels, nonfiction, screenplays, and TV/movie scripts.

Contact: By referral only. Responds in 1 mo.
Commission: 15%; foreign 20%; dramatic rights 15%.
Fees: Charges office expenses and other negotiable expenses.

WENDY SHERMAN ASSOCIATES, 27 W. 24th St., Ste. 700B, New York NY 10110. (212) 279-9027. Fax (212) 279-8863. Website: www.wsherman.com. Agents: Wendy Sherman, Kimberly Perel. Open to unpublished authors and new clients. General agents. Handle adult spiritual nonfiction.

Contact: Query by mail/SASE or send proposal/1 chapter. No phone/fax/e-query. Guidelines on website.
Commission: 15%; foreign 25%.

***MICHAEL SNELL LITERARY AGENCY,** PO Box 1206, Truro MA 02666-1206. (508) 349-3718. E-mail: snell.patricia@gmail.com. Website: http://michaelsnellagency.com. Agent: Patricia Snell. Estab. 1978. Represents 200 clients. Open to unpublished authors and new clients. General agent: handles adult religious.

Contact: Query with SASE. No simultaneous submissions. Responds in 1-2 wks.
Commission: 15%; foreign 15%.

***SPENCERHILL ASSOCIATES, LTD./KAREN SOLEM,** Chatham NY. (518) 392-9293. Fax (518) 392-9554. E-mail: submissions@spencerhillassociates.com. Website: www.spencerhillassociates.com. Agent: Karen Solem. Member of AAR. Recognized in the industry. Estab. 2001. Represents 15-20 clients with religious books. Not currently open to unpublished authors; very selective of new clients. Primarily handles adult Christian fiction; no YA, children's, or nonfiction.

Contact: By e-mail.
Commission: 15%; foreign 20%.
Fees: Photocopying and Express Mail charges only.
Tips: "Check website for latest information and needs and how to submit. No nonfiction."

LESLIE H. STOBBE, 300 Doubleday Rd., Tryon NC 28782. (828) 808-7127. E-mail: lhstobbe123@gmail.com. Website: www.stobbeliterary.com. Agent: Les Stobbe. Assoc. agent for children and YA: Sally Apokedak. E-mail: sally@sally-apokedak.com. Website: www.sally-apokedak.com. Well recognized in the industry. Estab. 1993. Represents more than 100 clients. Open to unpublished authors and new clients. Handles adult fiction, nonfiction, and crossover books.

Contact: By e-mail. Considers simultaneous submissions; responds within 12 weeks.
Commission: 15%.
Fees: None.
Tips: "I will not accept clients whose theological positions in their book differ significantly from mine."

SUITE A MANAGEMENT TALENT & LITERARY AGENCY, 120 El Camino Dr., Ste. 202, Beverly Hills CA 90212. (310) 278-0801. Fax (310) 278-0807. E-mail: suite-A@juno.com. Agent: Lloyd D. Robinson. Recognized in the industry. Estab. 2001. Several clients. Open to new and unpublished clients (if published in other media). Specializes in screenplays and novels for adaptation to TV movies.

Contact: By mail or fax only. For consideration of representation, send current bio, and for each screenplay, your WGA registration number, log line, and two-paragraph synopsis only. Complete scripts or e-mail submissions are not read; attachments are deleted. Responds only if interested.

Commission: 10%.

Comments: Representation limited to adaptation of novels and true-life stories for film and television development. Work must have been published for consideration.

MARK SWEENEY & ASSOCIATES, 28540 Altessa Way, Ste. 201, Bonita Springs FL 34135. (239) 594-1957. Fax (239) 594-1935. E-mail: sweeney2@comcast.net. Agents: Mark Sweeney; Janet Sweeney. Recognized in the industry. Estab. 2003. Open to new clients on a restricted basis. Handles adult religious/inspirational nonfiction, crossover books, general books. No new fiction at this time.

Contact: E-mail.

Commission: 15%; foreign 15%.

Fees: None.

***TALCOTT NOTCH LITERARY SERVICES,** 276 Forest Rd., Milford CT 06461. (203) 877-1146. Fax (203) 876-9517. Website: www.talcottnotch.net. Agent: Gina Panettieri (gpanettieri@talcottnotch .net). Not yet recognized in the industry; building a Christian presence. Estab. 2003. Represents 25 clients (3 with religious books). Open to unpublished authors and new clients. Handles nonfiction & fiction, crossover & general market books for all ages.

Contact: By e-mail (editorial@talcottnotch.net). Accepts simultaneous submissions; responds in 8 wks.

Commission: 15%; foreign or with coagent 20%.

Fees: None.

Tips: "While Christian and religious books are not our main focus, we are open to unique and thought-provoking works from all writers. We specifically seek nonfiction in areas of parenting, health, women's issues, arts & crafts, self-help, and current events. We are open to academic/scholarly work as well as commercial projects."

***3 SEAS LITERARY AGENCY,** PO Box 8571, Madison WI 53708. (608) 221-4306. E-mail: threeseaslit@aol.com. Website: www.threeseaslit.com. Agent: Michelle Grajkowski. Estab. 2000. Represents 40 clients. Open to unpublished authors and new clients. General agent; handles adult religious/inspirational novels & nonfiction.

Contact: E-query only with synopsis & 1 chapter (queries@threeseaslit.com). Considers simultaneous submissions. Responds in 2-3 mos.

Commission: 15%; foreign 20%.

TRIDENT MEDIA GROUP, LLC, 41 Madison Ave., 36th Fl., New York NY 10010. (212) 262-4810. Fax (212) 262-4849. E-mail: dfehr@tridentmediagroup.com. Website: www.tridentmediagroup.com. Agent: Don Fehr. Open to unpublished authors and new clients. General agent. Handles adult religious nonfiction.

Contact: No unsolicited mss. Query/SASE first; send outline and sample chapters on request. Responds to queries in 3 wks.; mss in 6 wks.

Commission: 15%.

***VAN DIEST LITERARY AGENCY,** PO Box 1482, Sisters OR 97759. (541) 549-0477. Fax (541) 549-1213. E-mail through website: www.ChristianLiteraryAgency.com. Agents: David & Sarah Van

Diest. Estab. 2004. Represents 20 clients. Open to unpublished authors and new clients. Recognized in the industry. Handles teen & adult novels, nonfiction for all ages, crossover books.

Contact: By e-mail. Use online form. Responds in 4 wks.

Commission: 15%; 25% for first-time authors.

***VERITAS LITERARY AGENCY,** 601 Van Ness Ave., Opera Plaza Ste. E, San Francisco CA 94102. (415) 647-6964. Fax (415) 647-6965. E-mail: submissions@veritasliterary.com. Website: www.veritasliterary.com. Agent: Katherine Boyle (kboyle@veritasliterary.com). Member AAR. Handles serious religious nonfiction (no New Age).

Contact: Query with SASE; e-query OK (no attachments); no fax queries.

***WATERSIDE PRODUCTIONS INC.,** 2055 Oxford Ave., Cardiff-by-the-Sea CA 92007. (760) 632-9190. Fax (760) 632-9295. E-mail: admin@waterside.com. Website: www.waterside.com. Agent: William E. Brown (webrown@waterside.com). Christian agent in a highly regarded general agency. Interested in handling Christian books, or books which otherwise challenge and engage readers from a Judeo-Christian perspective. Prefers nonfiction, but will look at fiction (the bar is very high). In addition to spiritually oriented books, devotions, theology, chick lit, and mom lit; list includes business books: leadership, marketing, sales, business development.

Contact: Query via online form (see website). Considers simultaneous submissions.

Commission: 15%; foreign 25%.

***WINTERS & KING, INC.,** 2448 E. 81st St., Ste. 5900, Tulsa OK 74137-4259. (918) 494-6868. Fax (918) 491-6297. E-mail: dboyd@wintersking.com. Website: www.wintersking.com. Agent: Thomas J. Winters. Estab. 1983. Represents 100+ clients. Recognized in the industry. Rarely open to unpublished authors; open to qualified new clients with a significant sales history/platform. Handles adult religious/inspirational novels & nonfiction for all ages, screenplays, TV/movie scripts, gift books, e-books, crossover books, secular w/ underlying Christian theme.

Contact: By fax (918) 491-6297. No more than 10 pages.

Commission: 15%; foreign 15%.

Fees: None.

Tips: "Unsolicited proposals/manuscripts will not be acknowledged, considered, or returned. Solicited proposals/outlines/samples/manuscripts that are not in proper format will not be reviewed or considered for representation. No handwritten submissions."

***WOLGEMUTH & ASSOCIATES INC.,** 8600 Crestgate Cir., Orlando FL 32819. (407) 909-9445. Fax (407) 909-9446. E-mail: rwolgemuth@wolgemuthandassociates.com. Agent: Robert D. Wolgemuth; Andrew D. Wolgemuth (awolgemuth@wolgemuthandassociates.com); Erik S. Wolgemuth (ewolgemuth@wolgemuthandassociates.com); Austin Wilson (awilson@wolgemuthandassociates.com). Member AAR. Well recognized in the industry. Estab. 1992. Represents 85 clients. No new clients or unpublished authors. Handles mostly adult nonfiction; most other types of books handled only for current clients.

Contact: By letter.

Commission: 15%.

Fees: None.

Tips: "We work with authors who are either bestselling authors or potentially bestselling authors. Consequently, we want to represent clients with broad market appeal."

WORDSERVE LITERARY GROUP, Denver CO. (303) 471-6675. E-mail: admin@wordserveliterary.com ("Query" in subject line). Website: www.wordserveliterary.com. Agents: Greg Johnson (greg@wordserveliterary.com), Alice Crider (alice@wordserveliterary.com), and Sarah Freese (sarah@wordserveliterary.com). Estab. 2003. Represents 120 clients. Recognized in the industry. Open to new clients. Handles novels & nonfiction for all ages, gift books, crossover books, general books (memoir, military, self-help, adult fiction).

Contact: By e-mail (no attachments). Visit website for submission guidelines. Responds in 4-8 wks.
Commission: 15%; foreign 15-20%.
Fees: None.
Tips: "Nonfiction: First impressions count. Make sure your proposal answers all the questions on competition, outline, audience, felt need, etc. Fiction: Make sure your novel is completed before you submit a proposal (synopsis, plus 5 chapters)."

WRITERS HOUSE, 21 W. 26th St., New York NY 10010. (212) 685-2400. Fax (212) 685-1781. E-mail: dlazar@writershouse.com. Rebecca Sherman, Sr. Agent Juv & Yng Adult. E-mail: rsherman@writershouse.com. Website: www.writershouse.com. Agent: Dan Lazar. Founded 1974. Represents trade books of all types, fiction & nonfiction, including all rights. Handles film & TV rights. No screenplays, teleplays, or software. No unsolicited mss, query first with an intelligent one-page letter stating what's wonderful about the book, what it's about, & what background & experience you, as an author, bring to it. Queries generally responded to within 2 weeks & mss within 4 weeks. No reading fee.

YATES & YATES, 1100 W. Town and Country Rd., Ste. 1300, Orange CA 92868-4654. (714) 480-4000. Fax (714) 480-4001. E-mail: email@yates2.com. Website: www.yates2.com. Agents: Sealy Yates, Matt Yates, Curtis Yates, Esther Fleece. Estab. 1989. Recognized in the industry. Represents 50+ clients. No unpublished authors. Handles adult nonfiction.
Contact: E-mail.
Commission: Negotiable.

***ZACHARY SHUSTER HARMSWORTH LITERARY AND ENTERTAINMENT AGENCY,** 1776 Broadway, Ste. 1405, New York NY 10019. (212) 765-6900. Fax (212) 765-6490. Or 535 Boylston St., Ste. 1103, Boston MA 02116. (617) 262-2400. Fax (617) 262-2468. E-mail: mchappell@zshliterary.com. Website: www.zshliterary.com. Agent: Mary Beth Chappell (Boston office). Recognized in the industry. Represents 15-30 religious clients. Open to unpublished authors and new clients. Handles adult religious/inspirational novels & adult nonfiction, crossover books, general books.
Contact: E-mail with online form only; no unsolicited submissions.
Commission: 15%; foreign & film 20%.
Fees: Office expenses only.
Tips: "We are looking for inspirational fiction, Christian nonfiction, especially that which focuses on the emerging/emergent church or that which would appeal to readers in their 20s and 30s, and teen/YA series."

12

Contests

A listing here does not guarantee legitimacy. For guidelines on evaluating contests, go to www.sfwa.org/beware/contests.

CHILDREN/YOUNG-ADULTS CONTESTS, WRITING FOR

THE CHILDREN'S WRITER CONTESTS. Offers a number of contests for children's writers. Website: www.childrenswriter.com.

HIGHLIGHTS FOR CHILDREN FICTION CONTEST. (570) 253-1080. Website: www.highlights.com. Offers 3 prizes of $1,000 each for stories up to 800 words for children; for beginning readers up to 500 words. See website for guidelines and current topic. (To find contest info put "Contest" in search field.) No crime, violence, or derogatory humor. No entry fee or form required. Entries must be postmarked between January 1 and January 31.

CORETTA SCOTT KING BOOK AWARD. Coretta Scott King Task Force, American Library Assn. Toll-free (800) 545-2433. E-mail: olos@ala.org. Website: www.ala.org. Annual award for children's books by African American authors and/or illustrators published the previous year. Books must fit one of these categories: preschool to grade 4; grades 5-8; grades 9-12. Deadline: December 1 each year. Guidelines on website (click on "Awards & Grants"/click on contest name on list). Prizes: a plaque, a set of encyclopedias, and $1,000 cash. Recipients are authors and illustrators of African descent whose distinguished books promote an understanding and appreciation of the "American Dream."

LEE & LOW BOOKS NEW VOICES AWARD. E-mail: info@leeandlow.com. Website: www.leeandlow.com. Annual award for a children's fiction or nonfiction picture book story by a writer of color; up to 1,500 words. Deadline: between May 1 and October 31. Prizes: $1,000 plus publication contract; $500 for Honor Award Winner. Guidelines on website (click on "Creators"/"New Voices Award"). Sign up on website for their newsletter, which will include details for the next contest.

MILKWEED PRIZE FOR CHILDREN'S LITERATURE. Milkweed Editions. (612) 332-3192. E-mail: editor@milkweed.org. Website: www.milkweed.org. Annual prize for unpublished novel intended for readers 8-13; 90-200 pgs. Prize: $10,000 advance against royalties and publication. Guidelines on website (Click on "Submissions Guidelines & Prizes").

POCKETS WRITING CONTEST. (615) 340-7333. Fax (615) 340-7267. E-mail: pockets@upperroom.org. Website: www.pockets.org. United Methodist. Lynn W. Gilliam, ed. Devotional magazine for children (6-11 yrs.). Fiction-writing contest; submit between March 1 and August 15 every yr. Prize: $500 and publication in *Pockets*. Length: 750-1,000 words. Must be unpublished and not historical fiction. Previous winners not eligible. Send to Pockets Fiction Contest at above address, designating "Fiction Contest" on outside of envelope. Send SASE for return and response. Details on website (click on "Breaking News"/"Annual Fiction Contest").

SKIPPING STONES 25TH ANNIVERSARY AWARDS. PO Box 3939, Eugene OR 97403 USA. (541) 342-4956. E-mail: editor@skippingstones.org. Website: www.skippingstones.org. Interfaith/multicultural/nature. Arun N. Toké, exec. ed.; literary, multicultural, and nature awareness magazine for young people, worldwide. Now in 25th year. The 25th Anniversary awards are for students 8-18.

Deadline October 2, 2013, Winners announced in January 2014. Guidelines and prizes on website (click to "AWARDS/ 25TH ANNIVERSARY AWARDS" in the sidebar) or e-mail the editor.

SKIPPING STONES YOUTH HONOR AWARDS. PO Box 3939, Eugene OR 97403-0939. Phone/fax (541) 342-4956. E-mail: editor@skippingstones.org. Website: www.skippingstones.org. Annual awards to "promote creativity as well as multicultural and nature awareness in youth." Prize: publication in the autumn issue, honor certificate, subscription to magazine, plus 5 multicultural and/or nature books. Categories: short stories, nonfiction, and poetry. Entry fee: $3; make checks payable to *Skipping Stones*. Cover letter should include name, address, phone, and e-mail. Deadline: June 20. Entries must be unpublished. Length: 1,000 words maximum. Open to any writer between 7 and 17. Guidelines available by SASE, e-mail, or on website. Accepts inquiries by e-mail or phone. "Be creative. Do not use stereotypes or excessive violent language or plots. Be sensitive to cultural diversity." Results announced in the September–October issue. Winners notified by mail. For contest results, visit website. Everyone who enters receives the issue that features the award winners. Acquisitions: Arun N. Toké. Editorial Comments: *Skipping Stones* is a winner of the 2007 NAME award and now in its 25th year.

SOCIETY OF CHILDREN'S BOOK WRITERS & ILLUSTRATORS GOLDEN KITE AWARDS. Website: www.scbwi.org. Details on website (click on "Awards & Grants"/"Golden Kite Awards").

FICTION CONTESTS

AMAZON BREAKTHROUGH NOVEL AWARD. In cooperation with Penguin and Hewlett-Packard. Penguin will publish winning novel with a $25,000 advance. November deadline.

AMERICAN CHRISTIAN FICTION WRITERS CONTESTS. Phone/fax (321) 984-4018. E-mail: genesis@ACFW.com, boty@acfw.com, or vp@acfw.com. Website: www.acfw.com/genesis. Sponsors a fiction contest and others. See website for current contests and rules (scroll down to "Contests"/ click on name of contest).

ATHANATOS CHRISTIAN MINISTRIES BOOK LENGTH NOVEL CONTEST. (202) 697-4623. E-mail: director@athanatosministries.org. Website: www.christianwritingcontest.com. Novel 40,000-90,000 words. Prizes: 1st prize $1,500 and a possible book contract; 2nd prize $1,000 and a possible book contract. Entry fee: $69.95. Deadline: September 1.

BARD FICTION PRIZE. Awarded annually to a promising, emerging young writer of fiction, aged 39 years or younger. Entries must be previously published. Deadline: July 15. No entry fee. Prizes: $30,000 and appointment as writer in residence for one semester at Bard College, Annandale-on-Hudson NY. E-mail: bfp@bard.edu. Website: www.bard.edu/bfp.

BOSTON REVIEW SHORT STORY CONTEST. *Boston Review*. Website: www.bostonreview.net. Prize: $1,500 (plus publication) for an unpublished short story up to 4,000 words. Entry fee: $20. Deadline: October 1. Details on website (click on "About"/scroll down to "Contest"/"Aura Estrada Short Story Contest").

BULWER-LYTTON FICTION CONTEST. For the worst opening line to a novel. Deadline: April 15. Website: www.bulwer-lytton.com. Rules on website.

CANADIAN WRITER'S JOURNAL SHORT FICTION CONTEST. White Mountain Publications, PO Box 1178, New Liskeard ON P0J 1P0, Canada. (705) 647-5424. Canada-wide toll-free (800) 258-5451. E-mail: cwc-calendar@cwj.ca. Website: www.cwj.ca. Sponsors semiannual short fiction contests. Deadline: April 30. Length: to 1,500 words. Entry fee: $5. Prizes: $150, $100, $50. All fiction needs for CWJ are filled by this contest. Click on "CWJ Short Fiction Contest."

ALEXANDER PATTERSON CAPPON PRIZE FOR FICTION. New Letters, UMKC, University House, 5101 Rockhill Rd., Kansas City MO 64110. (816) 235-1168. E-mail: newletters@umkc.edu. Website: www.newletters.org. Deadline: May 18. Entry fee: $15. Prize: $1,500. Click on "Awards for Writers."

THE CHRISTY AWARDS. Phone/fax (734) 663-7931. E-mail: CA2000DK@aol.com. Website: www .christyawards.com. Awards in 9 fiction genres for excellence in Christian fiction. Nominations made by publishers, not authors. For submission guidelines and other information, see website (click on "Forms"/"Official Guidelines"). Awards are presented at an annual Christy Awards Banquet held Friday prior to the annual ICRS convention in July.

JACK DYER FICTION PRIZE. Crab Orchard Review, Fiction Contest, Dept. of English, Mail Code 4503, Southern Illinois University–Carbondale, 1000 Faner Dr., Carbondale IL 62901. (618) 453-5321. Website: www.siuc.edu/~crborchd. Entry fee: $10. Prize: $1,500. Deadline: submit between March 1 and May 10 (may vary). Submit fiction up to 6,000 words. See website for guidelines.

GLIMMER TRAIN PRESS FICTION CONTESTS. Glimmer Train Press. Website: www.glimmer train.com. Sponsors a number of contests. Check website for current contests (click on "Writers' Guidelines").

JAMES JONES FIRST NOVEL FELLOWSHIP. (570) 408-4547. E-mail: cwriting@wilkes.edu. Website: www.wilkes.edu/pages/1159.asp. Deadline: March 1. Entry fee: $25. Prizes: $10,000 first prize; $750 for two runners-up. Submit a 2-page outline and the first 50 pages of an unpublished novel. Guidelines on website.

THE MARY MCCARTHY PRIZE IN SHORT FICTION. Sarabande Books. E-mail: sarabandeb@ aol.com. Website: www.sarabandebooks.org. Prize: $2,000 and publication of a collection of short stories, novellas, or a short novel (150-250 pgs.), plus a standard royalty contract. Deadline: submit between January 1 and February 15. Entry fee: $25. Guidelines on website (click on "Submission Guidelines"/scroll to bottom and click on name of contest).

SERENA MCDONALD KENNEDY AWARD. Snake Nation Press. Website: www.snakenationpress.org. Novellas up to 50,000 words, or short-story collection up to 200 pgs. (published or unpublished). Deadline: July 30 (check website to verify). Entry fee: $25. Prize: $1,000 and publication. Guidelines on website (click on "Contests").

NATIONAL WRITERS ASSOCIATION NOVEL-WRITING CONTEST. The National Writers Assn., 10940 S. Parker Rd., #508, Parker CO 80134. (303) 841-0246. Website: www.nationalwriters.com. Check website for current contests and guidelines (click on "Contests"/then name of contest).

NATIONAL WRITERS ASSOCIATION SHORT-STORY CONTEST. The National Writers Assn., (303) 841-0246. Website: www.nationalwriters.com. Check website for current contest and guidelines (click on "Contests"/then name of contest).

THE FLANNERY O'CONNOR AWARD FOR SHORT FICTION. University of Georgia Press. Website: www.ugapress.uga.edu. For collections of short fiction, 50,000-75,000 wds. Prize: $1,000, plus publication under royalty book contract. Entry fee: $25. Deadline: between April 1 and May 31 (postmark). Guidelines on website (click on "About Us"/"For Prospective Authors"/"Flannery O'Connor Award for Short Fiction").

OPERATION FIRST NOVEL. Sponsored by the Jerry B. Jenkins Christian Writers Guild and Worthy Publishing. For unpublished novelists who are students or annual members of the Christian Writers Guild. Winner receives $15,000 and publication. Length: 75,000-100,000 words. For contest rules, go to www.christianwritersguild.com.

GRACE PALEY PRIZE FOR SHORT FICTION. (703) 993-4301. E-mail: awp@awpwriter.org. Website: www.awpwriter.org. Prize: $4,000 & publication. Entry fee: $25. Deadline: Postmarked between January 1 and February 28, 2012.

KATHERINE ANNE PORTER PRIZE FOR FICTION. Literary Contest/Fiction, *Nimrod Journal*, University of Tulsa. (918) 631-3080. E-mail: nimrod@utulsa.edu. Website: www.utulsa.edu/nimrod /awards.html. Quality prose and fiction by emerging writers of contemporary literature, unpublished.

Deadline: submit between January 1 and April 30. Entry fee: $20. Prizes: $2,000 and publication; $1,000 and publication. Guidelines on website (click on "Nimrod Literary Awards").

THE SILVER QUILL SOCIETY SHORT FICTION 2013 CONTEST. Website: www.thestoryteller magazine.com/. Entry fee: $5. Deadine: September 25, 2013. Prizes: 1st place: $50, 2nd place: $25, 3rd place: $15, 4th place: $10. Open genre contest. Writers may enter as often as they wish, but entry fee must accompany each entry. Name, address, phone, e-mail, title of story, and word count should be on cover page. Name should not appear anywhere else on ms. No pornography, graphic anything, New Age, or children's stories will be accepted.

TOBIAS WOLFF AWARD IN FICTION. Western Washington University, Bellingham WA. E-mail: bhreview@cc.wwu.edu. Website: www.bhreview.org. Short story or novel excerpt up to 8,000 words. Deadline: postmarked between December 1 and March 15. Entry fee: $18 for first story/chapter; $10 each additional. Prize: $1,000, plus publication. Details on website.

WRITER'S JOURNAL ANNUAL FICTION CONTEST. E-mail: writersjournal@writersjournal.com. Website: www.writersjournal.com. Sponsors several contests; see website (click on "Contests"/scroll down to "Contest Entry Manuscript Format").

WRITE TO INSPIRE. July 19–20, 2013. Elk Grove CA. Contact Elizabeth Thompson. Inspire Christian Writers, PO Box 276794, Sacramento, CA 95827. (916) 607-7796. Limited to writers unpublished by traditional publishers, or published only in anthologies, compilations, or periodicals.

NONFICTION CONTESTS

AMY WRITING AWARDS. Cosponsored by The Amy Foundation and WORLD News Group. The awards are designed to recognize creative, skillful journalism that applies biblical principles to stories about issues and lives. The goal is for non-Christian readers to see the relevance of biblical truth and for Christian readers to become disciples. First prize is $10,000 with a total of $34,000 given annually (additional prizes of $1,000-5,000). To be eligible, a .pdf of your article, as published, must be submitted using an online submission form. Deadline for submitting entries published in the first six months is July 15th. Deadline for submitting entries published in the second six months is January 15th. You may make both first half and second half submissions, but the total number of entries for the year cannot exceed ten. Visit www.worldmag.com/amyawards for an online submission form and to see the judging rubric. Submitted articles must be published in a secular journalistic outlet and must be reinforced with at least one passage of Scripture. Winners are notified by May 1. For questions contact via e-mail at amyawards@worldmag.com. Website: www.worldmag.com/amyawards.

AWP CREATIVE NONFICTION PRIZE. Assoc. of Writers and Writing programs, George Mason University, Fairfax VA. E-mail: awp@awpwriter.org. Website: www.awpwriter.org. For authors of book-length manuscripts; submit only 150-300 pgs. Deadline: February 28. Entry fee: $15 for members; $30 for nonmembers. Prize: $2,000. Guidelines on website (click on "Contests"/"AWP Award Series").

THE BECHTEL PRIZE. *Teachers and Writers Magazine* Contest. E-mail: info@twc.org. Website: www.twc.org/publications/bechtel-prize. Contemporary writing articles (unpublished) to 3,500 words. Deadline: June 30 (varies). Entry fee: $20. Prize: $1,000, plus publication.

DOROTHY CHURCHILL CAPON PRIZE FOR ESSAY. New Letters, UMKC, University House. (816) 235-1168. E-mail: newletters@umkc.edu. Website: www.newletters.org. Deadline: May 18. Entry fee: $15. Prize: $1,500. Guidelines on website (scroll down and click on "New Letters Writing Contests").

ANNIE DILLARD AWARD IN CREATIVE NONFICTION. Essays on any subject to 8,000 words. Deadline: between December 1 and March 15. Entry fee: $18 for first; $10 each additional. First prize: $1,000. Unpublished works only, up to 8,000 words. E-mail: bhreview@cc.wwu.edu. Website: www.wwu.edu/~bhreview. Details on website (click on "Contests"/"Contest Submission Guidelines").

EVENT CREATIVE NONFICTION CONTEST. Deadline: mid-April, annually. $1,500 in prizes. Judges reserve the right to award either two prizes valued at $740 or three at $500. Plus winners get published in *EVENT*. Must be creative nonfiction and must not exceed the 5,000-word limit. Entry fee is $34.95, including a one-year subscription to *EVENT*. See www.eventmags.com for details.

GRAYWOLF PRESS NONFICTION PRIZE. (651) 641-0036. Website: www.graywolfpress.org/Company_Info/Submission_Guidelines/Graywolf_Press_Nonfiction_Prize_Submission_Guidelines. For the best literary nonfiction book by a writer not yet established in the genre. Deadline: between June 1 & June 30 (varies). Entry fee: none. Prize: $12,000 advance and publication. Guidelines on website (click on "Submission Guidelines").

GUIDEPOSTS CONTEST. Website: www.guideposts.org. Interfaith. Writers Workshop Contest held on even years, with a late June deadline. True, first-person stories (yours or someone else's), 1,500 words. Needs one spiritual message, with scenes, drama, and characters. Winners attend a weeklong seminar in New York (all expenses paid) on how to write for *Guideposts*.

HALO MAGAZINE WRITING CONTEST. Deadline July 31. Maximum of 1,000 wds. on topic of "How I Found Jesus." $25 entry fee. 1st prize $150, 2nd prize $100, 3rd prize $50. All participants receive a one year subscription. Send submissions to Halo Magazine Writing Contest, 1643 Pinnacle Dr. SW, Wyoming MI 49519. All entries become property of *Halo Magazine* and may be used in future issues.

RICHARD J. MARGOLIS AWARD. Blue Mountain Center, Margolis & Assocs. E-mail: hsm@margolis.com. Website: www.award.margolis.com. Given annually to a promising young journalist or essayist whose work combines warmth, humor, wisdom, and concern with social justice. Deadline: July 1. Prize: $5,000. Guidelines on website.

MASTER BOOKS SCHOLARSHIP ESSAY CONTEST. PO Box 726, Green Forest AR 72638. (870) 438-5288. Fax (870) 438-5120. E-mail: submissions@newleafpress.net. Essay contest; $3,000 college scholarship; website: www.newleafpublishinggroup.com/scholarship.php. Details on website.

WRITE TO INSPIRE. July 19–20, 2013. Elk Grove CA. Contact Elizabeth Thompson. Inspire Christian Writers, PO Box 276794, Sacramento, CA 95827. (916) 607-7796. Limited to writers unpublished by traditional publishers, or published only in anthologies, compilations, or periodicals.

PLAY/SCRIPTWRITING/SCREENWRITING CONTESTS

AMERICAN ZOETROPE SCREENPLAY CONTEST. E-mail: contests@zoetrope.com. Website: www.zoetrope.com/contests. Deadline: August 1 (early), September 6 (final). Entry fees: $35 (early), $50 (final). Prizes: First prize $5,000. That winner and 10 finalists will be considered for film option and development.

AUSTIN FILM FESTIVAL SCREENWRITERS COMPETITION. (512) 478-4795. E-mail: info@austinfilmfestival.com. Website: www.austinfilmfestival.com. Offers a number of contest categories for screenplays. See current details on website.

BAKER'S PLAYS HIGH SCHOOL PLAYWRITING COMPETITION. Plays may be about any subject and any length as long as the play can be reasonably produced by high school students on a high school stage. Deadline: January 30. Prizes: $500, $250, and $100. Guidelines on website: www.bakersplays.com (go down to "Information" box & click on "Contests & Festivals").

KAIROS PRIZE FOR SPIRITUALLY UPLIFTING SCREENPLAYS. John Templeton Foundation. E-mail: contact@kairosprize.com. Website: www.kairosprize.com. Annual. For first-time screenwriters with a religious message. Prizes: $25,000, $15,000, $10,000. Guidelines on website (click on "Guidelines").

MOONDANCE INTERNATIONAL FILM FESTIVAL COMPETITION. E-mail: director@moondancefilmfestival.com. Website: www.moondancefilmfestival.com. Open to films, screenplays, and features. Deadline: May 30. Entry fees: $50-100. Prize: winning entries screened at festival. Details on website.

NICHOLL FELLOWSHIPS IN SCREENWRITING. (310) 247-3010. E-mail: nicholl@oscars.org. Website: www.oscars.org/nicholl/index.html. International contest held annually, open to any writer who has not optioned or sold a treatment, teleplay, or screenplay for more than $5,000. Up to five $30,000 fellowships offered each year to promising authors. Deadline: May 1. Entry fee: $30. Guidelines/required application form on website (scroll down to "About the Competition" and click on "More").

MILDRED & ALBERT PANOWSKI PLAYWRITING AWARD. Award Coordinator, Forest Roberts Theatre, Northern Michigan University, Marquette MI. Website: www.nmu.edu/theatre. Unpublished, unproduced, full-length plays. Deadline: September 1. Prizes: $2,000, a summer workshop, a fully mounted production, and transportation to Marquette. Guidelines on website (click on "Playwriting Award").

SCRIPTAPALOOZA ANNUAL INTERNATIONAL SCREENPLAY COMPETITION. (323) 654-5809. E-mail: info@scriptapalooza.com. Website: www.scriptapalooza.com. Over $25,000 in prizes and over 90 producers reading all the entries. Entry fees are from $40-55, plus you can get feedback on your entry now. Deadlines: January 7th, March 5th, and April 15th.

POETRY CONTESTS

ANHINGA PRIZE FOR POETRY. E-mail: info@anhinga.org. Website: www.anhinga.org. A $2,000 prize for original poetry book in English. Winning manuscript published by Anhinga Press. For poets trying to publish a first or second book of poetry. Submissions: 48-80 pgs. Number pages and include $25 reading fee. Deadline: between February 15 and May 1 each year. Details on website (click on contest name).

MURIEL CRAFT BAILEY MEMORIAL POETRY AWARD. E-mail: poetry@comstockreview.org. Awarded annually. Deadline: July 1. Prizes: $100 to $1,000. Finalists published in the *Comstock Review*. Unpublished poems up to 40 lines. Entry fee: $5 for each poem (no limit on number of submissions). Details on website: www.comstockreview.org.

BALTIMORE REVIEW POETRY CONTEST. All styles and forms of poetry. April 1–July 1. Entry fee: $10. Prizes: $300 & publication; $150; $50; plus publication in the *Baltimore Review*. Details on website: www.baltimorereview.org. Click on "Contests" on main menu.

BLUE MOUNTAIN ARTS/SPS STUDIOS POETRY CARD CONTEST. (303) 449-0536. E-mail: poetry contest@sps.com. Website: www.sps.com. Biannual contest. Next deadlines: June 30, December 31. Use online form for submissions. Rhymed or unrhymed original poetry (unrhymed preferred). Poems also considered for greeting cards or anthologies. Prizes: $300, $150, $50. Details on website ("Poetry Contest").

BOSTON REVIEW ANNUAL POETRY CONTEST. Deadline: June 1. First prize: $1,500, plus publication. Submit up to 5 unpublished poems. Entry fee: $20 (includes a subscription to *Boston Review*). Submit manuscripts in duplicate with cover note. Website: www.bostonreview.net. Details on website (click on "About"/"Contests"/name of contest).

CAVE CANEM POETRY PRIZE. Supports the work of African American poets with excellent manuscripts who have not found a publisher for their first book. Deadline: April 30 (varies). Prize: $1,000, publication by a national press, and 15 copies of the book. Entry fee: $15. Details on website: www.cavecanempoets.org (click on "Book Awards"/click on name of contest/scroll down and click on "Competition Guidelines"). E-mail: ccpoets@verizon.net.

49TH PARALLEL POETRY AWARD. Mail Stop 9053, Western Washington University, Bellingham WA. (360) 650-4863. E-mail: bhreview@cc.wwu.edu. Website: www.wwu.edu/~bhreview. Poems in any style or on any subject. Deadline: submit between December 1 and March 15. Entry fee: $18 for first entry; $10 for each additional entry. First prize: $1,000 and publication. Details on website.

FLO GAULT STUDENT POETRY COMPETITION. Sarabande Books. E-mail: info@sarabandebooks.org. Website: www.sarabandebooks.org. Prize: $500. Submit up to 3 poems. Deadline: October 30. Details on website (click on "Student Poetry Prize").

GRIFFIN POETRY PRIZE. (905) 618-0420. E-mail: info@griffinpoetryprize.com. Website: www.griffinpoetryprize.com. Prizes: two $65,000 awards (one to a Canadian and one to a poet from anywhere in the world) for a collection of poetry published in English during the preceding year; plus additional prizes ($200,000 in prizes total). All submissions must come from publishers. Deadline: December 31. Details on website.

DONALD HALL PRIZE FOR POETRY. (703) 993-4301. E-mail: awp@awpwriter.org. Website: www.awpwriter.org. Prize: $4,000 & publication. Entry fee: $25. Deadline: postmarked between January 1 and February 28, 2012.

TOM HOWARD/JOHN H. REID POETRY CONTEST. Website: www.winningwriters.com/tompoetry.htm. Deadline: between December 15 and September 30. Poetry in any style or genre. Published poetry accepted. Entry fee: $7 for every 25 lines. Prizes: $3,000 first prize; total of $5,550 in cash prizes. Details on website.

THE LEDGE ANNUAL POETRY CHAPBOOK CONTEST. E-mail: info@theledgemagazine.com. Website: www.theledgemagazine.com. Submit 16-28 pages of poetry with title page, bio, and acknowledgments. Entry fee: $12 for first three poems; $3.00 each additional. Prizes: $1,000, $250, and $100, plus publication. Deadline: April 30.

BARBARA MANDIGO KELLY PEACE POETRY AWARDS. Nuclear Age Peace Foundation. (805) 965-3443. E-mail: wagingpeace@napf.org. Website: www.wagingpeace.org. Annual series of awards to encourage poets to explore and illuminate positive visions of peace and the human spirit. Deadline: July 1. Prizes: $1,000 for Adult; $200 for Youth 13-18 years; and $200 for Youth ages 12 and under. Adult entry fee: $15 for up to 3 poems; $5 for youth; no fee for 12 and under. Details on website (see right-hand column).

NARRATIVE MAGAZINE SIXTH ANNUAL POETRY CONTEST. Website: www.NarrativeMagazine.com. Submission fee: $22. Prizes $1,500/$750/$300 plus 10 finalists $75 each. Complete guidelines on website.

NEW LETTERS PRIZE FOR POETRY. New Letters, UMKC. (816) 235-1168. E-mail: newletters@umkc.edu. Website: www.newletters.org. Deadline: May 18. Entry fee: $15 for first entry; $10 ea. for additional. Prize: $1,500 for best group of 3 to 6 poems.

PEARL POETRY PRIZE. Pearl Editions. Website: www.pearlmag.com. Deadline: submit between May 1 and June 30. Entry fee: $20. Prizes: $1,000 and publication in *Pearl Editions*.

RICHARD PETERSON POETRY PRIZE. *Crab Orchard Review*, Poetry Contest, Dept. of English, Mail Code 4503, Southern Illinois University–Carbondale, 1000 Faner Dr., Carbondale IL 62901. (618) 453-5321. Website: www.siuc.edu/~crborchd. Entry fee: $15. Prize: $1,500. Deadline: submit between March 1 and May 10 (may vary). Submit up to 3 poems; 100-line limit.

POETRY SOCIETY OF VIRGINIA POETRY CONTESTS. Website: www.poetrysocietyofvirginia.org. Categories for adults and students. Prizes: $20-250. Entry fee per poem for nonmembers: $4. Deadline: March 15. List of contests on website.

SLIPSTREAM ANNUAL POETRY CHAPBOOK COMPETITION. Website: www.slipstreampress.org/contest.html. Prize: $1,000, plus 50 copies of chapbook. Deadline: December 1. Send up to 40 pages of poetry. Reading fee: $20. Guidelines on website.

SOUL-MAKING LITERARY COMPETITION. National League of American Pen Women. E-mail: pennobhill@aol.com. Website: www.soulmakingcontest.us. One-page poems only (single- or double-spaced). Up to 3 poems/entry. Deadline: November 30. Entry fee: $5. Prizes $25, $50, $100.

HOLLIS SUMMERS POETRY PRIZE. Ohio University Press. (740) 593-1155. E-mail: oupress@ohio.edu. For unpublished collection of original poems, 60-95 pgs. Entry fee: $25. Deadline: October 31. Prize: $1,000, plus publication in book form. Details on website: www.ohioswallow.com/poetry_prize (scroll down to "About OU Press" and click on "Poetry Prize").

SUMMERTIME BLUES POETRY CONTEST. Website: www.thestorytellermagazine.com/. Entry fee $5 per 3 poems. Deadline: July 15, 2013. Prizes: 1st place: $25; 2nd place: $15; 3rd place: $10. Poems may be rhyming or nonrhyming, any style. Writers may enter as often as they wish, but entry fee must accompany each entry. Name, address, phone, e-mail, title of poem, and word count should be on cover page. You may include only one cover page per 3 poems. Name should not appear anywhere else on ms. No pornography, graphic anything, New Age, or children's poetry will be accepted.

THE MAY SWENSON POETRY AWARD. Utah State University Press. (435) 797-1362. Website: www.usu.edu/usupress. Collections of original poetry, 50-100 pgs. Deadline: September 30. Prize: $1,000, publication, and royalties. Reading fee: $25. Details on website ("Swenson Poetry Award").

KATE TUFTS DISCOVERY AWARD. Claremont Graduate University. (909) 621-8974. E-mail: tufts@cgu.edu. Presented annually for a first or very early work by a poet of genuine promise. Prize: $10,000. Deadline: September 15. Details and entry form on website: www.cgu.edu/tufts.

KINGSLEY TUFTS POETRY AWARD. Claremont Graduate University. (909) 621-8974. E-mail: tufts@cgu.edu. Presented annually for a published book of poetry by a midcareer poet. Prize: $100,000. Deadline: September 15. Details and entry form on website: www.cgu.edu/tufts.

UTMOST NOVICE CHRISTIAN POETRY CONTEST. Utmost Christian Writers Foundation, Canada. E-mail: nnharms@telusplanet.net. Website: www.utmostchristianwriters.com/poetry-contest/poetry-contest-rules.php. Nathan Harms. Entry fee: $10/poem. Prizes: $500, $300, $200; Best Rhyming Poem $150. Deadline: August 31. Details and entry form on website.

MULTIPLE-GENRE CONTESTS

AMERICAN LITERARY REVIEW CONTESTS. University of North Texas. E-mail: americanliteraryreview@yahoo.com. Website: www.engl.unt.edu/alr. Now sponsors three contests: short fiction, creative nonfiction, and poetry. Prize: $1,000 and publication in spring issue of the magazine. Entry fee: $15. Deadline: October 1. Details on website ("Contest").

BAKELESS LITERARY PUBLICATION PRIZES. Bread Loaf Writers' Conference, Middlebury College. E-mail: bakelessprize@middlebury.edu. Website: www.bakelessprize.org. Book series competition for new authors of literary works of poetry, fiction, and nonfiction. Entry fee: $10. Deadline: between September 15 and November 1. Details on website.

BEST NEW CANADIAN CHRISTIAN WRITING AWARDS. The Word Guild, Canada. E-mail: admin@thewordguild.com. Website: www.thewordguild.com. Sponsors a number of contests annually. Check website for any current contests and guidelines (click on "Awards"/"Contests").

BLUE RIDGE CONFERENCE WRITING CONTEST. (760) 220-1075. E-mail: alton@ganskycommunications.com. Website: http://brmcwc.com. Sponsors three book contests. First prize: a trophy plus $200; scholarship toward conference. Fiction or nonfiction. Unpublished Writers, Director's Choice, and the industry-wide Selah Awards. See website for information.

CHRISTIAN SMALL PUBLISHER BOOK OF THE YEAR. Website: www.christianbookaward.com. Christian Small Publisher Book of the Year Award is designed to promote small publishers in the Christian marketplace as well as to bring recognition to outstanding Christian books from small publishers. Publishers and authors nominate titles for the award and Christian readers vote to determine the winners. www.christianbookaward.com.

COLUMBIA FICTION/POETRY/NONFICTION CONTEST. Website: www.columbiajournal.org/contests.htm. Length: 20 double-spaced pgs. or up to 5 poems. Prize: $500 in each category, plus publication. Deadline: January 15 (varies). Details on website.

ECPA CHRISTIAN BOOK AWARD. (480) 966-3998. E-mail: info@ecpa.org. Website: www.ChristianBookExpo.com. Presented annually to the best books in Christian publishing. Awards recognize books in 6 different categories: Bibles, Fiction, Children, Inspiration, Bible Reference, Nonfiction, and New Author. Only ECPA members in good standing can nominate products. Submit between September 1 and October 2 (verify on website). Books submitted must have been published between October 2011 and October 2012. Awards are presented annually at the ECPA Executive Leadership Summit. Verify all details on Evangelical Christian Publishers Association website: www.ecpa.org.

EVANGELICAL PRESS ASSOCIATION ANNUAL CONTEST. PO Box 20198, El Cajon CA 92021. (888) 311-1731. E-mail: director@evangelicalpress.com. Website: www.evangelicalpress.com. Sponsors annual contest for member publications. Deadline: early January.

WILLIAM FAULKNER–WILLIAM WISDOM CREATIVE WRITING COMPETITION. Offers significant cash prizes in seven categories: Novel, Novella, Novel-in-Progress, Short Story, Essay, Poem, and Short Story by a High School Student. For details, visit www.wordsandmusic.org and download guidelines and entry form. Or e-mail the Society at Faulkhouse@aol.com.

GOD USES INK NOVICE CONTEST (for nonpublished writers). Opens in September of 2010. Prizes are available in three age categories: ages 14 to 19; 20 to 39; and age 40 and over. First prize: Registration to Write! Canada Christian Writers' Conference (approximate value nearly $400.00), held in June. (Please check website for details: www.writecanada.org.) Second prize: A $100 gift certificate for The Word Guild (can be used for conference registration, membership, etc.). Third prize: A $50 gift certificate for The Word Guild (can be used for conference registration, membership, etc.).

ERIC HOFFER AWARD. *Best New Writing.* E-mail: info@hofferaward.com. Website: www.HofferAward.com. Submit books via mail; register online. Submit prose online only. The prose category is for creative fiction and nonfiction less than 10,000 words. Annual award for books features 17 categories including e-books and older books. Pays $250-2,000. Guidelines at www.HofferAward.com.

INSCRIBE CHRISTIAN WRITERS' CONTEST. Edmonton AB, Canada. (780) 542-7950. Fax (780) 514-3702. E-mail: query@inscribe.org. Website: www.inscribe.org. Sponsors contests open to nonmembers; details on website.

INSIGHT WRITING CONTEST. (301) 393-4038. Fax (301) 393-4055. E-mail: insight@rhpa.org. Website: www.insightmagazine.org. Review and Herald/Seventh-day Adventist. A magazine of positive Christian living for Seventh-day Adventist high schoolers. Sponsors short story and poetry contests; includes a category for students 22 or under. Prizes: $50-250. Deadline: June 1. Submit by e-mail. Details on website (click on "Writing Contest").

GRACE IRWIN AWARD. Website: canadianchristianwritingawards.com. All shortlisted finalists in fiction and nonfiction book categories in The Word Guild Canadian Christian Writing Awards will contend for the Grace Irwin Award. Prize $5,000. A separate round of independent judging will determine the prizewinner.

MINISTRY & LITURGY VISUAL ARTS AWARDS. (408) 286-8505. Fax (408) 287-8748. E-mail: vaa@rpinet.com. Website: www.rpinet.com/vaaentry.pdf. Visual Arts Awards held in 4 categories throughout the year. Best in each category wins $100. Entry fee: $30. Different deadline for each category (see website).

NARRATIVE MAGAZINE SPRING 2014 STORY CONTEST. Website: www.NarrativeMagazine.com. Fiction and nonfiction. Submission fee: $22. Prizes $2,500/$1,000/$500, plus 10 finalists at $100 each. Also sponsors a fall contest. Complete guidelines on website.

NARRATIVE MAGAZINE 30 BELOW CONTEST—2014. www.NarrativeMagazine.com. Fiction, nonfiction, poetry, graphic novels, graphic art, audio, video, and photography. Submission fee: $22. Prizes $1,500/$750/$300, plus 10 finalists will receive $100 each. Complete guidelines on website.

NARRATIVE MAGAZINE WINTER 2014 STORY CONTEST. Website: www.NarrativeMagazine.com. Fiction and nonfiction. Submission fee: $22. Prizes $2,500/$1,000/$500, plus 10 finalists will receive $100 each. Also sponsors a spring contest. Complete guidelines on website.

NEW MILLENNIUM AWARDS. Website: www.newmillenniumwritings.com/awards.html. Prizes: $1,000 award for each category. Best Poem, Best Fiction, Best Nonfiction, Best Short-Short Fiction (fiction and nonfiction 6,000 words; short-short fiction up to 1,000 words; 3 poems to 5 pgs. total). Entry fee: $17 each. Deadline: June 17. Guidelines on website. Enter online or off.

NEW MILLENNIUM WRITINGS SEMIANNUAL WRITING CONTESTS. Contact: Steve Petty (stevepetty@live.com). Website: www.newmillenniumwritings.com. Includes fiction, short-short fiction, poetry, and creative nonfiction. Entry fee: $17. Prizes: $1,000 in each category. Deadlines: June 17 & November 30.

ONCE WRITTEN CONTESTS. Fiction and poetry contests. Website: www.oncewritten.com.

OREGON CHRISTIAN WRITERS CASCADE WRITING CONTEST. Sponsors a multiple genre contest for both published and unpublished works (fiction, nonfiction, young adult, poetry, children's, and short entries: columns, stories, and devotionals). E-mail cascades@oregonchristianwriters.org. Guidelines on website: www.oregonchristianwriters.org. Cascade Awards presented at annual OCW summer conference August 6, 2014, Portland. Deadline: April 30.

THE EUPLE RINEY MEMORIAL AWARD. Website: www.thestorytellermagazine.com. Entry fee $5. Deadline: June 20, 2013. Prizes: 1st place: $50; 2nd place: $25; 3rd place: $15; 4th place: $10. Plus an Editor's Choice Award. Open genre contest, but must be about family—good or bad. Can be fiction or nonfiction. Writers may enter as often as they wish, but entry fee must accompany each entry. Name, address, phone, e-mail, title of story, and word count should be on cover page. Name should not appear anywhere else on ms. No pornography, graphic anything, New Age, or children's stories will be accepted.

MONA SCHREIBER PRIZE FOR HUMOROUS FICTION AND NONFICTION. E-mail: brad.schreiber@att.net. Website: www.brashcyber.com or www.bradschreiber.com. Humorous fiction and nonfiction to 750 words. Prizes: $500, $250, and $100. Entry fee: $5 per entry. Foreign entries, please include US currency. Deadline: December 1. Details on website (click on contest name at bottom of illustration).

SOUL-MAKING KEATS LITERARY COMPETITION. Entering its twentieth year, Soul-Making Keats Literary Competition consists of thirteen categories with cash prizes awarded to first, second, and third place in each. Annual deadline is November 30th (postmarked), and winners and honorable mentions are invited to read at the Awards Event at the Koret Auditorium, San Francisco Mail Library, Civic Center. Complete details are available at the website: www.soulmakingcontest.us or via an SASE to The Webhallow House, 1544 Sweetwood Dr., Broadmoor Vlg., CA 94015.

THE STORYTELLER CONTESTS. (870) 647-2137. E-mail: storytellermag1@yahoo.com. Contest website: www.thestorytellermagazine.com. Fossil Creek Publishing. Offers 1 or 2 paying contest/yr., along with People's Choice Awards, and Pushcart Prize nominations.

TICKLED BY THUNDER CONTESTS. Canada. (604) 591-6095. E-mail: info@tickledbythunder.com. Website: www.tickledbythunder.com. Sponsors several writing contests each year in various genres. Entry fee $10 for nonsubscribers. Prizes: Based on point system. See website for details.

THE WORD GUILD CANADIAN CHRISTIAN WRITING AWARDS. (For published writers.) Thirty-five awards, encompassing 19 book categories and 16 article/short piece categories, including song lyrics, scripts or screenplays, and blog posts. Round One deadline is September 30 and Round

Two deadline is December 31. The fee structure is available on the website for members and nonmembers. Categories of books and articles, etc., can be found on the website: http://canadianchristian writingawards.com.

WRITER'S DIGEST COMPETITIONS. (715) 445-4612, ext. 13430. E-mail: WritersDigest WritingCompetition@fwmedia.com. Website: www.writersdigest.com. Sponsors annual contests for articles, short stories (multiple genres), poetry, children's and young adult fiction, inspirational writing, memoirs/personal essays, self-published books, and scripts (categories vary). Deadlines: vary according to contest. Prizes: up to $3,000 for each contest. Some contests also offer a trip to the annual Writer's Digest Conference in New York City. See website for list of current contests and rules.

WRITERS-EDITORS NETWORK ANNUAL WRITING COMPETITION. E-mail: editor@writers-editors.com. Website: www.writers-editors.com. Open to all writers. Deadline: March 15. Nonfiction, fiction, children's, poetry. Prizes: $100, $75, $50. Details on website (see right-hand column).

WRITERS' UNION OF CANADA AWARDS & COMPETITIONS. Canada. (416) 703-8982. Fax (416) 504-9090. E-mail: info@writersunion.ca. Website: www.writersunion.ca. Various competitions. Prizes: $500-10,000. Details on website.

RESOURCES FOR CONTESTS

ADDITIONAL CONTESTS. You will find some additional contests sponsored by local groups and conferences that are open to nonmembers. See individual listings in those sections.

FREELANCE WRITING: WEBSITE FOR TODAY'S WORKING WRITER. Website: www.freelance writing.com/writingcontests.php.

OZARK CREATIVE WRITERS CONTESTS. E-mail submissions only: ozarkcreativewriters@earth link.net. Website: www.ozarkcreativewriters.org. Lists a number of contests on website.

THE WRITE PLACE BY KIMN SWENSON GOLLNICK. Contest listings. Website: www.KIMN.net /contests.htm.

THE WRITER CONTEST. *The Writer* magazine. (262) 796-8776. E-mail: editor@writermag.com. Website: www.writermag.com. General. How-to for writers. Occasionally sponsors a contest and lists multiple contests. Check website.

MAJOR LITERARY AWARDS

AUDIES: www.audiopub.org

CALDECOTT MEDAL: www.ala.org

CAROL AWARDS: www.acfw.com/carol

EDGAR: www.mysterywriters.org

HEMINGWAY FOUNDATION/PEN AWARD: www.pen-ne.org

HUGO: http://worldcon.org/hugos.html

NATIONAL BOOK AWARD: www.nationalbook.org

NATIONAL BOOK CRITICS CIRCLE AWARD: www.bookcritics.org

NEBULA: http://dpsinfo.com/awardweb/nebulas

NEWBERY: www.ala.org/alsc/awardsgrants/bookmedia/newberymedal/newberymedal

NOBEL PRIZE FOR LITERATURE: www.nobelprize.org

PEN/FAULKNER AWARD: www.penfaulkner.org

PULITZER PRIZE: www.pulitzer.org

RITA: www.rwanational.org/cs/contests_and_awards

13

Denominational Book Publishers and Periodicals

ASSEMBLIES OF GOD
Book Publisher
My Healthy Church

Periodicals
Enrichment Journal
Live
Pentecostal Evangel
Testimony

BAPTIST, FREE WILL
Book Publishers
Randall House
Randall House Digital

BAPTIST, SOUTHERN
Book Publishers
B&H Publishing
New Hope Publishers

Periodicals
Mature Living
On Mission

BAPTIST (OTHER)
Book Publishers
Earthen Vessel Publishing
Judson Press (American)

Periodical
Secret Place (American)

CATHOLIC
Book Publishers
American Catholic Press
Canticle Books
HarperOne (Cath. bks.)
Loyola Press
Our Sunday Visitor
Pauline Books

Periodicals
America
Catholic New York
Columbia
Diocesan Dialogue
Leaves
Our Sunday Visitor
Parish Liturgy
Prairie Messenger
Priest
Share
St. Anthony Messenger

CHRISTIAN CHURCH/ CHURCH OF CHRIST
Book Publisher
CrossLink Publishing

CHURCH OF GOD (HOLINESS)
Periodicals
Church Herald and Holiness Banner
Gems of Truth

CHURCH OF GOD (OTHER)
Periodicals
Bible Advocate (Seventh-day)
The Gem
Now What? (Seventh-day)

JEWISH
Periodicals
The Messianic Times

LUTHERAN
Book Publishers
Concordia
Langmarc Publishing
Lutheran University Press

Periodicals
Canada Lutheran (ELCC)
Canadian Lutheran
Lutheran Digest

MENNONITE
Periodicals
The Messenger
Purpose
Rejoice!

METHODIST, FREE
Periodicals
Evangel
Light and Life

METHODIST, UNITED
Book Publisher
Abingdon Press

Periodicals
Mature Years
Pockets
Upper Room

NONDENOMINATIONAL
Subsidy Publisher
Healthy Life Press

PRESBYTERIAN
Periodicals
Presbyterians Today
These Days

REFORMED
Periodical
Perspectives

SEVENTH-DAY ADVENTIST

Book Publisher

Pacific Press

Periodical

Guide Magazine

WESLEYAN CHURCH

Book Publisher

Wesleyan Publishing House

Periodicals

Light from the Word

Vista

MISCELLANEOUS DENOMINATIONS

Antiochian Orthodox

Conciliar Press

Church of God (Anderson IN)

Warner Press

Grace Brethren Churches

BMH Books

BONUS SECTION

Writer's Helps

Marketing

Following Trends

by Jerry B. Jenkins

RESIST THE TEMPTATION to jump on the bandwagon with a manuscript in a trendy category unless you're certain the topic will still be hot eighteen to twenty-four months from now. That's how far in advance many houses look to acquire projects. Their current lists are already set.

"We are filled up for fiction through next year," one acquisitions editor at a large Christian publisher recently told an agent. "I'm looking now for the year after that and beyond."

Trying to follow the crowd almost guarantees you'll get lost in it. Another agent I know was recently listed in an e-mail blast by a writers magazine. Inside a week he got more than one hundred inquiries.

Many who pitched him were trying to capitalize on the success of the Twilight series, or *The Hunger Games*, or a combination. But who knows how long vampires and wolves and kids killing kids will be hot?

What's Next?

In Christian publishing the market rallied around prairie romances, then spiritual warfare, then end times fiction, and now bonnet fiction.

But something new is coming.

What will it be? As with all breakout novels, no one will know till it seems to strike everyone's fancy.

A recent Dean Fetzer article proclaims, "Mermaids are the New Vampires—for Girls and Women." Are you "sick of vampires?" he writes, "been Twilighted beyond sense? Well, it looks like blood suckers are passé for a lot of female readers—they've been replaced by, of all things, mermaids!"

At the front of this newest wave is Brenda Peterson, author of *The Drowning World.* "Are mermaids the next big thing?" Fetzer says. "I'd bet a lot of traditional publishers think so. We're more than likely to see a number of new releases in the coming months based on the legends."

And so it goes. Trend-watching writers will grind out mermaid stories, and agents will be deluged with proposals. Then the shelves will be flooded with mermaid stories. Until the next trend. . . .

Be Yourself

My friend McNair Wilson once helped the team at Disney design theme parks. Today he's a creativity specialist at large, coaching corporate groups and individuals in ways to release the ideas within. At the Writing for the Soul conference, he challenges people not to try to be another Francine Rivers or Frank Peretti.

"Don't try to be somebody else," he says, "they've already been done."

"If you don't be you," McNair says, "*you* doesn't get done."

Neither do your stories. They're ones no one else could write.

What's my next novel? I didn't get any bites on *Chicken Soup for the Left Behind Amish Vampire.* But what if she were a mermaid?

This first appeared in the May 2013 issue of *Christian Communicator.*

Fighting the Tide

by Jerry B. Jenkins

How LONG SHOULD you look for a publisher for your novel, especially if it's in a category editors and agents say isn't selling?

If you put the manuscript back on the shelf, you can be certain no one will ever buy it.

If you keep trying to sell it, you may still find no success—or you may get a surprise. Like Peter Bekendam did.

"Eight years ago," Bekendam says, "fresh out of medical school I found myself wandering the halls of the hospital at two in the morning when I passed a guy mopping the floor. I was working eighty hours a week as a woefully underpaid intern, while he was listening to his headphones and dancing with his mop. As I glanced at him with genuine envy, the premise for *Prime of Life* planted itself in my tired brain."

The story was the fifth manuscript for Bekendam, who is an eye surgeon in Southern California. "I worked on it during my spare time throughout residency," Bekendam says. "I knew this one had a chance."

He gave himself every opportunity to sell the story. He attended the San Diego Christian Writers Guild's fall conference, where he took advantage of a "Thick-skinned Manuscript Critique" session I conducted. In the workshop I edited the first two pages of Bekendam's novel the way I would if I were editing it for publication. My cutting was extensive, but it showed him how his prose would look without needless words—and set the bar for his next 350 pages.

His resulting work was good enough to convince a top Christian literary agent to take him on. The agent shopped his novel for three years—with no success. Peter was told his writing and the story were good, but it didn't fall into a category publishers were able to sell.

Bekendam's novel isn't a historical. It's not a romance. It doesn't involve bonnets. It tracks a surgeon who abandoned his career and has become a janitor at a retirement home. Eventually his past catches up with him, forcing him to face deep issues of his life and faith.

As an unpublished member of the Christian Writers Guild, Bekendam entered the novel in the 2009 Operation First Novel contest. It placed as a semifinalist, but that didn't give his agent enough leverage to land him a contract.

Despite the age of the Baby Boomer generation—and their parents—it wasn't yet time for publishers to look for stories set in retirement homes. But that was three years ago.

"Last year I dusted off the manuscript, subjected it to its fifth rewrite, said my millionth prayer, and entered it into the contest again," Bekendam says.

In December 2012 he learned it was a semifinalist again. In January 2013, a finalist. And in February at the Writing for the Soul conference, he learned that Worthy Publishers and the Christian Writers Guild had selected *Prime of Life* that year's winner—which includes publication by Worthy.

How will the story be received? The publisher will do its best to publicize the novel and show how the story—involving a quirky cast of retirement home residents and employees—will connect with readers.

Maybe it will spark the next trend. I know at least one other agent who represents a novel largely set in a retirement home. At the conference he asked several acquisitions editors about their potential interest, and they weren't encouraging. Not yet.

Maybe when *Prime of Life* is released by Worthy, the market will change.

This first appeared in the June 2013 issue of *Christian Communicator*.

Establishing Your National Platform

by Dennis E. Hensley

I AM CONSTANTLY ASKED, "Why do people like Dr. Phil, Donald Trump, and Laura Bush get books published? They aren't even writers. I've worked on a manuscript for years, but I can't get a publisher. What's with that?"

The answer? *Visibility*. Those people have platforms. They're known.

Become known, and you too can attract interest from publishers. How?

Bill yourself as an expert in your field and get out there, speaking on your topic.

Start Small

Don't overlook the obvious matters: business cards; brochures including your photo, titles of your speaking topics, and endorsements; a website promoting your writing and speaking. Additionally, make available a CD of one of your talks or a DVD of one of your workshops.

In Your Backyard

Years ago I pitched a Saturday half-hour radio show called "Freelance Writing Made Easy." I lined up two bookstores willing to sign fifteen-week contracts to underwrite the show. After a year I was so busy with speaking engagements, I ended the radio program and went on the road.

Contact independent TV outlets; create your own promotional blog; speak to public service groups (Kiwanis, Lions, Elks); speak at banquets and retreats or teach college night school courses. At first, you may have to do some of this pro bono. Later you can charge a fee, as well as set up your book sale table.

The Success Factor

None of this prep work amounts to anything unless your presentations are stunning. Amazing. Rocko-socko. Your next two bookings are sitting in each audience. When you knock a crowd for a loop, people talk. This will lead to more invitations. Nothing will boost your career as much as positive word of mouth. Never allow yourself to give anything less than a phenomenal presentation.

Each year I meet dozens of people (80 percent of them women) who hand me a business card that says *Susan Smiley, author/speaker.* They have taken a three-day crash course in how to dress for success and prepare a speech. Bingo—they're ready to go on tour. They land a gig or two at a ladies' luncheon or PTA meeting. But, oddly enough, their phone doesn't ring off the hook thereafter. Clearly there was no pizzazz in the presentation. All the promotional trappings were in place, but no one got excited about the speaker.

Prepare and Deliver

Avoid this by writing a content-heavy, highly entertaining speech. Rehearse it, hone it, revise it until it's a knockout. Then, prepare another one. If you are a great orator, you'll be booked at massive venues. That leads to large on-the-spot book sales and additional speaking engagements.

A big platform results in lots of books sold—and publishers love that.

This previously appeared on the Christian Writers Guild blog: www.christianwritersguild.com/blog/establishing-your-national-platform/.

Social Media Works

by T. Suzanne Eller

YOU KNOW YOU NEED to create a social media platform, but the prospect is daunting. I know. I've been there.

I wrote the Christian Writers Guild's *Building Your Social Media Platform* course, and to prove it works, I created a new blog from scratch.

That's what the course teaches students to do, but could I start over with a new topic and audience? Could I really design an inviting blog from the ground up? Could I get the word out effectively?

Passion and Purpose

I'm passionate about healthy living, especially now in my fifties. So I started a personal fifty-day challenge and began keeping a journal. I decided to use this passion and my journal to launch my new blog.

My first task was to come up with a great title. I decided on *50 Days to Looking (and Feeling) Great After 50*. Then, based on the criteria in the social media course, I came up with a core message and tagline.

I went to WordPress.com and created a new blog: *50daystoagreat50.wordpress.com*. (I later purchased the domain.)

Get Creative

I played with several themes and decided on a super clean one that allows my title and images to pop. I also found some cool tools. WordPress.com has several options for widgets (tools you can add to your page). I chose the following:

- an RSS (Really Simple Syndication) feed
- a counter
- an option for readers to subscribe to the blog by e-mail
- the ability to show the last five comments on the main page

The RSS feed and e-mail options make it easier for people to read and interact. The counter helps me keep up with the number of visitors, and the comments widget is just cool—and gives a brief view of the conversations taking place.

My goal was to connect with one hundred readers (real people with real needs) in the first week. Then the blog exploded. . . .

Lightning Strikes

In the social media course, we talk about synergy. That means a combined effort greater than its individual parts. It happens when one action—like a single blog post—takes on new life through word of mouth in online communities.

I began by sharing a link to my first *50 Days* blog post on my personal Facebook page. I also tweeted about it. Soon the news was showing up in my friends' newsfeeds. By day five I had received more than 4,000 unique hits, 150-plus subscribers by e-mail, and twice that on my RSS feed!

Why did this happen? I see three reasons:

1. The topic hit an apparent felt need. Lots of people over fifty want to feel and be at their best.
2. People were excited and shared the information with their friends on Facebook and Twitter.
3. The new blog offered community. Living healthy is easier if you do it with others.

Easy for You to Say

Perhaps you think I received results like these because I'm already an author. I'm far from well known, but just in case, I did not link or talk about *50 Days to Looking (and Feeling) Great* on my ministry blog or any of my ministry Facebook pages.

I would have been ecstatic if I had hit my original goal of one hundred people, because I was connecting with a targeted audience and could build community from there. But four thousand?

I am having a blast in this experiment! Best of all, it proves that you *can* use social media to reach real people with real needs through the passion on your heart.

Design Concerns

Facebook has changed multiple times in the past year. WordPress.com offers regular updates with new tools and fixes for old glitches. As I launched my new blog, I ran into technical issues you might face.

My first challenge was the new options for design in WordPress. My ministry blog was designed by a professional four years ago. Adding and deleting design elements was new territory for me.

Scanning the themes, I found designs for a price, as well as for free. Some seemed a good fit; others had more options. I chose a free theme that was clean with a strong title section. It looks great, but it's bare bones.

So I went back to the dashboard (think of it as the brain of your blog site). This is where you write blog posts, publish them, and add media. It's also where you add or delete pages, change the theme, add widgets, and more.

Banish Fear and Try It

In the dashboard sidebar I chose Appearances and clicked on Widgets (automated applications in the form of on-screen tools). There were so many that this became my second challenge: choosing what works.

I played with different widgets, clicked on the preview option, and *voilà*, I could see what they looked like. Some just cluttered my site. Others were a perfect fit. I'm still experimenting. I just added a drop-down widget allowing visitors to choose archived blog posts by month.

The key is to explore without fear. Technology and programs change often. Be willing to try new options and use the Help section.

Finding Like-Minded People

The *50 Days to Looking (and Feeling) Great* blog was a personal challenge. When more than four thousand people visited in the first ten days, suddenly my challenge didn't seem like such a huge endeavor. I no longer felt alone.

Visitors signed up for the blog by e-mail and RSS feed. Several shared their struggles and successes. What emerged was encouragement, information, and a combined interest—in other words, community.

That's the Goal

This was an experiment, but I've now purchased the domain and have created PDF files to offer as freebies on the Resource page. My hope is that this site will inspire me—and others—to live our best lives after fifty.

Social media works. When you know why and what you are doing, it gives you the tools to connect with those searching for you and your message.

It can work for you, too. Don't allow fear of technology to keep you from diving in.

This previously appeared as a multipart article on the Christian Writers Guild blog: www.christianwritersguild.com /blog/social-media-does-it-work-part-1/.

Going Up: Preparing Your Elevator Pitch

by T. Suzanne Eller

I CLIMBED INTO the airport shuttle and realized I was sitting next to an editor. When she discovered we were attending the same event, she asked, "What's your book about?"

Ten minutes later I was still explaining and the editor sat glassy-eyed. Thankfully, I learned from my mistake, discovering three simple principles to a successful elevator pitch.

You get on an elevator and just as the doors are closing, Editor Marvella, the one you've wanted to meet, gets on too. You have until the elevator doors open on her floor to sell your idea. This is your elevator pitch: a three- to four-sentence overview of your article or book idea.

Be Yourself

In real life I rarely stumble over words or talk on and on. We often place editors on a different level than a potential friend who loves words, just like we do. This makes us nervous. Be yourself, but with a touch of professionalism. Editors aren't just buying manuscripts; they are creating relationships that will last long term.

Be Prepared

Before the conference, write a one-paragraph pitch.

For nonfiction, answer these questions:

- Who is my audience?
- What value does this book or article offer?

This was the pitch for my parenting book, which was published:

How can you be a good mom if no one shows you how? In *The Mom I Want to Be,* I come alongside moms raised in dysfunction and show how to forgive, how to let go, how to leave parenting baggage in the past, and how to give their children a greater legacy than they received.

For fiction, share these elements:

- Who
- The situation
- The conflict

This is my pitch for a recent historical novel:

In 1964, psychotherapist Dr. Caroline Bergen counsels a patient, Liza, who reveals that she lost her husband in the Mauthausen concentration camp two decades earlier. As her story unfolds, it unlocks secrets in Caroline's own family past. When she discovers that her beloved Grandpa is a former SS guard, will she ever trust again?

Be Ready to Answer

We often attempt to answer all of the questions editors might ask, or think to ask, long before they are hooked by the idea and value to their audience. Now that they are intrigued, be prepared to answer follow-up questions succinctly.

This previously appeared on the Christian Writers Guild blog: www.christianwritersguild.com/blog/going-up-preparing-your-elevator-pitch/.

Meeting an Editor or Agent

by Jennifer Slattery

It's your first agent appointment at your first conference and as you watch other authors give pitches, you feel you're going to lose your lunch.

Ephesians 2:10 tells us we are "God's handiwork, created in Christ Jesus to do good works, which God prepared in advance for us to do" (NIV). Tuck this truth into your pocket and relax. No editor or agent appointment, no matter how disastrous, can thwart God's plan for you.

Make Every Word Count

You'll have ten to fifteen minutes to make an impression so you can hear those coveted words, "Send me your proposal." Every word counts. Focus on what makes you and your writing unique. Know your hook, your brand, and your audience.

"I want to hear a strong marketable hook," says Jan Stob, senior acquisitions editor at Tyndale. "Is it unique? Is it something that will resonate with our core market?"

Kathy Willis, owner of KCW Communications, agrees that the hook is vital. "Make it good, rich prose, laden with the full weight of your writer's voice. Raise questions with the first sentence. Start at the first dramatic or crucial moment."

Know Your Stuff

Practice your pitch. Ane Mulligan, women's fiction writer and an editor for the Novel Rocket website, says, "My critique partners and I called each other with no notice. The moment we answered the phone, the other would say, 'Tell me about your book.' It took a few times before we could do it coherently, but it made us ready for anything."

Pitching editors and agents can be unnerving. So present your best self and sell your novel with a well-rehearsed, attention-grabbing pitch, and be prepared for whatever God has planned.

This previously appeared on the Christian Writers Guild blog: www.christianwritersguild.com/blog/take-your-thoughts-captive/.

Preparing a Winning Book Proposal

by Karen O'Connor

YOU'VE SIGNED UP for a writers conference where you can present your book ideas to editors and agents. But how can you present your material in a professional way? Here's a list of the items to include in a nonfiction book proposal that has worked for thousands of writers over the years. (For fiction, see the end of this piece.)

Page One: Your name and contact information centered at the top of the page, and the title of your book and byline (by Sue or Sam Smith) centered, midway down the page.

Following pages: Include the following headings:

Concept: Describe the book idea in one or two succinct paragraphs, using lively language to engage the editor.

Approach/Structure: State the format you will use: how-to, self-help, human interest stories with prayers and quotations or whatever style you've planned.

Audience: Name the group of readers you want to target, i.e., parents, business owners, women in recovery, teens, etc. Be as specific as possible.

Reader Benefits: List the ways your book will help readers. Example: information about your topic, inspiration from real life stories, reader involvement through journaling and prayers, or whatever applies. Be specific so editors can envision the book.

Competition: Record the titles, authors, and publishers of two or three books that may compete with yours, describing in one sentence for each how yours is different. Stay positive in talking about your book's differences; avoid bashing the competition.

Publicity: Provide in short paragraphs ways you'll cooperate with promoting the book. Example: blogging, Facebook, author appearances, radio and television interviews, etc. Include the addresses for your website, blog, and social media pages.

Author Bio: Create a brief bio of your professional and/or personal qualifications for writing this book. Are you a teacher, counselor, pastor, business owner? You want to inspire confidence in the editor that you are the one to complete this work.

Chapter Outline: Write two or three sentences describing what each chapter will cover.

Introduction (optional)**:** Start a new page and write a short introduction to the book. You can change or add to it later.

Sample Chapters (one to three)**:** Include at least one chapter. If you receive encouragement and interest from an editor, he or she may ask for a few more.

Novel Proposals

If you're presenting an idea for fiction, instead of a chapter outline include a two- to three-page synopsis of the plot, including all major characters, plot points, twists, turns, surprises, and the ending, and three sample chapters. Most fiction editors will also want to know that your book is completed.

Even if your book is not yet finished, take advantage of the opportunity at the conference to meet with editors and agents. You will receive great information on the current market and encouragement to get to "The End."

Take time to put together a focused proposal and print several copies to have available. Don't miss this excellent opportunity to introduce yourself and your ideas to editors who can help you move from beginning writer to published author. It starts with showing up.

This previously appeared on the Christian Writers Guild blog: www.christianwritersguild.com/blog/preparing-a-winning-book-proposal/.

How to Find a Publisher for Your Nonfiction Book

by Kevin Scott

Overview of the Key Pieces and Players

Writing an excellent book is one thing; convincing the right publisher is quite another.

As you undertake the quest, it helps to know what the acquisitions process looks like. Here's an overview of some necessary elements, the gatekeepers, and the typical phases a nonfiction book project must pass through.

The Proposal

1. One-sheet

A three-minute summary of your book proposal that tells

- what the book is about,
- who it's for, and
- why you're the person to write and help market it.

2. Full proposal

A detailed look at the contents of your book, your marketing plan, and the competition.

3. Sample chapters

Two or three complete chapters from the book that represent your best writing.

Acquisitions Gatekeepers

1. Agent

Your partner in finding the right publisher for your book.

2. Initial reviewer

The first gatekeeper at the publishing company.

3. Acquisitions editor

The person who needs to champion your project for it to survive the acquisitions process.

4. Marketing director

The person who has to be convinced the book will sell sufficient copies.

5. Publisher

The final gatekeeper at the publishing company.

Stages of the Acquisitions Process

1. Securing an agent

You find and contract with the agent who can best represent your work to potential publishers.

2. Polishing the proposal

You work with your agent to prepare a convincing summary of your writing to submit to publishers.

3. Submission to the editor

You consult with your agent in choosing one or more publishers to whom your agent will submit your proposal.

4. Responding to the editor's queries

If the acquisitions editor is interested, he or she may have questions or request revisions to the proposal.

5. Submission to the publisher
If the acquisitions editor likes your proposal, he or she may submit it to a publishing board.

6. Responding to the publisher's queries
If the publishing board likes your proposal, they may have additional questions or revision suggestions.

7. Contract offer and negotiation
If the publishing board approves your proposal, they will initiate the process of contract negotiation.

What Must You Fit into a One-Sheet?

Your one-sheet—a single page intended to pique an agent or editor's interest so they want to see your full proposal—serves as a marketing tool that provides a concise overview of your book.

Typical information in a one-sheet includes:

Title and Subtitle
Although these will likely change before publication, they are significant elements that should immediately engage the agent or editor. Ideally the title and subtitle should

- grab the reader's attention,
- tell what the book is about, and
- identify the reader benefit.

Contact Information
Give the agent or editor the best ways to reach you.

Description
Consider this advertising copy or a condensed version of what will appear on the back cover. Describe your book and tell why people read it.

Target Audience
As specifically as you can, describe your primary and secondary readerships.

Features or Benefits
Describe what is unique about your book. What does it offer that is not found in others on this topic?

Author Bio
Provide your credentials, especially those that provide legitimacy for you as an author for this book.

Author Platform
This section addresses why you have people's attention on this topic and what means you have to make your voice heard.

Previous Publications
To establish your legitimacy, list some or all of what you've had published in books, magazines, journals, or other periodicals.

That's a lot to fit in one single-spaced page. Resist the urge to reduce the font size or margins. If agents or editors have to strain to read it, they will quickly lose interest. Each section can be no longer than one paragraph or a few bullet points.

Whittling to one page everything you could say about your book will help you communicate clearly why an agent or editor should be interested in reading your full proposal.

What Goes into Your Proposal?

Crafting an excellent book proposal may be the most significant step in finding a publisher. I recommend investing as much time and energy researching, writing, editing, and proofing your proposal as you do for your book's first chapter. It's that important.

Your proposal must immediately capture the acquisitions editor's attention—then give him or her all the information to decide whether your project is a good fit for the publishing house.

A good proposal contains these key elements:

1. Title Page

Start with a clean, easy-to-read title page that includes your manuscript's title and subtitle, as well as your contact information. At this point most editors are not impressed with graphics. So unless design serves a key element in your book, just make sure your title page is clean and error-free.

2. Description

Give a detailed overview of the book. This typically includes the following:

- a three- to four-paragraph summary
- an overview of the structure with an annotated table of contents
- a list of the unique features and benefits
- the status of the manuscript (how much is written)
- an estimated completion date (if the manuscript is not yet finished)

3. Market Analysis and Plan

The publisher will make a decision based on whether they believe they can sell enough copies of your book. So make your case that it will have a sufficient market. Your evidence includes the following:

- a description of your target audience
- your relevant biography and platform
- the competition
- your personal plans for marketing

4. Sample Chapters

The acquisitions editor will want to see at least two completed chapters. Include those you feel represent your best work, regardless of where they fall in the outline. While the first three elements are vital, they will get you nowhere if your sample chapters fail to impress.

Will Your Sample Chapters Make Them Ask for More?

Excellent writing can rescue an average proposal. So make sure your sample chapters are as polished as can be. Your prospective agent or editor will assume you're sending your best work.

As an acquisitions editor, here's what I look for:

Compelling Prose

Even before considering your message, an editor wants to know how well you communicate. The sample chapters must attract your target readers and compel them to keep reading.

Compelling nonfiction gets to the point quickly. I look for economy of language.

I also check whether the language matches the target audience. If you're writing to an average person, your writing should feel at home in their neighborhood, not a seminary classroom.

Clear Message

A great book begins with your passion. Each sample chapter must clearly convey its message. And your proposal's annotated table of contents should make plain how that chapter fits into the book's flow and supports its overall message.

Consistent Structure

This is one of the biggest mistakes I see. Nonfiction chapters need to be guided by an internal structure. And that structure should remain generally consistent through all chapters. A typical chapter structure will follow these steps:

1. introduce a need or challenge
2. explain it in more detail
3. identify the solution
4. guide the reader to apply the solution
5. summarize and conclude

You don't have to make the structure obvious, but readers will sense when it's there—and become frustrated when it's not.

Do Your Best

If the rest of your proposal serves as the interview before the audition, your sample chapters are the actual audition. So make sure they are as good as you can make them.

But there comes a time when you must release them to your prospective agent or editor. You may worry that they're not perfect; they never are and never will be. But be sure you've sent the best work you can do.

Do You Need an Agent?

A literary agent can serve many useful roles as you seek a publisher. Two of the most valuable roles are that of expert guide and advocate:

Expert Guide

An experienced agent knows the publishing industry. He or she can help you

- polish your one-sheet, full proposal, and sample chapters,
- know which publishing houses may be a good fit for your book,
- navigate the process of negotiating and contracting with a publisher, and
- learn how to market your book.

Advocate

An experienced agent has relationships in the industry that can open doors for you. He or she will

- make the initial contact with publishers,
- pitch the full proposal to the acquisitions editor, and
- negotiate with the publisher.

Having an experienced agent in your corner can be a huge benefit. But for many first-time authors, securing an agent can be as challenging as finding a publisher. This leads many to wonder if it's really necessary.

The answer depends on your goals. Many people will tell you that having an agent is essential to getting published—because many publishing houses accept proposals only through agents. For these houses, the agent serves as a gatekeeper to ensure they review only the best proposals.

Yet there are a few other pathways.

Self-Publishing

This has become easier and less expensive. And because more sophisticated self-publishing options have emerged, the stigma it endured in its early years has been reduced.

Authors who succeed in selling a self-published book will merit a closer look by a traditional publisher for their next book. But there are two caveats:

- If the self-published book does not sell well, it will be more of a negative than a positive.
- It's highly unusual for a traditional publisher to republish a self-published book. A self-published title will likely always remain one.

If you go this route, you won't need an agent. But know what you're getting into—and make sure you're equipped to do your own marketing.

Smaller Publishers

Some smaller houses (such as where I work) still accept manuscripts without agents. Before you submit, review their submission guidelines and publishing interests. Make sure your proposal fits what they seek so you don't waste your time and theirs.

Contacts at Conferences

Some writers conferences offer opportunities to meet acquisitions editors from larger publishers. This is the one time they will review a proposal from an author who doesn't have an agent.

If you ultimately decide to secure an agent, do your due diligence. Also, remember that your agent works for you. While they have experience and connections, it's your book—and your writing career. Your agent can give you great advice, but the important decisions are always yours.

Ways to Help Your Proposal Survive the Initial Review

When you send your proposal to a publisher, it will likely go through an initial screening. If that first reviewer determines the proposal is not a good fit, it may not even make it to the acquisitions editor.

To help you avoid that disappointment, here are five things the initial reviewer wants to see.

A Clear and Compelling Title

A jazzy title might capture attention, but don't forget, its most important function is to indicate who it's for and what it's about.

If your title is merely catchy, include a subtitle that answers those questions.

A Concept that Fits the Publisher

I think of a book's concept as the hook plus the promise. The hook is what sets the book apart from all the others at Amazon. The promise is what your readers can expect. The overall idea must align with the publisher's interests and market.

A Proposal that Follows the Publisher's Guidelines

A publisher will not reject a great proposal on a technicality. But by following a publisher's guidelines, you can be sure to provide everything its people need to make an informed decision.

An Error-Free Document

A publisher also won't reject a great proposal over a few typos. But one riddled with minor errors will probably not survive. This is your opportunity to impress, so put your best foot forward.

A Writing Sample that Reveals Your Talent

Some editors jump directly to the writing sample. If they aren't immediately captured by its quality and readability, the rest of the information won't salvage the proposal.

Surviving the initial review is an important hurdle to getting your book published. Once your proposal makes it to an acquisitions editor, you can be sure it will receive serious consideration.

Ways to Turn an Acquisitions Editor into an Advocate

If you clear the first hurdle to getting your book published—surviving the initial review—your proposal will receive more serious consideration by an acquisitions editor.

This is the person who will present your proposal to the publishing board, answering their questions and responding to any objections. To get your book published, you need the acquisitions editor to present a convincing case.

To turn an acquisitions editor into a strong advocate for your proposal, give him or her everything needed to make an outstanding presentation to the publishing board.

Acquisitions editors love a well-constructed proposal that makes it easier for them to prepare to meet the publishing board.

This includes

- a great title and subtitle;
- a book description that offers an accurate and compelling snapshot of the manuscript;
- a depiction of the target audience—and tailoring every element to match that; and
- demonstrating how you will take ownership for marketing the book.

Two People to Convince

The key publishing board members the acquisitions editor has to convince that your book is worthy are the marketing director and the accountant.

The marketing director needs to be convinced the book will connect with a significant audience. Evidence includes more than the title and content; it's also about the author's platform—his or her established audience. Increasingly, the question is what the author can and will do to build that audience.

The accountant wants to know that the book is likely to provide a significant return on investment. Publishing is a business, with people's livelihoods on the line. The acquisitions editor needs to convince the accountant that the book will be good for the company's bottom line.

In Their Shoes

Try to think like a publisher. In your proposal, provide all the requested information. If you appreciate why the publisher needs the information, you can write to persuade.

Think like a publisher, equip your acquisitions editor to make a great presentation, and you are likely to gain a powerful advocate for your proposal.

Five Key Things the Marketing Director Wants to See

Without the marketing director's support, your book will likely be rejected. Here are five key areas the marketing director focuses on when your proposal goes before the publishing committee:

Concept

To build awareness of your book, the marketing director needs your concept to be fresh, clear, and compelling and distinctive from similar books.

To satisfy this need, craft your title and book description to clearly communicate the following:

- the need your book addresses
- how it meets that need
- the promise it makes to the reader

Biography

The marketing director wants to know who you are. Share your

- experience,
- degrees,
- titles,
- awards, and
- anything else that makes you the right person to write this book.

Platform

To get your book published, you must have built a significant relationship with your audience, the people already paying attention to you.

Your platform includes where you regularly speak and where you are being published: online and in print. When you write or speak, who reads and listens?

Platforms come in all sizes. Generally, the larger the publishing house, the larger the platform the marketing director wants to see.

Marketing Strategy

Aside from the marketing opportunities the publishing house will create, the marketing director wants to know what you plan to do to market your own book.

This is not about what you are *willing* to do if the publishing house creates the opportunity, but what you will *initiate* and accomplish. These are things like

- writing magazine articles,
- setting up speaking engagements,
- seeking specific endorsements, and
- using existing networks to get out the word about your book.

Competition

Finally, the marketing director wants a list of current books that most closely compete with yours, but also a description of what sets yours apart.

This previously appeared as a multipart article on the Christian Writers Guild blog: www.christianwritersguild.com/blog/find-a-publisher-for-your-nonfiction-book-part-1/.

Prepare for Your Author Interviews

by Heather Kreke

ONCE YOUR NOVEL has been released, be prepared for media interviews.

Where to Look

The chances that Oprah will call are slim, but opportunities for author interviews abound. Contact your local newspaper or radio or television station and see if they would be interested in interviewing a local author. Because your book is a novel, the subject of the interview will likely be you and not much about the story.

Look for blogs that interview new authors or even other authors who might be willing to interview you on their website. Interview yourself and put it on your website.

Don't wait for the phone call. Prepare now.

Create Questions

Few interviewers write their own questions, so awaken your inner Boy Scout and be prepared. Send questions that will work whether the interviewer has read your book or not. Too few do, and there's nothing worse than an interview that begins, "So, what's your novel about?"

Know Your Story

Be able to succinctly explain your plot and why people will want to read your book. Remember the elevator pitch that secured that appointment with your dream editor? Pull that out and polish it.

Know *Your* Story

You also need to know the story behind your book. Why did you write it? How did you come up with the idea? Is any of it based on real events? A great story will have a great backstory.

Now go tell the world about your novel.

This previously appeared on the Christian Writers Guild blog: www.christianwritersguild.com/blog/preparing-for-your-author-interviews/.

Planning a Successful Book Signing

by Deborah Raney

AUTHOR BOOK SIGNINGS ARE HIT OR MISS. Retailers spend time and money advertising. Authors spend time and money traveling to the store. Results are often less than successful. But planning can increase your odds of success.

- Schedule your signing far in advance and stay in contact with the store.
- Do your part to advertise the event to your readers/community via your website, newsletter, and social media.
- E-mail photos and book covers (both high resolution) and a bio to the store for advertising purposes.
- Consider a multi-author event. Help the retailer by connecting them with other authors. Designate one of you to serve as store liaison.
- Notify your publishers about the event in time for them to send promotional materials—or, if your publisher does not provide materials, produce them yourself. Bookmarks, postcards, posters, and bag-stuffers are great ways to advertise the event ahead of time. Check with the store so you don't duplicate each other's efforts.
- Customers are often confused about who that person sitting behind the stack of books is, so prepare a name tag and table sign, and ask for someone to direct people to you.
- Arrive early enough that you can freshen up, visit with the staff, and acquaint yourself with the store.
- Bring something to share with customers. Free bookmarks, pens, reader's guides, or a piece of chocolate helps the signing feel less a marketing ploy and more a conversation with readers. If the retailer approves, hold a drawing for a book or other giveaway.
- Offer to do a reading, give a speech, or hold a Q&A time for readers. Be creative in tying into the theme of your book.
- Go prepared to pray with customers. Have ears to hear the needs of those who come to your book table, but don't be tempted to take on the role of psychologist.
- If traffic is light, ask how you can help the staff. Straighten shelves. Entertain customers' children. Go with a servant's heart and be a blessing to the staff.
- Ask if you may autograph stock before you leave, but don't be offended if the staff declines. Most publishers don't allow returns on signed books.
- Express gratitude for the invitation, for stocking your books, and for hosting the signing.
- Pray for the store and for a successful signing.

Above all, communicate. When author and retailer have both planned ahead, a book signing can be pleasant and profitable.

This previously appeared on the Christian Writers Guild blog: www.christianwritersguild.com/blog/planning-a-successful-book-signing/.

14

Resources for Writers

The Jerry B. Jenkins Christian Writers Guild does not endorse the following organizations, websites, articles, or services, but we hope this listing will be a good starting place as you develop your writing as well as your platform.

Book Publicity Firms (Christian and General Markets)
Some of these are not specifically Christian. Also, be sure you interview the firm as well as the individual who will be promoting you and your work to be confident that this is the best fit for you. Take your time, and ask for references. And do your homework on the specific firm.

Author Echo: http://www.authorecho.com/
DeChant Hughes Public Relations: http://www.dechanthughes.com/index.htm
Litfuse Publicity: http://litfusegroup.com/
PR by the Book: http://www.prbythebook.com/
Pure Publicity Inc.: http://www.purepublicity.com/
Christian Authors Network: http://christianauthorsnetwork.com/
Rocky Mountain Media Group: http://rm2g.com/
We Grow Media: http://wegrowmedia.com/

Helpful Websites (Christian and General Markets)
These are a sampling of the variety of sites of potential interest to you as a writer looking to develop a platform. A Google search for the specific topic on which you need guidance will provide additional options. Some of these are not geared toward the Christian market.

Bestseller Labs: Practical Advice on How To Get Published and Grow Your Readership: http://bestsellerlabs.com/how-to-find-readers-on-twitter/
eBook-Pub.com: e-publish today!: http://www.ebook-pub.com/
Writer's Relief: Author's Submission Service: http://www.writersrelief.com/
Christian Fiction Blog Alliance: Where People Come Together to Further the Lord's Kingdom by Supporting Christian Fiction: http://www.christianfictionblogalliance.com/
The Savvy Book Marketer: The Tools You Need to Sell More Books: http://bookmarketingmaven.typepad.com/resources/2009/11/book-marketing-resources.html
Body and Soul Publishing: http://www.bodyandsoulpublishing.com/advertising-for-christian-authors/ (Offers a section where authors can post their books for free to get reviews. Other advertising opportunities available.)
Grammar Girl: Quick and Dirty Tips for Better Writing: http://grammar.quickanddirtytips.com/
The Writer: http://www.writermag.com/
Poets & Writers: http://www.pw.org/magazine
Jonathan Gunson, Bestseller Labs: http://bestsellerlabs.com/7-free-photo-libraries/
eBook-Pub.com: http://www.ebook-pub.com/
Jeff Goins: http://goinswriter.com/resources/

Blogs (Christian and General Markets)

These are a sampling of current writers' blogs. A Google search for the specific topic on which you need guidance will provide other options.

Jerry B. Jenkins Christian Writers Guild: http://www.christianwritersguild.com/blog/
Michael Hyatt, Intentional Leadership: http://michaelhyatt.com/
Rob Eagar, WildFire Marketing: http://www.startawildfire.com/blog
Dan Blank: http://wegrowmedia.com/blog/
Author Media: Growing Your Platform Online: http://www.authormedia.com/blog/
Where Writers Win: Marketing, Websites, Training and Tools for Emerging Authors: http://writerswin.com/blog/#axzz2KfJ5InsG
Rachelle Gardner: http://www.rachellegardner.com/category/popular-posts/
The Quick and Dirty: The Latest From Your Experts: http://blog.quickanddirtytips.com/
Godly Writers: http://www.godlywriters.com/tag/social-media-2/

Webinars

A Google search for the topic on which you need guidance will provide other options.

Using Social Media to Build Your Online Platform (CWG): http://www.christianwritersguild.com/store/webinars/using-social-media-to-build-your-online-platform
Shameless Networking (CWG): http://www.christianwritersguild.com/store/webinars/shameless-networking-9-27-2012
Shameless Self Promotion (CWG): http://www.christianwritersguild.com/store/webinars/shameless-self-promotion-9-11-2012
Ten Ways to Increase Your Platform Using Facebook (CWG): http://www.christianwritersguild.com/store/webinars/ten-ways-to-increase-your-platform-using-facebook
Publicity 101: Waiting for the Limo (CWG): http://www.christianwritersguild.com/store/webinars/publicity-101
Selling What You Write (CWG): http://www.christianwritersguild.com/store/webinars?product_id=238

Facebook Pages

There are many pages and groups on Facebook for writers of various genres and levels. Search for these and other pages to find ones that best fit your needs. Also, search for your favorite authors and join their Facebook pages so you can watch how they use this social media option.

Christian Writers Guild
Christian Speakers Services
Blogging Bistro, LLC: A full menu of Social Media Services
Inspire Christian Writers
Ebookmybook

Online Articles

These are a small sampling of how-to and advice articles geared toward developing your platform.

Are You Ready to Blog? (CWG): http://www.christianwritersguild.com/blog/are-you-ready-to-blog/
Your Web Domain Name Matters (CWG): http://www.christianwritersguild.com/blog/your-web-domain-name-matters/
Social Media: Does It Work? Part 1, 2, 3, and 4 (CWG): http://www.christianwritersguild.com/blog/social-media-does-it-work-part-1/

Planning a Successful Book Signing (CWG): http://www.christianwritersguild.com/blog/planning-a-successful-book-signing/
Market Your Book Now (CWG): http://www.christianwritersguild.com/blog/market-your-book-now/
Improve Your Proofreading (CWG): http://www.christianwritersguild.com/blog/improve-your-proofreadng/
Building a Facebook Community (CWG): http://www.christianwritersguild.com/blog/building-a-facebook-community/
Top 5 Tips: Writing for the Web (CWG): http://www.christianwritersguild.com/blog/top-5-tips-writing-for-the-web/
How to Build your Author Platform (Writer's Digest): http://www.writersdigest.com/writing-articles/by-writing-goal/get-published-sell-my-work/how-to-build-your-author-platform
The Basics of Building a Writer's Platform (Writer's Digest): http://www.writersdigest.com/writing-articles/by-writing-goal/build-a-platform-start-blogging/building-a-writers-platform
Book Publicity: A Labor of Love (Christian Fiction Online Magazine): http://www.christianfictiononlinemagazine.com/aug-08-buzz_publicity.html
Are You Social Media Savvy or Social Media Awkward?: http://altongansky.typepad.com/writersconferences/2013/01/are-you-social-media-savvy-or-social-media-awkward.html
Social Media and Christian Authors: http://keikihendrix.com/social-media-etiquette-and-christian-authors/

Books

Note: Some of these are not specifically geared to the Christian market.

GENERAL TITLES

Bird by Bird by Anne Lamott (Doubleday Anchor Books, 1994)
Culture Making: Recovering our Creative Calling by Andy Crouch (IVP, 2008)
How to Write What You Love and Make a Living at It by Dennis E. Hensley, PhD (Shaw/Random House, 2000)
I Know What You're Thinking by Lillian Glass, PhD (John Wiley & Sons, 2002)
No Mentor but Myself: A Collection of Articles, Essays, Reviews, and Letters by Jack London on Writing and Writers edited by Dale L. Walker (Kennikat Press, 1979)
On Writing Well (30th Anniversary Edition) by William Zinsser (Harper Perennial, 2006)
Scribbling in the Sand by Michael Card (IVP, 2002)
Stein on Writing by Sol Stein (St. Martins, 1995)
The Craft of Writing by William Sloane (Norton, 1979)
The Creative Call by Janice Elsheimer (Waterbrook Press, 2001)
The Synonym Finder by J. I. Rodale (Rodale Press, 1986)
The Write Way by Richard Lederer and Richard Dowis (Simon & Schuster Pocket Books, 1995)
The Writer's Little Helper by Jim Smith (Writer's Digest Books, 2012)
Word Painting by Rebecca McClanahan (Writer's Digest Books, 1999)
Writers on Writing edited by James N. Watkins (Wesleyan Publishing House, 2005)
Writing for the Soul by Jerry B. Jenkins (Writer's Digest Books, 2006)

CHILDREN'S BOOKS

Writing Books for Children by Jane Yolen (The Writer, Inc., 1973)

FICTION

Characters, Emotion, and Viewpoint by Nancy Kress (Writer's Digest Books, 2005)
Characters & Viewpoint by Orson Scott Card (Writer's Digest Books, 1988)

Dialogue by Gloria Kempton (Writer's Digest Books, 2004)
Dynamic Characters by Nancy Kress (Writer's Digest Books, 2004)
Elements of Fiction Writing: Conflict and Suspense by James Scott Bell (Writer's Digest Books, 2012)
Fiction Attack! by James Scott Bell (Compendium Press, 2012)
Fiction Writing Demystified by Thomas Sawyer (Ashleywilde, Inc., 2003)
Getting into Character by Brandilyn Collins (John Wiley & Sons, 2002)
Goal, Motivation, and Conflict by Debra Dixon (Gryphon Books for Writers, 1996)
How Fiction Works by Oakley Hall (Writer's Digest Books, 2003)
How to Grow a Novel by Sol Stein (St. Martin's Griffin, 1999)
Mastering Point of View by Sherri Szeman (Story Press, 2001)
On Writing by Stephen King (Scribner, 2010)
On Writing Romance: How to Craft a Novel That Sells by Leigh Michaels (Writer's Digest Books, 2007)
Plot and Structure by James Scott Bell (Writer's Digest Books, 2004)
Revision and Self-Editing by James Scott Bell (Writer's Digest Books, 2012)
Self-Editing for Fiction Writers by Renni Browne and Dave King (William Morrow, 2004)
Spider, Spin Me a Web by Lawrence Block (William Morrow, 1996)
Story by Robert McKee (ReganBooks, 1997)
Techniques of the Selling Writer by Dwight Swain (University of Oklahoma Press, 1982)
Telling Lies for Fun and Profit by Lawrence Block (William Morrow, 1994)
The Art of Character by David Corbett (Penguin Books, 2013)
The Art of War for Writers by James Scott Bell (Writer's Digest Books, 2009)
The Dance of Character and Plot by DiAnn Mills (Bold Vision Books, 2013)
The Emotion Thesaurus by Becca Puglisi and Angela Ackerman (CreateSpace Independent Publishing Platform, 2012)
The Fire in Fiction by Donald Maass (Writer's Digest Books, 2009)
The First 50 Pages by Jeff Gerke (Writer's Digest Books, 2011)
The Liar's Bible by Lawrence Block (Open Road Media, 2011)
The Moral Premise by Stanley D. Williams (Michael Wiese Productions, 2006)
The Power of Body Language by Tonya Reiman (Gallery Books, Reprint Edition 2008)
The Scene Book by Sandra Scofield (Penguin Books, 2007)
Writing Dialogue by Tom Chiarella (Story Press, 1998)
Writing the Breakout Novel by Donald Maass (Writer's Digest Books, 2002)
Writing the Breakout Novel Workbook by Donald Maass (Writer's Digest Books, 2004)

GRAMMAR & STYLE

Formatting & Submitting Your Manuscript by Cynthia Laufenberg and the editors of *Writer's Digest* (Writer's Digest Books, 2004)
Garner's Modern American Usage (3rd Edition) by Bryan A. Garner (Oxford, 2009)
Grammar Girl's Quick and Dirty Tips for Better Writing by Mignon Fogarty (Holt, 2008)
Nitty-Gritty Grammar by Edith H. Fine and Judith P. Josephson (Ten Speed Press, 1998)
Punctuate It Right by Harry Shaw (HarperCollins Reference Library, 2010)
The Associated Press Stylebook and Briefing on Media Law (46th Edition) (Associated Press, 2013)
The Chicago Manual of Style by the University of Chicago Press Staff (University of Chicago Press, 2010)
The Christian Writer's Manual of Style (Updated and Expanded Edition) edited by Robert Hudson (Zondervan, 2004)
The Elements of Style by William Strunk, Jr. and E. B. White (Macmillan, 2009)
Woe Is I (3rd Edition) by Patricia T. O'Conner (Riverhead Books, 2009)

MARKETING

Book Proposals That Sell by W. Terry Whalin (Write Now Publications-ACW Press, 2005)
Create Your Writer Platform: The Key to Building an Audience, Selling More Books, and Finding Success as an Author by Chuck Sambuchino (Writer's Digest Books, 2012)
Get into Bed with Google by Jon Smith (The Infinite Ideas Company, 2008)
Get Known Before the Book Deal: Use Your Personal Strengths to Grow an Author Platform by Christina Katz (Writer's Digest Books, 2008)
Guerrilla Marketing for Writers: 100 No-Cost, Low-Cost Weapons for Selling Your Work by Jay Levinson, Rick Frishman, Michael Larsen, and David L. Hancock (Morgan James Publishing, 2010)
Guerrilla Social Media Marketing: 100+ Weapons to Grow Your Online Influence, Attract Customers, and Drive Profits by Jay Levinson and Shane Gibson (Jere L. Calmes, Publisher, 2010)
How to Write a Book Proposal by Michael Larsen (Writer's Digest Books, 2004)
Internet Marketing Made Easy by Jo-Anne Vandermeulen (The Laurus Company, 2012)
Platform: Get Noticed in a Noisy World by Michael Hyatt (Thomas Nelson, 2012)
Premium Promotional Tips for Writers by Jo-Anne Vandermeulen (The Laurus Company, 2009)
Promote Your Book: Over 250 Proven, Low-Cost Tips and Techniques for the Enterprising Author by Patricia Fry (Allworth Press, 2011)
Sally Stuart's Guide to Getting Published by Sally E. Stuart (Harold Shaw Publishers, 1999)
Sell More Books by J. Steve Miller and Cherie K. Miller (Wisdom Creek Press, 2011)
Sell Your Book Like Wildfire: The Writer's Guide to Marketing and Publicity by Rob Eagar (Writer's Digest Books, 2012)
Shameless Self Promotion and Networking for Christian Creatives by Paula K. Parker, Mike Parker, and Torry Martin (WordCrafts Press, 2011)
Small Time Operator: How to Start Your Own Business, Keep Your Books, Pay Your Taxes, and Stay Out of Trouble by Bernard B. Kamoroff (Taylor Trade Publishing, 2013)
Social Media Just for Writers: The Best Online Marketing Tips for Selling Your Books by Frances Caballo (ACT Communications, 2012)
The Christian Writer's Market Guide by Jerry B. Jenkins (Tyndale House Publishers, 2014)
The Sell Your Novel Tool Kit by Elizabeth Lyon (Penguin Books, 2002)
The Social Media Bible: Tactics, Tools, and Strategies for Business Success by Lon Safko
The Ultimate Guide to Marketing Your Business with Pinterest by Gabriela Taylor (CreateSpace Independent Publishing Platform, 2013)

PERIODICALS

Effective Magazine Writing by Robert C. Palms (WaterBrook Press, 2000)
Feature & Magazine Writing: Action, Angle and Anecdotes (2nd edition) by David E. Sumner and Holly G. Miller (Wiley-Blackwell, 2009)
Writer's Digest Handbook of Magazine Article Writing (2nd edition) edited by Michelle Ruberg (Writer's Digest Books, 2005)
Writing Articles from the Heart: How to Write and Sell Your Life Experiences by Marjorie Holmes (Writer's Digest Books, 1993)

SCIENCE FICTION

World-Building by Stephen L. Gillet (Writer's Digest Books, 1996)

E-Books

Secrets to E-book Publishing Success (Kindle edition) by Mark Coker (Smashwords Guides, 2013)

Magazines

Christian Communicator by American Christian Writers (monthly)
Writer's Digest by F&W Publications (monthly)

DVDs

Grabbing the Reader in the First 10 Pages (audio CD) by Michael Hauge and James Mercurio (Producer) (2005)
The Hero's 2 Journeys by Michael Hauge and Christopher Vogler (Writer's Audioship, 2001)

Organizations and Services

These services and organizations can help you develop your craft and establish your platform.

Full Manuscript Critique: http://www.christianwritersguild.com/full-manuscript-critiques/
Partial Manuscript Critique: http://www.christianwritersguild.com/partial-manuscript-critiques/
Jerry B. Jenkins Christian Writer's Guild: www.ChristianWritersGuild.com
Advanced Writers and Speakers Association: http://www.awsa.com/
Somersault Group: http://somersaultgroup.com/home
Constant Contact (E-mail Marketing Service): http://www.constantcontact.com/index.jsp

Glossary

Advance: Amount of money a publisher pays to an author up front, against future royalties. The amount varies greatly from publisher to publisher and is often paid in two or three installments (on signing contract, on delivery of manuscript, and on publication).

All rights: An outright sale of your material. Author has no further control over it.

Anecdote: A short, poignant, real-life story, usually used to illustrate a single thought.

Assignment: When an editor asks a writer to write a specific piece for an agreed-upon price.

As-told-to story: A true story you write as a first-person account but about someone else.

Audiobooks: Books available on CDs or in other digital formats.

Avant-garde: Experimental; ahead of the times.

Backlist: A publisher's previously published books that are still in print a year after publication.

B & W: Abbreviation for a black-and-white photograph.

Bar code: Identification code and price on the back of a book read by a scanner at checkout counters.

Bible versions: AMP—Amplified Bible; ASV—American Standard Version; CEV—Contemporary English Version; ESV—English Standard Version; GNB—Good News Bible; HCSB—Holman Christian Standard Bible; ICB—International Children's Bible; KJV—King James Version; MSG—The Message; NAB—New American Bible; NAS—New American Standard; NEB—New English Bible; NIrV—New International Reader's Version; NIV—New International Version; NJB—New Jerusalem Bible; NKJV—New King James Version; NLT—New Living Translation; NRSV—New Revised Standard Version; RSV—Revised Standard Version; TLB—*The Living Bible*; TNIV—Today's New International Version.

Bimonthly: Every two months.

Bio sketch: Information on the author.

Biweekly: Every two weeks.

Bluelines: Printer's proofs used to catch errors before a book is printed.

Book proposal: Submission of a book idea to an editor; usually includes a cover letter, thesis statement, chapter-by-chapter synopsis, market survey, and 1-3 sample chapters.

Byline: Author's name printed just below the title of a story, article, etc.

Camera-ready copy: The text and artwork for a book that are ready for the press.

Chapbook: A small book or pamphlet containing poetry, religious readings, etc.

Circulation: The number of copies sold or distributed of each issue of a publication.

Clips: See "Published clips."

Column: A regularly appearing feature, section, or department in a periodical using the same heading; written by the same person or a different freelancer each time.

Concept statement: A 50-150 word summary of your proposed book.

Contributor's copy: Copy of an issue of a periodical sent to the author whose work appears in it.

Copyright: Legal protection of an author's work.

Cover letter: A letter that accompanies some manuscript submissions. Usually needed only if you have to tell the editor something specific or to give your credentials for writing a piece of a technical nature. Also used to remind the editor that a manuscript was requested or expected.

Credits, list of: A listing of your previously published works.

Critique: An evaluation of a piece of writing.

Defamation: A written or spoken injury to the reputation of a living person or organization. If what is said is true, it cannot be defamatory.

Derivative work: A work derived from another work, such as a condensation or abridgement. Contact copyright owner for permission before doing the abridgement and be prepared to pay that owner a fee or royalty.

Devotional: A short piece that shares a personal spiritual discovery, inspires to worship, challenges to commitment or action, or encourages.

Editorial guidelines: See "Writers' guidelines."

Electronic submission: The submission of a proposal or article to an editor by electronic means, such as by e-mail or on disk.

Endorsements: Flattering comments about a book; usually carried on the back cover or in promotional material.

EPA/Evangelical Press Assn.: A professional trade organization for periodical publishers and associate members.

E-proposals: Proposals sent via e-mail.

E-queries: Queries sent via e-mail.

Eschatology: The branch of theology that is concerned with the last things, such as death, judgment, heaven, and hell.

Essay: A short composition usually expressing the author's opinion on a specific subject.

Evangelical: A person who believes that one receives God's forgiveness for sins through Jesus Christ, and believes the Bible is an authoritative guide for daily living.

Exegesis: Interpretation of the Scripture.

Feature article: In-depth coverage of a subject, usually focusing on a person, an event, a process, an organization, a movement, a trend or issue; written to explain, encourage, help, analyze, challenge, motivate, warn, or entertain as well as to inform.

Filler: A short item used to "fill" out the page of a periodical. It could be a timeless news item, joke, anecdote, light verse or short humor, puzzle, game, etc.

First rights: Editor buys the right to publish your piece for the first time.

Foreign rights: Selling or giving permission to translate or reprint published material in a foreign country.

Foreword: Opening remarks in a book introducing the book and its author.

Freelance: As in 50% freelance: means that 50% of the material printed in the publication is supplied by freelance writers.

Freelancer or freelance writer: A writer who is not on salary but sells his or her material to a number of different publishers.

Free verse: Poetry that flows without any set pattern.

Galley proof: A typeset copy of a book manuscript used to detect and correct errors before the final print run.

Genre: Refers to type or classification, as in fiction or poetry. Such types as westerns, romances, mysteries, etc., are referred to as genre fiction.

Glossy: A black-and-white photo with a shiny, rather than matte, finish.

Go-ahead: When a publisher tells you to go ahead and write up or send your article idea.

Haiku: A Japanese lyric poem of a fixed 17-syllable form.

Hard copy: A typed manuscript, as opposed to one on disk or in an e-mail.

Holiday/seasonal: A story, article, filler, etc., that has to do with a specific holiday or season. This material must reach the publisher the stated number of months prior to the holiday/season.

Homiletics: The art of preaching.

Honorarium: If a publisher indicates they pay an honorarium, it means they pay a small flat fee, as opposed to a set amount per word.

Humor: The amusing or comical aspects of life that add warmth and color to an article or story.

Interdenominational: Distributed to a number of different denominations.

International Postal Reply Coupon: See "IRC."

Interview article: An article based on an interview with a person of interest to a specific readership.

IRC or IPRC: International Postal Reply Coupon: can be purchased at your local post office and should be enclosed with a manuscript sent to a foreign publisher.

ISBN: International Standard Book Number; an identification code needed for every book.

Journal: A periodical presenting news in a particular area.

Kill fee: A fee paid for a completed article done on assignment that is subsequently not published. Amount is usually 25-50% of original payment.

Libel: To defame someone by an opinion or a misquote and put his or her reputation in jeopardy.

Light verse: Simple, lighthearted poetry.

Little/Literary: Small circulation publications whose focus is providing a forum for the literary writer, rather than on making money. Often do not pay, or pay in copies.

Mainstream fiction: Other than genre fiction, such as romance, mystery, or science fiction. Stories of people and their conflicts handled on a deeper level.

Mass market: Books intended for a wide, general market, rather than a specialized market. These books are produced in a smaller format, usually with smaller type, and are sold at a lower price. The expectation is that their sales will be higher.

Ms: Abbreviation for manuscript.

Mss: Abbreviation for more than one manuscript.

Multiple submissions: Submitting more than one piece at a time to the same publisher, usually reserved for poetry, greeting cards, or fillers, not articles. Also see "Simultaneous submissions."

NASR: Abbreviation for North American Serial Rights.

Newsbreak: A newsworthy event or item sent to a publisher who might be interested in publishing it because it would be of interest to his particular readership.

Nondenominational: Not associated with a particular denomination.

Not copyrighted: Publication of your piece in such a publication will put it into the public domain and it is not then protected. Ask that the publisher carry your copyright notice on your piece when it is printed.

Novella: A short novel starting at 20,000 words—35,000 words maximum. Length varies from publisher to publisher.

On acceptance: Periodical or publisher pays a writer at the time the manuscript is accepted for publication.

On assignment: Writing something at the specific request of an editor.

Onetime rights: Selling the right to publish a story one time to any number of publications (usually refers to publishing for a nonoverlapping readership).

On publication: Publisher pays a writer when his or her manuscript is published.

On speculation/On spec: Writing something for an editor with the agreement that the editor will buy it only if he or she likes it.

Overrun: The extra copies of a book printed during the initial print run.

Over the transom: Unsolicited articles that arrive at a publisher's office.

Payment on acceptance: See "On acceptance."

Payment on publication: See "On publication."

Pen name/pseudonym: Using a name other than your legal name on an article or book in order to protect your identity or the identity of people included, or when the author wishes to remain anonymous. Put the pen name in the byline under the title, and your real name in the upper, left-hand corner.

Permissions: Asking permission to use the text or art from a copyrighted source.

Personal experience story: A story based on a real-life experience.

Personality profile: A feature article that highlights a specific person's life or accomplishments.

Photocopied submission: Sending an editor a photocopy of your manuscript, rather than an original. Some editors prefer an original.

Piracy: To take the writings of others just as they were written and put your name on them as the author.

Plagiarism: To steal and use the ideas or writings of another as your own, rewriting them to make them sound like your own.

Press kit: A compilation of promotional materials on a particular book or author, usually organized in a folder, used to publicize a book.

Print-on-Demand (POD): A printing process where books are printed one at a time instead of in quantity. The production cost per book is higher, but no warehousing is necessary. Bookstores typically will not carry POD books.

Public domain: Work that has never been copyrighted, or on which the copyright has expired. Subtract 75 from the current year, and anything copyrighted prior to that is in the public domain.

Published clips: Copies of actual articles you have had published, from newspapers or magazines.

Quarterly: Every three months.

Query letter: A letter sent to an editor telling about an article you propose to write and asking if he or she is interested in seeing it.

Reporting time: The number of weeks or months it takes an editor to get back to you about a query or manuscript you have sent in.

Reprint rights: Selling the right to reprint an article that has already been published elsewhere. You must have sold only first or onetime rights originally, and wait until it has been published the first time.

Review copies: Books given to book reviewers or buyers for chains.

Royalty: The percentage an author is paid by a publisher on the sale of each copy of a book.

SAE: Self-addressed envelope (without stamps).

SAN: Standard Account Number, used to identify libraries, book dealers, or schools.

SASE: Self-addressed, stamped envelope. Should always be sent with a manuscript or query letter.

SASP: Self-addressed, stamped postcard. May be sent with a manuscript submission to be returned by publisher indicating it arrived safely.

Satire: Ridicule that aims at reform.

Second serial rights: See "Reprint rights."

Semiannual: Issued twice a year.

Serial: Refers to publication in a periodical (such as first serial rights).

Sidebar: A short feature that accompanies an article and either elaborates on the human interest side of the story or gives additional information on the topic. It is often set apart by appearing within a box or border.

Simultaneous rights: Selling the rights to the same piece to several publishers simultaneously. Be sure everyone is aware that you are doing so.

Simultaneous submissions: Sending the same manuscript to more than one publisher at the same time. Usually done with nonoverlapping markets (such as denominational or newspapers) or when you are writing on a timely subject. Be sure to state in a cover letter that it is a simultaneous submission and why.

Slander: The verbal act of defamation.

Slanting: Writing an article so that it meets the needs of a particular market.

Slush pile: The stack of unsolicited manuscripts that have arrived at a publisher's office.

Speculation: See "On speculation."

Staff-written material: Material written by the members of a magazine staff.

Subsidiary rights: All those rights, other than book rights, included in a book contract such as paperback, book club, movie, etc.

Subsidy publisher: A book publisher who charges the author to publish his or her book, as opposed to a royalty publisher who pays the author.

Synopsis: A brief summary of work from one paragraph to several pages long.

Tabloid: A newspaper-format publication about half the size of a regular newspaper.

Take-home paper: A periodical sent home from Sunday school each week (usually) with Sunday school students, children through adults.

Think piece: A magazine article that has an intellectual, philosophical, or provocative approach to a subject.

Third world: Reference to underdeveloped countries of Asia and Africa.

Trade magazine: A magazine whose audience is in a particular trade or business.

Traditional verse: One or more verses with an established pattern that is repeated throughout the poem.

Transparencies: Positive color slides, not color prints.

Unsolicited manuscript: A manuscript an editor didn't specifically ask to see.

Vanity publisher: See "Subsidy publisher."

Vignette: A short, descriptive literary sketch of a brief scene or incident.

Vitae/Vita: An outline of one's personal history and experience.

Work-for-hire: Signing a contract with a publisher stating that a particular piece of writing you are doing for the publisher is work-for-hire. In the agreement you give the publisher full ownership and control of the material.

Writers' guidelines: An information sheet provided by a publisher that gives specific guidelines for writing for the publication. Always send an SASE with your request for guidelines.

About the Contributors

Sandra P. Aldrich, an international speaker and the author or coauthor of nineteen books, is a writing mentor for the Christian Writers Guild. Her five-hundred-plus articles have appeared in Focus on the Family, *Moody* magazine, *Today's Christian Woman*, *Discipleship Journal*, and others.

James Scott Bell is the author of *Plot & Structure* and numerous thrillers, including *Deceived, Try Dying*, and *Watch Your Back*. He is a winner of the Christy Award and has served as the fiction columnist for *Writer's Digest*. His craft books include: *Revision & Self-Editing, The Art of War for Writers,* and *Conflict & Suspense*. His website is www.jamesscottbell.com.

Judy Bodmer is a mentor, author, and freelance editor who enjoys working with new writers and seasoned veterans, including as a mentor for the Christian Writers Guild. Visit her at judybodmer.com.

Sandra Byrd has published more than forty books. Her adult fiction debut, *Let Them Eat Cake,* was a Christy Award finalist, as was her first historical novel, *To Die For: A Novel of Anne Boleyn.* Sandra has also published dozens of books for tweens and teens.

Deborah Christensen has been freelancing since 1989. She works as a writer/editor for Lighthouse Christian Products and serves as a mentor for the Christian Writers Guild. She writes the blog *Plowing the Fields* to help writers glean ideas from everyday life.

T. Suzanne Eller (Suzie) is a Proverbs 31 Ministries speaker and has authored six books and contributed to thirty others, as well as hundreds of articles on family, feelings, and faith. Suzie hosts the Facebook community Moms Together (*facebook.com/MomsTogether*).

Joyce K. Ellis is an award-winning author, coauthor, and ghostwriter of more than a dozen books, as well as hundreds of articles in numerous national publications. A columnist for the *Christian Communicator* magazine, she also mentors students for the Christian Writers Guild.

Lindsey A. Frederick is communications manager at Future Business Leaders of America and a freelance writer and editor in the DC metro area.

Danielle Grandinetti is a graduate of the Christian Writers Guild's *Apprentice, Journeyman,* and *Craftsman* courses. She also received an MA in Communication and Culture from Trinity International University. Danielle especially enjoys writing teen fiction.

Deborah Dee Harper writes inspirational, humorous books for kids and adults. A former newspaper columnist and a member of American Christian Fiction Writers, she is a graduate of the Christian Writers Guild's *Apprentice*, *Journeyman*, and *Craftsman* courses. Visit her at www.deborahdeeharper.com.

Dennis E. Hensley, PhD, directs the professional writing program at Taylor University, Upland, Indiana. A Christian Writers Guild board member, he is the author of more than fifty books, the most recent of which is *Jesus in the 9 to 5* (AMG Publishers).

Gary A. Hensley is a thirty-five-year veteran in the fields of accounting, auditing, and federal taxation. He has had numerous articles in publications such as *Writer's Digest, Writer's Yearbook, Christian Communicator,* and *Writers Journal.*

Michele Huey takes time from working on her current manuscript, a historical fiction, to find a cozy corner and read. She also writes an award-winning column, is a Christian Writers Guild mentor, and preaches for a small congregation between pastors. Visit her at www.michelehuey.com.

Angela Hunt, a Christy Award winner, is the bestselling author of more than one hundred works ranging from picture books and nonfiction books to novels. Her website is www.AngelaHuntBooks.com.

Julie-Allyson Ieron is a journalist whose passion is to open God's Word alongside readers to equip them to apply its riches to daily joys, questions, and challenges. Her books include *The God Interviews: Questions You Would Ask; Answers God Gives*. Julie recently celebrated twenty-five years as an author, writing coach, editor, and conference speaker.

Dallas Jenkins is an award-winning producer and director who worked in Hollywood for ten years. He is president and CEO of Jenkins Entertainment and visual media director for Harvest Bible Chapel. He loves to interact with those interested in filmmaking and is open to questions via e-mail anytime at djenkins@harvestbiblechapel.org.

Jerry B. Jenkins is the author of more than 180 books with sales of more than seventy million copies, including the bestselling Left Behind series. Twenty of his titles have reached the *New York Times* Best Sellers List (seven debuting #1).

Virelle Kidder is an internationally-known conference speaker and the author of six books and countless articles published in *Today's Christian Woman*, *Moody Magazine*, *In Touch*, *Focus on the Family Pastor's Magazine*, and *Decision*. She loves training writers of all levels. Visit her at www.VirelleKidder.com.

Matthew Koceich completed the Christian Writers Guild's *Apprentice, Journeyman,* and *Craftsman* courses. He and his wife, Cindi, have four children and live in Mansfield, Texas.

Heather Kreke is a graduate of the Christian Writers Guild's *Apprentice, Journeyman,* and *Craftsman* courses. She lives in Pittsburgh with her husband and two daughters. Heather is an avid reader and hopes to inspire youth to seek God's will for their lives through her writing.

Jennifer E. Lindsay draws much of her writing inspiration from the scenic Northwest. She began the Guild's *Apprentice* course while earning her bachelor's degree in English and writing and has since completed the *Journeyman* and *Craftsman* courses. A full-time editor, Jennifer also enjoys volunteering with local youth.

Jeanette Gardner Littleton, a writer as well as an editor, has served on staff with eight publications, including *Moody* magazine, and also a book publisher. Books she has written or coauthored include *When Your Teen Goes Astray, What's in the Bible for Teens*, and *Hugs for Coffee Lovers.*

Kathryn Mackel is a published novelist and produced screenwriter who has worked with Showtime, Disney, and Twentieth Century Fox. Her most recent novel is *To Know You* (Thomas Nelson Fiction), written with Shannon Ethridge.

DiAnn Mills is an award-winning author who believes her readers should always "expect an adventure." She is a popular teacher at writers conferences and the craftsman mentor for Jerry B. Jenkins Christian Writers Guild. Her website is www.diannmills.com.

Bill Myers is a best-selling author and award-winning filmmaker. His books have sold more than eight million copies. Visit him at www.BillMyers.com.

Karen O'Connor is a mentor for the Christian Writers Guild and an award-winning author of books and articles for children and adults. Her titles include *God Bless My Senior Moments.* Visit her at www.karenoconnor.com.

Roger Palms, former editor of *Decision Magazine,* is the author of fifteen books and hundreds of newspaper and magazine articles. He has written and mentored writers throughout the world and has helped many authors develop their books.

Deborah Raney's first novel, *A Vow to Cherish,* inspired a World Wide Pictures film and launched her writing career after twenty happy years as a stay-at-home mom. Her books have won the RITA Award, ACFW Carol Award, HOLT Medallion, National Readers' Choice Award, Silver Angel, and twice been Christy Award finalists.

Gayle Roper, a Christian Writers Guild mentor, is the award-winning author of more than forty-five books. She has been a Christy Award finalist three times for her novels *Spring Rain, Summer Shadows*, and *Winter Winds*. Visit her at www.gayleroper.com.

Andy Scheer, the Christian Writers Guild's editor-in-chief, also works as a freelance writer and editor. A frequent teacher at writers conferences, he formerly served as managing editor of *Moody Magazine.*

Kevin Scott is an acquisition editor for Wesleyan Publishing House and author of *ReCreatable: How God Heals the Brokenness of Life* (Kregel, March 2014). As a freelance writer, Kevin has published hundreds of devotions and dozens of small group studies for twentysomethings. He blogs at www.kevinscottwrites.com.

Jennifer Slattery writes and edits for Christ to the World Ministries, and also writes for the *ACFW Journal, The Christian Pulse, Internet Cafe Devotions, Jewels of Encouragement,* and reviews for *Novel Reviews*. She also cohosts Living by Grace, a Facebook community.

Les Stobbe has worked in Christian publishing as an editor, consultant, and literary agent for more than fifty years. Les has authored or coauthored fourteen books and more than five hundred feature articles, as well as provided editorial leadership at six publishers. He is a member of the Christian Writers Guild's editorial board.

James N. Watkins is the author of sixteen books and over two thousand articles, an editor with Wesleyan Publishing House, a conference speaker, a writing instructor at Taylor University, and a beloved child of God. Visit him at www.jameswatkins.com.

Estee B. Wells is a writer, photographer, and artist. A student at Taylor University, Upland, Indiana, Estee is majoring in Professional Writing and minoring in Public Relations with the goal of becoming an editor. Her writing has appeared in magazines including *Clubhouse* and *Oncourse.*

PeggySue Wells, a graduate of the Christian Writers Guild's *Craftsman* program, is a speaker and the author of a dozen books including *Rediscovering Your Happily Ever After* (Kregel). Contact her at www.PeggySueWells.com.

Terry White, EdD, is a writer, editor, educator, and journalism entrepreneur. He has founded and published newspapers and magazines including the *Minnesota Christian Examiner, The Christian Communicator,* and *GraceConnect*. He has taught journalism, magazine writing, and related courses at eight Midwest colleges and is currently adjunct faculty at Grace College, Winona Lake, Indiana, and Indiana Wesleyan University.

Index

This index includes periodicals, distributors, greeting cards/specialty markets, and agents, as well as some of the organizations/resources you may need to find quickly. Conferences and groups are listed alphabetically by state in those sections.